INCLUSION OF EXCEPTIONAL LEARNERS IN CANADIAN SCHOOLS

FIFTH EDITION

A PRACTICAL HANDBOOK FOR TEACHERS

INCLUSION OF EXCEPTIONAL LEARNERS IN CANADIAN SCHOOLS

FIFTH EDITION

A PRACTICAL HANDBOOK FOR TEACHERS NANCY L. HUTCHINSON

QUEEN'S UNIVERSITY

PEARSON

Toronto

Editorial Director: Claudine O'Donnell
Acquisitions Editor: Kimberley Veevers
Marketing Manager: Michelle Bish
Program Manager: John Polanszky
Project Manager: Jessica Mifsud
Developmental Editor: Stephen Kass
Media Developer: Bogdan Kosenko
Production Services: Cenveo® Publisher Services
Permissions Project Manager: Erica Mojzes
Photo and Text Permissions Research: Integra-CHI US
Art Director: Alex Li
Interior and Cover Designer: Anthony Leung
Cover Image: Lightspring/Shutterstock

Vice-President, Cross Media and Publishing Services: Gary Bennett

7   18

Library and Archives Canada Cataloguing in Publication

Hutchinson, Nancy Lynn, author
     Inclusion of exceptional learners in Canadian schools : a practical handbook for teachers / Nancy L. Hutchinson.—Fifth editon.

Includes bibliographical references and index.
ISBN 978-0-13-409588-2 (paperback)

     1. Inclusive education—Canada. I. Title.

LC3984.H88 2015   371.9'0460971   C2015-905770-1

ISBN 978-0-13-409588-2

For my friend, Linda, who has believed in me always, and for all the graduate students who have taught me so much over my years at Queen's—this one is for you!

Brief Contents

Contents

Preface

Preparing this edition of *Inclusion of Exceptional Learners in Canadian Schools* has once again made me a learner. During this process, I learned by doing background research in areas with which I was less familiar; by discussing current issues with colleagues, graduate students, parents, teacher candidates, and individuals with exceptionalities. And, always, I learn by challenging my assumptions about teaching exceptional children and adolescents. I continue to believe that, when we accept the challenges of teaching exceptional students in inclusive settings, we must be prepared to challenge assumptions about what exceptional students can and cannot do and to find new ways to help them reach their potential. I hope this book will help you to challenge your assumptions and to reflect critically on what it means to include exceptional students in the classroom.

I am proud of Canadian approaches to inclusion and inclusive education, and aware that we cannot rest on our laurels: educators in other countries look to Canada's commitment to inclusion as a model and an inspiration. Our 1982 *Constitution Act* has served as a model for countries developing constitutions since the early 1980s. Even Britain's charter of rights, approved by its upper and lower chambers in 2000, was compared with our *Canadian Charter of Rights and Freedoms* and found to contain fewer guarantees of individual rights. At the same time, I am aware of the incredible challenges facing parents, educators, employers, and exceptional individuals in making inclusion a reality. I hope that this book may serve as a research-based, practically-focused resource on inclusive education for teacher educators and pre-service and in-service teachers.

I have tried to include many references to Canadians—exceptional individuals, schools, educators, and educational researchers—including their locations in the country. I believe it is critical that we know our history, stories, legislation, and heroes. Perhaps we are too self-effacing—I have observed that Canadians are among those least likely to be aware of how we lead by example in our field. I have tried to point to the contributions of individuals such as Terry Fox and Rick Hansen, heroes and leaders of advocacy for the disabled, and of organizations such as the Canadian National Institute for the Blind, winner of national and international awards for advocacy and service. I believe that Aboriginal students, learners from diverse cultures, and students at risk can benefit from inclusive environments, universal design for learning, and differentiated teaching. I have tried to draw attention to significant recent developments in Aboriginal education that coexist with the crisis of disappearing Aboriginal languages. Whenever possible, I have given Canadian examples and cited Canadian research. I hope that the extensive listings of Canadian books, websites, and programs will help teacher candidates, teacher educators, and parents to locate our resources and our experts, of which there are many.

Perspective

For many years I have organized my pre-service and in-service teaching about exceptional learners around topics such as planning, classroom organization and climate, and differentiating teaching and assessment—using a non-categorical approach. I am reminded each year, as I work in the university and in schools in our community, how much is expected of beginning teachers. If they are to meet these expectations, I think they must begin, from the first lesson they plan, by thinking about the range of strengths, needs, and interests of the individuals in the class. The first question they need to ask is, "How do I use universal design for learning and differentiated instruction to include all students?" Given the recent emphasis on well-being, the second question they need to ask themselves is, "How do I ensure that what I am doing contributes positively to my students' mental health and to my own well-being?" That is the perspective you will find in this book. I have tried to focus on the kinds of information, skills, and strategies that recent teacher candidates have reported they found both thought-provoking and practical, and have included current information about mental health in every chapter. I have taught in elementary and secondary schools, and I teach classes that include teacher candidates from both panels; I have tried to acknowledge the different challenges in these two settings.

Organization

This textbook is informally divided into two main sections.

The first section provides fundamental background knowledge in the field of exceptional education in Canada.

- Chapter 1 describes the current situation in Canada and provides a brief history of how we came to be where we are. It also introduces universal design for learning and differentiated instruction and includes a step-by-step strategy for adapting instruction, called ADAPT, that will help teachers to meet the needs of exceptional students.

- Chapter 2 introduces the individual education plan, and describes the role of the classroom teacher in the education of exceptional learners and the kinds of partnerships that teachers forge with parents, educational assistants, and other professionals.

- Chapter 3 focuses on students with learning and behaviour exceptionalities—that is, teaching gifted students as well as students with learning disabilities, attention deficit hyperactivity disorder, emotional and behaviour disabilities—and includes discussion of school-based mental health.

- Students with intellectual disabilities (mild intellectual disabilities and developmental disabilities) as well as students with autism spectrum disorder are the focus of Chapter 4; the characteristics of these students and strategies to meet their learning needs are discussed.

- Chapter 5 provides information about characteristics of and differentiated teaching for students with communication exceptionalities (students with speech and language disorders and students who are hard of hearing or deaf), physical exceptionalities (including vision loss, cerebral palsy, epilepsy, fetal alcohol syndrome, and many other disabling conditions), and chronic health conditions (such as diabetes, allergies, and asthma).

- Chapter 6 turns attention to equity and diversity. There are strategies for differentiating teaching for Aboriginal students; culturally diverse students; English language learners; and students at risk for a variety of reasons, including poverty and abuse.

The second section of the book presents the heart of any course on inclusive practices: instructional approaches that emphasize teaching students effectively regardless of exceptionality or other forms of diversity.

- Chapter 7 focuses on the climate, organization, and management of inclusive classrooms.

- Chapter 8 provides approaches to using universal design for learning and differentiating teaching.

- Chapter 9 focuses on differentiating assessment. There are many examples representing a range of grades, exceptionalities, and teaching subjects.

- In Chapter 10, you will find information on enhancing social relations of exceptional students.

- Chapter 11 deals with the many transitions that challenge teachers of exceptional learners; these include transitions within the school day, the transition from early childhood education into school, and transitions between schools and out of school into post-secondary education and the workplace.
- The Conclusion turns the focus from exceptional learners to those who teach them most successfully and how they thrive on challenges and cope with stress in their professional lives.

Features

This book offers the following features designed to help readers learn effectively:

- Chapter-opening vignettes serve as introductory cases to help readers relate the chapter content to the real world of Canadian schools.
- Learner objectives at the beginning of each chapter point to key content within that chapter.
- Key terms throughout the chapters appear in boldface type, and easy-to-understand definitions often appear in the text and always appear in the Glossary at the back of the book.
- Chapter summaries at the end of each chapter highlight important information in the chapter.
- Margin notations are designed to stimulate critical reflection and to introduce additional resources, including weblinks, that have been researched and tested for quality and relevance.
- *Focus* boxes offer readers inspiring examples of Canadian schools, programs, and educators that may serve as models.
- *Theory and Research Highlights in Educational Psychology* boxes provide a theoretical grounding in the psychology that informs the education of exceptional students and their inclusion in Canadian society.
- *Challenges for Reviewing . . .* features at the end of each chapter present review questions to help students apply what they have learned in the chapter.
- *Activities for Reviewing . . . with Your Peers* features at the end of each chapter present review questions for students to work on collaboratively with peers to apply their learning.
- *New Annotated Bibliographies* in each chapter provide brief descriptions of current resources on school-based mental health resources relevant to the focus of the chapter.
- Canadian references throughout help students locate practical supports, resources, research, curricula, people, and websites within the exceptional education community in Canada.

Highlights of This Edition

This edition has been updated to include new, cutting-edge information.

- Chapters 1 and 8 are excellent resources for using universal design for learning (UDL) and differentiated instruction (DI) to make classrooms welcoming and efficient for all learners.
- Chapters 3, 4, and 5 provide an extensive discussion of the spectrum of exceptionalities which many students experience. This discussion looks at chronic illnesses,

emotional exceptionalities, and mental health issues. Chapter 6 includes a discussion of environmental exceptionalities such as poverty, homelessness, and abuse.

- Chapter 4 includes an extensive discussion of intellectual disabilities, providing in-depth information on mild and severe intellectual disabilities and autism spectrum disorder (ASD), providing teachers with accurate descriptions of the students' needs, and tips for ways in which they can be successfully integrated into classrooms settings.

- Chapter 11 focuses on transitions, one of the most challenging aspects of inclusive education.

- Throughout, there is a focus on creating safe, functional environments to discourage bullying.

- NEW Throughout, there is a focus on well-being of students and teachers; every chapter includes an annotated bibliography on school-based mental health resources relevant to the topics in the chapter.

Student Supplements

Pearson eText Pearson eText gives students access to the text whenever and wherever they have access to the Internet. eText pages look exactly like the printed text, offering powerful new functionality for students and instructors. Users can create notes, highlight text in different colours, create bookmarks, zoom, click hyperlinked words and phrases to view definitions, and view in single-page or two-page view. Pearson eText allows for quick navigation to key parts of the eText using a table of contents, and provides full-text search. The eText may also offer links to associated media files, enabling users to access videos, animations, or other activities as they read the text.

Instructor Supplements

The following supplements are available to instructors on Pearson Canada's password-protected online catalogue (**http://pearsoncanada.ca/highered**):

Instructor's Manual Each chapter of the Instructor's Manual includes an overview outline, teaching ideas, activities, discussion questions, transparency masters, and handout masters.

Learning Solutions Managers Pearson's Learning Solutions Managers work with faculty and campus course designers to ensure that Pearson technology products, assessment tools, and online course materials are tailored to meet your specific needs. This highly qualified team is dedicated to helping schools take full advantage of a wide range of educational resources, by assisting in the integration of a variety of instructional materials and media formats. Your local Pearson sales representative can provide you with more details on this service program.

Acknowledgments

Many people have contributed to the completion of this project, so many that, out of necessity, I will name only a few. First, thanks to my family—Jen, Deb, Jim, and Sandy—for understanding. And then to my friend, Linda, who has sustained me in the rough times and laughed with me in the good times. To my outstanding graduate students, for their persistence in locating elusive references and for their positive perspectives no matter how much work was left to be done; and to my colleagues, for collaboration, stimulation, and endless support. The awesome graduate students and colleagues include Kyle Robinson, Ian Matheson, Jeff MacCormack, Glenda Christou, Jenn Dods, Connie Taylor, CJ Dalton, Angela Pyle, Marcea Ingersoll, Wanda Beyer, Toni Thornton, Kate Walker, Nicole Lévesque, Jenny Taylor, Shelley Gauthier-McMahon, Cinde Lock, Lara Smith, Karin Steiner, Beth Noble, Cheryl Schmid, Jolene Wintermute, Jenn deLugt and Andrea Martin, Derek Berg, and John Freeman. To those I have left out, I apologize and I thank you too. Many, many library searches over the years were made easier by the generous work of our excellent reference librarian in the Queen's Faculty of Education, Brenda Reed. Finally, many thanks to the professionals at Pearson Canada—to Cliff Newman, who started me on this odyssey, and to all the folks who have guided me at every stage. For this edition—thank you to John Polanszky, Stephen Kass, and Jessica Mifsud for your all your work.

Finally, heartfelt thanks to thousands of parents, pre-service and in-service teachers, and exceptional students–especially to those who have taken the time to contact me with your suggestions and expressions of appreciation for the book. You have been my teachers. I hope I have learned well and that this book does justice to your fine practice and your high ideals for including exceptional students in Canadian society and in Canadian classrooms.

Nancy L. Hutchinson
Queen's University
Kingston, Ontario, Canada

Introduction

So You Want to Be a Teacher

You may have heard educators in Canadian schools say, "I didn't realize there would be so many exceptional students in my classes." Or "I wanted to teach English literature, not special education." Allow me to begin talking directly with teachers, using the second person "you"—so you want to be a teacher. One of the purposes of this book is to help you become more knowledgeable about the realities of teaching all your students. In Canada, early in the twenty-first century, being a classroom teacher means you are certain to have exceptional children or adolescents in your classes, and you may feel like a special education teacher some days—even if you were hired to teach classes in advanced physics. This is because, as a country, we have made a commitment to the inclusion and participation of persons with disabilities in Canadian society. This commitment is expressed formally through federal and provincial legislation and has been supported by many court decisions. Although you and your teaching colleagues were not consulted individually about inclusion, all Canadian citizens have repeatedly participated in this decision—through elections, public debates, polls, and research.

The polls and research studies suggest that Canadians support inclusion, but individuals who must fulfill these expectations, whether they are employers or teachers, report that they need guidance and support. They repeatedly express that, while they want to treat everyone fairly, they simply don't know enough about disabilities and about the changes that must be made in schools, workplaces, and society.

My intent in writing this book has been to help you and your fellow educators to access the information you need to be confident and competent when you teach in inclusive classrooms. Research has shown that when regular classroom teachers use differentiated teaching practices within inclusive classes, the result is increased achievement for typical students, low achievers, and students with disabilities. These studies are cited throughout this book. The differentiated teaching practices used in these studies included guided inquiry, group work, monitoring and facilitating student thinking, and recursive opportunities for students to develop and refine investigative processes. Actions that you can take to differentiate instruction include attending to the dynamics of students working effectively with peers; conferencing with students about how they are thinking and why they are making specific decisions; providing a variety of presentation and practise opportunities for students so they have choices; and accepting multiple methods for students to show what they know. A number of studies that you will learn about in upcoming chapters point to the same conclusion: the teaching approaches used to increase the learning of exceptional students—universal design for learning and differentiated instruction—also increase the learning of students who are low achievers, average achievers, or gifted.

These teaching approaches represent a paradigm shift, from educators' belief that "one size fits all" to ensuring that variety and flexibility for diverse learners, including exceptional learners, are built into instructional design, delivery, and assessment. No one would say that such approaches are without dilemmas or that we have all the research we need to inform our teaching decisions. However, many researchers are focused intently on advancing our understanding of the issues associated with these approaches to teaching. You are joining the profession at an exciting time for advances in practice and in research in the field of inclusion.

The Role of Classroom Teachers

As you have probably already deduced, schools and classroom teachers have a pivotal role in the creation of an inclusive society. First, unlike other institutions, schools are legally responsible for preparing children and adolescents with disabilities to participate meaningfully as educated adults in a democratic society. This means that as teachers we are expected to teach exceptional children and adolescents the same kinds of knowledge and skills that we teach all other students, in ways that are meaningful to them. In recent years we have adopted policies in every jurisdiction in Canada that reflect our commitment to carrying out this teaching in regular classrooms alongside peers without exceptionalities whenever possible. (This topic is explored fully in Chapter 1.) Second, schools have a legislated responsibility to prepare all children and adolescents to participate in an inclusive society and to accept individuals with disabilities as peers, co-workers, employees, employers, and so forth. This responsibility follows from one of the primary purposes of public education: preparing citizens to live in the democratic society that we have shaped, with its values, laws, and high expectations for participation. This means that Canadian educators, educational researchers, and policy-makers have to direct their efforts to understanding and reconciling these potentially conflicting responsibilities. As the discussion below suggests, it is impossible to hold dialogues in Canada about inclusive education without acknowledging and matching the extensive efforts of other institutions to include persons with disabilities.

While teachers are central to the Canadian project of inclusion, it is important for you as an individual teacher to remember that you are neither the cause of nor the solution to all of the problems that arise in your classroom. You can come to feel overwhelmed by guilt about your inability to be all things to all people. Crucial to your survival is judicious and frequent use of the resources provided to support classroom teachers and their exceptional students, the focus of much of this book. You also need to think about your advancement as inseparable from the advancement of the collective of educators in your school, your school district, and your province or territory. Both seeing yourself as part of a collective and learning to collaborate are essential to your effectiveness and to your well-being as an inclusive educator.

The Place of Inclusion in Canadian Society

In Canada inclusive education is an issue within the context of Canadian society, not just within the context of Canadian schools. In 1982 the Canadian constitution was patriated from Britain. At that time we adopted the *Canadian Charter of Rights and Freedoms*, which has influenced every aspect of our society. The Charter guarantees rights for minorities and specifically names persons with disabilities. The Charter not only guarantees rights but also specifies responsibilities of the Canadian government, of provincial governments, and of institutions to ensure that these rights are attained and maintained. This means that in Canada inclusion is closely related to equity: inclusion of exceptional persons follows from our commitment to equitable treatment guaranteed in the Charter.

Inclusive Schools

Inclusive schools are a natural part of inclusive society, and equitable treatment of students regardless of (dis)ability is closely related to equitable treatment of students regardless of gender, race, and so on. In Canada, if we choose to teach, we are choosing to teach in inclusive settings.

Dilemmas in Inclusive Schools

I am sure you are aware that dilemmas are a constant and pressing feature of teachers' lives. Rarely do we get through a day, let alone a week, of inclusive teaching without confronting some kind of a dilemma. Many of these may look, at first analysis, like they only involve decisions about teaching methods. However, upon critical examination, they frequently turn out to have implicit ethical dimensions. Do I allow a student's insensitive comment to an exceptional classmate to go unanswered? How far can I push my commitment to every student participating in hands-on learning when some can only complete the activities with so much assistance that finishing makes them feel more helpless rather than more empowered? How much differentiation of assessment is fair, and why is it easier for us and our students to accept these changes for blind students than for students with learning disabilities? The reality is that we live on the horns of complex ethical dilemmas every day of our teaching lives and that these dilemmas are only intensified by our commitment in Canada to an inclusive society and inclusive classrooms.

Becoming a Teacher

Throughout this book you will hear the voices of exceptional children, their parents, and teachers who are working together to enhance the learning experiences of exceptional students in regular classrooms. I hope that their words will strengthen and inspire you to use all your available resources to meet the challenges of inclusive teaching.

Exceptional Students, Universal Design for Learning, and Differentiated Instruction: The Canadian Experience

Racorn/Shutterstock

LEARNER OBJECTIVES

After you have read this chapter, you will be able to:

1. Describe the current state of social inclusion in Canadian society.

2. Describe the current state of inclusive education for exceptional students in Canada.

3. Discuss the concepts of universal design for learning (UDL), differentiated instruction (DI), and progress monitoring, including response to intervention (RTI), and how they are used in inclusive education.

4. Trace highlights in the development of inclusive education in Canada.

5. Describe briefly various exceptionalities that are identified across Canada.

6. Discuss what it means to differentiate or adapt teaching and classrooms to meet the needs of exceptional learners, and describe the steps of a strategy for adapting teaching to include exceptional learners.

GURJIT IS A BRIGHT AND ARTICULATE GIRL IN GRADE 3 WHO WAS IDENTIFIED AS GIFTED IN GRADE 1. On the first day of the social studies unit about Canada, Gurjit answered all of Ms. Wang's questions about the provinces. She asked questions the teacher had not thought of, especially about Nunavut, which became a separate territory on 1 April 1999. In a bored voice, Gurjit asked how long they would have to "do Canada." Gurjit read reference books independently, surfed the Internet on her family's computer, and wrote pages while most of her classmates penned a few sentences. Gurjit had already met the unit's outcomes and needed a challenge. The next day, Ms. Wang assigned a province or territory to each group of students. She challenged Gurjit to research the human and physical geography of Nunavut and to work closely with the small group who were focusing on the adjacent Northwest Territories. Gurjit found information about Nunavut on the Web, and contributed many ideas to the small group about life in the Northwest Territories.

While the rest of the class prepared booklets about their provinces, Gurjit developed activities for her classmates to complete at a centre on Nunavut, which remained available to the grade 3 class for the next two months.

BEN HAS A LEARNING DISABILITY THAT WAS IDENTIFIED IN GRADE 9. His grade 9 teachers said he rarely handed in assignments or contributed to class discussions, but when he did speak he had good ideas. Ben was often late for classes and forgot his books. His report card comments included, "Could work harder" and "Ben is disorganized." An assessment showed that Ben's reading comprehension was below grade level. He skipped over words he didn't understand and could not answer interpretive questions. At Ben's request and with the approval of his teachers, Ben transferred from the academic to the applied stream at the beginning of grade 10. The resource teacher, who then began to work with Ben and his teachers, focused on organizational strategies. She showed him how to use an agenda book to keep track of activities, classes, and assignments, and how to break an assignment into parts and set a date for the completion of each part. The resource teacher also taught Ben to use the RAP strategy—Read, Ask yourself questions, Paraphrase—for comprehending one paragraph at a time. She encouraged Ben's teachers to make adaptations, that is, to differentiate their teaching. One teacher used a paired reading strategy, another taught RAP to the entire class, and the chemistry teacher adopted occasional open-book tests. Ben passed all his applied courses in grade 10 but says that the courses were too easy. Now he wants to return to the academic stream.

1. Why are both Gurjit and Ben considered exceptional students?

2. How common do you think it is to teach an exceptional student like Gurjit and Ben in your classroom?

3. What should teachers be expected to do to meet the learning needs of students like Gurjit and Ben?

4. What expectations might Gurjit have after engaging in the enriched experience about Nunavut, while her classmates completed more traditional projects?

5. How do you think Ben's teachers and parents should respond to his request to return to the academic stream?

Introduction

As a classroom teacher, you will find students like Gurjit and Ben in every class you teach, because learning disabilities and giftedness are common exceptionalities. Occasionally you will teach students with less common exceptionalities, perhaps students who are deaf or blind. This book will prepare you to include exceptional students in the life and learning of your classroom. You will find that kids such as, Gurjit and Ben are like other students in most ways: first, they are children or adolescents; second, they have exceptionalities.

This chapter introduces you to the context in which we educate exceptional students: the current state of inclusion of persons with disabilities and of inclusive education, policies across the country, and historical and legal roots. We discuss how instructors can help exceptional students to reach their potential, using universal design for learning and differentiated instruction. The chapter includes brief descriptions of exceptionalities and closes by introducing a strategy for differentiating or adapting teaching to include exceptional learners: ADAPT.

Exceptional Education in Canada

In Canada, **exceptional students** include both pupils who are gifted and those who have disabilities. These students are entitled to **special education programming** which means "programming and/or services designed to accommodate students within the public school system whose educational needs require interventions different from, or in addition to, those which are needed by most students" (Prince Edward Island (PEI) Department of Education and Early Learning; http://www.gov. pe.ca/eecd/). Many provinces, including Ontario, use two terms to describe these changes: accommodations (changes to *how* a student is taught) and modifications (changes to *what* a student is taught). Increasingly, to ensure inclusion, teachers use universal design and plan proactively to meet the needs of all their students, including those who need special education programming (Robinson, 2015).

Accommodations include alternative formats (e.g., Braille or books on tape), instructional strategies (e.g., use of interpreters, visual cues, cognitive strategy instruction), and changes to assessment (e.g., highlighting the important words in a question on a test). **Modifications** are changes made to the grade-level expectations (or *outcomes*) for a subject or course to meet a student's learning needs. These changes to outcomes draw on outcomes from a different grade level in the curriculum, or increase or decrease the number and complexity of the regular grade-level curriculum expectations. Gifted grade 3 students may have modifications that include outcomes from the grade 5 math curriculum. A third type of adaptations, **alternative expectations**, focus on the development of skills in areas not represented in the curriculum, such as mobility training for blind students and anger management for students experiencing mental health challenges. You will see examples in upcoming chapters of a grade 5 student learning to use the telephone and a secondary school student learning life skills like making a sandwich.

You will need to become familiar with your provincial and school district documents about exceptional students because, since Confederation, provinces have had the authority to pass laws about education. These laws must be consistent with the *Constitution Act,* which contains the **Canadian Charter of Rights and Freedoms** (Government of Canada, 1982; http://laws-lois.justice.gc.ca/eng/charter). The

Weblinks

SNOW (SPECIAL NEEDS OPPORTUNITY WINDOWS): EDUCATION, ACCESS, AND YOU
http://snow.idrc.ocad.ca

COUNCIL FOR EXCEPTIONAL CHILDREN
www.cec.sped.org

PUBLIC HEALTH AGENCY OF CANADA
www.publichealth.gc.ca

equality rights that apply to education are contained in section 15(1): "Every individual is equal before and under the law and has the right to the equal protection and equal benefit of the law without discrimination and, in particular, without discrimination based on race, national or ethnic origin, colour, religion, sex, age or mental or physical disability."

Canada: Inclusive Society, Inclusive Schools

Participating in all facets of society, including educational institutions, is a fundamental right of all Canadians. Many developments worldwide contributed to Canada's adoption of the *Canadian Charter of Rights and Freedoms* in 1982. For example, all members of the United Nations adopted the Universal Declaration of Human Rights in 1948. Education was one of the fundamental human rights listed in the Declaration; however, there was no mention of people with disabilities. In 1975, the United Nations declared that disabled persons had the same rights as other people (including community living, education, work, voting, etc.) in the Declaration of the Rights of Disabled Persons. The *Canadian Human Rights Act* of 1977 states that no one should be discriminated against for reasons of physical or mental ability. Subsequently, 1981 was proclaimed the International Year of Disabled Persons, causing heightened awareness of disabilities and enhancing the self-advocacy of people with disabilities. That year, the Canadian parliament was debating the terms of the *Canadian Charter of Rights and Freedoms*. When people with disabilities were not named in an early draft of the Charter, they protested on Parliament Hill and got their story into the newspaper headlines and *Maclean's* magazine. The result was that when the Charter was passed, Canada became one of the first countries to guarantee rights to people with disabilities in its constitution.

The United Nations continued to champion the rights of persons with disabilities, and in 1993 it adopted the Standard Rules on the Equalization of Opportunities for Persons with Disabilities, targeting eight areas for **equal participation**, including education. "Persons with disabilities are members of society and have the right to remain within their local communities. They should receive the support they need within the ordinary structures of health, education, employment and social services" (United Nations Enable; www.un.org/disabilities).

Then on 13 December 2006, the Convention on the Rights of Persons with Disabilities was adopted by the United Nations; it came into force on 3 April 2008, after it had received its twentieth ratification. You can read the text of the Convention at www.un.org/disabilities/default.asp?id=259. The United Nations has described the Convention as a paradigm shift in attitudes and approaches to persons with disabilities because it views them as "subjects" with rights who are capable of claiming those rights and making decisions for their lives based on their free and informed consent as well as being active members of society. The Convention clarifies how all categories of rights apply to persons with all types of disabilities and

Eric Hayes

Activists with intellectual disabilities at the People First Conference. In 1981, blind people and people with physical disabilities and intellectual disabilities held conferences and rallied on Parliament Hill demanding equality.

identifies areas where adaptations have to be made so persons with disabilities can exercise their rights.

Canada's policy on persons with disabilities emphasizes **inclusion**. In 2013, the federal, provincial, and territorial ministers responsible for social services (except the minister from Québec) released a document titled *In Unison: A Canadian Approach to Disability* (on the website of the Council of Canadians with Disabilities; www.ccdonline.ca/en/socialpolicy/poverty-citizenship/income-security-reform/in-unison#sec-canadian-approach). The document includes a vision: "Persons with disabilities participate as full citizens in all aspects of Canadian society. The full participation of persons with disabilities requires the commitment of all segments of society." This vision reflects the views of Canadians expressed in the executive summary of the *Advancing Inclusion* (Government of Canada, 2008) report: "Canadians feel that people with disabilities should have the opportunity to participate in life to their fullest potential—that this is part of the 'Canadian way' of doing things. Most feel that while the solutions might be expensive, they are necessary and the social benefit is worth it." However, our aspirations for inclusion still outstrip our accomplishments. And as educators, we have an important role: schools prepare the next generation to honour our national commitment to inclusion of persons with disabilities in all aspects of Canadian society.

What do you think?

As you read this text, search for current newspaper articles on issues related to social inclusion in Canadian society. Discuss with your peers the progress we have made as a country and what we can do in our role as educators to advance inclusion in Canada, so all people are valued participants in our society.

The Current State of Inclusive Education for Exceptional Students: Universal Design for Learning and Differentiated Instruction

It is challenging for us as educators to consider the implications of broad social movements for the policies and procedures that guide our work with exceptional learners. As you think about the expectations our society holds for inclusive education, for students with disabilities and gifted students learning the same content as their typical peers, you may be asking yourself how this can be accomplished effectively. It is clear that more research needs to be conducted in regular classrooms, research that focuses on how to include exceptional students successfully while teaching all the other students. And you will experience dilemmas of practice as you learn your role as an inclusive educator and have to make decisions about how to teach.

Three concepts that are receiving increasing attention will help you to ensure "education for all." This phrase served as the title of a 2005 report in Ontario that introduced these three concepts to teachers. These concepts are universal design for learning (UDL), differentiated instruction (DI), and progress monitoring (with one specific form called response to intervention (RTI)).

Universal Design for Learning and Differentiated Instruction

Universal design for learning (UDL) was inspired by work in architecture on designing buildings, right from the start of the design process, that can be accessed by all people, including those with physical disabilities. This eliminates the need for retrofitting when a person with accessibility needs arrives; for example, the building already has ramps and wide doorways to accommodate wheelchairs. As it turns out, wide doorways and ramps are advantageous for many people, not just for those with physical disabilities. UDL involves a set of principles for developing curriculum and teaching that give all students equal opportunity to learn (New Brunswick Department of Education and Early Childhood Development, 2013; www.gnb.ca/0000/pol/e/322A.pdf). As per Burgstahler and Chang (2009) and Katz (2012), here are eight guidelines for planning teaching and activities that will be accessible for all:

1. Adopt practices that value diversity and inclusiveness to create a positive climate.
2. Communicate so everyone can understand to enhance interactions among students and between students and the teacher.
3. Make the physical environment safe for everyone and its products available to all.
4. Communicate high expectations and provide a high level of support for all.
5. Vary instructional methods so learning is accessible in many ways.
6. Make course materials and technology engaging and flexible so they can be understood by all.
7. Provide specific feedback frequently.
8. Assess student progress frequently and flexibly so everyone can show what they know.

In her book *Teaching to Diversity,* Jennifer Katz of the University of Manitoba (2012) considers UDL to be an overarching concept composed of three main blocks that are all essential to making inclusion work. The most fundamental block is social and emotional learning, which demands that we develop compassionate learning communities. The role of teachers in social-emotional learning of students is the theme of the annotated bibliography in Figure 1.1. Students' social-emotional well-being is the focus of Chapters 7 and 10 and a recurring theme in this book. The second block is inclusive of instructional practice, and is often called differentiated instruction and differentiated assessment, which is the focus of Chapters 8 and 9. The third block in Katz's three-block model focuses on systems and structures, from policy to planning teams. Many of these administrative aspects essential for inclusive education have been introduced in this chapter and are elaborated in Chapter 2.

Rather than developing a unit and making changes after the fact for exceptional students, English language learners (ELL), or students from diverse cultures, UDL encourages teachers to make a class profile and then plan from the beginning to provide means and pedagogical materials that meet the needs of all students. Of the three blocks in Katz's model, the one that generally receives the most attention is block two, which she identifies as inclusive instructional practice and which others often call differentiated instruction.

Differentiated instruction (DI) acknowledges that students differ in many important ways that contribute to learning in our classrooms: interests, strengths, needs, modalities on which they rely (especially students with vision or hearing loss), current level of knowledge, level of functioning, ability to read fluently, ability to use visual arts to express their understanding of the world, and many others. While UDL can be seen to operate at the overarching level, DI helps teachers to make decisions at the student level to address specific characteristics, experiences, backgrounds, skills, and difficulties. The aspects of teaching that teachers can differentiate are often described as content, process, and product (Ontario Ministry of Education, 2005; Tomlinson, 2014). You will learn throughout this text about using such strategies as tiered assignments (created at varying levels of difficulty), small-group instruction in which intensity is increased, learning centres at which students can engage with a

What do you think?

Read two of the following Canadian resources and contrast their perspectives on disabilities. Think about why we need a range of perspectives to fully understand the experience of life with a disability and to understand how to ensure valued recognition and social inclusion for individuals with disabilities. Talk with your peers about your differing points of view.

Tichkosky, T. (2011). *The question of access: Disability, space, meaning.* Toronto, ON: University of Toronto Press.

Bendall, L. (2008). *Raising a kid with special needs: The complete Canadian guide.* Toronto, ON: Key Porter Books.

Prince, M.J. (2009). *Absent citizens: Disability politics and policy in Canada.* Toronto, ON: University of Toronto Press (Google eBook).

A Vision Paper Federal/Provincial/Territorial Ministers Responsible for Social Services SP-113-10-98E. (2013). *In unison: A Canadian approach to disability issues.* Retrieved at www.ccdonline.ca/en/socialpolicy/poverty-citizenship/income-security-reform/in-unison#sec-canadian-approach (website of Council of Canadians with Disabilities).

FIGURE 1.1 ANNOTATED BIBLIOGRAPHY ON TEACHERS' ROLE IN THE WELL-BEING AND MENTAL HEALTH OF STUDENTS

Students do not leave their concerns and uncertainties about mental health at the door of the school. This can prove challenging for teachers who feel they are not experts and fear "doing the wrong thing."

Improving Mental Health in Schools (2014)

by Eric Rossen & Katherine Cowen, *Phi Delta Kappan, 96*(4), 8–13.

There is a solid foundation of research for schools to use to provide a multi-tiered system of supports for students. Such interaction between students and teachers enhances student well-being, but also promotes student learning and reduces stigma.

Building Mental Health as a School Community (2014)

by Suzanne Hughes, *Nurture, 48*(3), 16–18.

This paper gives a brief description of the actions taken by one school to enhance student mental health, including making the topic a focus, creating committees to address health issues, and providing professional development to help staff recognize mental illness.

Emotional Health and Well-Being in Schools: Involving Young People (2013)

by Lindsey Coombes, Jane Appleton, Debby Allen, & Paul Yerrell, *Children and Society, 27*(3), 220–232.

When asked, adolescents suggested that issues of mental health and well-being should be addressed more in the curriculum but also cautioned that teachers determine the effectiveness of these lessons through their enthusiasm and creativity. They expressed concerns about confidentiality, and they were more comfortable having these conversations with peers. Seeking student input might be an important first step for a secondary school developing an intervention for mental health and well-being.

Dr. James Gallagher's Concern for Gifted Learners Beyond Academics (2015)

by Del Siegle, *Journal for the Education of the Gifted, 38*(1), 58–63.

We may not associate mental health issues with students who are gifted. However, especially if they are bored in school, gifted students may not thrive unless their teachers take an active role in both challenging and supporting them.

A Combined Intervention Targeting Both Teachers' and Students' Social–Emotional Skills (2014)

by Cristina Iizuka, Paula Barrett, Robyn Gillies, Clayton Cook, & Welber Marinovic, *Australian Journal of Guidance and Counselling, 24*(2), 152–166.

Teachers working in a school in a disadvantaged community received professional development to teach social and emotional skills to students and participated in a resilience program for themselves. The intervention was well received by the teachers and it helped students to decrease their anxiety. The FRIENDS program has shown positive results in other schools as well.

range of tasks, and varied pacing (Chappuis, 2014). Katz (2012) describes planning for an entire school year and provides many examples of how the three blocks, including the block on inclusive instructional practices—that is, DI—can be used together to ensure that UDL is implemented effectively. Strategies for making DI work in your classroom will be our focus in Chapter 8. As an introduction, I offer the following ten principles that are often used to guide DI:

1. Use respectful tasks; consider the perspective of all students.

2. Make groupings flexible, purposeful, and short-term.

3. Use heterogeneous groupings.

4. Choose multi-level texts so everyone is reading something they understand.

5. Offer varied response formats that enable everyone to respond meaningfully and offer choice.

6. Demonstrate how students can make connections between what they know and what they are learning.

7. Model strategies, that is, make the invisible visible, to students who will not develop those strategies on their own.

8. Consider student interests and try to engage everyone; offer choice.

9. Begin where students are and ensure that everyone learns and recognizes they are learning.

10. Develop diverse assessments that show you and the students what they have learned.

The Special Education Association of BC suggests that teachers begin small (using DI for a lesson or unit and work up to using UDL to plan all their teaching for the year) and suggests you collaborate with a colleague who teaches at the same grade level. Having well-established routines and a safe and positive environment will make it easier to embrace DI and UDL. The more you help students to understand themselves as learners, that is, to be metacognitive and to advocate for their own learning (ideas developed throughout this book), the easier it will be for students to make good choices of tasks. Help them to know themselves as learners, understand what they are good at, and recognize what they need to work (at http://seabc.pbworks.com).

Think of DI as the basis for offering learning opportunities in varied, adapted, and engaging ways so you can ensure that everyone learns and demonstrates their learning in meaningful ways. And approach it as one key part of using UDL to inform all aspects of your practice so that, right from the initial planning, you are focusing on making learning accessible to all.

As the website of Alberta Education reminds teachers, "Differentiated instruction is a philosophy and an approach to teaching in which teachers and school communities work to support the learning of *all* students through strategic assessment, thoughtful planning and targeted, flexible instruction" (n.d.; http://education.alberta.ca/media/1233952/4_ch1%20intro.pdf). So when you use UDL and DI, you will not disadvantage any students; this approach gives all students multiple opportunities to make sense of what they are learning and to demonstrate what they are learning.

Progress Monitoring: Response to Intervention

When the Ontario Ministry of Education introduced its teachers to UDL and DI in *Education for All* (2005), it included a third key concept that can contribute to this approach to teaching, learning, and assessment: continual **progress monitoring**. Progress monitoring is important for learners of all ages. One specific form of progress monitoring, more often focused on primary students until recently, has received considerable attention; it is called **response to intervention (RTI)**. RTI is a way of thinking about how we can intervene before students fail by intensifying and improving teaching for struggling learners. It is often described as tiered intervention or a multi-tiered system of supports (MTSS; Witzel & Clarke, 2015). Children who are struggling after receiving excellent instruction (tier 1) are given a different type of instruction, which is more intense and of longer duration than regular classroom instruction (tier 2). For example, if some students in a grade 1 class are not learning to read with their peers, they could be taught in a small group of two to five; this may take place for ten to twenty weeks for forty-five minutes on most days. At the end of this intervention, those who have learned to read return to regular classroom

Weblinks

ONTARIO MINISTRY OF EDUCATION/ EDUGAINS WEBSITE PROVIDES RESOURCES, INCLUDING LESSON PLANS
www.edugains.ca

ALBERTA EDUCATION: MAKING A DIFFERENCE: MEETING DIVERSE LEARNING NEEDS WITH DIFFERENTIATED INSTRUCTION PROVIDES A TEACHER RESOURCE
http://education.alberta.ca/teachers/resources/cross/making-a-difference.aspx

SPECIAL EDUCATION ASSOCIATION OF BC HOSTS A WIKI FOR TEACHERS USING DI: FIRST STEPS
http://seabc.pbworks.com

instruction, while those who are still struggling move to the next tier (tier 3) of more intense, more individualized teaching, and perhaps to short-term placement in special education.

A 2007 Canadian study by Marcia Barnes of the University of Guelph and Lesly Wade-Woolley of Queen's University suggests that learning disabilities can be decreased by up to 70 percent by a combination of early screening, progress monitoring, and intensive teaching. RTI has received much attention in the past decade, and many states in the United States have already recognized it as an appropriate means of identifying learning disabilities. A review by Kent McIntosh and colleagues from UBC (2011) describes the state of implementation of RTI for identifying students with learning disabilities in New Brunswick, Saskatchewan, Alberta, and British Columbia. Ontario's *Education for All* (2005) describes UDL, DI, and RTI in a document for teachers and administrators.

The Current State of Exceptional Education in Each Province and Territory

This section provides snapshots of exceptional education policies and practices in all the jurisdictions, from west to east.

BRITISH COLUMBIA (www.bced.gov.bc.ca/specialed)

Special Education Services: A Manual of Policies, Procedures and Guidelines (2011; www.bced.gov.bc.ca/specialed/ppandg.htm) states: "Inclusion describes the principle that all students are entitled to equitable access to learning, achievement and the pursuit of excellence in all aspects of their education." It continues, "The practice of inclusion is not necessarily synonymous with integration and goes beyond placement to include meaningful participation and the promotion of interaction with others." Individual education plans (IEPs) are developed for exceptional learners to identify learning goals and support services. Of all the provinces, British Columbia provides the most comprehensive set of practical documents to support teachers working with exceptional students, including four documents on teaching students with mental health challenges (e.g., *Teaching Students with Mental Health Disorders, Volume 2, Depression*) and documents on topics as diverse as giftedness and fetal alcohol syndrome disorder (FASD). These are available at the website www.bced.gov.bc.ca/specialed under Special Education Resource Documents. The Ministry of Education has recently partnered with Ministry of Children and Family Development, and Ministry of Health in the Child and Youth with Special Needs Framework for Action to provide more co-ordinated services for children and their families.

YUKON (www.education.gov.yk.ca)

Yukon's *Student Support Services Manual* (November, 2015; http://www.education.gov.yk.ca/manual.html) describes its guiding principles as stressing "success of all learners through inclusive education." It continues: "To succeed, some students may require adaptations in methodology, materials or assessment techniques; or modifications or enhancements of programs; or compensatory skill development." Students' strengths and challenges are to be central to all decisions and there are numerous assertions that all students can learn and that teachers and parents must work together. No special education categories are defined but a "pyramid of intervention" shows problem solving and intervention moving from what is universal and provided to all

Further Reading

About RTI:

National Center on Response to Intervention. *Essential components of RTI: A closer look at response to intervention.* Washington, DC: National Center on Response to Intervention. http://www.rti4success.org

National Center on Response to Intervention. *Tiered interventions in high schools.* Washington, DC: National Center on Response to Intervention. http://www.rti4success.org

Witzel, B., & Clarke, B. (2015). Benefits of using a multi-tiered system of supports to improve inclusive practices. *Childhood Education, 91*(3), 215–219.

Turse, K.A., & Albrecht, S.F. (2015). The ABCs of RTI: An introduction to the building blocks of response to intervention. *Preventing School Failure, 59*(2), 83–89.

students by classroom teachers, to targeted interventions for those who need more to meet their needs, to intensive intervention for the few who require it. At the latter two levels of the pyramid, students may receive additional supports from school-based professionals in addition to the instruction of the regular classroom teacher.

ALBERTA (http://alberta.ca/educationtraining.cfm)

In 2008, Alberta began a broad examination of how it could meet the educational needs of students with disabilities and those who are gifted and talented. *Setting the Direction* (2009; https://education.alberta.ca/media/1082136/sc_settingthedirection_framework.pdf) was undertaken as part of an extensive consultation process to build an inclusive education system. The process has been working through four phases to achieve a system in which all students' learning begins with Alberta Programs of Study, recognizes strengths as well as needs, and is enabled by educators' changing the environment: "At the core of inclusion is the concept of making differences ordinary so that all students have a place, feel valued and welcomed, and are equipped by success." Individual program plans (IPPs) are developed for students with special needs and are expected to meet *Standards for Special Education* (2004; https://education.alberta.ca/department/policy/standards/sestandards). Many resources are being developed for teacher professional development. For example, nine videos on the website (each three to five minutes long) explain topics like using respectful language, differentiated instruction, and UDL. Each video is accompanied by a conversation guide. There are also guides for teachers on topics like teaching students with ADHD and with FASD.

NORTHWEST TERRITORIES (www.ece.gov.nt.ca)

The *Ministerial Directive on Inclusive Schooling* (2006; www.ece.gov.nt.ca) stated that inclusive schooling, defined by equal access, means more than the right of all students to participate in education programs offered in regular instructional settings with their age peers. "It also means the provision of support services as necessitated by the needs of individual students" including accommodations to how students are taught, modifications in what students are taught, or an IEP when they are working on outcomes not in the curriculum or have significant needs. In response to widespread concerns about lack of support services, an independent review was conducted, *Review of Minister's Directive of Inclusive Schooling* (Dean, 2014; www.ece.gov.nt.ca/files/ERI/independent_review_of_inclusive_schooling_2014.pdf). Students with learning difficulties who were not receiving remediation, the highest needs students, and those experiencing mental health challenges were identified as being served least well. The report recommends introduction of screening and early intervention, RTI, a tiered approach to flexible intervention for academic and behavioural needs, as well as a self-regulation framework and UDL. Immediately the Department of Education, Culture and Employment developed a three-year action plan, including eighteen areas for action, based on the recommendations, with implementation to occur over three years (www.ece.gov.nt.ca).

NUNAVUT (www.edu.gov.nu.ca)

Given that most of the inhabitants of Nunavut are Inuit, it is not surprising that this territory of 30 000 has developed educational policies embedded in Inuit culture (www.edu.gov.nu.ca). *Inuglugijaittuq–Foundation for Inclusive Education in Nunavut*

Schools illustrates why Nunavut's approach has been described as "culturally defined inclusive education" (Philpott, 2007, p. 14). It asserts, "Inclusion is an attitude and a belief, a way of life, and a way of living and working together in schools. In Nunavut, inclusion builds on the Inuit belief that each individual is valuable, belongs and contributes to the group. Inclusion infuses all aspects of school life." The document makes no specific reference to exceptional learners. Practices described include accepting that students learn at different rates, including all students in regular classrooms, being resourceful to provide supports, and showing respectful pride for Inuit culture. A tiered model includes Tumit 1 for the majority of students, Tumit 2 and 3 (accommodations and group or individual interventions), and Tumit 4 and 5 (specialized individual interventions and an IEP). Teachers are expected to differentiate instruction and work collaboratively with school teams.

SASKATCHEWAN (www.education.gov.sk.ca)

Saskatchewan education policy emphasizes inclusive learning environments. Since 2012 school divisions in Saskatchewan have used service delivery rubrics to review their student support services. The first rubric is inclusionary philosophy and beliefs, while the other two focus on instruction and collaboration. Saskatchewan Education also describes intensive supports as promoting "the success of students who have learning needs that impact several areas of development and who require intense and frequent supports to optimize their learning achievement" (www.education.gov.sk.ca/IntensiveSupports). Intensive supports that receive funding include assistive technologies, student support teachers, and community-based services. School teams involve parents in a process to complete an inclusion and intervention plan (IIP) that includes student outcomes and a plan for supports, strategies, and interventions. A list of categories and definitions, which states that identified needs are more important than labels, includes mental health disorders and intellectual disability, but does not name learning disabilities or autism spectrum disorder. The website also describes early childhood intervention programs and family intervention programs which are designed to prevent school failure, and includes practical documents to guide teacher practice when including students with exceptionalities such as learning disabilities and ASD.

MANITOBA (www.edu.gov.mb.ca/k12/specedu/index.html)

On its Student Services website, Manitoba Education states: "Inclusion is a way of thinking and acting that allows every individual to feel accepted, valued, and safe. An inclusive community consciously evolves to meet the changing needs of its members." It asserts that inclusion goes beyond physical location to incorporate a belief system and values that promote participating and belonging. Going beyond most provincial websites, Manitoba includes the expectation that educators will enhance students' abilities to "deal with diversity." A number of documents report the regulations that ensure "appropriate educational programming" and describe expectations for areas including IEPs, assessment, discipline, and dispute resolution. Many practical documents are available to inform teacher practice such as *Positive Behaviour Support* (www.edu.gov.mb.ca/k12/specedu/planning/index.html) which includes a tiered approach, protocols for collaborating with other government agencies and departments, and extensive information on promoting positive mental health. A series of publications on safe and caring schools was revised in 2015 and deals with diversity in a wide range of areas including sexual and gender identity. *Independent Together: Supporting the Multilevel Learning Community* (www.edu.gov.mb.ca/k12/docs/support/multilevel) is a valuable resource that helps teachers to implement differentiation.

ONTARIO (www.edu.gov.on.ca/eng/general/elemsec/speced/speced.html)

Students who require additional supports beyond those ordinarily received in the school setting and who meet definitions for behaviour or communication disorders or intellectual, physical, or multiple disabilities, or who are gifted may be formally identified as exceptional pupils. The identification is carried out by an **Identification, Placement, and Review Committee (IPRC)**, a committee unique to Ontario. The regular classroom with appropriate services is the first choice for placement and IEPs outline expectations, programs, and services. Recently Ontario has begun developing IEPs for students who have not had an IPRC but require accommodations. In 2004 *The Individual Education Plan (IEP): A Resource Guide* (www.edu.gov.on.ca/eng/general/elemsec/speced/guide/resource/iepresguid.pdf) was developed, containing a thorough description of the IEP process. Then in 2005, Ontario released *Education for All* which focused on differentiating instruction and on using UDL and RTI to informally and quickly identify struggling learners in elementary years, and to put tiered interventions into practice before labels were applied, without the delay and bureaucracy of IEPs and IPRC meetings. This process has continued with the release of *Learning for All* (Ontario Ministry of Education, 2013; www.edu.gov.on.ca/eng/general/elemsec/speced/learning.html) which promotes differentiation for K to 12.

QUÉBEC (www4.gouv.qc.ca)

In 1999, Québec released a policy on special education, *Adapting Our Schools to the Needs of All Students* (Ministère de l'Éducation, 1999), which recommends that before a student is formally identified as having special needs, the focus should be on early intervention and prevention. When that is not adequate to meet a student's needs, those who are deemed to have special needs, by an evaluation, are identified as having handicaps, social maladjustment, or learning disabilities (acronym EHDAA) as defined by Ministère de l'Éducation (2000). The first choice is to integrate students with EHDAA into a regular class or group and into school activities if that will facilitate the student's learning and social integration while not significantly undermining the rights of other students. Services and instruction are to be adapted based on an IEP, and differentiated instruction is recommended as a strategy for teachers' meeting these challenges effectively along with teamwork and complementary educational services. Within Québec's English-sector school boards, about 85 percent of the special needs population is integrated into regular classes (Hobbs, 2015).

NEW BRUNSWICK (www.gnb.ca/0000/index-e.asp)

New Brunswick has a long history of commitment to integration. In 1986, the province introduced legislation to ensure integration of exceptional students, and in 2002 it published guidelines to ensure a consistent method for the development and application of special education plans (SEPs) for exceptional students. In 2007, the *MacKay Report* (www.gnb.ca/0000/publications/mackay/mackay-e.asp) described inclusive

---

Cross-Reference
Chapter 2 describes IEPs, your role in the IEP process, and collaboration with parents.

Further Reading

Read three recent educational documents produced in Canada that raise questions about the approach to teaching exceptional learners that has developed here over the past twenty-five years. Discuss your thoughts about the directions for change in inclusive education in Canada.

MacKay, W. *MacKay Report (Inclusive education: A review of programming and services in New Brunswick).* www.gnb.ca/0000/publications/mackay/mackay-e.asp.

Ontario Ministry of Education. (2013). *Learning for all: A guide to effective assessment and instruction for all students, kindergarten to grade 12.* www.edu.gov.on.ca/eng/general/elemsec/speced/learning.html.

Philpott, D. (2007). Assessing without labels: Inclusive education in the Canadian context. *Exceptionality Education Canada, 17*(3), 3–34.

education as "an approach not a place," emphasizing accommodating all children in learning so as to maximize their potential and foster their sense of belonging to the school community and to the society. The Porter–Aucoin report (2011), *Strengthening Inclusion, Strengthening Schools* (www.gnb.ca/0000/publications/comm/Inclusion.pdf), made specific recommendations about how to implement McKay's report, and in 2013 New Brunswick adopted *Policy 322 on Inclusive Education* making these recommendations the law for all students. The common learning environment is expected to enable each student to participate fully, through the application of UDL and the implementation of accommodations in a timely way. The definitions in the policy contain no reference to exceptionalities although there is a definition for a personalized learning plan (PLP) for a student who requires strategies and supports to meet individual needs.

NOVA SCOTIA (www.ednet.ns.ca)

Nova Scotia has also been experiencing change. In 2014, the report of the minister's panel on education was titled *Disrupting the Status Quo: Nova Scotians Demand a Better Future for Every Student* (www.ednet.ns.ca/files/reports/report_minister_panel_on_education.pdf). The compilation of the survey responses of over 19 000 citizens addresses seven themes which the report says demonstrate "a compelling case for change": (1) the curriculum, (2) teaching, (3) transitions, (4) inclusion, (5) school climate, (6) student health and well-being, and (7) the system structure. We discuss many of these themes in this text, especially (3) through (6). The report contains thirty recommendations and urges the government to act immediately. In January 2015, the government released an action plan, *The 3Rs: Renew, Refocus, Rebuild* (www.ednet.ns.ca/files/2015/Education_Action_Plan_2015_EN.pdf). The plan puts heavy emphasis on early screening and intervention, emphasizing literacy and numeracy to catch students before they fail, and on comprehensive assessments of individual students. It also requires use of consistent criteria for placing a student on an individual program plan (IPP) and monitoring progress of students on IPPs at the school, board, and provincial levels through use of technology.

PRINCE EDWARD ISLAND (www.gov.pe.ca/eecd)

The Department of Education, Early Learning and Culture oversees education in PEI. The *Minister's Directive on Special Education,* originally issued in 2001 (No. MD 01-08; www.gov.pe.ca/eecd/index.php3?number=1027961&lang=E), describes special education as programming and services that accommodate students who need interventions in addition to or different from those needed by most students. An IEP is defined as "a written record that documents the collaborative process for the development of an individualized plan for a student with special educational needs. . . . The IEP outlines support services and educational program adaptations and/or modifications." (Prince Edward Island (PEI) Department of Education and Early Learning; http://www.gov.pe.ca/eecd/) All policies emphasize that all students are to be educated in inclusive settings. In an inclusive classroom, the student should participate at some level in all classroom activities, ranging from full participation, through partial participation, to parallel participation. There are specific resources on the provincial website for teachers to inform their work, for example, meeting behavioural challenges (www.gov.pe.ca/photos/original/ed_bestaff.pdf) and a 2015 resource on working with students with autism developed through an Atlantic partnership (www.apsea.ca/aie).

Since 2008, Newfoundland and Labrador has been moving through phases toward inclusive education. On their website, they emphasize that inclusive education is for all students, not just those with exceptionalities, and assert that inclusion involves more than student placement. It promotes a welcoming school culture in which some students may need individualized or small group instruction periodically for their needs to be met. A recent document, *Roles of Teachers in Inclusive Schools* (Newfoundland and Labrador Department of Education and Early Childhood Development, 2010; www.ed.gov.nl.ca/edu/forms/studentsupport/teacherroles.pdf), is intended to help educators assume new roles as they change their practice to make schools more inclusive. It emphasizes collaboration, co-teaching, and a range of learning environments to meet all students' needs. The Department of Education site provides definitions of twelve exceptionalities or conditions that entitle students to access special education services including mental health and acquired brain injury, as well as specific learning disorder and intellectual disability. There is also information about students who are gifted and talented. Embedded in the information about these exceptionalities are links to other sources of information.

Cross-Country Summary: Individual Education Plans and Dilemmas in Inclusive Education

After reviewing the provincial and territorial documents, you will have noticed that an **individual education plan (IEP)** is used across Canada as an administrative structure to help individual teachers and **in-school teams** to plan an exceptional student's program. The IEP is a formal document described in provincial legislation. Although the name may vary slightly (e.g., individual program plan or special education plan), the intent is similar. Goals are laid out, and the means of reaching those goals are described—usually as accommodations (change how things are taught), modifications (change what is taught), or alternate expectations (change what is taught to expectations outside the school curriculum). These have already been described in this chapter. The development of an IEP usually requires that you, as the classroom teacher, participate on an in-school or **school-based team** with a special educator, an administrator, the child's parent or guardian, and others who can contribute to the problem solving involved in developing a plan to help this student learn successfully. Chapter 2 includes a full description and many examples to help you to become familiar with this process. Often the IEP process involves designating the student as an exceptional or special needs student (identifying that the student has learning disabilities or documenting the extent and implications of the student's hearing loss, for example) and may also involve making recommendations for the student's placement, that is, where the services and changes in program will be delivered to the student.

You can see from the discussions in this chapter that we aspire in Canada to have schools that embrace inclusion for all students, including exceptional students. The means for accomplishing these goals include universal design for learning, differentiated instruction, and regular progress monitoring—in contexts taught by regular classroom teachers, complemented by opportunities for more intense instruction in a timely fashion. However, educators and researchers are experiencing tension between such nimble, responsive teaching and assessment consisting of continuous progress monitoring and tiered, preventive interventions beginning as soon as students begin to struggle (UDL and DI), on the one hand, and, on the other hand, our traditional, laborious process of school-based team meetings, IEP development, and intensive funding supports based on verified student characteristics (Philpott & Dibbon, 2007). It appears that yet again, or still, "change in exceptional education is everywhere" (Hutchinson, 2007), and yet, for many exceptional students and their families, "everything remains the same." Our aspirations are growing and remain beyond our grasp. The expectations are high, our classrooms and our society are diverse; inclusion is the driving social value. These dilemmas—that accompany legislating universal design, differentiation, and inclusion alongside identification and labelling in IEPs—require our best problem solving and teamwork informed by research and goodwill. As educators in Canada in the early twenty-first century, we must embrace these challenges.

How We Got Here: Recent Highlights in the Development of Inclusive Education in Canada

Over the past few decades, inclusive education has evolved rapidly (for a better understanding of this evolution within a broad social context, see Table 1.1). From the 1800s to 1950, there was no obligation for schools to educate students with disabilities.

TABLE 1.1 EVOLUTION TOWARD INCLUSION

1800s: Establishing a Country, Establishing Institutions	
Developments in Canadian Society	**Developments in Education**
1815–50 The Great Migration brings thousands of new settlers to Upper and Lower Canada	1830–60 Orphanages open in Halifax, Montreal, Kingston, and Toronto
1850s Railway building joins the colonies together	1831–86 Schools for blind and deaf children open in Québec, Ontario, Nova Scotia, and Manitoba
1867 Confederation; education becomes a provincial responsibility	1893 Children's Aid Societies start in Ontario

1900–50: Change and Growth	
Developments in Canadian Society	**Developments in Education**
1914–18 First World War, followed by the economic boom of the 1920s and the Great Depression of the 1930s	By the 1920s, special education classes are offered in urban elementary schools
1939–45 Second World War increases Canada's international reputation	By 1923, summer courses for teachers of special classes are available
1945 Fifty-one nations meet to establish the United Nations, which has among its goals the promotion of equality among peoples	1940s Residential institutions are "home" to many people with disabilities (e.g., Weyburn, SK; Smiths Falls, ON); small groups of parents of children with what was then called mental retardation form local associations for mutual support

1950–70: The Impact of the Baby Boom Generation	
Developments in Canadian Society	**Developments in Education**
1950s Baby boomers and immigrant families cause population increases, cultural diversity, and the construction of suburbs	Formation of the Canadian Association for Retarded Children (1958) and the Canadian Association for Children with Learning Disabilities (1963)
Cold War and *Sputnik* lead to huge developments in technology	Parent associations establish schools and developmental centres for the education of retarded children
Television brings global events into Canadian homes; youth movement for civil rights and social justice worldwide	Growth of segregated programs for gifted students and students with disabilities

(continued)

TABLE 1.1 (*continued*)

1964 Pearson government funds the Company of Young Canadians to give young activists the opportunity to work toward social change in local programs	Growth of post-secondary education: universities and community colleges

1970–80: Advocacy and Rights

Developments in Canadian Society	**Developments in Education**
1975 United Nations Declaration of the Rights of Disabled Persons	1970 *One Million Children* (Roberts & Lazure) advocates for the integration of exceptional children and instruction based on individual learning needs; in 1971 *Standards for Education of Exceptional Children in Canada* (Hardy et al.) sparks teacher education on exceptional children at Canadian universities
1977 *Canadian Human Rights Act*	1977 Deinstitutionalization became the priority of the Canadian Association for the Mentally Retarded
12 April 1980 Terry Fox begins his "Marathon of Hope" to promote public awareness of the abilities of persons with disabilities and to raise funds for cancer research	1978 Alberta's Supreme Court rules that the Lamont County school board must accommodate the physical and educational needs of Shelley Carrière, a student with cerebral palsy; in 1979 Bill 188 (*An Act to Provide for the Rights of Handicapped Persons*) was advanced and then withdrawn in Ontario in response to pressure from a coalition of disability groups, who described it as "separate and unequal"
1981 United Nations Year of the Disabled	1980 Bill 82 in Ontario guarantees the right of all exceptional students to an appropriate education with a new funding model
1981 Demonstrations by Canadians with disabilities on Parliament Hill to demand rights for people with disabilities in the Charter	Early 1980s Provinces develop IEPs; Ontario phases in the IPRC
21 March 1985 Rick Hansen sets out on his "Man in Motion" tour of thirty-four countries to raise money for spinal cord research	Mid-1980s Integration is adopted as the prevailing approach to educating exceptional students
1988 People with mental disabilities receive the right to vote	Late 1980s Educational reviews begin across Canada, including reviews of special education

1990s: Inclusion, Reform, and Challenges

Developments in Canadian Society	**Developments in Education**
Cutbacks in government funding to schools, social services, and universities	Parents demand inclusion in regular classroom settings
August 1994 First inclusive Commonwealth Games, hosted by Victoria, British Columbia	10 October 1996 Supreme Court of Canada rules that Emily Eaton receive appropriate education to meet her individual needs in a segregated setting, reversing an earlier decision of a lower court
1997 Release of the Report of the Royal Commission on Aboriginal Peoples	Reviews and changes in exceptional education policies across Canada make inclusion the dominant policy

2000–2015: Social Inclusion and Differentiated Classrooms

Developments in Canadian Society	**Developments in Education**
2002 Release of the Laidlaw Foundation's *Working Papers Series on Social Inclusion*	2005 Ontario Ministry of Education releases *Education for All*, promoting differentiated instruction
2006 Convention on the Rights of Persons with Disabilities is adopted by the United Nations	2006 SET-BC, which focuses on technology in classrooms, begins initiative to advance practice in BC based on Universal Design for Learning
2008 Exhibit at the Royal Ontario Museum titled Out from Under: Disability, History, and Things to Remember	Large growth continues in every province in numbers of students identified with ASD
2008 Canadian government formally apologizes to Aboriginal peoples for treatment during era of residential schools	Increasing emphasis on curriculum development and on policy frameworks for Aboriginal education, including Manitoba's (2007) *Curriculum Framework of Outcomes for Aboriginal Languages and Culture*, kindergarten to grade 12

During the 1950s, Canadian parents began schools for children with intellectual disabilities. The Canadian Association for Retarded Children was formed in 1958, and the Learning Disabilities Association of Canada in 1963. Between 1950 and 1970, parents lobbied hard, and many school districts developed segregated programs for exceptional students.

By 1970, researchers and parents in North America were beginning to question a special education system that paralleled regular education. In the United States, Dunn (1968) published an influential paper asking whether the ends (what was learned) justified the means (separate education for students by category of disability). In 1970 the first of a series of reports—the CELDIC report, *One Million Children* (Roberts & Lazure, 1970)—was released in Canada. Radical for 1970, it recommended integration, the right to free public education, and teaching based on an exceptional child's learning needs rather than on the category of exceptionality. In 1971 the SEECC report, *Standards for Education of Exceptional Children in Canada,* recommended that universities include courses about exceptional children in teacher education (Hardy et al., 1971). Within a few years, such courses were being taught to classroom teachers in many provinces.

During the 1970s, a number of influential developments took place in the United States. In 1972, the federal courts ordered the Commonwealth of Pennsylvania and the District of Columbia to provide free public education to students with disabilities in the same schools as children without disabilities. In 1975, Congress enacted a federal special education law entitled *Education of All Handicapped Children Act,* better known as Public Law (PL) 94-142. The Act governed how students with disabilities were educated in publicly funded schools. The law required that free appropriate public education be made available to all students with disabilities and required procedural safeguards so that students with disabilities could challenge schools that did not live up to the provisions of the law.

Cases also began to appear in the Canadian courts. In 1978, an Alberta Supreme Court decision ordered the Lamont County school board to widen doors, build a ramp, and educate Shelley Carrière, a student with cerebral palsy, in her community school. In 1980, the *Ontario Education Act* was amended to recognize the rights of students with disabilities to receive an appropriate education at public expense, and to permit parents to appeal both the identification of their child as exceptional and the placement of their child.

In 1981, with the imminent possibility of people with disabilities being overlooked in the *Canadian Charter of Rights and Freedoms,* people with disabilities and parents of children with disabilities advocated vigorously, including protesting on Parliament Hill and taking their case to *Maclean's* magazine. The Charter was passed in 1982, and section 15, which named persons with disabilities as an equity group, came into force in 1985. Since then, several court cases have been heard, mainly disputing a school district's decision to place a student with a severe disability in a segregated special education classroom. In 1991, in a case in Québec (*Re: David M. and Commission scolaire Saint-Jean-sur-Richelieu*), a 9-year-old boy was found to be the victim of direct and indirect discrimination under the Québec Charter. The school district was ordered to integrate him into a regular classroom with the necessary adaptations and support (Smith, 1992).

In the 1995 case *Eaton v. Brant County Board of Education*, the Ontario Court of Appeal stated: "unless the parents of a child who has been identified as exceptional by reason of a physical or mental disability consent to the placement of that child in a segregated environment, the school board must provide a place-ment that is the least exclusionary from the mainstream and still reasonably capable of meeting the child's special needs" (*Eaton v. Brant Board of Education,* 1995, pp. 33–34).

Then in 1996, the Supreme Court of Canada overturned the Ontario Court of Appeal's ruling on this case. While many saw this decision as a major setback for the equity of people with disabilities, Lepofsky (1996, p. 393), in a lengthy analysis, dis-agreed. Lepofsky argued that the Supreme Court's approach rested on the founda-tion that the decision to remove a child from an integrated setting (always the preferred setting) must be governed solely by an individualized, case-specific con-sideration of what is in the best interests of that child. Such a decision cannot be made simply because of the existence of a disability.

In Canada, we have reached our commitment to inclusive education through a complex set of circumstances, including United Nations proclamations; the repatria-tion of our constitution during the International Year of the Disabled; protests, innovative legislation and human rights codes; and our idealistic notions of a multi-cultural, diverse, and equitable society. Canadian heroes and ordinary people with disabilities alike have advocated for themselves and raised public awareness that people with disabilities are "People First." When we choose to teach in Canada in the first decades of the twenty-first century, we are choosing to teach in inclusive schools in a society committed to inclusion. Although our reach exceeds our grasp, Canadian classrooms include exceptional learners, and we must *embrace* this chal-lenge and *value* all our students.

Community and Inclusive Education

There are a number of ways in which community is important to inclusive educa-tion. A **community** is a group of people who have shared interests and who mutually pursue the common good. Usually community members share an acceptance of group standards and a sense of identification with the group (Dewey, 1916; McCaleb, 1995). A community ensures that students are well known and that they are encouraged by adults who care about them. Canadian educators Faye Brownlie and Judith King of British Columbia (2000) demonstrate how schools provide the advantage of a community; we can move beyond being a col-lection of individuals looking out for their individual rights to being a welcoming community that works, learns, and experiences together. As discussed earlier, inclusion involves the acceptance and participation of all, a way of being together rather than a place, and inclusive classrooms ought to be communities. There are many ways that we can act on our belief that community is important. For example, we can conduct classroom meetings and develop what Katz (2012) describes as a democratic classroom in her three-block model of UDL. We can use a sharing chair when teaching younger children, teach active listening, pro-vide students with choices, and build mentoring relationships with older students (Hall, 2014). High school practices that facilitate community and social connect-edness include teachers' adopting shared approaches to teaching, focusing on stu-dent well-being, and using technology for community building (Bower et al., 2015). Ensuring that everyone experiences belonging in our classrooms and schools and that everyone learns to be part of a diverse community is an import-ant responsibility of public education in a democracy.

Further Reading

Learn more about inclusive edu-cation in many parts of the world:

India—Sharma, U., & Das, A. (2015). Inclusive education in India: Past, present and future. *Support for Learning, 30*(1), 55–68.

Australia—Anderson, J., & Boyle, C. (2015). Inclusive education in Australia: Rhetoric, reality and the road ahead. *Support for Learning, 30*(1), 4–22.

Asia-Pacific Region (Hong King, Malaysia, New Zealand, Thailand)—Bevan-Brown, J., Heung, V., Jelas, Z., & Phongaksom, S. (2014). Why is inclusive education important to my country? *International Journal of Inclu-sive Education, 18*(10), 1064–1068.

Europe (Austria, Czech Republic, Ireland, Spain)—Smyth, F. et al. (2014). Inclusive education in prog-ress: Policy evolution in four European countries. *European Journal of Special Needs, 29*(4), 433–445.

Terry Fox

Newscom

Terry Fox is a Canadian hero. When Canadians were asked to name their heroes in 1999, Terry Fox was voted Canada's Greatest Hero. This young man won Canadians' admiration and raised our awareness of people with disabilities. Fox, from Coquitlam, BC, was only 19 years old when he lost his right leg to cancer in 1977. While he was recovering, he dreamed of inspiring others with cancer and raising money to fight the disease.

In April 1980 Fox set out from St. John's, Newfoundland, to run across Canada on a "Marathon of Hope." All summer he ran forty kilometres a day, ignoring the pain, heading for the Pacific Ocean. Newspaper reporters described his run as "lift, hop, lift, hop, lift, hop" because he rocked back and forth between his left leg and his prosthetic right leg. Television cameras reported his daily progress and all of Canada began to watch. Thousands lined the streets as he passed through towns and cities. Money for cancer research poured in. Then in September, after running 5300 kilometres and raising $2 million, Terry Fox stopped running on the north shore of Lake Superior. The cancer had returned; Fox died less than a year later.

Canadians were inspired by Terry Fox and his Marathon of Hope. In the months following the end of his run, they donated $25 million for cancer research. Every fall people all over the world hold marathons in his name to raise funds, and annually thousands visit the memorial marking the site where he halted his run. Since 1980 athletes with disabilities have become much more prominent in our communities and in the news, but Terry Fox was one of the first and has become a Canadian hero.

Who Are Exceptional Learners?

Earlier we defined exceptional learners as both students who are gifted and students with disabilities. There are many definitions of disability. The World Health Organization (WHO) (1980) set out three definitions related to disability that focus on interactions with the environment: *impairment, disability,* and *handicap.* Later WHO replaced these terms with the neutral terms of *body, activities,* and *participation* in the International Classification of Functioning (ICF) (2010). While some provinces refer to students with special needs, I have chosen to use *exceptional students* and *exceptionalities,* more neutral terms.

This section contains brief descriptions of exceptionalities. These generic descriptions will not apply to all students with these exceptionalities, and they should be quickly replaced by your description focusing on the most relevant characteristics of an individual learner. Exceptional learners are not their exceptionalities; rather, they are children and adolescents with exceptionalities. That is why we use person-first language (see Table 1.2).

Put into Practice

Go to the website of the Canadian Association for Community Living (www.cacl.ca) and investigate the section of their website called 10 Steps to Inclusive Communities. In a group, divide the list up so each person is responsible for becoming an expert on one or two sections. Inform each other about what you have learned on the website generally and in your own section(s) especially.

TABLE 1.2 USING PERSON-FIRST LANGUAGE: STUDENTS WITH DISABILITIES

Terminology Guide Concerning Persons with Disabilities

Do not use or say	Do use or say
The blind; visually impaired	Person who is blind; person with a visual impairment
Confined to a wheelchair; wheelchair-bound	Person who uses a wheelchair; wheelchair user
Crippled	Person with a disability; person who has a spinal cord injury; etc.
The deaf	Person who is deaf; when referring to the entire deaf population and their culture, one can use "the Deaf"
The hearing impaired	Person who is hard of hearing
Epileptic	Person who has epilepsy
Fit	Seizure
The handicapped	Person with a disability
Insane; mentally diseased	Person with a mental health disability; person who has schizophrenia; person who has depression; etc.
Mentally retarded	Person with an intellectual disability
Normal	Person who is not disabled
Physically challenged	Person with a physical disability

Source: Based on Human Resources and Social Development Canada's website, *A Way with Words and Images* (www.hrsdc.gc.ca/en/disability_issues/reports/way_with_words/index.shtml).

The box entitled Theory and Research Highlights from Educational Psychology introduces you to the concept of executive function, which refers to cognitive processes responsible for higher-level action control. These include our capacity to plan, display self-control, follow multistep directions even when interrupted, stay focused despite distractions, and multitask. These functions are important for academic learning in school, where students learn in groups in social contexts. Executive function begins developing at an early age and continues to increase into the adult years; executive function difficulties are characteristic of students with many exceptionalities during childhood and adolescence.

Cross-Reference
Chapters 3, 4, and 5 provide detailed information about the exceptionalities discussed in this chapter.

Descriptions of Exceptional Students

STUDENTS WHO ARE GIFTED OR DEVELOPMENTALLY ADVANCED

Students who are **gifted** show exceptionally high abilities in one or several areas, including specific academic subjects, overall intellect, leadership, creativity, or the arts. Gurjit, described in the opening of this chapter, is gifted; she is eager to learn, sometimes reaches the outcomes for a unit before it has begun, and learns quickly.

STUDENTS WITH LEARNING DISABILITIES

Students with **learning disabilities (LD)** have lower achievement than one would expect and dysfunctions in processing information. They may have disabilities in reading, writing, or arithmetic calculations. LD is often defined as a discrepancy between ability and achievement despite average or above-average intelligence, although there is controversy about this means of defining LD. Learning disabilities

Weblinks

THE LEARNING DISABILITIES ASSOCIATION OF CANADA
www.ldac-acta.ca

THE LEARNING DISABILITIES ASSOCIATION OF ONTARIO
www.ldao.ca

CHILDREN AND ADULTS WITH ADD (CHADD CANADA, INC.)
www.chaddcanada.com

are not a result of another disabling condition or of socio-economic disadvantage. Ben, described at the beginning of this chapter, has a learning disability with difficulties in reading comprehension and organization.

STUDENTS WITH ATTENTION DEFICIT HYPERACTIVITY DISORDER

Students with **attention deficit hyperactivity disorder (ADHD)** show a persistent pattern of inattention and impulsiveness or of hyperactivity or of both, and this hinders their social, academic, and vocational success. ADHD is usually identified by physicians, and students with this exceptionality may take medications to help them focus their attention and to make them more responsive to interventions.

> **Cross-Reference**
> Chapter 3 has information about medications prescribed to students with ADHD. Read about the potential benefits and side effects so you can ask questions about this common practice.

THEORY AND RESEARCH HIGHLIGHTS FROM

EDUCATIONAL PSYCHOLOGY

The Development of Executive Function and Its Role in Learning at School

How often do you find yourself switching your attention from the assignment you are working on to your friend (or family member) who has just entered the room, only to return to the assignment and pick up where you left off? And do you recall the last time you took a deep breath and talked to the person next to you in line instead of criticizing the lone cashier trying to check out everyone's purchases? Have you recently had to remember a page number, telephone number, or address until you could enter it into your phone or jot it down for future reference? All of these are examples of occasions when you have used executive function. While there are limits to our abilities to multitask, display self-control, or remember relevant information, we use these executive functions in our daily life in order to succeed at home, work, and school.

The concept of executive function refers to cognitive processes responsible for higher-level action control—directing, connecting, and organizing information in the brain (Blasco et al., 2014). These include our capacity to plan, display self-control, follow multistep directions even when interrupted, stay focused despite distractions, and multitask. As you can understand, all of these functions are important for academic learning in school, which usually takes place in groups within social contexts with a small number of adults and a large number of students. Recent research suggests that executive function begins developing at a very early age and continues to increase into the adult years; as well, research points to executive function difficulties as characteristic of students with many exceptionalities—both during childhood and adolescence.

The Center on the Developing Child (at Harvard University) describes executive function as "the brain's air traffic control system" at

a busy airport, managing the arrivals and departures of many planes on multiple runways. Research on executive function (EF) at the centre and at other universities and hospitals is showing that:

1. EF skills are critical "building blocks" for early development of cognitive and social capacities;

2. How EF unfolds in any individual is affected by differences in the nature and pace of their "developmental trajectories," and if they experience significant adversity (e.g., neglect or abuse), EF can be affected; and

3. Interventions that support development of specific executive functions are beginning to show effectiveness.

The three executive functions that have received the greatest attention are working memory, inhibitory control, and cognitive flexibility. Working memory in adults refers to our ability to remember many tasks, rules, and strategies for the many different situations in which we participate. By contrast, 3 year olds can hold in mind two rules (e.g., red cards go here, blue cards go there) and act on the basis of these rules. But if you suddenly change the rules, they will probably follow the initial rules.

Inhibitory control in adults refers to consistent self-control that is appropriate to the situation, while adolescents (10 to 18 years) continue to develop the flexibility required to decide what to pay attention to (for example, road signs and pedestrians while driving, rather than billboards for fast-food restaurants).

Cognitive flexibility in adults refers to their ability to revise their plans and accompanying actions when the circumstances change. Teens 10 to 12 years old are developing cognitive flexibility and can

(continued)

(continued)

adapt to changing rules, so they recognize, for example, that it is acceptable to use a louder voice on the schoolyard than in the classroom (that is, if you have taught this as the expected behaviour).

Think about the brief descriptions of exceptional students provided in this chapter and consider how even the limited characteristics provided suggest that many exceptionalities are characterized by challenges in executive function. Think about the potential role EF might play in their classroom challenges and strengths. Return to this Theory and Research box after reading Chapters 3, 4, and 5, where you will learn much fuller information about students with exceptionalities and about how we can teach them effectively.

Sources consulted:

Center on the Developing Child at Harvard University. (2011). *Building the brain's "air traffic control" system: How early experiences shape the development of executive function*. Working Paper No. 11. (www.developingchild.harvard.edu).

Perner, J., & Lang, B. (1999). Development of theory of mind and executive control. *Trends in Cognitive Science, 3*(9), 337–344.

Best, J.R., Miller, P.H., & Naglieri, J. (2011). Relations between executive function and academic achievement from ages 5 to 17 in a large representative national sample. *Learning and Individual Differences, 21,* 327–336.

Blasco, P., Saxton, S., & Gerrie, M. (2014). The little brain that could: Understanding executive function in early childhood. *Young Exceptional Children, 17*(3), 3–18.

STUDENTS WITH BEHAVIOUR AND EMOTIONAL EXCEPTIONALITIES

Students who show behaviour that varies markedly and chronically from the accepted norm and that interferes with the student's own learning and the learning of others are usually described by educators as having an **emotional or behaviour exceptionality**. Increasingly they are seen as within the fourth tier within models of school-based **mental health**. At the first three tiers, the emphasis is on enhancing strengths of all students, reducing risk factors for all students, and targeting students with recognized risk factors. The fourth tier consists of treatment interventions for students experiencing mental health problems or diagnosable disorders.

STUDENTS WITH INTELLECTUAL DISABILITIES: MILD AND SEVERE

Students with **intellectual disabilities (ID)** develop cognitive abilities and adaptive behaviours at a much slower rate than do their peers, which results in significant limitations in these areas. Despite these limitations, they can often participate in their communities and neighbourhood schools, and can lead productive adult lives if supported in employment. There are mild levels of intellectual disabilities (usually called MID for mild intellectual disabilities) and severe levels of intellectual disabilities (sometimes called developmental disabilities [DD] or severe cognitive disabilities).

STUDENTS WITH AN AUTISM SPECTRUM DISORDER

Autism spectrum disorder (ASD) is the current name in the new, fifth edition of *Diagnostic and Statistical Manual of Mental Disorders* (American Psychiatric Association [APA], 2013) for four previously separate disorders: **autistic disorder**, **Asperger's disorder or Asperger's syndrome (AS)**, childhood disintegrative disorder, and pervasive developmental disorder not otherwise specified (PDDNOS). *DSM-5* describes people with ASD as having social communication and social interaction deficits. Additionally, they demonstrate restrictive repetitive behaviours, interests, and activities (RRBs). Combining four disorders into one continuum has been controversial: two contentious issues have arisen. First, there has been much discussion about whether children previously diagnosed under the criteria for *DSM-IV* would still be

Cross-Reference
Chapter 10 focuses on promoting social relationships and handling challenging behaviours. It will help you to respond to students with behaviour exceptionalities.

Further Reading

A first-person account of life with intellectual disabilities:

Kingsley, J., & Levitz, M. (2007). *Count us in: Growing up with Down syndrome* (2nd ed.). New York, NY: Mariner Books (A Harvest Book).

Family members' accounts of life with a child with intellectual disabilities:

Palmer, G. (2005). *Adventures in the mainstream: Coming of age with Down syndrome*. Bethesda, MD: Woodbine House.

Hemminger, D. (2014). *Reflections from Holland: A new mother's journey with Down syndrome*. (available as an e-book from Amazon Digital services)

diagnosed under the criteria for *DSM-5*. Second, there are questions about the lack of robust data to support one autism continuum, and about the differences between autistic disorder and Asperger's disorder. Given that there are many children and adolescents in schools who have been diagnosed with Asperger syndrome or disorder, I include it.

STUDENTS WITH COMMUNICATION DISORDERS (SPEECH AND LANGUAGE)

Students with **speech and language disorders** may have a speech impairment (e.g., lisp or stutter) or an impairment in expressive or receptive language. Students with other disabilities (e.g., autistic disorder) may also receive services to enhance communication.

STUDENTS WHO ARE HARD OF HEARING AND STUDENTS WHO ARE DEAF

Students who are **hard of hearing** or **deaf** have partial or complete hearing loss that interferes with the acquisition and maintenance of the auditory skills necessary to develop speech and oral language. They depend on visual sources of information to supplement or replace hearing.

STUDENTS WITH VISUAL IMPAIRMENTS AND STUDENTS WHO ARE BLIND

Students with **visual impairments** or who are **blind** have partial or complete loss of sight and depend on auditory and tactile sources of information to supplement or replace sight.

STUDENTS WITH PHYSICAL DISABILITIES AND CHRONIC HEALTH CONDITIONS

Physical disabilities are a range of conditions restricting physical movement or motor abilities as a result of nervous system impairment, musculoskeletal conditions, or chronic **medical conditions**. I have included descriptions for a number of these, because each is slightly different in cause, characteristics, and implications for the classroom.

Students with Cerebral Palsy. **Cerebral palsy** is a group of disorders impairing body movement and muscle coordination as a result of an interference in messages between the brain and the body (nervous system impairment).

Students with Spina Bifida. **Spina bifida** is a condition developed prenatally that disturbs proper development of the vertebrae or spinal cord and results in varying degrees of damage to the spinal cord and nervous system (nervous system impairment).

Students with Epilepsy. **Epilepsy** is a neurological disorder that occasionally produces brief disturbances in normal electrical functions in the brain that lead to sudden, brief seizures. Seizures vary in nature and intensity from person to person (nervous system impairment).

Put into Practice

Many people who are deaf view themselves as belonging to the Deaf culture and see themselves as different but not disabled. Find resources about Deaf culture and about American Sign Language (ASL), the language of Deaf culture.

Cross-Reference

Chapter 4 includes information on physical disabilities and chronic health conditions, along with websites about medical aspects and implications for mobility and classroom learning.

Newscom

Roisin Hartnett was the first blind page to serve in Ontario's legislature.

Students with Tourette Syndrome. Students with **Tourette syndrome** have a neurological disorder involving motor tics and uncontrollable vocal sounds or inappropriate words. These are often accompanied by obsessions and hyperactivity (nervous system impairment).

Students with Brain Injury (BI). Students with **brain injury** have sustained damage to their brain tissue, most often as a result of a blow to the head or an accident. Brain injury can cause physical difficulties (such as paralysis) and cognitive problems (including memory loss). The nature of school challenges varies widely, depending on the extent and location of the brain injury (nervous system impairment).

Students with Fetal Alcohol Spectrum Disorders. Students with **fetal alcohol spectrum disorders (FASD)** have physical and physiological abnormalities caused by prenatal exposure to alcohol. Children with FASD have developmental delays and central nervous dysfunction, and often show a characteristic pattern of facial features. They experience learning and behavioural challenges in school (nervous system impairment).

Students with Muscular Dystrophy. **Muscular dystrophy (MD)** is a group of muscle disorders characterized by progressive weakness and wasting away of the voluntary muscles that control body movement (musculoskeletal condition).

Students with Juvenile Arthritis. **Juvenile arthritis (JA)** is a chronic arthritic condition with continuous inflammation of one or more joints. Students report stiffness and pain, and the eyes can become involved (musculoskeletal condition).

Students with Diabetes. Students with **diabetes** have a condition of the pancreas that results in failure to produce a sufficient amount of the hormone insulin, required for proper sugar absorption in the body. They may have restrictions on their physical activity at school (health condition).

Students with Allergies. Students with **allergies** have an abnormal reaction to a normal substance (such as peanuts). Those with life-threatening allergies usually carry an EpiPen to provide an injection and need to be taken to the hospital immediately if they go into anaphylaxis (health condition).

Students with Asthma. Students with **asthma** experience obstructed airways that hinder the flow of air into and out of the lungs. An attack—characterized by persistent wheezing, chest tightness, and excess phlegm—can be life threatening and requires that the student be rushed to hospital (health condition).

Students with Cystic Fibrosis. **Cystic fibrosis (CF)** causes increasingly severe respiratory problems and often involves extreme difficulty in digesting nutrients from food. Students may have to do breathing exercises during school to clear their lungs and air passages (health condition).

Students with Crohn's and Colitis. **Crohn's disease (CD)** and **ulcerative colitis (UC)** are the two forms of inflammatory bowel disease (IBD). Both involve inflammation in specific parts of the gastrointestinal (GI) tract. Symptoms that affect life at school include abdominal pain, frequent trips to the bathroom with little warning, weight loss, and lack of energy (health conditions).

Students with Cancer or Leukaemia. **Cancer** is characterized by uncontrolled division of cells and the ability of these to spread; **leukaemia** is a type of cancer that forms in the bone marrow, causing abnormal white blood cell development. Students may miss periods of school for treatment. Yet they often return to school as soon as possible because school may play a normalizing role in a young life suddenly full of traumatic medical experiences, pain, and fear of the unknown (health conditions).

Using the ADAPT Strategy for Adapting Teaching to Include Exceptional Learners

This chapter introduces you to a systematic strategy called **ADAPT**, for adapting or differentiating teaching to include exceptional learners. This strategy is similar to others that serve the same purpose, but it includes considering the perspectives of those influenced by the decision to ADAPT and the consequences for them of the adaptation. This approach is elaborated on throughout the text with many examples, especially in Chapters 3, 4, 5, 8, and 9. This strategy recognizes that both the characteristics of the student (**strengths** *and* **needs**) and the demands of the classroom environment have to be considered when devising adaptations.

The ADAPT strategy for adapting teaching to include exceptional learners has the following five steps:

- Step 1: **A**ccounts of students' strengths and needs
- Step 2: **D**emands of the classroom on students
- Step 3: **A**daptations
- Step 4: **P**erspectives and consequences
- Step 5: **T**each and assess the match

These five steps constitute a procedure that you can use in both elementary and secondary classrooms with learners who have a variety of exceptionalities.

Step 1: Accounts of Students' Strengths and Needs

This first step requires that you know each exceptional student well. Start with the student's confidential file—it usually contains the IEP, assessment reports, teachers' anecdotal comments, and relevant medical information. It is your responsibility to be familiar with this file from the first day the student is a member of your class. Do not fear that the file will prejudice you. You are a professional and have to learn to be above being influenced in this way. Your observations will quickly complement the views of others. The IEP includes specific statements of strengths and needs, usually in three general areas: social, emotional, and behavioural; physical; and academic.

Social, emotional, and behavioural strengths may include carrying on a conversation with peers, turn-taking in a group activity, controlling anger, or being highly motivated to improve. You can use a strength such as high motivation to help a student focus on meeting personal goals. Conversely, social, emotional, and behavioural needs could mean that a student requires significant instruction and support because she taunts peers or cries when frustrated by academic tasks.

Physical strengths and weaknesses include motor skills, neurological functioning, and vision. A student may have strong mobility skills in spite of low vision and may be able to move around the school independently; however, her low vision may mean she needs significant instruction or adaptation to read, using a communication aid such as Braille or large print.

Academic strengths and weaknesses include the basic skills of reading, mathematics, and so forth. They also include strategies for studying and problem solving.

What do you think?

The ADAPT strategy and other similar strategies have most often been used for carrying out DI, rather than UDL. Why do you think this is the case? How could you use ADAPT to help with adopting UDL as your approach to curriculum planning?

Cross-Reference
Chapter 8 focuses on differentiating teaching, and Chapter 9 focuses on adapting assessment.

Cross-Reference
In Chapter 2 you will find strengths and needs as described in a student's IEP. The IEP will supplement your own observations of a student.

Students can demonstrate strengths in completing calculations (with or without a calculator), organizing themselves, and answering questions orally. Student needs can include requiring significant instruction and support to develop beginning reading, comprehend a textbook, or solve word problems in mathematics.

The IEP is a working document, but it is usually confidential and therefore should not be left where students can access it. Some teachers prepare a brief description of the strengths and needs of each exceptional student and tape it into their agenda. Focus on strengths and needs that are most relevant for your classroom environment and for the way you teach.

Step 2: Demands of the Classroom on Students

Next, consider the social, emotional, and behavioural demands of your classroom. Do students learn individually or are they working with peers most of the time? A student with attention difficulties may find it hard to focus on and remember the steps in complex assignments without peer support but may also be distracted by learning groups that are never really quiet. How long is the lecture or information-sharing section at the beginning of the class, and is it reasonable to expect a student with behavioural challenges to listen for that amount of time? Do you model positive interactions with and respect for all students?

When you consider physical demands, think about the frequency with which you move the furniture in the classroom. Could changes be dangerous to anyone—especially to a student who is blind or in a wheelchair? Do you rely on projecting images, and might some students experience difficulty seeing the projected images from where they sit in the classroom? What are the demands of your physical education classes, and could they endanger a student with asthma?

The academic demands of the classroom are manifested in the instructional materials you use, including textbooks, audiovisual aids, and manipulative devices. Do all of the children in grade 1 have the same basal readers, or do some have readers, others chapter books, and others instruction to learn the sounds in words, followed by reading of highly predictable rhyming books?

The academic demands of the classroom are also shown in your assessment and evaluation methods. Written reports, oral reports, drawings, three-dimensional models, and reports produced on iPads represent different forms of assessment. Do you look for means of assessment that enable exceptional learners to show what they know rather than to show their disabilities?

Step 3: Adaptations

In this step you compare a student's learning needs to the demands of the classroom and identify potential mismatches and adaptations or ways to differentiate teaching and assessment that will eliminate these mismatches. As we saw earlier, it is almost impossible to develop an account of a student's strengths and needs and to assess the demands of the classroom without thinking about adaptations that would bridge this gulf by taking advantage of the student's strengths. There are a number of ways to make adaptations, as we saw in the examples.

You can ADAPT the fundamental organization and instruction of the classroom. For example, in a secondary history class one group may read speeches made by Canadian politicians during the Second World War and articles that appeared in Canadian newspapers of the same era to study divergent views on conscription.

Students who are less competent readers may study political cartoons and view videos of historians discussing the issue of conscription. Both groups could use combinations of visual, oral, and written means to communicate their findings (with the emphasis on written communication varying between 20 and 80 percent of the assignment).

Bypassing a student's learning need is another way to ADAPT. For example, Chung has not mastered the multiplication tables. In grade 5, his teacher shows the class how to use a calculator efficiently. The teacher reminds Chung to use his calculator and to request a "booster session" if he has forgotten any procedures. Bypassing his weakness in calculations enables Chung to work on the same authentic problems as the rest of the class. A peer editor or computerized spell checker bypasses poor spelling, and Braille bypasses lack of vision. Bypass strategies minimize the impact of a disability.

Teaching students basic learning skills is also a way to ADAPT. Chung was taught two basic skills to use a calculator well: how to identify the series of operations required to solve a math problem and how to estimate the answer so he can check that his result is reasonable. Secondary teachers teach basic skills about note taking and test taking. While study skills may be an urgent need for students with LD, there are likely to be others in the class who will benefit.

Step 4: Perspectives and Consequences

Reflect critically on adaptations and consider them from many perspectives. What is your experience of the adaptation? How time-consuming is it? Whereas step 2 focuses on the demands on students, it is also important to ask at step 4: What demands does this adaptation make on you? Does it change the fundamental nature of the teaching for you? Are you likely to find it satisfying? Your point of view is important because if you are uncomfortable with an adaptation, it is unlikely that you will continue with it. You have limited time and energy, so you want to choose the simplest adaptation that is effective. To get the most return for your effort, choose adaptations whenever you can that are beneficial for many (if not all) students in your class, and choose adaptations that have demonstrated effectiveness. Validated practices are described in textbooks and in professional journals, as well as on websites.

Next, take the perspective of the exceptional student. How does or will this make the student feel? For example, does the change draw too much unwanted attention to the student, in the student's view? Is the adaptation age appropriate? Can you communicate to the student that you are "paying attention to him without drawing attention to him"? Is the return for effort worthwhile for the student? Will the student feel competent, connected to others in the classroom, or autonomous if you make him part of a well-functioning group working on a project together? If you don't consider the student's perspective, you may find yourself putting in great effort, while the student is investing little. Observe and listen to the student to understand his point of view. Ask the student, and ADAPT in a way that is respectful of the student.

There are other perspectives to consider. How does the rest of the class view the adaptation? Do they notice? Are they concerned, involved, and respectful? If you find them mocking a student because she is using a book usually associated with younger students, your adaptation may not be effective. Do other students feel ignored when you spend large amounts of time explaining assignments to one

Chris Schmidt/Getty Images

Activities that enable pairs and small groups to work co-operatively help students to learn cognitive strategies and to improve social skills.

student, or are they bored while you speak slowly to accommodate another student? How do the parents of the exceptional student view your adaptations? For example, can they see the benefits of the intense reading instruction in their child's willingness to read at home? What do other parents say to you about the changes you are making? Are they expressing concern that their child is being ignored or receiving too little of your time and attention, or are they delighted by the caring community you have created that includes students with Down syndrome in all activities? Broaden the circle of concern to think about how the community views adapting teaching for exceptional students. How can your school contribute to community acceptance of inclusion?

Consider consequences, intended and unintended. What are the consequences for the exceptional student—are participation and learning evident? Are there drawbacks? Pat, who has physical disabilities, may need more time and help to finish seasonal crafts in December. However, too much assistance may make Pat dependent, and the additional time may cause him to fall behind in math. Perhaps completing one craft well is more realistic and rewarding than asking Pat to make as many crafts as the other students. What are the consequences of the adaptation for others in the class? Do any dilemmas arise? Are some students providing too much assistance to classmates when they should be completing their own assignments? If you provide an open-ended assessment, you may be disappointed when students capable of writing an essay choose to develop a graphic representation of what they learned. Giving choice requires that we help students to know themselves and to make good choices for themselves, with an appropriate degree of challenge; otherwise we will experience unintended consequences.

Step 5: Teach and Assess the Match

Ask how well the adaptation has matched student strengths and needs to classroom demands. This analysis will help you decide whether to alter the adaptation while it takes place and whether to use the adaptation again in the future. Remember that "things take time"; it is important to persevere and give an adaptation time to be effective. If you have tried everything, you may not have stayed with any one thing long enough. You can assess the match by observing how engaged the student is, asking how she finds the changes, charting the student's marks, analyzing any errors, and talking with her parents. You will think of many other sources of information to help you decide whether to continue or to rethink an adaptation.

Evaluating Internet Resources

Internet sites are identified throughout this book. I have visited these sites and found them useful; however, websites can change. Site addresses also change, but most Web browsers will automatically forward you to the new link. Each site address was verified shortly before this book went to press. Before beginning to use any new information resource—print, online, or Web-based—take a few minutes to examine and evaluate the resource. This is particularly necessary for Web-based resources because they have

@

Weblinks

CORNELL UNIVERSITY LIBRARY: EVALUATING WEB PAGES
http://guides.library.cornell.edu/evaluating_Web_pages

MEMORIAL UNIVERSITY LIBRARIES: HOW TO EVALUATE WEB PAGES
www.library.mun.ca/researchtools/guides/doingresearch/evaluateweb

BERKELEY UNIVERSITY: EVALUATING WEB PAGES
www.lib.berkeley.edu/TeachingLib/Guides/Internet/Evaluate.html

QUEEN'S UNIVERSITY: EVALUATING WEB SOURCES
http://library.queensu.ca/inforef/tutorials/qcat/evalint.htm

not undergone the same rigorous process of review by experts in the field as have most books and articles. Barker (2005) describes a famous cartoon that was published in the *New Yorker* magazine on 5 July 1993. Two dogs are looking at a computer screen, and one says to the other, "On the internet, nobody knows you're a dog." Barker goes on to remind us that there are "some real 'dogs' out there" on the Internet amongst all the rich offerings by people exchanging ideas and sharing valuable resources.

Summary

Exceptional education refers to the adapted teaching and specialized services that thousands of exceptional students in Canada receive every day. Current practices have developed out of our history, legislation, research, and commitment to an equitable society. The dominant approach is inclusive education—with educators currently experiencing expectations that are a hybrid of our focus on IEPs for the past twenty-five years and recent demands for responsive teaching and assessment that embrace universal design for learning (UDL), differentiated instruction (DI), and response to intervention (RTI). With these expectations come dilemmas of practice for classroom teachers. Many exceptionalities are recognized across Canada, including students who are gifted and those with learning disabilities, emotional disabilities, or sensory disabilities. As a teacher, you will be expected to differentiate your teaching and your assessment for exceptional learners. The ADAPT strategy will help you meet the needs of exceptional students as you teach, and it will guide you as you learn strategies for the inclusive classroom in the upcoming chapters.

Key Terms

accommodations (p. 3)

ADAPT (p. 25)

allergies (p. 24)

alternative expectations (p. 3)

Asperger's disorder or Asperger's syndrome (AS) (p. 22)

asthma (p. 24)

attention deficit hyperactivity disorder (ADHD) (p. 21)

autism spectrum disorders (ASD) (p. 22)

autistic disorder (p. 22)

blind (p. 23)

brain injury (p. 24)

Canadian Charter of Rights and Freedoms (p. 3)

cancer (p. 24)

cerebral palsy (CP) (p. 23)

community (p. 18)

Crohn's disease (CD) (p. 24)

cystic fibrosis (CF) (p. 24)

deaf (p. 23)

diabetes (p. 24)

differentiated instruction (DI) (p. 6)

emotional or behaviour exceptionality (p. 22)

epilepsy (p. 23)

equal participation (p. 4)

equality rights (p. 4)

exceptional students (p. 3)

fetal alcohol spectrum disorder (FASD) (p. 24)

gifted (p. 20)

hard of hearing (p. 23)

Identification, Placement, and Review Committee (IPRC) (p. 12)

in-school teams (p. 14)

inclusion (p. 5)

individual education plan (IEP) (p. 14)

intellectual disabilities (ID) (p. 22)

juvenile arthritis (JA) (p. 24)

learning disabilities (LD) (p. 20)

leukemia (p. 24)

medical conditions (p. 23)

mental health (p. 22)

modifications (p. 3)

muscular dystrophy (MD) (p. 24)

needs (p. 25)

physical disabilities (p. 23)

progress monitoring (p. 8)

response to intervention (RTI) (p. 8)

school-based team (p. 14)

special education programming (p. 3)

spina bifida (p. 23)

universal design for learning (UDL) (p. 5)

speech and language disorders (p. 23)

strengths (p. 25)

visual impairment (p. 23)

Tourette syndrome (p. 24)

ulcerative colitis (UC) (p. 24)

Challenges for Reviewing Chapter 1

1. Describe to an acquaintance what social inclusion means in the context of Canadian society and why educators have a particularly important role in relation to this issue.

2. Describe what Canadians mean by inclusive education on the level of policy and on the level of practice, acknowledging that there are differences from province to province and that dilemmas accompany this ambitious approach.

3. Prepare a brochure for the various communities associated with a school with which you are familiar (including families and educators). Your topic is the highlights—as you see them—of the path to inclusive education in Canada.

Activities for Reviewing Chapter 1 with Your Peers

4. Describe the role of community in inclusion in Canadian education, and clarify what schools can do now to be inclusive of all students, not just those with disabilities. Debate with your peers the importance of ensuring that students with disabilities and gifted students feel that the intensive instruction they receive (e.g., UDL, ID, RTI) in the regular classroom and in contexts other than the regular classroom makes them feel like they belong and are part of the community. Discuss what you can do as a teacher to ensure that such strategies are not experienced as exclusion by students and their families.

5. Make a list of the various exceptionalities identified across Canada. Then make a personal list of these exceptionalities, from the most challenging for you to include to the least challenging. Identify the three that you think are most challenging for you. Given what you know about yourself as a teacher, research these three and develop an approach to teaching that makes you feel more confident about teaching students with these exceptionalities. Compare your list and your strategies with those of your peers. Make a plan for how you can implement this approach in classrooms at the level you teach.

6. Develop an example of using UDL and DI to plan teaching for a class that includes an exceptional learner. Use the ADAPT strategy implicitly or explicitly, and justify the actions it led you to. Compare your ideas with those of your peers. Translate your example into a series of classes that enable this student to succeed. Add more complexity to the classroom by describing groups of students in the class as well as individuals who need differentiated instruction. Then develop a plan for including all these students through the use of UDL and DI. Discuss with your peers how to make the plan feasible for implementation.

CHAPTER 2

The Teacher's Role in an Inclusive Classroom

Iakov Filimonov/123RF

LEARNER OBJECTIVES

After you have read this chapter, you will be able to:

1. Describe the role of the classroom teacher in identifying the needs of exceptional learners.

2. Discuss the role of the classroom teacher in carrying out pre-referral adaptations.

3. Describe collaboration with your colleagues and outline how an in-school team collaborates to meet the needs of exceptional students.

4. Describe the process of developing an individual education plan (IEP).

5. Describe your responsibilities in working with educational assistants to enhance the learning of exceptional students.

6. Discuss how you can work effectively with parents in the education of exceptional students.

JOAN HUGHES TELEPHONED SILVER BIRCH SCHOOL TO MAKE AN APPOINTMENT WITH HER SON ANDY'S GRADE 2 TEACHER, MS. SAUVÉ. Joan told Ms. Sauvé that Andy's report card—with many ratings of "needs improvement" and "is progressing with close supervision"—seemed poor for a bright young boy who likes to read, gets his friends to take part in plays, and is intensely curious. One comment sounded familiar: "Cannot listen to instructions and complete his work independently. Is easily distracted and has a difficult time organizing his work and his belongings." Joan's older son, who is now in grade 7, had brought home similar report cards and was subsequently identified as having attention deficit hyperactivity disorder. Joan suggested to Ms. Sauvé that Andy be referred to the in-school team. Having an individual education plan (IEP) had helped her older son—classroom teachers had adapted teaching and a resource teacher had taught him strategies to focus his attention and complete tasks. Ms. Sauvé was reluctant to make a referral based on a parent's request. As a new teacher, she was not certain if parents could request such referrals, or if teachers had to act on them. Ms. Sauvé kept thinking about the three students who seemed to have more difficulty learning than Andy did. She wondered, "How can I take Andy's case to the in-school team, if I don't take their cases too?" Ms. Sauvé does not want the principal to think she cannot resolve her own challenges. She is not sure how she would feel about sharing her students with a resource teacher. Ms. Sauvé doesn't know what to do.

BRENDA PIET HAS A LEARNING DISABILITY AND AN IEP. It is September and she is hoping to complete grade 11 this year. Brenda has asked her homeroom teacher, Mr. Bogg, to help her to refine and act on the brief transition plan in her IEP. She is worried about what she should do after secondary school. She has always wanted to be an architect, but she has heard recently that the local community college offers a program in architectural technology. She is wondering whether that might be a better option for her. It is not clear to Mr. Bogg how much he needs to know about all of these career options. He understands that exceptional students have a transition plan, but he does not yet know the extent of his responsibility for helping Brenda to implement hers. There are so many changes taking place in schools, and teachers are expected to take on so many new roles. Mr. Bogg used to feel that he knew what was expected of him. Now he's not so sure. He decides to consult his peers, confident that they can help him meet this challenge.

1. What is a teacher's responsibility when a parent or student asks for an assessment, a referral to an in-school team, or help in developing a transition plan?

2. What steps should Ms. Sauvé and Mr. Bogg take to respond to the requests made of them?

3. Whom should each of these teachers consult to help them decide what to do?

4. As the classroom teacher, what role might Ms. Sauvé expect to play if the in-school team decided to develop an IEP for Andy?

5. What can classroom teachers like Mr. Bogg do to advise students effectively about academic and career planning?

Introduction

"Inclusion is for life, not just for a class or a term or a year. In order to prepare our students with special needs to live within society as contributing adults, and in order to prepare society to accept them as an integral part of the community, we need to structure our educational organization to best serve all students" (Hobbs, J. (2011) Inclusive education: Lessons from Quebec's English sector. Education Canada, 51(4). [www.cea-ace.ca/education-canada/article/web-exclusive-inclusive-education-lessonsquebec%E2%80%99s-english-sector]). These words of a retired Québec teacher remind us of the important role of schools and teachers in Canadian society.

As a classroom teacher, you know your students well. In an elementary classroom you may be with them all day. In middle or secondary school, you may meet more than a hundred students each day, but you will come to know their interests, their friends, and their strengths as learners. When you encounter students in difficulty, you may wonder if they should be identified as exceptional students and have IEPs. What is your role in this process? How do teachers, parents, and educational assistants work together for students? You are introduced here to the many roles of classroom teachers in inclusive education. Following one teacher, this chapter describes the procedure used in most parts of Canada after a teacher recognizes that a student may have special education needs. The teacher's roles on the in-school special education team and in the assessment of the student are emphasized. Depending on the assessment findings and on how successfully the student's needs are met, an IEP could be developed for the student. The teacher has key responsibilities to inform and support parents as well as to direct the duties of educational assistants assigned to work with the child, the teacher, or the class.

The Role of the Classroom Teacher in Identifying Needs of Exceptional Learners

Weblinks

PROVINCIAL ASSISTIVE TECHNOLOGY SITES:

SPECIAL NEEDS ONTARIO WINDOW (SNOW)
http://snow.idrc.ocad.ca

SPECIAL EDUCATION TECHNOLOGY BRITISH COLUMBIA
www.setbc.org

NOVA SCOTIA ASSISTIVE TECHNOLOGY
http://novascotia.ca/news/release/?id=20120503001

Classroom teachers and parents usually have the most detailed knowledge about the strengths and needs of students with documented or suspected exceptionalities. Many exceptionalities, especially those that occur rarely—called low-incidence exceptionalities—are identified early in a child's life. These include developmental disabilities, blindness, deafness, and physical disabilities such as cerebral palsy. Teachers are usually informed about these exceptionalities before the students enrol in their classrooms, can read the student files and the IEPs, and are responsible for carrying out the recommended accommodations and modifications. Observing these students, and talking to previous teachers and to parents will be informative. You will also be involved in regular reviews of the IEPs of these students.

High-incidence, or more frequently occurring exceptionalities, such as learning disabilities, attention deficit hyperactivity disorder, and giftedness are most often identified after students enrol in school. All teachers need to be aware of the characteristics associated with these exceptionalities and of the key teaching strategies. Secondary teachers frequently find that these students have already been identified and have IEPs. Usually, the challenge for secondary teachers is adapting complex curricula and teaching approaches to provide accommodations or modifications. Thus, while any teacher may be involved in recognizing students' exceptionalities, elementary teachers, especially those in the primary grades, have a key role in the initial identification of exceptional students. Teachers and parents bring individual students

FIGURE 2.1 FIRST STEPS

1. Document the student's characteristics, behaviours, and needs that led to your concern (or to the parent's concern). Also document the student's strengths. Analyze the demands of your classroom. Observe the student in your classroom.

2. Re-read the student's file, test results, psychological reports, attendance records, and comments by previous teachers. Consult the protocol for identifying exceptional students.

3. Talk with the resource teacher. Share your observational notes, documentation, and ideas about how to address the student's needs.

4. Ask the resource teacher for suggestions and resources, including community associations. Plan pre-referral interventions. Inform the principal or the student's counsellor. The resource teacher may observe the student in your classroom.

5. Contact the parents to share your concerns and ideas for pre-referral interventions. Listen to the parents. The resource teacher may take part in this meeting. The protocol may recommend that you contact the parents before meeting with the resource teacher.

6. Make pre-referral adaptations or differentiations, keeping brief records of these and the student's responses. Use ADAPT and stay with any adaptation long enough for it to be effective. Reflect on your teaching. Could you be contributing to the student's learning needs? (This step may take from three weeks to three months.)

7. Analyze your records and make recommendations. Focus on the clearest examples of needs and strengths and the most effective adaptations. Look for patterns. Is there a need for further assessment or additional services?

to the attention of the principal and other professionals when they suspect that a student needs intervention beyond the regular program.

When teaching at any level, you may encounter a student who is reading below grade level and cannot get meaning from a textbook or a student who is restless and cannot focus on classroom tasks. A student's social interactions may be so different from those of the rest of the class that you suspect an emotional or behaviour disability. In the case at the beginning of this chapter, Ms. Sauvé recognized that Andy was not thriving in the classroom, but she was not confident that Andy was experiencing enough difficulty to warrant a referral. With experience, she will recognize that the first steps she can take focus on collecting relevant information to help in decision making. These steps are described in Figure 2.1.

Making Classroom Adaptations and Keeping Records

Ms. Sauvé described her meeting with Joan Hughes to the teacher assigned as her mentor. Her mentor gave Ms. Sauvé a copy of the school's protocol, similar to Figure 2.1, and encouraged her to talk with the principal and the resource teacher. Ms. Sauvé began recording the times when Andy did not follow instructions or complete assigned work. She noted when he seemed most distracted. By collecting samples of his work, she understood his organizational needs better. Ms. Sauvé also recorded what Andy did well and the times when he did not experience attention difficulties. Three weeks later, Ms. Sauvé showed the resource teacher her notes, which confirmed that most of Andy's inattentive behaviours and inability to follow instructions occurred at three times: during mathematics lessons, late in the day, and when other children were off task. She began to cue Andy during oral instructions, especially in mathematics, and to help him monitor his own behaviour. The resource teacher gave Ms. Sauvé two books to read and observed Andy in the classroom. With her own observations and the suggestions of the resource teacher, Ms. Sauvé telephoned Joan Hughes to report what she would be doing to differentiate for Andy. They agreed to meet in six weeks.

Mentoring and Induction of New Teachers

Ms. Sauvé's school had a formal mentoring program. Many early-career teachers in Canada benefit from mentoring or induction programs that link them with experienced colleagues. Ontario has the New Teacher Induction Program and Prince Edward Island has the Beginning Teachers Induction Program. The successful induction program in Prairie Valley School District in Saskatchewan involves principals and senior teachers mentoring beginning teachers for one year with clear roles for the mentors (Boggan et al., 2009). Research shows that induction programs benefit mentors as well as enhance the confidence of beginning teachers (Conway, 2006). If your school does not have a formal mentoring or induction program, look for a "soulmate" on staff who is willing to mentor you throughout your first year.

Using the ADAPT Strategy

Ms. Sauvé and the **resource teacher** made **pre-referral interventions** to meet Andy's needs by following the steps of the ADAPT strategy in Chapter 1. First, it suggests you develop an **A**ccount of the student's strengths and needs. Andy has many strengths, social and academic. For example, he likes to read (academic), and he has friends in the class (social). Andy also needs to learn to concentrate on his assigned work and complete it more independently (academic). He is easily distracted and needs to learn to ignore other children when they are off task (social). He also needs strategies for organizing his work and belongings (academic). Developing this account of strengths and needs involves informal assessment of the student's current knowledge and learning approaches.

Second, the ADAPT strategy suggests that you describe the **D**emands you make of students in the way you teach in your classroom. Ms. Sauvé read the questionnaire (shown in Figure 2.2) given to her by the resource teacher. Afterward, she wrote the following list:

- Most math classes start with a fifteen-minute "lecture" that introduces a new concept. Andy interrupts by talking, or I have to ask him to sit still.
- I expect students to work in groups, and sometimes the noise is distracting. I often have to ask Andy to move to the quiet table at the back of the room because he "clowns around" when in a group.
- During "catch-up time," the last half-hour of the day, I want the children to finish anything not completed and ask about anything they don't understand. Andy wanders around the classroom and talks to his friends.

The third step in ADAPT is making **A**daptations that help to eliminate the kinds of mismatches in Ms. Sauvé's list. After talking with the resource teacher, Ms. Sauvé reduced the introduction to her math lessons from fifteen to ten minutes.

Ms. Sauvé told Andy to check with his friend Chen that he understood all instructions. She arranged a cue with Andy—snapping her fingers was a reminder to him to "sit up straight and listen." During group work, Andy had to "work hard" or

Further Reading

For more information about mentoring and teacher induction, consult:

Ontario Ministry of Education. (2006). *Partnering for success: A resource handbook for new teachers.* Toronto: Ontario Ministry of Education.

www.edu.gov.on.ca/eng/teacher/induction.html

Prince Edward Island Department of Education. (2007). *Beginning teachers induction program handbook.* Charlottetown: PEI Ministry of Education.

Northwest Territories Education, Culture and Employment. (2008). *Teacher induction: A program for beginning teachers.* Yellowknife, NW: Education, Culture and Employment. www.newteachersnwt.ca

Kane, R. G., & Francis, A. (2013). Preparing teachers for professional learning: Is there a future for teacher education in new teacher induction? *Teacher Development, 17*(3), 362–379.

Abu Rass, R. (2012). Supporting newly recruited teachers in a unique area, the Northwest Territories in Canada. *Journal of Education for Teaching, 38*(2), 141–161.

Put into Practice

Interview a resource teacher from the panel in which you teach (elementary or secondary) about the pre-referral interventions that the teachers on that panel might make if they were in Ms. Sauvé's position.

Informal assessment includes asking a child to think aloud while solving a problem.

FIGURE 2.2 ASSESSING THE DEMANDS YOU MAKE OF STUDENTS IN YOUR CLASSROOM

Teacher _____ Classroom/Course _____

Student _____

1. For what percentage of class time do students typically listen to lectures or instructions?
2. How many pages of in-class reading do you assign to be done in a typical class?
3. How many pages of out-of-class reading do you assign to be done in a typical evening?
4. List typical classroom activities (e.g., lectures, demonstrations, labs, co-operative learning, independent work, discussion, pairs, videos, etc.).
5. How many hours of homework do you typically assign in a week?
6. Describe the typical assignment and the number of days from assignment given to assignment due.
7. Do you assign projects or long-term assignments? (If so, how much structure or guidance is given?)
8. Do you give a final test at the end of each unit?
9. How are grades assigned?
10. What are your expectations for student behaviour in class?

After answering these questions, star up to three items where you perceive a mismatch between the strengths of the named student and the demands of your classroom or course.

Source: N.L. Hutchinson, *Teaching exceptional children and adolescents: A Canadian casebook*, p. 142. Copyright © 2004 by Prentice Hall. Reprinted with permission by Pearson Canada Inc.

What do you think?

Ms. Sauvé knows that Chen can help Andy by reviewing the teacher's instructions with him to ensure that he understands. What are the advantages and disadvantages of this strategy for each boy?

move to the quiet table before Ms. Sauvé asked him to move. Andy was to consult with Ms. Sauvé at the beginning of catch-up time and to sit with a quiet friend.

Every day, Ms. Sauvé jotted informal observations about Andy on yellow sticky notes. At the end of the day, she copied all of these observations onto one page. Below is her summary for one day:

- Snapped my fingers three times in ten minutes when introducing the math activity. Andy didn't understand until I explained it one-on-one.
- Andy moved to the quiet table by himself during math. He stayed quiet for five minutes. Then he argued with the next child who came to the quiet table. Quiet table only works when Andy is there alone.
- Andy fidgeted through the Halloween story but he had great ideas for a play after Chen told him what had happened in the story.
- Andy spent catch-up time discussing the play with two children. No catching up.

The fourth step in ADAPT is to consider **P**erspectives and consequences. Ms. Sauvé wondered what the other students thought about what she was doing and what their parents would think. She thought about the effects of the changes on the other students. Generally, she thought the changes were improving the experience for other students (e.g., shorter lectures at the start of math class), but she questioned the impact on Chen of constantly explaining things to Andy, and made a note to ensure there were no negative consequences for him.

The fifth step is to **T**each and assess the match. Ms. Sauvé felt that the changes had helped Andy, but that he needed even better strategies for staying focused. Andy told her he was trying to work hard, but that he didn't know how. Ms. Sauvé was concerned that the consequences of pushing Andy to work harder would be frustration and self-criticism.

By the next parent–teacher meeting, Ms. Sauvé had recognized the need for further assessment and services. Although he had tried to follow Ms. Sauvé's cues and to monitor his own attention, Andy continued to be distracted and to distract others. This occurred mainly during math and following a disruption. Andy needed more consistent and intensive intervention to learn **self-monitoring** strategies than Ms. Sauvé could provide within her grade 2 classroom. Joan Hughes agreed. Ms. Sauvé informed the resource teacher and the principal about her observations, documentation, parent meeting, and recommendations. Together they decided it was time for more collaboration—time for a meeting of the in-school team.

Self-monitoring is a specific instance of **self-regulation**, a key concept in educational psychology. To learn more about self-regulation, see the box entitled Theory and Research Highlights from Educational Psychology.

THEORY AND RESEARCH HIGHLIGHTS FROM

EDUCATIONAL PSYCHOLOGY

Self-Regulated Learning

One of the overall goals of education is to help all children and adolescents become self-regulated learners. Our understanding of self-regulation has been advanced by the work of many Canadian researchers, including Phil Winne of Simon Fraser University (e.g., Winne, 2014), Nancy Perry of the University of British Columbia (e.g., Perry et al., 2007), Allyson Hadwin of University of Victoria (e.g., Hadwin & Jarvela, 2011), and Rob Klassen formerly of University of Alberta (e.g., Klassen et al., 2008). Self-regulated learners have a combination of academic learning skills and self-control that makes learning easier. That is, they have the *skill* and the *will* to learn. Their *skill* or knowledge about learning includes knowing about themselves, so they recognize which tasks they do best, the strategies upon which they can rely, and the contexts in which those strategies apply. They are knowledgeable about the subjects they are learning and about how they can use what they know to learn more. They recognize when a task requires them to rehearse or to make a concept map of the relationships among complex ideas (Schunk & Zimmerman, 2007). They understand that academic learning is challenging and effortful, and over time they come to use their repertoire of strategies automatically. Their *will* to learn, or motivation, is reflected in their initiative, independence, commitment, and effort. Usually they are able to sustain learning, no matter what distractions or setbacks they encounter. When they complete tasks successfully, they recognize their accomplishments, and this increases their sense of self-efficacy for similar tasks in the future.

Self-regulated learners "proactively direct their behavior or strategies to achieve self-set goals" (Cleary & Zimmerman, 2004, p. 538). Self-regulated learning emphasizes autonomy and control by the individual. Measurement of self-regulated learning has been addressed through quantitative means using surveys, interview schedules, and inventories; for example, the Learning and Strategies Study Inventory (LASSI) (Weinstein et al., 1987) and the Motivated Strategies for Learning Questionnaire (MSLQ) (Pintrich et al., 1991). These methodologies have produced correlations showing a strong relationship between self-regulated learning and academic achievement (Winne & Perry, 2000). Qualitative methods have been used to expand our understanding of self-regulated learning (Perry et al., 2007), providing rich descriptions of individuals as they engage in self-regulated learning.

Recent research suggests that gifted students demonstrate high potential for self-regulation of learning (Mooij, 2008), while many children and adolescents with disabilities require help to become more self-regulated learners. For example, Robert Klassen and colleagues (2008) reported that students with learning disabilities demonstrated less self-regulation and more procrastination than those without learning disabilities. There is also research on the self-regulation of children with intellectual disabilities (Nader-Grosbois & Lefevre, 2011), and ADHD (Barkley, 2010) as well as interventions for at-risk adolescents (e.g., Cleary et al., 2008).

Throughout this text you will find examples of instructional approaches for teaching self-regulation and learning strategies. Research

(continued)

(continued)

is beginning to demonstrate the significance of self-regulation for understanding and enhancing the learning of exceptional students.

References

Barkley, R. A. (2010). Differential diagnosis of adults with ADHD: The role of executive function and self-regulation. *The Journal of Clinical Psychiatry, 71* (7), e17–e23.

Cleary, T.J., Platten, P., & Nelson, A. (2008). Effectiveness of the Self-regulation Empowerment Program with urban high school students. *Journal of Advanced Academics, 20* (1), 70–107.

Cleary, T.J., & Zimmerman, B.J. (2004). Self-regulation empowerment program: A school-based program to enhance self-regulated and self-motivated cycles of student learning. *Psychology in the Schools, 41,* 537–550.

Hadwin, A., & Jarvela, S. (2011). Where social and self meet in the strategic regulation of learning. *Teachers College Record, 113,* 235–239.

Klassen, R.M., Krawchuk, L.L., Lynch, S.L., & Rajani, S. (2008). Procrastination and motivation of undergraduates with learning disabilities: A mixed methods inquiry. *Learning Disabilities Research and Practice, 23,* 137–147.

Mooij, T. (2008). Education and self-regulation of learning for gifted pupils: Systematic design and development. *Research Papers in Education, 23* (1), 1–19.

Nader-Grosbois, N., & Lefevre, N. (2011). Self-regulation and performance in problem-solving using physical materials or computers in children with intellectual disability. *Research in Developmental Disabilities, 32,* 1492–1505.

Perry, N.E., Hutchinson, L., & Thauberger, C. (2007). Mentoring student teachers to design and implement literacy tasks that support self-regulated reading and writing. *Reading and Writing Quarterly, 23,* 27–50.

Pintrich, P.R., Smith, D.A.F., Garcia, T., & McKeachie, W.J. (1991). *A manual for the use of the Motivated Strategies for Learning Questionnaire (MSLQ).* (Tech. Rep. No. 91-B-004). Ann Arbor, MI: University of Michigan School of Education.

Schunk, D.H., & Zimmerman, B.J. (2007). Influencing children's self-efficacy and self-regulation of reading and writing through modeling. *Reading and Writing Quarterly, 23,* 7–25.

Weinstein, C.E., Schulte, A., & Palmer, D. (1987). *LASSI: Learning and Study Strategies Inventory.* Clearwater, FL: H&H Publishing.

Winne, P.H. (2014). Issues in researching self-regulated learning as patterns of events. *Metacognition and Learning, 9* (2), 229–237.

Winne, P.H., & Perry, N.E. (2000). Measuring self-regulated learning. In M. Boekaerts, P.R. Pintrich, & M. Zeidner (Eds.), *Handbook of self-regulation* (pp. 531–566). San Diego, CA: Academic Press.

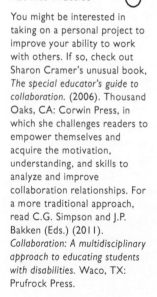

Put into Practice

You might be interested in taking on a personal project to improve your ability to work with others. If so, check out Sharon Cramer's unusual book, *The special educator's guide to collaboration.* (2006). Thousand Oaks, CA: Corwin Press, in which she challenges readers to empower themselves and acquire the motivation, understanding, and skills to analyze and improve collaboration relationships. For a more traditional approach, read C.G. Simpson and J.P. Bakken (Eds.) (2011). *Collaboration: A multidisciplinary approach to educating students with disabilities.* Waco, TX: Prufrock Press.

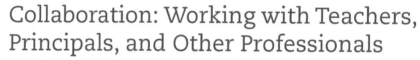

Collaboration: Working with Teachers, Principals, and Other Professionals

Critical factors in meeting the needs of exceptional students include the beliefs and actions of teachers and administrators (Jordan et al., 2010) and their willingness to collaborate (Levine & Marcus, 2010). **Collaboration** entails teachers and other professionals learning from each other's experiences and working in teams where all members feel that their contributions are valued. This involves joint planning, decision making, and problem solving directed toward a common goal. As a classroom teacher, you are central to collaboration—you are the expert on the curriculum, organization, and management of your classroom. However, you do not have to be an expert on every aspect of the exceptional student's needs. Collaboration enables you to draw on the expertise and resources of many individuals. You will work closely with resource teachers, special educators, classroom teachers, guidance counsellors, district consultants, and your principal. Other professionals you could find yourself collaborating with include speech therapists, occupational therapists, social workers, and psychologists.

Studies conducted in Canada demonstrate elements that contribute to collaboration:

- Professionals (like teachers and occupational therapists) with shared goals and clear responsibilities for intervening with exceptional students and communicating with families.

- Classroom teachers and resource teachers who maintain regular contact, build strong relationships, and communicate frequently.
- Classroom teachers and educational assistants who respect each other's contribution and communicate daily.
- Principals and resource teachers who set a positive tone for inclusion, expect collaboration to be effective, and support classroom teachers.
- Principals who provide leadership to build trusting relationships based on shared norms of safety, risk-taking, and a positive orientation to change.
- Classroom teachers who learn together to change their practices and improve teaching for students who struggle to learn.
- An in-school team that provides classroom teachers with information, effective strategies, and moral support.

Source: Based on Cranston (2011); Egodawatte et al. (2011); Ramsay (2007); Villeneuve & Hutchinson (2012); Villeneuve et al. (2013).

Cross-Reference
Chapter 8 focuses on adapting teaching, and Chapter 10 describes best practices for enhancing social relations, including collaborative learning and peer tutoring.

The Classroom Teacher and the In-School Team

To support inclusive education, school districts develop **in-school teams** that share responsibility for exceptional students, usually composed of members of the school staff and parents. Professionals from the district or community may be added when they have relevant expertise.

Suggesting a Meeting of the In-School Team

When should you suggest that the in-school team meet to discuss a student? You and the resource teacher have carried out all of the steps in the pre-referral stage (see Figure 2.1 on page 34), and you feel that the adaptations you have tried are not sufficient to meet the student's needs. That suggests that the in-school team should consider the student's case. For example, Andy engaged in more self-regulated learning, paid more attention, and completed more assignments; however, Ms. Sauvé was sure that he would benefit from more intensive teaching and practice of strategies. She recognized that she did not have time for such concentrated work with Andy.

Ms. Sauvé worked closely with the resource teacher. A resource teacher can have many titles, including learning assistance teacher, tutor, and curriculum resource teacher. Resource teachers support classroom teachers and exceptional students, usually by consulting with teachers and offering some direct services to exceptional students, either in the classroom or in the resource room (AuCoin & Porter, 2013).

If you and the resource teacher believe that the first level of intervention has not been effective, then you will approach the in-school team. In many jurisdictions you will complete a form similar to Figure 2.3 prior to making a referral to the in-school team. This is a collaborative problem-solving team that assists classroom teachers to implement instructional or management strategies and coordinate resources for students who may have special education needs. As the classroom teacher or referring teacher, you are a key member of the in-school team, along with the principal and the resource teacher. Usually the parents are invited to take part, and sometimes the student is invited. Parental consent is sought for decisions that significantly alter the education of an exceptional student. Usually in-school teams work better when they are small and focused.

Put into Practice
There are a variety of names for problem-solving teams that meet before an IEP is considered for a student. Talk with educators and principals to learn what such a team is called in your school district and how its role is described.

FIGURE 2.3 FORM TO BE COMPLETED PRIOR TO MAKING A REFERRAL TO THE SCHOOL-BASED TEAM

Student name: Student #:

Grade: Date of birth:

Reason for referral:

Student's strengths and needs:

Brief listing of colleagues consulted:

Brief description of contact with family:

Relevant classroom assessment:

Please check off and list the interventions that have been tried in the classroom:

Environmental	Instructional	Assessment
❏ Preferential seating	❏ Intensive individual instruction	❏ Oral assessment
❏ Proximity to instructor	❏ Intensive small group instruction	❏ Alternative test/ assignment
❏ Frequent breaks	❏ Graphic organizers	❏ Scribe
❏ Alternative workspace	❏ Calculator	❏ Shorter assignments
❏ Study partner	❏ Taped texts	❏ Extended time
	❏ Copy of notes	
	❏ Tracking sheets	
	❏ Repeated instructions	

Additional comments:

Teacher's signature: Date:

The Work of the In-School Team

The in-school team "provides support through extended consultation on possible classroom strategies . . . referrals and resource decisions" (British Columbia Ministry of Education, 2012, Section C). Usually the team appoints a case coordinator and problem-solves informally. You will likely be asked to present the student data from the pre-referral interventions. The team brainstorms and suggests additional assessment strategies and teaching strategies, including **informal assessment** conducted by you or the resource teacher and, perhaps, formal assessment conducted by the resource teacher, a psychologist, or another professional.

When the team recommends that you and the resource teacher continue with assessment and intervention, the team usually monitors and supports your actions. In some jurisdictions the team would prepare an IEP at this point. As the referring teacher, you supply the relevant classroom information. Regardless of the decision to pursue an IEP at this time, members will confer with you, and another meeting of the team will take place to assess what has been accomplished.

The in-school team is the cornerstone of the process of identification, assessment, and planning. The team could recommend that other **formal assessments** be conducted, such as an intelligence test; behaviour observation checklists; vision, hearing, or language assessments; or medical tests. In some school districts there is a long waiting list for assessment services, and parents may choose to pay for assessments administered privately outside the school system. When results are available, the in-school team, including the parents, usually meets to consider the recommendations. In most provinces the IEP (or equivalent) would be written at this stage; again, you will likely play a large role in this. In Ontario there is a two-stage process in which an **Identification, Placement, and Review Committee (IPRC)** usually meets to consider whether the child is exceptional and recommends a placement. This is followed by an IEP, usually written by the teacher and the resource teacher in elementary schools and by the resource teacher or guidance counsellor with input from the classroom teachers in secondary schools. In Newfoundland and Labrador an **individual support services plan (ISSP)** is developed in a collaborative process that involves the child, parent(s), school personnel, and personnel from other agencies, including the departments of Health, Human Resources and Employment, and Justice. An IEP may also be developed. Ask about the procedures in your school, because there are variations even within a district.

THE IN-SCHOOL TEAM AND THE IEP PROCESS

The IEP process addresses areas of student need, including adaptations in the regular classroom, supports and services to be provided there, and other services the student may receive. With inclusive education as the predominant approach, services are increasingly offered within the neighbourhood school, and within the regular

Chris Schmidt/Getty Images

Teachers with experience in collaboration say it is worth the effort. In-school teams share the responsibility for exceptional students.

classroom. However, some students still require and receive services outside the neighbourhood school. For example, an IEP may recommend that a violent student attend a board-wide program for anger management until able to cope with the social demands of the classroom. Sometimes an itinerant teacher or a resource teacher can meet a student's needs best by removing the student from the regular classroom for intensive and direct instruction. For a discussion of the issues associated with teaching Braille outside the regular classroom, see papers by Cooper and Nichols (2007) and by Cay Holbrook of the University of British Columbia (Emerson et al., 2009).

The educators on the in-school team share with the teacher the ongoing responsibility for the student's program when they hold brief, frequent, and informal meetings, even after the IEP has been established. Participating on in-school teams has benefits for teachers, especially when teachers have a strong knowledge base and beliefs that are aligned with the approach. Participation on the in-school team can be a professional development experience that teachers view as contributing to better instruction for exceptional students. Figure 2.4 contains suggestions for participating in an in-school team meeting.

FIGURE 2.4 PREPARING FOR AND PARTICIPATING IN AN IN-SCHOOL TEAM MEETING

Communicate Regularly with Parents

- Send out a monthly newsletter with space for parents' comments.
- Host a class curriculum night to communicate your curriculum and expectations.
- Make a positive contact with parents of exceptional students before you make a negative contact.
- If you have not met the parents, make telephone contact before an in-school team meeting.
- Respond to parents' notes and telephone calls promptly.

Look at Each Student as an Individual

- Read all of the student files before the term starts.
- Make notes on the files, reports, IEPs, and medical information of exceptional students.
- Make written observations of all exceptional students early in the term.
- Meet with the resource teacher, ask questions, secure resources, and learn strategies to adapt teaching; make written notes.
- Collect work samples that demonstrate the student's strengths and needs in your class.

Prepare for the In-School Team Meeting

- Ask for and read the information about responsibilities of the members at in-school team meetings.
- Ask the chair of the meeting what will be expected of you.
- Discuss the student's case thoroughly with your best source of information, probably the resource teacher; ask his opinion on what you plan to say.
- Prepare to give a brief summary of the student's history in the school as well as in your classroom.
- Bring all of your written notes to the in-school team meeting.
- Bring work samples to show the student's strengths and needs in your classroom.

During the In-School Team Meeting

- Approach the meeting in a spirit of goodwill.
- Think about how stressful these meetings can be for parents.

(continued)

FIGURE 2.4 *(continued)*

- Listen actively to what others have to say; take notes; do not interrupt.
- Answer questions briefly and honestly without becoming defensive.
- Ask questions if you do not understand; do not agree to commitments you cannot keep.
- Make your presentations brief, clear, and to the point; be positive and realistic in saying what you can do to meet the student's needs.
- Ensure that the meeting is summarized and ends on a positive note; thank the parents and other team members for their participation.
- Clarify when the next meeting is likely to occur and what is expected of you.

The Teacher and the Individual Education Plan

The individual education plan (IEP) is the formal document that is used to plan an exceptional student's program and serves as the blueprint for that student's education.

The term *IEP* is used in most provinces (Alberta, British Columbia, Manitoba, Nunavut, Ontario, Prince Edward Island, Québec, and Yukon). In other provinces different terms are used: **individual program plan (IPP)** in Nova Scotia, **personal program plan (PPP)** in Saskatchewan, and **special education plan (SEP)** in New Brunswick. The Northwest Territories (NWT) requires a **student support plan (SSP)** if a student has a modified education plan based on outcomes in the NWT curriculum and an IEP if a student has a unique, student-specific plan. An individual support services plan (ISSP) is used in Newfoundland and Labrador to record and coordinate the services provided to a child by more than one government agency (which often includes the Department of Education); and an IEP is an "education only" document for students who have a modified, alternate, or functional life skills program (what are called Pathways 3, 4, and 5). Across Canada, whenever significant changes in learning expectations, curriculum, or teaching approaches are made to a student's educational program over the long term, an IEP or an equivalent is prepared.

Planning to Meet Individual Needs

The IEP demands that you and your colleagues make an individual plan for an exceptional student. However, that does not mean that you must teach the student one-on-one. We recognize that students want to be part of the class and that that is what their parents desire as well. This means we need to ascertain the extent to which the exceptional students can learn the content we are presenting to the class.

The documents of a number of provinces, including Saskatchewan, Manitoba, and Ontario, increasingly use the term *differentiated instruction*. Carol Tomlinson (2010) urges us to differentiate by using a range of teaching and learning modes that help all students to learn. Differentiated instruction ensures that all students have optimal learning opportunities within the core academic curriculum through the use of assessment and flexible grouping. Assessment identifies students' needs, and flexible grouping allows teachers to form learning groups customized to students' needs. The composition of such groups varies on an as-needed basis. Then intensive, focused instruction can be tailored to the groups, including instruction above and beyond what the rest of the class requires. Differentiated instruction is the focus of Chapter 8.

Put into Practice

Obtain a copy of the IEP form used in your school district. Compare it with the IEP shown in Figure 2.5.

Cross-Reference
In Chapter 11, you can read about strategies for encouraging independence and for helping exceptional students to make successful transitions into and out of each level of schooling.

The amount of time students take to learn a skill can be changed. As well, the content may be modified so that certain skills are selected for the exceptional students and other skills are deleted from their program plans. In rare cases the entire content may be replaced with more appropriate learning experiences. Again, the question to ask is, "To what extent can the exceptional student learn in the same way as the rest of the class, and how can I differentiate the way I teach, based on the student's unique learning needs?"

Exceptional students sometimes need a different way to demonstrate the learning outcomes they have accomplished. Whenever the same outcome is appropriate, maintain that outcome. When necessary, choose alternative formats or products that enable students to show what they have learned rather than showing the impact of their disabilities. Widely used adaptations are more time for tests, speaking into a tape recorder, and using a scribe. Adapting assessment is the focus of Chapter 9.

Example of an IEP for a Student with a Learning Disability

Barbara Bylsma has a learning disability. It is October, and she is in grade 11. She is telling the counsellor who meets with her once a month about the challenges she is facing in her classes. "Sometimes I get to class late, usually because I am mixed up about what day it is. Or which floor the room is on. And sometimes I get there with the wrong books. I really find it hard to get all my assignments done. The teachers give me extra time but there are only so many hours in the day. So I end up working late on my assignments, and having no sleep or else no time to do anything but schoolwork." When the counsellor asks Barbara about the assignments she has not submitted in her English class, Barbara explains that she didn't finish them and was embarrassed to hand in a half-completed assignment, so she handed in nothing on

FIGURE 2.5 EXAMPLE OF AN IEP (USING ONTARIO TEMPLATE)

This IEP contains AC ☑ MOD ❏ ALT

REASON FOR DEVELOPING THE IEP

☑ Student identified as exceptional by IPRC

❏ Student not formally identified but requires special education program/services including modified/alternative learning expectations and/or accommodations

STUDENT PROFILE

Student OEN: 444444

Last Name: Bylsma   **First Name:** Barbara

Gender: F   **Date of Birth:** March 1, 1998

School: Brock Secondary

School Type: Secondary   **Principal:** Ms. Yung

Current Grade/Special Class: Grade 11 School Year: 2014–2015

Exceptionality (identified): Learning disability

Placement: Regular class with withdrawal

(continued)

FIGURE 2.5 *(continued)*

Student (secondary only) is currently working toward attainment of the:

√ Ontario Secondary School Diploma | Ontario Secondary School Certificate | Certificate of Accomplishment

STUDENT'S AREAS OF STRENGTH AND AREAS OF NEED

Areas of Strength	Areas of Need
1. Problem-solving skills	1. Expressive language skills—writing
2. Self-advocacy skills	2. Receptive language skills—writing
3. Expressive language skills	3. Organizational skills
4. Keyboarding skills	4. Processing speed

SUBJECTS, COURSE/CODES, OR ALTERNATIVE SKILL AREAS TO WHICH THE IEP APPLIES

Accommodated only (AC), Modified (MOD), Alternative (ALT)		
1. English	ENG 3C	AC
2. Math/Personal Finance	MBF 3C	AC
3. Health/Physical Education	PPL 30	AC
4. History/Canadian & Politics	CHH 3C	AC
5. Biology	SBI 3C	AC
6. Learning Strategies/ Advanced	GLE 30	AC
7. Information Technology Applications/Business	BTA 30	AC
8. Dramatic Arts	ADA 30	AC

ACCOMMODATIONS FOR LEARNING, INCLUDING REQUIRED EQUIPMENT

Accommodations are assumed to be the same for all program areas unless otherwise indicated

Instructional Accommodations	Environmental Accommodations	Assessment Accommodations
Assistive technology: text-to-speech	Access to outlet for assistive technology	Additional time
Word processing for spell check		Computer with spell check
Extra time		Speech-to-text software
Graphic organizers		Verbatim scribing of responses
Organizational coaching		
Laptop		

HUMAN RESOURCES (teaching/non-teaching)

Type of Service	Frequency or Intensity for Staff	Location
Special education teacher	Daily during CLE	Resource room
Guidance counsellor	Monitor one time per month	Resource room
Support for computer programs	Minimum once per semester	Resource room

Source: Based on sample IEPs available on the Ontario Directors of Education website, www.edu.gov.on.ca/eng/general/elemsec/speced/guide/resource/iepresguid.pdf.

the days the assignments were due. "I always think that I will get my English assignments done somehow, and then I get working on the next thing and I never get back to it. Not like my math homework, which I love and can always get done on time. And not like having to give a speech in English or History—I love that! It's completely different than writing a paper!" When the counsellor asks Barbara how her assistive technology is working, Barbara replies, "I think I need more help using the programs efficiently. That is what I want to work on with you today. I want to figure out a strategy to get more help using my speech-to-text and text-to-speech software. When you help me prepare what I am going to say, I do a better job of convincing people of what I need to be successful. We should do this now." Excerpts from Barbara's IEP appear in Figure 2.5.

Changing Context of IEPs in Canada

Recent provincial documents suggest that the expectations for IEPs are changing; these documents recommend that teachers develop profiles of individual students and of the entire class to aid in planning assessment and instruction that is good for all and necessary for some (Alberta Education, 2010a; Ontario Ministry of Education, 2013). Individual profiles may include information about student learning preferences (e.g., learning from a book or a DVD; working alone or with a partner); interests (animals, sports); previous assessment information, and so forth. A class profile consists of a compilation of the information gathered about each student on an aspect that informs your teaching of the class. The CAST website (www.cast.org) is a multimedia resource for teachers where they can learn about using universal design for learning (UDL) to create flexible goals, methods, materials, and assessments to meet the needs of diverse learners. Besides UDL, recent provincial documents suggest differentiated instruction (DI) and tiered approaches to intervention where the intensity and duration of intervention increase for students who have not responded to the previous intervention (RTI).

The Teacher and the Educational Assistant

Put into Practice

Look for provincial and district policies about educational assistants. Interview an educational assistant about his or her working relationship with teachers and in-school teams.

In-school teams may include **educational assistants (EAs)**, also referred to as teacher assistants, teacher aides, teacher associates, or paraeducators. These staff members are employed to assist teachers in carrying out the program and to support the personal care, behaviour management, and instruction of exceptional students. The role generally includes (Canadian Teachers' Federation, 2009):

- helping students with learning activities under the supervision of the teacher
- assisting by providing accommodations and services described in the IEP
- maintaining ongoing communication with the student's teachers

The Role of the Educational Assistant

Sometimes educational assistants are assigned to work full-time or part-time with one or more exceptional students in your classroom, while other times they are assigned to support your work with the entire class while monitoring the progress of

These students with physical disabilities are included with the support of an educational assistant.

Put into Practice

Read two of the following resources that are relevant to your teaching assignment and develop a plan for working with an EA in a class that you are presently teaching or will be teaching:

Haegele, J.A., & Kozub, F.M. (2010). A continuum of paraeducator support for utilization in adapted physical education. *Teaching Exceptional Children Plus, 6*(5), Article 2. http://journals.cec.sped.org/tecplus

Binger, C., et al. (2010). Teaching educational assistants to facilitate the multisymbol message productions of young students who require augmentative and alternative communication. *American Journal of Speech-Language Pathology, 19*(2), 108–120.

Mackenzie, S. (2011). Yes, but . . . : Rhetoric, reality and resistance in teaching assistants' experiences of inclusive education. *Support for Learning, 26*(2), 64–71.

Devecchi, C., & Rouse, M. (2010). An exploration of the features of effective collaboration between teachers and teaching assistants in secondary schools. *Support for Learning, 25*(2), 91–99.

Carnahan, C.R., et al. (2009). A systematic approach for supporting paraeducators in educational settings: A guide for teachers. *Teaching Exceptional Children, 41*(5), 34–43.

the exceptional students and offering them assistance at key moments. Who assigns these responsibilities to teacher assistants and how you can know what to expect? Often the IEP includes information about the role of the educational assistant in the program of an exceptional student. The EA could work in one or all of the following places: in the classroom (e.g., supporting completion of assigned work), at a separate workspace in the classroom (e.g., teaching a strategy for organizing an essay), or in a space outside the classroom (e.g., administering medication). The principal is responsible for assigning roles in your school to an educational assistant, but usually the principal will consult with you when one of your students is involved, and normally the EA works under the direction of a teacher.

A recent review found that the responsibilities of educational assistants have become increasingly focused on instruction (Giangreco et al., 2010), extending an earlier Canadian study which reported that over half of EAs' time was spent on instructional tasks (Hill, 2003). Research suggests that in successful inclusive schools, educational assistants and teachers collaborate effectively, meet frequently before and after school to discuss happenings in the classroom, and are engaged teaching partners (Devecchi & Rouse, 2010). Jennifer Ramsay, a teacher in Ontario, found that teachers and EAs shared beliefs about what was most important for inclusive education, recognized that their roles were distinct, and received direct and indirect support from the principal and the resource teacher (2007). An EA in your classroom can provide continuity and contribute to the planning and delivery of services. Ensure that the EA has a workstation in the classroom and that the two of you have a shared understanding of her role. If the procedures permit it, include EAs in the discussions of the in-school team; otherwise you must relay the team's discussion and decisions to EAs who work with you.

Your Role in Working with an Educational Assistant

It is important to clarify your role before beginning a partnership with an educational assistant (see Figure 2.6). When you learn that you will be teaming with an educational assistant, read the job description and expectations of EAs in your province and in your school district. Also reread the IEPs of any exceptional students in your upcoming classes for information about the role of the EA with these students.

You may need to prepare materials for the EA to use; provide informal training to the EA about programs and strategies; and inform this partner about the expectations, routines, and transitions you set for the class (Carnahan et al., 2009). Many teachers have never supervised another team member; some find it difficult to assign tasks they feel they should do themselves. While there may be more of these challenges when you work closely with an EA, you can also share the responsibility and ideas with an enthusiastic partner. Many provinces (e.g., Manitoba; www.edu.gov.mb.ca) and school districts (e.g., Peterborough Victoria Northumberland and Clarington Catholic District School Board; www.pvnccdsb.on.ca) have prepared resource guides to clarify the roles of educational assistants.

FIGURE 2.6 ROLE OF CLASSROOM TEACHERS IN WORKING WITH EDUCATIONAL ASSISTANTS

Classroom teachers who receive support from educational assistants have the following responsibilities:

- communicating effectively as the team leader in the classroom
- developing a shared philosophy for the classroom
- establishing a pattern of regular meetings
- informing EAs of classroom procedures and rules, and methods of classroom management
- assigning appropriate responsibilities and tasks to EAs, taking into consideration their training, knowledge, and skills as well as student needs
- documenting identified responsibilities and tasks with EAs, and providing copies for principals (and special education supervisors, where appropriate)
- providing input regarding the supervision and evaluation of EAs
- informing principals when students whom EAs support are absent so that the EAs' schedules can be changed
- ensuring that time is allocated for EAs to meet with teachers regularly
- ensuring communication with EAs through communication books, logs, regular meetings for collaborative monitoring, and ongoing discussion
- recommending training and resources to support EAs in their roles
- modelling the confidentiality of the student–school relationship
- helping EAs to develop skills they need, such as observation and data-collection strategies and effective behaviour management strategies
- encouraging high standards of practice
- resolving conflicts with EAs at the classroom level first, school level second, and regional school board level third

Sources: Alberta Teachers' Association (2007). *Teachers and teachers' assistants: Roles and responsibilities*. Edmonton: Alberta Teachers' Association; Carnahan, C.R., Williamson, P., Clarke, L., & Sorensen, R. (2009). A systematic approach for supporting paraeducators in educational settings: A guide for teachers. *Teaching Exceptional Children, 41*(5), 34–43; Manitoba Education. (2009). *Educational assistants in Manitoba schools*. Winnipeg: Manitoba Education; Nova Scotia Teachers Union. (2006–2007). *NSTU guidebook*. Halifax: Nova Scotia Teachers Union; Warger, C. (2003). *Supporting paraeducators: A summary of current practices*. ERIC/OSEP Digest #E 642.

Sometimes EAs may work with the same exceptional students for years and know the students better than the classroom or subject teacher. Remember that EAs should always complete their job assignments under the supervision of qualified classroom teachers. It is important that EAs contribute to the participation of exceptional children in regular classrooms and do not come between the children and their classmates, teachers, or learning tasks (Giangreco et al., 2010). In a Canadian study, eight children and adolescents with developmental disabilities reported feeling that at times their EAs compromised their social participation and networking with peers (Tews & Lupart, 2008). To make the partnership work smoothly, establish clear communication and a good working relationship with each EA who works in your classroom. EAs say that the teachers with whom they work "make or break" the year (Mackenzie, 2011). Look for the EA's unique strengths and then work together; the students will benefit.

Further Reading

About working with paraeducators:

French, N.K. (2007). *A paraeducator's resource guide*. Port Chester, NY: National Professional Resources, Inc.

Giangreco, M.F., Suter, J.C., & Doyle, M.B. (2010). Paraprofessionals in inclusive schools: A review of recent research. *Journal of Educational and Psychological Consultation, 20*, 41–57.

Peterborough Victoria Northumberland and Clarington Catholic District School Board. (2003). *Educational assistants: Resource guide*. www.pvnccdsb.on.ca.

The Teacher and the Parents

In recent years, parents have developed increasing awareness of their own and their children's legal and social rights and are asserting themselves more with school personnel. Being aware of these rights and making an effort to understand and support parents who exercise them is likely to enhance your relations with parents. These families have to meet the challenges that accompany the disability as well as all the normal pressures of family life. Families of children with disabilities spend significant amounts of time interacting with educational and other professionals. By becoming sensitive to parents' needs, you can ensure that your meetings with families go more smoothly.

Understanding the Parents' Perspective

A recurring theme in this text is the importance of taking others' perspectives. This section focuses on the perspectives of parents of exceptional students. Living with an exceptional child or adolescent creates challenges for a family, with both positive and negative effects. Lily Dyson of the University of Victoria has studied how a child's disability influences parents and siblings (2010), while Patricia Minnes and her colleagues at Queen's University have reported that families experience both empowerment (Nachshen & Minnes, 2005), and high levels of stress when caring for exceptional children and adolescents (Nachshen et al., 2005).

CARING FOR EXCEPTIONAL CHILDREN AND ADOLESCENTS

Coming to terms with a child with disabilities is not a linear process but rather a recurring one, so that difficult questions that parents deal with at the time of diagnosis reappear at critical junctures and major developmental stages (Callen, 2009). Parents of children with disabilities in Ontario and parents of gifted children in Alberta report challenging transitions from preschool to kindergarten (Villeneuve et al., 2013; Sankar-DeLeeuw, 2007), and emphasize the importance of teachers listening to parents. Many families receive comprehensive early intervention at a child development centre (e.g., Yukon Child Development Centre; www.cdcyukon.com), and may find the programming in their neighbourhood school less intensive. Sometimes parents' expectations for accomplishment in school are shattered following the identification of a child's disability.

What do you think?

Recently contrasting perspectives on our work with parents have emerged. Some researchers have argued that educators must strive to identify shared values with families. For example, see Parent engagement: Building trust between families and schools in *Education Canada*, 53(2), 48–50 by Lorna Constantini (2013). At the same time, educators have begun to receive advice on how to deal with aggressive parents. For example, see *The difficult parent: An educator's guide to handling aggressive behavior* by Charles Jaksec (Corwin Press, 2005) and *Working with challenging parents of students with special needs* by Jean Cheng Gorman (Corwin Press, 2004). Are these perspectives contradictory or complementary? What do you think?

Parents often find fewer opportunities for children and adolescents with disabilities to participate in social, recreational, and leisure activities in the community, although such participation is a widely used means of promoting friendships among children without disabilities. Recent Canadian studies have reported that children and adolescents with autism spectrum disorders, intellectual disabilities, and physical disabilities participated in fewer social, recreational, and leisure activities than their typically developing peers. And, when they did participate, it was more likely to be with parents and other adults (Jamieson et al., 2009; Law et al., 2006; Solish et al., 2010). Such restricted opportunities may contribute to families' frustrations and stress.

Parental challenges in caring for exceptional children and adolescents vary. Some children require physical and personal care daily and need to be lifted frequently. Others have life-threatening allergies that require parents to be constantly vigilant. Some children look different from their peers, and families may have to provide emotional support to overcome the potentially destructive effects of rejection. Others, with behaviour disorders, behave differently, even unacceptably, although they look like everyone else. It is important for us, as educators, to listen and understand the family's perspective when a child has a disability.

Because learning disabilities are an invisible handicap, parents may not receive the same support as they would if their children had more visible disabilities (Dyson, 2010). For some children, learning disabilities are identified when they struggle to

Letter to Andrew

Families of exceptional children in Calgary published a book entitled *Letters to Our Children*.

Here is the letter to Andrew Ziebell, who was born three weeks prematurely with cerebral palsy that affects all four limbs. Andrew has some hearing and vision loss.

Dear Andrew,

You, my love, turned seven years old on March 3, 1993. In your short lifetime you have had a long, hard road to follow. And that road will not get any easier. Always know, Andrew, that I love you more than anything in the world and I will always be there right beside you, helping your every step, sharing in your dreams, your hopes, your tears and your fears.

You have a circle of friends who love you and love to share in your life. These friends are special in every way because they see you as Andrew, a person first and foremost, and your disability doesn't matter.

The sky was the limit when you entered preschool. Your teachers, Jill, Jo-Anne, and Val took you through two years of learning, socializing, and fun-filled experiences. Your summer program there was just as wonderful because I could see the look of excitement on your face each and every day when you came home from the Leisure Centre. You had a great year at your community school where you moved mountains and acquired lifelong friendships.

In the beginning of 1993, another chapter opened in your life. You entered the world of Scouting. In full uniform you and your brother proudly stand united with all Boy Scouts of Canada. We are all proud to feel your sense of belonging.

Your world is not always full of joy and not all people see your strength, but dwell on your disabilities. The most difficult challenge began in June 1992 when you were not allowed to continue in your community school placement. Not only did this cost you a year of education, but the emotional devastation this inflicted on your brother and sister, who could not understand why you were not allowed to go to school with them, has been very traumatic. We will continue to fight to obtain your right to a fair and equal education in your community school, no matter how long it takes.

What your future holds for you, my son, I cannot say; but what I hope it holds for you is full acceptance into society and a world that is kind and full of love; a circle of friends and independence.

Lovingly,
Your Mom, Dad, Jennifer-Lea, Christopher and last, but not least, your watchful puppy Kelsey

Source: Excerpted from D.E. Badry, J.R. McDonald, & J. LeBlond (Eds.), *Letters to Our Children*. Copyright © 1993 by University of Calgary Press. Used by permission.

learn in French Immersion (FI) programs, and their parents often experience frustration because of the paucity of research on inclusive teaching approaches for FI (Mady & Arnett, 2009). Gifted children and adolescents also feel different and can be teased and ridiculed at school. A parent who tells you there is no time or energy for a parent–teacher meeting may have good reason to feel tired and discouraged.

PARENTS' TEACHING AND ADVOCATING FOR EXCEPTIONAL YOUTH

Parents assume the roles of teachers and advocates (Hutchinson et al., 2014). They often spend long hours helping their children with disabilities complete unfinished schoolwork. One parent expressed it this way: "He has me working with him, up reading every night, constantly, even on the weekends." Some exceptional children and adolescents cannot communicate effectively with their parents about school, which causes parents to say, "The best part of an ideal school would be clear communication, feeling comfortable to call the teacher after school and ask, 'What kind of day did my kid have?'" A communication book for children or an agenda book for adolescents, which the students carry between school and home each day, can help remind the students about assignments and enable parents to see what is expected. Sometimes parents report that their teaching role interferes with their parenting role and they have to work teaching into the normal home routines as much as possible. It seems more important for exceptional children and adolescents to have accepting and supportive parents than to have another academic teacher. Teaching is, after all, your role. Many parents also assume the role of **advocate**, believing their child's success depends on their ability to advocate for him. Advocating can be a transformative, emotional, and satisfying experience for parents (Hutchinson et al., 2014).

CONCERN FOR THE FUTURE

Focusing on the future enables individuals and their families to consider what might be and how they can use their energy to make the possible real. Kim Anderson, a Cree/Métis writer, editor, educator, and storyteller, has written about why it is especially important for Aboriginal people to engage in "future-oriented stories . . . envisioning where we want to go in the future" (2004, pp. 126–127). Depending on the nature and severity of their disabilities, some individuals may not be able to live independently and may face an uncertain future in career and work. The case of Brenda Piet, in the chapter opening section, illustrates that, increasingly, IEPs contain transition plans that include workplace experience.

Collaborating with Parents

Many teachers recognize that the real experts on a student are usually the parents (Constantini, 2013). In turn, some parents recognize the pressure that teachers are under and can be a source of support and advocacy for additional resources. In a recent study, a teacher described herself as "a co-advocate" with the parent of a child with developmental disabilities; the mother advocated outside of school, and the teacher advocated daily at school because, as she said, "I am here with him every day; I see what he needs at school" (Hutchinson et al., 2014). Intensive case study research shows that the more extensive the collaboration between schools and families, the more successful children with exceptionalities are likely to be (Villeneuve & Hutchinson, 2012). Not all parents choose to collaborate with teachers and schools, and

Further Reading

On parents' planning for the future of their children with disabilities:

Pike, K., & Steinemann, P. (1997). *Connections: A planning guide for parents of sons and daughters with a mental handicap.* Brampton, ON: Brampton Caledon Community Living. (available from 34 Church St. West, Brampton, ON L6X 1H3)

The "Special Needs" Planning Group (SNPG). www.specialneedsplanning.ca/tools.html

Weblinks

CANADIAN NATIONAL INSTITUTE FOR THE BLIND (CNIB) (FOR HELP WITH ADVOCACY)
www.cnib.ca

NATIONAL EDUCATIONAL ASSOCIATION OF DISABLED STUDENTS (NEADS) (ADVOCATES FOR ACCESS TO COLLEGE AND UNIVERSITY)
www.neads.ca

ADVOCACY RESOURCE CENTRE FOR THE HANDICAPPED (ARCH) (A LEGAL RESOURCE CENTRE IN ONTARIO)
www.archlegalclinic.ca

not all parents are good at collaborating (Kidder, 2011), but parents are more likely to co-operate with educators if the school and teacher make them feel welcome.

What will parents of exceptional students expect of you? Many Canadian parents believe that excellence in teaching leads to school success for children with special needs. The qualities they look for in teachers include patience, approachability, comfort, flexibility, a positive attitude, and adequate training. Parents feel that teacher–parent communication and co-operation are important and that the teacher must accept the child's disability. There are a number of Canadian guides developed for parents of exceptional children who wish to work closely with teachers—including one for parents of young children (Lucas & Smith, 2004) and one for Aboriginal parents (Crowchief-McHugh et al., 2000). Canadian parents have articulated that inclusion means exceptional children are fully participating, valued, and contributing members of regular classrooms where they feel safe, accepted, and encouraged in a rich learning environment (Villeneuve et al., 2013).

Parent–Teacher Conferences

Parent–teacher conferences are one of the most commonly used methods to facilitate partnerships between parents and professionals. To ensure strong working relationships with the parents of exceptional students, try to communicate effectively with them at every opportunity. In spite of your busy schedule, you should make calls to these parents yourself, rather than ask the school secretary to do it. Prepare well by being informed about the student and the resources available in the school and community.

BEFORE PARENT-TEACHER CONFERENCES

If possible, contact the parents of exceptional students prior to the start of term. Introduce yourself and assure the parents that you are concerned about their child and want to work with them to ensure a positive working relationship. Remember that a face-to-face conversation with you, the teacher, is most parents' first choice of means of communication and that successful alliances can be established by adhering to three assumptions:

1. Assume goodwill—that the parents, like you, have a deep desire to see the child or adolescent do well.

2. Assume competence—that parents whose input is welcomed and valued will make constructive suggestions.

3. Assume a shared responsibility—that everyone needs to co-operate and actively participate in making and carrying out plans toward a common goal.

Set up parent–teacher conferences in a way that communicates effectively to your school's community. Be flexible with time, with inviting the child if that is likely to help reach the goals, and with using child-produced invitations as well as formal announcements in newsletters, on Twitter, by email, on the radio, and in local newspapers (in the languages most used in the community). A recent Canadian study suggests that it is critical to understand the expectations of ESL parents before a parent–teacher conference or parents' night and to use bilingual assistants or liaisons to minimize parents' feelings of intimidation and to ensure effective communication (Guo, 2010). Constantini (2013) describes a principal who went to a mosque in his school's neighbourhood to talk about the school and help parents to understand how they could participate. Reach out to parents.

Cross-Reference
Chapter 6 describes many situations that place families at risk—homelessness, unemployment, discrimination, poverty, violence—and that might reduce their collaboration with schools.

DURING PARENT–TEACHER CONFERENCES

The message you want to convey is that there is a team approach between home and school, between students and teachers, and among teachers. Parents report that they find an "us versus them" atmosphere to be a serious impediment to communication (Staples & Dilberto, 2010) and that teachers sometimes seem to be speaking "a different language" (jargon that is unfamiliar to parents) (Constantini, 2013). Create a comfortable atmosphere. Use adult chairs. Parents prefer to receive information about their children informally, in conversational meetings with teachers, so avoid jargon and give examples to show what you mean. While you may want to focus on teaching methods, parents are usually most interested in the outcomes for their children, so be prepared to discuss frankly the goals for the next week, month, and term. Begin by talking about strengths and then move to discussing needs or weaknesses. You may need to remind parents gently about what the student is accomplishing now and what is reasonable to expect in the upcoming months. Rather than forecasting far into the future, focus on what is feasible in your classroom if everyone makes a concerted and collaborative effort. All of this will be easier, if you make a plan and ensure that you have all the information and examples that you need to communicate effectively. If you are not familiar with a disability, read up on it prior to the meeting to ensure you can contribute to the discussion. Then, while communicating, invite parents to talk and remember to look at the parents and listen attentively to what they say. After consensus has been reached, make a plan that supports the student in age-appropriate and culturally sensitive ways.

It is not always easy to reach consensus, so you should be aware of approaches for solving problems if they arise (see *Shared Solutions* from Ontario Ministry of Education for ways to prevent and resolve conflicts). Be honest but tactful. Let the parents know that you like their child. If there are responsibilities to be shared, discuss what you can do, what the parents can do, and what the exceptional student can do. Sometimes it is helpful to include the student in the conference. But don't surprise anyone by doing this without prior discussion with the family members.

Exceptional adolescents are expected to learn **self-advocacy**. Figure 2.7 provides an annotated bibliography on self-advocacy. Then they can negotiate with their teachers for accommodations consistent with the IEP and with the recommendations of the resource teacher or case manager. Adolescence is a period of development toward autonomy and personally relevant life goals. Participating in parent–teacher conferences may contribute to this development. Prepare students to take part and prepare their parents for the idea that the adolescent should join the conference. In a study in a Halifax school, Versnel (2005) found that grade 6 students learned a strategy for participating in parent–teacher conferences during ten one-hour group strategy lessons. The students used the strategy to advocate with teachers, sports coaches, parents, and classmates, as well as to discuss their classroom needs, and they highly recommended the program for other students. Versnel recently notified me that she had met some of these students when they were advocating for themselves at Dalhousie University—almost ten years after they had been participants in her study. Some school districts have found that implementing student-led, teacher-supported conferences, beginning with students in the middle years, has improved communication with parents and improved student learning (for an example, see Goodman, 2008). Chapters 7 and 11 describe strategies for helping students to engage in effective self-advocacy.

Put into Practice

Read about the challenges of creating welcoming parent–teacher conferences in schools with diverse student populations. Then develop a plan for engaging parents who may be reluctant to attend or uncomfortable in meetings with educators. Put yourself in the parents' place and think about what they might find helpful. Resources you could consult include:

Allen, J. (2007). *Creating welcoming schools: A practical guide to home–school partnerships with diverse families.* Newark, DE: International Reading Association.

Guo, Y. (2010). Meetings without dialogue: A study of ESL parent–teacher interactions at secondary school parents' nights. *School Community Journal, 20*(1), 121–140.

Staples, K.E., & Dilberto, J.A. (2010). Guidelines for successful parent involvement. *Teaching Exceptional Children, 42*(5), 58–63.

Brandt, S. (2003, Summer). What parents really want out of parent-teacher conferences. *Kappa Delta Pi Record,* pp. 160–163.

Ontario Ministry of Education. (2007). *Shared solutions: A guide to preventing and resolving conflicts regarding programs and services for students with special education needs.* Toronto, ON: Ontario Ministry of Education (retrieved from www.edu.gov.on.ca/eng/general/elemsec/speced/shared.pdf).

FIGURE 2.7 ANNOTATED BIBLIOGRAPHY OF RECENT SOURCES ON ENHANCING SELF-ADVOCACY, A KEY CONTRIBUTOR TO MENTAL HEALTH AND WELL-BEING, OF STUDENTS WITH DISABILITIES IN ELEMENTARY, SECONDARY, AND POST-SECONDARY EDUCATION

Because being able to advocate for oneself and feeling in charge of one's own life contribute to mental health and well-being, it is critical for educators to support students' self-advocacy.

Framing the Future: Self-Determination (2015)

by Michael Wehmeyer, *Remedial and Special Education, 36*(1), 20–23.

Reviews recent history of teaching self-determination and argues that to make progress we need to: (a) teach all students to self-advocate; (b) embrace strengths-based models of disability; (c) focus on teaching pre-service teachers about promoting self-advocacy.

Promoting Self-Determination: A Model for Training Elementary Students to Self-Advocate for IEP Accommodations (2013)

by Juliet Hart & Julianne Brehm, *Teaching Exceptional Children, 45*(5), 40–48.

Describes a ten-step process for teachers to use to help young students follow five cues when asking for the accommodations to which they are entitled.

Effectiveness of the IMPACT: Ability Program to Improve Safety and Self-Advocacy Skills in High School Students with Disabilities (2014)

by Eileen Dryden, Jeffrey Desmarais, & Lisa Arsenault, *Journal of School Health, 84*(12), 793–801.

Reports on an intervention that increased self-advocacy and safety knowledge, confidence, and speaking up for themselves in students enrolled in special education programs. More focused on self-advocacy for safety than for academic purposes.

Providing Support to Postsecondary Students with Disabilities to Request Accommodations: A Framework for Intervention (2014)

by Jean Ann Summers, Glen White, E. Zhang, & Jeffrey Gordon, *Journal of Postsecondary Education and Disability, 27*(3), 245–260.

Describes a training program to enhance knowledge and skills for self-advocacy which includes an online module and a self-assessment to help students identify their needs.

AFTER PARENT–TEACHER CONFERENCES

After a conference, you have several responsibilities. First, write notes to remind yourself of the important points discussed. Second, if you and the parents have made any major decisions, you may want to write a brief note to the parents to confirm what was decided. Third, if you agreed to take any action (such as consulting the resource teacher), carry it out as soon as possible. Provide other educators who work with the child with a brief update on the outcomes of the meeting. Some schools require that an update be entered in the parent–teacher conference log so the principal and other educators who were not present can access it.

Try to look at the situation from the parents' perspective when reflecting on the conference. Although you may find it challenging to include their child or adolescent in your classroom for one year, the parents have this challenge for their entire lives. While you have an important job—to teach this child and include him or her in your classroom—these parents also have an important job. Theirs is to love and care for this child and to be the child's advocate. This is the basis from which you can expect them to communicate with you. Partnerships are built over time; both you and the parents may have to challenge long-held beliefs and even live through a few mistakes. If you find that you need to prevent or resolve conflict, consult a document called *Shared Solutions,* developed by the Ontario Ministry of Education (www.edu. gov.on.ca/eng/general/elemsec/speced/shared.pdf).

There may be families who will not form partnerships with you. Because of situations families face—including unfamiliarity with the Canadian school system, homelessness, unemployment, discrimination, poverty, and violence—parents may not engage in collaboration. As educators, we have to respect their decisions and encourage them to attend the next parent–teacher conference.

Summary

The role of the classroom teacher in the education of exceptional children is increasing. Teachers identify the needs of exceptional students, carry out pre-referral adaptations, and collaborate with school-based teams to facilitate inclusion. Teachers also play a central role in developing IEPs and carrying out these IEPs by ADAPTing or differentiating their teaching, assessment, and classroom organization. Just as Ms. Sauvé recognized her responsibility to refer Andy Hughes to the in-school team, Mr. Bogg came to understand his role in advising Brenda Piet on her transition to college. Strategies for meeting these challenges appear in upcoming chapters. Both parents and educational assistants are partners in the education of exceptional students and can work with you to share the responsibility in these changing times.

Key Terms

advocate (p. 51)

collaboration (p. 38)

educational assistant (EA) (p. 46)

formal assessments (p. 41)

Identification, Placement, and Review Committee (IPRC) (p. 41)

individual program plan (IPP) (p. 43)

individual support services plan (ISSP) (p. 41)

informal assessment (p. 40)

in-school team (p. 39)

parent–teacher conferences (p. 52)

personal program plan (PPP) (p. 43)

pre-referral interventions (p. 35)

resource teacher (p. 35)

self-advocacy (p. 53)

self-monitoring (p. 37)

self-regulation (p. 37)

special education plan (SEP) (p. 43)

student support plan (SSP) (p. 43)

Challenges for Reviewing Chapter 2

1. Why is your role as a classroom teacher so important in identifying the needs of exceptional students, especially students with high-incidence exceptionalities such as learning disabilities?

2. Identify the steps a teacher would take before referring a child to an in-school team.

3. Identify three aspects of your role as a classroom teacher working with an educational assistant at the grade level at which you teach.

4. Return to the opening cases of Andy and Brenda and answer the five questions that follow the cases.

Activities for Reviewing Chapter 2 with Your Peers

5. Prepare to assume the role of one of the members of a school-based team (e.g., teacher, parent, resource teacher, principal, or special education consultant) for a meeting about Andy Hughes, whose case was described in the opening of this chapter. List (a) the resources you would use to prepare for the meeting, (b) the contributions you plan to make in the meeting, and (c) the reasons why you think these contributions are important. Participate with your peers in a role-play of the school-based team meeting about Andy.

6. Using Figure 2.5 on pages 44–45 as a model and working in a small group, develop an IEP for Andy Hughes. Refer to sources identified in this chapter as well as the information provided in this chapter.

7. Describe the actions you would take at the beginning of the school year to ensure collaborative working relationships with the parents and guardians of exceptional students in your class or classes. Participate with your classmates in role-playing a parent–teacher meeting for one of the two students described in the cases at the beginning of this chapter—Andy Hughes or Brenda Piet.

Exceptional Students: Learning and Behaviour Exceptionalities, and Mental Health Challenges

Cathy Yeulet/123RF

LEARNER OBJECTIVES

After you have read this chapter, you will be able to:

1. Identify exceptionalities, including giftedness, learning disabilities, attention deficit hyperactivity disorder (ADHD), behaviour exceptionalities, and mental health challenges.

2. Describe ways you can differentiate teaching in regular classrooms for students who are gifted or developmentally advanced.

3. Discuss differentiated teaching to meet the needs of students with learning disabilities.

4. Describe classroom differentiations for students with ADHD.

5. Discuss differentiated teaching for students with behaviour and emotional exceptionalities, as well as supporting students experiencing mental health challenges.

URJO is 15 YEARS OLD AND IN GRADE 10. His teachers describe him as non-compliant and underachieving. Their observations report a boy who fails to complete assignments in class, refuses to do his homework, has difficulty following instructions, and rarely co-operates with teachers or classmates. Teachers see him muttering under his breath, folding his arms across his chest, and shouting at peers. However, he excels in art class. While he engages in loud, verbal power struggles with most teachers, Urjo is quiet and engrossed when drawing or painting. The counsellor who interviewed him suggests that Urjo uses power struggles to avoid work he finds boring and pointless and to exert control over others. In an interview, Urjo's parents report that he initiates the same battles at home and that his younger brothers are starting to engage in the same behaviours. When teachers pressure Urjo to comply, he bad-mouths them and indulges in negative self-talk. Achievement tests show that Urjo is slightly below grade level in reading, written expression, and mathematics and is easily distracted but does not have a learning disability. His difficulties have been described as a behaviour exceptionality, with a focus on defiant behaviours and disruptions to the classroom.

CONNIE IS IN GRADE 3 AND IS READING AT THE GRADE 1 LEVEL. Her file contains a psychologist's report that indicates that she scored in the average range on a test of general intelligence (Wechsler Intelligence Scale for Children [WISC]). However, on a test called Early Reading Assessment, she had low scores on the core subtests—identifying written words, identifying letters, and matching letters and words. Her score on phonological awareness (discriminating among and manipulating sounds) was also low. But Connie showed a high level of receptive vocabulary, understanding words in common use. Her teacher believes that this is why everyone keeps expecting Connie to be a strong reader—she expresses herself well orally and loves to participate in class discussions. By contrast, her reading is hesitant as she guesses at the sounds of the letters and at the words. Earlier this year, Connie ran out of the classroom in tears when asked to read orally. The psychologist's report states that Connie has a learning disability in reading. Connie has begun attending tutoring in reading with the resource teacher, and her classroom teacher is beginning to make accommodations in the classroom, for example, when Connie has to read test questions.

1. Which of the characteristics of each student are most likely to affect learning and participation in the regular classroom? What learning needs are implied by these characteristics?

2. With such a range of characteristics and learning needs, what do exceptional students like Urjo and Connie, who are learning in inclusive classrooms, have in common?

3. How frequently is a teacher likely to be teaching a student with each of these exceptionalities?

4. What types of differentiation does each student need in order to be included in the social life and the group learning activities of the classroom?

Introduction

This chapter focuses on the characteristics and needs of students with a range of **learning and behaviour exceptionalities** and on classroom differentiations that help these students to learn. We use person–first language: exceptional students are children and adolescents *first* and they also have *some* characteristics associated with their exceptionality. We describe these students as *having* exceptionalities second. The exception to this general rule, for the exceptionalities described in this chapter, is the expression "children who *are* gifted."

Each section on an exceptionality begins with the personal story of a child or adolescent, followed by characteristics and then implications for learning and for differentiating in the classroom. There are examples of teachers differentiating in elementary and secondary classrooms. The implications for participation of exceptional learners in employment and community life as adults are explored briefly because these are important in a society committed to inclusion.

Learning and behaviour exceptionalities include students who are gifted, students who have learning disabilities (LD), attention deficit hyperactivity disorder (ADHD), or emotional and behaviour disabilities or exceptionalities (EBD), and we contextualize students with EBD within the larger topic of school-based mental health. The definitions for these four exceptionalities appear in Table 3.1. Prevalence estimates appear in Table 3.2. These students are often difficult to

TABLE 3.1 STUDENTS WITH LEARNING AND BEHAVIOUR EXCEPTIONALITIES

Exceptionality	Description
Gifted or developmentally advanced	Demonstrated or potential abilities; show exceptionally high capability in specific disciplines, intellect, or creativity.
Learning disabilities	Low school achievement usually paired with dysfunctions in processing information. Often defined as a discrepancy between ability and school achievement. Difference in ability/achievement not due to (a) visual, hearing, or motor disability; (b) emotional disturbance; or (c) environmental, cultural, or economic disadvantage. General intellectual functioning within normal range.
Attention deficit hyperactivity disorder	Persistent pattern of inattention and impulsiveness, or of hyperactivity, or of all of these.
Emotional and behaviour exceptionalities	Dysfunctional interactions between a student and his or her environment, including the classroom, home, and community. Can be seen in inability to build or maintain satisfactory interpersonal relationships with peers and teachers.

TABLE 3.2 ESTIMATED PREVALENCE OF LEARNING AND BEHAVIOUR EXCEPTIONALITIES

Exceptionality	General Prevalence in Research
Gifted	200 to 500 per 10 000 (Belanger & Gagne, 2006; Winzer, 2007)
Learning disabilities	400 to 700 per 10 000 (Dirks et al., 2008)
ADHD	400 to 800 per 10 000 (Zuvekas & Vitiello, 2012)
EBD	200 per 10 000 (Lane et al., 2005)

Further Reading

About gifted students and twice exceptional students:

Johnsen, S.K., Parker, S.L., & Farah, Y.N. (2015). Providing services for students with gifts and talents within a response-to-intervention framework. *Teaching Exceptional Children, 47*(4), 226–233.

Yssel, N., Adams, C., Clarke, L.S., & Jones, R. (2014). Applying an RTI model for students with learning disabilities who are gifted. *Teaching Exceptional Children, 46*(3), 42–52.

Baldwin, L., Omdal, S.N., & Pereles, D. (2015). Beyond stereotypes: Understanding, recognizing, and working with twice-exceptional learners. *Teaching Exceptional Children, 47*(4), 216–225.

Lee, S-Y., Olszewski-Kubilius, P., & Peternel, G. (2010). The efficacy of academic acceleration for gifted minority students. *Gifted Child Quarterly, 54*, 189–195.

Blanco, M., Carothers, D.E., & Smiley, L.R. (2009). Gifted students with Asperger syndrome: Strategies for strength-based programming. *Intervention in School and Clinic, 44*, 206–215.

Cross-Reference

Chapter 4 focuses on descriptions of and differentiated teaching for students with autism spectrum disorders and intellectual disabilities. Chapter 5 describes characteristics of and differentiated teaching for students with communication and physical exceptionalities, as well as students with chronic health conditions.

distinguish from peers without exceptionalities, especially outside school settings. In school, they frequently show a combination of behavioural, social, and academic needs. Gifted students usually benefit from differentiation, challenges, and opportunities to work with developmentally advanced peers. Other students described in this chapter usually benefit from differentiation and systematic, structured, instructional interventions such as those described in this chapter and throughout the book. The concept of **intelligence** is referred to in the definitions of some of these exceptionalities. In the Educational Psychology box, this term is discussed.

THEORY AND RESEARCH HIGHLIGHTS FROM

EDUCATIONAL PSYCHOLOGY

The Concept of Intelligence

Definitions of some of the exceptionalities in this chapter include references to intelligence (gifted and learning disabilities). However, controversy persists about what is meant by *intelligence* and how it should be measured. Early theories about intelligence referred to capacity to learn and knowledge already learned. In 1986 twenty-four psychologists attended a symposium on intelligence and provided twenty-four distinct views about the nature of intelligence (Sternberg & Detterman, 1986). There was little agreement about whether it was composed of a single, general ability or of many separate, domain-specific abilities. However, they agreed about the importance of higher-order thinking (e.g., abstract reasoning and problem solving), as well as metacognition—that is, thinking about thinking and knowledge of oneself.

An early theorist supporting general ability, Charles Spearman (1927), advocated g, or general intelligence, which he thought combined with specific abilities to enable us to perform mental tasks such as memorization. In contrast, Edward Thurstone (1938) theorized a number of distinct "primary mental abilities" for memory, numerical ability, reasoning, word fluency, and so forth, and no general intelligence. Howard Gardner (1993) postulated eight multiple intelligences: verbal, spatial, logico-mathematical, naturalist, musical, bodily-kinesthetic, interpersonal, and intrapersonal. He argued that intelligence is the ability to solve problems valued by one's culture.

Recent work in cognitive psychology has focused on how we gather and use information to solve problems, sometimes called cognitive processing or information processing. Robert Sternberg (1990) developed a triarchic theory of intelligence with three components: analytic or componential intelligence (abstract thinking abilities, verbal abilities, etc.); creative or experiential intelligence (emphasizing the ability to formulate new ideas and deal with novel situations); and practical or tacit intelligence (the ability to adapt to changing environments).

For recent work by Canadian researchers on intelligence and the processing that contributes to this elusive phenomenon, read about the PASS theory by J.P. Das of the University of Alberta in two new publications by Papadopoulos, Parrila, and Kirby (2014) and Das and Misra (2015). The latter looks at the role of cognitive planning and executive functions in intelligence.

The irony is that while these theoretical developments proceed, schools, for the most part, continue to use standardized tests to measure children's and adolescents' intelligence in a completely atheoretical way. In 1904 Alfred Binet developed a test with his collaborator, Theophile Simon, intended to measure mental age. By this they meant that a child who passed the tests normally passed by an 8 year old had a mental age of 8, regardless of chronological age. The Stanford–Binet Intelligence Scale has been revised many times, and while the concept of mental age has been altered somewhat, no one has developed theoretical underpinnings for the test. The most-used intelligence test in Canada and the United States is the Wechsler Intelligence Scale for Children (WISC test) developed by Jerome Sattler, which was designed to predict school achievement. It is similar to the Stanford–Binet in design and concept, and is also atheoretical. Most intelligence tests are designed so an average score is 100, and 68 percent of the population will earn scores between 85 and 115. Only about 16 percent of the population will receive scores either above 115 or below 85. The tests are less reliable as one gets away from the normal range, and yet they are most often used to identify those students with high scores (gifted students) or low scores (students with developmental disabilities), as well as students with learning disabilities. The tests are not likely to be valid for students from culturally diverse backgrounds for whom English is a second language or for Aboriginal students.

Controversy about IQ testing persists. For example, Sternberg (2010) has suggested an alternative model, WICS, referring to wisdom, intelligence, and creativity synthesized. Recent research suggests that working memory tests are better predictors of school achievement than IQ tests (Alloway & Alloway, 2010) and, for both clinical and non-clinical samples, attention may interact with intelligence to predict achievement (Steinmayr et al., 2010). Debates continue over whether intelligence is more a matter of nature (born with it, cannot do anything about it) or nurture (can be developed through stimulation and education). Today most psychologists believe both are important. Because we, as educators, can do little about nature, we must make every effort to influence nurture—to produce stimulating, caring classrooms in which students take risks and are willing to use and develop their intelligence.

References

Alloway, T.P., & Alloway, R.G. (2010). Investigating the predictive roles of working memory and IQ in academic attainment. *Journal of Experimental Child Psychology, 106*, 20–29.

Das, J.P., & Misra, S.B. (2015). *Cognitive planning and executive functions.* Thousand Oaks, CA: Sage.

Gardner, H. (1993). *Multiple intelligences: The theory in practice.* New York: Basic Books.

Papadopoulos, G., Parrila, R., & Kirby, J. (Eds.). (2014). *Cognition, intelligence, and achievement.* Waltham, MA: Academic Press (Elsevier).

Spearman, C. (1927). *The abilities of man: Their nature and measurement.* New York: Macmillan.

Steinmayr, R., Ziegler, M., & Trauble, B. (2010). Do intelligence and sustained attention interact in predicting academic achievement? *Learning and Individual Differences, 20*, 14–18.

Sternberg, R.J. (1990). *Metaphors of mind: Conceptions of the nature of intelligence.* New York: Cambridge University Press.

Sternberg, R.J. (2010). WICS: A new model for school psychology. *School Psychology International, 31*, 599–616.

Sternberg, R.J., & Detterman, D.L. (Eds.). (1986). *What is intelligence? Contemporary viewpoints on its nature and definition.* Norwood, NJ: Ablex.

Thurstone, E.L. (1938). Primary mental abilities. *Psychometric Monographs, No. 1.*

Teaching Students Who Are Gifted or Developmentally Advanced

Teacher: How can I help you stay out of trouble?

Brian: I don't want to be bored. Challenge me. Let me work ahead on things that really interest me.

Brian is a gifted Aboriginal boy in grade 3. This exchange took place after his teacher had intervened in a scuffle between Brian and a classmate for the third time in a week.

Teacher: Why did you push Larry?

Brian: When I have nothing to do, he gets to me. He calls me "brainer" and tells me that I'm weird. When I'm busy, I don't notice as much. I need more stuff to do . . . please.

Description of Gifted Students

Students who are advanced in one area or in many areas and exceed the expectations of parents or of the school curriculum in specific areas of development are described as gifted or talented. While it may seem odd to consider these students to have learning exceptionalities, research shows that many of them do not thrive in regular classrooms when their learning needs are not met (Reis & Renzulli, 2010). Historically, gifted students have been identified by high scores on intelligence tests and often were assumed to be advanced in all areas (McBee et al., 2012). Research conducted in Ontario schools emphasizes that gifted learners are **developmentally advanced** in specific **domains**. Dona Matthews and her colleagues (Matthews & Dai, 2014; Foster & Matthews, 2012) recommend that teachers differentiate curriculum to challenge students and meet their learning needs in the subjects in which they demonstrate advanced ability.

Weblinks

COUNCIL FOR EXCEPTIONAL CHILDREN (SEARCH FOR "GIFTED")

www.cec.sped.org

GIFTED CANADA

www3.telus.net/giftedcanada

GIFTED AND TALENTED EDUCATION (GATE) PARENT ASSOCIATION

www.gatecalgary.ca

Students who are gifted often demonstrate outstanding abilities in more than one area. They may demonstrate extraordinary intensity of focus in their particular areas of talent or interest. However, they may also have accompanying disabilities, and they should not be expected to have strengths in all areas of intellectual functioning. Gifted students who also have disabilities, such as learning disabilities, are often called "twice exceptional" (Baldwin et al., 2014; Yssel et al., 2014). When differentiating for these students, it is critical to ensure that they are challenged while meeting their need for structure and support in the areas of their learning disabilities.

Characteristics of Students Who Are Gifted

No gifted student will show all of the characteristics described here. Often gifted students' vocabularies are advanced and sophisticated. They may show an unusual degree of curiosity, of ingenuity in seeking answers, and of persistence with tasks they enjoy (Reis & Renzulli, 2010). The same students may surprise you with their ordinary performance in subjects in which they do not excel. Although some gifted students can be easily identified because they use their abilities and are willing to be recognized for them, some gifted students go unnoticed. These are most likely to be young boys, students from diverse cultural groups including Aboriginal students, those with disabilities, and adolescent women (e.g., Gentry & Fugate, 2012; Matthews & Kirsch, 2011).

COGNITIVE CHARACTERISTICS

Students gifted in academic skills and cognitive functioning are thought to differ from their classmates in four key ways: (1) the rate at which they learn new knowledge or skills, (2) the depth of their comprehension, (3) the range of their interests, and (4) their enhanced **metacognition**, or ability to decide when and where to use their knowledge and skills (Hannah & Shore, 2008; Yildiz et al., 2011). Characteristics teachers see that suggest advanced cognitive development also include

- communication—a large vocabulary and high verbal fluency
- memory—an excellent retention of new knowledge
- insight—a facility for learning quickly and easily
- reasoning—a demonstrated ability to make abstractions readily
- observation—the capacity to identify similarities, differences, and relationships
- motivation—advanced interests and intensity for learning

Reis and Renzulli's Enrichment Triad Model (2010) describes giftedness as an interaction among three primary clusters of characteristics: (1) above-average **cognitive abilities**, as described above; (2) high levels of task commitment; and (3) high levels of creativity. **High task commitment** is found in students who work hard and need little external motivation, especially in areas that interest them. They set their own goals, embrace new challenges, and persevere. However, high task commitment can result in perfectionism when students chastise themselves when they make a mistake. High levels of **creativity** are demonstrated by students' contributing many ideas, transforming and combining ideas, asking questions, and being insatiably curious.

BEHAVIOUR CHARACTERISTICS

The behaviour of gifted students varies. Sometimes gifted students are more advanced intellectually than emotionally (Peterson, 2015). They may show enhanced concern

Further Reading

About teaching gifted students:

Angelova, V. (2014). Aspects of teaching mathematics to gifted students in the context of inclusive education. *International Journal on New Trends in Education & Their Implications, 5*(3), 104–116.

Yildrim, R., & Akcayoglu, D.I. (2015). Strategy-based English language instruction: The impact on the language proficiency of young gifted learners. *Education, 43*(2), 97–114.

Callahan, C., Moon, T., Oh, S., Azano, A., & Hailey, E. (2015). What works in gifted education: Documenting the effects of an integrated curricular/instructional model for gifted students. *American Educational Research Journal, 52*(1), 137–167.

Maker, C.J., & Schiever, S.W. (2010). *Curriculum development and teaching strategies for gifted learners.* Austin, TX: PROED.

Ford, D.Y. (2011). *Multicultural gifted education* (2nd ed.). Waco, TX: Prufrock Press.

Rakow, S. (2011). *Educating gifted students in middle school: A practical guide.* Waco, TX: Prufrock Press.

Gifted students are challenged by authentic problem solving in places such as the Toronto Zoo. These students examine specimens in the butterfly meadows, a natural habitat area at the zoo.

for justice and awareness of complex ethical, environmental, and societal issues (Foster & Matthews, 2012). Parents and teachers can listen to children's concerns, acknowledge that there are troubles in the world, focus on how problems are being addressed, and help children to set reasonable goals for what they can do (Foster & Matthews, 2012).

Implications for Learning and Differentiating in the Classroom for Students Who Are Gifted

Differentiated education was first developed to meet the needs of gifted learners (Tomlinson, 1999; 2014) and then was recognized as appropriate for all learners. When differentiating for gifted learners, look for curriculum areas where students are not challenged and consider how to remedy that. Assessment to inform differentiation for gifted students may include RTI (discussed in Chapter 1; e.g., Johnsen et al., 2015) and embedded *assessment for learning* (discussed in Chapter 9; e.g., Miedijensky & Tal, 2009). Strategies that are often suggested include enabling students to pursue their interests (e.g., Gentry et al., 2007) and using tiered assignments, as discussed throughout this book (see examples for physics in Geddes [2010], math in Tretter [2010] and Barger [2009], reading in Preddy [2009], and general examples in Rakow [2007]).

Other strategies include introducing technologies, such as spreadsheets, to increase the sophistication of student projects (Siegle, 2005); assigning self-directed research projects (van Deur, 2011); designing multicultural literature units (Pedersen & Kitano, 2006); and developing accelerated programs (Renzulli, 2008). **Acceleration** refers to placing students based on readiness and potential to succeed rather than on chronological age (Kanevsky, 2011; Kanevsky & Clelland, 2013). Some acceleration strategies involve changing the placement of the student, such as moving the student into the next grade for math class, having the student move to the next grade in all subjects, creating combined classes, giving early entrance to kindergarten or grade 1, or early graduation from secondary school. Some acceleration strategies involve changing the curriculum while the student stays for all or most of the day with same-age peers; examples include correspondence courses, subject-matter acceleration, curriculum compacting, continuous progress, access to a mentor, self-paced instruction, advanced placement, and the International Baccalaureate program. Kanevsky (2011) found wide variation in the use of acceleration practices across Canada.

Research suggests that gifted learners need to be with their intellectual peers for at least part of the school day so they are stimulated in areas in which they are advanced (Reis & Renzulli, 2010). However, they also benefit from learning with same-age peers during each school day. Some gifted students prefer to work independently and learn alone, and it may be important to honour this preference at some time during each day. Online learning has also been shown to be effective for differentiating learning for gifted students (Thomson, 2010). Teaching self-advocacy encourages gifted students to become partners in differentiation (Douglas, 2004). Strategies for differentiating the curriculum to meet the needs of gifted students appear in Table 3.3. Figure 3.1 on page 65 provides an example of an **open-ended assignment**.

TABLE 3.3 ENRICHMENT STRATEGIES FOR TEACHING GIFTED STUDENTS

Strategies	Descriptions and Examples
Authentic problem solving	Students apply their knowledge and skills to problems that are significant to their own lives. *Example:* When studying watersheds, students test the water quality of a stream that collects runoff from a parking lot in their community and prepare a report for the town council.
Independent studies	Students pursue an area of personal interest or investigate a topic from the curriculum on their own. *Example:* Students select a character from *Hamlet* and prepare a résumé for that character based on their knowledge of the play.
Telescoping	Taking advantage of the overlap in curricula of adjacent grades, students do two curricula in a year. *Example:* Students complete grades 7 and 8 science in one year.
Compacting	After discerning what students already know of the unit, the teacher provides assignments so students can master unfamiliar material and then provides enrichment activities. *Example:* Students who have already understood many of the events and issues of the Second World War presented in the curriculum complete readings and written synopses on unfamiliar topics. They choose topics of interest about how the war changed Canadian society, contact the War Museum, use the Internet, talk with the teacher, and prepare multimedia presentations on their chosen topics.
Ability grouping	Students work with their intellectual peers on a regular, part-time basis in the classroom or outside the classroom, providing social and emotional support, as well as intellectual stimulation. *Example:* An advanced math work group, perhaps with peers from other classes, for enrichment.
Mentor programs	Students apply their knowledge and skills in a hands-on, real-life setting under the supervision of an adult in the community. *Example:* A student who is a skilled artist is partnered with a painter who invites the student to her studio to share the experience of preparing for an upcoming show.
Open-ended assignments	Students are given options for completing an assignment and deciding how far to take their learning. *Example:* In a kindergarten unit on whales, the teacher provides required assignments to be completed by all students about the habitat and diet of the whales studied and provides optional assignments that require more writing, allowing children to create games for whales based on knowledge of whales' characteristics. Figure 3.1 shows an open-ended assignment.
Tiered assignments	Teacher prepares a range of distinct assignments, from simple to complex, focusing on key learning outcomes. Students may be assigned particular activities, the teacher may select one activity to be completed by everyone and allow students to choose another, or students may choose the level of assignments they will complete. *Example:* In a secondary drama unit, the tiers for a culminating assignment include preparing a scene, an act, or a short play while employing two, three, or more actors, and embodying one or more of the themes from a list.

Source: Hutchinson, N.L. (2004). *Teaching Exceptional Children and Adolescents: A Canadian Casebook* (2nd edition), p. 144. Copyright Prentice Hall. Used by permission.

FIGURE 3.1 AN OPEN-ENDED ASSIGNMENT FOR A KINDERGARTEN CLASS CONTAINING GIFTED STUDENTS

A Whale of a Party!
Kindergarten Independent Project
Due Date: January 29

Dear Parents,

The following is an outline of the Independent Project for term two. The format I have set out does not have to be followed strictly, so if you or your child has something to add or change, please feel free to do so. The items that are starred (*) are optional. The written sections may be typed on a computer, but I would encourage student printing wherever possible. Obviously, I would like the students to do as much of the work as possible and to be making the decisions regarding their projects. However, this should be an enjoyable experience, so if they have reached their limit, feel free to give extra help or to cut something out. Stress quality over quantity and the experience/process over the final product. Finally, if you have any questions, don't hesitate to ask me in person or via the homework books.

You are going to throw a party, and all of your friends are whales. Pick two different kinds of whales to invite (three, if you are feeling extra keen) and fill out the following party plan. Plan on having ten whale guests.

The Guest List

(a) What kind of whales did you choose to invite and why? Make sure you invite whales that will get along (i.e., whales that will not eat each other!).
(b) Make a list of their names (e.g., Ollie Orca, Mandy Minke, etc.).
(c) *List the general address you would send an invitation to in January for each type of whale (e.g., Arctic Ocean).

The Invitation

Hand in a sample of the invitation you would send out to your guests.
Your invitation should include
(a) A cover design.
(b) The name and type of whale (e.g., Ollie Orca) to whom the invitation is addressed.
(c) *Location of the party (consider the size of your guests, but you can pretend that the whales can be out of the water for your wingding).
(d) Date and time of the party.
(e) RSVP address or telephone number.

The Party

(a) Draw me a picture of how you would decorate the party location to make your guests feel at home.
(b) Draw and/or print a menu of the food you will serve your guests.
(c) On another piece of paper, list the following:
(d) *The kind of music you will listen to at your party (this can be people music)
(e) *Will you ask your guests to do any tricks or play any games at your party (find out if your guests are especially good at something)?
(f) *Will you send your guests home with a party favour? What will it be?

The Party's Over

(a) Draw me a picture of what a photograph taken at your party might look like.
(b) *Write a thank-you letter that you think one of your guests might have sent you after the party.

Source: Courtesy of Jennifer Taylor. Used with permission.

Implications for Social and Career Participation of Students Who Are Gifted

Gifted adolescents often find it difficult to focus their career aspirations and to make appropriate course selections, perhaps because they have so many talents and interests. For example, Allen is a talented musician and a top student in almost every subject. He has been invited to audition for the Canadian Youth Orchestra (CYO). If Allen attends CYO, he cannot take part in an archaeological dig for which only eight students have been accepted. Allen says that every cello lesson reinforces his desire to be a professional musician.

However, after spending a day at the dig, he is just as passionate about becoming an archaeologist. Allen's guidance counsellor invites him to a seminar on careers, where Allen learns that there are prerequisite courses for entering a university program in archaeology. Allen also enrols in a co-operative education placement with an archaeologist, for which he receives a secondary school credit. Gifted students benefit from career development programs that build on their interests and connect them with individuals who share their passions (Gentry et al., 2007; Muratori & Smith, 2015).

Teaching Students with Learning Disabilities (LD)

Frank watched his teacher write the afternoon schedule on the board. The list included reading, social studies, and journal writing. Did that mean oral reading? Frank had not practised the next story in the book. If the teacher asked him to read, he would die, the other kids would laugh, and . . . He tried to think of a way to get out of class before oral reading. He felt his chest tightening and his stomach flipping. Frank hated to stutter and stumble. He slouched down in his seat and worried. He kept asking himself, "How bad can it be?" But he knew the answer: "Bad!" When you can't read in grade 6, it's bad. Frank is a grade 6 student with learning disabilities in reading.

Description of Students with Learning Disabilities

Students with learning disabilities have been described in recent years as having dysfunction in **information processing** or **executive function**. They may have disabilities in reading (**dyslexia**), writing (**dysgraphia**), or arithmetic (**dyscalculia**). In the provincial documents the term *learning disabilities* (LD) is usually used to refer to exceptional students with a **discrepancy** between ability (measured by an intelligence test) and achievement in one or more of the following areas: reading, writing, language acquisition, mathematics, reasoning, and listening (Kozey & Siegel, 2008). In most provinces the documents specify that this discrepancy is not primarily the result of a visual, hearing, or motor disability; emotional or behaviour disability; or environmental, cultural, or economic disadvantage. Usually the term LD is used to describe students who have at least average ability and from whom we would ordinarily expect better achievement (Klassen, 2002; Philpott & Cahill, 2007).

Controversies surround definitions of LD. In 2008 Michelle Kozey and Linda Siegel of University of British Columbia (UBC) described the inconsistencies in provincial definitions and procedures for identification. The 2002 definition developed by the Learning Disabilities Association of Canada (LDAC) (re-endorsed March 2, 2015; www.ldac-acta.ca) emphasized four aspects: learning disabilities are neurobiological, genetic, lifelong, and felt in all areas of life. The definition of the Learning Disabilities Association of Ontario (LDAO) (2001; www.ldao.ca) emphasized impairments in executive function or psychological processing related to learning that can cause difficulties in oral language, reading, written language, and mathematics.

These definitions have also referred to the "unexpected" aspects of learning disabilities: that difficulties learning in specific areas are discrepant with an individual's overall ability. Many researchers (including Canadians such as Siegel [1999] and Stanovich [2005]) have argued against using discrepancy formulas, arguing that all students who show disabilities in learning (in word recognition, reading comprehension, reading fluency, mathematics computations or problem solving, or written expression) should be identified as having LD (see Fletcher et al., 2007; Gresham & Vellutino, 2010).

This is essentially what has happened recently to the clinical definition used by psychiatrists and psychologists for diagnosing LD: the most recent definition emphasizes low academic achievement. In the American Psychiatric Association's *Diagnostic and Statistical Manual of Mental Disorders* (*DSM-5*; 2013), a specific learning disorder is described as a neurodevelopmental disorder of biological origin. This disorder is manifested in learning difficulties and problems in acquiring academic skills; the affected academic skills are below those expected for the individual's chronological age (and interfere with academic or occupational performance and activities of daily living) or academic achievement can be maintained only with extremely high levels of effort. The difficulties must have persisted for at least six months despite the provision of interventions for the difficulties, and not be explained by intellectual disabilities, visual or auditory disabilities, lack of language, or inadequate opportunity to learn.

Areas of academic skill difficulties include:

1. word decoding and word reading fluency
2. reading comprehension
3. spelling
4. writing difficulties such as organization, clarity, grammar, and punctuation
5. number sense, number facts, calculation
6. mathematical reasoning

In addition, clinicians are expected to synthesize information about the individual's development, medical history, family circumstances, educational reports, and standardized psycho-educational tests. According to *DSM-5*, an IQ test is not required but the individual must not have identified intellectual disabilities. Individuals are to be identified as having a learning disorder, and then the clinician can specify whether there is impairment in reading (dyslexia), in written expression (dysgraphia), in mathematics (dyscalculia), or in more than one of these areas, and specify the current severity: mild, moderate, or severe.

Controversies will continue to abound because now the guidelines that clinicians are expected to follow are substantively different than the definitions of most

Further Reading

Related to controversies surrounding evolving definitions of LD:

Ontario Ministry of Education. (2014, August 26). *Identification of and Program Planning for Students with Learning Disabilities: Policy/Program Memorandum (PPM) No. 8.* Toronto, ON: Ontario Ministry of Education. www.edu.gov.on.ca/extra/eng/ppm/ppm8.pdf

Malow, M.S. (2013). Learning disabilities and the *DSM V. Strategies for Successful Learning, 7*(1), www.ldworldwide.org

Tannock, R. (2014, January). *DSM-5* Changes in diagnostic criteria for specific learning disabilities (SLD): What are the implications? *Newsletter of the International Dyslexia Association: Promoting Literacy Through Research, Education and Advocacy,* http://dyslexiahelp.umich.edu

Tannock, R. (2013). Rethinking ADHD and LD in *DSM-5*: Proposed changes in diagnostic criteria. *Journal of Learning Disabilities, 46*(5), 5–24.

Hale, J., Alfonso, V., Berninger, V., Bracken, B., et al. (2010). Critical issues in response-to-intervention, comprehensive evaluation, and specific learning disabilities identification and intervention: An expert white paper consensus. *Learning Disability Quarterly, 33,* 223–236.

Students with learning disabilities often find written work in the classroom challenging.

provincial ministries and departments of education and of the major LD associations in Canada. Most provinces employ definitions based on the LDAC definition (2002, 2015). However, the Ontario Ministry of Education adopted a new definition of LD in *Policy/Program Memorandum No. 8* (August 26, 2014) which came into effect January 2, 2015. The definition of LD in these revised requirements for the identification of and program planning for students who have learning disabilities is similar to, and uses much of the language of, *DSM-5*. The major difference is that Ontario continues to compare a student's achievement to intellectual abilities (IQ) rather than to chronological age (www.edu.gov.on.ca/extra/eng/ppm/ppm8.pdf). The document states specifically that the program planning section also applies to "Any other students who demonstrate difficulties in learning and who would benefit from special education programs and/or services that are appropriate for students with learning disabilities" (Ontario Ministry of Education, 2014, p. 4). Approaches to assessment and intervention are to include universal design for learning, differentiated instruction, and tiered approaches.

Many American states use response to intervention (RTI) to identify students with learning disabilities, which is consistent with *DSM-5*. Following research-informed classroom instruction and screening, students who do not benefit adequately from increasingly intense instruction are identified as having LD (Gresham & Vellutino, 2010). Some researchers have raised concerns about this approach to identification and intervention (see Hale et al., 2010). Canadian provinces have been less quick to embrace RTI for identification (McIntosh et al., 2011). New Brunswick, Ontario, and Saskatchewan all refer to RTI in one or more provincial documents (Mattatall, 2008), and Ontario's recently adopted definition of LD moves close to that in *DSM-5* (Ontario Ministry of Education, 2014).

A number of provinces state that learning disabilities are apparent in both academic and social situations. Three key skill areas in social-emotional learning have been identified by Canadian researchers as most likely to pose difficulties for students with LD: recognizing emotions in self and others, regulating and managing strong emotions, and recognizing personal strengths and areas of need (Bloom & Heath, 2009; Galway & Metsala, 2011). These aspects are not specifically delineated in the new clinical guidelines of *DSM-5*, raising another area for controversy.

Characteristics of Students with Learning Disabilities

Teachers are most likely to suspect learning disabilities when the characteristics exhibited by the students interfere with classroom learning. However, characteristics vary greatly from student to student. According to Statistics Canada, more children in this country have learning disabilities than all other types of disabilities combined. Boys outnumber girls, although the reasons for this are unclear (Whitley et al., 2007).

COGNITIVE CHARACTERISTICS

Students with LD demonstrate lower-than-expected achievement in one or more areas. You will also see academic strengths that you can praise and build on. Frequently these students perform poorly on tasks requiring memory, focused attention, organization, metacognition, and information processing (Fuchs et al., 2011; Maehler & Schuchardt, 2011).

Cross-Reference
Chapter 8 contains practical strategies to implement phonemic awareness interventions.

CHARACTERISTICS: READING DISABILITIES OR DYSLEXIA

The most common learning difficulty for students with LD is experiencing difficulties learning to read, usually called dyslexia. Research supports insufficiently developed phonemic awareness as a characteristic of primary children with reading disabilities. **Phonemic awareness** includes the awareness that words can be segmented into component sounds, identifying sounds in various positions in words, and manipulating sounds in words (Ryder et al., 2008). Explicit, systematic instruction of phonemic awareness is necessary for most children and does no harm to those for whom it is redundant, and phonemic awareness interventions are effective in helping most children with LD to learn to read (Frijters et al., 2011; O'Brien et al., 2011). Canadian researchers such as John Kirby of Queen's University (Kirby et al., 2010) have demonstrated that **naming speed** or **rapid naming** also plays a significant role in learning to read. When children demonstrate deficits in both phonemic awareness and rapid naming, this has been called the **double-deficit hypothesis**. Other critical reading skills include phonics, fluency, vocabulary development, and text comprehension (National Reading Panel, 2010).

Some students with LD experience challenges in **reading comprehension**, including missing the main idea, getting events out of sequence, and deducing content that is not there (Davis & Guthrie, 2015; Guthrie et al., 2009). The areas of difficulty seen in adolescents weak in reading comprehension can include word recognition, language comprehension, and executive processes. Those poor in word recognition may struggle to sound out words and not recognize words by sight that their peers recognize automatically. In language comprehension difficulties, we see students who have difficulty expressing background knowledge related to what they are reading because they lack knowledge, vocabulary, or text structures. Their executive processes, cognitive and metacognitive, may be inefficient and poorly chosen. (For a thorough discussion of these issues, see Davis & Guthrie, 2015; Faggella-Luby & Deshler, 2008.)

The printed or written letters of students with LD can be distorted in size and shape, reversed, or barely legible (Berninger et al., 2006; Wise Berninger, 2012). Because all students tend to reverse letters until about age 8, reversals are only a problem when they persist past that age. Some students also have difficulty learning to spell (Berninger & May, 2011). The typical characteristics of young children with learning disabilities appear in Figure 3.2 and those of older students in Figure 3.3.

Weblinks

LEARNING DISABILITIES ASSOCIATION OF CANADA

www.ldac-acta.ca

LEARNING DISABILITIES ASSOCIATION OF ONTARIO

www.ldao.ca

COUNCIL FOR EXCEPTIONAL CHILDREN (CEC)

www.cec.sped.org

LD ONLINE (TEACHING LD)

http://teachingld.org

CHARACTERISTICS: LEARNING MATH

Recent research points to **number sense** being the mathematical equivalent of phonemic awareness (Jordan et al., 2010), with scores on a screening measure in kindergarten and grade 1 predicting later learning difficulties in math. Number sense refers to children's flexibility with numbers, the sense of what numbers mean, and the ability to make mental comparisons about quantities. Many recent studies have compared the executive functions of students with math disabilities or disorders (MD)

FIGURE 3.2 CHARACTERISTICS OF LD IN YOUNG CHILDREN

Problems in Reading

- often lacks awareness of sounds that make up words, does not "attack" a new word but guesses or waits for the teacher to say the word
- loses meaning of sentence before getting to the end; loses sequence of what has been read
- is painful to listen to, finds reading painful and finds creative ways to avoid reading

Difficulty in Copying

- copies better from a page beside him than from the board, appears careless
- loses his place frequently and ignores organizational cues

Difficulty with Alphabet

- has difficulty remembering sounds of letters and names of letters
- confuses letter names and sounds if learning both at once
- shows poor penmanship with frequent reversals or distorted shapes or sizes of letters (or numbers)

Strengths

- often shows strengths in some areas and weaknesses in others, and really benefits from recognition of his strengths
- often expresses ideas better orally than in writing
- often highly motivated by small successes and willing to work very hard to succeed again
- often shows imagination and complex ideas when asked to draw or act out his ideas, but reverts to simpler ideas when writing to avoid errors or embarrassment

Source: Hutchinson, N.L. (2004). *Teaching exceptional children and adolescents: A Canadian casebook* (2nd ed.), p. 60. Copyright Prentice Hall. Reprinted with permission by Pearson Canada Inc.

to those with reading disorders (RD), and to those with math and reading disorders (MD + RD); generally, all groups function poorly on working memory tasks in addition to tasks that are specific to their area(s) of disorder (see Andersson, 2010; Desoete & De Weerdt, 2013).

Challenges often arise in learning addition facts and multiplication tables, and students may ignore columns in computations and carry or borrow incorrectly, issues addressed in research by Derek Berg of Queen's University (Berg, 2006, 2008; Berg & Hutchinson, 2010). Older students with LD often find it challenging to represent mathematical relations in word problems (Montague et al., 2011). Students unable to grasp algebra may not understand they must use symbols to replace numbers, and may treat algebra as if it were the same as arithmetic. They may memorize procedures when what is needed is to represent word problems (Jitendra & Star, 2011), and they may need more concrete methods of representation than are usually available in algebra classrooms (Hughes et al., 2014).

SOCIAL AND BEHAVIOURAL CHARACTERISTICS

Research findings about social competence are inconsistent. Some students' social and behavioural needs are expressed in social withdrawal, frustration, and **depression** (e.g., Bloom & Heath, 2009; Galway & Metsala, 2011). Jess Whitley and colleagues (2007) of the University of Ottawa found that teachers reported that *most* students

FIGURE 3.3 CHARACTERISTICS OF STUDENTS WITH LD IN GRADES 4 TO 6 AND IN JUNIOR AND SENIOR HIGH SCHOOL

Characteristics in Grades 4 to 6

- avoids reading aloud
- has difficulty understanding and representing word problems
- experiences difficulty expressing ideas, especially in a meaningful sequence
- may be scapegoated by classmates because not socially aware
- knows content from watching movies and television, not from classes and reading
- may show less self-regulation than peers
- may be easily discouraged about lack of success

Characteristics in Junior and Senior High School

- spelling difficulties persist and now interfere with written expression
- reads slowly and experiences severe difficulties in comprehension, especially of textbooks
- difficulties persist in written expression and affect quality of written assignments
- difficulties with organization persist and now may affect grades (not submitting work)
- shows weak grasp of abstract concepts; cannot read to understand nuanced meanings
- benefits from having models of what is expected in assignments
- benefits from guided practise and needs more independent practise than peers
- learns well in intensity of small group where teacher is responsive to lack of comprehension
- can be encouraged and engaged by caring, attentive teacher
- may be much more successful in some classes than others
- may not have a realistic understanding of own strengths and weaknesses

Source: Hutchinson, N.L., & Martin, A.K. (2012). *Inclusive classrooms in Ontario schools*, p. 60. Copyright Prentice Hall. Reprinted with permission by Pearson Canada Inc.

with LD experienced social skills difficulties and peers reported that *many* had low **social status**. But only a *few* children with LD reported low social **self-concept** (Walker & Nabuzoka, 2007). Hutchinson et al. (2004) recommended that interventions recognize the extent to which adolescents' social competence is context-dependent and capitalize on adolescents' interests. Womack and colleagues (2011) recommended literature-based social skills interventions.

Klassen (2007) reported that adolescents with LD tend to overestimate their efficacy for spelling and writing. He also found that teachers who knew adolescents with LD well thought these adolescents were overconfident about their academic ability (Klassen & Lynch, 2007). Nancy Heath of McGill University and her colleagues (2013) also reported that adolescents with LD overestimated their performance in math. This can be challenging for teachers because we must encourage realistic self-assessments without discouraging students by continually pointing out how incompetent they are.

Implications for Learning and Classroom Differentiation: Students with Learning Disabilities

Most students with LD require differentiations in instruction and in the learning environment. They are usually taught in inclusive classrooms and may receive services in resource rooms.

ESTABLISHING AN INCLUSIVE CLASSROOM

It is important to establish a safe classroom where students with LD feel accepted. Strategies that will help include interactive teaching and frequent checks that individual students understand your instructions. Also try to eliminate bullying. Stough and Palmer (2003) reported that teachers who were expert at teaching exceptional students demonstrated knowledgeable, reflective, and concerned responsiveness to individual students. Long and her colleagues (2008) emphasized the importance of teachers' empathy, approachability, and willingness to differentiate instruction in promoting the confidence and engagement of students with learning disabilities. Kyle Robinson (2015) found that Ontario secondary teachers reported that they created an inclusive classroom by getting to know their students well and using that knowledge to differentiate instruction.

DIFFERENTIATING TEACHING

You can build on an inclusive learning environment by differentiating your instructional techniques to make them more accessible to students with LD. Differentiations include

- providing overviews of lessons in chart form
- varying the mode of presentation (oral, visual, activity-based)
- cueing students to listen to, or make notes about, important points
- relating material to students' lives and using experiential teaching approaches
- making directions short and reinforcing oral directions with visual cues
- clarifying definitions and ensuring understanding by having students repeat definitions
- breaking a large topic or task into manageable parts with individual deadlines
- using collaborative and co-operative learning approaches
- offering assistance when it is needed, after students have asked their peers
- preparing study guides of key words and concepts so students have clear notes from which to study
- using colour-coded materials to make organization easier
- using partially filled in tasks to guide students
- encouraging students to audio-record a lecture or listen to a recording of a book
- using cross-age tutoring both of younger students by those with LD and of those with LD by older role models
- using tiered assignments and tasks that are differentiated and differ in reading demands

TEACHING STRATEGIES

It is important that you demonstrate how to learn and allow students with LD time to practise the skills they find difficult. General organizational skills, highlighting main ideas, and note-taking strategies can be taught to the whole class; then provide additional practise for those who need it in a way that is respectful and does not make them feel less competent than their classmates. For example, introduce agenda books, model how to make entries, and put a daily agenda on the board. Teach outlining by providing a partial outline of your notes for students to complete, and teach highlighting by having pairs of students decide what main ideas should be highlighted. Model on a projector before the students begin an activity and debrief with reasons at the end of the lesson.

In a meta-analysis, Swanson and Deshler (2003) reported that eight instructional factors—(1) questioning, (2) sequencing and segmentation, (3) skill modelling, (4) organization and explicit practise, (5) small-group setting, (6) indirect teacher activities (e.g., homework), (7) technology, and (8) scaffolding—captured the majority of successful intervention programs for adolescents with LD. Most important was the organization and explicit practise factor, which included two important instructional components: advance organization and explicit practise. Find a way to teach more intensely—to students in a small group, where you can be more responsive when an individual does not understand—and if that is not enough, arrange for yourself, a special educator, an educational assistant, a volunteer, or an older student to provide individual tutoring and practise. Figure 3.4 includes strategies for helping students with LD to improve their organizational skills.

Students with LD are frequently taught **cognitive strategies** (Hughes, 2011). These strategies may focus on reading comprehension (Ciullo et al., 2015; Tejero Hughes & Parker-Katz, 2013), writing (Kadivar et al., 2010), or math problem solving (Pfannenstiel et al., 2015). Similar strategies are used to teach social competence

FIGURE 3.4 HELPING STUDENTS WITH LD TO IMPROVE THEIR ORGANIZATIONAL SKILLS

Strategies for Building Organizational Skills in Students with Learning Disabilities

- Post an agenda at the front of the class; follow it and give warning before you make changes
- If necessary, post a personal agenda on a student's desk until the class agenda is sufficient
- Post a calendar of deadlines on a bulletin board in the classroom
- Encourage the student (and parents, if necessary) to post a calendar of deadlines at home
- Teach students to record homework, deadlines, etc. in an organizer/planner
- Provide checklists so students can track their progress through activities and assignments
- Teach students to date and title notes and assignments
- If students move from room to room, provide a mobile schedule
- Help students to organize their desk or locker containing books and other necessities
- Suggest students carry books for two classes; they won't have to go to their lockers as often
- Teach students to use sticky notes and highlighters as reminders
- Provide time checks for the whole class at five- or ten-minute intervals so students self-monitor
- Provide clear, concise instructions and check that students understand what to do
- Teach appropriate help-seeking behaviour and encourage increasing independence
- Put organizational goals on IEPs so teachers must make accommodations focus on improvement
- Explicitly teach time management skills; follow up with students with LD regularly
- Remember that students with LD require more guided and independent practise to reach mastery of skills
- Be clear with students and parents about your expectations for organizational skills
- Emphasize that organizational skills are important and everyone can learn to be organized
- Be vigilant and persistent, especially at the beginning; changes in behaviour are worth it

Source: Hutchinson, N.L., & Martin, A.K. (2012). *Inclusive classrooms in Ontario schools*, p. 62. Copyright Prentice Hall. Reprinted with permission by Pearson Canada Inc

(Gumpel, 2007). Alan Edmunds (1999) of Western University suggested that teachers "talk out" a strategy for social cues with individual students and print the cues on a credit card–sized piece of paper. By laminating the card, punching a hole in one of its corners, and affixing a cable tie, you enable students to attach the cognitive credit cards to their pencil cases or backpacks.

In a thorough review of research on dyslexia, Shaywitz and her colleagues (2008) describe effective interventions as explicit, intense, systematic, and developmentally appropriate. They describe three important kinds of accommodations, which we considered in Chapter 1: those that bypass reading difficulties by providing information through the auditory mode; those that provide compensatory assistive technologies (access to recorded materials, computers, and print-to-speech software); and those that provide additional time so that dysfluent readers can demonstrate their knowledge (on examinations, in particular).

For many students with LD in reading, the challenges persist beyond learning to read and are manifested in comprehension difficulties when these students are reading to learn. Faggella-Luby and Deshler (2008, p. 76) describe a six-tiered continuum of literacy instruction:

Level 1: Enhance content instruction of critical content for all students.

Level 2: Embed strategy instruction in your large-group teaching.

Level 3: Provide more intense instruction in learning strategies and more time for practise for those who need it.

Level 4: Develop and provide, as a team, intensive basic skill instruction for students with severe deficits.

Level 5: Access therapeutic intervention for students with significant deficits in basic language competencies.

Level 6: Work with your colleagues and the students' families to extend instructional time through strategic before- and after-school tutoring.

For teaching mathematics to adolescents with LD, Witzel and his colleagues (2008) developed a **concrete-to-representational-to-abstract (CRA)** sequence of instruction. This approach takes students through **C**oncrete hands-on instruction with manipulative objects, then through pictorial **R**epresentations of the manipulatives used in the concrete stage, to learning through **A**bstract notation including operational symbols. They describe seven steps for implementing CRA:

1. Choose the math topic to be taught.

2. Review procedures to solve the problem.

3. Adjust the steps to remove notation or calculation tricks.

4. Match the abstract steps with an appropriate concrete manipulative.

5. Arrange concrete and representational lessons.

6. Teach each concrete, representational, and abstract lesson to student mastery.

7. Help students generalize what they learn through word problems.

Many researchers are developing tiered interventions to differentiate instruction for students with learning disabilities. Use the journal resources available through your school district or at the university where you take courses to keep up with changes in the field of LD. Access journal articles online through organizations and associations that subscribe to the journals or through your membership in such organizations as the Council for Exceptional Children.

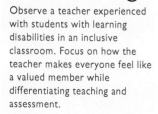

Put into Practice

Observe a teacher experienced with students with learning disabilities in an inclusive classroom. Focus on how the teacher makes everyone feel like a valued member while differentiating teaching and assessment.

Implications for Social and Career Participation of Students with Learning Disabilities

Although there are many successful adults with learning disabilities, many other adults with LD experience underemployment (Versnel et al., 2008; Shaywitz et al., 2008). **Career development** programs have used cognitive strategies to teach employment readiness and career awareness explicitly. Canadian programs for adolescents with LD include *The BreakAway Company: A Career Readiness Program for At-Risk Youth* (Campbell et al., 1994) and *Pathways* (Hutchinson & Freeman, 1994), which provide teachers with collaborative activities that accommodate heterogeneity. Although these programs were developed two decades ago, they are still used in Canadian classrooms. The research my colleagues and I have conducted shows that adolescents with LD benefit from workplace experience and through learning to negotiate workplace accommodations (Hutchinson et al., 2008).

Teaching Students with Attention Deficit Hyperactivity Disorder (ADHD)

I have ADHD and my Dad always says that I have eagle eyes. He means that I notice everything, even things that are not important at the moment. Dad also says that eagles know when to stop looking around and zoom in on their prey; I am learning this.

Once when Dad and my sister and I were hiking, a thunderstorm came up and we started to run back to the car. Dad tripped and twisted his knee. He could not walk, so he asked if my sister or I would go for help. My sister was not sure of the way.

"I can find it, Dad!" I said, and I told him the whole route. "Ben, I knew those eagle eyes of yours would come in handy," Dad replied. "Hurry, Ben! I need you." Swift as an eagle, I went to the ranger station and got help for Dad. I was the one who could do it. That's when I realized it's good to be me.

Based on Gehret, 1991, p. 11.

Description of Students with Attention Deficit Hyperactivity Disorder

Children and adolescents with ADHD have been described as displaying some or all of the behaviours of **inattentiveness**, **hyperactivity**, and **impulsivity** (e.g., *DSM-IV*; American Psychiatric Association, 2000). In the past, the condition was sometimes called ADD (attention deficit disorder). Although controversy has long surrounded the definition of ADHD (Barkley, 2010; Valo & Tannock, 2010), clinicians, educators, and parents have tended to focus on the behaviours these children display, such as having difficulty staying focused on schoolwork and chores, being easily distracted and forgetful, and being constantly on the go. Recent research suggests that there are unique underlying cognitive characteristics specific to ADHD that should be included in the criteria (Barkley, 2012; Gupta & Kar, 2010).With the release of *DSM-5* (APA, 2013), ADHD is viewed as a neurodevelopmental disorder, whereas it had been classified as a disruptive behaviour disorder in *DSM-IV*. However, the core diagnostic criteria remain essentially unchanged; we often overlook the strengths of individuals with ADHD like Ben in the vignette above.

> ### Further Reading
>
> About teaching students with ADHD:
>
> DuPaul, G., & Stoner, G. (2014). *ADHD in the schools* (3rd ed.). New York, NY: Guilford Press.
>
> Reid, R., & Johnson, J. (2012). *Teacher's guide to ADHD.* New York, NY: Guilford Press.
>
> Harlacher, J.E., Roberts, N.E., & Merrell, K.W. (2006). Classwide interventions for students with ADHD. *Teaching Exceptional Children, 39*(2), 6–12.
>
> Nadeau, K. (2015). *Understanding girls with ADHD: How they feel and why they do what they do.* Washington, DC: Advantage Books
>
> Evans, S., Owens, J., & Bunford, N. (2014). Evidence-based psychosocial treatments for children and adolescents with attention deficit/hyperactivity disorder. *Journal of Clinical Child and Adolescent Psychology, 43*(4), 527–551.

FIGURE 3.5 ANNOTATED BIBLIOGRAPHY ON MENTAL HEALTH AND ADHD

Recently researchers, practitioners, and clinicians have begun to focus on the aspects of ADHD that may cause children and adolescents with ADHD to experience mental health issues and stigma at school.

<u>Children's Attitudes Toward ADHD, Depression and Learning Disabilities</u> (2013) by Faye Francesca Bellanca & Helen Pote, *Journal of Research in Special Education Needs, 13*(4), 234–241.

Children responded to vignettes describing children with ADHD, depression, LD, or a child with none of these conditions. Children generally displayed more negative attitudes towards the ADHD vignette. Younger children and those with previous contact with children with ADHD were more positive.

<u>Adolescents' Beliefs about the Fairness of Exclusion of Peers with Mental Health Conditions</u> (2015) by Claire O'Driscoll, Caroline Heary, Eilis Hennessy, & Lynn McKeague, *Journal of Adolescence, 42,* 59–67.

Group interviews with adolescents revealed that they generally judged excluding peers with ADHD or depression from dyads and groups at school as unfair. However, evaluations were influenced by personal beliefs about the social and personal costs of excluding the target person. Understanding youths' perspectives may help reduce stigma.

<u>Educational Outcomes of a Collaborative School–Home Behavioral Intervention for ADHD</u> (2013) by Linda Pfiffner, Miguel Villodas, Nina Kaiser, Mary Rooney, & Keith McBurnett, *School Psychology Quarterly, 28*(1), 25–36.

A collaborative school–home intervention for children from grades 2 to 5 provided training to parents, intervention in the classroom, and a skills group for the children focused on social and independence skills. Large improvements were found in ADHD symptoms, organizations skills, and homework, as well as academic achievement and engagement.

<u>ADHD and Adaptability: The Roles of Cognitive, Behavioural, and Emotional Regulation</u> (2014) by Emma Burns & Andrew Martin, *Australian Journal of Guidance & Counselling, 24*(2), 227–242.

Adaptability has been viewed as cognitive, behavioural, and emotional regulation that helps individuals respond to change and uncertainty. This is particularly applicable to students with ADHD who struggle when cognitive and behavioural regulation are required to deal with change. This paper suggests how to help with adaptability.

Weblinks

TEACHING STUDENTS WITH ATTENTION-DEFICIT/HYPERACTIVITY DISORDER: A RESOURCE GUIDE FOR TEACHERS (2007, BC EDUCATION)

www.bced.gov.bc.ca/specialed/adhd

FOCUSING ON SUCCESS: TEACHING STUDENTS WITH ADHD (2006, ALBERTA EDUCATION)

http://education.alberta.ca/admin/special/resources/adhd.aspx

HEALTH IN FOCUS: ADHD (SICK KIDS HOSPITAL, TORONTO)

www.sickkids.ca/HealthInFocus/ADHD

CH.A.D.D.: CHILDREN AND ADULTS WITH ATTENTION DEFICIT DISORDERS (CANADIAN SITE)

www.chaddcanada.com

ONTARIO LITERACY AND NUMERACY SECRETARIAT: WHAT WORKS? RESEARCH INTO PRACTICE, RESEARCH MONOGRAPH #3, THE EDUCATIONAL IMPLICATIONS OF ATTENTION DEFICIT HYPERACTIVITY DISORDER

www.edu.gov.on.ca/eng/literacynumeracy/inspire/research/Tannock.pdf

Many provincial ministries of education have no separate category of ADHD, so to receive services at school, some students identified with ADHD may be identified as having LD or behaviour exceptionality; and ADHD criteria and identification processes are inconsistent across the provinces (Edmunds, 2008). The Centre for ADHD Awareness Canada (CADDAC) has criticized Ontario, British Columbia, and Québec because they do not include ADHD as a category of exceptionality (CBC News, 2010). In 2011 (December 19), the Ontario Ministry of Education distributed a memorandum reminding directors of education that students with ADHD should receive special education services based on need and could be identified within the LD category or one of the other categories such as behaviour. Both British Columbia and Alberta have well-developed resources for teachers about ADHD (see Weblinks). Figure 3.5 provides information about the mental health issues that may be experienced by individuals with ADHD.

Boys are more likely to have ADHD than girls, and generally have more severe ADHD, although girls may be at higher risk for psychological effects (e.g., anxiety, depression) (Arnett et al., 2015; Hinshaw et al., 2006). Usually information is gathered from the child, parents, and teachers through behavioural checklists, interviews, and observations; physicians and psychologists are considered qualified to make this diagnosis.

Characteristics of Students with ADHD

The characteristics and learning needs of students with ADHD vary. *The Diagnostic and Statistical Manual of Mental Disorders* (*DSM-5*) (APA, 2013) currently describes three presentations of ADHD: Predominantly Inattentive, Predominantly Hyperactive-Impulsive, and Combined Presentation. The new guidelines require that clinical judgment should be used to specify the severity level as mild (no or few more symptoms than required for diagnosis, no more than minor impairment in function), moderate (functional impairment between mild and severe), or severe (many symptoms in excess of those required for diagnosis or marked impairment resulting from symptoms).

CHARACTERISTICS OF ADHD, PREDOMINANTLY INATTENTIVE

Students with ADHD, Predominantly Inattentive, display more characteristics of inattention than hyperactivity-impulsivity. They may ignore details, make careless errors, or have trouble staying on task while working or playing. They may not seem to listen when you speak to them directly and may not follow through on instructions or complete tasks and homework. Students who are predominantly inattentive may have difficulty organizing their activities, and they may lose or forget things. They dislike or try to avoid work that requires them to concentrate for long periods of time, and may be easily distracted by movement, objects, or noises in the classroom. They may daydream and may rush through tasks.

CHARACTERISTICS OF ADHD, PREDOMINANTLY HYPERACTIVE-IMPULSIVE

Students with ADHD, Predominantly Hyperactive-Impulsive, display more characteristics of hyperactivity-impulsivity than of inattention. They may fidget and squirm, leave their desks, and run and climb at inappropriate times. They usually find it challenging to play or work quietly, they move constantly, and they talk excessively. Impulsivity characteristics include blurting out answers before you have finished asking a question, not waiting for their turn or not following other classroom rules, and disturbing or interrupting others. Their impatience can cause them to demonstrate unsafe behaviour and to neglect to consider the consequences of their actions. Transitions within the school day can be challenging. Impulsivity has been positively related to academic attainment, while inattention has been related to under-attainment (Tymms & Merrell, 2011).

CHARACTERISTICS OF ADHD, COMBINED PRESENTATION

Many students with ADHD have the Combined Presentation, perhaps as many as 50 percent (Lee et al., 2008). They display many characteristics of both inattention and hyperactivity-impulsivity. This type of ADHD involves major challenges with (1) sustained attention, (2) persistence toward goals, (3) resisting distractions, (4) inhibiting task-irrelevant activity (hyperactivity), and (5) inhibiting actions, words, thoughts, and emotions that are socially inappropriate or inconsistent with one's long-term goals and general welfare (Barkley, 2012).

What do you think?

There are a number of recent, controversial books that are critical of the identification and treatment of students with ADHD and other disabilities. Form a group with some of your colleagues and each read one of the sources listed below, representing different sides of the debate. Discuss the critiques and debate current practices with your peers. Arrive at a well-informed opinion so you can respond if a parent, administrator, or colleague asks: what do you think?

Root, E.E. (2009). *Kids caught in the psychiatric maelstrom: How pathological labels and "therapeutic" drugs hurt children and families.* Santa Barbara, CA: Praeger.

Gnaulati, E. (2013). *Back to normal: Why ordinary childhood behavior is mistaken for ADHD, bipolar disorder, and Autism Spectrum Disorder.* Boston, MS: Beacon Press.

Hawthorne, S. (2014). *Accidental intolerance: How we stigmatize ADHD and how we can stop.* Oxford, UK: Oxford Press.

Honos-Webb, L. (2010). *The gift of ADHD: How to transform your child's problems into strengths.* Oakland, CA: New Harbinger Publications.

Barkley, R. (2013). *Taking charge of ADHD: The complete, authoritative guide for parents.* New York, NY: Guilford Press.

Nass, R.D. (2011). *100 questions and answers about your child's ADHD: From preschool to college.* Sudbury, MA: Jones & Bartlett Learning.

Put into Practice

Consult Chapter 7. Develop a plan for a lesson; describe the cognitive characteristics of a student with ADHD and how you would differentiate instruction to ensure that the student with ADHD would understand and learn. Use resources such as these:

Anderson, K.M. (2007). Differentiating instruction to include all students. *Preventing School Failure, 51*(3), 49–54.

Nowacek, E.J., & Mamlin, N. (2007). General education teachers and students with ADHD: What modifications are made? *Preventing School Failure, 51*(3), 28–35.

Rotter, K.M. (2004). Simple techniques to improve teacher-made instructional materials for use by pupils with disabilities. *Preventing School Failure, 48*(2), 38–43.

EMERGING CONCEPTION OF ADHD: THE ROLE OF EXECUTIVE FUNCTIONING AND SELF-REGULATION

Recently, researchers including Rosemary Tannock and Rhonda Martinussen in Canada and Russell Barkley in the United States have begun to focus on executive functioning (EF) and self-regulation (SR) and their relationship with ADHD. While executive function has been defined in a number of ways, in the field of ADHD, it usually refers to those cognitive or neuropsychological processes needed to sustain problem solving toward a goal (Barkley, 2012; Tannock & Martinussen, 2001). This future-oriented, goal-directed process is similar to **self-regulation**, the means by which individuals manage themselves to attain their goals. These self-directed actions and cognitions include self-awareness, inhibition of distractions, managing attention, visualizing the goal, problem solving to reach the goal, and even encouraging oneself (self-motivation). This perspective emphasizes the cognitive sources of ADHD rather than the behavioural manifestations (e.g., Barkley, 2012; Karalunas & Huang-Pollock, 2011; Martinussen & Major, 2011). Tannock (2007) argues that ADHD should be reconceptualized as a learning disorder, but one that is distinct from LD.

CHARACTERISTICS OF SOCIAL INTERACTIONS

ADHD influences all aspects of an individual's life, including social interactions (McConaughy et al., 2011). Their social and emotional characteristics can cause peers and teachers to react negatively when students with ADHD show limited self-confidence, are unable to contribute to a team, misinterpret social cues, have difficulty with anger management, or overreact emotionally (Marton et al., 2009; Normand et al., 2011; Zentall et al., 2011). Treating students with ADHD respectfully and patiently can enhance your relationship with them and can serve as a model so they receive better treatment from their peers. Programs designed to improve the social problem solving of students with ADHD can be group-facilitated (Gresham, 2002) or computer-mediated (Fenstermacher et al., 2006). Chapters 7 and 10 include information about implementing such programs with the assistance of special educators and student services personnel.

Implications for Learning and for Differentiating in the Classroom: Students with ADHD

Because students with ADHD have underlying processing difficulties that give rise to their inattentive/distractible and impulsive/hyperactive behaviours, we must understand these processing difficulties to differentiate in the classroom. Barkley (2012) argues that these difficulties represent a delay and not a loss of executive function (as we see in students with brain injury). We need to structure the context to help them overcome or compensate for these delays by making accommodations. The goal is that they can more effectively manage themselves, focus on their tasks and goals, and prepare for their future. Barkley argues that changes need to be made in the natural setting, where the individual is not using what they know about SR and EF; in many cases, that is the classroom. Some general principles for accommodations include:

1. Externalize forms of information (because internally represented information, in working memory, for example, is not used effectively); for example, putting up posters with the steps to follow to use effective strategies.

2. Externalize time and structures needed for timeliness (to help with organization of cognition and behaviour and to make them aware of future as well as immediate plans and consequences); for example, setting out the day's schedule for young students and deadlines for daily progress toward assignment completion for older students.

3. Externalize sources of motivation (because of deficits in internal sources of self-regulation and the observed depletion of the resources for effort in students with ADHD after they have engaged in SR); for example, during SR-demanding situations, taking ten-minute breaks, ensuring routine physical activity, visualizing rewards, using self-affirming statements, and even offering concrete rewards if necessary. (Adapted from Barkley, 2012.)

These principles suggest that we use external supports to help students with ADHD to begin tasks and offer checkpoints for project completion. Provide homework journals for nightly assignments, as well as clear numbered and written instructions, in addition to verbal instructions.

Teachers who were interviewed reported using a range of approaches to promote acceptance of students with ADHD by their peers; one "hit problems head-on," while another reported using "subtle" means, but all said they modelled patience and acceptance, tried to "ward off" situations, and focused on accepting differences in discussions of course content (e.g., novel study) whenever possible (Nowacek & Mamlin, 2007). These teachers demonstrated awareness of key elements of differentiated instruction: flexibility, choice, creativity in differentiating the content, how students develop understanding of concepts, and how students demonstrate what they have learned (Anderson, 2007; Bellanti, 2011; Harlacher et al., 2006). Teachers can make teacher-designed materials more accessible to learners with ADHD: leave more white space on the page, use large fonts on the computer instead of handwriting tasks, and make the key information clear to students by bolding, colour-coding, or highlighting (Rotter, 2004).

ADAPTING CLASSROOM ORGANIZATION

Classroom organization can enhance learning for students with ADHD and their classmates. Externalize expectations and classroom organization. Provide a predictable, structured environment so students know what you expect of them and what they can expect of you. Communicate explicitly to ensure all students understand prior to starting an activity (DuPaul et al., 2011). Use the ADAPT strategy (discussed in Chapter 2), maintain the students' interest, model by **thinking aloud**, and ensure adequate opportunities for practise. Don't remove recess privileges from students with ADHD when they fail to complete their work; don't require them to "stay in" and finish. That increases levels of inappropriate behaviour for the remainder of the day (Ridgway et al., 2003). Look for other ways to help students complete their assigned work, and enable them to exercise and socialize with their classmates during recess. Table 3.4 provides examples of cognitive characteristics of students with ADHD and actions you can take to meet their needs.

RESPONDING TO INAPPROPRIATE BEHAVIOUR

Place the class rules in a prominent place and refer to them often to prevent inappropriate behaviour. Do all you can to help students to self-regulate. If you have to respond to inappropriate behaviour, give it as little attention as possible; instead, provide attention for appropriate behaviour as soon as it occurs (DuPaul et al., 2011).

TABLE 3.4 PROMOTING ACADEMIC SUCCESS FOR STUDENTS WITH ADHD

Current treatment approaches have focused on medication and behavioural interventions. However, emerging data on cognitive characteristics and executive function have implications for the classroom.

Cognitive Characteristics	Cognitive Adaptations in the Classroom
Difficulty understanding words such as *before*, *after*, *more than*.	Make language clear at beginning of task.
Lack of understanding of passage of time and of temporal events.	Post a list of items to be completed. Strike through items as they are finished.
Mismatch of student needs to lesson content and delivery.	Model what is to be done, repeat, and explain instructions and tasks.
Difficulty understanding and using language used in teaching and materials.	Rephrase to help with understanding and rephrase student's language when that helps others to understand student's meaning.
Lack of understanding about taking turns, working co-operatively.	Teach social skills (e.g., use microphone to show children whose turn it is to talk).
Difficulty understanding the process expected in practise activities following direct teaching.	Provide as much support as necessary for the student to begin the activity—guided practise. Gradually reduce support and increase self-direction.
Difficulty focusing on the needed information to complete tasks.	Reduce demands on working memory by providing external memory aids, mnemonics, graphic reminders, lists of steps, and strategies.
Lack of self-regulation.	Model strategies that can be used to self-regulate. Teach one strategy thoroughly and then another, helping students to discern when each is useful. Cue strategy use.

Sources: Information drawn from Tannock, R., & Martinussen, R. (2001). Reconceptualizing ADHD. *Educational Leadership*, 20–25; Mariage, T.V., Englert, C.S., & Garmon, M.A. (2000). The teacher as "more knowledgeable other" in assisting literacy learning with special needs students. *Reading and Writing Quarterly, 16*(4), 299–336.

A **verbal reprimand** may be necessary when behaviour gets out of hand. Effective reprimands are immediate, unemotional, brief, and backed up with a loss of privileges if that was the agreed-upon consequence. For a clear description of ways to use consequences effectively in the classroom, read DuPaul et al. (2011), *ADHD in the Classroom: Effective Intervention Strategies.*

STRATEGIES FOR SELF-REGULATION OR SELF-MANAGEMENT

Self-regulation strategies are implemented by the student and designed to increase self-control of behaviour (Burns & Martin, 2014; DuPaul & Weyandt, 2006). They teach students to use cognition to control behaviour or to take positive action. You and the student agree on a problem that is getting in the way of learning (e.g., looking around instead of completing assignments). You develop steps for the student to follow, put these on a cue card, and model their use. The student practises using the steps aloud, and gradually covertly, to solve the problem. The student monitors his performance of the steps. Some teachers use a signal to remind the student to begin using the steps. The student must know the steps and be able to carry them out individually. At first, the student can be cued, but eventually she must initiate the steps. Students can be taught self-regulated strategies for such academic tasks as writing (e.g., Jacobson & Reid, 2010; Mason et al., 2011) and math calculation (Iseman & Naglieri, 2011). Chapters 7 and 10 contain examples of such programs. These strategies take considerable thought and time in the early stages but are worth the effort when they are effective. Other ways to encourage SR and to overcome EF deficits are to explicitly teach goal-setting by incorporating it into academic tasks along with student self-monitoring to see if explicit goals are met (like doing five questions in five minutes) (Johnson & Reid, 2011). You can also give students with ADHD responsibilities they can handle so they feel they are contributing.

MEDICATION

Medication is one of the most controversial issues surrounding ADHD, and researchers estimate that about two-thirds of children diagnosed with ADHD receive pharmacological treatment. **Stimulants** such as methylphenidate (Ritalin) and amphetamines are the most commonly used medications prescribed for ADHD, and in recent years new formulations with controlled release have been introduced (Zuvekas & Vitiello, 2012). **Antidepressants** are also used (about 10 percent of the medication prescribed; Scheffler et al., 2009). Use of medications has continued to rise along with concerns about abuse and addiction. However, research has produced mixed results on the positive association between medication use and academic achievement (Langberg & Becker, 2012; Scheffler et al., 2009). The most common side effects of stimulants are insomnia, decrease in appetite, gastrointestinal problems, irritability, and increase in heart rate.

Current best practice for ADHD requires combining a focus on enhancing executive function and self-regulation with medical intervention (Barkley, 2012). Many suggest interventions that focus on the family as well as the classroom, and individual psychotherapy for the child if depression occurs. Figure 3.6 contains questions for parents and teachers to ask physicians about medication.

FIGURE 3.6 QUESTIONS FOR TEACHERS AND PARENTS TO ASK ABOUT MEDICATION FOR CHILDREN WITH ADHD

1. What is the medication that is prescribed? What do I need to know about it?
2. Why is this medication prescribed for my child? What changes should there be at home? At school?
3. What behavioural program or therapy is being implemented along with this drug therapy?
4. How long will this medication be prescribed for my child?
5. What are the side effects in the short term? In the long term?
6. What is the dosage? What is the schedule on which the medication should be taken?
7. How often will my child be seen by the prescribing physician for re-evaluation?
8. Should the medication be stopped for a short period of time to see if it is still required? When?
9. Are there foods, beverages, or other substances that should not be consumed when my child is taking this medication?
10. What kind of communication is necessary among home, school, and the student to evaluate whether the medication is having the desired effect?
11. What procedures should we follow if my child accidentally ingests an overdose?
12. What does my child need to know and who will provide the explanation?

Source: Hutchinson, N.L. (2004). *Teaching exceptional children and adolescents: A Canadian casebook.* Toronto: Prentice Hall. Reprinted with permission by Pearson Canada Inc.

Implications for Social and Career Participation of Students with ADHD

The account by Ben at the beginning of this section illustrates that people with ADHD have many strengths and plenty of energy. *DSM-5* acknowledges that ADHD is not likely to go away in adulthood. Like people with LD, adults with ADHD may find themselves undereducated and underemployed as adults unless they have opportunities for hands-on learning and for acquiring career awareness through explicit teaching and work-based education (DeLuca et al., 2012). The large number of adults with ADHD who attain successful careers reminds all of us that individuals with ADHD need to choose careers that are well-suited to their characteristics and enable them to use their considerable strengths.

Teaching Students with Emotional and Behaviour Exceptionalities and Students Experiencing Mental Health Challenges

> I don't like the work we do here. It is easy and boring. I can figure out the questions and after that I don't feel like doing them, so I don't. Most of the teachers back off when a student yells at them. They don't make me do it then. Other guys leave me alone when they see I can make the teacher afraid. I don't know what good this boring stuff is. I like to draw. I'm awesome at drawing. I should just do drawing all day at school so I can be an artist. I want to draw comic books and stuff like that.
>
> *From Urjo's interview with a counsellor about his experiences at school. Urjo, who is 15 years old, was identified as having a behaviour exceptionality.*

The Changing Context for Emotional and Behaviour Exceptionalities: School-Based Mental Health

What have traditionally been described as emotional and behavioural exceptionalities are among the most challenging to manage in classrooms. In interviews, educators in Ontario said, "student mental health . . . is our number one concern," and "student mental health and academic achievement go hand in hand" (Short et al., 2009). Researchers agree with educators that "student mental health needs exceed the current capacity of school systems to respond adequately" and report that one in five students in K to 12 has experienced mental health problems (Santor et al., 2009). Consensus is emerging that what is needed is wide adoption of prevention and intervention in the school context—that is, a school-based mental health strategy.

Child and adolescent mental health refers to the social, emotional, and behavioural well-being of children and adolescents and is considered an integral part of healthy development. While mental illness refers to diagnosable mental disorders, mental health problems include signs and symptoms of insufficient intensity or duration to meet the criteria for any mental disorder. However, mental health problems warrant active health promotion, prevention, and treatment (Santor et al., 2009).

The current approach emphasizes starting with fostering the well-being of students rather than simply targeting specific classroom problems in a reactive way (Morrison & Peterson, 2013). The intent is to enable students to thrive; and thriving is viewed as a process that takes place when youth are on a path to realize their potential and are successful in a number of areas (Heck et al., 2010). Recent models of school-based mental health are guiding urgent discussions across Canada (for a national report on mental health issues, see Bourget & Chenier [2007]). Models of school-based mental health generally include three or four tiers, the first of which is intended to enhance strengths of all students through positive strategies that foster healthy development, such as managing emotions, setting goals, and maintaining positive relationships (health promotion). The second tier is generally intended to reduce risk factors for all students, for example, information programs about substance abuse (universal prevention). The third tier generally targets students who have been identified as sharing a significant risk factor with preventive interventions to counter that risk (selective prevention). The second and third tiers are sometimes combined. The last tier consists of treatment interventions for students experiencing mental health problems or diagnosable disorders. (See, for example, Adelman & Taylor, 2006; Kutash et al., 2006; Weisz et al., 2005.) In most provinces, this fourth group includes students identified with emotional and behaviour disabilities.

Description of Students with Emotional and Behaviour Exceptionalities

Urjo was described at the opening of this chapter as refusing to do his homework; engaging in loud, verbal disagreements with teachers; and having a behaviour exceptionality. Don Dworet and Kimberly Maich of Brock University (2007) demonstrated the range of meanings held by the provinces across Canada for the term *behaviour exceptionality*. While students like Urjo are said to be externalizing, others may internalize their anxiety and possibly depression; these students are much less likely to be identified, although they may be withdrawn, not complete schoolwork, and be absent. Educators generally refer to behaviour that varies markedly and chronically from the accepted norm and that interferes with the student's own learning or the learning of others. That is, educators refer to educationally relevant characteristics. In contrast, psychologists and psychiatrists tend to focus on more clinical characteristics (Heath et al., 2006). Who makes the identification—educators or clinical personnel—varies, and expectations for social behaviour also vary across communities; both contribute to inconsistencies in definitions and estimates of the prevalence of behaviour exceptionalities.

The guidelines in British Columbia provide the following definition:

> Students can experience behaviour, social/emotional, or mental health problems that range from mild to serious. Most students with social/emotional difficulties can be supported in school through regular discipline, counselling, and school-based services. A smaller number of students require more intensive support. Students who require behaviour supports are students whose behaviours reflect dysfunctional interactions between the student and one or more elements of the environment, including the classroom, school, family, peers and community. This is commonly referred to as behaviour disorders. (British Columbia Ministry of Education. (2011). Special education services: A manual of policies, procedures and guidelines. Victoria, British Columbia Ministry of Education.)

What do you think?

Many have raised concerns about the experiences of exceptional children in military families and the challenges they experience because (a) they and their families tend to move frequently and there is little consistency in services for exceptional learners across the provinces, and (b) they are often separated from their parents who may be serving in dangerous locations around the world. Read one of the resources listed below and discuss with your peers the role that you think teachers can play in assuring the well-being of these children.

On the Homefront: Assessing the Well-Being of Canada's Military Families in the New Millennium (www.ombudsman.forces. gc.ca/en/ombudsman-news-events-media-news/military-families.page)

Iris the Dragon (www. iristhedragon.com) a charity that paired with the Canadian Forces to produce a book for children in military families to encourage them to talk about their feelings and mental health; www.cbc. ca/news/politics/mental-health-of-military-kids-focus-of-new-book-1.1189999

Davis, J., & Finke, E. (2015). The experience of military families with children with autism spectrum disorders during relocation and separation. *Journal of Autism & Developmental Disorders*, 45(7), 2019–2034. (American study)

Hisle-Gorman, E., Harrington, D., Nylund, C., Tercyak, K., Anthony, B., & Gorman, G. (2015). Impact of parents'

(continued)

(continued)

wartime military deployment and injury on young children's safety and mental health. *Journal of the American Academy of Child and Adolescent Psychiatry, 54*(4), 294–301. (American study)

Sometimes educators and clinicians forget that, like all other exceptional learners, children and adolescents with EBD and with mental health problems also have strengths; the extent to which they are able to showcase their strengths depends in part on what we do to change the context at school. As the Hincks-Dellcrest Centre for children's mental health says on its website, everyone experiences some mental health problems as a normal part of life, but children and adolescents require adult awareness and guidance to learn and grow from such problems. For some, these problems are serious enough that specialized assistance is needed. Without this, they and the people around them will experience stress and hardship, and such problems can lead to more serious mental health issues in adulthood (www.hincksdellcrest.org, search for "ABCs of Mental Health").

Challenges that Lead to the Behaviours We See in Classrooms

In *The ABCs of Mental Health*, the Hincks-Dellcrest Centre suggests that teachers have a key role in promoting student mental health because they know what their students typically do and can observe changes in mood and behaviour that seem unusual or excessive. They suggest that you think about mental health on a continuum from developmentally normal, through problems that you can address in the classroom, to problems that require assessment by experts and clinical intervention. You will grow concerned when a behaviour goes beyond a normal part of a particular student's development because of its intensity or frequency. Beyond that are behaviours that interfere to a significant extent with the student's functioning at school, or with normal development and activities. At each of these points on the continuum, you need to ask yourself: What is behind this behaviour? What might the underlying reasons be for this behaviour? Examples of underlying reasons include:

- family context (doing what has been taught or modelled at home)
- social context (doing what has been necessary for survival outside of school)
- differences between school and home/neighbourhood expectations (e.g., structure, routines, rules)
- need to "build a wall" or push people away to protect oneself
- fear or threat, especially for students who have experienced any form of maltreatment or abuse; what looks like overreacting is adaptive in the face of real threat but maladaptive in the absence of threat
- need for attention, recognition; seeking these in ways that may have worked elsewhere (but are not acceptable at school)
- poor interpersonal skills; may misread facial cues, other non-verbal communication, or verbal communication; not taking the current context into account; impulsive reactions; may not know how to act in the current situation
- cover for weakness; acting in a way that makes others see them as "bad" rather than "dumb"
- inaccurate self-perception (concerning ability, guilt, responsibility, etc.)

These students experience challenges in executive functioning and cognitive processing not unlike those experienced by many students with learning disabilities or ADHD. These include difficulties in:

- self-monitoring and prompting
- activation and effort (getting started and persisting)
- tolerating frustration (thinking before acting when frustrated)
- using "self-talk" to control present and future actions
- analyzing a situation by using complex problem-solving strategies
- organizing and planning ahead (managing time, materials)
- inhibiting and shifting (stopping one activity and beginning another)
- working memory (holding information in mind while manipulating it)
- recall (accessing information stored in long-term memory)

For more information about the classroom challenges that may arise from these processing difficulties, consult www.chrisdendy.com/executive.htm.

Weblinks

FOR LEARNING ABOUT MENTAL HEALTH AT SCHOOL IN CANADA:

HINCKS-DELLCREST CENTRE: *THE ABCS OF MENTAL HEALTH*

www.hincksdellcrest.org (search for "ABCs of Mental Health")

CHILD AND YOUTH MENTAL HEATH INFORMATION NETWORK: *EDUCATORS' GUIDE TO CHILD AND YOUTH MENTAL HEALTH PROBLEMS*

www.cymhin.ca

TAKING MENTAL HEALTH TO SCHOOL

www.excellenceforchildandyouth.ca/sites/default/files/position_sbmh.pdf

Characteristics of Students with Behaviour Exceptionalities

Recent research provides a description of the demographic characteristics and the social and academic experiences of a sample of Canadian students with EBD, compared to students without EBD, based on data drawn from the National Longitudinal Survey of Children and Youth (NLSCY) (Whitley et al., 2009). The EBD group contained a greater proportion of boys and of students from low-income families. Students in the EBD group reported having greater difficulty making friends and reported liking school less than the other students. Parents and teachers of students with EBD reported lower expectations than parents and teachers of the other group. Many students with emotional and behaviour disorders report being less satisfied with their quality of life in all domains (general, self, relationships, and environment) than their peers without disabilities (Sacks & Kern, 2008). Because students who experience behaviour exceptionalities are an extremely heterogeneous population, we must remember that no student would exhibit all of the characteristics discussed in this section of the chapter.

Students with behaviour disorders are likely to benefit from some or all of the following in the classroom (Reithaug, 1998):

- **structure**, predictability, and consistency
- immediate, frequent, and specific **feedback** with consequences
- academic success
- responsibility and independence
- positive problem solving
- positive alternatives to current behaviours
- enhanced self-confidence
- positive school-to-home support systems
- evidence that he is making changes for the better

Most students with EBD need challenging, respectful, and cognitively engaging activities. Sometimes we think we must lower expectations or excuse the student from learning; however, as

Help all students to participate constructively. This girl is demonstrating puppets she has made.

KidStock/Getty Images

Urjo suggests, boredom often contributes to students' acting out in class. Recent research suggests that when students, especially adolescents, experience positive emotions during school, they demonstrate higher levels of engagement (Gilman, et al., 2009; Reschly et al., 2008). Our challenge is to create a classroom milieu in which students feel valued and have positive experiences. It is important to focus on the behaviour you want to see the student engage in, and even explicitly teach the skills necessary for that behaviour, rather than assume that the student knows what to do and how to do it—they may not until we teach them. If their needs are not addressed, students with EBD fail more courses, miss more days of class, and are more likely to drop out of school than students with other exceptionalities (Sugai & Horner, 2008).

One group of students that has recently gained the attention of educators and mental health professionals is those who have experienced trauma. They could be dealing with traumatic stress due to experiencing or witnessing neglect; abuse or violence; war, illness, injury, or death. These situations can lead to emotional distresses that challenge a person's ability to cope. Intrusive symptoms include distressing memories of the event and sleep disturbances. Avoidance symptoms include persistent avoidance of the thoughts, memories, and reminders of the event or experience. Negative alterations in cognitions and mood include persistent negative emotional state, diminished interest in significant activities, feeling of detachment from others, and persistent inability to experience positive emotions. Alterations in arousal and reactivity include irritable behaviour or angry outbursts, hypervigilance, and problems with concentration (APA, 2013). These symptoms become maladaptive if the threat persists and may be at the root of emotional and behavioural needs seen in the classroom.

Implications for Learning and Differentiation in the Classroom: Students with Behaviour Exceptionalities

Students with emotional and behaviour exceptionalities, like Urjo, can be a disruptive force in the classroom and affect everyone present. You can help students improve their behaviour in many ways, ranging from preventive measures to direct responses. Table 3.5 describes strategies for preventing and responding to the challenging behaviour of any student, but especially those with EBD or who have experienced trauma. Focus on People describes a teacher who is effective in teaching students with EBD.

DIFFERENTIATING THE CURRICULUM AND STRUCTURING THE CLASSROOM

Differentiate the curriculum and structure the classroom environment to take advantage of "getting off to a good start." Apply procedures, rules, and consequences consistently and discuss any changes (reasons and implementation) with the class. Research suggests that you should use differentiated teaching for academic instruction without waiting for students' behaviour problems to be resolved (de Lugt, 2012; Gable et al., 2002). In fact, recent studies suggest that, for some students, academic difficulties contribute to students' behavioural problems (Morgan et al., 2008). The Manitoba Department of Education provides resources to help teachers develop behaviour intervention plans at its Student Services

What do you think?

About the mental health and well-being of Canadian students?
Read the OSDUHS Highlights (*The OSDUHS Mental Health and Well-Being Report for 2013*) published by the Centre for Addiction and Mental Health.
www.camh.net
Why do you think this report contains data on students' views of school climate? Are you surprised that overall 82 percent of students rate their teachers as excellent?
At the same website, access *Drug Use Among Ontario Students 2013 Report.*
Does it surprise you that alcohol is the most commonly used drug (by about 55 percent of students)?
Discuss these findings with your peers. Why is this information relevant for teachers?

Cross-Reference
Chapter 7 focuses on preventive classroom organization and classroom management, while Chapter 10 describes proactive ways of ensuring a positive milieu in which students respect and value one another.

TABLE 3.5 TEN STRATEGIES FOR PREVENTING AND RESPONDING TO CHALLENGING BEHAVIOUR

Strategies	Descriptions and Examples
Build rapport	Until you build rapport, some students will see any action you take as unfair and punitive. Students who need relationships the most may be the poorest at building them. No matter how many times they rebuff your efforts, they want you to reach out to them.
Make a personal connection	Get to know students as individuals by asking about their interests or hobbies. Learn about these topics from them. Ignore small problems; to students who see themselves as having "big" problems, the small things like swearing seem insignificant.
Include them in the plan	Ask questions, during a neutral conversation, about what would help them most and how you can help them manage themselves. When discussing behaviour and consequences, remain calm and ask what they would do in the situation and what seems fair to them.
Find something to like about them and tell them	Find their real strengths and competencies and point these out. Be specific and be sure they see what you say as genuine. Remind them of past success and of their progress, how far they have come. Give sincere praise.
Figure out how much space they need	Some students need you to be near; proximity can be a valuable strategy. At other times and for other students, giving them space is more effective. Observe and ask to figure out how much space is the right amount.
Iron fist in a velvet glove	Be firm and predictable. But couple your high expectations with a high level of support and caring. Communicate both expectations and support clearly. Being respectful, caring, and understanding does not mean that students can take advantage of you. Expect respect in return.
Talk to the student	If you anticipate a challenging situation, talk to the student beforehand to develop a strategy together. Put the onus on the student to tell you how a good choice will be made. Don't be afraid to raise the hard issues. Even if they don't respond, they know you care.
Avoid power struggles	Be aware of your body language, tone of voice, and language. Could any of these be perceived as a threat? Don't back students into corners and do de-escalate any conflict. Whenever possible, give choices and allow students to save face. Avoid an audience if a confrontation is inevitable. Give the student a chance to explain and apologize if you don't model appropriate behaviour.
Use humour to diffuse a situation	If a situation is escalating and you have good rapport with the student, you may be able to appeal to their sense of humour. Especially if the student is spunky and mischievous, they may see the humour in a situation and that may help you to de-escalate rising tensions.
Show respect and flexibility	Call students by name, treat them respectfully, avoid using sarcasm, especially in front of peers. Build flexibility into your classroom rules and use small slips (like forgetting a book or pencil) as an opportunity to build rapport rather than creating an issue. Invite students to tell you privately why they have not completed an assignment, etc. Remember that they may be giving you their best even though it seems less than adequate to you. And showing them respect and flexibility is much more likely to elicit their very best effort in your class.

Source: Based on a resource developed by Jenn Dods of Queen's University, for use in her teaching.

website (www.edu.gov.mb.ca/k12/specedu/bip/index.html). These plans help teachers to understand

- what a student is trying to accomplish with problem behaviours
- what the student needs from his or her teachers so the negative behaviour is not necessary
- proactive interventions to prevent reoccurrences
- reactive interventions to end the incident and minimize the disruption to learning

You can develop a behaviour or learning **contract** with a student with EBD that is specific to her greatest challenge, and ensure that it is realistic and immediate. Both of you should sign it. Contracts are described in Chapter 7.

Milly Fraser, Grade 4, Alexander Forbes School, Grande Prairie, Alberta

A teacher who catches students being good and much more.

"Stop, Drop, and Phone" Award

Milly Fraser will drop everything in the middle of the school day and phone parents, even at work, to let them know their child did especially well on a test. Milly Fraser might even suggest that mom or dad make the child a favourite meal as a reward.

Best Supporting Role

When Nancy Goheen's son, Taylor, was in a church play, Milly Fraser took in a rehearsal—because she couldn't make the performance. On skate night, she showed her support by attending, even though she doesn't skate. And when she heard that a local missionary group was going to help children in Nicaragua, Milly Fraser organized a class bake sale to raise money for school supplies for them. The kids saw their charitable efforts in action when the missionaries returned with a video of the Nicaraguan schoolchildren.

A Rewarding Experience

Taylor Goheen, a bright but troubled boy, was in danger of becoming the class outcast, but Milly Fraser brought him into the fold by establishing rapport with Taylor and employing savvy reinforcement techniques that engaged the whole class. When Taylor behaved well, he got to choose an enjoyable activity for everyone in the class—not just himself. Fraser also rewarded him, personally, with stickers and other little gifts. "She has given so much to my son," says Nancy Goheen, "that it has totally changed the person he is."

Source: Based on Nixon, D. (2000). Inspiring teachers. *Today's Parent Online*, September 4, 2000. www.todaysparent.com.

Further Reading

About interventions for students with behavioural exceptionalities:

Landrum, T., & Sweigart, C. (2014). Simple, evidence-based interventions for classic problems of emotional and behavioral disorders. *Beyond Behavior, 23*(3), 3–9.

Lane, K.L., Menzies, H.M., Barton-Arwood, S.M., Doukas, G.L., & Munton, S.M. (2005). Designing, implementing, and evaluating social skills interventions for elementary students: Step-by-step procedures based on actual school-based investigations. *Preventing School Failure, 49*(2), 18–26.

Gresham, F. (2015). Evidence-based social skills interventions for students at risk for EBD. *Remedial and Special Education, 36*(2), 100–104.

Cahit, K., Blake, J., & Chan, F. (2015). Peer-mediated interventions with elementary and secondary school students with emotional and behavioural disorders: A literature review. *Journal of Special Educational Needs, 15*(2), 120–129.

Doll, B., & Cummings, J.A. (Eds.) (2008). *Transforming school mental health services: Population-based approaches to promoting the competency and wellness of children.* Thousand Oaks, CA: Corwin Press.

Use the resources of the school, the district, and the community—to secure group intervention for the class—to teach **prosocial behaviours** and to develop co-operation. Topics typically include peer pressure, responsible citizenship, and interpersonal skills. Persist to secure individual therapy, counselling, or instruction in self-management strategies, consistent with the group intervention. Differentiate your teaching so all your students are fully engaged. For example, provide students with a choice of activities or at least of the order in which activities will unfold; and choose high-interest activities based on students' stated preferences, your observations, or informal polls. As Karen Hume of the Durham District School Board in Ontario (2008) says, "Start where they are." Notice, and offer sincere praise, when students respond well to differentiated teaching and choice. Praise is an easy and effective intervention when it is genuine (Landrum & Sweigart, 2014; Sprouls et al., 2015).

The ADAPT strategy can help you differentiate your teaching and ensure that a student with EBD finds classes meaningful; collaborating with a resource teacher, educational assistant, or volunteer can ensure that individual tutoring reinforces your adaptations. These actions can get a challenging student "onside" from the first day of term.

THE IMPORTANCE OF CLASSROOM PROGRAMS IN PROSOCIAL BEHAVIOUR (TIER 1 AND TIER 2 INTERVENTIONS)

Many programs that use literature have been effective in helping students with behavioural difficulties to learn about themselves and about others. For example, Regan and Page (2008) used the "Circle of Courage Model" (Brendtro et al., 1990; 2014). Cuccaro and Geitner (2007) describe a targeted intervention for a group of grade 5 students who had persistent problems at lunch and recess. They received direct instruction and practise in social skills at lunch every day for two weeks, with positive results. This action research may inspire you to develop a systematic approach to those students who require intensive help learning appropriate behaviour and respectful treatment of peers.

If you think that your efforts with these students are insignificant compared with the work of psychologists and psychiatrists, you are underestimating your importance. Recent Canadian reports (Buchanan et al., 2010; Dods, 2012) confirm earlier American reports (Mihalas et al., 2009; National Institute for Mental Health, n.d.) showing that teachers are key people who cultivate caring relationships with students with EBD and "make a difference," according to the students. We can prevent antisocial behaviour through interventions aimed at peers and other key people in the student's social environment. Our challenge is to alter adolescent norms so an aggressive reputation is no longer positively related to peer popularity. The primary strategy currently employed to achieve this goal is the use of classroom and school-based programs in social problem solving, conflict management, violence prevention, and more broad-based curricula for promoting emotional and social development in the total school population.

Implications for Social and Career Participation of Students with Behaviour and Emotional Exceptionalities

Historically, students with EBD and mental health problems have tended to lack advocates, perhaps because of the stigma associated with these conditions. In June 2008 the *Globe and Mail* ran an extensive series of newspaper articles, online contributions from readers, and question-and-answer opportunities with mental health experts with the aim of reducing the stigma associated with mental health conditions. They reported what the research has shown in recent years: adolescents and young adults are particularly vulnerable to depression, anxiety, schizophrenia, and other mental health problems. Stereotypes abound and make it difficult for these young people to make a successful transition into adult responsibilities and employment. However, since 2008, there have been many concerted efforts in Canada to address these issues and to point out the strengths of these individuals. Increasingly, organizations like the local branches of the Canadian Mental Health Association provide employment support to adolescents and adults.

Further Reading

On teaching students with emotional and behaviour disorders:

Jensen, M.M. (2005). *Introduction to emotional and behavioral disorders: Recognizing and managing problems in the classroom.* Upper Saddle River, NJ: Pearson Merrill Prentice Hall.

Morris, R.J., & Mathers, N. (Eds). (2008). *Evidence-based interventions for students with learning and behavioral challenges.* New York: Routledge.

Sprouls, K., Mathur, S.R., & Upreti, G. (2015). Is positive feedback a forgotten classroom practice? Findings and implications for at-risk students. *Preventing School Failure, 59*(3), 153–160.

Hickman, P., & Verden, C. (2009). "Teacher, it's just like what happens at my house." *Teaching Exceptional Children Plus, 5*(6), 1–20.

Further Reading

About the challenges for adolescents and their families:

Mojtabai, R., & Olfson, M. (2008). Parental detection of youth's self-harm behavior. *Suicide and Life-Threatening Behavior, 38*(1), 60–73.

Silver, R. (2008, May). Identifying children and adolescents at risk for depression and/or aggression. *Online submission*, ERIC Document Reproduction Service No. ED501283.

Crowell, S.E., Beauchaine, T.P., McCauley, E., Smith, C.J., Vasilev, C.A., & Stevens, A.L. (2008). Parent–child interactions, peripheral serotonin, and self-inflicted injury in adolescents. *Journal of Consulting and Clinical Psychology, 76*(1), 15–21.

Spoth, R., Randall, G.K., & Shin, C. (2008). Increasing school success through partnership-based competency training: Experimental study of long-term outcomes. *School Psychology Quarterly, 23*(1), 70–89.

Summary

Students with learning and behaviour exceptionalities include students who are gifted or who have learning disabilities, attention deficit hyperactivity disorder, and behaviour exceptionalities, or who experience mental health challenges. The prevalence rates for these exceptionalities mean that you will be teaching these students frequently.

In fact, many educators say that it is unusual, these days, to teach a class that does not contain at least one student with a learning disability or ADHD. These students may be inefficient at making sense of what you are teaching and may require encouragement and learning strategies that help them stay on task and complete assignments.

Gifted students will thrive with assignments that offer choice, challenge them, and enable them to go beyond regular curriculum expectations. When you see inappropriate or concerning behaviour in the classroom, remember to ask yourself what is behind the behaviour you are seeing, what might the underlying cause be. Expect to seek the assistance of other team members for students who have behaviour exceptionalities or mental health issues. They can be very challenging to teach and often require individual counselling that you simply cannot provide in a classroom setting. Asking for help when you really need it is a sign of strength, not weakness.

It is often difficult to distinguish students with the exceptionalities discussed in this chapter from their peers because their exceptionalities are not always obvious. Using the ADAPT strategy, in combination with students' IEPs, will help you to differentiate elements of the classroom so that you can meet individual needs. Most of these students will benefit from a structured, predictable, engaging class with a positive tone, in which everyone is treated with respect by you and taught that that is how they are expected to treat one another.

Weblinks

MINDYOURMIND.CA

This site says: "mindyourmind.ca is an award winning site for youth by youth. This is a place where you can get info, resources and the tools to help you manage stress, crisis and mental health problems. Share what you live and what you know with your friends. That's what we're about."

Visit this site and think about what makes it unique and why it might be more effective with youth than a site designed by adults. Can you find other similar sites for youth by youth?

Key Terms

acceleration (p. 63)
antidepressants (p. 81)
career development (p. 75)
cognitive abilities (p. 62)
cognitive strategies (p. 73)
concrete-to-representational-to-abstract (CRA) (p. 74)
contract (p. 87)
creativity (p. 62)
depression (p. 70)
developmentally advanced (p. 61)
discrepancy (p. 66)
domains (p. 61)
double-deficit hypothesis (p. 69)

dyscalculia (p. 66)
dysgraphia (p. 66)
dyslexia (p. 66)
executive function (p. 66)
feedback (p. 85)
high task commitment (p. 62)
hyperactivity (p. 75)
impulsivity (p. 75)
inattentiveness (p. 75)
information processing (p. 66)
intelligence (p. 60)
learning and behaviour exceptionalities (p. 59)
metacognition (p. 62)

naming speed (p. 69)
number sense (p. 69)
open-ended assignment (p. 64)
phonemic awareness (p. 69)
prosocial behaviours (p. 88)
rapid naming (p. 69)
reading comprehension (p. 69)
self-concept (p. 71)
self-regulation (p. 78)
social status (p. 71)
stimulants (p. 81)
structure (p. 85)
thinking aloud (p. 79)
verbal reprimand (p. 80)

Challenges for Reviewing Chapter 3

1. Read the brief description of Brian, a gifted student, at the beginning of the section on teaching students who are gifted. How could you differentiate instruction for Brian so that he is fully engaged in what he is learning and ensure that he is less likely to be taunted by his peers and to retaliate?

2. Write a description of a student with learning disabilities who is at a grade level you are likely to teach in the near future. Then describe the greatest challenges

you will face in differentiating your teaching so this student learns successfully, and consider the possibility of intensive tiered instruction outside your classroom to complement what you are doing.

3. Look back at the description of Urjo at the beginning of this chapter. He has been identified as having a behaviour and emotional exceptionality. Develop a chart to show his needs and strengths, and ways in which you can use his strengths to overcome his difficulties. Include intrapersonal, interpersonal, academic, and community aspects of Urjo's education. Think about whose support you might want to enlist for Urjo and for yourself while the two of you work together to improve these aspects of his education and to increase his likelihood of a successful transition to adulthood. If you are an elementary teacher, change Urjo's age to the age of students you teach.

Activities for Reviewing Chapter 3 with Your Peers

4. Return to the cases of Urjo and Connie, from the beginning of this chapter. Answer the four questions that follow the cases, and discuss your ideas with your peers. Identify the most surprising thing you have learned in this chapter and the most practical thing. What dilemmas about teaching stick in your mind after reading this chapter? What resources could you use or actions could you take that might help you to deal with these dilemmas?

5. Discuss with your peers why it is important to be prepared to differentiate the social aspects of your classroom as well as the academic instruction, especially for students experiencing mental health challenges.

6. You are currently a member of the in-school team for a student who has been identified as having ADHD, Predominantly Inattentive. Prepare to assume the role of one member of the team: classroom teacher, special educator, parent, or principal. Make a reading list and, after you have completed the readings, write a script for your contribution to a meeting occurring after differentiation of instruction has begun. Role-play the meeting with your peers. Generate a plan for keeping the student engaged in learning, now that she has experienced some success. Take the perspective that some of the student's characteristics are strengths unique to people with ADHD. How does this change what you say and do in the meeting and in your teaching?

CHAPTER 4

Exceptional Students: Intellectual Disabilities and Autism Spectrum Disorder

LEARNER OBJECTIVES

After you have read this chapter, you will be able to:

1. Describe students with mild intellectual disabilities and the ways in which you can differentiate, making accommodations and modifications, to meet their learning and social needs.

2. Describe how you can differentiate in classrooms for students with severe intellectual disabilities, including meeting alternative expectations.

3. Describe students with a range of autism spectrum disorder (ASD).

4. Describe how you can differentiate classroom teaching to meet the learning and social needs of students who are diagnosed with autistic disorder.

5. Describe accommodations and modifications that you would use to differentiate teaching to build on strengths and meet the social and learning needs of students with Asperger's disorder/high functioning autism (AS/HFA).

Maskot/Getty Images

PAMELA IS IN SENIOR KINDERGARTEN AT GROVE ELEMENTARY SCHOOL. She likes playing with water, making towers of blocks, being near the teacher, and exploring the materials the teacher is demonstrating. The classroom is often busy and noisy. For example, today a visitor is teaching the children to drum on the tomato-juice can drums they made last week. While the others sit in a circle, Pamela is running from one side of the room to the other, waving her arms. She has a short attention span for activities with a social component and becomes agitated when the classroom is too busy or too noisy. Pamela wants to sit on the chair beside the visitor and touch his drum. When she can't have her way, she has a tantrum. She repeats, "I like the big chair, I like the big chair," and "Thump the drum, thump the drum," both lines that she has heard the visitor say to the class. Pamela communicates through **echolalia** (echoing what is said), gestures, and limited functional speech, including, "No," "Help me," and "Get that one." Pamela's individual education plan (IEP) states that she has autistic disorder.

SCOTT IS INCLUDED IN A GRADE 3 CLASS AND LEARNS TO READ IN A SMALL GROUP IN THE RESOURCE ROOM. Scott was born with Down syndrome. His family has always involved him in all their activities, and he has always been in regular education programs. After participating in early intervention (from the age of 2 months to 4 years) and attending the neighbourhood early childhood education program, Scott moved with his classmates to kindergarten. Each year he has moved to the next grade, staying with the same classmates. Like many people with Down syndrome, Scott learns much by watching. For the past two years, he has watched and asked Billy, a friend and classmate with Attention deficit hyperactivity disorder (ADHD), whenever he didn't know what to do. Scott's parents and teachers know that the gap between Scott's academic achievement and that of his classmates will gradually increase. However, Scott works hard, likes school, and especially likes learning to read. Scott recognizes and sounds out many words, is reading small books with predictable stories, and for the past year has recognized the names of all the students in his class. In math, Scott can add and subtract numbers less than ten and hopes to learn to use his new calculator this year. He loves environmental science, discusses issues such as recycling, watches nature programs on television, and attends the "young naturalists" program in his community. Scott hopes to work in environmental protection when he grows up. His IEP (part of which appears in Figure 4.2 on page 98) lists his exceptionality as mild intellectual disabilities and refers to Scott's lower-than-average intellectual, social, and adaptive functioning.

1. Which of the characteristics of each student are most likely to affect learning? What learning needs are implied by these characteristics?

2. What do exceptional students like Pamela and Scott have in common?

3. How frequently is a teacher likely to be teaching a student with each of these exceptionalities?

4. What types of differentiation does each of these students need in order to be included in the social life and the learning activities of the classroom?

5. What community resources can a teacher draw on to supplement in-school resources to teach each of these students?

Introduction

Cross-Reference
For descriptions of and differentiations for students with learning and behaviour exceptionalities, see Chapter 3.

In this chapter, you will learn about the characteristics, needs, and strengths of students with two levels of **intellectual disabilities (ID)** and of students with **autism spectrum disorder (ASD)**. The two levels of intellectual disability are: (1) mild intellectual disabilities (MID) and (2) more severe intellectual disabilities, often called developmental disabilities (DD) (for example, DD is the term used by the Ontario Ministry of Education). We will discuss ASD under two headings: autistic disorder and Asperger's disorder/high functioning autism. The emphasis in this chapter is on how you can differentiate instruction in the classroom. Students with some of the exceptionalities described in this chapter are identified soon after birth because their needs are high and their disabilities or conditions are severe.

Some children with severe disabilities, such as Angelman syndrome (http://ghr.nlm.nih.gov/condition/angelman-syndrome), identified early in life, often start school with a detailed IEP. Labels give us a shared language, but it is important that we use language that is respectful and professional. Labels never capture the essence of the individual's experience of a disability or the family's experience. Sometimes labels can serve to limit our expectations, and cause us to focus too much on students' limitations and needs. We should make the effort to find ways these students can learn when we build on their strengths and we should consider what they contribute to the classroom.

As you read about students in this chapter, consider the parents' perspective. The parents of children with intellectual disabilities and ASD tend to be very involved in the lives of their offspring (Jansen et al., 2013). They may assume the role of **case coordinator** and are often better informed than classroom teachers about particular exceptionalities and conditions. You may teach a child with Prader-Willi syndrome (www.geneticdiseasefoundation.org/genetic-diseases/prader-willi-syndrome) once or twice in your career. The parents teach this child every day. I have used person-first language, for example, for students *with* ASD. This means we refer to the student first and describe the student as *having* an exceptionality or disability second.

TABLE 4.1 STUDENTS WITH INTELLECTUAL DISABILITIES AND AUTISM SPECTRUM DISORDER

Exceptionality	Description
Intellectual Disabilities	
Mild intellectual disabilities	Lower-than-average intellectual functioning and adaptive behaviour. Knows much about living in the community; requires instruction to be differentiated under supportive conditions
Severe intellectual disabilities	Severe limitation in both intellectual functioning and adaptive behaviour; individuals need support to function in the community
Autism Spectrum Disorder	
Autistic disorder	Impairments in verbal and non-verbal communication and reciprocal social interaction; restricted, repetitive patterns of behaviour; and intellectual disability
Asperger's disorder/high functioning autism (HFA)	Severe and sustained impairment in social interaction, and development of restricted, repetitive patterns of behaviour and interests (communication impairments in HFA)

TABLE 4.2 PREVALENCE OF INTELLECTUAL DISABILITIES AND AUTISM SPECTRUM DISORDER

Exceptionality	General Incidence in Research (Little Agreement Among Researchers for Incidence of ASD)
Mild intellectual disabilities	200 to 300 per 10 000 (BC Education, 2006; Christianson et al., 2002)
Developmental disabilities	13 per 10 000 (Arvio & Sillanpaa, 2003)
Autistic disorder	ASD: 36 per 10 000 (Fombonne et al., 2006); 50 to 90 per 10 000 (Schechter & Grether, 2008)
Asperger's disorder/high functioning autism	4 per 10 000 (Fombonne et al., 2006)

Each section begins with the words of a child or adolescent. Each entry follows a pattern: the exceptionality is described with information about its prevalence or frequency, followed by characteristics, classroom implications, and often implications for career participation. For some conditions discussed in this chapter, teachers must seek information on a need-to-know basis. However, the principles of inclusion, differentiation, accommodation, and modification always apply. Table 4.1 introduces the exceptionalities discussed in this chapter, and Table 4.2 provides data on the prevalence of ID and ASD.

Teaching Students with Mild Intellectual Disabilities

To Ms. Starr: I want to work in recycling. Because I want to help the environment and I won't need to read too much. I'm not too good at reading or writing, but I am learning this year. I like this class. You and Mr. T. [Mr. Tymchuk, the resource teacher] make me want to learn. You let me try my way. Thank you. That's why I want to be in recycling. The end.

Dictated to the resource teacher, following a lesson about careers, by Scott, who is in grade 3 and has mild intellectual disabilities.

Description of Intellectual Disabilities

Intellectual disability is a term widely used in Canada to replace *mental retardation*, a term now considered unacceptable. Intellectual disability is characterized by significant limitations both in intellectual functioning and in adaptive behaviour, which includes many everyday social and practical skills. This disability originates before age 18 (American Association of Intellectual and Developmental Disabilities [AAIDD], www.aaidd.org).

By intellectual functioning, the AAIDD means a general mental capability that involves the ability to learn, reason, solve problems, and so on. **Intelligence** is usually represented by intelligence quotient (IQ) scores obtained from standardized tests given by a trained professional. Generally an IQ test score of around 70 or as high as 75 indicates a limitation in intellectual functioning. Standardized tests can also be used to determine limitations in **adaptive behaviour**. Adaptive behaviour is thought to be comprised of the following three types of skills:

- conceptual skills (including language, literacy, number concepts, and self-direction)

- social skills (including interpersonal skills, social responsibility, social problem solving, and ability to follow rules and avoid being victimized)
- practical skills (such as activities of daily living, personal care, occupational skills, safety, and use of the telephone and transportation)

On its website, AAIDD stresses that professionals must take additional factors into account, such as the community environment typical of the individual's peers and culture, as well as linguistic diversity and cultural differences in the way people communicate, move, and behave. Assessments should focus on an individual's strengths as well as limitations, and recognize that level of life functioning will improve with personalized supports over a sustained period of time.

In recent years in educational and community service contexts in Canada, the term **developmental disabilities** has sometimes been used instead of the terms *mental retardation* or *intellectual disabilities* (e.g., Ontario Ministry of Community Services, www.mcss.gov.on.ca). However, across North America developmental disabilities is generally used to refer to a broad collection of disabilities, attributed to a mental or physical impairment or a combination of the two, which may not necessarily involve intellectual impairment. There are usually limitations in three or more of the following areas: self-care, receptive and expressive language, learning, mobility, self-direction, capacity for independent living, and economic self-sufficiency; examples include ASD, brain injury, cerebral palsy, Down syndrome, fetal alcohol syndrome, and spina bifida (University of Minnesota Institute for Community Integration, www.ici.umn.edu). The Ontario Ministry of Education uses the term *developmental disabilities* to refer to severe intellectual disabilities. These contradictory uses of a term can be very confusing for parents, teachers, and other professionals. If someone uses the term *developmental disabilities*, be sure to ask what characteristics she is referring to.

TWO LEVELS OF INTELLECTUAL DISABILITIES: MILD AND SEVERE

In the past, four categories—mild, moderate, severe, and profound—were used to describe ID, primarily associated with IQ score ranges. Recently, practitioners have begun to use two levels of functioning—mild and severe—to describe individuals with intellectual disabilities, primarily associated with level of adaptive functioning. **Mild intellectual disabilities (MID)** are discussed first, followed by severe intellectual disabilities.

MILD INTELLECTUAL DISABILITIES

The Ontario Ministry of Education describes MID as characterized by the ability to profit educationally within a regular classroom with modifications; by slow intellectual development; and by potential for academic learning, independent social adjustment, and economic self-support (2001b, p. A20). Research over the past twenty-five years has dispelled the earlier belief that individuals with **Down syndrome** necessarily function at a moderate level of developmental disability. Many individuals with Down syndrome have MID (Jones et al., 2014), similar to Scott, whose case is highlighted at the opening of this chapter. Figures 4.1 and 4.2 provide information about Down syndrome and an excerpt from Scott's IEP, respectively.

Weblinks

CONNECTING TO THE WHEEL: A CULTURAL RESOURCE TOOLKIT (ABORIGINAL FAMILIES AND DOWN SYNDROME)

www.cdss.ca/information/general-information/connecting-to-the-wheel-pdf.html

CANADIAN DOWN SYNDROME SOCIETY

www.cdss.ca

FIGURE 4.1 INFORMATION ABOUT DOWN SYNDROME

Down syndrome (DS) is a genetic condition in which a person has forty-seven chromosomes instead of the usual forty-six; this extra genetic material is usually associated with the twenty-first chromosome (trisomy). DS causes limitations in physical and cognitive development. About one in 800 live births in Canada is affected by Down syndrome. Though the likelihood of having a child with Down syndrome increases to some degree with the age of the mother, three-quarters of all children with the syndrome are born to mothers under 35.

Although children with Down syndrome have some degree of intellectual disability, factors such as, environment and low expectations also affect their learning potential. Generally, progress is slow, and some complex skills may be difficult to master. Each individual has unique strengths and weaknesses. Learning differences are highly variable and individualistic, like physical characteristics and health concerns.

Physically, children with Down syndrome have low muscle tone and a generalized looseness of the ligaments. There is also a strong susceptibility to hearing and vision difficulties. About one-third of the children will have heart defects.

Classroom Strategies: Teaching

- Discuss scheduling and activities before they happen; use wall charts, calendars, photos of a single activity or a single day.
- Allow time to finish a task.
- Use high interest, low vocabulary materials whenever possible.
- Break up tasks into small steps; use short blocks of time.
- Give more concrete assignments on a related topic.
- Make statements in short sentences and phrase questions simply. Allow response time.
- Encourage speech; ask the student with DS to express wants rather than answering "yes" or "no."
- Gain attention by making eye contact and using simple commands. Be clear.
- Help the child focus on the task—seat the child away from distractions.
- Expect appropriate behaviour. All students are accountable for their behaviour.
- Collaborate with parents to integrate activities of daily living, e.g., shopping, renting a DVD, travel. Be mutually aware of what the student knows and is learning.
- Learn about and use technology designed to facilitate reading and communication.

Classroom Strategies: Social

- Help the student to develop independence, and enhance self-esteem and social relations.
- Conduct awareness sessions with students to help dispel myths about people with disabilities. Initiate discussion about individual differences in abilities. Your behaviour and acceptance serve as a model to students.
- Seat the student with DS next to supportive peers. Encourage interaction and involvement with other students through play and classroom activities.

Sources consulted: British Columbia Ministry of Education. *Students with intellectual disabilities: A resource guide for teachers.* Canadian Down Syndrome Society (www.cdss.ca).

Incidence of Mild Intellectual Disabilities

It is estimated that roughly 2 to 3 percent of the general population has mild intellectual disabilities, depending on how the term ID is defined. In a school of 400 students, this would be eight to twelve students; however, there is variation from one community to another, with a higher rate associated with psychosocial disadvantage.

FIGURE 4.2 SECOND PAGE OF INDIVIDUAL EDUCATION PLAN (GOALS FOR THE YEAR/DIFFERENTIATIONS)

Student: Scott Boudin **Teacher:** Pat Kostas

Exceptionality: Mild intellectual disability (Down syndrome)

Long-Term Goals for the Year

1. Reading: Scott will continue to develop phonemic awareness and reading comprehension.
2. Writing: Scott will improve his written expression and use full sentences.
3. Listening: Scott will improve listening to and following instructions.
4. Speaking: Scott will speak clearly in social and learning situations, asking questions when he does not understand.
5. Math: Scott will improve counting, use of money, addition and subtraction of numbers to 10.
6. Social and environmental studies: Scott will participate in a collaborative learning group.
7. Motor development: Scott will engage in games, increase independence in eating lunch, increase hand–eye coordination.
8. Art and music: Scott will gain experience with various art media.
9. Self-management: Scott will follow lunch routines, join an extracurricular activity.
10. Social: Scott will develop relationships with peers and participate in group activities.

Accommodations and Modifications

1. Incorporating materials at his level; individualized instruction (resource teacher).
2. Using drawings or pictures from magazines as necessary (educational assistant).
3. Using comprehension check (repeating instructions to educational assistant or classroom buddy).
4. Asking educational assistant or classroom buddy about what to say.
5. Using coins, other concrete materials for addition and subtraction.
6. Asking educational assistant or classroom buddy when unsure of what to do.
7. Assistance with eating lunch, using computer (educational assistant).
8. Tasks at level.
9. Watching and following positive actions of peers (encouraged by educational assistant).

Source: Adapted from Hutchinson, N.L. (2004). *Teaching exceptional children and adolescents: A Canadian casebook*, p. 30. Copyright Prentice Hall. Reprinted with permission by Pearson Canada Inc.

Characteristics of Students with Mild Intellectual Disabilities

DELAYED DEVELOPMENT: COGNITIVE AND PHYSICAL

Put into Practice

Read the document *Down Syndrome and You* (www.dsaso.org/files/Down_Syndrome_and_You.pdf), written for young people with Down syndrome. How could you use it to help a young person with Down syndrome to gain self-knowledge? To help other students understand a classmate with Down syndrome?

Usually, students with mild intellectual disabilities learn to meet the everyday demands of life and develop into self-sufficient adults. However, they may have difficulty attaining the academic skills at their grade level because they pass through the developmental stages at a slower rate. Delays can be seen in physical, cognitive, language, and social development. In physical development, fine motor coordination, that is manual dexterity, may be delayed, affecting cutting, colouring, and printing (Vuijk et al., 2010). Cognitive delays affect short-term memory, attention, and ability to generalize and to recognize similarities and differences (e.g., Van der Molen et al., 2014). They may be less interested in letters, words, reading, and numbers than their classmates in the early school years. They are likely to find reading comprehension, arithmetic reasoning, and problem solving the most difficult, but they may attain lower levels of achievement in all curriculum areas (e.g., Jones et al., 2014). They often do best in curriculum areas where they can use experiential learning, such as Scott's expertise about recycling.

DELAYED DEVELOPMENT: COMMUNICATION AND SOCIAL ADJUSTMENT

In speech and language, you may see delay, with expressive language less developed than receptive vocabulary. Students with MID may not understand long sentences or complex ideas initially. Characteristics include articulation disorders and use of concrete language. Challenges in social adjustment are common, including lack of initiative and **learned helplessness**. They are often less socially prepared to pay attention, initiate conversation, and recognize emotions (Ališauskaitė & Butkienė, 2013).

TEACHER REFERRALS

Some students with MID will be identified before they start school—for example, those with Down syndrome, who have physically distinguishing characteristics. Other students with MID may be identified after they start school. Teachers frequently make pre-referral adaptations, consult with resource teachers, and refer these students for assessment (as described in Chapter 2). Sometimes school districts describe these students as "slow learners." They often are advised to register in the **applied or workplace stream** in secondary schools. When there is no clear evidence of an **organic cause** for delay, the suspected causes include disadvantage—poverty, inadequate nutrition, family instability, and lack of stimulation and opportunity to learn.

Implications for Learning and Differentiating in the Classroom

DIFFERENTIATING TO SUPPORT COGNITIVE DEVELOPMENT

To promote cognitive development, encourage students with intellectual disabilities to interact with other students. Arrange the environment to provide sensory and intellectual stimulation, as well as structure and consistency (Bennett et al., 2008). Set cognitive goals and use action-oriented activities and concrete materials (Smith et al., 2008). Recent research suggests that these students develop similar working memory skills to other children, just at a slower rate of development (Van der Molen et al., 2014).

Other ways to differentiate include colour-coding notebooks, reducing choices, and highlighting key text; these make learning easier because students can focus on the important parts of a lesson (Newfoundland and Labrador Department of Education, *Programming for Individual Needs: Communication Disorders Handbook*; www.ed.gov.nl.ca). Some ways to differentiate described in the BC resource *Students with Intellectual Disabilities: A Resource Guide for Teachers* (www.bced.gov.bc.ca/specialed/sid) include having the student arrive early to go over the day plan and preview materials before the lesson; preparing a summary of important information with blanks for the student to fill in while listening; and giving more concrete assignments on a related topic. Many of these differentiations may make learning easier for other students as well. This BC resource guide reminds us that "when making

Further Reading

About collaborative and co-operative learning:

Sapon-Shevin, M. (2010). *Because we can change the world: A practical guide to building cooperative, inclusive classroom communities.* Thousand Oaks, CA: Corwin Press.

Gillies, R.M., Ashman, A., & Terwel, J. (Eds.). (2008). *The teacher's role in implementing cooperative learning in the classroom.* New York, NY: Springer.

Hom, I.S. (2012). *Strength in numbers: Collaborative learning in secondary mathematics.* Reston, VA: National Council of Teachers of Mathematics.

Stahl, R., VanSickle, R., & Stahl, N. (Eds.) (2009). *Cooperative learning in the social studies classroom.* Washington, DC: National Council on the Social Studies.

Duyson, B., & Casey, A. (2012). *Cooperative learning in physical education: A research-based approach.* New York, NY: Routledge.

modifications teachers should change only that which is necessary to meet the needs of the student, with a view to fostering inclusion."

Extending deadlines and arranging for peers to create social opportunities can improve the learning environment for students with mild intellectual disabilities. Seek alternative resources such as parallel textbooks at lower reading levels, audio-taped texts, manipulatives that appeal to the senses, and games to practise important concepts. Students with MID will benefit from reteaching, practise, and application of skills and concepts. They often experience difficulty learning mathematics, and using money and other authentic manipulatives may prove helpful. Cognitive strategy instruction, in combination with worked examples, has been effective in teaching mathematics (Chung & Tam, 2005). Structured interventions have been used to teach decoding skills to middle school students with mild to moderate ID (Bradford et al., 2006), and reciprocal teaching has been found to improve reading comprehension for adolescents with MID (Lundberg & Reichenberg, 2013).

ADAPTATIONS TO SUPPORT LANGUAGE DEVELOPMENT

Simplify the language you use in instructions and relate new ideas to the student's experiences. Provide opportunities for students to use speech and language, without fear of correction or criticism, for a variety of communication purposes. Ensure that classmates treat the student with MID with respect, and create many contexts in which students learn by collaborating and using strengths other than traditional academic knowledge. Canney and Byrne (2006) provide an example of teachers using circle time in primary classrooms, and the BC resource guide on ID has many suggestions for working with adolescents (www.bced.gov.bc.ca/specialed/sid). To adapt assessment procedures for students with MID, look for ways to simplify, shorten, and clarify what you are looking for in an answer. Alternatives may also include oral exams, portfolios, or interviews.

Implications for Social and Career Participation of Students with Intellectual Disabilities

During the secondary years the focus usually shifts to functional, vocational, or applied learning. For example, there are many structured interventions for teaching skills such as supermarket shopping skills (Bouck et al., 2013). Students may learn in the community and in specialized classes as well as in regular classes. Adolescents and young adults with MID benefit from learning through experience in co-operative education and on-the-job training. Hutchinson et al. (2008) reported that Max, an adolescent with mild intellectual disabilities, benefited from a series of workplace experiences with gradually increasing demands for independence and productivity. Ensure that workplaces provide social opportunities and interdependent job designs that foster social interaction (Eisenman, 2007).

Some youth with intellectual disabilities participate in programs in community colleges and universities. Wintle (2012) provides an account of a young woman with MID who attends a university class. H'Art Centre in Kingston, Ontario has developed the H'Art School Inclusive Post Secondary Education program, which allows adults with intellectual disabilities to take university classes matched to their abilities and interests and work towards a five-year certificate of participation. Students also participate in literacy and arts classes at H'Art Centre for social support and learning skills. People with MID are primarily disadvantaged in formal school settings and usually thrive in the community, where they can use their life experience and are not required to use literacy skills or grapple with abstract concepts. In my community, young adults with mild intellectual disabilities attend university and community college, deliver mail in a large institution, organize audio-visual equipment in a university department, do cleaning in a small business, and work in food preparation. They have found niches as volunteers or employees in the service sector or in predictable jobs that don't require high levels of problem solving or literacy.

It is thought that the vast majority of adults with MID can obtain and maintain gainful employment if they develop personal and social behaviours appropriate to the workplace through transition experiences that prepare them for the expectations of employers. And employers must be aware of the contributions these individuals can make as well as of their needs for accommodations. A survey of adults in Ontario suggests that most respondents believe people with intellectual disabilities would not negatively affect the image of workplaces, but most thought lack of employment training for people with ID was a major obstacle to increased inclusion (Burge et al., 2008). To be successful, inclusion must prepare youth with intellectual disabilities for inclusion in the workplace and in the community, and not focus only on their learning of school subjects (Bouck & Satsangi, 2014).

Adults with intellectual disabilities benefit from participating in structured activities with peers.

Teaching Students with Severe Intellectual Disabilities

My dream: My name is Reid. I am 17 and I have developmental delay. Caused by a genetic condition—called Coffin–Lowry syndrome. Some people say I am retarded. I don't like to hear that. I am in a life-skills class at Campbell Collegiate. My favourite part is my work placement. Every morning, I clean the cages and walk the animals for a pet store. I also sweep the floors, and do odd jobs. Sometimes I sell kittens. My boss is my neighbour, Ms. Boychuk. I have known her all my life. That makes it easier. My goal is to live in my own place with my friend Dan. I want to move out like my older brother did. My mom says she hopes that I can do that, but she will miss me. We need people to help us. I use my wheelchair more than I used to. But I think we can do it. That's my dream.

Generated by Reid Ford and his mother in conversation.

Description of Severe Intellectual Disabilities

Intellectual disabilities are conditions originating before the age of 18 that result in significant limitations in intellectual functioning and conceptual, social, and practical adaptive skills (see the AAIDD website, www.aaidd.org). Intellectual disabilities are often the result of conditions described in Chapter 5 on physical disabilities and health conditions. For example, among the leading causes of intellectual disabilities are fetal alcohol spectrum disorder, cerebral palsy, and spina bifida, as well as fragile X, and other **chromosomal abnormalities**. Individuals with **severe intellectual disabilities** have greater limitations in intellectual abilities and adaptive functioning than individuals with mild intellectual disabilities. Intellectual abilities include reasoning, planning, solving problems, and thinking abstractly. They are assessed by means of a standardized intelligence test. Reid is clear about his need for supports—Reid can read environmental print (e.g., the symbol for Coke) and functional signs (like EXIT) but not labels on pill bottles. Adaptive behaviour refers to social and practical skills—Reid needs paid assistants to help him with bathing, taking medications, and so forth.

Sometimes people use the term **developmental disabilities** or **cognitive disabilities**. Some of the adaptive skills in which one would expect to see individuals challenged by the expectations of their environment include participation, interaction, and social roles; physical and mental health; and environmental context. Using Reid as an example may clarify the meaning of these adaptive skills. *Participation, interaction, and social roles* bring to mind the notion of "adaptive fit" and the individual taking advantage of strengths to take part in the community. Reid has many strengths—he communicates well orally, is a hard worker, knows himself, and uses this self-knowledge to make good decisions. With excellent support at home, at school, and in the neighbourhood, his life functioning has surpassed early predictions, but he is aware that he will increasingly need his wheelchair for mobility. He wants to be as independent as possible but accepts that he will always need support to participate in his environment. *Physical and mental health* influence functioning, and Reid recognizes that his participation depends on staying well. *Environmental context* refers to the school setting, the neighbourhood, and the patterns of culture and society. Reid has learned much about independence and responsibility by reporting to his work placement every morning, where he is comfortable, feels he makes a contribution, and increases his independence.

Characteristics of Students with Severe Intellectual Disabilities

The category of severe intellectual disabilities now includes students considered at times in the past to have moderate, severe, or profound disabilities. They span a wide range of abilities, from those who can acquire academic skills to those who require assistance with **self-care** for their entire lives.

An Intentional, Inclusive Community

Rougemount Co-operative (known as Deohaeko) is a 105-unit, non-profit apartment-style housing co-operative in Pickering, Ontario. Of the approximately 250 residents, six have an intellectual disability (Canadian Mortgage and Housing Corporation, www.cmhc.ca/en/inpr/rehi/rehi_011.cfm). It is an example of an intentional, inclusive community that includes units accessible for those with disabilities and residents committed to sharing their lives.

Tiffany Dawe was born with severe intellectual and physical disabilities. She moved into her own apartment in the Rougemount intentional community where she lives a full and rewarding life (with the aid of paid support workers, family, and friends), visiting friends, shopping, and participating in the Rougemount choir.

The idea for the co-operative was founded by local families of youth with severe disabilities, based on the knowledge that their offspring were accustomed to living in a neighbourhood, attending school and church, and being part of the community. The families applied for and obtained joint federal–provincial funding to build a co-op, which the governments are recouping through the Canada Mortgage and Housing Corporation. Of 105 units, twenty-five are designed for disabled residents; these special units are spread throughout the building to ensure full integration of those residents.

People who live in the "intentional" community must agree to be helpful, supportive, accepting, and friendly to all the residents of the co-op, including those who have severe disabilities. Then a second community was created, called the Deohaeko Support Network, taken from the Iroquois word for "spirit-supporters of life." Each

family has created a volunteer support network specifically to meet the needs of the individuals with severe intellectual disabilities. In 1997 the Rougemount Co-op won a Caring Community Award, given by the Ontario Trillium Foundation.

You usually find in their psychological reports and IEPs that students' strengths and needs have been assessed across four dimensions:

- intellectual or cognitive and adaptive behaviour skills
- psychological, emotional, and social considerations
- physical and health considerations
- environmental considerations

Cognitive characteristics of this group include difficulties focusing attention and getting information into memory; however, long-term memory may be excellent. Language is likely to be delayed, and in the most severe cases, verbal language may not develop. Adaptive behaviours refer to coping with the demands of daily living. Psychological characteristics often include frustration and impulsivity. Students with severe intellectual disabilities find social interactions challenging; often they do not know how to make friends, even though they may be loyal and caring. They may withdraw or develop repetitive behaviours that seem bizarre to their peers.

Physical and health considerations may depend on concomitant conditions such as cerebral palsy. Less physical dexterity and co-ordination than others of the same age are to be expected, and in the most severe cases there may be limited locomotion. Environmental considerations refers to such things as requiring a wheelchair that holds the head in a specific position or using a **voice synthesizer** to produce speech.

Focus on the strengths, not simply on the needs in the functional and educational assessments of students with severe intellectual disabilities, and look for teaching strategies that can make a difference; these students can contribute and learn in truly inclusive classrooms with differentiated instruction.

Differentiating Curriculum and Teaching for Students with Severe Intellectual Disabilities

Many of the ways of differentiating instruction discussed in Chapter 3 for students with learning and behaviour exceptionalities, as well as in this chapter for students with MID and ASD, are suitable for some students with severe intellectual disabilities.

Accommodations are likely to be needed in materials and presentation. For example, you can make accommodations in the environment by positioning the student where there are the fewest distractions, and the desk may be adapted to suit a wheelchair or a laptop computer. An agenda and list of assignments may be taped to the student's desk. You can highlight key points in the text, break information into steps, and complete the first example with the student. Use concrete examples. You could videotape a lesson so the student can review it at home. Allow extra time to complete tasks. The student may draw or write individual words rather than sentences and paragraphs to communicate his or her understanding (for an example of differentiated instruction, see Nel et al., 2011).

Recently, researchers (Jimenez et al., 2012) demonstrated the effectiveness of scripted lessons for teaching grade 3 and 4 science to students with moderate to severe intellectual disabilities. The topics were Rock Cycle, Life Cycle, and Senses. The nine elements of the scripted lessons were:

1. A brief introductory story to promote interest and personal relevance.
2. Teaching of two to three key vocabulary words.
3. Prediction of experiment outcomes.
4. Discrimination training for key concepts.
5. Experiment conducted by the teacher and observed by the students.
6. Description of observations.
7. Re-examination of predictions.
8. Reporting together on a chart the big idea or main findings.
9. Completion of science quiz with teacher individually.

MODIFYING CURRICULUM AND DEVELOPING ALTERNATIVE EXPECTATIONS

You will also probably need to modify the learning outcomes for students with severe developmental disabilities, deriving curriculum expectations from those at a lower grade in the curriculum document. Accommodations will likely be needed as well. Students with severe intellectual disabilities often require alternative expectations that are not derived from curriculum documents. Your guide for generating alternative outcomes is the goals section of the student's IEP. Consult with other members of the in-school team.

Two principles often guide the development of alternative curriculum for these students. The first is the principle of a **functional curriculum**, in which the goals for a student are based on life skills (Bouck, 2013). At his co-op placement in the pet store, Reid learned to be punctual and how to interact with customers, co-workers, and pets. Employers are often more willing to offer work experience to (and to employ) individuals with severe intellectual disabilities if they have experience with a family member with a disability or have experienced difficulty learning themselves (Hutchinson et al., 2008; Luecking, 2011). Schools need to locate such sympathetic employers to ensure that students like Reid can learn from experience in workplaces.

The second principle is that education should be **community-based** and relate what is learned in school to what occurs in the community (Pickens & Dymond, 2014). While other students in Reid's high school economics class are learning about the role of the Bank of Canada, Reid benefits from learning to cash a cheque, pay bills at the ATM, and withdraw cash from his account at the neighbourhood bank. Researchers report that activities such as using money take considerable practise for

FIGURE 4.3 MODIFIED AND ALTERNATIVE EXPECTATIONS FOR STUDENTS WITH SEVERE INTELLECTUAL DISABILITIES

When developing modified or alternative curriculum for a student, change only that which is necessary to meet the needs of the student, with a view to fostering inclusion.

- Give more concrete assignments on a topic related to that being studied by the class.
- Simplify learning tasks on a similar topic by providing more structure or examples for the student to use as a model.
- Ask easier questions related to the same concept.
- Assign the same materials to be used for a different purpose, for example, for addition instead of multiplication.
- Use high interest/low vocabulary resources on the same topic. With adolescents, choose age-appropriate topics and avoid texts written for primary students that may cause embarrassment.
- Provide community preparation, such as:
  - ❏ trips to community locations such as stores
  - ❏ opportunities to apply functional skills in different settings
  - ❏ job-related experiences, such as running a small business
- Individualize community tasks for each student based on need.

youth with severe intellectual disabilities (e.g., Xin et al., 2005). Special Olympics events that involve youth with and without disabilities offer many opportunities for both groups of students to learn social skills and other valuable community-based skills (e.g., soccer; Ozer et al., 2011). Hughes and colleagues (2011) used a similar approach to involve general education peers and high school students with intellectual disabilities in a social skills intervention that increased the conversational initiatives between the students.

There is great variation from one IEP to the next. Each IEP includes a detailed description of strengths and needs; the goals of an alternative program usually include

- functional academic skills
- physical development and personal care
- communication skills and social interaction skills
- community living skills
- career development, work experience, and transition planning

Figure 4.3 contains examples of ways to generate modified and alternative curriculum.

How can you explain to other students why someone like Reid has learning activities that differ from theirs? Younger children sometimes ask about this out of curiosity, whereas older students are likely to raise issues of fairness. If you have set a climate of inclusion in which differences are seen as normal, expected, and valued, you may have fewer questions and may find them easier to answer.

Explain the **principles of fairness** so that your students, no matter how young they are, understand that fairness does not mean sameness. You might use examples of different but fair treatment for exceptionalities not represented in your class. Ask whether it is fair to expect a student with no legs to climb stairs, or whether it is fair to expect a blind student to read a paper-and-pencil test. Most students can see that not everyone needs the elevator or Braille, and in fact most would be disadvantaged by Braille. To ensure equity, use routines for exceptional students that are similar to the routines you use for the rest of the class. Students with severe developmental disabilities should be assigned homework, tests, and projects at the same time as the rest of the class, and theirs should be as challenging for them as the assignments given to the rest of the class are for them.

Recent research suggests that inclusive education, when appropriately funded and supported, is more likely than segregated education to enable students with intellectual disabilities to engage with learning and to participate in independent living in adulthood (e.g., Dessemontet et al., 2012; Downing & Peckham-Hardin, 2007). A survey in Ontario found that a majority of adults viewed some degree of inclusive education in regular schools as best for students with intellectual disabilities (Burge et al., 2008).

Teaching Students with Autism Spectrum Disorder

I love buses. I know all the routes. And I can tell you anything about buses in Fredericton— the history, the kinds of buses, how they are serviced. But I wish there were no other people on the buses. The people bug me. When I ride the bus, I always get into trouble because of the people. They make noise and come near me. And I get mad at them. My favourite thing is to ride the bus with my dad while all the people are at work and school.

From the journal of Jason, who is 12 and was identified with Asperger syndrome but would currently be identified as having ASD (high functioning).

This section focuses on autism spectrum disorder (ASD). ASD is the current name in the new 5th edition of *Diagnostic and Statistical Manual of Mental Disorders* (*DSM-5*) for four previously separate disorders (American Psychiatric Association [APA], 2013; see www.dsm5.org). These four disorders were previously called autistic disorder, Asperger's disorder or Asperger's syndrome (AS), childhood disintegrative disorder, and pervasive developmental disorder not otherwise specified (PDDNOS) in *DSM-IV*. Combining four disorders into one continuum has been controversial. Even before this change, ASD were described as the fastest growing disorders in North America. See *Nature* (November 2011; www.nature.com/news/specials/autism/index.html) for a series of papers on ASD, with the introductory paper titled, "The Autism Enigma."

DSM-5 describes people with ASD as having social communication and social interaction deficits. These deficits can be seen when they respond inappropriately in conversation and misread non-verbal interactions, as well as when they experience difficulty forming friendships appropriate to their age. Additionally, they demonstrate restrictive repetitive behaviours, interests, and activities (RRBs). These characteristics are in play when people with ASD are overly dependent on routines, extremely sensitive to changes in their environment, or intensely focused on objects that are not appropriate. Both components are required for diagnosis of ASD. If no RRBs are present, a social communication disorder is to be diagnosed.

Under these criteria, the symptoms must be present from early childhood even if not recognized until later. *DSM-5* emphasizes that the symptoms of people with ASD will fall along a continuum from mild to severe symptoms. This spectrum is intended to allow clinicians to account for the variations in symptoms and behaviours from one person to another.

Two contentious issues have arisen with the collapsing of what were four distinct disorders into one continuum. First, there has been much discussion about whether children previously diagnosed under the criteria for *DSM-IV* would still be diagnosed under the criteria for *DSM-5*. Huerta and her colleagues (2012) reported that, in a recent study, 91 percent of children receiving a clinical diagnosis under *DSM-IV* would be identified by *DSM-5* criteria. In a paper in the same issue of *American Journal of Psychiatry*, Tsai (2012) raises questions about the lack of robust data to support one autism continuum, and suggests that there are important differences between autistic disorder and Asperger's disorder. In a 2013 paper, Tsai goes so far as to suggest that in the future, Asperger's disorder will return to *DSM*.

Most students with ASD, in schools at present, were identified under the criteria of *DSM-IV* because *DSM-5* has only recently been adopted. For that reason, the following sections discuss autistic disorder followed by a discussion of Asperger's disorder and high functioning autism (HFA), recognizing that in the future both groups will be identified with the label ASD.

Autistic Disorder: Description and Prevalence

One of the cases at the beginning of this chapter describes Pamela, a kindergarten student who has autistic disorder. Pamela communicates mainly by echoing the words of others, socializes little with her classmates, and sometimes runs from one side of the room to the other waving her arms.

Prevalence of ASD has been a contested subject for some time. Most studies conducted in the 1960s to 1980s reported prevalence ranging from 2 to 5 in 10 000; however, those studies typically focused on the more narrowly defined condition of autistic disorder (e.g., Burd et al., 1987). In studies published in the early 2000s, prevalence ranged from 30 to 60 in 10 000 (more than ten times the previous rate) (e.g., Gurney et al., 2003). More recent US studies reported rates from 50 to 90 in 10 000 children (Schechter & Grether, 2008). In a nationally representative US study, Kogan and colleagues (2009) reported that prevalence of ASD based on parental rate of reporting was 110 per 10 000 children, with four times as many boys as girls. Those with moderate or severe ASD were more likely than those with mild ASD to have at least one co-occurring condition (e.g., ADHD, developmental delay affecting ability to learn, anxiety, behavioural or conduct problems, or depression). Factors contributing to increased prevalence may include recognition of ASD co-occurring with other conditions and greater awareness of ASD (Gillberg & Fernell, 2014).

Autistic Disorder: Characteristics

There is wide variation in the characteristics of individuals with **autistic disorder**. Most have some level of intellectual disability, ranging from mild to severe. Language often shows **perseveration** on one topic or is characterized by echolalia. It is estimated that roughly fifty percent never develop functional speech. It is *not* that they do not want to interact reciprocally with others; rather, they are unable to understand or "read" social situations (Ryan et al., 2011). They may be unable to understand or even acknowledge the perspective of others; this has been described as lacking a **theory of mind** (Lombardo & Baron-Cohen, 2011). It seems that they are unaware that people have intentions, emotions, and so forth. Unusual and distinctive behaviours you might observe include:

- a restricted range of interests and a preoccupation with one specific interest or object
- an inflexible adherence to non-functional routine

Weblinks

GENEVA CENTRE FOR AUTISM (TORONTO)

www.autism.net

SASKATCHEWAN EDUCATION: *TEACHING STUDENTS WITH AUTISM: A GUIDE FOR EDUCATORS*

www.education.gov.sk.ca/ASD

MANITOBA EDUCATION, CITIZENSHIP AND YOUTH: *SUPPORTING INCLUSIVE SCHOOLS: A HANDBOOK FOR DEVELOPING AND IMPLEMENTING PROGRAMMING FOR STUDENTS WITH AUTISM SPECTRUM DISORDER*

www.edu.gov.mb.ca/k12/specedu/aut/pdf/acknowledgements.pdf

AUTISM SOCIETY CANADA

www.autismsocietycanada.ca

Further Reading

Read the articles about controversial issues related to ASD in *Nature* (November 2011; www.nature.com/news/specials/autism/index.html). Find related papers in educational sources. What are the implications of these controversies for educators like you?

- stereotypic and repetitive motor mannerisms, such as hand flapping, finger licking, rocking, spinning, walking on tiptoes, spinning objects
- a preoccupation with parts of objects
- a fascination with movement, such as the spinning of a fan or wheels on toys
- an insistence on sameness and resistance to change
- unusual responses to sensory stimuli

THEORY AND RESEARCH HIGHLIGHTS FROM

EDUCATIONAL PSYCHOLOGY

Theory of Mind

In attempting to explain the typical characteristics of children with autism spectrum disorder (impaired communication skills; impaired reciprocal social interaction; restricted, repetitive, and stereotypic patterns of behaviour), some researchers have developed unifying theories. The best known of these is *theory of mind* (ToM) (Baron-Cohen, 1995; Lombardo & Baron-Cohen, 2011). The other two grand theories of ASD are *executive functioning* (Ozonoff, 1997) and *central coherence* (Frith, 2003).

In locating the basis of autism, the term used at the time, Baron-Cohen et al. (1985) postulated that all people have a cognitive model of the world, or a theory of mind, which is the ability to appreciate other people's mental states. However, children with autism look at the world differently. They don't see others' intentions, needs, or beliefs and therefore demonstrate a mindblindness.

Theory of mind is a cognitive capacity that represents epistemic mental states such as pretending, thinking, knowing, believing, imagining, dreaming, guessing, and deceiving. Theory of mind ties together mental-state concepts (the volitional, perceptual, and epistemic) into an understanding of how mental states and actions are related. Basically, this cognitive capacity is described as the ability to attribute mental states to others and to oneself, to recognize these states, to understand they may differ from one's own, and to predict future behaviour from reading these mental states (Baron-Cohen, 1995).

False belief. A well-known test of theory of mind is called the false-belief test. The best-known false-belief task, the Sally-Ann task, studied by Baron-Cohen et al. (1985), involves a child and represents a story of a character's false belief that an object is in one location when it is actually in another. Three groups of children were tested: 4 year olds with normal development, children with autism, and children with Down syndrome. The story of Sally and Ann is enacted individually to each child. Sally has a marble that she places inside a basket. Sally leaves the room and Ann takes the marble and places it in a box while Sally is away and Sally cannot see that the marble has been moved. The child who is watching this scenario is asked three questions: a memory

question, "In the beginning where did Sally put the marble?" (correct answer: basket); a reality question, "Where is the marble now?" (correct answer: box); and a prediction question, "Where will Sally look for her marble?" (correct answer: in the basket where she placed it because, remember, she did not see Ann move the marble). Only 20 percent of children with autism attributed a false belief to Sally and predicted that she would look in the basket. The other 80 percent failed to recognize that Sally's previously correct belief that the marble was in the basket was now incorrect (a false belief). According to the researchers, not understanding a change in mental state and not ascribing false belief implies a lack of theory of mind. In contrast, 85 percent of the children with normal development and 86 percent of children with Down syndrome were able to predict correctly where Sally would look, recognizing that she falsely believed the marble was still in the basket (Baron-Cohen, 1995; Surian & Leslie, 1999).

Communication deficits. Deficits in communication are evident during the early years. They usually limit a child's ability to interact socially. When normally developing people talk to one another, they are aware of meanings behind messages and why a specific message was sent. Communication is a co-operative act in which each person attends to message and meaning. Charman and colleagues (1997) focused on communication deficits of empathy, pretend play, joint attention, and imitation. Their study included ten boys with autism, nine boys with developmental delays, and nineteen normally developing boys. Five tasks assessed empathic response, spontaneous play, structural play, joint attention, and imitation. The study of empathy involved the experimenter playing with the child, pretending to hurt himself with a toy hammer, and displaying facial and vocal expressions of distress. Children with autism were observed to see whether they looked to the experimenter's face, the experimenter's hand, or stopped playing with or touching the toy. The child's facial affect was also observed as (a) concerned or upset, (b) indifferent or neutral, or (c) positive. They found that on tasks of empathy, fewer autistic children looked to the experimenter's face and none expressed facial concern in response to another's distress. These data also suggest children with autism lack a theory of mind.

Reservations. A major characteristic of ASD evades explanation by theory of mind: restricted, repetitive, and stereotypic patterns of behaviours, interests, and activities. Researchers like Prior and Ozonoff (2007) question whether every child with autism lacks a theory of mind, and suggest that theory of mind deficits are not specific to autism and that theory of mind may be part of larger problems with executive function.

References

Baron-Cohen, S. (1995). *Mindblindness: An essay on autism and theory of mind.* Cambridge, MA: Bradford/MIT Press.

Baron-Cohen, S., Leslie, A.M., & Frith, U. (1985). Does the autistic child have a theory of mind? *Cognition, 21*, 37–46.

Charman, T., Swettenham, J., Baron-Cohen, S., Cox, A., Baird, G., & Drew, A. (1997). Infants with autism: An investigation of empathy, pretend play, joint attention, and imitation. *Developmental Psychology, 33*, 781–789.

Frith, U. (2003). *Autism: Explaining the enigma* (2nd ed.). Malden, MA: Blackwell.

Lombardo, M.V., & Baron-Cohen, S. (2011). The role of self in mindblindness in autism. *Consciousness and Cognition, 20*, 130–140.

Ozonoff, S. (1997). Causal mechanisms of autism: Unifying perspectives from an information-processing framework. In D.J. Cohen & F.R. Volkmar (Eds.), *Handbook of autism and pervasive developmental disorders* (pp. 868–879). New York: John Wiley & Sons.

Prior, M., & Ozonoff, S. (2007). Psychological factors in autism. In F.R. Volkmar (Ed.), *Autism and pervasive developmental disorders* (2nd ed) (pp. 69–128). New York: Cambridge University Press.

Surian, L., & Leslie, A.M. (1999). Competence and performance in false belief understanding: A comparison of autistic and normal 3-year-old children. *British Journal of Developmental Psychology, 17*, 141–155.

Autistic Disorder: Implications for Learning and Differentiating in the Classroom

The IEPs of students with autistic disorder usually include goals in the areas used to identify the exceptionality—communication, social interaction, stereotypic behaviours—as well as in functional and academic skills.

ENHANCING COMMUNICATION

To enhance communication, it may be necessary to teach the student to listen by facing the speaker, remaining still, and focusing on what is being said. Speak in sentences to the student; if you are not understood, use more concrete words and repeat as often as necessary. Use visual aids at an appropriate level; objects are the most concrete, followed by photographs, and then line drawings. For guidelines to develop and use a wide array of visual supports, consult Meadan et al. (2011), Shane et al. (2012), or Ganz et al. (2014):

1. Identify the purpose of the visual support (e.g., visual schedule, visual script, visual rule reminder).

2. Identify the type of visual representation to meet the student's needs (objects, photographs, line drawings, technology such as a tablet).

3. Create the visual support (e.g., chart, laminated cards to Velcro to a chart, images on a tablet).

4. Teach the child to use the visual support (e.g., direct instruction with practise and praise, making the connections between visuals and actions very clear).

5. Assess and adjust the visual support (e.g., child may need fewer steps or may be ready for visual supports for other purposes).

A digital camera, or even your phone, enables you to "catch the student doing good" and record the action. You can make a personalized schedule showing the

> **Further Reading**
>
> About teaching students with ASD:
>
> British Columbia, Ministry of Education, Special Programs Branch. *Teaching students with autism: A resource guide for schools.* Victoria, BC: Ministry of Education, Special Programs Branch. (www.bced.gov.bc.ca/specialed/docs/autism.pdf)
>
> Spencer, V.G., Evmenova, A., Boon, R., & Hayes-Harris, L. (2014). Review of research-based interventions for students with autism spectrum disorders in content area instruction: Implications and considerations for classroom practice. *Education and Training in Autism and Developmental Disabilities, 49*(3), 331–353.
>
> Kluth, P. (2010). *"You're going to love this kid": Teaching students with autism in the inclusive classroom.* Baltimore, MD: P.H. Brookes.
>
> Canavan, C. (2015). *Supporting pupils on the autism spectrum in secondary schools: A practical guide for teaching assistants.* New York, NY: Routledge.
>
> Wilkinson, L.A. (Ed.). (2014). *Autism spectrum disorder in children and adolescents: Evidence-based assessment and intervention in schools.* Washington, DC: American Psychological Association.

Put into Practice

Read about social stories in the resources listed below and develop a social story for Pamela, the kindergarten student with autistic disorder described in the case study opening this chapter. Choose a focus different from that illustrated in Figure 4.4.

Howley, M., & Arnold, E. (2005). *Revealing the hidden social code: Social stories for people with autistic spectrum disorders.* London and Philadelphia: Jessica Kingsley Publishers.

Flores, M., Hill, D., Faciane, L., et al. (2014). The Apple iPad as assistive technology for story-based interventions. *Journal of Special Education Technology, 29*(2), 27–37.

Xin, J., & Sutman, F. (2011). Using the Smart Board in teaching social stories to students with autism. *Teaching Exceptional Children, 43*(4), 18–24.

Scattone, D. (2008). Enhancing the conversation skills of a boy with Asperger's disorder through social stories and video modelling. *Journal of Autism and Developmental Disorders, 38,* 395–400.

(continued)

student completing each activity of the day, or a sequence of photographs or a video of the student carrying out the steps of a complex activity. To encourage oral language expression, accept limited verbal attempts and non-verbal behaviour as communication. Use specific praise. Video modelling provides an effective intervention; the videos may be of the focal child, but can also show others modelling the desired skill. Targeted skills may include communication as well as self-help, behavioural, and social objectives. The steps include (1) identifying the target skill(s), (2) producing or locating the videos, and (3) implementing the video modelling intervention. Ganz and her colleagues (2011) provide considerable detail and many examples.

For children with autistic disorder who have not developed verbal skills, Picture Exchange Communication System (PECS) offers a means of developing fundamental language skills, eventually leading to spontaneous communication (www.pecs.com; Lerna et al., 2014). Recently, many apps have been developed making iPads effective as a means of communication. Hill and Flores (2014) studied the two communication strategies and suggest that a developmental approach using PECS followed by iPads may be most effective.

ENHANCING SOCIAL COGNITION AND BEHAVIOUR

To improve social interaction, social skills, and social cognition, students with ASD require explicit teaching and practice. Carol Gray (2002) has developed first-person **social stories** that describe a situation from the perspective of the student and direct the young person to practise the appropriate behaviour. Each page in Gray's booklets—which can be up to five pages long—contains one or two sentences. There is a directive behaviour on one of the five pages. For an example of a social story, see Figure 4.4. Interventions have been developed using video to explicitly teach children with autistic disorder that others have intentions and emotions. You can also model for other children how to interact with their classmate with ASD. Ogilvie (2011) describes the steps in using video models and peer mentors to teach social skills, and encourages teachers to show the videos repeatedly to students with ASD who learn through visual repetition. She describes traditional role-playing using videos, using videos to prompt a student to complete the next step in a task, using video of the focal student completing the desired correct behaviour, and showing a video of someone else modelling task completion or desired behaviour.

GENERAL ADAPTATIONS AND MODIFICATIONS

Get to know students with ASD well and use that knowledge to guide differentiated instruction. Approaches that have been found effective include visual supports, technology-based instruction, concrete representations of the content, and direct instruction with content at a level that does not frustrate the student. Behavioural interventions are effective, especially when you use reinforcers that you know work for the individual (Spencer et al., 2014). As far as possible, keep the theme of the learning consistent with the lesson for the whole class.

Jules Selmes/Pearson Education

Getting to know the strengths and interests of students with intellectual disabilities or ASD helps teachers to differentiate instruction and assessment.

FIGURE 4.4 A SOCIAL STORY FOR PAMELA

(continued)

A social story describes a social situation and includes social cues and appropriate responses. It is written for a specific situation for an individual student. The story can be used to

- facilitate the inclusion of the student in regular classes
- introduce changes and new routines
- explain reasons for the behaviour of others
- teach situation-specific social skills
- assist in teaching new academic skills

Stories can be read, listened to on audio, or watched on video. The language must be understood by the child. The story should be from the child's perspective, using "I," and should direct the child to perform the appropriate behaviour. Social stories use descriptive sentences (which provide information on the setting and people), directive statements (i.e., positive statements about the desired response for a specific situation), and perspective statements (which describe the possible reactions of others).

Use two to five descriptive statements and one directive statement. Put only one or two sentences on a page. Symbols, drawings, or pictures can be included to support the meaning for the student.

Pamela tends to run and wave her arms while the other children sit on their chairs in a circle. Her teacher has made a social story for Pamela. The first page includes a photograph of the children smiling, sitting in a circle while the teacher reads a story. The second page shows Pamela smiling, sitting on her chair while the teacher holds a book. Page three shows a smiling child sitting on each side of Pamela, one speaking to her and the other offering her a toy. Each day, before the children sit in their circle, the teacher reads the story twice to Pamela and then reads each sentence and waits for Pamela to repeat it. Pamela has a video of the story at home that she watches with her mother.

Page 1: Other kids like to hear the teacher.

Page 2: I will sit on my chair when the teacher talks.

Page 3: Everyone talks to me and plays with me when I sit on my chair.

Source: Based on Gray, C. (1993). *The social story book.* Jenison, MI: Jenison Public Schools.

Bernad-Ripoll, S. (2007). Using a self-as-model video combined with social stories to help a child with Asperger syndrome understand emotions. *Focus on Autism and Other Developmental Disabilities, 22,* 100–106.

Dev, P. (2014). Using social stories for students on the autism spectrum: Teacher perspectives. *Pastoral Care in Education, 32*(4), 284–294.

If others are writing about highlights of the day in a daily journal, then try teaching the child with autistic disorder to cut a picture or symbol from a magazine or to use a digital photograph that communicates "something fun" that she has done today. She can name the picture or dictate a sentence. Whenever you can, use hands-on activities and allow as much time as the child requires.

It helps to provide a structured, predictable classroom environment. Make a customized visual daily schedule, and give advance warning of any changes from the usual schedule and of transitions from one activity to another. Four structured teaching components have been recommended by many researchers and practitioners (e.g., Azano & Tuckwiller, 2011; Hume & Odem, 2007; Simpson, 2005):

1. consistent, organized physical structure and organization of the workspace
2. visual schedules, including details about the required task
3. clear expectations of the individual during a task, including small steps to check off
4. immediate acknowledgement of accomplishments and gentle correction when needed

To maintain a calm learning environment, minimize auditory stimuli like noisy fans, reduce distracting visual stimuli, and remove textures the student finds aversive.

Weblinks

SUPPORTING AUTISM SPECTRUM (INCLUDES SOCIAL STORIES AND VISUALS)

http://supportingautismspectrum.weebly.com/social-storiesvisuals.html

VIDEO SOCIAL STORIES FROM CAROL GRAY, MARK SHELLEY, AND THE SPECIAL MINDS FOUNDATION

www.dttrainer.com/files/storymovies-handout.pdf

CAROL GRAY: WHAT ARE SOCIAL STORIES? (YOUTUBE)

www.youtube.com/watch?v=vjlIYYbVlrl

Put into Practice

Read three of the following papers and learn about the use of hand-held computing devices and other assistive technology with students with ASD. Consider how such technologies could help you meet the needs of a student in your class.

Mechling, L.C. (2011). Review of twenty-first century portable electronic devices for persons with moderate intellectual disabilities and autism spectrum disorders. *Education and Training in Autism and Developmental Disabilities, 46*(4), 479–498.

Newton, D.A., & Dell, A.G. (2011). *Assistive technology in the classroom: Enhancing experiences of students with disabilities* (2nd ed.). Toronto, ON: Pearson.

Walter, E.A., & Baum, M. (2011). Will the iPad revolutionize education? *Learning & Leading with Technology, 38*(7), 6–7.

Flores, M., Hill, D., Faciane, L., et al. (2014). The Apple iPad as assistive technology for story-based interventions. *Journal of Special Education Technology, 29*(2), 27–37.

Xin, J., & Sutman, F. (2011). Using the Smart Board in teaching social stories to students with autism. *Teaching Exceptional Children, 43*(4), 18–24.

FIGURE 4.5 ANNOTATED BIBLIOGRAPHY ON AUTISM SPECTRUM DISORDER AND MENTAL HEALTH

Depression and anxiety—and the serious mental health issues that accompany them—are often experienced by individuals with ASD and sometimes by their teachers and members of their families, depending on how they cope with the challenges associated with children with ASD.

Emotional and Behavioral Problems in Children with Language Impairments and Children with Autism Spectrum Disorders (2015) by Tony Charman, Jessie Ricketts, Julie Dockrell, Geoff Lindsay, & Olympia Palikara, *International Journal of Language and Communication Disorders, 50*(1), 84–93.

Teachers reported that children with ASD show elevated levels of emotional, conduct, and hyperactivity problems in the classroom. These problems often result in challenges when relating to peers and forming friendships. Teachers who monitor these aspects of their classroom interactions can prevent many difficulties from arising.

Evidence-based Classroom Strategies for Reducing Anxiety in Primary Aged Children with High-functioning Autism (2013) by Fran Hoffman, *New Zealand Journal of Teachers' Work, 10*(1), 25–42.

A preventive, multi-faceted approach appears to be most effective for reducing anxiety, including using social stories to teach social skills and creating a classroom context that provides social support. Paper includes a checklist of strategies that can be used at school and at home.

Mental Health Issues of Adolescents and Adults with ASD: Depression and Anxiety (2012) by Kathleen M. McCoy, *Counseling and Human Development, 45*(1), 1–16.

Depression, anxiety, and other mental health disorders appear more often in adolescents with ASD than in the general population. They usually involve abnormal happiness or sadness which affects daily functioning to some degree. Given their difficulties with communication and awareness of emotion, these youth may be unable to express their feelings or understand them. Families and educators are most likely to recognize these conditions, and may need to refer the student for mental health intervention or medication.

The Impact of Child Problem Behaviors of Children with ASD on Parent Mental Health: The Mediating Role of Acceptance and Empowerment (2012) by Jonathan Weiss, Catherine Cappadocia, Jennifer MacMullin, Michelle Viecili, & Yona Lunsky, *Autism: The International Journal of Research and Practice, 16*(3), 261–274.

Raising a child with ASD has been associated with high levels of parent stress. Parents who demonstrated high acceptance of the child and felt empowered reported less stress. These findings suggest that rather than using problem-focused coping, parents should engage in positive coping, focusing on their personal growth and strategies to reach their goals, being proactive rather than reactive.

Do everything you can to reduce anxiety, especially for adolescents with ASD. They need your help to overcome their challenges with executive function—that is, planning, thinking about their own thinking, and orchestrating. Plan transitions well and provide clear signals such as turning the lights off and on again, ringing a bell, and giving a three-minute, two-minute, and one-minute warning. Use graphic organizers to help all students organize information (and to especially meet the needs of students with ASD). As well, model think-alouds and use differentiated assessments. For descriptions of how to use these strategies with adolescents, see Azano and Tuckwiller (2011). Figure 4.5 provides an annotated bibliography on ASD and mental health.

Asperger's Disorder and High Functioning Autism: Description and Incidence

It may be helpful to begin this section by drawing attention to what has changed in the identification of individuals with ASD who have average or better intellectual functioning since the release of *DSM-5* (APA, 2013). A group of Canadian researchers led by Theresa Bennett (2014) of McMaster University explain that *DSM-5* has added "accompanying language impairment" as a clinical requirement for every diagnosis of ASD. This is a major change from the previous diagnosis of Asperger's disorder, which did not include the presence of early language delay. **Asperger's disorder or Asperger's syndrome (AS)** (the latter was the term more widely used in the past), was described as a lifelong developmental condition, characterized by a severe and sustained impairment in social interaction and the development of restricted, repetitive patterns of behaviour, interests, and activities, without significant delays in the acquisition of language. In the past, many researchers have argued about whether there were differences between individuals diagnosed as having Asperger's syndrome (AS) and those diagnosed as having high functioning autism (HFA). For example, Donaldson & Zager (2010) argued that they were the same condition, while Szatmari et al. (2003) argued that they were different conditions. The World of Psychology website (http://psychcentral.com/blog/archives/2015/03/06/top-10-aspergers-blogs-of-2015) discusses how the removal of AS as a category has "caused commotion among the Asperger's community, many of whom fought to get a diagnosis in the first place."

Incidence for Asperger's disorder has been unclear for the past ten years, with large increases and wide variation in the reported numbers; for example, in recent publications, Eric Fombonne and his colleagues at McGill University suggested rates of 10 per 10 000 (2006) and of 4 per 10 000 (2007). Similarly, Matilla and colleagues (2007) used four sets of diagnostic criteria to get prevalence rates ranging from 16 to 29 per 10 000.

Asperger's Disorder and High Functioning Autism: Characteristics and Teaching Strategies

Because of the recent changes introduced by *DSM-5*, this section includes information about **high functioning autism (HFA)** as well as AS, using the abbreviation AS/HFA when referring to both, a convention that has been adopted by many researchers in the field in the past few years (e.g., Markoulakis et al., 2012; Schohl et al., 2014). Students diagnosed with Asperger's disorder have been characterized by a qualitative impairment in social interaction and emotional relatedness, including difficulty with facial recognition and with recognizing social initiatives of others. They are generally enthusiastic about relating to others but often approach others in unusual ways. They misinterpret social cues, lack empathy, appear socially awkward, and are unaware of the rules of conversation. They need explicit instruction in social skills. With average or better intelligence, they tend to excel at learning facts but need intensive teaching in reading comprehension, mathematics in some cases, problem solving, organizational skills, and inference making. Those with HFA could be expected to also show impaired language development.

Frequently, students with AS/HFA are **hypersensitive** to sensory stimuli and may engage in unusual behaviour to obtain a particular sensory stimulation. The lighting and sounds in the classroom can be annoying, distracting, and even painful for these students. Flickering and fluorescent lights are particular irritants, while subdued lighting may be calming. Loud, unexpected noises bother some, and the buzz of heaters and of other students' voices can prove problematic; allowing students to be seated away from the noise or to wear earphones to reduce the sound may help.

What do you think?

Recently many people with ASD have written books about their experiences. Some have highlighted their strengths, challenging traditional views of disability and sharing insights to help teachers differentiate teaching and assessment. You can read a researcher's view of these accounts: Kluth, P. (2004). Autism, autobiography, and adaptations. *Teaching Exceptional Children, 36*(4), 42–47.

What do you think teachers can learn from first-person accounts by persons with ASD? Here is a list of books on ASD written by people with ASD (mainly with AS): Robison, J.E. (2012). *Be different: My adventures with Asperger's and my advice for fellow Aspergians, misfits, families, and teachers.* Guildhall, VT: Broadway Books.

Kraus, J.D. (2012). *The Aspie teen's survival guide: Candid advice for teens, tweens, and parents from a young man with Asperger's syndrome.* Slacks Creek, AU: Future Horizons.

Grandin, T. (2006). *Thinking in pictures, expanded edition: My life with autism.* New York: Vintage Books.

Top 10 Asperger's Blogs of 2015: http://psychcentral.com/blog/archives/2015/03/06/top-10-aspergers-blogs-of-2015

Further Reading

About AS/HFA (for teachers):

Winter, M., & Lawrence, C. (2011). *Asperger syndrome: What teachers need to know.* London, UK: Jessica Kingsley.

Frankel, F., & Wood, J.J. (2011). *Social skills success for students with autism/Asperger's: How to teach conversation skills, prevent meltdowns, and help kids.* San Francisco, CA: Jossey Bass.

Barnard-Brak, L., & Fearon, D.D. (2012). Self-advocacy as a predictor of student IEP participation among adolescents with autism. *Education and Training in Autism and Developmental Disabilities, 47*(1), 39–47.

McCafferty, K.R. (2011). How-to guide for autism. *Exceptional Parent, 41*(4), 16–17.

Hart, J.E., & Whalon, K.J. (2011). Creating social opportunities for students with autism spectrum disorder in inclusive settings. *Intervention in School & Clinic, 46*(5), 273–279.

Wilkinson, L.A. (2010). *A best practice guide to assessment and intervention for autism and Asperger syndrome in schools.* Philadelphia, PA: Jessica Kingsley.

Reducing class noise by putting tennis balls on the chair and desk legs is also a good strategy. Kluth (2004) suggests using music as a tool for instruction and support. These students tend to have unusual patterns of narrow interests and unique, stereotyped behaviour. Sometimes they exhibit motor clumsiness, overactivity, and inattention. These characteristics can be accompanied by depression and other emotional problems.

Students with AS/HFA may be inattentive, easily distracted, and anxious. Get to know each student well, consider each student's unique learning characteristics, and build on their considerable strengths. It is critical to create a climate of acceptance in the classroom and with the parents (Lindsay et al., 2014). Draw on the expertise of the in-school resource team too. These students appreciate having a safe space in the classroom or somewhere in the school (Kluth, 2004).

Recently, researchers have begun to focus on the implications of AS/HFA for students' learning in specific curriculum areas in the classroom. The cognition of these students can have direct effects on their development of literacy; they usually have strengths in decoding and difficulty with reading comprehension (Whalon & Hart, 2011; Williamson et al., 2012). To truly understand character development and character involvement within a story, the reader must take on the character's perspective; understanding both the rules and the meaning of language are critical to students' comprehending text. Strategies for success include developing a highly organized learning environment and organized learning materials, beginning with students' interests, linking the text to relevant background knowledge, adapting the text to meet learner needs, and using visual cues whenever possible. For more detailed suggestions regarding literacy, see Carnahan and colleagues (2011).

A number of strategies have proven successful for teaching mathematics to students with AS/HFA. These include giving the students checklists to complete as they perform computations which provide reminders for each step, and using direct instruction to teach students the steps in mathematical procedures and in solving word problems. Goal setting and rewards have been shown to be effective. Because these students are challenged in their processing of abstract concepts, the strategy called concrete-representation-abstract has been used to teach fractions. Students see concrete examples first (two halves of a paper or foil pie plate), followed by a representation of two halves of a square, and finally the abstract depiction of a fraction (1/2). More information about these math strategies is available in Donaldson and Zager (2010). Simpson and her colleagues (2010) and Menear and Smith (2011) provide instructional strategies for including students with AS/HFA in physical education. Get to know the student and use their interests when developing exercise and activities; provide clear and simple rules; use consistent reinforcement systems; demonstrate what is expected; and provide a private or quiet spot for the student when he is frustrated or overwhelmed. Use a visual schedule and give advance warning of changes from the routine. Both papers, by Simpson and Menear, provide many other practical strategies. Similar recommendations emerge in work by Saunders et al. (2011) on teaching science to students with AS/HFA. Rosetti and Goessling (2010) describe how educational assistants (EA) can facilitate friendships for secondary students with AS/HFA; they can bring students together and also fade into the background, when that is appropriate, so they do not come between exceptional adolescents and their classmates. And Schohl et al. (2014) address the social and mental health needs of adolescents with AS/HFA, describing the effective PEERS program designed specifically for these young people.

Implications for Social and Career Participation of Students with Autism Spectrum Disorder

Because ASD affects social awareness and understanding, children and adolescents with autistic disorder and with AS/HFA are vulnerable to bullying. Social skills, anxiety, anger, behaviour problems, and social vulnerability have all been shown to contribute to these students being bullied at school (Sofronoff et al., 2011). Teachers have found that teaching these students strategies for self-management is effective (Shogren et al., 2011). This may be a way to reduce their social vulnerability, a major predictor of being bullied. Advocacy, recreation, and relationships with family and friends are also important. Transition planning from secondary school to adult life should begin early in the high school years. Areas to consider, depending on functioning level and need, include employment options, post-secondary training or education options, residential options, transportation and medical needs, as well as income support opportunities. Work experiences, participation in co-curricular activities, and help with developing hygiene, appropriate dress, and self-management may be necessary during the secondary years. A recently developed strategy involves high school students with AS/HFA developing a career path binder that builds on their self-awareness and self-management (Hurlbutt & Handler, 2010). It includes steps to help the student develop a possible and realistic career path without narrowing too early. The students identify interest areas, research those areas to identify possible jobs or careers, gain work experience or exposure in those fields, and outline a plan for reaching the employment goal in a systematic way. Follow-up studies of adults with ASD show that individual characteristics such as intelligence and language ability are important. However, school experiences and especially teachers who ensure differentiated teaching, effective transition planning, supported work experience, and career development make a difference in life outcomes for students with ASD (Howlin, 2007).

Summary

Students with intellectual disabilities and ASD are increasingly participating in inclusive classrooms. Two levels of intellectual disability are usually recognized in provincial documents: students with mild intellectual disabilities and students with severe intellectual disabilities, sometimes referred to as *developmental disabilities* (a confusing term with different definitions in different contexts). These students have lower than average intellectual capacity and adaptive functioning skills. ASD usually refers to students with autistic disorder or to students with Asperger's disorder or high functioning autism (AS/HFA). Regardless of functioning level, students with ASD have difficulty with peer relationships, understanding social situations, and tend to engage in restricted repetitive patterns of behaviour, interests, or activities. Many also have communication difficulties. While accommodations will be adequate for many, some will require modified or alternative curriculum, especially students with severe intellectual disabilities and autistic disorder. Meeting the social and emotional needs of these students is important, because inclusion means making them feel part of the social and academic life of the class.

Key Terms

adaptive behaviour (p. 95)

applied or workplace stream (p. 99)

Asperger's disorder or Asperger's syndrome (AS) (p. 113)

autism spectrum disorder (ASD) (p. 94)

autistic disorder (p. 107)

case coordinator (p. 94)

chromosomal abnormalities (p. 102)

cognitive disabilities (p. 102)

community-based (p. 104)

developmental disabilities (p. 96)

Down syndrome (p. 96)

echolalia (p. 92)

functional curriculum (p. 104)

high functioning autism (HFA) (p. 113)

hypersensitive (p. 113)

intellectual disability (ID) (p. 94)

intelligence (p. 95)

learned helplessness (p. 99)

mild intellectual disability (MID) (p. 96)

organic cause (p. 99)

perseveration (p. 107)

principles of fairness (p. 105)

self-care (p. 102)

severe intellectual disabilities (p. 102)

social stories (p. 110)

theory of mind (p. 107)

voice synthesizer (p. 103)

Challenges for Reviewing Chapter 4

1. Read the brief description of Reid at the beginning of the section on teaching students with severe intellectual disabilities. How could you differentiate instruction for Reid so that he develops both his literacy skills and his workplace skills for the challenges he will meet as an adult trying to live as independently as possible?

2. Write a brief scenario that includes some of the greatest challenges to your teaching and management in a classroom with students with ASD—like Pamela in the opening case, who has autistic disorder, and Jason, described in this chapter, who has Asperger's disorder. Describe how you could differentiate instruction to meet their needs.

3. Alisha has Down syndrome and has been placed in your classroom. She shares an educational assistant with another student who has a severe intellectual disability. This means that Alisha receives little attention from the EA. You recognize that this situation does not allow Alisha to have her needs met in your classroom. Prepare a script for your conversation with your principal about the dilemma that has arisen in this situation.

Activities for Reviewing Chapter 4 with Your Peers

4. You are currently a member of the in-school team for a student who has Angelman syndrome, and last year you fulfilled a similar role for a student who had Prader-Willi syndrome. The team includes a classroom teacher, a resource teacher, a principal, and a parent. Use the information in this chapter to develop

a systematic approach to differentiating teaching and ensuring social participation of the student with Angelman syndrome. Consider how this approach is similar to and different from what was done last year for the student with Prader-Willi syndrome. Role-play this scenario with some of your peers, each assuming the role of a member of the team.

5. One of the students you teach has ASD. With your peers, develop a reading list that will help you to differentiate teaching and the social organization of the classroom, so this student will feel like a valued member, will not be bullied, and will learn each day. Consider what resources are most helpful for very young children and for adolescents.

6. Jason was described in this chapter. He has AS/HFA. How can you take advantage of Jason's interest in buses to improve his reading comprehension and math problem solving? With your peers, describe ways to differentiate in grades 1 to 3, grades 4 to 6, and in the high school years. Describe the process of gradually moving Jason toward other topics without losing his interest in what you are teaching.

CHAPTER 5

Exceptional Students: Communication Exceptionalities, Physical Exceptionalities, and Chronic Health Conditions

LEARNER OBJECTIVES

After you have read this chapter, you will be able to:

1. Describe a range of communication exceptionalities, physical exceptionalities, and chronic health conditions that may affect learning and social participation in the classroom.

2. Describe ways you can differentiate instruction for students with communication exceptionalities, both speech and language disorders.

3. Discuss differentiation of teaching for students with hearing loss, that is, students who are hard of hearing and students who are deaf.

4. Describe how you can differentiate classroom teaching for students with a range of physical exceptionalities.

5. Describe adaptations that would meet the needs of students with visual impairments.

6. Explain how you could differentiate teaching for students with chronic health conditions.

Phanie/Alamy

FARES IS A 7-YEAR-OLD BOY WITH MODERATE HEARING LOSS IN BOTH EARS. His hearing loss was acquired when he experienced meningitis at 9 months of age. Fares wears hearing aids in both ears, enabling him to hear most speech sounds when he is in a quiet environment. However, his grade 2 classroom is rarely quiet, and even low levels of noise interfere with his ability to concentrate and to hear. His language development is about 18 months behind that of his peers, and his speech is described as about 50 percent intelligible to his teachers who are familiar with his speech patterns. Fares is less mature socially than his classmates, although his social skills have been improving steadily since he started school. He often forgets to tell his teacher that the batteries in his hearing aids are dead, and says that he enjoys the quiet when he "can't hear all the noise" in his classroom. His teacher usually notices Fares' inattentive behaviour and then checks and replaces the batteries.

BRITTANY HAS CYSTIC FIBROSIS AND COUGHS CONSTANTLY. Although she is in grade 7, she is as small as most girls in grade 4. She has just returned to school after being hospitalized for two months. Brittany has told teachers and students in previous classes about how her body produces abnormally thick and sticky secretions that cause problems in her respiratory and digestive systems. This mucus builds up in her lungs and also makes it difficult for her to digest her food. Brittany has always agreed to leave class to take her medication and receive therapy to clear her airways; however, increasingly, teachers find that Brittany needs encouragement to follow her regime of medication and treatment. This year she also needs emotional support to deal with the recent insertion of a feeding tube that will ensure that she continues to grow and has enough energy. Brittany's health condition has an impact on her school life, mainly on her social and emotional well-being, and causes her to miss many classes each term.

1. Which of the characteristics of each student are most likely to affect learning? What learning needs are implied by these characteristics?

2. With such a range of learning needs, what do exceptional students like Fares and Brittany have in common?

3. How frequently is a teacher likely to be teaching a student with each of these exceptionalities?

4. What types of differentiation does each of these students need in order to be included in the social life and the learning activities of the classroom?

5. What community resources can a teacher draw on to supplement in-school resources to teach each of these students?

Introduction

Cross-Reference
For descriptions of and differentiations for students with learning and behaviour exceptionalities, see Chapter 3. For descriptions of and differentiations for students with autism spectrum disorders (ASD) and intellectual disabilities (ID), see Chapter 4.

In this chapter, you will learn about the characteristics, needs, and strengths of students with **communication exceptionalities**, **physical exceptionalities**, and **chronic health conditions**. Communication exceptionalities include speech and language disorders, often described as communication disorders. However, communication is also viewed as the main challenge resulting from hearing loss, whether children are hard of hearing or deaf. Physical exceptionalities include visual impairment and physical conditions such as cystic fibrosis and cerebral palsy, which may affect many areas of a child's functioning, just as chronic health conditions such as asthma can affect a child's life in many ways. While reading this chapter, think about children and adolescents you have known with these conditions. Labels give us a shared language, but they never capture the essence of the individual's experience of an exceptionality or health condition.

Each section on an exceptionality or health condition begins with the words of a child or adolescent. Then the exceptionality is described in general terms, followed by more specific characteristics, classroom implications, and often implications for career participation. Often, teachers must seek information on a need-to-know basis because it is almost impossible for you to remember the details of fifteen or more physical disabilities and health conditions. Information is provided about responding to life-threatening and extremely disruptive conditions—for example, teachers who are knowledgeable about allergic reactions and asthma may save a student's life. Table 5.1 introduces the exceptionalities and conditions discussed in this chapter. Table 5.2 provides data on their prevalence, that is, frequency.

Teaching Students with Communication Needs

There are two groups of students whose main needs in the classroom focus on communication. The first group includes students with language disorders and students with speech disorders, conditions usually described generally as communication disorders. Some students have both disordered language and disordered speech. The other group consists of students whose communication abilities are affected by hearing loss—students who are hard of hearing as well as students who are deaf.

Communication Disorders

> Writing in my journal every day helps me feel better and write better. I used to go to speech therapy every week. Now my therapist comes to school once a month. In between, I practice my sounds with helpers. Today my speech therapist told me that I am really getting better at making my sounds. She recorded me talking and I listened to myself on the recording. I felt proud. I have to talk like that in my class so the other kids will stop saying that I talk like a baby. I am going to ask if I can be in the next play for social studies.
>
> *From the journal of Ruth, a grade 2 student with an articulation speech disorder.*

Description of Communication Disorders

Generally, **communication disorders** include disorders of speech (articulation, voice, and fluency) and disorders of language (expressive or receptive). The term

TABLE 5.1 STUDENTS WITH COMMUNICATION EXCEPTIONALITIES, PHYSICAL DISABILITIES, AND CHRONIC MEDICAL CONDITIONS

Exceptionality	Description
Communication	
Communication disorders	Refers to exceptionalities in speech or language. Speech is disordered when it deviates so far from the speech of other people that it calls attention to itself, interferes with communication, or causes the speaker or listeners distress. Language is disordered when the student has impairment in expressive or receptive language
Hard of hearing and deaf	Hearing loss that has significantly affected development of speech and/or language and caused students to need adaptations to learn
Physical Disabilities and Chronic Medical Conditions	
Visual impairments	Students who are blind or partially sighted who need adaptations to learn through channels other than visual
Nervous System Impairment	
Cerebral palsy	Disorders affecting body movement and muscle coordination resulting from damage to brain during pregnancy or first three years
Spina bifida	Neural tube defect that occurs during first four weeks of pregnancy causing vertebrae or spinal cord to fail to develop properly
Epilepsy	Neurological disorder involving sudden bursts of electrical energy in the brain
Tourette syndrome	Neurological disorder characterized by tics
Brain injury	Damage to brain tissue that prevents it from functioning properly
Fetal alcohol spectrum disorders	Neurological disorders caused by significant prenatal exposure to alcohol
Musculoskeletal Conditions	
Muscular dystrophy	Genetically based muscle disorders that result in progressive muscle weakness
Juvenile arthritis	Continuous inflammation of joints in young people under 16
Chronic Health Impairments	
Diabetes	Condition in which the body does not make enough insulin and has problems absorbing and storing sugars
Allergies	Sensitivity or abnormal immune response to normal substance, which can cause anaphylactic shock
Asthma	Chronic lung condition, characterized by difficulty breathing, in which airways are obstructed by inflammation, muscle spasms, and excess mucus
Cystic fibrosis	Incurable disorder caused by inherited genetic defect, affecting mainly the lungs and the digestive system
Crohn's disease and colitis	Incurable disorders comprising irritable bowel syndrome, characterized by nausea, diarrhea, abdominal pain, weight loss, and lack of energy, requiring frequent hospitalization
Cancer and leukemia	Characterized by uncontrolled division of cells and the ability of these to spread; leukemia is a type of cancer that forms in the bone marrow, causing abnormal white blood cell development

speech impairment is widely used to refer to a disorder that involves the perceptual motor aspects of transmitting speech or oral messages. The Ontario Ministry of Education (2001) describes language impairment as "an impairment in comprehension and/or use of verbal communication or the written or other symbol systems of communication, which may be associated with neurological, psychological, physical, or sensory factors" (p. A19). Usually **language impairment** is described as involving one or more of the form, content, and function of language in communication and is characterized by language delay. You may see delayed development of expressive language, receptive language, or both.

TABLE 5.2 PREVALENCE OF COMMUNICATION EXCEPTIONALITIES, PHYSICAL DISABILITIES, AND CHRONIC HEALTH CONDITIONS

Exceptionality	General Prevalence in Research
Communication Exceptionalities	
Speech disorders	300 to 500 per 10 000 (McLeod & Harrison, 2009)
Language disorders	740 to 1470 per 10 000 at 5 years of age; rate decreases with age (McLeod & Harrison, 2009)
Hard of hearing	up to 1500 per 10 000 (Niskar, 2001)
Deaf	10 per 10 000 (Ontario Public Health, 2000)
Physical Disabilities and Chronic Medical Conditions	
Blind and low vision	Low vision: 35 per 10 000; blind: 4 per 10 000 (Maberly et al., 2006)
Nervous System Impairment	
Cerebral palsy	20 per 10 000 (Robertson et al., 2007)
Spina bifida	4 per 10 000 (Shin et al., 2010)
Epilepsy	56 per 10 000 (Tellez-Zenteno et al., 2004)
Tourette syndrome	30 per 10 000 (Blumberg et al., 2007)
Brain injury	Serious brain injury in children: 22 per 10 000 (Kraus, 1986)
Fetal alcohol spectrum disorders	10 to 30 per 10 000 (Barr & Streissguth, 2006)
Musculoskeletal Conditions	
Muscular dystrophy	Duchenne muscular dystrophy: 2 per 10 000 males (Dooley et al., 2010)
Juvenile arthritis	5 to 11 per 10 000 (depending on country) (Cakmak & Bolukbas, 2005)
Chronic Health Impairment	
Diabetes	Pediatric: 30 per 10 000 (www.phac-aspc.gc.ca/cd-mc/diabetes-diabete/pub_stats-eng.php)
Allergies	Peanut allergy: 134 per 10 000 (Kagan et al., 2003)
Asthma	910 per 10 000 (Akinbami et al., 2009)
Cystic fibrosis	3 per 10 000 (www.cysticfibrosis.ca)
Crohn's disease and colitis	6 per 10 000 under 20 years of age (Kappelman et al., 2007)
Cancer and leukemia	Pediatric cancer: 850 children in Canada annually (Ellison & Wilkins, 2009)

Recent funding cutbacks have reduced services for communication exceptionalities across the country. Prevalence data for speech and language disorders are uncertain because criteria and levels of service vary widely from district to district and even across schools within a district. Sometimes services are provided by the health care system, and some parents seek private therapy rather than face waiting lists. Boys with communication disorders outnumber girls by roughly two to one.

Characteristics of Students with Communication Disorders

Many students with communication disorders experience difficulties with both speech and language, but some students have difficulty in only one of these areas. Many students with other exceptionalities (e.g., autism, learning disabilities, cerebral palsy, intellectual disabilities) have communication disorders as a secondary disability.

TABLE 5.3 SPEECH AND LANGUAGE DISORDERS AND THEIR CHARACTERISTICS

Communication Disorder	Example of Characteristics
Language delay	For young students, at least six months behind in reaching language milestones; a grade 2 student uses three words rather than full sentences.
Receptive language	Student in grade 6 consistently fails to understand an oral instruction, even when given individually.
Expressive language	Student in grade 10 begins each sentence four or five times and cannot be understood by peers; refuses to speak in front of class.
Aphasia	Student cannot understand speech or produce meaningful sentences.
Apraxia	Student cannot sequence muscle movements and thus does not produce meaningful speech.
Articulation	Student in grade 2 cannot produce the S sound. This results in teasing by classmates.
Dysfluency	Student in grade 12 stutters but persists to express ideas.
Voice disorders	Student speaks slowly and softly in a husky voice (does not speak with normal pitch, loudness, duration, or quality); is shy about expressing ideas.
Orofacial defects	Student in grade 5 with cleft palate has difficulties with speech and feeding.
Dysarthria	Grade 9 student's speech is distorted because of paralysis of speaking muscles.

The designation "communication disorders" is usually used when speech or language is the primary exceptionality. There is a wide variety of communication disorders. You may recognize students with communication disorders in your classroom from some of the characteristics listed in Table 5.3. If you suspect that a young child has a speech or language disorder, talk with the parents. Recommend a thorough evaluation by a speech-language pathologist to determine the child's communication strengths and weaknesses. This professional can provide a plan for meeting the child's needs and can recommend services within the school district, the local health department, or an agency in the community.

Implications for Learning and Classroom Differentiation: Students with Communication Disorders

In the past, speech and language disorders were the responsibility of speech and language therapists, and students were removed from the classroom for therapy. Teachers often carried out follow-up exercises. However, in the scenario presented at the opening of this section, Ruth practises with volunteers between visits by the therapist. The knowledge needed by speech-language therapists and teachers in order to collaborate effectively is described in papers by Bauer et al. (2010) and Watson and Bellon-Harn (2014).

You can assist students with communication disorders. Create an accepting atmosphere and never allow classmates to mock or tease. Collaborate with the

Put into Practice

Seek resources to help you understand and enhance the language development of young children:

Roseberry-McKibbin, C. (2013). *Increasing language skills of students from low-income backgrounds: Practical strategies for professionals.* San Diego, CA: Plural Pub.

Beaty, J.J. (2009). *50 early childhood literacy strategies.* Upper Saddle River, NJ: Pearson Education.

Thatcher, K.L. (2010). The development of phonological awareness with specific language-impaired and typical children. *Psychology in the Schools, 47*(5), 467–480.

student, the parents, and the speech and language specialist to obtain suggestions and goals. Be proactive: give students opportunities to answer questions that require brief responses, and teach them to monitor their speech.

You can help students who have difficulty responding orally. Be a good role model for all students in the class when speaking to students with communication disorders. Speak clearly and a bit slower than normal, pause at appropriate times, and use straightforward language and simple grammatical structures. When responding to a student with a communication disorder, respond to the meaning of his speech rather than to how he speaks. Resist the temptation to interrupt students or to finish their sentences when they stutter or pause. Make eye contact with the speaker, and wait for a few seconds before responding.

Early communication development underpins much of academic learning. Thus many children with communication disorders also experience difficulty with academics. Problems with speech sounds can result in underdeveloped phonemic awareness, which is required for learning to read and spell (Pieretti et al., 2015). Receptive language delays contribute to challenges producing narrative accounts and to delays in development of working memory (McClintock et al., 2014) and can contribute to difficulties in reading comprehension and in understanding specialized terms in mathematics and other subjects (Nation et al., 2010). Language disabilities can seriously impede content-area learning in upper grades, where lectures and independent reading provide complex conceptual information. Recent research describes effective vocabulary and comprehension interventions (Fien et al., 2011; McCartney et al., 2015), including shared reading and electronic books (Korat, 2010). Research suggests that children with both speech-sound and language disorders are at greater risk for reading and spelling difficulties during elementary and high school and less ready for independence at the end of high school (Conti-Ramsden & Durkin, 2008).

Many provinces include relevant information on their websites to help you teach students with speech and language disabilities. For example, teachers in Yukon can consult www.education.gov.yk.ca. The Newfoundland and Labrador Department of Education has developed a handbook, *Programming for Individual Needs: Communication Disorders Handbook* (www.ed.gov.nl.ca/edu/k12), which defines relevant terms, describes students' needs, and discusses the role of professionals and how communication needs can be met.

Weblinks

TYKETALK (A PARTNERSHIP OF AGENCIES IN THAMES VALLEY, ONTARIO)

www.tyketalk.com

CANADIAN ASSOCIATION OF SPEECH-LANGUAGE PATHOLOGISTS AND AUDIOLOGISTS

www.caslpa.ca

ONTARIO ASSOCIATION OF SPEECH-LANGUAGE PATHOLOGISTS AND AUDIOLOGISTS

www.osla.on.ca

Implications for Social and Career Participation of Students with Communication Exceptionalities

Being unable to communicate effectively can contribute to social needs. Children with speech and language disorders can feel neglected or even rejected if their peers cease to include them in games and classroom activities. These pressures can be felt acutely during adolescence, when peer acceptance is so highly valued. Many adults are able to overcome speech disorders if these are their only exceptionalities. However, not developing either comprehension or production of language may prevent adults from participating fully in the workplace unless adaptations are provided, reminding us of the potential ramifications of ignoring students' communication exceptionalities.

Teaching Students Who Are Hard of Hearing or Deaf

I am deaf and have always gone to school with kids who can hear. I lip read and learned some Sign last summer at camp. Ever since then I have wanted to go to a school where all the kids are deaf.

From Kaufman, 2005, p. 114.

Description of Students Who Are Hard of Hearing or Deaf

Students who have hearing loss that has significantly affected the development of speech or language or both and who require differentiated teaching to participate effectively and benefit from instruction are described as being **deaf** or **hard of hearing**. Hearing loss is grouped into four general categories: mild, moderate, severe, and profound or deaf, depending on the dB (decibel) hearing level an individual can hear. This includes children who have a hearing impairment at birth and those who develop hearing loss later, those with conductive hearing loss (caused by middle ear infection and amenable to treatment), and those with sensory neural hearing loss (resulting from damage to the sensory mechanism or cochlea). The Canadian Association of the Deaf (www.cad.ca/index_en.php) recognizes a person to be deaf when that person has little or no functional hearing and depends upon visual rather than auditory communication. This organization describes a person with hearing loss as a person whose hearing loss ranges from mild to profound and whose usual means of communication is speech. They consider hearing loss to be both a medical and a sociological term.

@

Weblinks

CANADIAN HEARING SOCIETY

www.chs.ca

CANADIAN ASSOCIATION OF THE DEAF

www.cad.ca

VOICE FOR HEARING IMPAIRED CHILDREN (CANADA)

www.voicefordeafkids.com

Characteristics of Students Who Are Hard of Hearing or Deaf

The main characteristics of students with hearing impairments are that they cannot hear well enough to use hearing as a primary channel for learning without significant assistance and that their language development is likely to be influenced.

A complex array of factors influences learning. Two students with similar hearing loss may have completely different experiences before they arrive at school and may communicate in quite different ways. Language development and communication can be affected by

- the age at the onset of the hearing loss, especially whether the student had already developed spoken language at that time
- the severity of the hearing loss

Marmaduke St. John/Alamy

Xinhua/Du Yubao/Newscom

Brian Mitchell/Corbis

Young classmates of students who are deaf or hard of hearing are taught sign language by an instructor from the Canadian Hearing Society.

- intelligence
- **hearing status** of the family (a student who is deaf tends to experience higher academic success if the parents are deaf as well)
- means of communication chosen by the family

Some young children experience hearing loss when fluid builds up in the middle ear. Characteristics you might see include children failing to respond to their name, asking for directions to be repeated, turning their head to hear, and speaking too loudly or too softly. You may also see a change in behaviour or academic performance or hear the child complain of recurring earaches. Physicians can insert ventilating tubes that drain fluid, reversing the temporary loss of hearing. However, recent Canadian research reports that temporary hearing loss may influence subsequent language development and literacy learning (Briand, 2011). Teachers of young children who spot these characteristics play an important role in preventing hearing loss and subsequent language delays.

While students who are hard of hearing or deaf tend to fall behind in reading and other language skills, they often meet or exceed expectations in subjects like science and math. As with other exceptionalities, difficulty with a subject does not necessarily imply lack of ability. When fatigued and frustrated by their difficulties in communicating, these students can be disruptive and inattentive.

Implications for Learning and Classroom Differentiation for Students with Hearing Loss

The implications for classroom learning and participation are related to the choices parents make for their children about methods of communication in the preschool years and the type of schooling (Shaver et al., 2014). Depending on the degree of the child's hearing loss and the advice they receive, parents may decide to focus on the child maximizing their use of residual hearing within a regular classroom or on the child learning sign language in a specialized school setting or class and developing a deaf identity (Gibbons, 2015). Be sensitive to parents' concerns about whether they have made the best choice for their child. It is unlikely that you will teach children who use only **American Sign Language (ASL)**. If children who use ASL are included in your classroom, they will probably be accompanied by an interpreter. There are concerns that children who are deaf and working with interpreters may not be receiving all of the information teachers communicate to hearing students (e.g., Langer, 2007). Many students who learn in inclusive classrooms use amplification to help them hear. At first, you may experience difficulty understanding their speech, but teachers usually grow accustomed to their manner of speaking in a few days. Ask a student who is reluctant to speak in front of the class to speak with you individually so you can learn the speech patterns. The spoken language of children who are deaf or hard of hearing improves as the amplification technology advances. Frequency modulation systems may be child-specific or can be used to enhance sound for all class members. For recent information about amplification considerations, consult McKay et al. (2008) and Weil (2011).

ENHANCING SPEECH-READING

There are many actions you can take to differentiate your teaching. For students who are **speech-reading**, arrange the classroom so the student can see your face at all

Weblinks

HARD OF HEARING AND DEAF STUDENTS: A RESOURCE GUIDE TO SUPPORT CLASSROOM TEACHERS (BC MINISTRY OF EDUCATION)

www.bced.gov.bc.ca/specialed/ hearimpair/toc.htm

EDUCATORS' RESOURCE GUIDE: SUPPORTING STUDENTS WHO ARE DEAF OR HARD OF HEARING (MANITOBA)

www.edu.gov.mb.ca/k12/ docs/support/dhh_resource/ index.html

ESSENTIAL COMPONENTS OF EDUCATIONAL PROGRAMMING FOR STUDENTS WHO ARE DEAF OR HARD OF HEARING (ALBERTA)

www.education.alberta.ca/ media/511693/ecep_deaf_or_ hard_of_hearing.pdf

ATLANTIC PROVINCES SPECIAL EDUCATION AUTHORITY REFERRAL SERVICES FOR STUDENTS WHO ARE DEAF, HARD OF HEARING, DEAFBLIND, BLIND OR VISUALLY IMPAIRED

www.apsea.ca

times, and get the student's attention before speaking to her. Allow the student to move during a lesson. Ensure that you don't turn your back to the class and don't put your hands in front of your face. Speak normally and avoid making distracting gestures. Some words, such as *bat*, *pat*, and *mat*, look the same when you pronounce them. Try to put words like this into context, especially during spelling dictation. If other students ask questions, repeat them so the student who is deaf or hard of hearing knows what was asked. Summaries at the end of lessons give all students a second chance to take in information. During group discussions, sit the class in a circle so the student who is speech-reading can always see the face of the person who is speaking.

You can convey important messages visually as well as orally—for example, many students will benefit from having an agenda and assignments listed on the board. Use visual aids, written summaries, and **manipulatives**. The student with hearing loss will benefit from your **preteaching** any new vocabulary. Pay attention to and try to diffuse the student's frustration. You can plan the day's work so periods of intense concentration are interspersed with less demanding activities. For more information about including a student who is deaf or hard of hearing, see Figure 5.1.

Recent research provides guidance for enhancing phonological awareness for young students who are deaf (Beal-Alvarez et al., 2012), improving the vocabulary of hard of hearing second graders (Dimling, 2010) and adolescents (Luckner & Cooke, 2010), and using tablets and wireless technology to enhance mathematics learning for junior high students (Liu & Hong, 2006). Research is emerging on how to teach students with

FIGURE 5.1 TIPS FOR TEACHERS OF STUDENTS WHO ARE DEAF OR HARD OF HEARING

Students with hearing loss need to see your face all the time to speech-read and get meaning clues. Non-verbal communication is also important. Encourage students with hearing loss by making eye contact and smiling.

Natural lighting is best, if it is available, but avoid standing in front of lights or windows because they cause your face to be in shadow.

Speaking naturally helps the student with hearing loss. Talking very loudly or over-enunciating does not help your student; in fact it makes it harder. Do not speak too fast. Be aware that accents are very difficult.

- Discuss the best seating arrangement in the room with the student. Choose the best place for the student to receive maximum information within the normal flow of classroom activities.
- Provide vocabulary lists with definitions of new terms and concepts to be used during the day to help the student to develop a personal dictionary of words learned.
- Post an outline of the class agenda—just three or four points jotted on the board; this really helps the student to see the purpose and timing for short-term tasks and how they fit into the longer-range planning.
- Provide an outline of the topics and kind of work to be done in each unit and over the term.
- Provide an outline of a typical school day with the student's own timetable. Include room numbers and a list of people who can assist (e.g., counsellor, school secretary).
- During class discussion or group work, ensure that only one person speaks at a time. Then summarize on the board or have the groups report their work on large paper that can be read by everyone.
- Use visuals, handouts, and outlines.
- Ask other students in the class to volunteer as a buddy to take notes and help you watch for the need for more clarification.

Source: Adapted from BC Ministry of Education (www.bced.gov.bc.ca/specialed/hearimpair/tip15.htm) and VOICE (www.voicefordeafkids.com).

Further Reading

Padden, C.A., & Humphries, T.L. (2005). *Inside Deaf culture*. Cambridge, MA: Harvard University Press.

Lee, C. (2012). Deafness and cochlear implants: A Deaf scholar's perspective. *Journal of Child Neurology, 27*(6), 821–823.

Dalton, C. (2011). Social-emotional challenges experienced by students who function with mild and moderate hearing loss in educational settings. *Exceptionality Education International, 21*(1), 28–45.

Snodden, K., & Underwood, K. (2014). Toward a relational model of Deaf childhood. *Disability & Society, 29*(4), 530–542.

Put into Practice

Read *Deaf Education in America: Voices of Children from Inclusion Settings* by Janet Cerney (Washington, DC: Gallaudet University Press, 2007). Consider the complex issues surrounding the integration of students who are deaf into the regular classroom and the steps that can be taken to ensure their success in an inclusion setting. List the three most important things you learned from this book. Compare what you have learned with the learning of your peers. Make brief guidelines that you could use for working with the family, the student, and your colleagues to include a student who is deaf or hard of hearing in your class.

hearing loss who also have learning disabilities by adapting strategies typically used with students with LD, including modelling and guided practise (e.g., Soukup & Feinstein, 2007). Two recent Canadian studies emphasize the social-emotional challenges experienced by adolescents with hearing loss and the importance of family support for these youth (Dalton, 2011; Jamieson et al., 2011). They may feel stigmatized and definitely need your attention and support, but do not want you to draw attention to them.

SYSTEMS OF AMPLIFICATION

Classrooms often have excessive background noise and reverberation, which interfere with accurate speech perception. Degradation of the speech signal can be reduced for children who are hard of hearing by using **frequency modulation (FM)** devices in the classroom to enhance the speech-to-noise ratio (S/N) of the teacher's voice. There are three types of S/N-enhancing FM devices currently used in classrooms: (a) FM systems linked to personal **hearing aids**, (b) sound field systems with speakers placed throughout the classroom, and (c) personal sound field systems placed on the student's desk. Carpeted classrooms are best for all these systems; alternatively, place tennis balls over the feet of the desks and chairs. **Amplification** makes speech louder, not clearer, and also amplifies background noise. Results of a study that compared these three kinds of FM devices indicated that the ceiling sound field FM did not provide increased benefit beyond that provided by students' hearing aids alone. Desktop and personal FM systems provided substantial improvements in access to the speech signal, and there were indications that listening ease was greater with personal FM systems than with the desktop FM (Anderson & Goldstein, 2004). Expect new devices based on technological advances, and remember to speak clearly, stay still while talking, and allow the student to see your face (McKay et al., 2008).

Implications for Social and Career Participation of Students with Hearing Loss

Social participation is challenging for students with hearing loss or deafness because their exceptionality affects communication. Their system of communication is also influential. As the opening of this section suggests, some adolescents and adults who are deaf or hard of hearing choose to learn ASL and to join the **Deaf community**, in spite of their parents' earlier choice of oral language. Adults who are deaf or hard of hearing have a higher rate of underemployment and unemployment than the general population (Perkins-Dock et al., 2015). There are strong lobby groups to assist adults who are deaf, and career education and co-operative education can help adolescents learn about themselves and about careers. Transition guidelines for teachers of students who are deaf include focusing on career development from grade 6 on, involving adolescents in individual education plan (IEP) and transition meetings, and involving the family in transition planning (Garay, 2003; Saunders, 2012).

Teaching Children with Vision Disabilities and Blindness

"See you tomorrow, Ms. Fine!" The grade 3 students shouted goodbye to Marie Fine. Marie watched Amber painstakingly packing her laptop, books on tape, and thick pages of Braille into her backpack. Marie stood nearby in case Amber needed help. However,

Amber did the same thing every day; she put everything into her knapsack herself and then asked, "Did I get everything I need to finish my work? I still have a lot of questions to do in math." Marie thought about how hard Amber would work at home to complete the day's school tasks. Her voice sounded as heavy as her backpack. Amber knew that when you can't see, everything takes longer.

Adapted from Hutchinson, 2004 (2nd ed.), p. 9.

Description of Students with Visual Impairment

Students with total or partial **visual impairment** who require differentiated teaching, even with correction, are described as having visual disabilities. For educational purposes, a student with visual impairment is one whose visual acuity is not sufficient "to participate with ease in everyday activities" and whose impairment "can result in a substantial educational disadvantage, unless adaptations are made" in the environment, learning materials, teaching, and assessment (www.setbc.org). The IEP usually includes the student's need for orientation and mobility skills; efficient use of vision, **Braille**, and alternative formats such as taped books; access to technology; and daily living skills. These are typically the responsibility of a vision teacher or educational assistant (Morris & Sharma, 2011). The IEP also refers to differentiations that are your responsibility.

Characteristics of Students with Visual Impairments

Children and adolescents can experience deteriorating vision at any age. Teachers often identify students who need to be assessed. Complaints of blurred print or headaches may signal a need for correction; they can also signal conditions such as brain tumours. Pay attention to the appearance of the eyes (e.g., reddened, encrusted, frequent sties or tears). Listen to student complaints (e.g., headaches, burning eyes after use, nausea, blurred print). Also observe behavioural signs (e.g., the student squints or closes one eye, tilts head extremely, rubs eyes, turns head while reading across a page) (Nottingham Chaplin et al., 2014). Record your observations and encourage the parents to seek a vision assessment.

Knowing the characteristics of students with visual exceptionalities helps you understand their actions, postures, and developmental histories. Because they cannot learn social skills through observation, they may need specific instruction in areas such as body language and eye contact (Salleh et al., 2011). Because of vision's role in young children's exploration of their environment, these students may have had limited experiences and restricted movement in their environment, resulting in global delays in development (cognitive, motor, social, and emotional) stemming from lack of experience rather than lack of ability.

Implications for Learning and Classroom Differentiation for Students with Visual Impairments

Students with visual disabilities and blindness are likely to need differentiation in three areas: presentation of information, classroom environment and organization, and learning resources and assessment.

Put into Practice

View the two-part video presentation by Dr. Mary Nelle McLennan, *Developing Organizational Skills in Learners with Visual Impairments* at www.setbc.org. With your peers, develop a plan for implementing these strategies at the grade level you teach. The SET-BC website (www.setbc.org) contains many informative videos. Dr. Ellen Trief of Hunter College in New York has been developing a library of video clips for teacher preparation in visual impairments (see Trief, Lengel, and Baecher, 2013, in *Journal of Visual Impairment and Blindness*, Volume 13, pages 55–59).

Further Reading

On students who are deafblind:

Nelson, C., Greenfield, R., Hyte, H., & Shaffer, J.P. (2013). Stress, behavior, and children and youth who are deafblind. *Research & Practice for Persons with Severe Disabilities, 38*(3), 139–156.

Kamenopoulou, L. (2012). A study on the inclusion of deafblind young people in mainstream schools: Key findings and implications for research and practice. *British Journal of Special Education, 39*(3), 137–145.

On students who are blind:

Schaefer, L.M. (2008). *Some kids are blind.* Mankato, MN: Capstone Press.

Arndt, K., Lieberman, L., & James, A. (2010). Supporting the social lives of adolescents who are blind: Research to practice. *Clearing House, 87*(2), 69–74.

DIFFERENTIATING PRESENTATION OF INFORMATION

In differentiating the presentation of information, you will work closely with a vision teacher, an educational assistant, or a resource teacher. The specific differentiations depend on how the student acquires information—substituting other senses for vision, using residual vision, or both. For students who do not acquire information visually, give directions and notes verbally as well as visually and provide opportunities to explore three-dimensional models of visual concepts (see Jones et al., 2006, for an example in teaching science). For students with partial vision, enlarge print (usually to 130 or 140 percent on a photocopier or 18-point font size on your computer) and enhance contrast of written materials. Experiment to see whether coloured acetate (e.g., yellow or pale blue) enhances the contrast or if particular contrasts of paper and print are easiest for the student to read. A peer may serve as a note taker. You can make large-print copies of chalkboard notes and PowerPoints.

You may need to order materials from a provincial resource centre that provides audiobooks and adaptive technology for students who are blind. Some sources are listed below.

- **Alberta:** www.education.alberta.ca/teachers/resources/prb/ssvi
- **Atlantic provinces:** www.apsea.ca
- **British Columbia:** www.prcvi.org
- **Manitoba:** www.edu.gov.mb.ca/k12/specedu/blind
- **Ontario** (W. Ross Macdonald School Resource Services): www.psbnet.ca/eng/schools/wross/index.html
- **Quebec** (Montreal Association for the Blind and MacKay Rehabilitation Centre): www.mabmackay.ca/?langue=en
- **Saskatchewan:** www.education.gov.sk.ca/Vision

DIFFERENTIATING CLASSROOM ENVIRONMENT AND ORGANIZATION

Organize your classroom and use a seating arrangement so that students with partial vision have the best view possible of chalkboard work and demonstrations. Enclosed (rather than open-concept) classrooms with reduced clutter are better for these students. Ensure that everyone keeps possessions off the floor. To ensure safety, move the furniture as little as possible and always warn the student who cannot easily see changes. The organization of learning activities can also foster the inclusion of students with visual impairments. Form groups that enable them to practise social and communication skills with empathic peers. Work closely with the vision or resource teacher who may be instructing them in eye contact, body language, facial expression, and alternatives to behaviour patterns such as rocking and eye poking. For more information on including students with visual impairment, see Figure 5.2.

DIFFERENTIATING TEACHING RESOURCES AND ASSESSMENT

There are many learning resources for students with visual impairments, including large-print books, Braille books, and adaptive technology (AT). AT includes Braillers combined with word processors, programs that convert print to audio output, tablets, and speech-activated word processors (Campaña & Ouimet, 2015). An IEP usually ensures provincial funding for technology, three-dimensional maps and tape measures, and other learning materials. You may need to plan six months ahead to ensure

Weblinks

TEACHING STUDENTS WITH VISUAL IMPAIRMENTS (SASKATCHEWAN LEARNING)
www.education.gov.sk.ca/Vision

SPECIAL EDUCATION TECHNOLOGY BRITISH COLUMBIA (SET-BC)
www.setbc.org

SPECIAL NEEDS OPPORTUNITY WINDOWS (SNOW) ADAPTIVE TECHNOLOGY ONLINE WORKSHOPS FOR EDUCATORS AND PARAEDUCATORS
http://snow.idrc.ocad.ca

FIGURE 5.2 TIPS FOR TEACHERS OF STUDENTS WHO ARE VISUALLY IMPAIRED

1. Point out the classroom rules to which the student must adhere.
2. Expect the same quality of work, rather than the same quantity.
3. Don't move furniture in the classroom without warning the student.
4. Reduce glare on boards, desks, etc.
5. Provide multi-sensory experiences, learning by doing, and support without dependence.
6. Stress legibility, not size, as student will tend to print or write in large size, if at all.
7. Remind individual speakers to name themselves (and remind the visually impaired student of who is speaking if individual students forget).
8. Help everyone in the class to provide non-visual feedback to the student with the visual impairment (like saying "well done" instead of smiling or nodding).
9. Encourage peers to be friends, not helpers.
10. Encourage the visually impaired student to share his experiences with you, so that you can understand the student's perspective. Help the student to feel like an integral part of the community in the classroom.

Source: Hutchinson, N.L. (2004). *Teaching exceptional children and adolescents: A Canadian casebook* (2nd ed.), p. 13. Copyright Prentice Hall. Reprinted with permission by Pearson Canada Inc.

receipt of Braille textbooks, books on tape, and large-print learning materials before they are needed by the student.

The work and learning of students with vision impairments and blindness can be assessed effectively by extending time frames for test taking and homework assignments, and by testing students orally. Braille or large-print formats may be necessary, or assessments can be completed on a computer or under supervision in a resource room.

Implications for Social and Career Participation of Students with Visual Impairment

Adults with visual impairments experience higher-than-average rates of unemployment and underemployment. Students with visual impairment need to explore a wide variety of career options while developing a realistic understanding of their potential through a transition plan, differentiated career education, job shadowing, and co-operative education (Crudden, 2012; Wolffe & Kelly, 2011). Extracurricular activities and leisure activities with peers during adolescence help youth with visual impairments with social participation and to feel comfortable in adult roles, including in the workplace (Zebehazy & Smith, 2011).

Teaching Students with Physical Disabilities and Chronic Health Conditions

Researchers estimate that 20 percent of students experience a serious illness or health condition before the age of 18, and many of these illnesses and conditions influence their social participation and learning at school (O'Connor et al., 2015). These conditions result from genetic, environmental, and unknown causes and may be transient,

Further Reading

Downing, J.E. (with invited contributors). (2008). *Including students with severe and multiple disabilities in typical classrooms: Practical strategies for teachers.* Baltimore, MD: Paul H. Brookes.

Haslam, R.H., & Valletutti, P.J. (2015). *Medical and psychosocial problems in the classroom: The teacher's role in diagnosis and management.* Austin, TX: PRO-ED.

Shaw, S.R., et al. (2010). Responding to students' chronic illnesses. *Principal Leadership, 10*(7), 12–16.

Irwin, M.K., & Elam, M. (2011). Are we leaving children with chronic illness behind? *Physical Disabilities: Education and Related Services, 30,* 67–80.

Further Reading

O'Connor, M., Howell-Meurs, S., Kvalsvig, A., & Goldfeld, S. (2015). Understanding the impact of special health care needs on early school functioning: A conceptual model. *Child: Care, Health, & Development, 41*(1), 15–22.

DePaepe, P., Garrison-Kane, L., & Doelling, J. (2002). Supporting students with health needs in schools: An overview of selected health conditions. *Focus on Exceptional Children, 35*(1), 1–24.

A'Bear, D. (2014). Supporting the learning of children with chronic illness. *Canadian Journal of Action Research, 15*(1), 22–39. (includes use of iPod technology)

Brown, R.T., Rickel, A.U., & Daly, B.P. (2014). *Chronic illness in children and adolescents.* Toronto: Hogrefe & Huber.

lifelong, or life threatening. Many students experience unpredictable changes due to deteriorating health, recurring surgery, **remission**, and increasing doses and side effects of medication. Each physical condition can present differently from case to case, and how well families and individuals cope interacts with the physical condition. When you are teaching a student with a physical disability or chronic health condition or illness, it is critical for you to familiarize yourself with characteristics, emergency responses, and teaching strategies on a need-to-know basis—and to remember that because Canada is culturally diverse, we must listen to our students and their parents to understand their cultural perspective on the student's physical disability or chronic health condition.

Increasingly, teachers are expected to communicate regularly with children and adolescents who are not attending school due to hospitalization and recuperation at home, and often contact is maintained by using a tablet (Hopkins et al., 2014), communicating with digital technology like Skype (Simeonsdotter Svensson et al., 2014), etc. Teachers and classmates can help the student with a chronic illness to keep up with lessons and feel included in the class; the effects on the student's learning and well-being are significant (A'Bear, 2014).

Physical and chronic health conditions are difficult to categorize. The focus can be on the area of dysfunction, the cause, or the impact. For example, muscular dystrophy can be described as a musculoskeletal impairment, a health disorder, or a motor disability. A student is considered to have a physical disability or chronic medical disorder, based on the need for differentiated teaching or special education services, because of one or more of the following: (1) nervous system impairment, (2) musculoskeletal condition, or (3) chronic health impairment (BC Special Education Branch, 2008).

Nervous System Impairment

Nervous system impairment or **neurological dysfunction** results from damage or dysfunction of the brain or spinal cord that may have occurred before, during, or after birth. The exceptionalities discussed are cerebral palsy, spina bifida, epilepsy, Tourette syndrome, brain injury, and fetal alcohol spectrum disorders.

CEREBRAL PALSY

On Wednesday, nobody understood what I wanted. Most days I can point at it or just wheel over in my walker. I've got lots of words inside my head but people don't seem to hear them like I do. Some days, even my mum doesn't know what I mean. Wednesday was a bad day. Nobody understood. My big yellow school bus was on my

Marcel Jancovic/Shutterstock

Increasingly, young adults with physical disabilities are completing university and graduate school, like Jenny Clement, who works at ARCH Disability Law Centre in Ontario.

top shelf and I wanted to play with it. Dad handed me the blocks instead. Bbbusss . . .
That's a hard word to say.

From Yates, 1994, pp. 3–5.

This young girl has **cerebral palsy (CP)**. Although she speaks little and cannot walk, she has thoughts to express and can become frustrated. She might enjoy reading or listening to someone read *On Being Sarah* (Helfman, 1992). Cerebral palsy describes a group of disorders affecting body movement and muscle coordination resulting from damage to the brain during pregnancy or before age three. This damage interferes with messages in both directions between brain and body. Many individuals with intellectual disabilities also have cerebral palsy.

The effects vary widely. Mild CP causes awkward movement or hand control. Severe CP may result in almost no muscle control, profoundly affecting movement and speech. Depending on which areas of the brain have been damaged, one or more of the following may occur:

- muscle tightness or spasm
- involuntary movement
- difficulty with gross-motor skills such as walking or running
- difficulty with fine-motor skills such as writing and speaking
- abnormal perception and sensation

The brain damage that caused CP may also lead to seizures, learning disabilities or intellectual disabilities, hearing loss, or impaired vision. The degree of physical disability experienced by a person with cerebral palsy is not an indication of level of intelligence.

Treat students with cerebral palsy as normally as possible and don't underestimate their ability to learn and participate. They may need more time to complete a task or to respond verbally, and they may need to repeat themselves when misunderstood. Some use voice output communication aids; this can make it challenging for naturally speaking students to take turns in conversation with the student with CP (van Schie et al., 2013). Learn to help to position and transfer students who use wheelchairs and learn how to push wheelchairs by asking the student, a parent, or a physiotherapist. Many students with CP receive physiotherapy interventions at school to increase strength and coordination. Felt-tipped pens and soft-lead pencils enable the student to exert less pressure when writing. A rubber grip around the shaft may help with holding a pencil. You can help the student set and reach realistic goals in your classroom. Collaborate with the student and the parents to make the best possible use of school and community supports. For classroom accommodations consult www.bced.gov.bc.ca/specialed/awareness/33.htm and the work of Bjorquist and colleagues (2015) for optimizing the transition out of high school.

SPINA BIFIDA

I am going to try out for the swim team this year, even though I may not be chosen. I have been swimming since I was very young because my parents thought I might get hurt in rough team sports. I have always swum by myself, but I really want to be part of a team.

Excerpt from the diary of a 15-year-old male with spina bifida who wears leg braces and uses crutches.

Put into Practice

Read research about students with spina bifida and discuss with your classmates the implications for teaching. For example, Barnes et al. (2004) reports that children with spina bifida who have hydrocephalus have particular difficulty comprehending text even when they can decode the words.

Rissman, B. (2011). Nonverbal learning disability explained: The link to shunted hydrocephalus. *British Journal of Learning Disabilities, 39*(3), 209–215.

Barnes, M.A., et al. (2004). Meaning construction and integration in children with hydrocephalus. *Brain and Language, 89*, 47–56.

Barnes, M.A., et al. (2006). Arithmetic processing in children with spina bifida: Calculation accuracy, strategy use, and fact retrieval fluency. *Journal of Learning Disabilities, 39*, 174–187.

Coughlin, J., & Montague, M. (2011). The effects of cognitive strategy instruction on the mathematical problem solving of adolescents with spina bifida. *Journal of Special Education, 45*(3), 171–183.

Lindsay, S. (2014). A qualitative synthesis of adolescents' experiences of living with spina bifida. *Qualitative Health Research, 24*(9), 1298–1309.

Weblinks

SPINA BIFIDA ASSOCIATION (AMERICA)
www.sbaa.org

SPINA BIFIDA AND HYDROCEPHALUS CANADA
http://sbhac.ca

Spina bifida is a neural tube defect that occurs within the first four weeks of pregnancy. The spinal cord fails to develop properly, causing damage to the nervous system. Spina bifida often results in paralysis of the lower limbs as well as loss of bladder control, and affects cognitive development. It is often accompanied by **hydrocephalus** (about 80 percent of the time), the accumulation of cerebrospinal fluid surrounding the brain. This fluid can cause brain injury if not treated immediately; usually a **shunt** is installed to drain the fluid for reabsorption. Recent research clarifies the link between shunted hydrocephalus and non-verbal learning disabilities frequently seen in individuals with spina bifida (Rissman, 2011).

Headaches, co-ordination difficulties, vomiting, and seizures, all evident in the classroom, are indications of shunt blockage. If the student lacks bladder or bowel control, this can be a barrier to peer acceptance. You can model acceptance and be sensitive to the student's need to leave the classroom unexpectedly. Encourage independence and ensure privacy. Usually an educational assistant helps young students with these functions. Because sitting in a wheelchair can cause sores and skin breakdown, students need to be positioned properly and moved periodically. They may use prone standers, braces, or crutches for part of the day. Treat changes in position as normal occurrences, assist students without drawing undue attention to them, and accommodate extended absences from school.

Students with spina bifida often experience non-verbal learning disabilities, especially difficulties learning arithmetic, including challenges calculating addition and subtraction, retrieving number facts, and using strategies (Barnes et al., 2006). However, cognitive strategy instruction has been shown to help adolescents with spina bifida learn to solve math word problems (Coughlin & Montague, 2011). Encourage students with spina bifida to use computers and calculators, and give them two copies of books: one for school and one for home. By working closely with the family, you can help minimize the impact of spina bifida on school participation. Young adults with spina bifida report struggling to transition to living independently from their families and report feeling stigmatized because of their condition (Ridosh et al., 2011). School counsellors can help you to enhance the social participation and social acceptance of students in your classes who have spina bifida (Brislin, 2008).

EPILEPSY

> I started high school, in grade 9, at a new school in September. Last Thursday, in the third week of school, I had a seizure in my history class. I am so happy that I had told my new best friend, Emily, what to do if I had a seizure. When the teacher was flustered, Emily got everyone calmed down and helped to lay me on the floor. The history teacher has been treating me differently ever since, and asking me over and over again if I am OK. My Mom and I have arranged to meet with my teachers next week. I think my classmates would forget about it if the teacher would just treat me normally.

Adapted from Hutchinson.

Epilepsy is a common neurological disorder involving sudden bursts of electrical energy in the brain, characterized by sudden, brief **seizures** lasting from ten seconds to five minutes. In many cases the causes are unknown, but they can include chemical imbalance and head injury (Reilly & Ballantine, 2011). Many individuals with intellectual disabilities or cerebral palsy also have epilepsy.

The two main categories of seizures are partial and generalized. **Partial seizures** involve one area of the brain, while **generalized seizures** involve the whole brain. In a partial seizure there may be strange sensations, possibly accompanied by inappropriate movements such as plucking at clothes, smacking lips, or aimless wandering. Complete consciousness is not lost, though confusion usually follows.

Generalized seizures are of two types—simple absence and tonic-clonic. The **simple absence seizure** (formerly known as **petit mal**) occurs in children; they stare or daydream for five to fifteen seconds. There may be small muscle movements in the face, the eyes may roll upward or to one side, and the child may be confused about the seconds "missed." If these seizures are not treated, serious learning problems can result. Teachers most often notice these seizures; when you do, urge parents to seek a neurological assessment (DePaepe et al., 2002).

The **tonic-clonic seizure** (formerly called **grand mal**) can be frightening when it occurs in the classroom. Sometimes the student gives a sharp cry before falling to the floor, and the muscles stiffen and begin to jerk rhythmically. There may be loss of bladder control and breathing difficulty, and saliva may gather at the mouth. In most cases the seizure will not hurt the student and there is no emergency; some school policies require that the student be taken to the hospital. Medical attention is required if the seizure "lasts more than five minutes or is repeated without full recovery" (Epilepsy Toronto; www.epilepsytoronto.org).

A child with seizures may experience the world as an unpredictable and scary place. Concerns regarding safety may lead to overprotecting the child or adolescent, making the individual feel dependent, helpless, and unworthy (Lewis & Parsons, 2008). You may perceive a student with epilepsy as being unmotivated, not realizing that seizures can have a profound cognitive impact, especially on concentration and on learning mathematics (Reilly & Ballantine, 2011). Many individuals with epilepsy feel embarrassed when a seizure occurs in public and may exhibit acting out behaviours, which could serve to distance them from their peers. Your support for the child or adolescent is critical, and you may need to consult a special educator or school psychologist to help with targeted interventions. Many children with epilepsy require daily administration of medication during the school day. Medications often have side effects, ranging from hyperactivity to sleepiness, and include clumsiness, difficulty thinking or talking, inattentiveness and distractibility, and rashes, depending on the medication (DePaepe et al., 2002). Because of seizures and side effects, students may be excused from activities such as climbing high ropes or operating power tools. Epilepsy is a spectrum condition and the severity of the effects at school may vary greatly. Recent research suggests that concern about seizures has caused us to overlook learning disabilities, depression, and anxiety which may accompany epilepsy (Reilly & Ballantine, 2011).

Familiarize yourself with the student's condition and medication's side effects. You also need to know what to do when a seizure occurs. Figure 5.3 lists the specific actions to take during a generalized seizure.

TOURETTE SYNDROME

> My name is Jared. I am eleven years old and I have TS. I have tics that really bother me. Sometimes they keep me awake at night. I get "buggie" when I am frustrated and then I can't concentrate. My teacher says I can leave the classroom when I need to settle and I get a drink. I know that I make funny noises but I can't help it. Some of the tics I have are twirling my hair, moving my arms, shrugging my shoulders, sticking my pinky finger in the air.

Tourette syndrome (TS) is a complex neurological disorder modulated by psychological and social factors. It is characterized by **tics**: involuntary, rapid, sudden

What do you think?

Many people with epilepsy feel they are discriminated against. View the website of Epilepsy Toronto (www. epilepsytoronto.org) and of Epilepsy Canada (www. epilepsy.ca) and then discuss with your classmates this charge of unfair treatment.

Further Reading

Epilepsy can have an impact on the family life of any child, but especially for an adolescent. The publication *Exceptional Parent* has included a series of articles on adolescents and epilepsy. Here are a few of these articles, which will give you a much greater understanding of the lives of adolescents (and children) who live with epilepsy and seizures.

Shafer, P.O., & Schachter, S.C. (2007, November). Seizures and teens: Using technology to develop seizure preparedness. *Exceptional Parent, 37*(11), 64–66.

Sundstrom, D. (2007, April). Seizures and teens: Maximizing health and safety. *Exceptional Parent, 37*(4), 77–79.

Weinstein, S.C. (2007, June). Seizures and teens: The impact of seizures and epilepsy on families. *Exceptional Parent, 37*(6), 61–62.

Shafer, P.O., & Israel, B. (2007, February). Seizures and teens: The practical aspects of managing seizure medications. *Exceptional Parent, 37*(2), 57–59.

Cross-Reference
Chapter 4 contains information about mild intellectual disabilities and severe intellectual disabilities.

FIGURE 5.3 STRATEGIES FOR HANDLING A GENERALIZED SEIZURE IN THE CLASSROOM

Before a Seizure

- Meet with the parents and student at the beginning of the year. Learn the characteristics of the student's seizures.
- Familiarize yourself with the school's policies.
- Discuss with the family how to inform the class that a seizure may occur.
- Keep the area surrounding the student's desk free of objects that could cause harm to the student during a seizure.

During a Seizure

- Stay calm, and keep the students calm. Remind them that the seizure is painless. Ask another teacher to remove excited students from the classroom.
- Ease the student to the floor and loosen clothing.
- Try to remove any hard, sharp, or hot objects that might injure the student.
- Place a blanket, coat, or cushion under the student's head to soften the impact of the seizure.
- Place the student on his or her side to allow saliva to flow from the mouth.
- Write down the time the seizure began. If a seizure lasts longer than five minutes, medical attention may be needed.
- Refrain from restraining the student or placing objects in the student's mouth.
- Refrain from giving the student food or drink.

After a Seizure

- Allow the student to rest or sleep and then offer the opportunity to resume classroom activities.
- Be attuned to the student's emotional state, as most but not all students can rejoin classroom activities.
- The student should not leave the school alone if weakness or convulsive behaviour persists.
- Refrain from "fussing over" the student with epilepsy. Foster an attitude of understanding and acceptance. The student with epilepsy needs support from you and peers.

Put into Practice

Watch a video on epilepsy to reduce your discomfort with intervening when a student has a seizure. Make a brief action plan and discuss it with your peers. Epilepsy Toronto has a comprehensive list of videos on its website (www.epilepsytoronto. org). Two that are highly recommended are *Understanding Seizure Disorders* (eleven minutes) and *Seizure First Aid* (ten minutes, including demonstrations of first aid for individuals with different types of seizures).

muscular movements; uncontrollable vocal sounds; and inappropriate words. Symptoms appear between the ages of 3 to 8 and change over time, usually being most severe during adolescence. Stress aggravates TS symptoms; thus, more structure and predictability result in fewer disruptions. Typically, tics decrease with concentration on an absorbing task, so engaging teaching will help students with TS. These children may also have learning disabilities, obsessive-compulsive behaviours, and attentional difficulties. Many individuals with autism also have tics and some have Tourette syndrome (Canitano & Vivanti, 2007).

More boys than girls have TS, and symptoms appear to be more severe in students with concomitant identifications, such as ADHD, who are more likely to demonstrate peer problems and aggression.

When teaching a student with Tourette syndrome in a classroom,

- be patient and engage all students fully;
- respond to tics with tolerance, not anger; the student with TS cannot control them;
- encourage the student to leave the room for a short time when tics become distracting;
- provide a quiet place for the student to work or take tests, preferably in the classroom;

- consider whether a scribe or tape recorder would help the student to overcome tics when writing tests;

- minimize stress by differentiating, offering additional time, using structure, and eliminating chaos;

- with the help of a psychologist, find out what stimuli may trigger tics in the classroom and minimize these triggers;

- seek assistance for yourself and the student with TS from counsellors, psychologists, and parents (Chaturvedi et al., 2011; Koutsoklenis & Theodoridou, 2012).

Tourette Canada has developed an educator resource kit which can be ordered from their website (www.tourette.ca).

BRAIN INJURY

> How I hated going to school! Almost a year after my brain injury, I was still relearning to read and write and even to remember. Most of my teachers were helpful, and I had a tutor who helped me write my assignments and read my textbooks. But I felt myself getting more and more down, and it was really the counsellor who got me through those "dark periods."

> *Mark, reflecting on returning to school after his brain injury.*

Brain injury happens when the brain's tissue is damaged or not able to function properly. It is called **acquired brain injury (ABI)**, **head injury**, or **traumatic brain injury**. Many brain injuries are acquired, the result of a blow to the head from a fall, a sports injury, an assault, or a cycling or motor vehicle accident

Symptoms fall into three broad areas—cognitive, physical, and psychosocial or behavioural (Trudel et al., 2011). Cognitive difficulties in remembering, understanding, organizing, and planning interfere with learning in school. Difficulties with speed of processing, a cognitive skill that underlies many academic tasks, mean that students need more time to finish tasks and require instructions to be broken down into smaller steps. Expressive language challenges can persist for two or more years (Yu et al., 2011). *Educating Educators about ABI: Resource Book* (Bennett et al., 2003) describes strategies for teaching students with ABI including redirecting (steering a student away from their preoccupation) and restructuring (focusing on the relevant, ignoring the irrelevant or inaccurate). Because they know themselves as they were prior to the brain injury, students with ABI may hold on to their pre-trauma academic and career aspirations; realistic goals are essential but can be discouraging. Physical effects such as paralysis and vision and hearing loss affect life both in and out of school. Socio-emotional effects include anti-social behaviour, impulsiveness, confusion, and often significant personality changes such as paranoia (Fowler & McCabe, 2011). Figure 5.4 contains strategies for physical, language, cognitive, and social differentiation in the classroom.

FETAL ALCOHOL SPECTRUM DISORDERS

> My son has a hard time in school. He has fetal alcohol syndrome (FAS), a disorder caused by prenatal exposure to alcohol, his birth mother's drinking during pregnancy. James has mild retardation, small stature, unusual facial features, and damage to his central nervous system. He doesn't have any close friends, maybe because he has a hard time learning the rules of life. He needs to be reminded how to behave around other people.

> *A mother speaking about her child with fetal alcohol syndrome.*

Further Reading

Bennett, S., et al. (2003). *Educating educators about ABI: Resource book.* St. Catharines, ON: Ontario Brain Injury Association. www.abieducation.com

Crylen, A.E. (2015). Socio-emotional support needs for re-entry to school after traumatic brain injury. *International Perspectives on Inclusive Education, 5*, 159–179.

Bullock, L.M., et al. (2005). Traumatic brain injury: A challenge for educators. *Preventing School Failure, 49*(4), 6–10.

Chesire, D., Canto, A., & Buckley, V. (2011). Hospital–school collaboration to serve the needs of children with traumatic brain injury. *Journal of Applied School Psychology, 27*(1), 60–76.

Weblinks

TOURETTE CANADA
www.tourette.ca

Weblinks

ONTARIO BRAIN INJURY ASSOCIATION
www.obia.on.ca

BRAIN INJURY ASSOCIATION OF NOVA SCOTIA
http://braininjuryns.com

NEUROSCIENCE FOR KIDS
http://faculty.washington.edu/chudler/neurok.html

FIGURE 5.4 STRATEGIES FOR TEACHING STUDENTS WITH BRAIN INJURY IN A CLASSROOM SETTING

Strategies for Physical Differentiation

- Schedule rest breaks; have a shortened day.
- Schedule more difficult classes early in the day.
- Provide adaptive technology and scribes, without drawing undue attention.

Strategies for Language Differentiation

- Use shorter, simpler sentences, with pictures and gestures to aid comprehension.
- Teach the student to ask for clarification or repetition at a slower rate.
- To aid student communication, use pictures, an alphabet chart, etc.

Strategies for Cognitive Differentiation

- Remove distractions and limit the amount of information on a page.
- Provide focusing cues and visual cues or a set of steps to follow.
- Adjust the length of assignments to the student's attention span; include fewer steps.
- Use rehearsal to improve memory; have the student practise aloud.
- Use an audio recorder instead of having the student write notes.
- Teach the student to compensate for word-finding problems by describing the function, etc. of items that cannot be recalled.
- Praise students once they begin a task; remind them they can do it.
- Give prior warning for transitions; make transitions clear and structured.
- Role-play appropriate responses and stop inappropriate responses when they begin.

Strategies for Social Differentiation

- Make asking for assistance a student goal and remind the student.
- Check work after a small amount is begun to reassure the student that she can do it.
- Emphasize personal progress; discourage comparisons to classmates.
- Arrange for counselling to deal with frustration.
- Model patience and understanding to the class.

Weblinks

ALBERTA EDUCATION: TEACHING STUDENTS WITH FETAL ALCOHOL SPECTRUM DISORDER: BUILDING STRENGTHS, CREATING HOPE
http://education.alberta.ca/teachers/resources/fasd.aspx

SASKATCHEWAN LEARNING: FETAL ALCOHOL SPECTRUM DISORDER (FASD): A LEARNING RESOURCE TO STRENGTHEN PLANNING FOR STUDENTS WITH FETAL ALCOHOL SPECTRUM DISORDER
www.education.gov.sk.ca/FASD

MANITOBA EDUCATION, TRAINING, AND YOUTH: TOWARDS INCLUSION: TAPPING HIDDEN STRENGTHS—PLANNING FOR STUDENTS WHO ARE ALCOHOL-AFFECTED
www.edu.gov.mb.ca/k12/specedu/fas

NATIONAL ORGANIZATION ON FETAL ALCOHOL SYNDROME: STAMP OUT STIGMA
www.nofas.org/stigma

Prenatal exposure to alcohol can lead to significant neurodevelopmental disabilities, now recognized as **fetal alcohol spectrum disorders (FASD)**. This includes both **fetal alcohol syndrome (FAS)**, a lifelong birth defect, and a wider range of enduring learning and behaviour deficits often called **partial fetal alcohol syndrome (pFAS)** and **alcohol-related neurodevelopmental disorder (ARND)**. Alcohol interferes with the development of the embryo as well as the central nervous system and physical development (Olson et al., 2007). For a description of the features of each disorder in FASD, see Table 5.4. At one time it was believed that only significant prenatal exposure to alcohol could cause FASD; however, recent research suggests that even occasional alcohol consumption during pregnancy can cause damage along the spectrum.

FASDs are difficult to diagnose. Reasons include the similarity of characteristics to those of other exceptionalities and the resistance of some mothers to the idea that they are responsible for their children's disabilities.

Students with FASD can be chatty and charming, and this may initially mask their learning and behaviour difficulties. They usually show impaired rates of learning, poor memory, and difficulty generalizing. They often act impulsively; exhibit

TABLE 5.4 CRITERIA FOR FETAL ALCOHOL SPECTRUM DISORDERS

Disorder	Diagnostic Features
Fetal alcohol syndrome (FAS)	Growth deficiency: height or weight < 10th percentile
	Cluster of minor facial anomalies: small eye slits, thin upper lip, smooth groove above the upper lip
	Central nervous system damage: evidence of structural or functional brain impairment
	Reliable evidence of confirmed prenatal alcohol exposure (not required if the cluster of facial anomalies is present)
Partial FAS (pFAS)	Some of the characteristic minor facial anomalies
	Growth deficiency: height or weight < 10th percentile
	Central nervous system damage: evidence of structural or functional brain impairment
	Reliable evidence of confirmed prenatal alcohol exposure
Alcohol-related neurodevelopmental disorder (ARND)	Central nervous system damage: evidence of structural or functional brain impairment
	Reliable evidence of confirmed prenatal alcohol exposure

short attention spans; and have difficulty staying focused, recognizing and understanding patterns, predicting common sense outcomes, and mastering mathematics and reading. Parents describe examples of fearlessness, lack of social judgment, and lack of internalization of modelled behaviour. Difficulty understanding cause and effect appears to be an integral part of learning and behaviour difficulties for individuals with FASD (Olson et al., 2007). Consistency in behaviour management across home and school usually helps these children and adolescents.

Figure 5.5 includes strategies for behaviour management at home and at school. There has been little research to indicate what kinds of interventions are most effective for students with FASD until recently. Bertand (2009) describes effective interventions, involving collaboration and consistency across teachers and parents to teach social skills that improve peer friendships, math, and self-regulation. These structured, collaborative interventions build on the recent interventions by Laugeson et al. (2007) and Coles et al. (2007). Cheryl Poth and colleagues at University of Alberta (2014) report that educators experienced with this population emphasized understanding the whole student and optimizing student-centred programming. Figure 5.5 also includes strategies for teaching students with FASD.

Musculoskeletal Conditions

Two **musculoskeletal conditions** that can affect all aspects of a student's life are muscular dystrophy and juvenile arthritis. They have different characteristics, treatments, and educational implications.

MUSCULAR DYSTROPHY

When I was in grade two, I started to fall down at school. My teacher gave me extra time to move to other classes like French and let me be scorekeeper in gym. I got very tired at school and needed breaks, and my teacher gave me shorter assignments.

Put into Practice

Recent papers report on teaching approaches that "work" for students with FASD. Consider the implications for regular classroom teachers with your peers. Make recommendations for teachers based on your reading.

Laugeson, E.A., Paley, B., Schonfeld, A.M., Carpenter, E.M., Frankel, F., & O'Connor, M.J. (2007). Adaptation of the children's friendship training program for children with fetal alcohol spectrum disorders. *Child and Family Behavior Therapy, 29*(3), 57–69.

Coles, C.D., Strickland, D.C., Padgett, L., & Bellmoff, L. (2007). Games that "work": Using computer games to teach alcohol-affected children about fire and street safety. *Research in Developmental Disabilities, 28*, 518–530.

Bertrand, J. (2009). Interventions for children with fetal alcohol spectrum disorders (FASDs). *Research in Developmental Disabilities, 30*, 986–1006.

Kable, J., Taddeo, E., Strickland, D., & Coles, C. (2015). Community translation of the Math Interactive Learning Experience Program for children with FASD. *Research in Developmental Disabilities, 39*, 1–11.

FIGURE 5.5 STRATEGIES FOR CLASSROOM MANAGEMENT AND TEACHING STUDENTS WITH FASD

- Place the student near the front of the room to help with focus.
- Allow the student to have short breaks when necessary.
- Review and repeat consequences of behaviours. Ask the student to tell you consequences.
- Do not debate or argue over rules already established. "Just do it."
- Notice and comment when the student is behaving appropriately.
- Redirect behaviour.
- Monitor the student carefully; intervene before behaviour escalates.
- Use concrete, hands-on learning methods.
- Establish routines; follow them or provide the student with ample warning.
- Post an agenda, illustrated if the student is preliterate.
- Give short and simple directions; ask the student to repeat directions.
- Whenever you can, use the same directions as in the past.
- Reduce the distractions in the classroom; limit the amount of information on each piece of paper.
- Notice and comment when the student is doing well.
- Work with the family to maintain consistency; communicate regularly with the family.

Put into Practice

Team up with three peers and each choose a chronic health condition that you may encounter in the students you teach. Develop a list of accommodations that you think would meet the needs of a student with the condition you have chosen. Share resources and discuss your ideas with your peers. Look for similarities and differences in your lists of accommodations.

She talked with my Mom and I went to the doctor. Some other boys in my family have DMD and the doctor diagnosed that I have DMD too. Now I use a wheelchair to get around, a computer to do my assignments, and I have a rest period at school every day.

Jeremy, in grade 5, describing his diagnosis of Duchenne muscular dystrophy.

Muscular dystrophy (MD) refers to a group of genetically based neuromuscular disorders that result in progressive muscle weakness. Muscle tissue is replaced by fatty tissue and connective tissue, which causes the muscles to weaken and eventually waste away, making it difficult to speak, breathe, or move. Each form of MD is caused by an error in a specific gene associated with muscle function; however, several individuals with the same disorder may experience the disorder and its symptoms quite differently. **Duchenne muscular dystrophy (DMD)** is the most common form of MD, with marked physical degeneration occurring during the school years, so students need differentiations, adaptive technology, and a supportive school environment (Wolff Heller et al., 2008).

Symptoms of DMD include difficulty in rising from the floor and climbing stairs. The calf muscles become prominent. A wheelchair is usually necessary by early adolescence, and breathing is increasingly affected. Children with DMD sometimes demonstrate poor social skills and delayed language (Hendriksen et al., 2009), both of which can have wide-ranging consequences for learning in highly social classrooms. The frequency of behavioural problems and learning difficulties in spelling, reading, and mathematics is higher than in the general population, especially for some types of muscular dystrophy (Hoskin & Fawcett, 2014). Most adolescents with DMD are prone to respiratory infections. Lifespan is shortened, with death typically occurring during the twenties although the lifespan is gradually increasing. Other forms of MD include Becker MD and myotonic MD (Steinert's disease), neither of which is as severe as DMD during the school years.

Physical therapy and exercise usually form part of the treatment, but care must be taken to avoid overactivity and fatigue. Because the disease is progressive, the needs of

Weblinks

MUSCULAR DYSTROPHY CANADA
www.muscle.ca

THE ARTHRITIS SOCIETY
www.arthritis.ca

CROHN'S AND COLITIS CANADA
www.ccfc.ca

the student are continually changing—including physical adaptations, needs for differentiated teaching, adjustment to a wheelchair, exercising to avoid obesity, and coping with the prospect of a reduced lifespan. Emotional support is critical. For information on all aspects of MD, including recent research developments and advice for educators, visit the website of Muscular Dystrophy Canada (www.muscle.ca; search on the site for the School Resource Guide).

JUVENILE ARTHRITIS

> My juvenile arthritis was diagnosed when I was eight. I was upset because I played sports, played the piano, and was good at art. My treatment team has helped me to take charge of my life. I play the piano even though I can't practise when my hands are swollen. I continue to play the sports with the least chance of body contact. Now I am 18. Some days I can't get out of bed, but those days are rare. With the help of my family, friends, and teachers I do well in school and will go to university next year. You can take charge of your arthritis, too.
>
> *From Helen's speech to children recently diagnosed with juvenile arthritis.*

Juvenile arthritis (JA)—continuous **inflammation** of one or more joints for which no other cause can be found—is a chronic arthritic condition present before the age of 16. Characteristics include joint swelling and loss of mobility from inflamed joints. Students may complain of stiffness or pain, walk with a limp, or have difficulty using an arm or leg. The immune system seems to be overactive, inflaming joints as if fighting an infection when none is present. Usually physiotherapy and occupational therapy are essential parts of the treatment (Sanzo, 2008).

Students with JA may feel stiffness and pain after sitting in one position, and should be encouraged to stand for part of a class period or move around. Because of low stamina, they may require a shorter day or rest breaks. They may have to take medication during the school day, usually with food to prevent adverse effects on the gastrointestinal tract. Fever is a symptom of JA and does not indicate an infectious disease. Because eyes can become involved in arthritis, be alert for any indications of a visual problem and notify the parents.

You may need to make differentiations. In physical education, take into account decreased stamina and limit strenuous games that put pressure on joints or limbs. Pain can interfere with concentration, so break tasks into shorter segments and check comprehension of the instructions. Students may have a limited range of motion and swollen fingers that prevent them from grasping pencils and pens. Writing may be difficult when arthritis affects the student's hands. Timed written tests may need to be extended. Other ways to protect hand joints:

- Use grips on pens and pencils.
- Give the student felt tip pens, which require less effort.
- Offer a computer or other electronic device for writing assignments.
- Record lectures or provide a copy of notes and visuals.
- Provide extra time for written tests or test the student orally.
- Shorten or modify long written assignments.

Because symptoms vary from day to day, you must be accepting of a wide range of variation in the student's functioning and independence. Encourage as much independence as possible while reassuring the student that support is available (Sanzo, 2008).

Further Reading

These sources can help you to develop an insider's perspective on arthritis.

Miller, D.D.L. (2002). *Taking arthritis to school.* Plainview, NY: JayJo Books.

The Arthritis Society (of Canada). (2009). *You, your child, and arthritis.* www.arthritis.ca/document. doc?id=79. (Contains a section on adolescents and a section on school.)

The Arthritis Foundation (of U.S.). www.arthritis.org. (Section titled Kids Get Arthritis Too has many resources.)

Put into Practice

Read Daniel L. Clay's *Helping Schoolchildren with Chronic Health Conditions: A Practical Guide* (2004, Guilford Press). How can you learn whether students in the class have chronic conditions that you don't know about? Plan the information you would leave for a substitute teacher about the student(s) with chronic health conditions in your class(es). Remember that, as the classroom teacher, it is your responsibility to ensure the safety, health, and continued well-being of all in your care.

What do you think?

Some people have argued that obesity is a chronic health condition. What do you think? How have you seen obesity affect student learning in the classroom?

Further Reading

Sparapani, V., et al. (2015). What is it like to be a child with type 1 diabetes mellitus? *Pediatric Nursing, 41*(1), 17–22.

Kucera, M., & Sullivan, A. (2011). The educational implications of type 1 diabetes mellitus: A review of research and recommendations for school psychological practice. *Psychology in the Schools, 48*(6), 587–603.

Brown, P., & Kent, M. (2000). *Guidelines for the care of students with diabetes in the school setting.* Trenton, NJ: New Jersey Dept. of Education. www.state.nj.us/education/edsupport/diabetes/diabetes.pdf

Living with arthritis adds to the challenges during adolescence of separating from family and learning to be independent. Adolescents usually take more responsibility for managing their arthritis—that is, taking medication, monitoring side effects, and following an exercise program. Be supportive, and remember that your guidance and encouragement may enable the student to adapt so arthritis has little or no impact on life at school, especially if the symptoms are mild to moderate (Erkolahti & Ilonen, 2005).

Chronic Health Conditions

Usually, students with chronic health conditions have been assessed by a qualified medical practitioner who certifies that they require medical procedures, beyond taking medication, while at school to ensure their health and safety. Often they require ongoing monitoring and differentiated instruction because of their limited school attendance or because the condition adversely affects their educational performance at school (Irwin & Elam, 2011; Shaw et al., 2010). The speed and accuracy with which teachers, office staff, and school administrators respond to a student health crisis has far-reaching implications (Bevans et al., 2011). Familiarize yourself with your school's Emergency Protocols Manual, request an orientation session, and sign up for a CPR and first aid course. Then you will be prepared and confident to respond to school health crises.

Two issues that arise in the education of students with chronic illnesses are the need for culturally competent interventions (McManus & Savage, 2010) and the challenges of hospital-to-school transitions (Shaw & McCabe, 2008). Clay (2007) argues that it is critical that we consider cultural issues in interventions, both in medical facilities and in educational contexts, for these students. Examples include prayer, rituals to cleanse the body, and rituals to establish harmony with the earth. The best way to understand the cultural issues at play may be to gently ask questions of the student and the family and to listen actively to learn what they *believe* might influence their decisions to adhere to the treatment and to choose complementary options.

The second issue is the need to facilitate smooth transitions from the hospital for students with chronic illnesses, when they return to school. While healthy students are typically absent from school about three days per year, students with chronic illness are absent on average sixteen days a year (Shaw & McCabe, 2008). At one time those with chronic illnesses, including cancer, would have endured an extended stay in hospital, a short stay at home, and a gradual reintroduction to school. Now they may spend only a day or two in hospital at a time, often on repeated occasions, to receive treatment, and then go home and return immediately to school. Parents may come to school to give medication and monitor progress. This puts children in school who are behind in their academic work, who are enduring treatment, and who are often dealing with impaired concentration and the side effects of powerful drugs. Teachers are likely to need to differentiate instruction, and these students may experience social and emotional difficulties, including behaviour problems, depression, withdrawal, anxiety, and poor peer relations. By adolescence, students with chronic illnesses may experience suicide ideation and engage in substance abuse. For an extended discussion of these issues, consult the work of Steven Shaw of McGill University (e.g., Shaw & McCabe, 2008). Discuss the student's needs with the student and the family; be sure to include the student in all stages of academic planning.

Conditions discussed in this section include diabetes, allergies, asthma, cystic fibrosis, Crohn's disease and colitis, and cancer and leukemia. There are many other chronic health impairments, including congenital and acquired heart disease and hemophilia. You can obtain relevant information from the family, community agencies, websites, pamphlets, and books.

DIABETES

> I stayed after school to talk to my homeroom teacher. I told her that I have diabetes. She already knew from my file. I told her that I keep juice in my backpack and that if I ask to leave class, it will be because I need sugar or insulin and she should let me go right away. Tomorrow I have to talk with my physical education teacher because I always need to eat after exercising. Today was good—a practice run for tomorrow.
>
> *Phil, describing his first day of high school to his parents.*

Students with **diabetes** do not make enough insulin and have problems absorbing and storing sugars (Mandali & Gordon, 2009). Treatment options include daily insulin injections or an insulin pump. Adolescents give themselves insulin injections and check their blood sugar regularly, but younger students may need assistance. Often parents will take an active role in their child's care throughout the day. Diabetes is affected by the food consumed, the amount of insulin, and regular physical activity.

There are three types of diabetic emergencies that you could face: low blood sugar, high blood sugar, and diabetic ketoacidosis. The symptoms appear similar, but only a glucose (finger prick) test will definitively determine what course of action should be taken. The causes of **low blood sugar (hypoglycemia)** include too much insulin, delayed or missed meals, and more exercise than usual without extra food. The symptoms occur suddenly: cold, clammy, or sweaty skin; trembling; confusion; difficulty speaking; and, if untreated, possibly fainting or unconsciousness. The student may report hunger, headache, dizziness, blurry vision, and abdominal pain. Take the student to a quiet place, and assist them with the blood glucose testing, then provide the student with a snack if they are experiencing a low. If the student is unconscious, call 911 and the parents immediately. Do not administer any treatment other than that which was discussed with parents (this may include a glucagon injection, but will not include sugar in a raw form). If the student is conscious, continue to treat, followed by a snack until blood sugar levels return to normal. Do not leave the student alone. Be sure to follow the school's protocol during, and inform the parents after, every episode.

High blood sugar (hyperglycemia) symptoms show more gradually, even over days. Causes include overeating, too little insulin, and stress. You may see thirst, flushed dry skin, nausea, drowsiness, and possibly unconsciousness. Follow school protocol, and contact the parents if you suspect that a student is experiencing high blood sugar. The student requires insulin to lower his blood sugar; however, in some cases, it may be necessary to take the student to hospital.

The third condition that you should be aware of, which is related to high blood sugar, is called diabetic ketoacidosis (DKA). DKA, which is a result of blood glucose being highly elevated over a long period of time, can lead to severe dehydration, loss of consciousness, and even death (Touchette, 2000). It occurs most often in children who have not yet been diagnosed with diabetes; we must watch for these symptoms in children who have been diagnosed with other conditions, such as a urinary tract infection, as it could in fact be diabetes (Canadian Diabetes Association Clinical Practice Guidelines Expert Committee, 2008).

Put into Practice

Make a contingency plan for when a student has low blood sugar and needs to be rushed to hospital. Consult A. Rosenthal-Malek & J. Greenspan (1999), A student with diabetes is in my class, *Teaching Exceptional Children*, *31*(3), 38–43; and the Canadian Diabetes Association website: www.diabetes.ca.

Students will have individual plans and protocols that you should be aware of; read the student's file carefully, meet with the parents, and make use of the tools provided by the Canadian Diabetes Association. Know the location in your school of **diabetes emergency kits** containing juice, raisins, or dextrose, and always take one on field trips. Most students with diabetes carry emergency food or juice in their backpack, but if they become weak and confused they may not consume what they need. Explain to younger children the importance of eating their own snacks, without focusing undue attention on the child with diabetes. Most students know about their condition and require your support and respect; they also need information about changes in the routine, especially in the timing of snacks and meals.

Diabetes affects students in the classroom. It can be life-threatening when students experience highs or lows, and they may also be irritable if they have had high or low blood sugar during the night. They might also be weak, tired, and unable to concentrate. Encourage students to speak with you confidentially, develop a sign to be used in class when the student needs to leave quickly (and check within one minute to be sure the student is safe), and talk regularly with parents of younger children about their child's changing condition. Beware of the following misconceptions about diabetes (Shaw & McCabe, 2008):

■ that the student will inform you of highs or lows—sometimes the student won't be aware

■ that only food affects the level of blood sugar—activity level also influences it

■ that bathroom privileges can wait—a few minutes can put a student into a coma

■ that all the effects are physical—attention, memory, learning, and processing speed in the classroom may be affected

In 2014, Canadian teachers, in provinces including Alberta, joined the international KiDS project (Kids and Diabetes in Schools) which has developed guidelines and training for educators to keep students with diabetes safe at school (Hare, 2014; www.idf.org/education/kids; get the app at the Apple app store). The information pack is available for free in eight languages at the website.

ALLERGIES

On 29 September 2003, Sabrina Shannon bought French fries for lunch at school, which she had purchased the week before after checking that they were cooked in vegetable oil and not peanut oil. Sabrina's allergy triggers were peanut, dairy products, and soy, all of which put her at risk of anaphylaxis. In class after lunch, Sabrina began to wheeze and headed toward the office saying, "It's my asthma." A teacher raced to Sabrina's locker to get her EpiPen® in case it was her food allergies. Sabrina went into cardiac arrest before the EpiPen® could be administered and before the ambulance arrived. She died one day later. The coroner posited that the allergic trigger was dairy protein and that Sabrina had been exposed to cross-contamination from cheese curds because the tongs had been used to serve poutine as well as fries.

Sabrina's mother, Sara, made a promise to her dying daughter that she would do whatever she could to prevent this from happening to any other child. The result was the passage of Sabrina's Law which requires all principals in Ontario school boards to implement anaphylaxis plans that include strategies to reduce exposure to allergens; procedures to communicate to parents, students, and employees about life-threatening allergies; and regular training on dealing with life-threatening allergies for all staff. Principals must also develop an individual plan for each student at risk of anaphylaxis, maintain a file that lists the student's prescriptions and emergency contacts, and ensure that parents supply information about a student's allergies when enrolling the student in school.

Adapted from Allergic Living (www.allergicliving.com).

An **allergy** is an abnormal immune response to a substance that is tolerated by non-allergic people. It results in individual signs and symptoms that vary in range and severity and that can occur up to seventy-two hours after exposure to the allergen. Allergies can become worse with a single exposure to an allergen. **Anaphylaxis** or **anaphylactic shock** is a sudden, severe allergic reaction that causes breathing difficulties. Death can occur within minutes unless an injection is administered. As many as 40 to 50 percent of those with a diagnosed food allergy are at high risk for anaphylaxis (Sheetz et al., 2004). And the number of individuals with allergies is increasing every year.

Allergens, which cause allergic reactions, can enter the body:

- if breathed through the nose or mouth—including dust; pollen; moulds; odours from chemicals, markers, perfumes, etc.
- if ingested through the mouth—including foods such as peanuts, shellfish, and milk; drugs such as aspirin (ASA), penicillin, and other antibiotics
- by contact with the skin—including powders, lotions, metals such as jean snaps, latex, peanut butter
- through insect stings—including the venom of bees and wasps

Further Reading

Gold, M. (Ed.) (2004). *The complete kid's allergy and asthma guide: Allergy and asthma information for children of all ages.* Richmond Hill, ON: Firefly Books.

Deutsch, A.L. (2014). Keeping students with food allergies safe in school. *Education Digest, 79*(5), 56–59.

Thelen, P., & Cameron, E. (2012). Food allergy concerns in primary classrooms. *Young Children, 67*(4), 106–112.

For the allergic student reactions often accompany changes in routine, and anaphylactic shock is more likely to take place at school than at home. Before the start of the school year, read the school policy on allergies and meet with the family. Discuss the policy (e.g., who can administer an injection), and the individual emergency plan for their child. Inform the principal about the meeting and invite others who teach the student. Because characteristics of allergic reactions vary, it is important to learn each student's signs and symptoms. The main symptoms are itchy, watery eyes and itchy, runny nose. Other signs include itching elsewhere, eczema, hives, dark circles under the eyes, headache, shortness of breath, wheezing, cough, diarrhea, and stomach cramps.

You should know the steps in the individual emergency plan that has been developed for each student with severe allergies and the location of the injector for each student (in the student's fanny pack, in a cupboard, etc.). The general steps in an emergency plan are as follows:

- Administer **epinephrine** immediately (**EpiPen**® or **Twinject**), following directions on the injector. This can save a life, but note that the injector is only first aid.
- Call 911 or an ambulance, or transport the student to the nearest emergency facility. Warn that there is anaphylaxis. More serious reactions may follow, so a hospital is essential.
- Ensure that you have additional epinephrine available in case it is needed. If breathing difficulties persist, it may be necessary to re-administer it every fifteen minutes until the patient reaches hospital.
- Call the parents or next of kin but only *after* administering the injection immediately. Don't delay by calling the parents first.
- You can take steps to avoid an allergic reaction occurring in your classroom. Know about your students' allergies, enlist the class to help keep the classroom

safe, and involve the parents of all your students. Take extra care with field trips and do not allow the sharing of personal snacks (Zuger, 2007).

Children and adolescents with severe allergies can feel anxious and isolated because they feel "different from everyone else." They usually wear a MedicAlert identification bracelet (www.medicalert.ca) and carry an injector in a fanny pack. Sometimes adolescents leave their "uncool" fanny packs in their lockers or engage in risky behaviours such as eating cafeteria food with their peers. You can enhance self-acceptance by respecting feelings, accepting differences, and supporting personal decisions. Try to include the student in all activities, even if this means providing an allergen–free alternative.

Weblinks

A TEACHER'S GUIDE TO ASTHMA
www.troydryerase.com/research/
TeachersGuideAsthma.pdf

THE LUNG ASSOCIATION

WWW.LUNG.CA (UNDER LUNG HEALTH, THEN LUNG DISEASES A–Z, SELECT ASTHMA)

THE LUNG ASSOCIATION: MY ASTHMA ACTION PLAN

WWW.LUNG.CA (SEARCH "ASTHMA ACTION PLAN"; PLAN WRITTEN SO STUDENTS CAN FOLLOW IT WITH ADULT HELP)

ASTHMA

Ms. Aboul, I need to talk with you. Grade 9 is hard. I'm so far behind. I've missed a lot of classes this year because of my asthma and doctors' appointments. I hate carrying my puffer around at school and trying to avoid stressful situations that make my wheezing worse. Most of all I'm afraid of having a really big attack and not making it to the hospital. I need to talk with you.

Meghan Lowie, 9D

A note left for a guidance counsellor by a student with asthma.

Asthma is a chronic lung condition that can develop at any age but is most common in childhood, especially in children with allergies. The most important characteristic is difficulty breathing. The airways are obstructed by inflammation, muscle spasm, and excess mucus. Close to 15 percent of the population has asthma (Basch, 2011), and it results in school absences (on average ten days per year) and hospitalizations. More boys than girls are affected in childhood, but more girls than boys develop asthma during adolescence.

Jennie Woodcock/Corbis

A young student with asthma administers a "reliever," a drug that offers short-term relief, during the onset of an asthma episode by using what is commonly called a puffer or inhaler.

The airways respond in an exaggerated way to common irritants (e.g., smoke, smog, scents in markers), allergens (e.g., pollen, foods such as nuts and shellfish), and other triggers (e.g., viral head colds, exercise, cold air). To treat asthma effectively, the individual must know what may trigger an attack and avoid contact with these triggers. Two categories of medication are used for treating asthma. **Preventers** are anti-inflammatory drugs taken regularly to prevent and treat inflammation. **Relievers** are used as rescue medications to relax the muscles of the airways and provide quick relief of breathing problems. They are usually inhaled with a **puffer**.

Symptoms of asthma include persistent coughing, **wheezing**, chest tightness, and shortness of breath. Individuals are affected to varying degrees, from mild (only during vigorous exercise) to severe (with daily symptoms that cause lifestyle restrictions). In Canada about twenty children die annually from asthma. An asthma episode can lead to life-threatening anaphylactic shock. If you can identify the warning signs, you can help prevent an episode. Such signs are

- wheezing;
- rapid shallow breathing;
- complaints of chest tightness;
- lips and nails greyish or bluish in colour; and
- contracted and bulging neck muscles, nasal flaring, and mouth breathing.

When you see these signs, start asthma first aid treatment (see Figure 5.6). Time is critical, so you must know what to do before an episode occurs. Your familiarity with the information in the file of a student with asthma could save the student's life. Read the school policy on asthma and advise the principal of your upcoming meeting; then meet with the student and parents before school begins. Learn the student's triggers, warning signs and symptoms, and how the asthma medications are administered. Ask the parents to detail the steps they follow in first aid treatment, and together compare these with the school policy. If the two are not the same, consult your principal. Many schools have a form that parents must complete to describe medications, symptoms, prevention, and first aid.

FIGURE 5.6 ASTHMA FIRST AID TREATMENT

In case of breathing difficulty:

- Have the student stop all activity.
- Help the student assume an upright position; sitting with legs crossed and elbows on knees may ease breathing somewhat.
- Stay with the student; talk reassuringly and calmly.
- Have the student take the appropriate medication; it is more detrimental to withhold medication than to give the student medication when it is not needed. This is usually taken by means of an inhaler or nebulizer.
- Notify the proper person, in accordance with school policy. This usually means contacting the parents; if the student's condition does not improve or becomes worse fifteen minutes after giving the medication, call an ambulance. Have the student keep taking the medication until the ambulance arrives.

Source: Based on information provided by The Lung Association at www.lung.ca (search for asthma).

Always believe students with asthma. Do not make them wait for medication; asthma can be life threatening. If you think a student with asthma is using asthma symptoms to get attention, discuss your concerns with the parents and encourage the student to talk with a counsellor.

Although the physical outcomes have garnered the most attention, the potentially serious academic, social, and psychological ramifications cannot be ignored. Students with asthma are frequently wakened during the night by their condition, leaving them tired the next day, which may detract from their school performance, and causing many absences, which can impact achievement. Social problems seem to increase with the seriousness of the condition, and internalizing behaviour disorders, feelings of fatigue and worthlessness, and anxiety have also been reported, as well as difficulties with concentration, memory, and hyperactivity. Some of these effects may arise from the medications. For a thorough account of these issues, see Bray et al. (2008).

Encourage physical activities and remind students to monitor their symptoms. Inform students and parents about potential triggers likely to be introduced into the classroom. Taking medication and having asthmatic episodes at school can make students self-conscious. You can help by arranging for the student to leave unobtrusively when necessary; providing a quiet, supervised location in which the student can relax and take medication; and finding someone to remain with your class while you monitor the student with asthma. Because asthma is increasing in minority group children, it is critical to be sensitive to the cultural expectations of parents (Basch, 2011; Kaul, 2011; McManus & Savage, 2010). Figure 5.7 focuses on mental health of students with chronic health conditions.

FIGURE 5.7 ANNOTATED BIBLIOGRAPHY ON THE ROLE OF FAMILIES AND TEACHERS IN THE MENTAL HEALTH OF STUDENTS WITH CHRONIC HEALTH CONDITIONS

Staying Engaged: The Role of Teachers and Schools in Keeping Young People with Health Conditions Engaged in School (2014) by Julie Green, John Henry, Brian Edwards, & Shanti Wong, *Australian Educational Researcher, 41*(1), 25–41.

Young people with chronic health conditions are at greater risk of mental health conditions such as depression and anxiety. Families and educators can help to prevent these mental health conditions by working together to enhance educational engagement of these vulnerable youth.

BRIDGES: Connecting with Families to Facilitate and Enhance Involvement (2015) by Mary Sawyer, *Teaching Exceptional Children, 47*(3), 172–179.

This practical strategy involves the steps—Build, Recruit, Individualize, Dialogue, Generate, Empower, and Strengthen—which educators can use to connect with parents and encourage their involvement in all aspects of the education of their children with disabilities.

Family Matters: Transitions from Pediatric to Adult Care Programs and Resources (2015) by Juliette Schlucter, Deborah Dokken, & Elizabeth Ahmann, *Pediatric Nursing, 41*(2), 85–88.

The transition from pediatric to adult care for young people with complex chronic conditions can be very challenging. This analysis highlights the role of family in adolescents' well-being at this critical time.

Lessons Learned from Designing and Leading Multidisciplinary Diabetes Educational Groups (2014) by Bethany P. Glueck & Brett H. Foreman, *Journal of Mental Health Counseling, 36*(2), 160–172.

Multidisciplinary programs have enabled adults to interact effectively with young people with diabetes to help them to increase exercise and make better nutritional choices, two major contributors to their physical and emotional well-being.

CYSTIC FIBROSIS

> Today my mom told me I had no choice, and here I am in the hospital again. I have
> pneumonia. I'm sorry I can't be in our class play. I was really looking forward to that.
> I probably got overtired from the rehearsals, but I'm still glad I tried out for the play.
> I don't want CF to get in the way of having a life.
>
> *From the diary of Brittany, a grade 7 student with CF.*

Cystic fibrosis (CF) is incurable, the result of an inherited genetic defect, and causes chronic lung problems and digestive disorders. The lungs become covered with sticky mucus that is difficult to remove and that promotes infection by bacteria. Most people with CF require frequent hospitalizations and continuous use of antibiotics. (Remember Brittany's experience described at the beginning of this chapter.) They take **enzyme supplements** so they can digest the nutrients in their food. Life expectancy, which was once only eight years, is now in the mid-thirties, and a lung transplant can extend that. Still, most persons with cystic fibrosis eventually die of lung disease (DePaepe et al., 2002).

Weblinks

CYSTIC FIBROSIS CANADA
www.cysticfibrosis.ca

CYSTIC FIBROSIS FOUNDATION
(AMERICAN)

WWW.CFF.ORG (UNDER LIVING WITH
CF, SEE CF AND SCHOOL)

CYSTIC FIBROSIS WORLDWIDE
www.cfww.org

The student with CF copes with a chronic cough and may require physical therapy during school to remove airway mucus. She will probably have an excessive appetite, combined with weight loss, and may need to eat during school. Bowel disturbances are common and embarrassing. Repeated bouts of pneumonia mean frequent absences, but communication with the family can ease the process of shifting learning to the hospital room. Cystic fibrosis can have a negative impact on learning. It may mean that a student requires differentiated instruction, because CF has been associated with depressed mood, anxiety, memory and concentration problems, as well as fatigue (Grieve et al., 2011). You might find it helpful to consult the website of Cystic Fibrosis Canada (www.cysticfibrosis.ca). During adolescence you may witness a rebellion against treatments. Adolescents often need counselling to deal with delayed puberty (Bucks et al., 2009) and to accept that their life expectancy may be shortened.

CROHN'S AND COLITIS

> I have missed so much school this year. I just get on a roll, figure out what is going on in
> all my courses, and I have another flare-up. Then I am in the hospital, exhausted, sur-
> rounded by people in white coats trying to adjust my medication—and I am once again
> defined by my colitis. I hate it! I just want to go to school, have energy, eat what I like,
> and hang out with my friends!
>
> *Paula, who has colitis, describing her experience in grade 11 to the school psychologist.*

Crohn's disease (CD) and **ulcerative colitis (UC)** are the two forms of inflammatory bowel disease (IBD). CD involves inflammation somewhere in the gastrointestinal (GI) tract, usually in the lower part of the small bowel and the upper end of the colon. The symptoms that affect life at school usually include abdominal pain, cramping, diarrhea, frequent trips to the bathroom with little warning, nausea, weight loss, and lack of energy. With UC, the only area of the GI tract affected is the large intestine, that is, the colon. Symptoms are similar to those accompanying CD. However, side effects can include arthritis, eye problems, and skin problems. Both conditions are characterized by periods of remission and flare-ups when individuals have the symptoms of the disease and feel sick. Flare-ups can be random or can stay with the individual until the right medication is found or surgery is performed to remove the inflamed area.

Weblinks

CROHN'S AND COLITIS CANADA
www.ccfc.ca

Further Reading

On including children with child-hood leukemia and cancer in the classroom:

Prevatt, F.F., et al. (2000). A review of school reintegration programs for children with cancer. *Journal of School Psychology, 38,* 447–467.

Sullivan, N.A. (2004). *Walking with a shadow: Surviving childhood leukemia.* Portsmouth, NH: Greenwood Publishers.

Herrmann et al. (2011). Childhood leukemia survivors and their return to school: A literature review, case study, and recommendations. *Journal of Applied School Psychology, 27,* 252–275.

Bauman, S. (2010). School counsel-ors and survivors of childhood can-cer: Reconceptualizing and advancing the cure. *Professional School Counseling, 14*(2), 109–115.

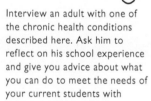

Put into Practice

Interview an adult with one of the chronic health conditions described here. Ask him to reflect on his school experience and give you advice about what you can do to meet the needs of your current students with chronic health conditions.

More people are diagnosed with IBD between the ages of 15 and 25 than at any other age. This makes it a particular concern for adolescents, their families, and their teachers. Two Canadian studies highlight the challenges. Wideman-Johnston (2011) studied the effects of these chronic illnesses on participation and learning of Canadian adolescents. She reports that every aspect of their life in high school can be affected by these conditions and urges teachers to take more responsibility for listening to these students and their parents; understanding their social needs and challenges; and differentiating teaching to accommodate their absences, hospital stays, and fatigue. Gordon (2012) found that children with IBD relied on the support of family and friends to manage the demands of school. The website of Crohn's and Colitis Canada offers extensive information about these chronic conditions (www.ccfc.ca).

CANCER AND LEUKEMIA

> When he was being treated for cancer, Garth appreciated returning to school after each treatment: "I really liked going back to school, being with my friends. And I really wanted to finish my work at school because I was missing so much and got so far behind every time I had a treatment." The following year, as a cancer survivor, Garth talked about how "nothing is the same as it was before; cancer changes everything."
>
> *Garth, a cancer survivor, when he was in grade 6.*

Because cancer changes everything during and following treatment, it is important that we, as teachers, educate ourselves about how to help students adjust at school to their changed world. Childhood **cancer**, particularly **leukemia**, is increasing. Cancer is the most common disease-related cause of death in this age group after the first year of life, with leukemia being the most commonly diagnosed cancer at 32 percent. Although survival rates for pediatric cancer and leukemia are much better than in the past, the effects of these chronic illnesses persist, and maintaining a normal lifestyle is essential to positive adaptation. This includes attending school whenever possible because school can serve as a normalizing factor (Herrman et al., 2011). Effective educational programs inform parents about what to expect, and findings suggest that well-informed patients and families show increased feelings of control over the individual's health (e.g., Aburn & Gott, 2014; Dragone et al., 2002). Prevatt and her colleagues (2000) reviewed school reintegration programs and suggest that the educators and peers of these students participate in structured programs that answer their questions and make them better informed. Differentiated instruction and frequent assessment (perhaps RTI) are essential (Herrmann et al., 2011) for students with leukemia and cancer who miss a considerable amount of school, may be vulnerable to communicable diseases circulating in the classroom, and are often both exhausted and changed by their treatments (for example, they may be bald or have an amputation). Educators must appreciate the serious nature of the illness and be sensitive; collaborate with the hospital, home schooling teacher, and school counsellor; provide opportunities for classmates to maintain contact during absences; and communicate frequently, proactively, and supportively with parents about the student's learning and psychosocial needs at school (Bauman, 2010).

Summary

The students discussed in this chapter have diverse strengths, challenges, and needs: communication exceptionalities, physical exceptionalities, and chronic health conditions. Many of them are already succeeding in your classroom, but want you to pay attention to their needs without drawing attention to them. You may teach only two or three students in your career who have, for example, cystic fibrosis; this means you will seek information when you need it. Many of the strategies you have already learned will be effective in teaching these students, and you should draw on the experience and expertise of parents and in-school team members. While accommodations will usually be adequate, on occasion you may need to modify the curriculum or develop an alternate curriculum.

It is customary to think of the physical and stamina limitations of students with physical and health conditions, as well as the possibility that they will need medication at school. However, meeting the social and emotional needs of these students is also important. Inclusion means more than the physical presence of these students in regular classrooms for all or part of the day. Inclusion means making them feel part of the social and academic life of the class and the broader community.

Key Terms

acquired brain injury (ABI) / head injury / traumatic brain injury (p. 137)

alcohol-related neurodevelopmental disorder (ARND) (p. 138)

allergy (p. 145)

American Sign Language (ASL) (p. 126)

amplification (p. 128)

anaphylaxis/anaphylactic shock (p. 145)

asthma (p. 146)

Braille (p. 129)

cancer (p. 150)

cerebral palsy (CP) (p. 133)

chronic health conditions (p. 120)

communication disorders (p. 120)

communication exceptionalities (p. 120)

Crohn's disease (CD) (p. 149)

cystic fibrosis (CF) (p. 149)

deaf (p. 125)

Deaf community (p. 128)

diabetes (p. 143)

diabetes emergency kits (p. 144)

Duchenne muscular dystrophy (DMD) (p. 140)

enzyme supplements (p. 149)

epilepsy (p. 134)

epinephrine (p. 145)

EpiPen® (p. 145)

fetal alcohol spectrum disorders (FASD) (p. 138)

fetal alcohol syndrome (FAS) (p. 138)

frequency modulation (FM) systems (p. 128)

generalized seizures (p. 134)

hard of hearing (p. 125)

hearing aids (p. 128)

high blood sugar (hyperglycemia) (p. 143)

hydrocephalus (p. 134)

inflammation (p. 141)

juvenile arthritis (JA) (p. 141)

language impairment (p. 121)

leukemia (p. 150)

low blood sugar (hypoglycemia) (p. 143)

muscular dystrophy (MD) (p. 140)

musculoskeletal conditions (p. 139)

nervous system impairment (p. 132)

neurological dysfunction (p. 132)

partial fetal alcohol syndrome (PFAS) (p. 138)

partial seizures (p. 134)

physical exceptionalities (p. 120)

prenatal exposure to alcohol (p. 138)

preventers (p. 147)

puffer (p. 147)

relievers (p. 147)

remission (p. 132)

seizures (p. 134)

shunt (p. 134)

simple absence (petit mal) seizure (p. 135)

speech impairment (p. 121)

speech-reading (p. 126)

spina bifida (p. 134)

tics (p. 135)

tonic-clonic (grand mal) seizure (p. 135)

Tourette syndrome (TS) (p. 135)

Twinject (p. 145)

ulcerative colitis (UC) (p. 149)

visual impairment (p. 129)

wheezing (p. 147)

Challenges for Reviewing Chapter 5

1. Amber, described at the beginning of the section on visual disabilities, is blind. Consider her learning needs. What are some of the most important things to remember when adapting teaching and assessment for Amber?

2. Consider what is meant by the term *chronic health condition*. Then compare the six chronic conditions described in this chapter, adding one more condition of which you are aware. Why must educators be knowledgeable about these chronic health conditions in order to meet their legal and ethical responsibilities?

3. Reread the opening case of Brittany, who has cystic fibrosis. Answer the questions that follow the case, focusing on Brittany. Consider the similarities and differences in answers that might be given by secondary and elementary teachers.

Activities for Reviewing Chapter 5 with Your Peers

4. Think about which physical and health conditions you expect to have to understand and differentiate teaching for in your next teaching experience. Discuss with your peers why it is just as important to understand the psychosocial aspects of these conditions as the physical aspects.

5. You are currently a member of the in-school team for a student who is hard of hearing, and last year you fulfilled a similar role for a student who is deaf. Prepare to assume the role of one member of the team. The team includes a classroom teacher, a resource teacher, a principal, and a parent. Describe how you would differentiate teaching and ensure social participation of the student who is hard of hearing. Contrast this with including the student who is deaf. Role-play this scenario with some of your peers, each assuming the role of a member of the team.

6. Many physical disabilities were described in this chapter. Develop a chart for these conditions (i.e., cerebral palsy, spina bifida, epilepsy, Tourette syndrome, brain injury, fetal alcohol spectrum disorders, muscular dystrophy, juvenile arthritis) and one other. Compare these disabilities on four dimensions, one of which is differentiating teaching. Compare your chart with those of your peers. What dimensions are most important to teachers?

Teaching for Diversity: Including Aboriginal Students, Students from Diverse Cultural Backgrounds, and Students Who Are at Risk

Dejan Ristovski/Getty Images

LEARNER OBJECTIVES

After you have read this chapter, you will be able to:

1. Discuss how teachers can address the needs of Aboriginal students.

2. Describe how teachers can address the needs of students from diverse cultural backgrounds and consider what role differentiated instruction might have.

3. Discuss strategies for teaching students who are English language learners (ELL students), including differentiated instruction.

4. Describe how teachers can respond to incidents of inequity in the classroom and foster equitable treatment of all class members.

5. Explain how classroom teachers can differentiate curriculum for students at risk for failure, including students who live in poverty, are homeless, or have been abused.

RAGU IS IN DAN BORENSTEIN'S GRADE 5 CLASS. Ragu experienced trauma in his home country before coming to Canada. This is Dan's fifth year of teaching but his first year working in the inner city. Ragu arrived in Canada recently after living in a refugee camp. Most days Ragu wanders the classroom or sits with his head on his arms. He enjoys his English as a second language (ESL) tutorial, where he is beginning to dictate stories to his tutor and read them back. All of Ragu's stories are about violence and killing, except one about games Ragu used to play with his best friend. Ragu told Dan that soldiers attacked them and his friend died. Ragu still has nightmares about it. Until he had to leave school two years ago, Ragu was a quick learner with high grades. Dan tries to communicate his high expectations to Ragu without pressuring him. Dan wonders how long he will have to wait for schoolwork to re-emerge as a priority for Ragu.

ANITA HARPER IS PROUD OF HER ABORIGINAL HERITAGE. She is a ceremonial dancer, and her mother is a leader in her nation. Anita always spoke openly about her heritage in elementary school and expected to do the same when she entered South River Secondary School two months ago. Now two grade 12 boys taunt Anita after school while she waits for the bus. They call her "squaw" and humiliate her. Anita asks her homeroom teacher, Betty Bird, who is also Aboriginal, for advice. Anita says, "I should be able to work this out myself, but I can't. Teachers don't usually do anything, but you're different. You're like me." Betty Bird knows that only with support will Anita report the racist incidents to the school administration. Betty wishes there were an Aboriginal counsellor at South River for the 120 Aboriginal students in this school of 700. There are still too few Aboriginal educators, and Betty knows they are fortunate to have three at South River. Betty looks at her agenda, knowing she must find a time when the three Aboriginal teachers can talk about how they will support Anita. They must also gain the support of their fellow teachers and the school administration to increase efforts to make South River Secondary more inclusive for Aboriginal students.

1. How can teachers respond to the situations of Ragu and Anita described in these case studies? What aspects of each situation are most likely to affect learning?

2. With such a range of characteristics and learning needs, what do students like Ragu and Anita have in common?

3. How frequently is a teacher likely to be teaching an Aboriginal student or a refugee student?

4. What does each of these students need in order to be included in the social and academic life of the classroom and of the school?

5. What community resources can a teacher access to ensure that each student learns?

Introduction

This chapter illustrates the conceptual and pragmatic ties between exceptionality and other manifestations of diversity in Canadian society. Equity is the common driving force, and differentiation is the common teaching approach. You will learn about differentiating teaching to meet the needs of students from Aboriginal cultures and students from other cultural backgrounds. Certain issues are unique to the education of Aboriginal students, including the threatened extinction of Aboriginal languages and cultures. You will be challenged to identify your perspectives and question your stereotypes about diversity. This chapter also focuses on students who are at risk for school failure for a variety of reasons. Poverty, homelessness, abuse, and other conditions are explored for their impact on learning and participation.

Differentiating teaching for these students is similar to the process explored in earlier chapters. However, fluctuations in students' circumstances and lack of documentation (e.g., no IEP) may mean that you receive less direction. School teams may not include these students in their mandates, although in some provinces funding is directed to the needs of diverse and at-risk students. While the specific causes of the need for sensitive and differentiated teaching vary greatly in the examples throughout this chapter, the process of ADAPTing is consistent, and equity and respect for diversity are central.

Diversity and Equity in Canadian Society

Canada is one of the most ethnically diverse countries in the world, and communities and schools in Canada are increasing in **diversity**. Sources of this diversity include immigration to Canada and our willingness to receive refugees. For example, according to the National Household Survey (NHS) of 2011, one in five people in Canada's population is foreign-born. In addition, more than 200 languages are spoken in Canada (Statistics Canada, 2011b; *Immigration and Ethnocultural Diversity*). Aboriginal families continue to move into urban areas, and the Aboriginal population increased by 20.1 percent from 2006 to 2011, compared with 5.2 percent for the non-Aboriginal population in that period (Statistics Canada, 2011a; *Aboriginal Peoples*). Other sources of the increasing diversity in Canadian schools include the growth of poverty, homelessness, and other social conditions that place Canadian youth at risk for failing to learn in school and for leaving school early.

In Chapter 1 we discussed the *Canadian Charter of Rights and Freedoms*. The equality rights that apply to education cover the rights of all students: "Every individual is equal before and under the law and has a right to the equal protection of and equal benefit of the law without discrimination and, in particular, without discrimination based on race, national or ethnic origin, colour, religion, sex, age, or mental or physical disability" (section 15[1]).

The Unique Role of Education, Schools, and Educators

Schools have a unique role in the creation of an inclusive society, for two reasons. First, schools are legally responsible for preparing all children and adolescents (including those who have disabilities or are members of minorities) to take meaningful roles as adults in our society. Second, schools have a legislated responsibility to prepare all children and adolescents to participate in an inclusive democracy. This means that you as a teacher are mandated to prepare our youth to accept all individuals (including those who have disabilities or are members of minorities) as fellow citizens.

TEACHING CHALLENGES

There are many reasons for including a broad discussion of teaching for **equity**. An inclusive classroom is a learning community in which *all* students feel accepted and safe. The students described in this chapter often benefit from differentiated teaching, a powerful reminder that many of the strategies you learn throughout this book apply to all of your students, not only those with IEPs.

Student needs are complex. For example, the gifted student Gurjit, described in Chapter 1, is also a member of a cultural minority and could be an English language learner (ELL). Children who live in poverty can also be at risk for other reasons, such as drug abuse in their family. To teach students with multiple needs, make use of all supports your community can provide—parents, cross-age tutors, volunteers, social workers, public health nurses, police officers, immigration counsellors, translators—in addition to school psychologists, consultants, and resource and ESL teachers. Our challenge is to create classrooms that respect diversity and foster learning for *all* students.

Aboriginal Education

Weblinks

ABORIGINAL AFFAIRS AND NORTHERN DEVELOPMENT CANADA
www.aadnc-aandc.gc.ca

HIGHLIGHTS OF THE REPORT OF THE ROYAL COMMISSION ON ABORIGINAL PEOPLES
www.aadnc-aandc.gc.ca/eng
(search for Highlights of the Report of the Royal Commission on Aboriginal Peoples)

FIRST NATIONS UNIVERSITY OF CANADA
www.fnuniv.ca

This section begins with a brief description of the history of **Aboriginal cultures** in Canada and of recent attempts to negotiate education that will help to preserve Aboriginal languages and culture. The focus then moves to strategies for teaching Aboriginal students and for teaching all Canadian students about Aboriginal cultures.

History of Aboriginal Cultures in Canada

Prior to the arrival of Europeans, the Americas were inhabited to their carrying capacities for the ways of life being followed (Dickason & Newbigging, 2010). In the part that is now Canada, there were eleven language families and roughly sixty languages. Several regional economies coexisted, based on hunting and gathering, agriculture, buffalo, and salmon and whales. They all emphasized the group as well as the individual (Dickason & Newbigging, 2010). When European settlers brought smallpox to Canada, the First Nations populations were decimated, and the traditional ways were altered forever. The *Indian Act of Canada*, passed in 1876, aimed to integrate First Nations people into mainstream society. It gave the federal government almost complete control over their lives. Throughout the twentieth century, the Act has been updated and, in recent years, many leaders have called for the *Indian Act* to be abolished.

Education for Aboriginal children and youth has always been intertwined with complex cultural issues. In 1972 the National Indian Brotherhood (now the Assembly of First Nations) presented the position paper *Indian Control of Indian Education* (ICIE) to the Minister of Indian Affairs and Northern Development. In 1991 four Aboriginal and three non-Aboriginal commissioners were appointed to investigate Aboriginal issues, including education, and to advise the federal government. In light of history, the first sentence of the **Report of the Royal Commission on Aboriginal Peoples (RCAP)** (1996) sounds conciliatory: "Canada is a test case for a grand notion—the notion that dissimilar peoples can share lands, resources, power and dreams while respecting and sustaining their differences." The central conclusion of RCAP was that the policy of assimilation must change. In a response to RCAP, *Gathering Strength: Canada's Aboriginal Action Plan* (1998), the federal government acknowledged that "much more attention still needs to be given to pressing issues." The Indian Residential Schools Truth and Reconciliation Commission was established in 2007 to act as an independent body and to provide a safe space for those affected by the residential school system to share their experiences. And in 2008, the prime minister offered a full apology on behalf of Canadians for the Indian Residential Schools system. However, 2011 saw the crisis in Attawapiskat, where housing conditions were abysmal and elementary school classes took place in portables because the school had been closed as a health risk in 2000 and never replaced with a permanent structure. News reports at the time showed that Attawapiskat was not an isolated case (Ivison, 2011).

In 2013, the federal government released a new act and accompanying policy, *First Nations Education Act*, which would have increased funding for education. However, the Act was rejected by individual First Nations and by the Assembly of First Nations (AFN). One of the three concerns of the AFN was that too little attention was paid to the role of language and culture in the education of First Nations students (Morcom, 2014). A revised act, Bill C-33, was brought forward in 2014; it was also rejected by many in the AFN, leading to divisions within Aboriginal leadership and to the resignation of the national chief of the AFN, Shawn Atleo. As Morcom writes in 2014, "Still, a mutually satisfactory approach to language and culture in First Nations schools has not been reached" (p. 11). (Figure 6.1 provides some terminology and information about Canada's Aboriginal peoples.)

FIGURE 6.1 ABORIGINAL PEOPLES IN CANADA

Who are the Aboriginal peoples in Canada?

They are descendants of the original inhabitants of North America. The Canadian *Constitution Act* (1982) recognizes three separate Aboriginal peoples with unique heritages: First Nations, Métis, and Inuit. In 2011 1.4 million people reported an Aboriginal identity representing 4.3 percent of the total Canadian population (Statistics Canada, 2011a).

What is a First Nation?

This is a term that came into use in the 1970s to replace the word *Indian*, which many people found offensive. No legal definition of *First Nation* exists. There are 609 First Nations in Canada. Statistics Canada (2011a) used the expression First Nations (North American Indian) in its 2011 report on the NHS titled *Aboriginal Peoples in Canada: First Nations People, Metis and Inuit*.

Who are Indians?

Although many Aboriginal people find the term *Indian* outdated and offensive, the *Constitution Act* (1982) used this term to describe all Aboriginal people in Canada who are not Métis or Inuit. In the 2011 NHS 61 percent of Aboriginal people identified themselves as a First Nations person.

Who are Métis people?

They are people of mixed First Nations and European ancestry who identify themselves as Métis people, as distinct from First Nations people, Inuit, or non-Aboriginal people. In the 2011 NHS 33 percent of Aboriginal people identified themselves as Métis.

Who are Inuit people?

They are Aboriginal people who live north of the treeline in Nunavut, Northwest Territories, northern Quebec, and Labrador. In the 2011 NHS 4 percent of Aboriginal people identified themselves as Inuit.

Put into Practice

Locate one of the following resources and develop a series of activities to introduce your students to the history of Aboriginal cultures in Canada.

Knopf, K. (Ed.). (2008). *Aboriginal Canada revisited.* Ottawa, ON: University of Ottawa Press.

Cardinal, T., Highway, T., Johnston, B., King, T., Maracle, B., Maracle, L., Marchessault, J., Qitsualik, R.A., & Taylor, D.H. (2004). *Our story: Aboriginal voices on Canada's past.* Toronto: Doubleday.

Dickason, O.P., & Newbigging, W. (2010) *A concise history of Canada's First Nations* (2nd ed.). Don Mills, ON: Oxford University Press.

Brazeau, C., & Charmly, S. (2014). *Hurt, help, healing, hope: Rethinking Canada's residential school history* (Primary resource teaching guide for the Ontario Curriculum, 2013, Grade 8 History; lesson plans and resources). Kingston, ON: QSpace at Queen's University. Retrieved at http://hdl.handle.net.proxy.queensu.ca/1974/12331

(continued)

FIGURE 6.1 (*continued*)

Who are Registered Indians?

A Registered Indian is a person who is registered under the *Indian Act*, while a non-Registered Indian is not registered as an Indian under the *Indian Act*. This may be because his or her ancestors were never registered or because he or she lost Indian status under former provisions of the *Indian Act*. A treaty Indian is a status Indian who belongs to a First Nation that signed a treaty with the Crown. Of the people who identified themselves as Aboriginal in the 2011 NHS, 46 percent reported being Registered Indians.

How many Aboriginal people live on reserves?

Among those who reported being a Registered Indian in 2001, about 45 percent (316 000) lived on a reserve.

How many Aboriginal people live in urban areas?

In 2006 about 54 percent of self-identified Aboriginal people lived in cities.

What is the age distribution of Aboriginal people?

The Aboriginal population in Canada has a lower mean age than the non-Aboriginal population. Twenty-eight percent of Aboriginal people are less than 15 years old (compared with 17 percent for non-Aboriginals). Similarly, there was a higher percentage of Aboriginal youth (15 to 24) at 18 percent compared to 13 percent of the non-Aboriginal population in the NHS of 2011.

Sources: Based on information from Statistics Canada (2011a; *Aboriginal Peoples in Canada*) and the *Report of the Royal Commission on Aboriginal Peoples* (1996).

Larry Pierre of the Okanagan on the occasion of the First Nations Constitutional Conference, 1980, demanding Aboriginal participation in constitutional talks.

Differences Between Issues in Aboriginal Education and Multicultural Education

Aboriginal issues are distinct from multicultural issues. Native peoples did not immigrate to a different cultural context thinking that they might have to change their ways to fit into the society of a foreign country (Bell, 2004). Rather, their country became foreign to them with the arrival of other peoples, and they had to deal with forced assimilation. Eber Hampton, of First Nations University of Canada in Saskatchewan, wrote of "the world-shattering difference [in perspective] between the conquered and the conqueror" (1995, p. 41). Binding treaties were ignored, spiritual activities were outlawed, and children were forced to attend residential schools (Roberts, 2006).

The Importance of Education and Community in Preserving Disappearing Cultures and Languages

George Erasmus, former chief of the AFN, has said, "The future of our people in Canada and the survival of our cultures, languages, and all that we value are directly linked to the education of our children" (1996). In an open letter to the minister of Aboriginal Affairs and Northern Development Canada rejecting the *First Nations Education Act* Shawn Atleo (2013), then national chief of the AFN, wrote that it is "imperative" that First Nations children be "nurtured in an environment that affirms their dignity, rights, and their identity, including their languages and cultures" (p. 3).

Across Canada, all but four of the approximately sixty Aboriginal languages are in danger of being lost (Ojibwe, Mi'kmaq, Inuktitut, and Cree) (UNESCO, 2014). Unlike other languages, these Aboriginal languages cannot be revitalized or supported in other countries. In recent years, the source of traditional knowledge and teaching has been dying with the elders. Brent Delaine (2010) of the University of Manitoba describes the role that schools play in the revitalization of First Peoples' languages while Lindsay Morcom (2014) of Queen's University argues that these languages enhance the education of Aboriginal youth. Morcom provides evidence of the effectiveness of "localized, culture-based and language-founded programming", such as the Mi'kmaw Kina'matnewey Agreement in Nova Scotia which has a graduation rate of 87.7 percent, far exceeding the national average and the First Nations average of 36 percent (p. 6). Self-Governing Agreements grant communities a degree of autonomy and teach students _through_ their cultural values rather than teaching students _about_ their traditional cultures (McCue, 2004, p. 6). Morcom shows that this distinction is at the base of the 2013 disagreement between the federal government and the AFN: the AFN advocates "Aboriginal languages and cultures as the medium of instruction through which the curriculum is delivered," that is, culture-based programming (2014, p. 20). While this approach may require more resources, Morcom argues convincingly that it has been demonstrated to produce better learning for Aboriginal students, and Delaine argues that it helps to preserve endangered Aboriginal languages.

Working with the Community

The AFN and the RCAP have emphasized that First Nations must assume responsibility for reserve schools. However, increasing numbers of Aboriginals live in urban areas and almost 70 percent of Aboriginal children attend neighbourhood schools, not reserve schools. Urban non-profit organizations often provide holistic education programs that provide hope to youth in safe, non-school environments (e.g., Parent, 2011). Neighbourhood schools face challenges in developing community-based programming collaboratively with Aboriginal parents and communities to ensure that children are proud of their heritage (Stelmach, 2009). Angelina Weenie (2009) of the First Nations University of Canada described how such knowledge of heritage comes from sacred stories, ordinary stories, ceremonies, and teachings of the elders. If these sources are to be included and valued in the education of Aboriginal children in neighbourhood schools, then Aboriginal parents, elders, and teachers must be true partners in curriculum decision making (Martell, 2008). To this end, the Alberta Department of Special Education has published _A Handbook for Aboriginal Parents of Children with Special Needs_, authored by members of the Aboriginal community (Crowchief-McHugh et al., 2000).

Strategies and Approaches: Putting Community at the Heart

Aboriginal peoples tend to view education, culture, and language as intimately related to each other and to community (e.g., Atleo, 2013). This section describes three approaches: culturally responsive teaching, infusion of Aboriginal studies throughout the curriculum for all, and direct support to Aboriginal students.

Weblinks

THE FIRST PERSPECTIVE, CANADA'S SOURCE FOR NEWS ABOUT INDIGENOUS PEOPLES
www.firstperspective.ca

WINDSPEAKER, CANADA'S NATIONAL ABORIGINAL NEWS SOURCE
www.ammsa.com/publications/windspeaker

SASKATCHEWAN SAGE, SASKATCHEWAN'S ABORIGINAL NEWS PUBLICATION
www.ammsa.com/publications/saskatchewan-sage

FIRST NATIONS DRUM: NEWS FROM CANADA'S NATIVE COMMUNITIES
www.firstnationsdrum.com

ABORIGINAL MULTI-MEDIA SOCIETY
www.ammsa.com

EAGLE FEATHER NEWS
www.eaglefeathernews.com

Weblinks

ASSEMBLY OF FIRST NATIONS
www.afn.ca

MÉTIS NATIONAL COUNCIL
www.metisnation.ca

Further Reading

Birch Bark Comics, an illustrated series put together to tell the Sacred Circles story, can be accessed from http://prairielibrarian.wordpress.com/2007/09/18/graphic-novels-and-comics-by-aboriginal-peoples

Joe, D. (1999). *Salmon boy: A legend of the Sechelt people.* Madeira Park, BC: Nightwood Editions. (Teaches respect for the environment. Primary grades.)

Plain, F. (1989). *Eagle feather: An honour.* Winnipeg, MB: Pemmican Publications. (A story of an Ojibwa boy. Primary grades.)

Thompson, S. (1991). *Cheryl Bibalhats/Cheryl's potlatch.* Vanderhoof, BC: Yinka Dene Language Institute. (Book written in Carrier and English about a Carrier child's naming ceremony and the potlatch in her honour. Primary grades.)

Carvell, M. (2004). *Who will tell my brother?* New York, NY: Hyperion Books. (Story of a boy trying to remove offensive mascots from his school. Junior high and secondary level.)

Monture-Angus, P. (1995). *Thunder in my soul: A Mohawk woman speaks.* Halifax, NS: Fernwood Press. (Autobiography. Grades 10 to 12.)

What do you think?

Preview some of the nine videos in the series *First Nations: The Circle Unbroken* (1993, 1998) or the videos in the series *Finding Our Talk* (2001), Episodes 1–13, and *Finding Our Talk II* (2002), Episodes 1–13 (both Montreal: Mushkeg Media Inc.). Do they help you understand the perspectives of Aboriginal peoples? If you are Aboriginal, do these videos represent your perspective?

Aboriginal students learn better and are more engaged in schooling when they can make connections to it (Castagno & Brayboy, 2008). Culture-based education or **culturally responsive teaching (CRT)** involves using the cultural knowledge, prior experience, frames of reference, and learning approaches of students to make learning more relevant and effective for them (Lewthwaite et al., 2014b). Gay (2000), who developed CRT, suggested that it involves teaching to and through the strengths of the students, as well as forming genuine and caring relationships with all students and maintaining high expectations for all learners. This requires that teachers of Aboriginal students be aware of and capable of using cultural learning patterns, multiple world views, and tribal languages in their teaching. Nicole Bell (2013) of Trent University describes an Anishinaabe culture-based program for Aboriginal children and youth designed to provide a sound education while developing a strong sense of identity and pride in self and Anishinaabe culture.

In their book, *Teaching Each Other: Nehinuw [Cree] Concepts and Indigenous Pedagogies*, Linda and Keith Goulet present a framework that they believe strengthens Indigenous identity. Their model of effective teaching for Indigenous students contains four relational categories of teacher actions that they describe as interacting to form an interactive whole: culturally responsive learning environment, culturally meaningful knowledge construction, culturally affirming interpersonal relationship (between teacher and student), and respectful social system (including relations among students) (2014, pp. 86–97).

Ann Pohl (1997), a non-Aboriginal, advises teachers like her to become informed about the local Aboriginal community and to, first, focus on the First Nation on whose traditional territory your school is located. It is a respectful protocol, when working with Aboriginal people, to acknowledge the traditional territory on which you are living and working (BC Ministry of Education, 2006). You can consult a local elder or band council for guidance in adopting such protocols.

Lewthwaite and his colleagues (2014a) conducted interviews to learn about the teaching practices that one Yukon First Nation community perceived as effective for its children. They designed a *Classroom Teaching Inventory* that they used in subsequent studies to help teachers develop more effective teaching practices. The eight-element *Inventory* included some elements that could be considered universal effective teaching practices (e.g., feedback, clear instruction) and some elements specific to the community and culture (e.g., need for extensive wait time, need for teachers to talk less). They wrote 300-word narrative "vignettes," to represent these elements for a booklet titled *Our Stories About Teaching and Learning*. Then Lewthwaite et al. (2014b) describe how they used this resource to help teachers to engage in more culturally responsive teaching. Students' learning behaviours also improved on a six-element rubric that included effort, self-image, and problem-solving skills. However, a recent study describes the efforts of a school district in BC to implement an agreement to enhance Aboriginal education and reports on its challenges in implementing holistic notions of student success that are consistent with Aboriginal values (White et al., 2012).

Teaching materials, such as the video series *First Nations: The Circle Unbroken* (Williams et al., 1998) and books (e.g., Roberts, 2006) will help you to bring Aboriginal voices into the classroom. The website of the Living Sky School

Division in Saskatchewan (www.lskysd.ca) includes insightful curriculum activities on Aboriginal issues. Harvey McCue of Trent University authored *The Learning Circle: Activities on First Nations in Canada* (2000). A recently developed curriculum resource may inspire you. Courtney Brazeau and Samantha Charmly (2014) aligned *Hurt, Help, Healing, Hope: Rethinking Canada's Residential School History* with the Ontario curriculum for grade 8 history, but their insightful lesson plans and resources serve as a model for CRT at many grade levels (available at QSpace at Queen's University).

"Non-Native teachers who are the most successful [teaching Aboriginal students] are those who are continually learning, who understand and accept Native ways, and who can then transmit values, beliefs, and behavioral norms which are consistent with those of the community" (Gilliland, 1999, p. 50). In this process, question your taken-for-granted assumptions; you might begin with a CD from the National Film Board, "Qallunaat! Why White People Are Funny," and with the strategies of critical analysis adapted from the guide for *First Nations: The Circle Unbroken* (Williams et al., 1998, p. 8):

- Ask how you know what you know.
- Search for the biases in your socialization and in what you have been told about Aboriginal peoples.
- Consider the competing interests and powers that might have influenced your learning.
- Ask whose interests are served by what you have learned about Aboriginal peoples.
- Identify social and political problems. Look for systemic sources of these problems.

You can show respect by adopting teaching approaches consistent with traditional Aboriginal experiential learning. Experiential learning includes field trips, role-playing, and designing and making. Oral presentations reflect the oral tradition of Aboriginal cultures. Do not assume that Aboriginal students are knowledgeable about the traditions of their people; invite **Aboriginal elders**, parents, and artists into your classroom. Table 6.1 presents strategies for Aboriginal education.

TABLE 6.1 STRATEGIES FOR ABORIGINAL EDUCATION

Strategy	Examples
Engage students in Aboriginal culture through the arts.	Invite storytellers, singers, dancers, painters, weavers, and other artists from the Aboriginal community to collaborate.
Help students to understand aboriginal perspectives.	Provide readings, etc., at the students' developmental level: fiction, reports, films from an Aboriginal point of view.
	Invite speakers who are comfortable telling their stories and providing their perspectives.
Use Aboriginal communication and participant structures.	Use the talking circle, where the right to speak is indicated by passing a concrete object, such as a feather.
Explicitly discuss Aboriginal values.	Teach environmental education through an Aboriginal perspective, "caring for the earth."
Help students to think critically about complex issues, such as racism and cultural identity.	Deal with sensitive issues and controversial topics in a caring and proactive way. Use video series like *First Nations: The Circle Unbroken* to teach about current issues.

Put into Practice

Develop an annotated bibliography of references for teaching and learning materials on Aboriginal education. To begin, consult:

Van Etten, J. (1996). *Resource reading list: An annotated bibliography of recommended works by and about Native peoples.* Toronto, ON: Canadian Alliance in Solidarity with Native Peoples.

Max, K.E. (2003). *Joining the circle: Working as an ally in Aboriginal education.* Ottawa, ON: National Library of Canada.

Roberts, J. (2006). *First Nations, Inuit, and Métis peoples: Exploring their past, present, and future.* Toronto, ON: Edmond Montgomery Publications. (Teacher's resource available.)

Indian and Northern Affairs Canada (2007). *Share in the celebration! National Aboriginal Day is June 21: Learning and activity guide.* Ottawa, ON: Minister of Public Works and Government Services Canada.

Munro, R. (2005). *Canada's first peoples.* Markham, ON: Fitzhenry and Whiteside.

Kainai Board of Education, Métis Nation of Alberta, Northland School Division, & Tribal Chiefs Institute of Treaty Six. (2004). *Aboriginal studies 10: Aboriginal perspectives.* Edmonton, AB: Duval House Publishing. (Teacher's resource available.)

Kainai Board of Education, Métis Nation of Alberta, Northland School Division, & Tribal Chiefs Institute of Treaty Six. (2005). *Aboriginal studies 20: People and cultural change.* Edmonton, AB: Duval House Publishing. (Teacher's resource available.)

Kainai Board of Education, Métis Nation of Alberta, Northland School Division, & Tribal Chiefs Institute of Treaty Six. (2005). *Aboriginal studies 30: Contemporary issues.* Edmonton: Duval House Publishing. (Teacher's resource available.)

The second approach overlaps with and strengthens the first. Learning about Aboriginal cultures, developing respectful teaching, and involving the local Aboriginal community will ensure the infusion of Aboriginal studies throughout the curriculum for all students. Many provinces have policies that reflect this approach. For example, the first goal in Alberta Learning's (2002) policy framework on First Nations, Métis, and Innu education is to "increase and strengthen knowledge and understanding among all Albertans of First Nations, Métis, and Innu governance, history, treaty, and Aboriginal rights, lands, cultures and languages" (p. 2).

Some recently developed resources can guide schools in this process:

- Manitoba Education. Aboriginal education, kindergarten to grade 12— *Incorporating Aboriginal perspectives: A theme-based curricular approach.* www.edu .gov.mb.ca/k12/abedu/perspectives
- Toulouse, P.R. (2008, March). *Integrating Aboriginal Teaching and Values into the Classroom* (What Works? Research into Practice). Toronto, ON: Ontario Literacy and Numeracy Secretariat. www.edu.gov.on.ca/eng/literacynumeracy/ inspire/research/whatWorks.html
- British Columbia Ministry of Education. (1998). *Planning Guide and Framework for Development of Aboriginal Learning Resources.* www.bced.gov.bc.ca/ abed/planguide/welcome.htm
- British Columbia Ministry of Education. (1998). *Shared Learnings: Integrating B.C. Aboriginal Content, K–10.* www.bced.gov.bc.ca/abed
- Manitoba Education. (2003). *Integrating Aboriginal Perspectives into Curricula: A Resource for Curriculum Developers, Teachers, and Administrators.* www.edu.gov. mb.ca/k12/docs/policy/abpersp/ab_persp.pdf
- Coalition for the Advancement of Aboriginal Studies (CAAS) www.anti-racism.ca/content/coalition-advancement-aboriginal-studies
- Lakehead Public Schools: *Aboriginal Presence in Our Schools.* www.lake-headschools.ca/?xs=Aboriginal+Presence+in+Our+Schools
- Saskatoon Catholic Cyber School: *Teacher Resources on Aboriginal Education* www.gscs.sk.ca/studentsandfamilies/fnme/Pages/default.aspx
- Living Sky School Division (Saskatchewan): *Treaty 6 Education* http://treat-y6education.lskysd.ca

For infusing Aboriginal studies throughout the curriculum, consider *The Learning Circle,* in three volumes, with activities for ages 4 to 7, 8 to 11, and 12 to 14 http://publications.gc.ca (search for The Learning Circle). For example, Unit 6 in the volume for students aged 8 to 11 is entitled "First Nations and the Environment." The two objectives are to learn how First Nations viewed their responsibilities to the land and to explore how students' behaviour and actions affect the environment. The activities range from writing poetry to planning sustainable development in an expanding community. Each activity is debriefed to communicate First Nations' perspectives as the Earth's stewards. *Shared Learnings* (www.bced. gov.bc.ca/abed/shared.pdf) is also made up of activities to integrate Aboriginal content into K–10 curricula. One activity, entitled "Using the Internet to Learn about Aboriginal Peoples," challenges secondary students to visit websites to learn about traditional stories, legends, and artwork and to answer questions about Aboriginal people in modern society.

Weblinks

THE INNU NATION
www.innu.ca

VIRTUAL MUSEUM CANADA:
TEACHERS' CENTRE
www.virtualmuseum.ca/home

TORONTO DISTRICT SCHOOL
BOARD: ABORIGINAL EDUCATION
www.tdsb.on.ca (under
"Community" see "Aboriginal
Education")

Weblinks

ON PREPARING TO TEACH ABOUT
ABORIGINAL CULTURE:

FOUR DIRECTIONS TEACHINGS (ON
THE BLACKFOOT, CREE, OJIBWE,
MOHAWK, AND MI'KMAQ BY THE
NATIONAL INDIGENOUS LITERACY
ASSOCIATION)
www.fourdirectionsteachings.com

STATISTICS CANADA: LESSON ON
DEMOGRAPHICS OF THE ABORIGINAL
POPULATION IN CANADA
www12.statcan.gc.ca (search
for Lesson on demographics of
the Aboriginal population)

NATIONAL FILM BOARD OF CANADA
(NFB) FILMS ON ABORIGINAL PEOPLES
www3.onf.ca/enclasse/
doclens/visau

THE CANADIAN ENCYCLOPEDIA
www.thecanadianencyclopedia
.com (search for Aboriginal
culture.)

COMMON CURRICULUM FRAMEWORK
FOR ABORIGINAL LANGUAGE AND
CULTURE PROGRAMS: KINDERGARTEN
TO GRADE 12
www.wncp.ca/english/
subjectarea/fnmi/
commoncurriculumframework
.aspx

DIRECT SUPPORT TO ABORIGINAL STUDENTS

The third approach, providing direct services to Aboriginal students, should include much more than the remedial strategies used to help some Aboriginal students in the past. Providing opportunities to learn or strengthen **heritage languages** is vital, as is a sense of community. You can view the *Common Curriculum Framework for Aboriginal Language and Culture Programs: Kindergarten to Grade 12* (Western Canadian Protocol for Collaboration in Basic Education) at www.wncp.ca/english/subjectarea/fnmi/commoncurriculumframework.aspx.

These school-based approaches demand teachers be knowledgeable about, sensitive to, and respectful of the cultures of individual Aboriginal students. Each of us can do this by learning about our students and their heritages—from them, their parents, and the community.

At University of Northern British Columbia a sense of community is fostered through the First Nations Centre, which provides a place where Aboriginal culture is the norm, not on the periphery. Most universities and colleges have such centres, but they are rare within secondary and elementary schools. Counselling, tutoring, and socializing can be provided in such a context. In an elementary classroom, you could create a place where Aboriginal symbols and ways are dominant, perhaps a "circle" for reflection and quiet talk. Secondary schools with Aboriginal counsellors can create a First Nations Centre. Providing Aboriginal counsellors is one of the recommendations of Ontario's *First Nation, Métis, and Inuit Education Policy Framework* (2007), because without them it is not possible to provide culturally responsive contexts for teaching and counselling (Long et al., 2006; Wihak & Merali, 2007). Paquette and Fallon (2014) identify the challenges to post-secondary institutions of simultaneously providing education grounded in Aboriginal culture while providing a reasonable degree of parity with the content and quality of mainstream post-secondary education.

Weblinks

ABORIGINAL YOUTH NETWORK
http://orgs.tigweb.org/aboriginal-youth-network

CENTER FOR WORLD INDIGENOUS STUDIES
www.cwis.org

Teaching Students from Culturally Diverse Backgrounds

Canadian classrooms have been increasing in racial, cultural, and linguistic diversity, and this trend is expected to continue. The percentage of Canadians who were visible minorities in the 2006 census report was 16.2 percent and was 19.1 percent in the NHS of 2011 (Statistics Canada, 2006, 2011b [*Immigration and Ethnocultural Diversity*]). In addition to English and French, the 2011 NHS estimated more than 200 languages as the mother tongue of Canadians.

The reasons that students from **culturally diverse backgrounds** can encounter difficulties in school are complex. They often experience discrimination in society and lack role models because most teachers are from the majority culture. Societal expectations and realities for these students are often contradictory. Although they are told to aim high, low teacher expectations can influence their effort and participation. Schools may use discriminatory assessment practices and textbooks that promote stereotypes and omit culturally important information. This section discusses measures that can begin to rectify discriminatory practices: cultural awareness, high teacher expectations, culturally responsive teaching, co-operative learning, and teachers as role models.

Being Culturally Aware and Questioning Assumptions

Teaching students who are members of diverse groups involves recognizing the nature of these students' experiences in Canada and of our own experiences. In a book with the poignant title . . . *But Where Are You Really From?*, Hazelle Palmer (1997) describes how this question "keeps us forever foreign, forever immigrants to Canada" (p. vi). Sometimes teachers' cultural insensitivity can contribute to miscommunication, distrust, and negative school experiences. Keren Brethwaite (1996) described a teacher who had not heard a grade 5 girl from the Caribbean read in class. She assessed the student as unable to read and informed the mother at a parent–teacher conference. The mother protested that the girl read fluently at home. "So she brought a Bible to the school, and to the amazement of the teacher, the student read from it fluently" (p. 109). The teacher's assumption that the student could not read is a powerful reminder of the need for **cultural awareness**. In their edited volume *The Great White North? Exploring whiteness, privilege, and identity in education*, Carr and Lund (2007) underline the importance of white people understanding not just the racialization of others, but their own whiteness and the privilege that it bestows. This is an important issue for teachers because the majority of teachers in Canada are white and Canadian schools tend to embody a culture of whiteness.

The implication is that white teachers must know their own whiteness before they can embrace social justice as allies of many of the students they teach. Teachers are responsible for developing an understanding of how their students might approach learning because of their backgrounds. For example, some students don't ask questions of the teacher, an authority figure, and some students don't participate in the classroom until they feel very comfortable. Samaroo and her colleagues (2013) describe the tendency to look at minority students with a "deficit" lens and to focus on what they cannot do (a form of blaming the student) when we need to create contexts that focus on helping students to show what they can do and what they do know. They suggest, we look for deficiencies in the system rather than looking for them in the students.

Not all students from a similar cultural background have similar characteristics. Jo-Anne Dillabough and her colleagues from the University of British Columbia (2005) interviewed adolescents about their experiences of exclusion in urban schooling and of gaining status in their youth subculture. They described in depth the struggles of individuals, of both sexes, from a range of ethnic backgrounds, including Afro-Caribbean students. In contrast, Henry Codjoe (2006) focused on the experiences of black students in an urban context who achieved academic success in spite of adversity; these students all showed pride and knowledge about their cultural heritage. We must be aware of the cultural backgrounds of our students while regarding them as capable individuals.

High Expectations Coupled with Support and Encouragement

What does it feel like to be a student from a visible minority? In interviews, black youth in Montreal expressed the importance of teachers who set high expectations and, in the words of the authors, "push them to succeed" (Livingstone et al., 2014, p. 298). One student reported, "You need a teacher that's going to pressure you and be, like, 'C'mon, c'mon, you gotta do this. You gotta do this!"; and another explained, "The thing that motivates me the most is when I get a lot of encouragement from my teacher and when the teacher wants me to succeed" (Livingstone et al., 2014, p. 298). Students expressed concern that some teachers set lower expectations for black students because of stereotyping, and one student described that, as the only black student in an advanced math class, she felt that "Each time you must prove that you are capable" (Livingstone et al., 2014, p. 298). In Lam's (1996) study, an Asian teacher described an experience when she was a student with a teacher who assumed from her appearance that she could not speak English. We have to confront the racism of low expectations and maintain high expectations for all students, including minority students. Such expectations can influence teaching approaches and student-teacher relations.

If we teach with low expectations and students are unchallenged, they are unlikely to learn. Students from some racial backgrounds are more likely to be streamed into less challenging courses (Lewis, 1992) or into particular subject areas and denied opportunities to develop in other important areas. Teachers who hold high expectations for their students have been found to spend more time providing better explanations, more challenging questions, more feedback, and more positive approaches to managing their students' behaviour (Rubie-Davies, 2007). A study conducted in Canada, Australia, and New Zealand reported that principals effective in culturally diverse schools had four common characteristics: (a) holding high expectations for all students and rejecting an "excuse culture"; (b) making a strong commitment to social justice principles, which they embedded in school practices and culture; (c) accepting and accommodating differences, using the diversity of cultures as a school strength; and (d) celebrating individual and group differences through a wide range of cultural and sporting activities (Billot, et al., 2007). Figure 6.2 includes a list of strategies for teachers to use in culturally diverse classrooms.

Culturally Responsive Teaching and Culturally Relevant Curriculum

Teachers who practice **culturally relevant pedagogy** in Vancouver described four main ways in which they supported students who are culturally diverse (Parhar & Sensoy, 2011). First, they described inclusive classrooms with a respectful classroom climate in which they had meaningful relationships with their students. They connected with their students based on their cultural background, learning about and, on occasion, attending cultural events in which their students participated. Respect extended to ensuring the classroom "felt safe" for every student. Second, they expanded "what counts as curriculum." As one teacher reported, "different languages and literature and parents' expectations are all a part of our school" (Parhar & Sensoy, 2011, p. 198). This enabled all students to see themselves portrayed and their culture validated in the curriculum. Bondy and colleagues (2007), who studied culturally responsive teachers in the United States, also found that they developed respectful, caring, and personal relationships with each student and built a community in the classroom where people trusted one another. They used what they had learned about their students' lives to make what they taught meaningful to the students—with language, examples, and challenges that the students recognized from their lives and related to. These teachers recognized that definitions of appropriate classroom behaviour were culturally defined, and they were well enough informed about their students to understand what this meant. They engaged their students in

Further Reading

About multiculturalism and science teaching:

Krugly-Smolska, E. (2013). Twenty-five years of multicultural science education: Looking backward, looking forward. *Encounters on Education, 14*, 21–31.

McMillan, B.A. (2013). Inuit legends, oral histories, art, and science in the collaborative development of lessons that foster two-way learning: The return of the sun in Nunavut. *Interchange, 43*, 129–145.

Saint-Hilaire, L.A. (2014). Multicultural literature for elementary science classrooms. *Ohio Journal of English Language Arts, 54*(1), 27–37.

Van Eijck, M., & Roth, W.-M. (2007). Keeping the local local: Recalibrating the status of science and traditional ecological knowledge (TEK) in education. *Science Education, 91*(6), 926–947.

Hines, S.M. (2007). *Multicultural science education: Theory, practice, and promise.* New York, NY: Peter Lang.

Mujawamariya, D., Hujaleh, F., & Lima-Kerckhoff, A. (2014). A reexamination of Ontario's science curriculum: Toward a more inclusive multicultural science education? *Canadian Journal of Science, Mathematics and Technology Education, 14*(3), 269–283.

FIGURE 6.2 STRATEGIES FOR TEACHERS IN CLASSES WITH HIGH DIVERSITY

- Ensure that all students can see themselves in the posters, encouragements, and adornments on your classroom walls.
- Learn about the cultures of all your students from the students and their parents. Be a good listener.
- Incorporate your students' cultures into the learning environment.
- Use non-threatening activities to find out how prepared your students are for the topics that you are about to teach.
- Become aware of the language proficiencies and needs of ELL students. Talk with them individually in a quiet place to help to understand their spoken language. Consult with a language resource teacher or your principal for information.
- Accommodate cultural diversity and ensure you make your teaching meaningful for all your students.
- Read about anti-racist education and actively look for ways to reduce the racism your students experience at school.
- Respond quickly and firmly when you see or hear racist behaviour in the school or on the schoolyard.
- Examine your topics, materials, and teaching methods for bias.
- Develop activities that truly engage students, and teach them by degrees how to take responsibility for their own engagement with learning. Don't assume they know how to collaborate or co-operate to learn. Teach them how.
- Establish legitimate standards for classroom work, and make the necessary efforts to ensure that all students reach these standards; this may mean making differentiations or accommodations.
- Help all students to relate their lives and issues to classroom learning.
- Model the kind of caring, respectful, and community behaviour that you expect of your students.
- Let your students know when they are meeting your expectations. Positive feedback is essential for enhancing appropriate behaviour and engagement with learning in the classroom.

Source: Hutchinson, N.L. (2004). *Teaching exceptional children and adolescents: A Canadian casebook* (2nd ed.), p. 116. Toronto: Allyn and Bacon. Reprinted with permission of Pearson Education Canada, Inc.

conversation, listened respectfully, and shared information about themselves, their families, their passions, and their backgrounds.

Parhar and Sensoy's (2011) findings go further. The third major approach described by these Vancouver teachers is their effort to develop a community resource network. Some emphasized collaborating with parents, and others focused more on collaborating with support workers (including language interpreters, multicultural workers, Aboriginal workers, school counsellors, and ELL teachers). To honour our students' heritage, we must address the values, history, current relations, and power relationships that shape a culture; invite representatives from local advocacy groups; and respect the diversity within any group. The black students in Livingstone's (2014) study valued a community worker who tutored them, brought culturally relevant activities into the school, and acted as a nurturing role model. The fourth approach involves educators committing to a "continual learning process embedded in teaching" (Parhar & Sensoy, 2011, p. 205), which includes feeling uncomfortable, reflecting critically on one's practice, and seeking information and professional development from scholarship and research. These Vancouver teachers also acknowledged the challenges of implementing CRT and culturally relevant curriculum, including helping students to develop a sense of critical consciousness, reconciling expectations with families of culturally diverse students, and the difficulties of collaborating with colleagues who do not share a willingness to reflect and to feel discomfort.

Cultural relevance may be more straightforward in subjects like social studies and literature. Continual under-representation of some cultural groups in science and mathematics, both in schools and in careers, suggests that culturally relevant curricula are necessary in these subjects. Culturally relevant pedagogy is grounded in an understanding of the role of culture and language in learning and involves advocating for and differentiating for the learning of all students (Villegas & Lucas, 2007).

Using Collaborative Learning and Co-operative Learning

Collaborative learning, or a "community of learning," was one aspect of the approach described by the Vancouver teachers in the study by Parhar and Sensoy (2011, introduced above) to ensure an inclusive classroom culture. These teachers described collaborative learning as a means of supporting student interaction and of promoting academic success. One teacher emphasized "mutual responsibility," which is also key to co-operative learning. Research demonstrates that co-operative learning improves student attitudes and behaviours toward diversity and boosts self-esteem in elementary and secondary classrooms (Kagan, 2013; McCafferty et al., 2006; Pedersen & Digby, 2014). Principles of **co-operative learning** include:

- Tasks are structured so no one can complete the learning task alone.
- Positive interdependence is fostered and developed.
- Students work in teams.
- Students learn language and social skills necessary for co-operation while learning content.

Begin with team-building activities, such as brainstorming in triads, interviews in pairs, or assembly-line craft projects (or writing activities) in which each person does one step (or writes one sentence) and passes the project along to the next person. Figure 6.3 provides step-by-step instructions for a number of co-operative learning activities.

FIGURE 6.3 CO-OPERATIVE LEARNING STRUCTURES

Brainstorming
This gives all students an opportunity to express their ideas.

- Generate as many ideas as possible.
- Record all ideas.
- Do not evaluate any ideas presented until after all have been used as basis for discussion.

Think-Pair-Share
Everybody gets a say.

- Everybody has time to think of an answer independently.
- Students then discuss their answers in pairs.
- After a signal for silence, students have a chance to share their ideas with the whole group.

Numbered Heads Together
One member speaks on behalf of the team.

- Students are placed in groups of four and number themselves from one to four.

(continued)

Put into Practice

Develop lesson plans to introduce your students to co-operative activities on the first day. See the following sources:

Roehlkepartain, J. (2013). *Spark student motivation: 101 easy activities for cooperative learning.* Minneapolis, MN: Search Institute.

Huffman, C. (2013). *Making music cooperatively: Using cooperative learning in your active music-making classroom.* (Electronic book text distributed by MyLibrary).

McCafferty, S.G., Jacobs, G.M., & DaSilva Iddings, C. (Eds.). (2006). *Cooperative learning and second language teaching.* Cambridge, UK: Cambridge University Press.

Bres, M., Weisshaar, A., Evers, C., Starr, C. & Starr, L. (2015). *Cooperative learning: Making connections in general biology.* Toronto, ON: Nelson.

Pederson, J.E., & Digby, A.D. (Ed.). (2014). *Secondary schools and cooperative learning: Theories, models, and strategies.* (Electronic book distributed by MyLibrary).

Strebe, J.D. (2014). *Engaging mathematics students using cooperative learning.* (Electronic book distributed by MyLibrary).

Jacobs, G.M., Power, M.A., & Wan Inn, L. (2002). *The teacher's sourcebook for co-operative learning: Practical techniques, basic principles, and frequently asked questions.* Thousand Oaks, CA: Corwin Press.

Vermette, P.J. (1998). *Making co-operative learning work: Student teams in K–12 classrooms.* Upper Saddle River, NJ: Allyn and Bacon.

Brownlie, F., Feniak, C., & Schnellert, L. (2006). *Student diversity: Classroom strategies to meet the learning needs of all students.* Markham, ON: Pembroke.

FIGURE 6.3 *(continued)*

- The teacher then asks a question for discussion, e.g., "What do you think . . . ?" or "Why would . . . ?" Try to frame questions that elicit discussion about current studies.
- Students "put their heads together" to figure out the answer as a team.
- The teacher calls a specific number (one to four) to respond on behalf of the team. Because no one knows which number will be called, all students must be prepared.

Jigsaw (also called expert groups)

A four-step structure:

Step 1 Students form a "home" group.
Step 2 Each student is assigned a number. The topic overview is presented.
Step 3 Students now move to form an "expert group" with other students who have same number. Each "expert group" works on one assigned part of the larger topic.
Step 4 When time is up, the experts regroup with their original home groups. Each expert now teaches the skills or content learned in the expert group about his subtopic to the home group. Quiz the students on what they have learned.

- All members contribute something to the topic, so everybody is an expert.
- Team members depend on one another to complete the overall task.
- Each team member must learn skills or content from the others.
- Evaluation depends on both an individual mark and a team effort mark.

Sources: Inspired by Meyers, M. (1993). *Teaching to diversity*. Toronto: Irwin Publishing, and Kagan, S. (2008). *Kagan cooperative learning*. San Clemente, CA: Kagan Publishing.

Cross-Reference
Chapters 7 and 10 focus on creating a positive classroom climate and helping students to work together.

Further Reading

Ontario Ministry of Education and Training. (2008). *Antiracism and ethnocultural equity in school boards*. www.edu.gov.on.ca/eng/document/curricul/antiraci/antire.html.

Joshee, R., & Johnson, L. (Eds.). (2007). *Multicultural education policies in Canada and the United States*. Vancouver, BC: UBC Press.

Ghosh, R., & Abdi, A.A. (2013). *Education and the politics of difference: Select Canadian perspectives* (2nd ed.). Toronto, ON: Canadian Scholars' Press.

Carr, P.R., & Lund, D.E. (Eds.). (2007). *The great white north? Exploring whiteness, privilege, and identity in education*. Rotterdam, The Netherlands: Sense Publishers.

Banks, J.A. (2014). *An introduction to multicultural education* (3rd ed.). Toronto, ON: Pearson Education Canada.

Saint-Hilaire, L.A. (2014). So, how do I teach them? Understanding multicultural education and culturally relevant pedagogy. *Reflective Practice, 15*(5), 592–602.

Kubota, R. (2015). Race and language learning in multicultural Canada: Towards critical antiracism. *Journal of Multilingual and Multicultural Development, 36*(1), 3–12.

Teachers as Role Models

In 1992, Stephen Lewis asked, "Where are the minority teachers?" Although more members of visible minorities are teachers today, this is still an important issue in a country as diverse as Canada. Teachers who are members of visible minorities serve as role models for students from diverse cultures (Duquette et al., 2007). Patrick Solomon

Teachers can serve as role models for students from minority cultures.

(1996) suggested that dominant-group students also benefit from experience with teachers of colour because it helps to modify their stereotypes about minorities.

This issue is important to every minority group in Canada. A black student interviewed by Dei (2003) said, "I've never had a black teacher. . . . But I think it would really help . . . having someone who's black up there [and] can share some of my experiences" (p. 52). Aboriginal teachers report that members of their community see them as role models (Duquette et al., 2007). Jim Grieve, director of education for the Peel District School Board, said of Canadian society and schools, "with this amazing diversity comes a responsibility to reflect the communities" in our teachers (Brown, 2008). Carl James (2012) highlights the importance of community for minority students and stresses the importance that identification and a sense of belonging have on a young person. However, his main message for us, as educators, is that teachers can make a world of difference by understanding the communities they serve.

Teaching English Language Learner Students

Some students from diverse cultures speak **English as a second language (ESL)** and are known as **English language learner (ELL) students**. Some are born in Canada to parents who speak limited English and others arrive in Canada as refugees or immigrants. Roughly 225 000 immigrants arrive in Canada each year; over 80 percent have a first language other than English, and half of those have no English proficiency. Ontario is the province chosen by over 50 percent of newcomers to Canada (Webster & Valeo, 2011). Although most are able to use English to communicate in social situations, many ELL students take between five and seven years to match the achievement levels of first-language English students on achievement tests (Early, 2005).

Research shows that many ELL students experience learning difficulties in school while developing competence and confidence in English usage in the classroom. On the Education Quality and Accountability Office (EQAO) of Ontario 2013–2014 grade 6 tests (http://www.eqao.com/en), the percentages of students achieving at or above provincial standard (levels 3 and 4) was

- Reading: 70 percent of ELL students; 79 percent of all participating students;
- Writing: 75 percent of ELL students; 78 percent of all participating students;
- Mathematics: 51 percent of ELL students; 54 percent of all participating students.

Teaching Students Who Are Immigrants or Refugees

Global migration affects millions of students worldwide every year. Each year, Canada accepts approximately 225 000 immigrants. Of these, about 20 000 are refugees. There are more than two hundred ethnic groups in Canada. Some researchers have begun to question Canada's success at absorbing immigrants, suggesting that recent immigrants are not faring as well as earlier ones, and asking how we can meet the challenges in our schools (Levin, 2008). Others suggest that it is time to focus on the benefits of cultural diversity and reframe these challenges as potentially rich learning opportunities for all students and teachers (Adams & Kirova, 2007).

Put into Practice

Consult the website for The Advocates for Human Rights (a program for K–12 students) at www. theadvocatesforhumanrights.org and read two of the following resources. Make a list of the kinds of challenges you would expect if a refugee student joined your class, at the level at which you usually teach. Then plan for how you would help this student to settle into your classroom, knowing that you will have to be sensitive to individual needs as you get to know the student. Also plan how you would educate your class about refugees and why they are forced to leave their homes. Discuss your ideas with your peers.

Brewer, C.A., & McCabe, M. (2014). *Immigrant and refugee students in Canada*. Toronto, ON: University of Toronto Press.

Stewart, J. (2011). *Supporting refugee children: Strategies for educators*. Toronto, ON: University of Toronto Press.

Behnia, B. (2007). An exploratory study of befriending programs with refugees: The perspective of volunteer organizations. *Journal of Immigrant and Refugee Studies*, 5(3), 1–19.

Reynolds, C. (2004). Children of war. *Maclean's*, 118(1), 78–81.

Magro, K. (2006/2007). Overcoming the trauma of war: Literacy challenges of adult learners. *Education Canada*, 47(1), 70–74.

However, for individual immigrant and refugee students, there are challenges. On arrival in a new country, **immigrants** begin a period of adjustment thought to consist of four stages: (1) arrival and first impressions, (2) culture shock, (3) recovery and optimism, and (4) acculturation (Kim, 2001). Joining a welcoming classroom may help students feel comfortable at school before they feel comfortable in other contexts; our actions and our non-verbal communication can make a difference. In some cases almost every aspect of our culture, all of which we take for granted, is different from what the student is used to; for example, in some cultures young children kiss one another when they greet, which is not a practice likely to be welcomed on a Canadian schoolyard. All students need to feel like they belong (Osterman, 2000), a tall order when one has no idea how to interact with peers (Adams & Kirova, 2007). Researchers at the University of Alberta helped immigrant children to explore their sense of belonging and peer relations through a fotonovela (Emme et al., 2006), which combines still photos taken by students and arranged in a narrative sequence with text, often in the form of text balloons (like those that appear in comics). Many factors contribute to adjustment and acculturation. These include whether the family immigrated by choice, the degree of family separation and emotional preparation, and environmental factors, such as the climate and size of the community (Hamilton & Moore, 2004). Some family characteristics, such as English proficiency, socio-economic status, and cultural conflict between home and school, are also influential. Additionally, 30 percent of immigrant families with children live in poverty.

Those who arrive as **refugees** may have lived through traumatic experiences, including war, violence, oppression, torture, and flight. Those who have experienced torture are at particular risk for mental health problems. Mental health researchers have described typical early stages in the adjustment of refugees to life in a new country. These include relief to be alive, guilt about surviving when others did not, recognition that they may not be able to return home, and stress associated with waiting for their refugee claims to be heard, which can take many years.

Canadian teachers describe refugee students as often withdrawn, restless, inattentive, and fearful of noises. Their drawings, like Ragu's in this chapter's opening case, may depict war, violence, bombs, guns, and soldiers. Some show symptoms of post-traumatic stress, including nightmares, disturbed sleep, crying, and depression, and many are still afraid of the government they fled, fearing that someone may be spying on them (Magro, 2006/2007). Some refugees have been child soldiers, and "it's hard to imagine what they must be going through trying to adjust to a normal life in the classroom" (Reynolds, 2004, p. 80). Others, such as female adolescent refugees from Afghanistan, may never have been to school, making the educational gap between them and their peers very large.

Recent research shows that talking about hope with refugee and immigrant students can empower them and help them to develop resilience in the face of adversity. Three sources of hope that researchers reported were secure relationships with teachers, peaceful relationships with nature, and engagement in physical and cognitive activities that gave them a calm feeling (Yohani & Larsen, 2009). Both immigrant and refugee students may need psychological support beyond a sensitive and aware teacher, but it is important to remember that when they receive support, most immigrant and refugee families are resilient and successful in their new lives. When interviewed, second language adolescents from immigrant families living in Ottawa discussed how multiculturalism gave them a sense of belonging and how important

@

Weblinks

CANADIAN MULTICULTURAL EDUCATION FOUNDATION
www.cmef.ca

MULTICULTURALISM (CITIZENSHIP AND IMMIGRATION CANADA)
www.cic.gc.ca/english/multiculturalism/index.asp

CANADIAN RACE RELATIONS FOUNDATION
www.crr.ca

MULTICULTURAL EDUCATION INTERNET RESOURCE GUIDE
http://jan.ucc.nau.edu/~jar/Multi.html

STOP RACISM AND HATE COLLECTIVE
www.stopracism.ca/pages/home.php

Further Reading

Early, C. (2005, Summer). Meeting the needs of ESL/ELD learners in the classroom. *ETFO Voice*, 21–24.

Quicho, A.L., & Ulanoff, S.H. (2009). *Differentiated literacy instruction for English language learners*. Boston: Allyn & Bacon.

Travers, P., & Klein, G. (Eds.) (2004). *Equal measures: Ethnic minority and bilingual pupils in secondary schools*. Stoke on Trent, UK: Trentham Books.

Adelman Reyes, S., & Vallone, T.L. (2008). *Constructivist strategies for teaching English language learners*. Thousand Oaks, CA: Corwin Press.

Soltero, S. (2011). *Schoolwide approaches to educating ELLs: Creating linguistically and culturally responsive K–12 schools*. Toronto, ON: Pearson Education Canada.

Arroyo, E. (2012). *A+RISE: Research-based instructional strategies for ELLs*. Toronto, ON: Pearson Education Canada.

it was for them to learn English and French in order to participate in the community and Canadian democracy (Bangou & Fleming, 2014).

Welcoming Students

Establish a procedure for welcoming ELL students, immigrants, and refugees and their parents to your classroom. Elementary schools often involve the principal and ESL teacher, while secondary schools may include a counsellor. Whenever possible, an ELL student should be placed in a class where another student speaks the same first language. Many schools hold an informal interview with the student, parents, and an interpreter in the home language. If you sense reluctance to answer particular questions, delay these questions until a later interview. Provide the family with information in a language that they can understand: school information (hours, special days, etc.) and community information (about adult ELL classes, daycare facilities, ethnic associations, and the Red Cross telephone number) (Hamilton & Moore, 2004). You can collect relevant information about the student's linguistic and academic background through the interview and through assessment. Using inclusive ways to engage parents of refugee students (such as cultural brokers or liaisons who speak their language) has proven very effective (Georgis et al., 2014). Before a new student arrives, try to teach your class and fellow teachers to say "Hello" in the new student's language. Teach your students about refugees and why they are forced to leave their homes (http://equitas.org/en/what-we-do/human-rights-defenders-and-educators/ghrep).

Teaching Strategies

The ELL students will be quiet, even silent, in their early days in your classroom. They may be figuring out how to fit in. Remain warm and accepting, even if they are silent for a few months. Observe how the student interacts with someone who understands her first language—a friend in the class or a translator. When ELL students understand little of what you are teaching, you can feel unsure about how to begin. The following list highlights what to focus on in the early weeks:

- Make the student feel comfortable; use non-verbal communication to show warmth.
- Encourage the student to continue speaking their first language at home.
- Seat the student with a classmate who speaks the same language, if possible.
- Seat the student with classmates you know will be welcoming; buddies and tutors can be very helpful.
- Teach frequently used vocabulary first.
- Use visual aids, gestures, concrete materials, games, puzzles (age-appropriate).
- Speak in short, simple sentences.
- Stress the use of first-language skills.
- Use student translators in teaching content areas.
- If a large number of students speak the same second language, place them in pairs (later singly) into co-operative learning groups so they interact with English speakers.
- Suggest that the new student bring maps, pictures, and articles from his home country, but don't push if you see reluctance. (Remember the case of Ragu from the opening of this chapter. He had many memories of his country that he wanted to forget. Be sensitive to this possibility.)

Weblinks

UNHCR, THE UNITED NATIONS REFUGEE AGENCY
www.unhcr.org

NEW HORIZONS FOR LEARNING: "THE MULTICULTURAL CLASSROOM: TEACHING REFUGEE AND IMMIGRANT CHILDREN"
http://education.jhu.edu/PD/newhorizons

STRANGERS BECOMING US (TEACHING MATERIALS FOR ELEMENTARY SCHOOLS)
www.classroomconnections.ca/en/sbuelementary.php

STRANGERS BECOMING US (TEACHING MATERIALS FOR SECONDARY SCHOOLS)
www.classroomconnections.ca/en/sbusecondary.php

Put into Practice

Read from the following list of resources. Consider how you could help to alleviate the fears of a child or adolescent about terrorism or of a student with a parent deployed in the military. Think about what you could do and then consider the limits to your expertise. Locate a national organization and a community organization that employ professionals with expertise in counselling children and adolescents who fear war or terrorism. Build a list of resources (books, videos, websites, and human resources) that you could share with your colleagues.

Moses, L.F., Aldridge, J., Cellitti, A., & McCorquodale, G. (2003). *Children's fears of war and terrorism: A resource for teachers and parents*. Olney, MD: Association for Childhood Education International.

Ellis, D. (2008). *Off to war: Voices of soldiers' children*. Toronto, ON: Groundwood Books.

Arond, M. (Ed.). (2006). *Feeling safe: Talking to children about war and terrorism*. Darby, PA: Diane Publishing Co.

Put into Practice

Some ELL students also have disabilities. Look for resources to help these students to succeed in the classroom. To get you started, here are three recent Canadian resources:

Cannon, J.E., & Guardino, C. (2012). Literacy strategies for deaf/hard-of-hearing English language learners: Where do we begin? *Deafness & Education International, 14*(2), 78–99.

Gunning, P., & Oxford, R.L. (2014). Children's learning strategy use and the effects of strategy instruction on success in learning ESL in Canada. *System, 43*, 82–100.

Paradis, J., Schneider, P., & Sorenson Duncan, T. (2013). Discriminating children with language impairment among English-language learners from diverse first language backgrounds. *Journal of Speech, Language, and Hearing Research, 56*, 971–981.

Cross-Reference
Chapter 9 focuses on adapting assessment to meet the needs of all students in your classroom.

Communicating High Expectations

You can communicate high expectations in many ways. Encourage group rehearsal before selecting individuals to respond to questions. Wait long enough for a response so students can ask peers for help with translation. Provide supportive feedback. Pay attention to, and interact with, all students. Try to group students heterogeneously for activities. Ensure that your expectations grow and that students have to stretch a bit more on each new assignment, and never provide more assistance than students need.

Adapting Assessment

Because language plays a large role in most means of assessment, this creates challenges for assessing ELL students equitably. Students may know what you have taught but be unable to verbalize their understanding. If you use essay questions, ELL students have difficulty with the writing demands, and if you use multiple-choice questions, they may have difficulty with the reading demands. In both instances their English language knowledge may prevent them from showing what they know. Try using true/false questions, completion questions, and identification questions in which a series of simple statements can be labelled with the concept they describe (see Reiss, 2008). You can observe ELL students or conference individually, use instructions like "point to," "draw," and "find the page about." A peer may be able to translate, or a translator may be able to tell you the contents of an assignment written in the student's first language. Use performance-based assessment or portfolio assessment and provide models of what is expected. In the early days you can implement a simple system of grades, such as: = (meets expectations), + (exceeds expectations), and − (does not meet expectations). Ensure that the student understands your feedback about what was done well and what was done poorly. Generally, ask students how they prefer to learn and consult an ESL teacher when you have questions.

Other Issues of Equity in the Classroom

Responding to Incidents in Your Classroom

In classrooms characterized by diversity, you may see incidents of racism, sexism, or bullying. When you set the class rules, be clear that such behaviours are unacceptable in your classroom; focus on equity. When students fail to meet your expectations for respectful and equitable treatment, you must act. If you do not have effective procedures for responding to such incidents, you will not have the safe community necessary for inclusive education. Figure 6.4 describes a problem-solving approach for responding to such incidents.

Proactive Teaching to Minimize Incidents in Your Classroom

It is important that you take action from the first day; that sets the tone of community and establishes how students are to treat one another. Model respectful and equitable treatment, and teach these ways of behaving and thinking. Students act differently in different situations depending on what is expected of them. That is why you may find a class to be co-operative and eager learners, while another teacher may describe

FIGURE 6.4 FRAMEWORK FOR ANALYZING EQUITY INCIDENTS IN THE CLASSROOM

Ask yourself:

1. Is _____ part of what is happening here? (Put in *racism*, *sexism*, etc.)

2. Who was present and/or involved in the situation? Who must be included in the intervention/response? (All who witnessed must see support given and see that the actions are not condoned.)

3. Who does this situation affect? How does it affect them? (Support the victims and teach all who witnessed. Punishment of the perpetrator may be required.)

4. Was the behaviour conscious or unconscious? Was malice involved? (Intervention should address intent, carelessness, or both.)

5. What can you achieve with an intervention? (Teach students what is unacceptable and what is acceptable, and the reasons.)

6. What actions must be taken and why? (Immediately support victim, address perpetrator. Over time teach for prevention.)

Equity education means tailoring teaching to challenge inequities and discrimination.

---

them as unmanageable. Implementing collaborative and co-operative learning may be the most effective proactive approach for secondary school classes (see Damini, 2014; Gillies et al., 2007; Pedersen & Digby, 2014).

Issues of Gender Equity

SEXUAL HARASSMENT

Both males and females can experience sexual harassment. The researchers in a large study in Ontario concluded that "the young women involved in this project experienced strong feelings of humiliation, fear, and suffering as a result of sexual harassment. They came together to express their anger that schools had done nothing to effectively prevent or penalize it" (Ontario Secondary School Teachers' Federation, 1995, p. 3). A decade later, Peter Joong and Olive Ridler (2005) of Nipissing University found that both middle school and secondary school students and teachers reported experiencing bullying and sexual harassment in their schools. Another decade later Deidre Pike (2012) of Hamilton, Ontario urges schools to take this issue seriously and ensure that schools are safe places for all students regardless of their gender or sexual orientation.

Sexual harassment refers to talking about and interacting with people as if they were sexual objects (Meyer, 2010). This includes put-downs and negative comments made about gender or sexual preference, sexist jokes, and calling someone gay or lesbian. Other examples include inappropriate staring, bragging about sexual ability, demanding dates or sexual favours, rating people on a scale, displaying sexually offensive pictures or graffiti, and intimidating behaviour such as blocking a person's way. Anne Lacasse and Morton Mendelson (2006) of McGill University found that 70 percent of Québec high school students reported experiencing at least one moderately offensive sexual behaviour, while over 25 percent experienced at least one severe non-coercive behaviour. A study in Newfoundland (Duffy et al., 2004) suggests that being sexually harassed has psychological consequences for high school students. Students say they don't report incidents because most teachers never do anything about them (Joong & Ridler, 2005). Ensure that you are a teacher

Cross-Reference
Chapters 7 and 10 discuss many effective, proactive programs, as well as co-operative and collaborative learning, and provide strategies for enhancing social relationships in the classroom.

Put into Practice

Develop a classroom activity for your students after reading one of the following:

Robertson, J., Andrews, B., Cook, S.A., & Stanley, T. (1998). *Words can change the world.* Toronto: OADE/OWD.

Wallace, J., & Harper, H. (1998). *Taking action: Reworking gender in school contexts.* Toronto: OADE/OWD (includes video).

Gay, Lesbian and Straight Education Network (GLSEN). (2012). *Playgrounds and prejudice: Elementary school climate in the United States.* New York, NY: GLSEN.

Further Reading

On teaching gay and lesbian students:

Southern Poverty Law Center. (2013). *Best practices: Creating an LGBT-inclusive school climate (A teaching tolerance guide for school leaders.)* Montgomery, AL: Southern Poverty Law Center. Retrieved at www.splcenter.org

Pike, D. (2012, Summer). The gift of positive space groups: A transformation for LGBTQ students. *Education Canada,* 28–30.

Pike, D. (2010). *Creating and supporting LGBTQ positive space groups in the Hamilton-Wentworth District School Board: A resource guide for secondary school administrators, teachers and support staff.* Retrieved at www.sprc.hamilton.on.ca/reports.php

Peterkin, A., & Risdon, C. (2003). *Caring for lesbian and gay people: A clinical guide.* Toronto, ON: University of Toronto Press.

Gay, Lesbian and Straight Education Network (GLSEN). (2012). *Playgrounds and prejudice: Elementary school climate in the United States.* New York, NY: GLSEN.

Lipkin, A. (2004). *Beyond Diversity Day: A Q & A on gay and lesbian issues in schools.* Boulder, CO: Rowman and Littlefield.

Baker, J.M. (2002). *How homophobia hurts children: Nurturing diversity at home, at school, and in the community.* New York, NY: Harrington Park Press.

Canadian Teachers' Federation. (2005). *Lessons learned: A collection of stories and articles about bisexual, gay, lesbian, and transgender issues.* Ottawa, ON: Canadian Teachers' Federation.

Elementary Teachers' Federation of Ontario. (2004). *Imagine a world free from fear: A K to grade 8 resource addressing issues related to homophobia and heterosexism.* Toronto, ON: Elementary Teachers' Federation of Ontario.

Rasmussen, M.L. (2006). *Becoming subjects: Sexualities and secondary schooling.* New York, NY: Routledge.

Planned Parenthood of Toronto. (2004). *Hear me out: True stories of teens educating and confronting homophobia.* Toronto, ON: Second Story Press.

Students who are gay or lesbian are at risk for identity confusion, bullying, and suicide. They need teacher support and safe spaces.

who acts. Urge your school and district to develop, display, and enforce anti-harassment policies. Recent research suggests that dating violence is a serious and prevalent threat for adolescents (Runciman, 2012; Wolfe et al., 2009). Resources to combat sexual harassment appear on the Still Not Laughing website (www.osstf.on.ca/SNL).

INEQUITABLE TREATMENT OF GAY, LESBIAN, BISEXUAL, AND TRANSSEXUAL YOUTH

"I was around thirteen when I realized what I was and the more I found out, the more scared I became" (the words of an 18-year-old lesbian; Baker, 2005). Gay and lesbian, bisexual, and transgender (GLBT) youth who are questioning and exploring their sexual identity are also targets of discrimination (Saewyc et al., 2006). Sexual orientation harassment or **homophobia** takes the form of taunts, ridicule, and physical assaults. Seeing the way others are treated causes many gay and lesbian youth to hide their sexual orientation. This can cause feelings of alienation, depression, self-abuse, and confusion about sexual identity (Baker, 2005; Williams et al., 2005), putting students at greater risk for poor school performance, criminality, substance abuse, dropping out, and suicide. Misunderstanding and rejection by their families can lead to homelessness. Attempted suicide rates are higher for gay and lesbian students than for their heterosexual peers (sometimes estimated as much as three times higher) (Borowsky et al., 2001). Do not tolerate teasing, bullying, or harassment based on sexual orientation.

The rainbow is a symbol understood by gay and lesbian students to indicate support for them. Many school boards offer "Safe Spaces" programs that teach teachers how to communicate that their classrooms are safe spaces for GLBT students and to ensure the safety of their classrooms. If your school district does not have such a program, you might talk with the youth officer in your local police force to learn about community supports. The National Film Board has released a film for elementary students called *Apples and Oranges* (2003). For ideas on how to use this video as a

FIGURE 6.5 SUPPORTING GLBT STUDENTS

- Provide safe, non-discriminatory environments in which all students are valued.
- Learn about the social, psychological, and educational needs of GLBT youth.
- Make no assumption about sexuality. Use language that is broad, inclusive, and gender neutral (e.g., "Are you seeing anyone?" rather than "Do you have a boyfriend?")
- Guarantee confidentiality with students. Respect their privacy.
- Challenge homophobia, heterosexism, and stereotyping in school and society.
- Help students obtain appropriate services from agencies and professionals who are sensitive and trained to deal with GLBT issues.
- Make it clear that language has power and that abusive language will not be tolerated.
- Provide role models, including gay adults.
- Do not advise youth to come out to their families or friends. They need to come out at their own pace. Many have to leave their family home after coming out, so it should be their decision.
- Discuss diversity in families and family structures.
- Enforce your school's policies on sexual harassment, anti-violence, and anti-discrimination.
- Encourage your school administration to implement clear policies on anti-homophobia. These are more effective for supporting GLBT students than general anti-discrimination policies. Get involved in helping to create and enforce such policies.

Sources consulted: Salend, S.J. (1998). *Effective mainstreaming: Creating inclusive classrooms* (3rd ed.) Toronto: Prentice Hall; Pike (2012), and Creating safe schools for lesbian and gay students: A resource guide for school staff (http://twood.tripod.com/guide.html).

teaching tool, consult Russell and Solomon (2004). Deidre Pike (2010) has developed a resource guide for *Creating and Supporting LGBTQ Positive Space Groups*. Baboudjan and colleagues (2011) report the experience of a teacher with a Positive Space sign in her classroom who had a student tell her that just seeing that sign there every day got him through the day. See Figure 6.5 for ways you can support GLBT students. One secondary school teacher reminded us all, "Teachers and administrators are professionals . . . they have to accept gays and lesbians for who they are and treat them with the same respect they treat everybody else" (Baker, 2005).

Weblinks

THE RAINBOW EDUCATORS' NETWORK
www.gol.com/users/aidsed/rainbow

WE ARE FAMILY
www.waf.org

PARENTS, FAMILIES, FRIENDS, AND ALLIES OF LESBIANS AND GAYS
www.pflag.org

BEING LGBTQ IN TODAY'S HIGH SCHOOL
www.cea-ace.ca/video (search videos using the tag "gender")

Teaching Students Who Are at Risk Due to Poverty, Homelessness, and Abuse

In this section the characteristics and needs of at-risk students are described. Poverty, homelessness, and abuse are explored for their impact on learning and classroom participation. Figure 6.6 provides an annotated bibliography of recent sources on the mental health of these at-risk students.

Teaching Students Who Live in Poverty

Living in **poverty** in Canada means having difficulty covering the basic essentials of food, shelter, and clothing. It means having to use food banks each month, and living in overcrowded or substandard housing. And for an increasing number of Canadians, including families with children, it may mean having no roof at all. In 2013 Statistics Canada reported that about 9 percent of Canadians had low enough incomes to be considered poor. These Canadian families do not have the amount of income that it takes to live and participate in Canadian society.

FIGURE 6.6 ANNOTATED BIBLIOGRAPHY OF RECENT SOURCES ON THE MENTAL HEALTH OF AT-RISK STUDENTS WHO EXPERIENCE POVERTY, HOMELESSNESS, BULLYING, AND ABUSE

The issues that place children and adolescents at risk in school have been shown to increase the likelihood that they will experience mental health challenges in school and in their life outside of school.

Academically At-Risk Students and Mental Health Issues: Information for Educators (2014)

by Steven Shaw, *Communiqué, 34*(1), 23.

This brief, highly readable summary makes six recommendations for educators: (a) spend time with students at risk, (b) teach social skills, (c) promote leisure activities, (d) enhance motivation, (e) use effective behaviour management, (f) emphasize parent involvement.

Mental Health and Poverty in the Inner City (2013)

by U. Anakwenze & D. Zuberi, *Health & Social Work, 38*(3), 147–157.

This review shows that there is a cyclical relationship between mental illness and poverty with each reinforcing the other. The authors argue that a comprehensive health care and educational approach is required to break this cycle.

The Prevalence of Mental Illness in Homeless Children: A Systematic Review and Meta-Analysis (2015)

by Ellen Bassuk, Molly Richard, & Alexander Tsertsvadze, *Journal of the American Academy of Child & Adolescent Psychiatry, 54*(2), 86–96.

School-age homeless children have a rate of mental health problems that is two to four times that of children living in poverty, which is already quite high. These problems frequently present as behaviour problems at school and may require sensitive and supportive interventions.

Cumulative Bullying Victimization: An Investigation of the Dose-Response Relationship between Victimization and the Associated Mental Health Outcomes, Social Supports, and School Experiences of Rural Adolescents (2014)

by Caroline Evans, Paul Smokowski, & Katie Cotter, *Children and Youth Services Review, 44*, 256–264.

The more the rural adolescents in this study were the victims of bullying, the more they exhibited negative mental health functioning, social relationships, and school experiences. Because bullying at school is accompanied by cyberbullying at home, adolescents could not escape it. They felt rejected by teachers and peers who did not intervene.

Impacts of Family and Community Violence Exposure on Child Coping and Mental Health (2015)

by Esror Tamim Mohammad, Esther Shapiro, Laurel Wainwright, & Alice Carter, *Journal of Abnormal Child Psychology, 43*(2), 203–215.

Family violence was associated with post-traumatic stress disorder, and community violence with anxiety and aggression. Interventions that focus on emotionally-regulated coping (ERC) may be effective because ERC appeared to play a protective role for children's mental health in contexts where they were exposed to violence.

We have associated poverty with poor academic performance, and data have suggested that students who perform poorly in school have difficulty changing their economic status and that of their children later in life (e.g., Berliner, 2009). In a recent study, Doug Willms of the University of New Brunswick and his colleagues reported a widening gap in achievement between students of higher and lower socioeconomic families as the students get older; from 7 to 11 years of age, the gap was consistent and then grew gradually for students from 11 to 15 (Caro et al., 2009).

In earlier studies Willms found that unfavourable cognitive and social outcomes in school were related to four factors in addition to family income: the "style" of parenting in the home, the cohesiveness of the family unit, the mental health of the mother, and the extent to which parents engage with their children in learning and play activities (2002a, 2002b).

Children in low-income families are more likely to experience parental neglect, to witness violence, and to change schools frequently, and these disruptions can affect their mental health and show up as behaviour problems at school (McKinney, 2014; Miller et al., 2014). Poor children often come to school tired and stressed. They may lack nutritious meals, a quiet place to do homework, basic school supplies, warm clothes in winter, and the footwear needed for gym class. However, research like that of Willms, discussed above, shows that children in some low-income families will not be vulnerable, so as educators we must be careful not to stereotype our students or their parents.

There are many things we can do to make children less vulnerable at school. Healthy snacks, such as apples and granola bars (beware of allergies), and school supplies (e.g., pencils and erasers) can be kept in the classroom for students who need them. Some elementary schools collect winter clothing and teachers invite children to stay after school to choose mittens or a warm hat. Sometimes students may be preoccupied about their families' circumstances. Older students may be expected to work weekends and evenings to support the family or to miss school to babysit younger siblings. All of these things can affect students' concentration and learning.

The view that poverty causes school difficulties may be questioned today (for controversy on the topic, see Rothstein, 2008), but it is important to remember that students who live in poverty are <u>more likely</u> to be at risk for health problems, inattention, friends who are poor role models, low achievement in math and vocabulary, not participating in organized sports, and dropping out of school without employment. Social support of parents, neighbourhood services, teachers, and well-behaved peers, along with persistence and understanding the value of educational attainment,

Further Reading

About Canadian research on resilience:

Kanevesky, L., Corke, M., & Frangkiser, L. (2008). The academic resilience and psychosocial characteristics of inner-city English learners in a museum-based school program. *Education and Urban Society, 40*(4), 452–475.

Kordich Hall, D., & Pearson, J. (2005). Resilience—giving children the skills to bounce back. *Education & Health, 23*(1), 12–15.

McMahon, B.J. (2007). Resilience factors and processes: No longer at risk. *The Alberta Journal of Educational Research, 53*(2), 127–142.

Grover, S. (2005). Advocacy by children as a causal factor in promoting resilience. *Childhood, 12*(4), 527–538.

DeLuca, C., Hutchinson, N. L., deLugt, J., Beyer, W., Thornton, A., Versnel, J., Chin, P., & Munby, H. (2010). Learning in the workplace: Fostering resilience in disengaged youth. *Work: A Journal of Prevention, Assessment & Rehabilitation, 36*, 305–319.

Put into Practice

Read a resource on poverty and its relationship to school engagement and success. Develop a plan that you could implement in your classroom to help students living in poverty to feel safe and to be successful learners. Here are some written resources. Search for relevant online resources as well. Exchange resources with your peers.

Berliner, D.C. (2009). *Poverty and potential: Out-of-school factors and school success*. Boulder, CO: Education and the Public Interest Center and Education Policy Research Unit. Retrieved at http://epicpolicy.org/publication/poverty-and-potential.

Miller, P., Pavlakis, A., Lac, V., & Hoffman, D. (2014). Responding to poverty and its complex challenges: The importance of policy fluency for educational leaders. *Theory Into Practice, 53*, 131–138.

McKinney, S. (2014). The relationship of child poverty to school education. *Improving Schools, 17*(3), 213–216.

Mandy Godbehear/Shutterstock

Schools continually seek ways to reduce bullying and cyberbullying.

The Concept of Resilience in Children and Adolescents

While it is generally agreed that the concept of resilience refers to positive adaptation in the face of adversity, there have been many distinct approaches to understanding this important idea. There have also been a number of waves of research within these approaches that have broadened our understanding. Researchers are currently embarking on a fourth wave.

One approach to understanding resilience, a developmental approach, is largely behavioural in focus, and probably best exemplified by the research of Ann Masten of the University of Minnesota. She argues that in the first wave, researchers generated a short list of potential assets or protective factors associated with resilience (good coping despite risk) in children and adolescents (Masten & Obradovic, 2006). These included personality and disposition of the child and supportive adults. Then in the second wave, researchers tried to uncover what enables these personal and environmental protective factors to function in a protective manner for the child or adolescent. In the third wave, researchers concentrated on the nature of actions that would promote resilience through prevention, intervention, and policy (e.g., helping families to raise their children in healthy ways even when they were facing difficult circumstances). Such programs have had names like Better Beginnings.

Much of the research referred to in Masten and Obradovic (2006) was conducted by clinical psychologists and researchers in psychiatry and human development. The threats they focused on included poverty, divorce, war, natural disasters, and bereavement. The criteria for positive adaptation were diverse, including school achievement, getting along with peers, psychological well-being, and success on tasks appropriate for the developmental period of the child or adolescent. The fourth wave of research involves more complex studies that use powerful statistical tools to identify positive pathways of development or recovery among groups who have experienced very high adversity exposure or trauma. The intent is to understand subgroups that follow different pathways.

A competing model has used a constructivist approach to understand the experience of individuals who have experienced adversity and demonstrated resilience in the face of great odds. Michael Ungar, a social worker conducting research at Dalhousie University, has taken a "practical" theoretical approach that focuses extensively on interventions. He has been associated with the Phoenix Youth Program in Halifax, which works with at-risk and homeless youth, an example of putting theory into action in effective interventions (2008). He emphasizes processes that build on individuals' strengths; the notion that there are many routes or pathways to resilience, including effective educational programs; and the need for social justice as a foundation for successful personal development. An issue that has recently come to prominence in Ungar's work is the need for culturally- and contextually-sensitive approaches to resilience (2011).

Ungar has reworked the definition of resilience to emphasize the need for individuals to exercise personal agency to navigate, or make their way to, the resources they require (2005a, 2005b). Social workers, educators, and others can intervene to help the individual youth to accomplish this. He describes these resources as psychological resources as well as community resources such as health care, school, and family. As well as navigation, Ungar emphasizes the importance of negotiation, that is, for communities to negotiate culturally meaningful ways for resources to be shared.

Recently Ungar has analyzed how educational institutions can develop pathways to resilience, build on strengths, and enable at-risk youth and their families and communities to navigate toward and negotiate for the individualized resources they need. He talks of substituting rather than suppressing behaviours (2006). Researchers have begun to analyze educational programs like work-based education (WBE) to identify whether they satisfy Ungar's criteria for enabling navigation and negotiation and substituting effective behaviours in a new context for ineffectual behaviours in classroom contexts experienced as adversity. DeLuca and his colleagues (2010) describe and compare the experiences of two at-risk youth, Ashley and Tim, enrolled in WBE who were learning in workplaces judged likely to promote resilience, and highlight how supportive adults and at-risk youth engage in interactions that facilitate the emergence of resilience in the workplace.

Joan Versnel of Dalhousie University (Versnel et al., 2011) argues that WBE programs, like co-operative education, where adolescents learn in workplaces, enable youth who have experienced the regular classroom as an adverse environment to thrive in an alternative learning context. Versnel brings together Ungar's concepts of navigation and negotiation in the field of resilience with cases of youth in WBE, and shows how students who experience the traditional academic program as adverse can act agentically and select WBE as a pathway to resilience. Versnel shows that WBE programs can harness the potential of the protective factors that are already known to foster resilience, including parental involvement, development of outside interests, and connection with a non-related adult.

Recent research suggests that the concept of resilience may be relevant for shaping and differentiating the education of at-risk children and adolescents in Canadian schools.

References

DeLuca, C., Hutchinson, N.L., deLugt, J., Beyer, W., Thornton, A., Versnel, J., Chin, P., & Munby, H. (2010). Learning in the workplace: Fostering resilience in disengaged youth. *Work: A Journal of Prevention, Assessment & Rehabilitation, 36*, 305–319.

Masten, A.S., & Obradovic, J. (2006). Competence and resilience in development. *Annals of the New York Academy of Science, 1094*, 13–27.

Ungar, M. (2005a). Pathways to resilience among children in child welfare, corrections, mental health, and educational settings: Navigation and negotiation. *Child and Youth Care Forum, 34* (6), 423–442.

Ungar, M. (2005b). Resilience among children in child welfare, corrections, mental health and educational settings: Recommendations for service. *Child and Youth Care Forum, 34* (6), 445–464.

Ungar, M. (2006). Strengths-based counseling with at-risk youth. Thousand Oaks, CA: Corwin Press.

Ungar, M. (2008). Putting resilience theory into action: Five principles for intervention. In L. Liebenberg & M. Ungar (Eds.), Resilience in action (pp. 17–38). Toronto: University of Toronto Press.

Ungar, M. (2011). The social ecology of resilience: Addressing contextual and cultural ambiguity of a nascent construct. *American Journal of Orthopsychiatry, 18*, 1-17.

Versnel, J., DeLuca, C., de Lugt, J., Hutchinson, N.L., & Chin, P. (2011). Work-based education as a pathway to resilience. *Journal of Educational and Vocational Research, 2* (5), 143–153.

contribute to better social and school outcomes (Mo & Singh, 2008; Molnar et al., 2008). When teachers and school counsellors create a culture of encouragement and participation where students feel they belong and can express their aspirations, students are more likely to overcome the challenges associated with their life circumstances (Uwah et al., 2008). Research by Michael Ungar of Dalhousie University has been directed at understanding resilience, what he has called "drifting toward mental health" and "the process of empowerment" (2000). He argues that communities, schools, and families can help at-risk children and adolescents to exercise personal agency and take responsibility (Ungar, 2004; see also Armstrong et al., 2005). And, among the more culturally pluralistic communities in Canada, we need to encourage many definitions of successful growth (Ungar, 2006, 2007). **Resilient students** tend to develop attributes, such as social competence, problem-solving skills, autonomy, and a sense of purpose and future. Families, schools, and communities that protect at-risk youth tend to be caring and supportive, have positive expectations, show humility, and provide opportunities for participation. See the Educational Psychology box for more on resilience.

Education is seen as part of the solution to poverty because good teaching raises achievement for all students. Good teaching includes targeted interventions, high expectations, programs that enhance family-school teamwork, collaborative learning, and effective teams of community professionals working with educators.

Teaching Students Who Have Experienced Homelessness

Some children and adolescents are **homeless**. A family's loss of its home is always traumatic; it can be sudden or can be experienced as "doubling up" with family and friends before going to a shelter or living on the street. They may move from shelter to shelter and eventually move to the street. The family is often thrust away from its community, friends, and support system, and the effects can be devastating. Canada's

> ### Further Reading
>
> Find a written resource and an online resource to supplement the book by Barone identified here. Describe three actions teachers can take, at the grade level that you teach, to ensure that they are part of the solution in supporting students in high-poverty schools.
>
> Barone, D.M. (2006). *Narrow the literacy gap: What works in high-poverty schools.* New York: Guilford Press.

homeless population is estimated to be 200 000 (Gaetz et al., 2013), while another 1.7 million people struggle with finding affordable housing (Laird, 2007). Often homeless children do not attend school regularly and, when they do attend, they feel unconnected to school and participate little in extracurricular activities (White, 2010). Obstacles to school attendance include health problems, hunger, lack of transportation, and lack of school clothes and supplies. When homeless children attend school, you may see socialization and behavioural problems, language delays, and self-esteem problems (Grant et al., 2013). They often face stigmatization and rejection by classmates and teachers. Mohan and Shields (2014) give voice to six children who live in a shelter, their family's car, or a hotel: Ramona, who is 13, says, "It is hard to concentrate on my schoolwork. I don't want anyone to know about my family; when I talk about it, it hurts" (p. 194); and Mariah (10 years old) says, "Finally things are starting to get better for me at school, and I am really worried that I will have to change schools again" (p. 193).

Students' academic achievement drops in the face of homelessness (Cutuli et al., 2013). Teachers can be a powerful force in their lives, helping them academically and emotionally (Kottler & Kottler, 2006). Be sensitive and accepting. When a student transfers into your class, be prepared with school supplies and find a private way for the student to choose clothes from a supply kept at the school. Communicate with the previous teacher; when a student transfers to another school, try to contact the next teacher. Refer students to counsellors and differentiate teaching to help students keep up in spite of absences. Do what you can to aid homeless students in making friends and do not tolerate bullying or victimization.

Adolescents may be homeless due to a history of negative experiences with their family; for example, one paper is titled "We're locking the door" (Alvi et al., 2010). Homeless adolescents often live a **transient lifestyle**, moving from shelter to shelter, in unstable conditions, without adult guidance except perhaps that of a concerned teacher. Others live on the streets and are vulnerable to using and pushing drugs and to mental health problems (Kirst et al., 2011). Sean Kidd of McMaster University has studied the social stigma experienced by street youth (Kidd & Evans, 2011) and factors that contribute to their suicide attempts (Cleverley & Kidd, 2011). Some make the brave move to return to school only to leave before obtaining credits for their courses. They need encouragement, support, and differentiated teaching. Often if they can connect with one teacher and one peer, they have enough support to persevere. Educational dreams can be a powerful motivator for youth trying to get off the streets (Brown & Amundson, 2010). School administrators and probation officers can be effective advocates for keeping youth in school if they communicate their belief in the young person to achieve their goals (Carter & Leschied, 2010).

Teaching Students Who Have Experienced Abuse

Reports of **child abuse**, **neglect**, psychological harm, sexual abuse, and children observing violence have increased (National Clearinghouse on Family Violence; www.phac-aspc.gc.ca/ncfv-cnivf/index-eng.php). Contributing factors are thought to be unemployment, poverty, unwanted pregnancy, substance abuse, and adults' history of abuse during childhood (Newland, 2014). Being abused may lead to higher rates of sexual promiscuity, alcohol use, other risky behaviours, and impaired intellectual functioning.

Figure 6.7 lists signs that may suggest a student is being abused. If you suspect child abuse or neglect, it is your responsibility to report your concerns to the child

Put into Practice

Consult resources about youth and homelessness, such as the following, and talk with your peers about what teachers can do to ensure that they connect with homeless students who choose to return to school:

Calos, M. (Producer, Director). (2004). *The fifth estate: No way home* [video recording]. Toronto: Canadian Broadcasting Corporation.

Grant, R. et al. (2013). Twenty-five years of child and family homelessness: Where are we now? *American Journal of Public Health, 103*(S2), e1–e10.

Weblinks

FOR INFORMATION ON BREAKFAST CLUBS, SEE:

THE HUMAN LEAGUE ASSOCIATION
http://humanleaguesudbury.com

BREAKFAST CLUB OF CANADA
www.breakfastclubcanada.org

FIGURE 6.7 SIGNS OF ABUSE

Note: These lists need to be used with caution as some of these indicators may reflect problems other than child abuse. Recognition of child abuse relies on the recognition of several indicators over a period of time.

Signs of Physical Abuse

If a child is being physically abused, you may see the following **physical indicators**:

- Unexplained bruises, welts, and abrasions; especially on the face, back, buttocks, or thighs; sometimes in the shape of a belt or hairbrush; most often after the child has been absent or after a weekend
- Unexplained burns; from cigarettes on hands, feet, buttocks, back; sometimes in the shape of an iron or electric burner; immersion burns from scalding water
- Unexplained fractures and dislocations; to the skull or facial structure; spiral fractures of the long arm or leg bones
- Inappropriate dress; especially long sleeves or pants in hot weather to cover bruises, burns, etc.
- Unexplained head injuries, including patches of hair pulled out
- Delays in seeking medical attention for any kind of injury

If a child is being physically abused, you may see the following **behavioural indicators**:

- Reports of injury by parents
- Extreme wariness of parents
- Extreme wariness of adults in general
- Wariness of physical contact, especially when initiated by an adult
- Resistance to being touched; pulling away when someone approaches or extends a hand
- Extreme watchfulness
- Fear of going home
- Unexplained prolonged absence; may be kept home while healing
- Unlikely explanations for bruises, burns, etc. or denial of these injuries
- Resistance to undressing to change clothes for physical education
- Poor social relations with peers
- Apprehensiveness when other children cry
- Appearing unhappy, anxious
- Extremes of behaviour from aggressiveness to withdrawal

Signs of Neglect

If a child is being neglected, you may see the following **physical indicators**:

- Attending school hungry or fatigued
- Poor hygiene, dirtiness, lice, skin disorders associated with poor hygiene
- Inappropriate dress; exposure symptoms including sunburn, frostbite, frequent colds, pneumonia
- Unattended health problems
- Inadequate supervision or abandonment
- Frequent absence from school

If a child is being neglected, you may see the following **behavioural indicators**:

- Theft
- Frequently forgets lunch; begging for or stealing food
- Verbal evidence of no caretaker in the home; child's explanations for arriving early, staying late
- Sleeping in class
- Delinquency, alcohol or drug use

Signs of Emotional Abuse

If a child is being abused emotionally, you may see the following **physical indicators**:

- Lags in emotional, mental, or physical development

(continued)

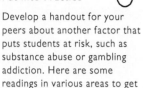

Put into Practice

Develop a handout for your peers about another factor that puts students at risk, such as substance abuse or gambling addiction. Here are some readings in various areas to get you started:

Verbeke, E.M., & Dittrick-Nathan, K. (2008). Student gambling. *The Education Digest, 73*(6), 60–63. (www.eddigest)

Walsh, S.P., White, K.M., & Ross, R.M. (2008). Over-connected? A qualitative exploration of the relationship between Australian youth and their mobile phones. *Journal of Adolescence, 31*(1), 77–92.

Gentile, D.A., & Anderson, C.A. (2006). Violent video games: The effects on youth, and public policy implications, in N. Dowd, D.G. Singer, & R.F. Wilson (Eds.). *Handbook of children, culture and violence,* (pp. 225–246). Thousands Oaks, CA: Sage.

Finn, K.V., & Willert, H.J. (2006). Alcohol and drugs in schools: Teachers' reactions to the problem. *Phi Delta Kappan, 88*(1), 37–40.

Walker, S., Sanci, L., & Temple-Smith, M. (2011). Sexting and young people. *Youth Studies Australia, 30*(4), 8–16.

Shiel, V. (2009, May 22). Indecent exposure. *Times Educational Supplement Magazine,* 16–21. (children's involvement with pornography)

Stone, D.M., et al. (2014). Sexual orientation and suicide ideation. *American Journal of Public Health, 104*(2), 262–271.

FIGURE 6.7 *(continued)*

- Extreme lack of confidence or withdrawal
- Inability to concentrate, continual procrastination
- Excessive desire for teacher's attention
- Has-to-win attitude
- Extreme aggressiveness or passivity when playing with other children
- Over-participation in too many activities

If a child is being abused emotionally, you may see the following **behavioural indicators**:

- Conduct disorders; anti-social and destructive behaviour
- Extreme depression, attempted suicide
- Constant apologies, even when not responsible
- Speech disorders, sleep disorders, inhibition of play
- Fear of failure
- Inappropriate adult behaviours, including "bossing" or disciplining others
- Inappropriate childish behaviours, including throwing tantrums, crying, and sulking
- Sucking, biting, rocking
- Fear of failure, giving up, unwilling to try after even small setbacks

Source: Hutchinson, N.L. (2004). *Teaching exceptional children and adolescents: A Canadian casebook* (pp. 101–102). Toronto: Pearson Education Canada. Reprinted with permission by Pearson Canada Inc.

welfare agency in your community. No province or territory requires the person who suspects abuse to collect evidence to support their suspicion. However, teachers who fail to report suspected abuse could face misconduct charges from their professional organization, be convicted of an offence, fined, or even jailed. As long as a report has been made in good faith, a teacher cannot be sued even if there was no abuse.

When a child tells you about or discloses abuse, listen calmly. Let the child tell the story in her own way. Tell the child that you believe her, that you will do your best to find help, and that you cannot keep this a secret because the law says you must report it. Do not probe for details, but take notes on what the child says, using the child's language. Report the disclosure to the child protection services, the local Children's Aid Society (CAS), immediately. Ask the intake worker if a case will be opened, if a case worker will come to the school, and when updates will be provided. The CAS will determine if the case meets the standard for abuse or neglect. If so, they will open a case and a social worker will have sixty days to investigate and reach a finding. Although it is the goal of CAS to keep children in their home and over 90 percent of children remain in the home, the child will be removed if deemed to be in immediate danger (Trocmé et al., 2010).

Consider that there may be emotional and behavioural repercussions and that such children may need the support and differentiated teaching usually provided for children with behaviour and emotional exceptionalities. Recent research suggests that empowering students by teaching them their human rights fosters resilience and higher engagement in school (Howe & Covell, 2011). Figure 6.8 suggests how you can teach abused students in sensitive and effective ways.

FIGURE 6.8 TEACHING ABUSED STUDENTS IN SENSITIVE AND EFFECTIVE WAYS

Weblinks

CANADIAN CENTRE ON SUBSTANCE ABUSE
www.ccsa.ca

YUKON EDUCATION POLICY ON SUBSTANCE ABUSE
www.education.gov.yk.ca/pdf/policy_substance_abuse.pdf

KIDS HELP PHONE (HAS INFORMATION ON SUBSTANCE ABUSE)
www.kidshelpphone.ca/Teens/InfoBooth/Emotional-Health/Alcohol-And-Drugs.aspx

REPORT ON SUBSTANCE ABUSE AMONG MANITOBA HIGH SCHOOL STUDENTS
http://afm.mb.ca/publications/an-inside-view-vol-7-no-2-2001

1. **Ensure that the classroom is a safe environment.**
   Exercise enough control to keep the student feeling that the classroom is a safe and predictable place. Minimize chaos. You will want to directly teach positive ways to resolve conflict. Do not tolerate violence of any kind (verbal taunts, gestures, or sexual harassment).

2. **Remember that abused children differ and avoid stereotypes.**
   Children's experiences of abuse differ widely, as do their needs. Factors like frequency, duration, and severity of abuse, as well as identity and role of the abuser (family member or other, such as camp counsellor) are influential. The child's characteristics, thoughts about the experience, and social support are all important. You should pay attention to the child in deciding what the child needs from you and support the child's individual development, no matter the rate. Respect the child's expressed need for privacy, quiet time, or time away from noisy, busy activities.

3. **Change takes time, so be patient.**
   Children may persist with inappropriate behaviours after the abuse has stopped. The problem behaviours may even get worse before they improve. Children who have been "spacing out" to avoid dealing with abuse will require time to drop this once-useful habit. Ask what the counsellor suggests the student do instead of "spacing out," and make the same suggestion. Consistency will be reassuring. Other once-useful responses to abuse may include running away or lying.

4. **Be supportive; the child may be under greater stress than ever.**
   Your reporting may have caused others to punish the child. Other possible consequences include ridicule or being called a liar. Sometimes increased violence takes place in the relationships among family members as they are required to take part in court appearances. Income may drop because a member leaves the family. Separation of the parents or incarceration of a family member are also possible as a direct consequence of your report. The child may be held responsible by the family.

5. **Be compassionate, but also be firm with problematic behaviours.**
   Most of the above suggestions include concrete examples of showing the child compassion, which is very important. It is also critical to be firm and address inappropriate behaviours when they occur. The child is still responsible for his actions even though there has been abuse; these actions include internalized and externalized problem behaviours.

6. **Teach the child, expect learning, and promote tangible skills.**
   Use many words of encouragement, support, and informational feedback to create positive experiences at school for the maltreated child. Experiences of maltreatment often cause children to have negative views of themselves. You can contribute to changing these views by helping the child to be able to say, "I am the smart one who is good at math," or "I am the creative one who is good at painting." Hold high expectations for the child and provide high levels of support (and differentiated instruction if it is needed) so the child can reach these expectations. Help the child to recognize small gains, to set realistic proximal goals, and to stay on track learning and moving toward goals.

Resources

Horton, C.B., & Cruise, T.K. (2001). *Child abuse and neglect: The school's response.* New York: Guilford Press.

Youngblade, L.M., & Belsky, J. (1990). Social and emotional consequences of child maltreatment. In R.T. Ammerman & M. Hersen, (Eds.), *Children at risk: An evaluation of factors contributing to child abuse and neglect* (pp. 107–146). New York: Plenum Press.

Source: Hutchinson, N.L. (2004). *Teaching exceptional children and adolescents: A Canadian casebook* (pp. 105–106). Toronto: Pearson Education Canada. Reprinted with permission by Pearson Canada Inc.

Summary

This chapter has dealt with many aspects of teaching for diversity. Aboriginal education has become a greater priority in Canada since the 1996 *Report of the Royal Commission on Aboriginal Peoples*. Because of issues like the preservation of almost-extinct languages and cultures, Aboriginal education is distinct from multicultural education. However, students from diverse cultures and students with English as a second language also require differentiated teaching. For all of these students, high expectations, co-operative learning, culturally responsive curricula, and sensitive teaching are appropriate. Other equity issues that arise in classrooms concern gender and students who are gay, lesbian, bisexual, or transgender. You can teach proactively to reduce the occurrence of inequitable incidents. We also teach students who are at risk for a range of other reasons, including poverty, homelessness, and abuse. However, many of these students are resilient and, with the support of a caring teacher and the friendship of a classmate, can overcome what appear to be great risks. We are challenged to create classrooms that respect diversity and foster learning for *all* students.

Key Terms

Aboriginal cultures (p. 156)
Aboriginal elders (p. 161)
child abuse (p. 180)
co-operative learning (p. 167)
collaborative learning (p. 167)
cultural awareness (p. 164)
culturally diverse backgrounds (p. 163)
culturally relevant pedagogy (p. 165)
culturally responsive teaching (p. 160)

diversity (p. 155)
English as a second language (ESL) (p. 169)
English language learner (ELL) students (p. 169)
equity (p. 156)
heritage languages (p. 163)
homeless (p. 179)
homophobia (p. 174)
immigrants (p. 170)

neglect (p. 180)
poverty (p. 175)
refugees (p. 170)
Report of the Royal Commission on Aboriginal Peoples (RCAP) (p. 156)
resilient students (p. 179)
sexual harassment (p. 173)
transient lifestyle (p. 180)

Challenges for Reviewing Chapter 6

1. Consider the case of Anita Harper, described at the beginning of this chapter. Think about the ways in which teachers can create a welcoming classroom climate and differentiate teaching so students like Anita feel safe and are engaged in our classrooms. What are some of the most important things you can do to ensure this at the grade level at which you teach?

2. Write a brief scenario in which you describe some of the greatest challenges that teachers experience when teaching in schools with high cultural diversity. Include yourself and an examination of your biases and assumptions in your scenario. Describe how you can ensure that all your students feel valued and learn successfully in your classroom. What is the role of differentiated

instruction in this classroom? What else is important for you to be mindful of? Chapters 8 and 10 may help you to answer these questions.

3. You are currently teaching in a school with many ELL students from a wide range of cultural backgrounds. Your principal has shown you the latest document on ELL, and it recommends differentiated instruction (DI). You are familiar with DI from your experience including exceptional learners. Describe how you can use DI to meet the needs of your ELL students. And consider how this approach might be different from using DI to include exceptional learners. How might it be similar?

Activities for Reviewing Chapter 6 with Your Peers

4. Ragu, who was described at the beginning of this chapter, is in your class. You see that he is taunted and treated unfairly by other students. What will you do to respond to these incidents of inequity? How can you ensure that everyone gets the message that this is unacceptable and begins to act differently? Discuss with your peers what you should do as a school as well as what you are doing individually to change situations like this one.

5. You have chosen to teach in a neighbourhood where there are many at-risk students, some of whom live in poverty, have been abused, have experienced family breakdown, or are homeless. Some have had all of these experiences. Describe your efforts to differentiate teaching to meet the needs of these students. Describe some of the schoolwide initiatives that have helped. What resources have been particularly helpful and what resources does your school still need? What are the most important lessons you would share with colleagues newly arrived at your school. With your peers, develop a plan for involving the community in your plans.

6. Return to the opening cases of Ragu and Anita and answer the five questions that follow the cases. Talk with your peers. Consider the differences in answers given by elementary and secondary teachers. Consider the similarities in the issues raised by elementary and secondary teachers.

CHAPTER 7

Climate, Community, and Classroom Management for Student Well-Being

LEARNER OBJECTIVES

After you have read this chapter, you will be able to:

1. Identify and describe the key elements of creating a classroom community that will enhance the well-being and mental health of all its members.

2. Describe developing an inclusive climate: developing relationships with students, physical layout, and norms for interaction.

3. Identify and describe the major parts of negotiating and enforcing classroom rules and procedures.

4. Understand some of the reasons for students' challenging behaviours and strategies for responding.

5. Describe the major components of managing behaviour in an inclusive classroom and explain how they can be differentiated to meet the needs of exceptional students.

6. Consider the advantages and disadvantages of punitive approaches (such as expulsion) and of more positive approaches (such as restorative justice) for classroom management and student well-being.

KidStock/Getty Images

MANDY HAS BEEN AT BAYSIDE SINCE SEPTEMBER. She is in Ms. Turner's grade 6 class. Ms. Turner tells visitors to her classroom how Mandy invited another student who has few close friends to play basketball in the schoolyard. This act of kindness assumes significance when you know the rest of the story. If you had visited Mandy's grade 5 class at another school the previous June, you might have seen Mandy scream at her teacher, punch another student, or storm out of the classroom. It was terrible for Mandy and for her previous teacher. What has changed? Mandy moved to a small school with a caring and involved principal and to Ms. Turner's classroom. Ms. Turner is described as an exemplary teacher—every year children hope they will be in her class. Pre-service teachers love interning with her. They say, "All the kids treat each other so well. There is never any bullying. She won't have it. Everyone belongs." Mandy says, "I like Ms. Turner. She always says 'good morning' to me and makes me feel important. I don't want to let her down. So I try my best. She never lets anyone hurt me and I don't have to hurt anyone back." At her last school, Mandy had been identified as having a behaviour exceptionality. Her principal thought that she needed a fresh start where the students and teachers were unaware of her reputation, with a teacher known for valuing and respecting every student—a teacher like Ms. Turner.

JACOB IS IN GRADE 10. He has cerebral palsy and a learning disability. He uses arm crutches to move around the school. To keep his energy up, Jacob has permission to eat healthy snacks in class. Recently he has been bringing chocolate bars and candy to his history class and has become very popular by handing out treats. Mr. Chan knows he will have to tackle this threat to his orderly classroom. Every day when the grade 10 students enter his history class, they find a "challenge" on their desks and have four minutes to determine, with a partner, which historical figure made the quoted statement. Recently some students have been too busy seeking a treat from Jacob to find solutions to the challenge. Mr. Chan does not approve of bribery, but he has noticed that recently more students talk with Jacob and invite him to join their groups for collaborative activities. Perhaps talking with the resource teacher who tutors Jacob will help Mr. Chan develop a response to the actions of Jacob and his classmates.

1. Under what circumstances could Mandy and Jacob be considered a challenge to the climate, organization, and management of their inclusive classrooms?

2. How can teachers develop classrooms that feel like communities, where all students are respected?

3. How can teachers discuss their approaches to classroom management with their classes and later refer to these discussions when responding to students who challenge order and learning in the classroom?

4. Whom might teachers like Ms. Turner and Mr. Chan turn to for assistance in teaching students to change their actions in the classroom?

5. How can Mr. Chan enable Jacob to eat a healthy snack when he needs it and to maintain his improved peer relations, while preventing bribery and chaos in the classroom?

Cross-Reference
Chapter I focuses on the general context for inclusion in Canadian society, while Chapter 6 emphasizes diversity arising from sources other than exceptionality. Chapter 10 examines social relations between students and how to enhance the inclusion of diverse students.

Put into Practice

Read about creating an inclusive climate. Develop an approach you might use from the first day of school.

Larivee, B. (2008). *Authentic classroom management: Creating a learning community and building reflective practice.* Boston: Allyn & Bacon.

Hensley, M., Powell, W., Lamke, S., & Hartman, S. (2007). *The well-managed classroom: Strategies to create a productive and cooperative social climate in your learning community.* Omaha, NE: Boys Town Press.

Brownlie, F., Feniak, C., & Schnellert, L. (2006). *Student diversity: Classroom strategies to meet the learning needs of all students.* Markham, ON: Pembroke.

Introduction

You can expect to meet exceptional students like Mandy and Jacob in almost every class you teach, which means you will meet challenges like those just described. The purpose of this chapter is to help you to establish relationships with all your students, create a positive classroom climate that contributes to well-being, and use negotiation and management effectively in your teaching. The goal is to create a community in which diversity is encouraged and all students feel their contributions are valued. Because students form their first impressions of their teachers within the first few minutes of meeting them, it is critical that you start off positively—with warmth and energy. These can be lasting impressions, so make the first few minutes of contact count.

Creating a Community

You will be teaching students with many exceptionalities and health conditions. Your classes may include Aboriginal students and others with a multiplicity of ethnic heritages. This diversity reflects our country, and as teachers we must shape an inclusive classroom community in which everyone belongs. Building community is a deliberate process that takes time. Many provinces have recently released documents supporting this process. Examples include *Caring and Respectful Schools: Ensuring Student Well-Being* in Saskatchewan (2004), New Brunswick's *Positive Learning Environment Policy* (2002b), and Newfoundland and Labrador's *Safe and Caring Schools Policy* (2006). Ontario passed the *Safe Schools Act* (2007) and in 2014 adopted *Safe and Accepting Schools* (2014). Schools and their neighbourhoods must work together to ensure that, when at school, students experience community, feel safe, and receive the social and emotional support they need. Many of the approaches described in this chapter are effective for reducing bullying and are appropriate as responses to bullying incidents (Jimerson et al., 2010). Bullying and cyberbullying are a major focus of Chapter 10. Preventing bullying begins with building community (Orpinas & Horne, 2010).

Community involves a sense of belonging, of the group's concern for each individual, of individual responsibility for the good of the group, and of appreciation for shared experiences (Noddings, 1996). This means that classrooms become places where teachers and students talk to each other, learn together, and enjoy each other's company. A supportive, relational community enables children and adolescents to take the risks involved in thinking for themselves and in assuming responsibility for their own learning. With a sense of belonging, students can seek the help of their teachers and learn through peer interaction (Naraian, 2011; Watson & Battistich, 2006). Many approaches contribute to the creation of community. They all emphasize mutual respect and teachers establishing, modelling, and insisting on caring relationships in the classroom. These approaches include a common vision; parents, teachers, students, and others functioning as partners; time for planning and collaboration; and clear communication without jargon. They may help us describe community at the classroom level.

Common Vision

To fashion a common vision, teachers can involve students meaningfully in setting classroom rules and the consequences for not following these rules. Don't assume that the consequences are obvious to all students; recent research suggests that even gifted students benefit from having the consequences of their actions explained clearly (Kaplan, 2008). Students have many ideas about what classrooms can and should be like and they have great energy to work toward their goals (Berry, 2006). Harnessing this energy requires that you provide leadership and a structure for productive student discussion, and that you listen and model behaviour that includes everyone. Ensure that exceptional students have opportunities to participate. Emphasize the importance of **climate**, that is, the general feeling we create when we treat each other respectfully.

Parents, Teachers, and Students as Partners

Many resources are available about team building. Some focus on parents and extended families as partners and on culturally responsive parental involvement (e.g., Goodwin & King, 2002). All students, even secondary students, are more successful when their parents are involved in their education (Jeynes, 2007), and parental participation is even more critical for exceptional learners. Many resources recommend sending letters to parents early in the year and meeting to talk about their priorities for their children's learning. Other strategies include inviting a parent to observe his or her child who is disrupting the class, in order to devise joint approaches for home and school; student-led parent–teacher conferences; and students as peer negotiators. Whatever strategies you choose, focus on creating an equitable community with high-quality communication among all partners (Azzopardi, 2011).

Time for Collaboration and Joint Planning

Set small amounts of scheduled time aside for your students to learn and practise collaboration and joint planning. Include learning outcomes from your curriculum, such as effective oral communication, planning and co-operating, and development of self-awareness. Write plans for these times, list them in your term's teaching plans, and be prepared to explain their role in creating community. Ms. Turner, described in one of the opening cases, spends considerable time during the first few weeks of the school year teaching her students what she expects of them and helping them to collaborate and plan together. She knows that she can easily catch up to the other classes, in the academic realm, in late September because her students know what she expects and she spends less time on management issues throughout the rest of the year. Vicki Gill, an award-winning teacher, agrees: "I spend a great deal of time in the first week creating a sense of community, generating excitement for the curriculum, and setting up classroom expectations" (2007, p. 24). Her two goals for the first week are that every student feels known and that all students understand what will cause a problem in her classroom and how she will react to that problem.

Clear Communication

Model clear use of language and ensure that what you say is understood by all members of the extended classroom community; avoid jargon. Listen to the language others use and point out when people are referring to the same phenomenon by different names. Communicate tactfully so parents don't feel they are being "talked

Further Reading

On creating community in the classroom:

Naraian, S. (2011). Seeking transparency: The production of an inclusive classroom community. *International Journal of Inclusive Education, 15*(9), 955–973.

Obenchain, K.M., & Abernathy, T.V. (2003). Twenty ways to build community and empower students. *Intervention in School and Clinic, 39*(1), 55–60.

Capuzzi, D., & Gross, D. (Eds.). (2004). *Youth at risk: A prevention resource for counselors, teachers, and parents* (4th ed.). Alexandria, VA: American Counseling Association.

Gill, V. (2007). *The ten students you'll meet in your classroom: Classroom management tips for middle and high school teachers.* Thousand Oaks, CA: Corwin Press.

Cross-Reference
Chapter 2 includes many examples of strategies for collaborating with parents.

Making the class inviting is part of your work as a teacher.

kate/Getty Images

down to." If you use a classroom website, maintain other means of communication for families without computer access. Effective teachers who demonstrated CRCM (see Bondy et al., 2007) used words and expressions that were familiar to the students and were used by their cultural group. These teachers also made references to popular culture—movies, musicians, and television programs that the students were familiar with. They gave straightforward directives that were explicit and used no jargon. One teacher said on the first day of school, "This is how it's going to work this morning. People will come in and I will have to go to the door to welcome them to the class. You will wait quietly" (Bondy et al., 2007, p. 344). Although the teachers were warm and funny, there was no question that they meant what they said. Building community should complement, rather than replace, the mandated curriculum and should enhance collaborative learning. The following Focus on Schools box gives tips for getting the school year off to a good start.

FOCUS ON SCHOOLS

First Day

The first day of school can be a harrowing experience—for teachers and students. Both are probably asking the same kinds of questions: Will my students like me? Will my teacher like me? Can I teach? Can I learn?

Experienced teachers advise novices to expect to be nervous on the first day, but to try to focus on four things:

1. Help your students to see you positively from the first minute they enter the classroom. You can greet them at the door with warmth and energy. Tell the class a bit about yourself so they know what interests you. Connect with their interests, such as television programs, movies, video games, sports teams, or books. If you have ELL students, you could try to greet them in their first language. I have put a letter on each student's desk on the first day and some students still had that note four years later—clearly it was important to them. Make sure everyone learns something on the first day; choose a learning task that students can engage with at their own level and in their own way. Remember that every parent, especially of younger students, will ask them what they learned at school on the first day. Adolescents will likely have a first day experience in three or more classes one after another, so try to make this a unique and engaging experience.

2. Begin to build community. Parents may accompany younger students, exceptional students, and students new to school. Greet parents warmly, but remember that it is usually best if they do not come into the classroom; that can increase separation anxiety for students. Learn your students' names and interests. Provide opportunities for students to get to know one another. Communicate that you expect everyone to succeed. This is a fresh start for all students no matter what their previous experience at school. (Make every day a fresh start for yourself and for every student. Carry no grudges forward.) Give the message that you will provide a high level of support while holding high expectations.

3. Establish rules and procedures. When these are discussed on the first day, usually the school year starts off more smoothly. Keep the number of rules to a minimum and be prepared to enforce them. Teach the rules and procedures; make no assumptions. Also establish with students your expectations for the daily schedule. Knowing the schedule helps students to predict how the day or class will unfold. It is usually best to post schedules and be especially attentive to exceptional students who have a high need for predictability. Communicate this information gently in ways that will be understood by all your students.

4. Help students to take some ownership and act with autonomy in the classroom. Ensure they have opportunities to make choices even on the first day. They could choose a place to sit, or a book to read, or a partner to play a game with, or an activity to complete. These do not need to be big or totally open-ended choices. Make them age-appropriate and help students to feel some ownership of the classroom, its routines, rules, schedules, and space.

Self-determination theory suggests that all human beings need a sense of relatedness, a sense of competence, and a sense of autonomy in order to thrive. These guidelines for the first day attend to all of these needs—connect with each student, ensure everyone learns something, and give all students opportunities to make choices.

Sources: Fredericks, A.D. (2010). *The teacher's handbook.* Toronto: Rowman & Littlefield Education.

Foley, D. (2012). *The ultimate classroom management handbook.* St Paul: Jist Works.

Ryan, R.M., & Deci, E.L. (2000). Self-determination theory and the facilitation of intrinsic motivation, social development, and well-being. *American Psychologist, 55*(1), 68–78.

Developing an Inclusive Climate and Developing Relationships with Students

Relationships are key to creating a positive climate. Research suggests that students form their first—and they can be lasting—impressions of their teachers in the first two or three minutes of contact (Johnson, 2011). So begin positively, with energy and warmth. As well, make sure that the physical space is inviting and inclusive for all students, including exceptional students, and works efficiently for learning. Classroom norms for interaction and discussion also contribute to an inclusive climate.

Caring Relationships

Relationships are viewed by students and teachers as one of the most important aspects of their experience at school. "There is ample evidence that school climate and quality of **child–teacher relationships** share a mutually reciprocal association" (Pianta, 2006, p. 697). Students have called caring teachers "the glue" that holds their life at school together, and have expressed that the most important things they need at school are teachers who take charge of the classroom so all students feel safe, and teachers who are willing "to be there for them, to listen, and to show concern for students' personal and academic lives—in short, to care" (Woolfolk Hoy & Weinstein, 2006, p. 183). The characteristics and actions of teachers who contribute to positive **teacher–student relationships** include (Dalton et al., 2009):

- having an affect or tone that minimizes disruptions and keeps the class moving in a positive direction
- demonstrating a caring personality in the classroom (students use words like kind, friendly, respectful, firm, patient, and understanding)
- being professional (described by students as showing enthusiasm for teaching and for the teaching profession, and as showing leadership)
- acting patient, calm, and respectful; tempering responses and decisions

Recent research documents how teachers begin, on the first day of school, to create safe and productive environments for diverse student populations through culturally responsive classroom management (CRCM) (Bondy et al., 2007; Weinstein et al., 2004). CRCM is characterized by teachers developing a respectful, caring, and personal relationship with each student, in addition to building a learning community with an emotional climate where students can take risks, laugh, and trust one another as well as their teacher. In Bondy's study (2007), each of the three teachers introduced herself to the students on the first day in a way that communicated genuine interest in the students and shared personal information about herself, her hobbies, and her family. They all engaged their students in activities to get to know one another, and communicated core lessons about the importance of respect and kindness, including this one: "We don't laugh at anyone in here. You can feel very secure in this classroom" (Bondy et al., 2007, p. 336).

Students say that teachers must choose their words and actions carefully so that they are not perceived as being biased by students' status, characteristics, race, ability/disability, or religion (Whitney et al., 2005). To form and maintain supportive reciprocal relationships with students, teachers need to treat all students well; students reported that they understood the need for differential treatment on occasion but expected it to be based on student need and not motivated by racism, sexism, or favouritism (Woolfolk Hoy & Weinstein, 2006).

Research confirms that positive relationships with teachers are especially important for exceptional students and for at-risk students. Supportive relationships with teachers engage these students who may feel challenged in the classroom. When teachers expect them to do well and provide support so they can succeed, these students are more likely to be successful and to feel successful (Dalton et al., 2009). This may be because they feel more willing to take risks when they feel they "belong" in their classroom. What you do to establish relationships with your students may be among the most important actions you take as a teacher in an inclusive classroom. These actions will be supported by making the classroom an inviting space and by teaching norms for how everyone interacts in the classroom.

Making the Physical Space Efficient, Inviting, and Accessible

The social environment you are creating should be supported by a physical arrangement that allows students to talk and collaborate for part of each class; it should also allow for learning in a whole-class setting and for learning individually. Arrange the **physical space** to make it inviting as well as accessible and efficient before the school year begins and revisit the arrangement frequently. Consider furniture (e.g., desks), audiovisual equipment, visual aids (e.g., bulletin boards), and any extra items you bring (e.g., plants). Think proactively about the physical needs of exceptional students for space, adapted desks, and adaptive technology. Jacob, described in an opening case study, can move around easily in Mr. Chan's classroom with his arm crutches. This helps Jacob to feel comfortable and conveys to Jacob that Mr. Chan cares enough about him to ensure the classroom meets his needs.

ARRANGING FOR EFFICIENCY AND ACCESSIBILITY

A classroom is a small workspace for up to thirty students and you, for many learning materials, and for a variety of activities using different structures and parts of the room. There may be exceptional students who need a predictable physical layout because of visual impairments and students who need wide aisles to manoeuvre wheelchairs. Keep pathways clear to permit orderly movement, keep distractions to a minimum, and make efficient use of the available space.

ARRANGING AN INVITING CLASSROOM

Ask yourself what you can do in the physical set-up to make each student feel that she is a valued member of your classroom. Students are more likely to be engaged in the classroom and in learning if they think their teachers are caring and sensitive. For ELL students, perhaps you can post a sign in their first language. For a student like Jacob, with a physical disability, a poster that includes someone in a wheelchair or using arm crutches will communicate a positive message. Students with learning difficulties will appreciate knowing exactly what is expected; write an agenda on the board or on chart paper to ensure that all students find the day predictable. If necessary, use a visual schedule, with a book to show story time, and so forth. If only a few students need a visual schedule, tape it to their desks to avoid embarrassment. Students with behaviour disabilities or ADHD may also benefit from a schedule taped to their desks.

On your bulletin boards, use inspirational posters and generate interest in an upcoming unit by connecting the topic to current events or popular culture. Post

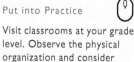

Put into Practice

Visit classrooms at your grade level. Observe the physical organization and consider how to ensure that the physical organization supports the classroom community you want to create.

student work or seasonal art. Change displays frequently, post classroom rules (discussed in the next section), and ask students for suggestions to enhance bulletin boards. Use colour, but avoid distracting students. Ensure that before the first day of school, you provide a welcoming message for students. One Aboriginal student commented, "I walked into the room and I saw that on his walls were pictures of Native American people. And I thought, 'Okay, I'm going to like this guy'" (Pewewardy & Hammer, 2003, p. 18.).

Desktops and tabletops should be clean and the room free of clutter. The appearance of order and organization in the physical environment communicates that you expect students to behave in an organized way. Place materials at a level where a student in a wheelchair can reach them independently to communicate that you value independence. Look at the classroom from the perspective of the students and of parents who come to visit; ensure that it is inviting.

Teaching Norms for Classroom Interaction and Learning

Teaching students **norms for classroom interaction** and learning is complex. First, be a model of effective communication and respectful interaction in all your dealings with students. You also need to establish norms for discussion and lead discussions effectively.

MODELLING COMMUNICATION AND LEADING DISCUSSION

You are responsible for making it safe for people to share ideas and for affirming them as part of the community. This means teaching students to engage in discussions. If you are teaching young children, you might consult Diane Levin's book, *Teaching young children in violent times: Building a peaceable classroom* (2003). Middle school teachers can see suggestions in *Classroom management for middle-grades teachers* (Charles & Charles, 2004), and teachers of high school students can consult *Classroom management for middle and high school teachers* (Emmer & Evertson, 2013). Lead discussions from the first day to deal with problems that arise. Be sure to prepare yourself for discussions and decide in advance how you will introduce them. Anticipate the biggest issues students will raise and prepare questions to stimulate a wider range of ideas. Anticipate possible outcomes so you can guide discussion toward them, but remain open to other resolutions.

When leading brainstorming sessions, listen to all ideas, and ask students to "tell us more" if their ideas are not clear; write all suggestions briefly on chart paper, and encourage a range of solutions. Don't evaluate at this stage, and model how to combine suggestions. Stop before everyone tires of the discussion, and acknowledge the group's accomplishments in specific terms; for example, "Thanks for listening to one another." Before you leave the topic, suggest what the class will do to complete the task and when this will happen. Make "discussion rules" one of the earliest topics for discussion. Figure 7.1 contains tips for leading successful discussions.

ESTABLISHING NORMS FOR DISCUSSION

Introduce and teach the norms that you expect students to adhere to in discussion. The *Tribes* program may help you; it is proactive in teaching discussion and community participation (Gibbs, 2001, 2006). The two groupings in *Tribes* are community circle (all members of the class) and small groups or tribes that are introduced

FIGURE 7.1 TIPS FOR LEADING SUCCESSFUL DISCUSSIONS

- Plan ahead the kinds of questions to ask as the discussion proceeds.
- Balance the needs of individual students and the needs of the group.
- Let the discussion flow and then bring the focus back to the main topic.
- Intervene to keep all the students engaged in the discussion.
- Plan ahead so you can re-direct the discussion if it begins to embrace values you do not want to promote.
- Introduce ideas and information that extend the students' thinking while acknowledging and accepting their input.
- End the discussion before students lose interest, and help the group see the progress they have made.
- Teach students how to participate in discussion; don't assume they know how.
- Ensure everyone feels safe and is heard.
- Re-focus the class when necessary.
- Clarify a student's contribution if it is not clear to the other students.
- Help the class apply the ideas raised during discussion to their everyday actions and experiences.

Sources: Adapted from Levin, D.E. (2003). *Teaching young children in violent times*. Cambridge, MA: Educators for Social Responsibility. Dalton, C., Hutchinson, N.L., & Dods, J.C. (2009). *Creating positive learning environments*. Prepared for the MISA Professional Network Centre. Kingston, ON: Queen's University.

Weblinks

CHECK OUT THESE SITES DESIGNED TO INFORM PARENTS AND HELP THEM DEAL WITH THEIR ADOLESCENTS.

INTERNET ARCHIVE: EDUCATIONAL FILM FROM THE 1950S ON DISCIPLINING ADOLESCENTS
www.archive.org/details/discipline_during_adolescence

ABOUT.COM: PARENTING OF ADOLESCENTS
http://parentingteens.about.com/od/disciplin1

gradually. For secondary students, you can refer to whole-class discussion and small-group discussion and use the *Tribes* approach flexibly. During the introductory session establish the **signal** you will use to get attention. *Tribes* recommends raising your hand, but some teachers flick the lights, play a few notes on the piano, or start rhythmic clapping and invite everyone to join in. Explain that, at this signal, everyone stops talking and raises his hand. With young students, practise the signal. Tell older students that if they are not successful at first, you will practise the signal with them.

Tribes begins with the whole group, or **community circle**. There are more than a hundred activities with detailed lesson plans, many of which are appropriate to the community circle. For younger students, you might start with "Five Tribes" (faces ranging from very sad to joyous), in which you ask everyone to report how they feel today. For adolescents, "Bumper Sticker" might be an appropriate introductory activity. One of the earliest discussions should be about what we need in order to feel safe in a group. From this discussion, settle on a maximum of four or five statements on which everyone can agree. Gibbs (2001, 2006) suggests four **community agreements**:

1. attentive listening
2. appreciation—no put-downs
3. right to pass and right to participate
4. mutual respect

Talking circles is an Aboriginal approach to experiential learning that stimulates awareness of and respect for individual differences as well as facilitating group cohesion. It incorporates traditions from various First Nations' council meetings. Triplett and Hunter (2005) describe how handing a feather around the circle to the student who is going to speak next helps students to listen to one another and ensures that only one person speaks at a time. An elementary teacher says, "I have Talking

Circle on Mondays because students are eager to share their weekend stories. Instead of seeing this as a classroom management dilemma, I see it as an opportunity to get to know my students better" (Triplett & Hunter, 2005, p. 5).

TEACHING AND PRACTISING CLASSROOM NORMS

The four community agreements listed above express norms for how students interact in the classroom, distinct from the classroom rules discussed in the next section. Attentive listening can be taught and practised with activities in paraphrasing and reflecting the feelings of the speaker. Look at *Tribes*, talking circles, and other programs for activities. Students can practise appreciating others by saying something positive about another student's role in the activity—model this for your students. Be specific; for example, "I admire you for the way you work so patiently with your reading buddy" or "I commend you for the way you persisted today to finish your math questions." Enforce your ban on put-downs vigorously. The **right to pass** means that students have the right to choose the extent to which they will participate in a group activity that requires sharing personal information. Acknowledge a pass by saying, "That is fine," but do not allow students to avoid doing class assignments by saying "Pass." You can offer a second chance to those who passed. Mutual respect means that everyone's beliefs, values, and needs are honoured. Students' property should be respected as well as their confidentiality. What is said in community circles should be treated in confidence and not become the basis for gossip. Remind students about this early in the year until it becomes an established norm.

The skills for working together need to be taught and practised. Make these skills explicit; for example, discuss and come to agreement on what listening *looks like* (e.g., eyes looking, leaning forward), *sounds like* (one person talking at a time, "good ideas"), and *feels like* (people care, "I'm being heard"). Post the four community agreements in a prominent place. Affirm students when you see them upholding the agreements, and refer to the agreements when you notice infringements.

What do you think?

Is it sound to allow students to pass when discussing personal feelings or information? How can you ensure that this privilege is not abused? What reading informs your thinking on this issue?

Negotiating and Enforcing Classroom Rules and Procedures

Rules and procedures enable the classroom to function smoothly and predictably. After negotiating and teaching rules and procedures, you must monitor students to ensure they are followed. Consistent application of consequences is critical.

Negotiating Rules

Rules help create a sense of order and predictability and enable you to be proactive in preventing difficulties. Teachers who are effective at managing their classrooms engage in community building and communicate the message that they care to each student, but they also have well-defined rules (e.g., Bondy et al., 2007). Effective classroom **rules** are brief and specific, positively worded, and clearly understood by students. They should be consistent with school rules, so you must become aware of the school code of conduct before the term begins. Then think about the general rules you hope to enforce for an orderly and predictable classroom. In Bondy's study (2007), the three effective teachers who used CRCM recognized that definitions of appropriate classroom behaviour are culturally defined; they therefore developed knowledge of their students' cultural backgrounds so they could use culturally appropriate classroom management strategies. This helped each of them to be an authoritative teacher but not an authoritarian one. They all introduced rules and procedures within the first two hours of school. One said, "It will probably take about two weeks [for my grade five class], so I'm going to keep going over rules and consequences" (Bondy et al., 2007, p. 338).

Although research supports both sides of this issue (DiClementi & Handelsman, 2005; Emmer & Evertson, 2013; Lewis & Burman, 2006), I recommend involving the students in the discussion about rules rather than deciding the rules alone. You might ask students to think of reasons for having rules and reasons for dispensing with rules, and ask what kind of class they want to have. Then ask students to talk in small groups to come up with three rules they think are important. It will help if you provide a general model—short, clear, and positively stated—such as "Respect and be polite to all people." Each group, in turn, states a rule it thinks is important that has not already been stated. Continue eliciting suggestions until no new ones emerge. To prevent key issues being overlooked, you could take a turn. After writing the suggestions on the board, group them into roughly five specific but broad rules and use other student suggestions as examples of the rules. Table 7.1 contains five rules with examples.

As soon as possible, write the rules on a poster and mount it in the classroom. Then you can point to the rules from the first day of class onward. Student input in setting rules usually helps to enhance classroom climate, build community, develop student understanding of the rationale for rules, and enhance the quality of your relationship with students. The standard to aim for is that there is no difference in student conduct when you leave the classroom briefly. This means that students are enforcing the rules and growing in self-discipline and respect for the rules. Before discussing the procedures that govern daily routines, I focus on how you can teach rules so they are integral to the life of the classroom.

There are three key aspects of teaching rules: demonstration, practise, and feedback. First, describe and demonstrate the desired behaviours. Be specific. If students may talk to one another in quiet voices while working in small groups, then use a quiet voice when you ask a student to speak quietly. Give feedback about the volume; if it was too loud, repeat the procedure. With adolescents, engage in teaching

Weblinks

SAFE POSITIVE SCHOOLS (GREATER SASKATOON CATHOLIC SCHOOLS)
www.gscs.sk.ca (look at the websites of individual schools)

SAFE AND CARING SCHOOLS (MANITOBA EDUCATION)
www.edu.gov.mb.ca/k12/safe_schools

TABLE 7.1 CLASSROOM RULES AND EXAMPLES

Rules	Examples
1. Be polite and helpful.	■ Wait your turn; say please and thank you. ■ Ask the teacher for help only after asking your group; offer help in your group. ■ Behave well for a substitute teacher.
2. Respect other people's property.	■ Keep the room clean. ■ Do not borrow without asking. ■ Return borrowed property.
3. Listen quietly while others are speaking.	■ During whole-class discussion, raise your hand. ■ In small groups, speak when the previous person is finished. ■ Don't call out.
4. Respect and be polite to all people.	■ Never call anyone a name or bully anyone. ■ Don't allow anyone to do these things to you or to another person. ■ Treat the teacher respectfully.
5. Obey all school rules.	■ Follow rules for the schoolyard, cafeteria, etc. ■ Remember that all teachers and students are expected to help with enforcement of school rules.

the rules with sensitivity to their age; perhaps ask each group to teach a rule to the class. Second, rehearsal means asking students to show that they understand. Younger students may need to practise standing up to a bully. Never have a student enact the role of the bully, because that amounts to you teaching someone to be a bully. Rather, ask students to imagine seeing a bully push their friend. Then have them practise asking the bully to stop and helping their friend report the incident to an adult (including asking the adult when they can expect a report on action taken). Again, feedback is important. Develop the habit of giving feedback after students have followed a rule. Make specific comments: "I like the way you were raising your hands in the large group and taking turns talking in your small groups."

If one student violates a rule, take him or her aside and say privately, for instance, "I heard you call John an unpleasant name. Next time that happens, I will call your name, and you will stand beside the door until I discuss this with you. I will not tolerate name-calling. We agreed that we would not treat one another that way. I expect you to behave better than this." This is **enforcing a rule**.

Monitoring is important to ensure that students engage in learning activities and internalize classroom rules and procedures. A discussion of monitoring follows the section on establishing procedures.

Some high school teachers recommend taking a different approach with adolescents and establishing one rule, such as "If you make it so I can't teach effectively, or you or other students can't learn effectively, then there is a problem" (Foley, 2012, p. 4).

Foley suggests that you have a student wad up a piece of paper and throw it in the waste basket, and have another wander up to the sharpener and sharpen a pencil. Ask students to notice how they all looked at these students. And then tell the class, "It doesn't take much to distract my classes because I am so boring." He recommends you continue by explaining that this means that if the students are going to learn anything, they will have to "just sit there when I'm teaching. I'll try to be funny and interesting. But you can see I have a long way to go" (Foley, 2012, p. 5). As Foley demonstrates, a sense of humour can help in winning adolescents over, especially if they recognize that you are trying to be funny and engaging. In handling the challenge to be consistent, Foley explains to students that, like a traffic cop, he won't catch every student who disrupts class, but all who are disruptive take the chance of being caught, just like all speeders take the chance they will be caught by the traffic cop. Foley suggests adolescents understand these concepts and can see that it is still fair, even if everyone is not caught, because the onus is now on each student who takes the risk.

Establishing Procedures

Teachers usually develop classroom procedures for using classroom space, seat work and teacher-led activities, transitions into and out of the room, small-group activities, and general procedures. Figure 7.2 contains examples of procedures. However, before you focus on rules and procedures, remember to start your days, especially your first day, positively. **Classroom procedures** are efficient ways of moving everyone along that are consistent with your goals for the classroom. Because procedures usually follow from the rules, making this connection will help most students understand them. Teach the most critical procedures first, introduce them as the need arises during the first few days, and introduce only as many in a day as the class can handle. In one of the opening cases, Mr. Chan had developed a procedure for getting his grade 10 class straight into academic work—they found a "challenge" on

Further Reading

On classroom management:

Emmer, E.T., & Evertson, C.M. (2013). *Classroom management for secondary teachers* (9th ed.). Boston, MA: Allyn and Bacon.

Vitto, J.M. (2003). *Relationship-driven classroom management*. Thousand Oaks, CA: Corwin Press.

Khalsa, S.S. (2014). *Teaching discipline and self-respect: Effective strategies, anecdotes, and lessons for successful classroom management* (2nd ed.). Thousand Oaks, CA: Corwin Press.

Jones, V., & Jones, L. (2012). *Comprehensive classroom management: Creating communities of support and solving problems* (10th ed.). Boston, MA: Pearson Education.

Put into Practice

Some resources for teachers seem to be especially written for beginning teachers. Locate one of the three resources listed below and read the sections that interest you most. List some strategies that seem well suited to the way you approach teaching. Try these strategies in your classroom.

For elementary teachers:

Jonson, K., Cappelloni, N., & Niesyn, M. (2011). *Flourishing in your first year: The new elementary teacher's handbook.* Thousand Oaks, CA: Corwin.

For secondary teachers:

Foley, D. (2012). *Ultimate classroom management handbook: A veteran teacher's instant techniques for solving adolescent student misbehavior.* St. Paul, MN: Just Works.

Johnson, L. (2011). *Teaching outside the box: How to grab your students by their brains.* San Francisco, CA: Jossey-Bass.

FIGURE 7.2 PROCEDURES FOR THE CLASSROOM

Procedures to Organize Use of the Room

Teacher's Desk and Storage Areas

- Normally, students remove items only with your permission.

Student Desks and Other Student Storage Areas

- Normally, students remove items from others' desks only with permission.

Storage for Common Materials

- Tell students if and when they may remove texts, paper, rulers, etc.

Drinking Fountain, Pencil Sharpener

- Normally, students use these one at a time, and not during large group presentations.

Centres, Stations, Equipment Areas

- Tell students when they may use these areas and how many students at a time, and post instructions for the use of any equipment.

Transitions into and out of the Room

Beginning of the School Day

- Establish a routine that you supervise. With young children, it may be a "sharing" time; with older students, it may be a "challenge" that they work on for a few minutes alone, in pairs, or in groups.

Leaving the Classroom

- Younger students leave quietly, in a line—and when you give the signal.
- Older students leave quietly and when you give the signal (not just when the bell rings).

Returning to the Classroom

- After a noisy activity, allow quiet talking and then request silence before you begin the next activity.
- After a quiet activity, provide a challenge to focus students and request silence before you begin the next activity.

Ending the Day or Period

- Review what was learned and look ahead to any homework, upcoming activities; end on a positive note.

- Tidy the room with all students doing their part; use procedures for leaving.

General Procedures

Distributing Materials

- Make it efficient; each week assign a student to this task for each group.

Interruptions or Delays

- Teach students that after an announcement on the public address system, they are to return immediately, without comment, to their work.
- If you leave the room, remind students you expect them to act the same as when you are present; leave them working.

Washrooms

- Tell students how many can leave class at a time and whether they need your permission.

Library, Resource Room, School Office, Cafeteria

- Review school rules.

Schoolyard

- Review school rules, prevent bullying, and help students include everyone.

Fire Drills

- Learn school procedures; practise with your class prior to the first drill (October is fire prevention month in Canada).
- Arrange to assist students with physical, visual, hearing, or developmental disabilities.

Classroom Helpers

- Share these privileges systematically; identify helpers (or pairs of helpers) at the beginning of the week.
- Demonstrate how helpers are to fulfill their roles; don't accept shoddy work.

their desks when they entered and had four minutes to determine with a partner which historical figure had made the quoted statement. Many teachers find that procedures that enable a productive and focused opening of class help them to set a positive tone and to be efficient.

Monitoring Student Actions

Monitoring involves being responsive to student action and learning. When you present information to the class, position yourself so you can see every student's face. Move around the classroom so you come close to all students. However, if there is a student in the class who has hearing loss and speech-reads, you must ensure this student can see your face straight on whenever you are talking; in this case, you will not be able to move around the classroom while presenting. Scan the whole class frequently; some teachers tend to focus on the middle front rows, but you should be aware of the reactions of students on the periphery. Some teachers use response cards to monitor the understanding of all students—students can write on a response card or hold up a preprinted response card. These can be as simple as yes/no in response to the question, "Are you ready for me to move to the next topic?" or can engage students in creating or selecting a brief answer to a mathematics question, dictated spelling word, and so on. Response cards promote high levels of teacher monitoring, active student response, and learning (Randolph, 2007). Some teachers use a thumbs-up or thumbs-down for students to show whether they are "cool" with what has just been taught and ready to move on to the next part of the lesson.

If you teach one small group while other groups are working independently, position yourself so you can see all the students and move around the room between working with one group and the next group. When you circulate, look closely to see that the students are completing the assigned work. During this break between your work with groups, ask if anyone has a question that could not be answered by a classmate. If there is a question, tell the students you will give a brief reply. After one minute of responding, name a peer for the student to direct any further questions to. Then call for the next small group to assemble. While you are engaged with a small group, keep monitoring; look up frequently and be alert for disruptions.

When all students are working on independent assignments, circulate and check each individual's progress. Avoid prolonged discussion with one student that interferes with alert monitoring. Remind students that they should ask you for help only after they have tried to obtain the assistance of a peer. If a student requires sustained assistance, the two of you should move to a location from which you can monitor the entire class. If you move to your desk, do not let students congregate there and block your monitoring of the room or distract students seated nearby.

After introducing a new lesson to the whole class, instruct students to take out the appropriate materials. Scan the class to ensure that every desktop has what is needed. You may want to have all students try the first example under your direction and then take this example up with the group. Scan the class to see that everyone is writing. Check on exceptional students to ensure that they understand the instructions. Keep checking when students move to the next example. Quietly and individually ask the students experiencing difficulty to join you for reteaching at an area from which you can monitor the rest of the class. To prevent these invitations from being seen as punishment, also ask the advanced students to join you at the reteaching area for challenge activities after they have completed the assigned work. Ensure that all students have opportunities to work with you at this location.

You will find it helpful to monitor student work by collecting assignments frequently, even if you have asked students to check their own work in class. Write brief comments so students see you have read their work, and keep your mark book current. You will see patterns of students who do not attempt assignments, leave assignments incomplete, or complete work only with assistance. When teaching

Chris Schmidt/Getty Images

Students learn to work collaboratively in small groups, enhancing social skills and social acceptance while meeting learning goals.

Put into Practice

Interview an experienced principal or teacher about how he or she maintains consistency in applying consequences and still retains the flexibility needed to treat exceptional students equitably. Ask how she talks with students about consistency and flexibility.

Weblinks

SAFE AND CARING SCHOOLS & COMMUNITIES
http://safeandcaring.ca

LEARNING RESOURCES CENTRE OF THE GOVERNMENT OF ALBERTA
http://education.alberta.ca
(go to Learning Resources Centre [LRC])

COOL QUOTES FOR TEENS
http://quotations.about.com/cs/inspirationquotes/a/Teens1.htm

BC RESPONSIBLE & PROBLEM GAMBLING PROGRAM (YOUTH GAMBLING)
www.bcresponsiblegambling.ca/prevention-education/high-school

ACTING TOGETHER: YOUTH GANG VIOLENCE (CANADIAN RESEARCH)
www.actingtogether.ca/training-education/youth-gang-violence

Cross-Reference
While this chapter focuses primarily on creating an inclusive classroom climate that is well managed and welcoming for exceptional students, Chapter 10 places more emphasis on schoolwide approaches.

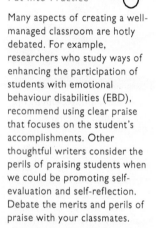

Put into Practice

Many aspects of creating a well-managed classroom are hotly debated. For example, researchers who study ways of enhancing the participation of students with emotional behaviour disabilities (EBD), recommend using clear praise that focuses on the student's accomplishments. Other thoughtful writers consider the perils of praising students when we could be promoting self-evaluation and self-reflection. Debate the merits and perils of praise with your classmates.

In favour of praise:

Sutherland K.S. (2000). Promoting positive interactions between teachers and students with emotional/behavioral disorders. *Preventing School Failure, 44*(3), 110–115.

Howell, A., Caldarella, P., Korth, B., & Young, K.R. (2014). Exploring the social validity of teacher praise notes in elementary school. *Journal of Classroom Interaction, 49*(2), 22–32.

Questioning praise:

Larivee, B. (2002). The potential perils of praise in a democratic interactive classroom. *Action in Teacher Education, 23*(4), 77–88.

Skipper, Y., & Douglas, K. (2012). Is no praise good praise? Effects of positive feedback on children's and university students' responses to subsequent failure. *British Journal of Educational Psychology, 82*(2), 327–339.

students to do long-term assignments, set quarter-way and half-way **checkpoints**. Devise a checklist for students to complete that shows what they have finished, and write brief, specific, and encouraging feedback on the checklist. You can conference with students who need guidance or **scaffolding** (support that can gradually be removed) to ensure that the differentiated outcomes set for exceptional students are appropriate.

Applying Consequences Consistently

You know how important it is for teachers to be consistent. **Consistency** and equity should be discussed together to eliminate misunderstanding about this important matter. Be consistent in your expectations from day to day. Also apply consequences consistently. For example, if you say students must move to the door and await a conversation with you for being disrespectful to a peer, then apply this consequence to all students; don't excuse one student because he begs or suspend another because she annoyed you earlier. Obvious inconsistencies confuse students about what is acceptable behaviour, and then students may test you to find the limits.

However, there are occasions when circumstances justify making exceptions. Consider the student who has been ill; it may make sense to compare his work with the quarter-way checkpoint when everyone else is at the half-way checkpoint, and to renegotiate the date for a half-way checkpoint. The student's participation in setting a new timeline increases the likelihood of staying on schedule. Students with IEPs, ELL students, and at-risk students may need adapted outcomes, differentiated instruction, and more scaffolding. Lead discussions that help students understand that fairness does not necessarily mean sameness. Mr. Chan may find it helpful to discuss with his grade 10 class Jacob's need to eat healthy snacks frequently to maintain his energy level, although eating during class is not allowed for those without a medical reason. Refreshing students' memories about a rule set at the beginning of term is helpful; such a discussion can remind Jacob that he and his family have agreed that only he can consume his healthy snacks. It will also serve as a reminder to Jacob's classmates that they are contributing to a problem by accepting food from Jacob.

Understanding and Responding to Behaviour in the Inclusive Classroom

Sometimes students do not act as we expect them to or wish they would. There are many possible **reasons why students act the way they do** (Dods, 2014). We should not assume that students are challenging our authority and should never take their actions personally. Some students have poor interpersonal skills and do not have the social skills to act in an appropriate way. Remember that some exceptional students, especially those with ASD, have difficulty reading facial expressions and that students with ADHD may act impulsively. Sometimes difficulties in executive functioning cause students to see a situation differently than we see it, and what they do may make sense to them and feel appropriate given the way they see the situation. Some students may experience fear or feel threatened and may overreact because their arousal system is overactive—if they have experienced maltreatment or threat in the past, such a reaction may have been adaptive in the face of real threat. However, it can be maladaptive when there is no threat (Dods, 2014).

Other reasons for a student's behaviour include seeking attention or validation, perhaps to meet a basic need for recognition. Sometimes people act out to cover a weakness they perceive in themselves, believing that others will not perceive them as struggling just as "bad" or will see them as in control. Acting out—by exhibiting defiant or oppositional behaviour—can be a defense mechanism that pushes people away; this is sometimes called "building a wall." Finally, if expectations in the home environment are very different than school expectations, students may be modelling what they have seen at home or what works in their neighbourhood. It is important to understand that the behaviours we see at school may serve a purpose for the student, may make sense to the student, or may be the only way the student can act in the situation until we teach them to behave differently (Dods, 2014). Figure 7.3 provides strategies for responding to challenging behaviour in the classroom. Figure 7.4 includes an annotated bibliography of programs designed to help teachers to enhance student well-being in the classroom and to respond to students' mental health and mental illness needs.

FIGURE 7.3 STRATEGIES FOR RESPONDING TO CHALLENGING BEHAVIOUR

1. Build rapport! – Often no strategies are successful until you have established rapport. Until then any action you take to address behaviour is simply seen as unfair and punitive.

2. A few strategies to build a good connection with a student:
   - Get to know them as a person, beyond knowing them as a student. Connect and converse on a topic that has nothing to do with behaviour—an interest, hobby, etc.
   - Give the person the opportunity to teach you or share knowledge with you—this can help them see you as human, not knowing how to do something. This might be with regards to technology, an athletic skill, current music, pop culture, anything that lets them know you learned something from them.
   - Ignore inappropriate behaviour where possible in the early stages of building rapport (e.g., attitude, swearing, etc.). Once you have rapport you can address these things but until then try to not react strongly unless it is blatantly inappropriate.

3. Include them in the planning. – Give them responsibility for their own actions and consequences. During a neutral conversation ask questions such as: What helps you? What can you do? What can I do? When discussing behaviour and consequences point out problems and issues in a matter-of-fact way and seek input into the solution: If you were me and I were you what would you do? What would be fair? What would make sense? What would I need to know to make the best decision possible?

4. Space. – There are situations in which proximity can be a valuable strategy and, for other people, giving them space is much more effective.

5. Point out competencies and strengths (real ones only, no lip service). – Point out and remind them of past successes. They need to see you and what you say as genuine. People are pretty good at figuring out who is being authentic and who isn't.

6. Be firm but caring and respectful. – Have consistent expectations and consequences. Follow through, taking into account all the factors that may be going on underneath. If people see you as indecisive, scared, or losing control they may take advantage of that. Being respectful, caring, and understanding does not mean they can walk all over you. Predictability and routine are good—avoid surprise transitions or changes.

7. Pre-empt difficult behaviour by addressing it before it happens. – Put the onus on the person to tell you how a good choice will be made. "You seem antsy today—is everything okay?" or "Last time group work was difficult for you. How are we going to manage this today?"

8. Avoid power struggles. – Watch your body language—don't tower over people. Anything perceived as threat (tone of voice, body language) may trigger someone to react. Avoid making people feel backed into a corner. Power struggles will almost always escalate. Whenever possible, give options—you set boundaries for options and they can make a choice. That way they still feel as though they have some control.

9. Use humour when you can to diffuse an escalating situation. – You need rapport to do this and to know the person to make sure it can work.

10. Respect. – Have high expectations and believe in the person's ability to meet those expectations. Notice them—use their name in the hallway. Avoid any statements, humorous or otherwise, that could be perceived as humiliating or embarrassing in front of others.

Developed by Jennifer Dods, in 2014, in *Ideas about why people act the way they do*. Unpublished document, Kingston, ON: Queen's University. Used with permission.

FIGURE 7.4 **ANNOTATED BIBLIOGRAPHY ON SCHOOL MENTAL HEALTH PROGRAMS**

In the past decade, many programs have been developed for educators to support and enhance the mental health of children and adolescents.

Supporting Minds: Educator's Guide to Promoting Students' Mental Health and Well-Being (School Mental Health ASSIST)

http://smh-assist.ca/supporting-minds

By Ontario Ministry of Education

School Mental Health ASSIST is a provincial implementation support team. For example, a working draft of a resource designed by school administrators for school administrators, titled Leading Mentally Healthy Schools, is available and feedback is requested.

ABCs of Mental Health (Teacher Resource)

www.hincksdellcrest.org/ABC/Welcome

By The Hincks-Dellcrest Centre

Practical information is organized by age of students (3–5 years, 6–12 years, 13–14 years, and 15–18 years). For early adolescence, 13–14 years, there are ten chapters on topics such as "The Angry and Aggressive Child." Within this topic there is background information and extensive practical information about how to understand how serious the adolescent's issues are and how to intervene. Outstanding resource for teachers. There is a parallel Parent Resource.

Talking About Mental Illness (T.A.M.I.) (Teacher's Guide)

www.camh.ca/en/education/Documents/www.camh.net/education/Resources_teachers_schools/TAMI/tami_teachersall.pdf

By Centre for Addiction and Mental Health

Thorough resources for helping teachers to understand mental illness beginning with understanding stigma. As well as being very informative, it has an extensive list of relevant websites.

Teen Mental Health

http://teenmentalhealth.org/care/educators

By teenmentalhealth.org (A Canadian research and practice organization)

Intended to increase mental health literacy for students, educators, and school staff. Contains a ToolBox of resources for each group. Unusual in that it speaks directly to adolescents as well as to their teachers.

KidsMatter (Australia)

www.kidsmatter.edu.au/primary/resources-schools

By Australian Primary Schools Mental Health Initiative

Thorough resources for creating a positive school environment including a component on helping children with mental health difficulties. Many additional resources to explore.

Managing Behaviour in the Inclusive Classroom

Managing student behaviour contributes to learning in the inclusive classroom. We focus on increasing appropriate behaviour, decreasing undesirable behaviour, and enhancing self-management. This section ends with a short discussion of positive behavioural supports followed by a brief consideration of harsh and inappropriate punishments. If you have the opportunity, you might want to take part in a course or workshop that coaches teachers on how to manage challenging behaviours in the classroom;

studies show that teachers show higher levels of positive classroom climate, sensitivity to students, and behaviour management after such coaching (e.g., Raver et al., 2008).

Increasing Appropriate Behaviour

There are a number of approaches to increasing appropriate behaviour and to helping students to assume responsibility for their actions, including anticipating and preventing inappropriate behaviour and focusing on helping students to be aware of and practise core virtues.

In effective classrooms, teachers and students respect and trust each other and students are engaged in learning. There are many actions you can take to increase students' appropriate behaviour. First, give positive attention to the behaviour you want to maintain or increase. (Lindberg and Swick [2006] call this common sense classroom management.) Provide verbal cues, prompts, and praise to indicate the behaviour you expect. And recognize social and academic achievement and qualities unique to individual students. Teachers who are effective and increase students' appropriate behaviour appear to have **"invisible" classroom management** techniques.

What do you think?

How does teaching awareness of core values differ from other approaches to promoting appropriate behaviour? With a peer, discuss how you might teach core values throughout the curriculum, and the benefits and disadvantages of this approach for Aboriginal and non-Aboriginal students.

REWARD SYSTEMS

In the past, **reward systems** were widely used in special education programs that served students with emotional and behaviour disabilities. They are much less common in today's inclusive classrooms, with the growing emphasis on intrinsic motivation and teaching students to regulate their own behaviour. Reward systems may distract teachers from looking for the causes of misbehaviour (Henley, 2006). Teacher attention and encouragement may be the most powerful rewards that have few drawbacks.

Wolford et al. (2001) argue that, while teacher praise and attention are powerful influences on student performance, classrooms are busy places. For this reason, Alber and Heward (1997) have developed a strategy for teaching exceptional students to "recruit" their teachers' attention in a positive way. Teachers begin by discussing how recruiting the teacher's attention can help students to be more successful; for example, you can say to students, "You will get more work done, your grades may improve, and the teacher will be happy you did a good job." Once students understand what is involved, then the teacher should model the steps in recruiting while thinking aloud. The steps are easy to remember using the acronym CLASS (Alber & Heward, 1997):

- **C**omplete your work.
- **L**ook it over for mistakes.
- **A**sk yourself if the teacher is available.
- **S**ignal the teacher and ask her to look at your work.
- **S**ay "Thank you."

Students need to practise and to receive feedback on how they are doing. Research has shown positive results for students with learning disabilities and with intellectual disabilities in recruiting praise and in student learning. There have also been increases in the amount of praise delivered by teachers. An educational assistant may be able to help a student learn to recruit teacher attention in a positive way.

ENCOURAGEMENT

Some researchers suggest encouragement is a healthier way for teachers to support and increase appropriate behaviour than praise (e.g., Larivee, 2006). **Encouragement** refers to giving courage or spurring someone on. Figure 7.5 describes encouragement, which can be provided to all students regardless of their achievement. Encouragement helps to alleviate the discouragement that exceptional students sometimes feel.

FIGURE 7.5 PROVIDING ENCOURAGEMENT TO EVERY STUDENT

Effective Encouragement

- Is specific, clear, and personal, requiring that we know each of our students
- Is genuine and expressed in a heartfelt way
- Is available to all, not just those who are achieving
- Discourages competition and helps students to focus on their own accomplishments
- Enhances willingness to try and gives courage to take risks, and contributes to renewed effort
- Helps students to accept themselves and evaluate their own progress
- Is catching—students tend to pass it on
- Tells students that how they feel about themselves is important
- Helps students to appreciate the successes of others
- Is embedded in trusting relationships, dialogue, and community
- Comes from teachers perceived as caring
- Is filled with meaning for the individuals involved
- Helps students to recognize their strengths
- Supports collaboration
- Contributes to internal motivation and values

Teachers Who Encourage

- Expect the best of everyone
- Pay attention, so they know their students and see even their small accomplishments
- Smile to communicate acceptance and caring, and make eye contact
- Use humour to put students and themselves at ease
- Personalize recognition
- Celebrate with students
- Set the example for their students
- Make all members of the class feel valued for what they contribute, and give credit to others
- Remember how good it feels to be acknowledged

The Language of Encouragement:

- I know you can do this. Let's get started.
- I see that you've thought of a new way to approach this problem. Let's see how well it works.
- I really liked the humour in your short story.
- What did you learn from that mistake?
- You've used many adjectives and it makes your writing interesting to read.
- I see you've decided to work alone instead of with a partner. Tell me at break how that worked for you.
- I can see that you've put a lot of work into this science project.
- How are these two experiences related?
- I like your new haircut.
- I appreciate the way you worked with your group members today.
- You've tried hard. What strategy could you use next time that might be more helpful?
- I know this is a difficult time for you.
- This sort of thing has happened to me, too. I was really hurt.
- I was moved by the way you responded to her feelings.
- I noticed you got right to work and completed the whole assignment.
- You must be proud of the work you did on this.

Sources: Larivee, B. (2002). The potential perils of praise in a democratic interactive class-room. *Action in Teacher Education, 23*(4), 77–88; McIntyre, E., Kyle, D.W., & Moore, G.H. (2006). A primary-grade teacher's guidance toward small-group dialogue. *Reading Research Quarterly, 41*, 36–66; Kouzes, J.M., & Posner, B.Z. (2007). *Encouraging the heart: A leader's guide to rewarding and recognizing others.* Somerset, NJ: John Wiley.

Motivation and Rewards

Motivation is a term educators use often. And we may worry about whether rewarding students makes them less motivated. Recent theory and research in educational psychology may help us to understand this contentious issue.

Motivation is frequently described as intrinsic or extrinsic. *Intrinsic* usually means that a person engaging in a task or behaviour develops internally satisfying consequences. Examples of intrinsic rewards include acquisition of knowledge, task completion, and sense of mastery. *Extrinsic* usually means that a person engages in a task or behaviour to reach satisfying consequences outside himself. Extrinsic rewards include token systems, social approval, and tangible objects.

What are the arguments against using extrinsic rewards? Many have argued that children should engage in learning for its own sake. Will children who receive external rewards for learning and behaviour come to depend on and expect these rewards (Greene & Lepper, 1974; Witzel & Mercer, 2003)? Extrinsic rewards are easily overused, are ineffective at teaching students how to regulate their behaviour, and may not generalize beyond the classroom. While we would prefer students be intrinsically motivated to learn and manage their own behaviour, we recognize that this is not the case for many students, some of whom are exceptional learners.

What are the arguments in favour of using extrinsic rewards? Teachers are often advised to use extrinsic motivation with young children and exceptional learners, perhaps because these students often rely on adults for guidance and reassurance. For example, Grolnick and Ryan (1990) found that students with learning disabilities had less internal control for academic work than their classmates without disabilities. In 1994 Cameron and Pierce of the University of Alberta conducted a meta-analysis on one hundred studies involving rewards. They found that, overall, participants receiving tangible rewards reported higher intrinsic motivation than non-rewarded participants. When students received contingent verbal praise, they demonstrated significantly higher motivation (measured by time on task and by attitude) than students who did not receive such praise. These analyses led Cameron and Pierce to conclude that rewards, tangible and verbal, increase positive behaviour and learning, and do not interfere with intrinsic motivation for low-interest activities.

Two aspects of Cameron and Pierce's findings may be key to understanding the role of extrinsic motivation and rewards: first, that extrinsic rewards did not interfere with motivation for *low-interest activities*; and second, that *pairing an external reward with information*, in the form of verbal praise, was most effective.

Why might student interest in the activity be important to understanding rewards and motivation? To answer this question, we turn to a specific theory of motivation called self-determination theory (SDT), developed by Edward Deci and Richard Ryan. They found that human beings have three motivational needs in order to be self-determining: competence (feeling effective), autonomy (feeling of acting in accord with one's sense of self), and relatedness (feeling connected to others). SDT postulates a continuum of motivation ranging from amotivation through four degrees of decreasing external motivation to intrinsic motivation. Intrinsic motivation is defined as engagement in a task for the pure joy and inherent satisfaction derived from doing the task (Ryan & Deci, 2000).

Ryan and Deci (2000) argue that many of the activities people are asked to engage in are not intrinsically motivating; thus people are not likely to engage in them fully without some external motivation. They also suggest that to move along the continuum toward intrinsic motivation, people need to experience competence, autonomy, and relatedness. According to SDT, the more that students feel effective at school tasks, feel they have chosen to engage in the tasks, and feel they belong in the classroom, the more likely they are to engage in school tasks for their own sake. And perhaps external rewards have a part in keeping students at uninteresting tasks long enough to develop feelings of competence, autonomy, and relatedness. Therefore, it may be that external rewards enhance motivation for learning that is not inherently interesting. Conversely, a classic study by Greene and Lepper (1974) found that giving preschoolers extrinsic rewards for drawing, an inherently interesting task for these children, led to decreased interest in drawing unless rewards were offered. Deci, Koestner, and Ryan (1999) found the same outcome in a meta-analysis of 128 studies on extrinsic rewards with tasks students found interesting. In summary, the theory and research suggest that rewards may be appropriate for increasing student motivation for tasks that students find uninteresting or very difficult. However, the function of rewards should be to move students toward the development of intrinsic motivation by increasing feelings of competence, autonomy, and relatedness.

Why might pairing an external reward with verbal praise be important? It may be that *how* a reward is delivered matters. Teacher praise can focus students' attention on the value and relevance of the task as well as inform students' self-perceptions of competence, autonomy, and relatedness. This information may be particularly important for exceptional students who look to others for guidance

(continued)

(continued)

and reassurance. The teacher may, in fact, be teaching the students how to judge themselves more positively and about the intrinsic interest and value of the activity. Although Deci and Ryan have argued against external rewards, they wrote that "the context within which they are administered has an important influence upon how they are experienced and thus upon how they affect intrinsic motivation" (1992, p. 22). "Rewards, when taken as informational rather than controlling, affect a person's autonomy and competence, leading to intrinsic motivation" (Witzel & Mercer, 2003, p. 91). A recent review of the literature suggests that the importance of intrinsic motivation to performance remained in place even when incentives were presented but that incentives or rewards had more effect when they were directly tied to performance; the authors conclude that rewards and intrinsic motivation are best considered simultaneously (Cerasoli et al., 2014). In summary, the relationship between motivation and rewards appears to depend on how rewards are delivered by the teacher and the best motivation appears to be a combination of intrinsic and incentives.

The research suggests that it is prudent to avoid overuse of rewards, while looking for opportunities to pair informational feedback and praise with rewards, especially for tasks that students do not find intrinsically motivating. Enhancing feelings of competence, autonomy, and belongingness—by teaching well, giving students choices, and creating a positive classroom climate—is likely to contribute to intrinsic motivation.

References

Cameron, J., & Pierce, W.D. (1994). Reinforcement, reward, and intrinsic motivation: A meta-analysis. *Review of Educational Research, 64,* 363–423.

Cerasoli, C.P., Nicklin, J.M., & Ford, M.T. (2014). Intrinsic motivation and extrinsic incentives jointly predict performance: A 40-year meta-analysis. *Psychological Bulletin, 140*(4), 980–1008.

Deci, E.L., Koestner, R., & Ryan, R.M. (1999). A meta-analytic review of experiments examining the effects of extrinsic rewards on intrinsic motivation. *Psychological Bulletin, 125,* 627–668.

Deci, E.L., & Ryan, R.M. (1992). The initiation and regulation of intrinsically motivated learning and achievement. In A. Boggiano & T. Pittman (Eds.), *Achievement and motivation: A social developmental perspective* (pp. 9–36). Cambridge, UK: Cambridge University Press.

Greene, D., & Lepper, M.R. (1974). Effects of extrinsic rewards on children's subsequent intrinsic interest. *Child Development, 45,* 1141–1145.

Grolnick, W.S., & Ryan, R.M. (1990). Self-perceptions, motivations, and adjustments in children with learning disabilities: A multiple group comparison study. *Journal of Learning Disabilities, 23,* 177–184.

Ryan, R.M., & Deci, E.L. (2000). Self-determination theory and the facilitation of intrinsic motivation. *American Psychologist, 55,* 68–78.

Witzel, B.S., & Mercer, C.D. (2003). Using rewards to teach students with disabilities. *Remedial and Special Education, 24,* 88–96.

Decreasing Undesirable Behaviour

Your actions to make everyone feel included and to increase positive behaviour may not be enough for some students. Sometimes you need to focus on decreasing undesirable behaviours. Think about why the student may be acting in this way (look back at the section titled Understanding and Responding to Behaviour in the Inclusive Classroom and at Figure 7.3). How can you help students to replace challenging and unhelpful behaviours with actions that will increase their participation and learning? Often we assume that students know what to do and are simply refusing to do it. This is not always the case. Try using the steps of the ADAPT strategy described in Chapter 1 and minimal interventions or low-key responses. When a student exhibits problem behaviour, refer to the classroom rules that were established. Remind the student which rule is being violated. This can be done with a pre-arranged gesture or signal, by using humour (with good judgment), or by verbally confronting the student (best done in private). Often it is best to positively tell the student what you expect, rather than dwelling on what the student has done wrong. Identify environmental factors that can be altered, such as the student's place in the classroom or the student's task. A quick tension- or energy-releasing activity may allow the student to return to work.

LOW-KEY INTERVENTIONS

Effective teachers appear to respond to misbehaviour at a moment's notice; however, they actually anticipate and act or **pro-act** almost before the behaviour occurs

Weblinks

CHECK OUT THESE SITES ON ANGER MANAGEMENT. COMPARE THE INFORMATION TO THAT AVAILABLE IN BOOKS AND ARTICLES. DO THE DIFFERENT SOURCES PROVIDE SIMILAR INFORMATION?

PARENTBOOKS CANADA: ANGER AND STRESS MANAGEMENT
www.parentbooks.ca (search for stress & anger)

AMERICAN PSYCHOLOGICAL ASSOCIATION: CONTROLLING ANGER BEFORE IT CONTROLS YOU
www.apa.org/topics/anger/control.aspx

FLORIDA DEPARTMENT OF EDUCATION: ANGER MANAGEMENT AND SCHOOLS
www.keystosaferschools.com/Reports/anger.pdf

FIGURE 7.6 LOW-KEY PROACTIVE RESPONSES TO DECREASE UNDESIRABLE BEHAVIOUR

Proximity: Move toward a misbehaving student immediately, but not so close that the student feels physically threatened. Usually there is no verbal exchange.

Touch: Check your school's policy on physical contact first. A quick, light, non-threatening touch to the shoulder without eye contact or verbal exchange shows that you are aware and care.

The look: As soon as attention-seeking begins, quickly and silently communicate to a student that the behaviour is inappropriate. This is not a glare.

Student's name: Use this positively to make the student feel included just before misbehaviour or as soon as misbehaviour occurs. Use a kind tone, not a nagging one. Don't overuse.

Gesture: Communicate expected behaviour, e.g., forefinger on the mouth to say "shhh" or a shake of the head to say "no." Ensure your meaning is understood by ELL students.

The pause: At the beginning of instructions, if a few are not listening, pause obviously. Combine with moving toward them, catching their gazes, and gesturing for quiet.

Ignore: Use with caution. Ignoring is best when the student's behaviour does not interfere with teaching or learning. If two students misbehave together, ignoring will be ineffective. Don't show agitation or the students will have won the attention they are seeking.

Signal to begin/signal for attention: Signal to get or refocus the attention of the class. Do not continue until you have their attention. Make the signal age-appropriate: a flick of the lights, a whistle, rhythmic hand clapping, or a sign you hold up. An elementary school teacher could call out a word ("baseball") and have the students give a choral response ("Blue Jays"); the students could choose a new word and response each week.

Deal with the problem, not the student: Quietly remove the object the student is tapping on her desk, or if two students are fighting over a book, say, "Book, please," and extend your hand. Say it as if you expect them to comply; if they do not, they have escalated the situation beyond a low-key proaction on your part.

(Henley, 2006). Such **low-key interventions** or minimal actions do not disrupt the flow of the class. They de-escalate rather than raise the stakes, and they communicate to the students that you are "with it" and that they cannot get away with anything. Over time, effective teachers develop a repertoire and match their "proaction" to the action they anticipate. If you overuse a proaction, it loses its effectiveness. Low-key proactions or responses are explained in Figure 7.6.

You may find it effective to combine these low-key responses. For example, one student is speaking to the class and a restless student catches your attention, although you are not certain why. You move silently toward this student, signalling to him to be quiet, touching the child lightly and briefly on the shoulder (if such a touch is allowed within your school's policies) to express calm, and smiling your appreciation when he begins to listen again. You did not disturb the flow of the class, and you prevented a distraction for the others. You can be "artful" in proactively noticing, selecting an effective

John Fedele/Blend Images/Newscom

Engaging in activities with peers helps to decrease inappropriate behaviour.

response, and carrying it out to refocus the student who was venturing into undesirable behaviour. For example, Mr. Chan could stand by Jacob's desk as soon as Jacob enters the classroom and point to direct his attention to the challenge Jacob should attack, while giving Jacob a signal to eat his snack himself. Many resources on classroom management provide guidance on how to implement low-key responses (e.g., Henley, 2006; Lindberg & Swick, 2006) and report data on the effectiveness of a proactive, caring approach, especially when it is relationship-driven and culturally responsive (Bondy et al., 2007).

Bullying is a pervasive problem in schools worldwide with negative consequences for the victim, the bully, and bystanders. We should always give the message to students that bullying is unacceptable. It requires an immediate and public response, usually beginning with a verbal reprimand. Low-key intervention is not enough. It is important to be clear with the bully and with all who were affected by the bullying incident, including those who witnessed the bullying, that it is not tolerated (Twemlow et al., 2010). Many children and adolescents say that they do not report bullying to adults because they do not believe that adults will "do anything about it." Jimerson and his colleagues (2010) suggest that much of our response to bullying must be proactive, including creating a positive classroom climate and school climate, as described in this chapter and Chapter 10 (Orpinas & Horne, 2010), understanding our role as the responsible adults in the school and on the schoolyard (Espelage & Swearer, 2010), and being vigilant about cyberbullying (Smith & Slonje, 2010). In addition to creating a caring community, we must intervene immediately. Recently, many schools have begun to use positive behaviour supports (discussed later in this chapter) to reduce the incidence and impact of bullying. Bullying receives a more thorough treatment in Chapter 10 along with more emphasis on schoolwide approaches to prevention and response.

GIVING THE CHOICE TO BEHAVE APPROPRIATELY

Sometimes you simply need to provide the choice to behave appropriately. For example, two students are discussing hockey rather than geography. Say, "You can choose either to work quietly together on the map you are making or to have your seating arrangement changed until the end of this unit." If the two students do not choose to work quietly on the map, then you must follow through and seat them apart. Do not offer any choice that you are unwilling to apply. One of my favourite choices when students play with toys, hair accessories, and such is, "In your pocket or mine—you choose." These choices are not ultimatums. They usually end problem behaviour without escalating conflict by using **natural consequences**. Stay calm, speak in a private-conversation voice, and offer to conference with the student. Help the student to feel respected rather than humiliated or overpowered. Thank the student sincerely as soon as the unacceptable behaviour stops (even smile or mouth your thanks). Keep your sense of humour; sometimes it is better to laugh and give a second chance than to prosecute, especially over small infractions.

HOLDING PATTERN

Sometimes you need to put a student in a **holding pattern**. Some teachers arrange to have a misbehaving student wait in an office, but I find it simpler to have a student stand beside the door in the classroom or, if I think she will distract others, in the doorway of the classroom (but in sight) until I come to talk to the pupil. Keep the

Further Reading

Consult resources on connecting behaviour interventions to IEPs. Here are four examples:

Hoyle, C.G., Marshall, K.J., & Yell, M.L. (2011). Positive behavior supports: Tier 2 interventions in middle schools. *Preventing School Failure, 55*(3), 164–170.

Mueller, T., Bassett, D., & Brewer, R. (2012). Planning for the future: A model for using the principles of transition to guide the development of behavior intervention plans. *Intervention in School and Clinic, 48*(1), 38–46.

Killu, K. (2008). Developing effective behavior intervention plans: Suggestions for school personnel. *Intervention in School and Clinic, 43*(3), 140–149.

Scott, T.M., Anderson, C.M., & Spaulding, S.A. (2008). Strategies for developing and carrying out functional assessment and behavior intervention planning. *Preventing School Failure, 52*(3), 39–50.

time brief and ensure the student's safety. If these talks are rare and heartfelt, they are likely to be taken seriously.

Enhancing Self-Management

The goal of this chapter is that your class conduct themselves the same way whether you are in the classroom or have stepped into the hall. Similarly, you want to help individual students develop self-control or self-management.

PROBLEM-SOLVING APPROACHES

Some educators develop a **problem-solving approach** that asks a student to answer a set of questions after engaging in unacceptable behaviour. Ask the student what they think the problem was, how they contributed to the problem, how they can make amends, and how they can prevent the problem from recurring. Sometimes the student and the teacher sign a form. What makes this an effective strategy is the follow-through, in which the adult and the student decide "who is going to do what" about the situation. If the two feel that they are on the same side and working together to overcome a common foe—such as an easily lost temper or peers who tease—then the student may work hard to honour the problem-solving solution.

INFORMAL CONFERENCES

In an **informal conference**, a teacher can often see that an exceptional student wants to change a troublesome behaviour but cannot do it alone. Such conferences require follow-through and involve the following steps:

- Greet the student to set a positive tone.
- Define the problem clearly and ensure that you agree before going to the next step.
- Generate solutions together, so you solve the problem mutually.
- Choose the best solution(s) together (and perhaps prioritize the other solutions); agree on what each of you will do to implement the solution(s); be sure you have a role as well as the student.
- Ensure that you have a shared understanding of the solution(s) to be undertaken.
- End positively by thanking the student.

Improving self-management is not easy for students. Provide support and encouragement, regular checks on progress, praise, additional informal, and positive chats. If the informal conference is no match for the problems that need to be solved, then provide a warning and try a formal contract the next time. Warnings are respectful ways to "raise the stakes" and remind students that what happens next is a consequence of what they do.

CONTRACTS

I found that young students enjoyed contracts and told their classmates about them, while adolescents appreciated private contracts. I informed parents so they would understand my rationale and the student's account of the consequences if the contract were broken. With a young child, a **contract** can be about a straightforward matter like hanging his coat on a hook when he enters the classroom instead of throwing it on the floor. Best to start with easily and quickly met agreements that provide immediate evidence of success and provide you with a way to give genuine praise.

After two successful contracts, move to your real objective. This might be the student beginning the day and getting to her desk without touching another student or having a verbal disagreement. A good start can make a difference to how a student conducts herself all day long. You may reap multiple benefits from start-of-day contracts; the student avoids getting into "a funk," and you sidestep the problem of that student's disruption of others. You can begin the day by praising the student sincerely instead of reprimanding her and build on this success to tackle bigger unacceptable behaviours that sabotage learning. I have seen adolescents thrive on private, individualized contracts. Word the contract simply to state what both you and the student agree to do and to specify the positive reward and the consequence for failure to live up to the agreement. Figure 7.7 shows a simple form for behaviour contracts.

SELF-MONITORING

Self-monitoring is a strategy for transferring responsibility to the student. It is particularly applicable for students who are off-task and require help focusing attention. Students observe and collect data on their own behaviour, which can change how frequently the behaviour occurs. Students need to understand the behaviour they are to monitor, and need an easy recording system and a reward. In the beginning, monitor closely and then give increasing responsibility to the student. Explain in advance: "Put a check on your tracking sheet when I say, 'Let's keep track,'" or "Put a check at the end of every page." A book of attractive forms and guidelines

FIGURE 7.7 BEHAVIOUR CONTRACT

CONTRACT BETWEEN _____ AND _____
                                (student)   (teacher)

DATE: _____
                 (may specify period in which contract applies)

_____ AGREES TO _____
           (student)   (describe behaviours)

AND _____ AGREES TO _____
          (teacher)   (describe behaviours)

CONSEQUENCES: _____

REWARDS: _____

_____

DATES FOR CHECKING PROGRESS: _____

COMPLETION DATE: _____

SIGNATURES: _____ AND _____
                     (student)   (teacher)

for making clear behaviour plans may be helpful (e.g., Reithaug, 1998a, 1998b). A simple self-monitoring card can be taped to the student's desk; the student makes a check mark at each signal or at the end of each task. After some successful self-monitoring, you could move to checklists taped to the desk or to sticky-note reminders. These strategies work well with young students, but I have also seen exceptional adolescents inconspicuously use self-monitoring cards taped inside their notebooks to help them focus their attention. An educational assistant can also signal the student and prompt the individual steps in a cognitive behaviour modification (CBM) strategy like SNAP (Figure 7.8).

Peers and paraprofessionals can help to implement cognitive behaviour modification programs.

FIGURE 7.8 IMPLEMENTING A COGNITIVE BEHAVIOUR MANAGEMENT PROGRAM

Cognitive behaviour modification (CBM) is a broad term that describes specific techniques that teach self-control. They increase a student's awareness of cognitive processes and knowledge of how behaviour affects learning.

CBM interventions require student evaluation of performance rather than teacher evaluation. This makes them practical for busy teachers and parents.

Self-instruction helps students to regulate their own behaviours. It uses self-statements to help students recall the steps required to solve a problem—whether social or academic. Examples of problems include rushing through assigned tasks, looking around instead of focusing on tasks, talking out of turn, and eating or giving food to others in the classroom. Initially, students say the steps out loud to a teacher or parent and then to a peer or themselves. Gradually they say the steps covertly.

The actions a teacher and student follow include:

1. They agree on a problem—social or academic—that is getting in the way of learning.
2. The teacher makes a cue card to prompt the student to use the steps of self-instruction.
3. The teacher models using the self-instruction steps to solve the problem impeding the student.
4. The student practises using the self-instruction steps aloud with the teacher to solve the problem.
5. The student practises with a peer and then alone, using the steps to solve the problem.
6. The teacher arranges booster practise regularly to review the strategy with the student. They use verbal rehearsal and practising in familiar and new situations.
7. The teacher and the student decide on a signal for the teacher to let the student know this is a time to use the steps. Use of the signal is then phased out as the student does the monitoring. For the SNAP strategy, snapping fingers may be a good signal.

Sample Cue Card to Tape to a Student's Desk or Book

> **SNAP** out of it!
>
> **S**ee my problem.
>
> **N**ame my best plan.
>
> **A**ct on my best plan.
>
> **P**at myself on the back. I solved my problem!

Further Reading

Recent research on PBS and the questions it raises:

Carr, E.G. (2006). SWPBS: The greatest good for the greatest number, or the needs of the majority trump the needs of the minority? *Research and Practice for Persons with Severe Disabilities, 31*, 54–56.

Morrison, J.Q., & Jones, K.M. (2007). The effects of positive peer reporting as a class-wide positive behavior support. *Journal of Behavioral Education, 16*, 111–124.

Caldarella, P., Shatzer, R.H., Gray, K.M., Young, K., & Young, R. (2011). The effects of school-wide positive behavior supports on middle school climate and student outcomes. *Research in Middle Level Education, 35*(4), online.

Pugh, R., & Chitiyo, M. (2012). The problem of bullying in schools and the promise of positive behavior supports. *Journal of Research in Special Education Needs, 12*(2), 47–53.

Chitiyo, M., Makweche-Chitiyo, P., Park, M., Ametepee, L.K., & Chitiyo, J. (2011). Examining the effect of positive behavior support on academic achievement of students with disabilities. *Journal of Research in Special Education Needs, 11*(3), 171–177.

Bohanon, H., & Wu, M-J. (2014). Developing buy-in for positive behavior support in secondary settings. *Preventing School Failure, 58*(4), 223–229.

(continued)

FIGURE 7.8 *(continued)*

Video self-modelling has been shown to decrease inappropriate behaviour, especially for adolescents with autism. Two elements are required for students to function as their own models. You need audiovisual technology that allows students to view themselves and they need to have the ability to change their behaviour so that they can function or appear to function beyond their present level. A cell phone might suffice. Buggey (2007) provides detail on how to capture video footage of students engaging in positive role modelling for themselves. Graetz and her colleagues (2006) describe using video footage of a student with autism engaging in inappropriate behaviours of which he was unaware, followed by self-modelling of appropriate behaviour. Buggey describes using self-modelling to motivate students with reading disabilities, who were discouraged by their inadequate reading. The teacher video recorded the students reading a practised text with accuracy and excellent intonation and then, after showing the students their video, found they tried harder and were more successful in reading.

Source of SNAP strategy: Hutchinson, N.L. (2004). *Teaching exceptional children and adolescents: A Canadian casebook* (2nd ed.). Toronto: Allyn and Bacon. Used by permission of Pearson Education Canada.

Positive Behavioural Supports and Classroom Management

Positive behavioural supports (PBS) refers to a tiered approach that can be implemented in a variety of contexts: schoolwide, classroomwide, non-classroom (such as the schoolyard), and individual. It is a problem-solving approach to managing problem behaviours by matching supportive strategies to the needs of the students to reduce or ideally eliminate targeted behaviours. This approach to dealing with problem behaviours focuses on the fixing of poor contexts that have been documented to be the source of the problems. The emphasis is on altering the environment before problem behaviour occurs or teaching appropriate behaviours as a strategy for eliminating the need for problem behaviours to be exhibited. Change should be systemic, build on students' strengths, and improve the quality and predictability of events in school, in the community, and at home. The intent is to make problem behaviours ineffective and to provide students with ways to reach their goals without resorting to inappropriate behaviours. Intensive supports, including functional assessments, are necessary for a small number of students with severe behavioural or cognitive disabilities.

Schoolwide programs are intended to establish a safe, positive climate for all students, but they do help students with behavioural exceptionalities in particular because they create predictable school environments (Caldarella et al., 2011). At the classroom level, PBS systems are used to create environments where students engage in work and to minimize disruptions. At the individual level, PBS provides a problem-solving process for students who do not respond to the first two levels, schoolwide and classroom (Chitiyo et al., 2011). Some teachers use daily behaviour report cards to record individual students' behaviour and progress within PBS (see Chafouleas et al., 2005, 2006). Recently researchers and educators have begun to consider PBS as a comprehensive approach to addressing bullying in schools on a number of levels simultaneously (Pugh & Chitiyo, 2012). For example, Ross and Horner (2009) have field-tested a three-tier program that addresses bullying systematically at the school level, with intensive small groups for those needing more intensity, and, finally, at the individual level in some cases. PBS has raised questions (e.g., Carr, 2006) and has many critics.

Put into Practice

Develop a tracking sheet for self-monitoring to be used by a student in grade 3 or a student in grade 10 who is trying to increase his focus in your class. Seek models in books and journals.

What do you think?

Debate with your peers whether harsh and inappropriate are always apt descriptors for the punishments described in this chapter. Defend the position opposite to what you believe. Why is this exercise a valuable experience for an educator?

Do Harsh Punishments and Inappropriate Punishments Ensure Safe Schools?

Punishment is usually defined as an unpleasant consequence aimed at reducing the likelihood of inappropriate behaviour. It is expected to work because it causes pain. Hall recently argued that "Punishment is when caregivers intentionally do things to children to make them feel guilty, humiliated, or fearful in an attempt to get them to change their behavior" (2013, p. 25). Paul Axelrod (2015) of York University recently reviewed the history leading to the Supreme Court of Canada ruling in 2004 that corporal punishment was an unreasonable application of force in the maintenance of classroom discipline. Assigning academic tasks as punishment is also an inappropriate punishment because it sends the message that schoolwork is something to be hated. The research indicates that punishment may control misbehaviour, but by itself it will not teach desirable behaviour or ensure safe schools (Findlay, 2010). Harsh punishment, like suspension or expulsion, also alienates students and tends to destroy the relationships you have built with your students.

DO SUSPENSIONS AND EXPULSIONS CONTRIBUTE TO SAFE SCHOOLS?

School policy may dictate that suspensions and even expulsions are used when a student's behaviour is so disruptive that teachers cannot meet their legal obligations to teach and keep the other students safe. These are drastic measures, so try every other possible avenue first. **Suspension** means temporary removal from the classroom (for a day or more), while **expulsion** means permanent removal. Many educators have argued that expulsion and suspension destroy the culture of caring (Cassidy, 2005) and are inconsistent with the commitment to inclusion that characterizes public education in Canada (James & Freeze, 2006). For many reasons, suspension and expulsion are not effective for teaching students, changing their behaviour, or ensuring safe schools. These reasons include the following (Boccanfuso & Kuhfeld, 2011; Browne-Dianis, 2011; Daniel & Bondy, 2008; Fenning et al., 2012; Sullivan et al., 2013):

- Racialized students, gay and lesbian students, and students with disabilities tend to be disproportionately affected by suspension and expulsion.
- The student misses the content you are teaching.
- The student does not receive assistance from school personnel, including teachers and counsellors.
- There may be adverse effects on students' social-emotional and academic status.
- Those who want to be out of school are rewarded.
- Some students who have been suspended or expelled come to school to "hang out," and school officials have little authority over them.
- As a general rule, behaviour does not improve as a result of suspensions or expulsions.

The exception to these drawbacks may be **in-school suspension**: a student is expected to attend school, complete assigned work, spend the day in a suspension room under supervision, and stay away from peers and social interactions. Haley and Watson (2000) developed what they called an in-school literary extension for students who had misbehaved. The researchers focused on helping students use

Further Reading

Readings and videos about alternative discipline:

Mergler, M., Vargas, K., & Caldwell, C. (2014). Alternative discipline can benefit learning. *Phi Delta Kappan, 96*(2), 25–30.

Wills, C., & Bradshaw, L. (2013). *Empowering voices for student success: Embedding restorative practice and circle process in school culture.* Brockville, ON: Upper Canada School District (to order: inquiries@ucdsb.on.ca).

Felesena, M.D. (2013). Does your district have a progressive discipline policy? *Education Digest, 79*(1), 39–42.

Restorative Justice Online www.restorativejustice.org

From Hostility to Harmony, International Institute for Restorative Practices

www.youtube.com/watch?v=LQWNyS4QSao (4.5 minutes)

Mending Conversations, A Step by Step Video Guide (Youth Diversion Program in Association with Limestone Education Foundation, Kingston, ON)

www.youtube.com/watch?v=aPHr65I8HqU

Riel, M. (2013). The Learning Circle Model: Collaborative Knowledge Building (Pepperdine University)

https://sites.google.com/site/onlinelearningcircles/Home/learning-circles-defined

Put into Practice

There is an extensive literature on using self-management and self-monitoring to enhance the attention, participation, and learning of children and adolescents with a range of exceptionalities. Choose three papers from the following list to read. Develop a simple strategy to help Mandy or Jacob, described in the opening case studies, to be more successful in an inclusive classroom.

Children with LD, speech and language exceptionalities, or emotional and behaviour disabilities:

Hoff, K.E., & Doepke, K.J. (2006). Increasing on-task behavior in the classroom: Extension of self-monitoring strategies. *Psychology in the Schools, 43*, 211–221.

Children with ADHD:

Ardoin, S.P., & Martens, B.K. (2004). Training children to make accurate self-evaluations: Effects on behavior and the quality of self-ratings. *Journal of Behavioral Education, 13*, 1–23.

Reid, R., Trout, A.L., & Schwartz, M. (2005). Self-regulation interventions for children with attention deficit/hyperactivity disorder. *Exceptional Children, 71*, 361–377.

Adolescents with ADHD:

Gureasko-Moore, S., DuPaul, G.J., & White, G.P. (2006). The effects of self-management in general education classrooms on the organizational skills of adolescents with ADHD. *Behavior Modification, 30*, 159–183.

Children and adolescents with emotional and behaviour disorders:

Mooney, P., Ryan, J.B., Uhing, B.M., Reid, R., & Epstein, M.H. (2005). A review of self-management interventions targeting academic outcomes for students with emotional and behavior disorders. *Journal of Behavioral Education, 14*, 203–221.

prewriting strategies (or discussion strategies) to reflect on their inappropriate behaviour and discover ways to improve their behaviour. Morris and Howard (2003) described an effective in-school suspension program that involved teaching middle school students organizational skills. Each student completed the work assigned in their regular classroom during the in-school suspension and received counselling for handling stressful situations and controlling their behaviour in the future. Flanagain (2007) conducted research on students' views of in-school and out-of-school suspensions. The students reported that out-of-school suspensions did not act as a deterrent and tended to antagonize relations of students with teachers and administrators. In-school suspensions were viewed somewhat more positively, although it was important that students received teaching and support for their difficulties during the in-school suspension. Research suggests teachers support in-school suspension although they believe they can be improved (Welch, 2010). Familiarize yourself with your school's policies and ask questions about a school's policies regarding suspension during an employment interview. It is usually easier to teach in a school when you agree with the policies.

CORPORAL PUNISHMENT, USING ACADEMIC TASKS AS PUNISHMENT, AND ATTENDANCE

Because we respect and value our students, we must ensure that we conduct our classes without **corporal punishment** or other cruel and dehumanizing techniques. In 2004 the Supreme Court of Canada reaffirmed that it is unacceptable to strike a student or threaten to strike a student (Axelrod, 2015). Corporal punishment violates students' rights and is ineffective in changing behaviour (Robinson et al., 2005). Students report that they perceive the practice of "hushing" the whole class as unfair and in conflict with the behaviour teachers expect of students. Whenever teachers blame and punish the whole class for the misdeeds of a few, they endanger the students' trust and respect that they have worked hard to earn (Thornberg, 2006). Besides alienating many students, punishment is ineffective at changing inappropriate behaviour and has been seen as "criminalizing kids" for minor offences (Thompson, 2011). Beware of assigning "lines" or mathematics problems as punishment. The contradictory message sent by assigning **academic tasks as punishment** only makes our job more difficult and students more resistant. However, requiring students to complete work missed due to absence is defensible; remember that some students may need support to accomplish this. When one student is absent, explore possible causes for that student's disengagement and academic difficulties. When many students have low attendance, look for a wider range of underlying causes. Ask what the contributing factors might be and look for complex solutions to what is usually a complex, multi-faceted problem. Your best strategy: make your classes so well taught and interesting that all students, including exceptional students with differentiated programs, hate to miss anything.

Alternative Approaches to School Discipline

Research conducted in the past decade suggests that alternative, more positive approaches to discipline do work. Rather than exclusionary approaches, like suspension and expulsion, schools can choose a **progressive discipline policy** which involves a sequence of gradually more stern responses from a classroom detention, through after-school detentions, to Saturday detentions, and eventually to in-school suspension (Felesena, 2013). Or schools can choose **restorative justice** (Mergler et al., 2014) which has the advantage of challenging students to hold themselves and each other accountable and to right wrongs as individuals and as a group. Restorative justice within schools focuses on developing relationships among students and the adults who work with them, teaching students how their actions affect the school community, and providing a platform for them to right the wrongs caused by their behaviour. An individual, either a student or an educator, mediates the discussion, called "the circle," so affected parties can reach a resolution acceptable to all involved (Wills & Bradshaw, 2013). This approach has been used extensively in the Upper Canada District School Board in Ontario (Wills & Bradshaw, 2013) and in the Ed White Middle School in San Antonio, Texas (Mergler et al., 2014). Wills and Bradshaw list many videos available on the topic and some of these appear in the previous Further Reading box.

Summary

It is important that classrooms in inclusive schools provide a sense of community so all members feel accepted and valued. Many elements contribute to developing an inclusive classroom climate, including developing relationships with students, the physical layout, and the norms of classroom interaction. Teachers negotiate and enforce classroom rules and procedures to ensure that all students, including exceptional learners, find the classroom predictable and safe. It is important to think about why a student might act the way she is acting and to use constructive approaches when responding to challenging behaviour. Managing behaviour in an inclusive classroom requires strategies for increasing appropriate behaviour, decreasing unacceptable behaviour, and enhancing self-management. Alternatives to exclusionary practices (such as suspension and expulsion) include positive behaviour support, progressive discipline, and restorative justice.

Key Terms

academic tasks as punishment (p. 214)
checkpoints (p. 200)
child-teacher relationships (p. 191)
classroom procedures (p. 197)
climate (p. 189)
community (p. 188)
community agreements (p. 194)
community circle (p. 194)
consistency (p. 200)
contract (p. 209)
corporal punishment (p. 214)
encouragement (p. 203)
enforcing a rule (p. 197)
expulsion (p. 213)

holding pattern (p. 208)
informal conference (p. 209)
in-school suspension (p. 213)
"invisible" classroom management (p. 203)
low-key interventions (p. 207)
monitoring (p. 198)
natural consequences (p. 208)
norms for classroom interaction (p. 193)
physical space (p. 192)
positive behavioural supports (PBS) (p. 212)
pro-act (p. 206)
progressive discipline policy (p. 214)

problem-solving approach (p. 209)
punishment (p. 213)
reasons why students act the way they do (p. 200)
relationships (p. 191)
restorative justice (p. 214)
reward systems (p. 203)
right to pass (p. 195)
rules (p. 195)
scaffolding (p. 200)
self-monitoring (p. 210)
signal (p. 194)
suspension (p. 213)
teacher-student relationships (p. 191)

Challenges for Reviewing Chapter 7

1. What does it mean for a classroom to have an inclusive climate? What contribution does the physical layout of a classroom make to an inclusive climate? Compare its importance with the importance of the norms for interaction that you teach to and expect of your students.

2. Write a brief scenario that includes some of the greatest challenges to your teaching and management in a classroom with a student like Mandy (in the opening case for this chapter), who has a history of losing her temper, punching, and screaming at her classmates. Look back through the chapter and identify the major differentiations you would make in your plan for managing the classroom. Describe how you would establish and maintain a positive relationship with Mandy.

3. Return to the opening cases of Mandy and Jacob and answer the five questions that follow the cases.

Activities for Reviewing Chapter 7 with Your Peers

4. How do teachers go about creating a classroom community in an elementary classroom? In a secondary classroom? Prepare a list of priority tasks you would undertake before the beginning of the school year, during the first day of school, and during the first week of school as either an elementary or secondary teacher. Compare your list with one of peers who teaches in the other panel and identify the common elements on your lists. Identify the priority tasks that differ for the two of you and try to identify whether the differences arise because of the panel in which you teach, because of your individual teaching philosophies, or for other reasons.

5. Prepare a series of lesson plans for negotiating and enforcing classroom rules and procedures. Take into account the age and grade level of the students you teach. Exchange plans with a peer and give each other feedback.

6. Organize a debate with your peers on the merits and drawbacks of restorative justice in the school context.

7. You are a member of the in-school team in Jacob's school (Jacob is described in one of the opening cases for this chapter). Prepare to assume the role of one member of the team. The team includes Jacob's history teacher, the resource room teacher, the principal, and two other teachers who teach Jacob in their classes this semester. Use the information in this chapter to develop a systematic approach that you recommend for curbing the problems that are emerging—without spoiling Jacob's improving relationship with his classmates. Why do you think that the approach that you recommend will be effective? You may want to role-play this scenario with your peers, each of you assuming a role of one of the members of the team.

CHAPTER 8

Using Universal Design for Learning (UDL) and Differentiated Instruction (DI)

Jani Bryson/Getty Images

MS. ASH TEACHES MATHEMATICS AT A LARGE INNER-CITY SECONDARY SCHOOL. A few years ago, she attended a workshop on UDL and DI. Since then, she has started every class with an example of how the day's math can be used—perhaps by engineers to design a heating system. When she teaches new mathematical content, she usually teaches to the whole class, with the students seated in pairs. First she reviews, pointing out explicitly how recent lessons relate to today's class. At the beginning of the term, she hands out a partially completed outline to every student and then projects the same outline on the screen. She demonstrates, questions, and fills in the outline while she explains the new content. She stops every few minutes for students to ask questions and complete their outlines. As the term progresses, Ms. Ash encourages students to create their own outlines and notes when they can show her that theirs are complete and accurate. Some do this within a few weeks and others opt to use her outline most of the term. She moves to guided practise by demonstrating an example on the overhead projector while students work in pairs on the same example. Then students complete two or three examples in pairs without Ms. Ash guiding them. She takes up these examples, guides students in practising another if necessary, and then asks students to work together on two or three examples and finally to complete two or three independently. Some students move to independent practise faster than others, and Ms. Ash respects students' thoughtful decisions about this. She moves to the round table and invites students who want to review the steps to join her while the rest complete a challenge task in collaborative groups or independently. Samuel has a learning disability and has always found math difficult. This term, Ms. Ash paired Samuel with a boy who answers his questions with explanations, and Samuel is learning in math class. He likes to go to the round table to hear Ms. Ash explain the concepts and the steps again and to have her correct his work. Ms. Ash has taught him how to use a calculator and encourages him to use it; it is one of the accommodations listed on his IEP. Now he feels that he is learning to solve problems rather than spending all his time trying to do calculations.

HEMA HAS AN INTELLECTUAL DISABILITY; SHE HAS A PACEMAKER, BUT IT DOES NOT RESTRICT HER ACTIVITIES. She is included in a grade 5 class and learns best with visual materials, hands-on activities, and preteaching. Hema reads common signs in the neighbourhood, recognizes the written names of family and friends, and reads calendar words. She prints her name on forms or applications, draws simple pictures, and types a couple of sentences on the computer while looking at a model. Her annual goals (on her IEP) include sustaining a conversation; maintaining socially appropriate behaviour; using a telephone; describing events, interactions, etc.; using money; and reading to get information. For the weather unit in Hema's science class, classroom teacher Mr. Carvello, along with the resource teacher, used the ADAPT strategy. While the other students completed a full-page chart on the weather each day using the class's weather station, Hema recorded only three aspects: she recorded the temperature, drew the cloud cover, and wrote the precipitation. To meet the IEP goals of using the telephone and relaying information, the two teachers designed a learning activity: in the company of a peer, Hema would go to the school office to telephone the regional weather office daily. Eleven peers volunteered to take turns accompanying Hema. Mr. Carvello demonstrated their role to the peer volunteers twice. Hema dialed the number, listened, and repeated what the meteorologist had said. The peer scribed as Hema repeated the information. Back in the classroom, Mr. Carvello printed it neatly and prompted Hema while she practised telling the class. Hema gradually used the telephone more independently, and the peer who had accompanied Hema provided any information she missed in her summary. Hema's daily goal was to give a full account, which she was soon able to do.

SALLY HAS ALWAYS STRUGGLED WITH COMPREHENDING AND INTERPRETING WHAT SHE READS. She no longer has an IEP, but she did have one for many years. This year she is in grade 11, and Yolanda Chiang is her language and literature teacher. The class is studying *Romeo and Juliet*. Yesterday Ms. Chiang taught the class elements of Shakespeare's tragedies, and Sally is worried because she knows that she can't yet identify all the elements of a Shakespearean tragedy. Sally is relieved when Ms. Chiang divides the class into three groups. Two groups are given clear instructions, oral and written, and begin to compare the elements of tragedy in *Romeo and Juliet* to the elements of tragedy in *A Doll's House* by Ibsen, a play the class read a month earlier. Each of these two groups is to create a poster using words and drawings, showing the elements in each tragedy, providing examples, and making comparisons. Sally is part of a group of eight students who are working with Ms. Chiang to review the elements of Shakespeare's tragedies as seen in *Romeo and Juliet*. Many of these students have IEPs, and others, like Sally, had an IEP for many years. Ms. Chiang leads Sally's group in charting and providing examples of the elements (in words and drawings) from *Romeo and Juliet*. Sally is pleased because she provides an example and suggests how it can be illustrated. After Sally's group is working well and understands the elements in *Romeo and Juliet*, Ms. Chiang moves on to check in with the other two groups. Sally is relieved that Ms. Chiang provides review and makes sure everyone understands each topic before the class moves on to the next topic.

1. How have these three teachers compared the strengths and needs of exceptional students—like Samuel, Hema, and Sally—with classroom demands?

2. How do these teachers use UDL and DI to ensure that everyone learns? How do these adaptations relate to the IEPs of exceptional students?

3. How have these teachers considered the perspectives of and consequences for others as well as for Hema, Samuel, and Sally?

4. Are these differentiations beneficial to students other than Sally, Hema, and Samuel? How?

5. How have these teachers ADAPTed teaching without unduly increasing their own workloads?

Introduction

In classrooms where teachers use universal design for learning (UDL) and differentiated instruction (DI), they begin where the students are and accept that students differ in important ways. Teachers can analyze their classroom environment and teaching in relation to students' academic and social needs and make adaptations or, in current terminology, differentiate to ensure success for all students, including exceptional students. The terms *differentiate* and *adapt* are used interchangeably in this chapter, as they are in the writings of Carol Ann Tomlinson, a well-known proponent of differentiated classrooms (e.g., Tomlinson, 2014). Essentially, differentiating instruction means structuring a lesson at multiple levels and in such a way that each student has an opportunity to work at a moderately challenging, developmentally appropriate level.

This chapter provides explicit examples of using the ADAPT strategy introduced in Chapter 1 to differentiate teaching. These examples represent many exceptionalities and many areas of the elementary and secondary curriculum. Individual teachers and students find that some ways of differentiating work better for them than others. For example, Ms. Ash finds it easy to model and provide guided practise, followed by independent practise, for the whole class. Samuel finds that the partially completed outline helps him follow her teaching. He benefits from using a calculator and from thoughtful pairing of students. Receiving immediate feedback on his completed work motivates Samuel. These accommodations (on the grade level curriculum) help other students as well. Hema is learning about weather at a level consistent with her strengths, prior knowledge, and needs, and is meeting goals from her IEP. She is also developing better social relationships with her peers. Mr. Carvello is making modifications (using goals from the curriculum for a lower grade) to meet Hema's learning needs without undue effort and helping Hema to meet alternate outcomes from her IEP that focus on social skills. In the case of Sally, Ms. Chiang is providing follow-up that is appropriate for all the students in her class. Two-thirds of the students demonstrated in discussion and in their written work yesterday that they understood the elements of Shakespearean tragedies. Ms. Chiang set them to work applying and extending what they had learned, while she helped the other one-third of the class to understand and illustrate the concept, rather than expecting them to apply it. She retaught the concept to these students and helped them to work together to demonstrate their understanding. Sometimes this is called tiering the lesson.

Using UDL and differentiating teaching and assessment are at the heart of inclusive education that honours diversity and strives for equity. The next section introduces universal design for learning and, following a brief history of this general approach, provides a description of a Canadian model for UDL that includes DI: Jennifer Katz's three-block model of UDL.

Universal Design for Learning (UDL)

Universal Design (UD) in Architecture

Universal design for learning (UDL) was inspired by work in architecture called universal design (UD), which advocated beginning the design process for buildings to ensure that they would be accessible by all people, including people with physical

Further Reading

Katz, J. (2012). *Teaching to diversity.* Winnipeg, MB: Portage & Main.

Tomlinson, C.A. (2014). *The differentiated classroom: Responding to the needs of all learners* (2nd ed.). Alexandria, VA: Association for Supervision and Curriculum Development.

Kluth, P., & Danaher, S. (2014). *From text maps to memory caps: 100 ways to differentiate instruction in K-12 inclusive classrooms.* Baltimore, MD: Paul H. Brookes Pub.

Dacey, L.S. (2013). *How to differentiate your math instruction: Lessons, ideas, and videos with common core support.* Sausalito, CA: Math Solutions [multimedia].

Plucker, J.A., & Callahan, C.M. (2014). *Critical issues and practices in gifted education: What the research says.* Waco, TX: Prufrock Press Inc.

Weblinks

MAKING A DIFFERENCE: ALBERTA DEPARTMENT OF EDUCATION. MEETING DIVERSE LEARNING NEEDS WITH DIFFERENTIATED INSTRUCTION
http://education.alberta.ca/teachers/resources/cross/making-a-difference.aspx

MANITOBA DEPARTMENT OF EDUCATION. DIFFERENTIATED INSTRUCTION: CURRICULUM DEVELOPMENT AND IMPLEMENTATION
www.edu.gov.mb.ca/k12/specedu/programming/universal.html

ONTARIO MINISTRY OF EDUCATION: LEADING MATH SUCCESS, GRADES 7–12
www.edu.gov.on.ca/eng/document/reports/numeracy/numeracyreport.pdf

THE ACCESS CENTER, OFFICE OF SPECIAL EDUCATION PROGRAMS (U.S.)
www.k8accesscenter.org/index.php

disabilities. This approach was intended to eliminate the need for retrofitting, an expensive and unsatisfactory approach of the 1990s. An American architect, Ronald Mace, challenged his colleagues to move beyond the barrier-free approach with its segregated accessible features, which were "special," expensive, and often unattractive. UD also responded to legislated rights for persons with disabilities and advances in assistive technology (Story et al., 1998). Because universal design and assistive technology had similar purposes, that is, to reduce physical and attitudinal barriers between people with and without disabilities, the two have intersected. This may explain why early understandings of UDL (and many current descriptions) tend to focus on using technology to accommodate all learners.

Story and her colleagues (1998) describe a full spectrum of human abilities that UD was intended to design for, not simply physical abilities. They describe how cognition affects design usability, considering variation in ability to receive, comprehend, interpret, remember, and act on information. They refer to many exceptionalities, including intellectual disabilities, learning disabilities, and brain injuries. They ask questions to assess the effectiveness of a design for cognition.

Is the design still usable and safe if you

- are using it for the first time without help or instruction?
- cannot read?
- perform steps out of order?
- try to use it much faster or slower than intended?
- are distracted or interrupted while using it?

They conduct a similar process to assess whether design is usable and safe for persons with a range of capabilities in vision, hearing, speech, and for physical disabilities affecting arm function, hand function, or mobility (e.g., cerebral palsy, muscular dystrophy, diabetes, arthritis, asthma).

The result of this analysis process has been seven principles for UD:

1. Equitable use: identical use when possible, otherwise equivalent use; appealing to all

2. Flexibility in use: accommodates many preferences and abilities; includes choice and adapts pacing

3. Simple and intuitive use: easy to understand regardless of user's experience, knowledge, literacy, concentration level; provides feedback

4. Perceptible information: communicates necessary information regardless of sensory or ambient abilities; is compatible with a range of devices

5. Tolerance for error: minimizes adverse consequences of accidental or unintended actions; most used elements are most accessible

6. Low physical effort: can be used efficiently and comfortably with minimal fatigue

7. Appropriate size and space for approach and use: for a range of body size, posture, grip, mobility

Technology in UD and UDL

Experience has demonstrated that UD can eliminate the need for retrofitting, and that wide doorways and ramps are advantageous for many people, not just those with physical disabilities. However, many applications of UD to education—that is, many approaches to UDL—have relied heavily on the association with assistive technology.

For example, the Center for Applied Special Technology (CAST) developed an approach called planning for all learners (PAL). This follows the basic principles:

- Use multiple or flexible representations of information and concepts (the what of learning);
- Use multiple or flexible options in expression and performance of learning (the how of learning);
- Use multiple or flexible ways to engage learners in the curriculum (the why of learning).

An example of the common emphasis on technology in UDL involves a free online tool, UDL Editions (http://udleditions.cast.org), which provides classic texts from world literature with comprehensive supports for struggling readers and offers challenging learning activities to engage expert readers. Gronneberg (2008) describes how to use these online texts with their three levels of support. For example, *Call of the Wild* (by Jack London, originally published in 1903) brings the gold rush to life with links to video, documents, letters, and maps, as well as strategy instruction. Students could choose to read the original text or could autonomously make selections at three levels to help them read and understand the text or to push them to engage at a higher level with the ideas. Other classic texts available include *How Coyote Stole Fire* (a Native American legend), *Sonnet XVIII* (by William Shakespeare), and *The Tell-Tale Heart* (by Edgar Allan Poe).

Katz's Three-Block Model of UDL

Canadian educational researcher Jennifer Katz (2012) of the University of Manitoba has also developed an approach to UDL, the **three-block model**, but this approach differs in that it does not assume that digital media are necessary. Katz argues that universal design can "help make inclusive education work" (2012, p. 13). Like in the original concept of universal design, Katz is committed to making the curriculum accessible to all and to enabling those who previously couldn't participate to participate. And she focuses on how we can do this in a way that does not disadvantage anyone else. She emphasizes the importance of classroom climate and of **differentiated instruction (DI)**, two ideas that are developed throughout this text. Based on Burgstahler and Chang (2009), Katz (2012, p. 15) lays out eight important aspects to keep in mind when planning teaching and activities so they will be accessible for all:

1. Classroom climate follows from practices that value diversity and inclusiveness.
2. Interactions among students and between students and the teacher are built on communication that can be understood by all.
3. Physical environment and products are available to all and safe for all.
4. Instructional standards hold high expectations for all and provide a high level of support for all.
5. Instructional methods are varied and ensure accessibility for all.
6. Information resources and technology (e.g., course materials) are engaging and flexible so they can be understood by all.
7. Feedback is provided regularly.
8. Assessment of student progress is frequent and adjusted so all can show what they know.

In her book *Teaching to Diversity*, Katz (2012) argues that UDL is an overarching concept composed of three main blocks, which are all essential to making inclusion

The Three-Block Model of Universal Design for Learning (UDL)

Block 1: Creating a Community; Social and Emotional Learning; consider using the Respecting Diversity Program (lessons in Katz, 2012)

Block 2: Planning for Diversity: Inclusive Instructional Practice

Plan for the whole school year

Plan for the terms and units (within the year)

Plan lessons (within the units)

In an extended example of her model (involving grade 7 social studies and science for Manitoba), Katz (2012) suggests and illustrates how to:

1. Align the topics in the curriculum with the school terms.

2. Integrate the curricula from social studies and science into thematic units.

3. Integrate and sequence the learning of skills, knowledge, and values from the other curriculum areas, such as language arts, mathematics, and fine arts, for the year within the themes already chosen above.

4. Develop learning outcomes by asking: What do I want my students to understand in a deep and profound way? What are the big ideas?

5. Pose inquiry questions, open-ended questions that use higher order cognitive processes.

6. Develop rubrics or adopt rubrics provided by the Ministry or Department of Education at four levels: beginning to develop; approaching expectations; fully meeting expectations; exceeding expectations.

7. Develop multiple modes of teaching and assessing, presenting the material in many ways: using work centres that draw on different student strengths (visual, verbal, numerical, written, spoken, hands-on); using a web for planning; the student developing ideas and seeking them online and from other resources.

8. Plan lessons, each focusing on one or two essential understandings and using a number of modes of learning; include "gradual release" (Katz provides many examples).

9. Plan an integrative inquiry project late in each unit, often including group co-operation and individual accountability.

Block 3: System and Structures; Leadership, Policy, and Practice; Inclusive Policy, Collaborative Practice, Team Planning, Assistive Technology

In a series of research reports, Katz examines students' emotional and behavioural outcomes in the Respecting Diversity Program (Katz & Porath, 2011); reports on students' increased academic and social engagement when experiencing the three-block model (2013); describes teachers' experiences with improved student learning and with barriers to implementation (2015); and the role of the principal when implementing the three-block model of UDL in a high school (Katz & Sugden, 2012).

Sources: Description of model adapted from Katz, J. (2012). *Teaching to diversity: The three-block model of universal design for learning.* Winnipeg: Portage and Main Press.

Katz, J. (2013). The three block model of universal design for learning (UDL): Engaging students in inclusive education. *Canadian Journal of Education, 36*(1), 153–194.

Katz, J. (2015). Implementing the three block model of universal design for learning: Effects on teachers' self-efficacy, stress, and job satisfaction in inclusive classrooms K–12. *International Journal of Inclusive Education, 19*(1), 1–20.

Katz, J., & Porath, M. (2011). Teaching to diversity: Creating compassionate learning communities for diverse elementary school students. *International Journal of Special Education, 26*(2), 29–41.

Katz, J., & Sugden, R. (2013). Three three-block model of universal design for learning implementation in a high school. *Canadian Journal of Educational Administration and Policy*, issue 141, 1–28.

work. The most fundamental block in her model is social and emotional learning, which demands that we develop compassionate learning communities. This is the focus of Chapters 7 and 10 and a recurring theme throughout the book. The second block is inclusive instructional practice, and is often called differentiated instruction and differentiated assessment, the topics addressed in Chapters 8 and 9. Every chapter of this book includes examples of DI, and many illustrate differentiated assessment. The third block in Katz's three-block model focuses on systems and structures, from policy to budget to planning teams. Many of these aspects essential for inclusive education were introduced in Chapter 1 and elaborated in Chapter 2, and examples appear in context in later chapters.

Using the ADAPT Strategy to Analyze and Differentiate Teaching for Individuals and Groups

West Coast Surfer/picture alliance / moodboard/Newscom

Talking with your students will help you know their strengths and needs and will enable them to trust you. This boy's father will be out of the country for the next six months.

You need strategies for differentiating teaching that are effective for exceptional students, are efficient for you, and become a regular part of your planning and teaching. Curriculum documents essentially tell teachers what to teach; DI helps teachers decide how to teach a range of learners by using a number of teaching approaches. Tomlinson has written about how you can differentiate one, two, or all three of the following elements: (a) the content (what the students are learning), (b) the process (the activities), and (c) the products (the accomplishments that show learning) (Tomlinson, 2014). Chapter 1 introduced ADAPT. This strategy is similar to many others, but it includes considering the perspectives of many people, including classmates, on the differentiation and on the consequences for them. The characteristics of the students (strengths *and* needs, interests, preferences for how they learn, prior knowledge, language proficiency, self-control in the classroom context, and many other characteristics that you have read about and experienced) and the demands of the classroom are important when devising adaptations to build on the student's strengths and either bypass areas of need or help the student strengthen these areas.

The ADAPT strategy has the following five steps:

- Step 1: **A**ccounts of students' strengths and needs
- Step 2: **D**emands of the classroom
- Step 3: **A**daptations
- Step 4: **P**erspectives and consequences
- Step 5: **T**each and assess the match

Step 1: Accounts of Students' Strengths and Needs

Cross-Reference
Chapters 7 and 10 focus on ways you can create a classroom community and help all students to feel like they belong in the classroom. Chapters 1 and 2 focus on aspects of policies and structural supports for teachers differentiating instruction.

This first step requires that you know your students well. From the first day of school you must be familiar with the content of the confidential file of each exceptional student you teach. Usually the file contains the student's IEP, test reports, comments from previous teachers, and medical information that could be critical to the student's well-being (e.g., indication of allergies, epilepsy, or asthma). If there is an IEP, it includes specific statements about strengths and needs, usually in three general areas: social, emotional, and behavioural; physical; and academic. It is important to quickly come to know your students as individuals with preferences and strengths that may not always coincide—students are not always best at what they say they enjoy most. Thus you will need to make the students collaborators with you because, as insiders, they can let you know, for instance, when tasks are too difficult or too easy and when activities are engaging or boring.

Social, emotional, and behavioural (SEB) strengths include such things as engaging in conversation. You can use strengths such as engaging in conversation or self-advocacy to help the student learn in a collaborative group. On the other hand, SEB needs could mean that a student requires supervision because he tends to get into fights when unsupervised. Physical strengths and needs include motor skills, sight, and hearing. One child may have strength in printing neatly and quickly, while another may need instruction and support to enter assignments into a computer. Academic strengths and needs include the basic skills of reading, writing, and mathematics, and learning strategies for test taking and problem solving. Students like Samuel have strengths such as using a calculator. Students like Hema have needs such as requiring instruction to develop beginning reading skills. Sally needs review and more than one opportunity to learn complex ideas, like the elements of a Shakespearean tragedy, but it is apparent in her case at the beginning of the chapter that she participates enthusiastically, especially in a small group. It is helpful to prepare a brief description of the strengths and needs, and other characteristics like interests and prior knowledge, of each student and consult these while planning and teaching.

Step 2: Demands of the Classroom on Students

Next consider the social, emotional, and behavioural demands of your classroom. Do students learn individually, work with peers, or do they do both? How long is the lecture portion of each lesson? Do you model positive interactions with all students? For physical demands, do you rely on projecting images, and can everyone see them clearly? The academic demands are manifested in things like the instructional materials you use (e.g., textbooks, computer programs, websites) and in the instructional approaches. Direct instruction followed by guided and independent practise benefits students with learning disabilities and many others in the class, while open-ended assignments challenge gifted students. Academic demands also appear in assessment methods.

Step 3: Adaptations

In this step you compare a student's learning needs with the demands of the classroom and identify potential mismatches and ways to differentiate that eliminate these mismatches. You can make adaptations in the fundamental organization and instruction that goes on in the classroom. In making adaptations, you can bypass a mismatch between a student and curriculum demands or you can teach through the mismatch. These strategies are discussed in the next section. You can use flexible grouping and make adaptations through flexible use of space, materials, time, and teacher contact to optimize learning for every student (like the three teachers in the case studies that open this chapter). Remember that you can give students choice and vary the means of representation, expression, and engagement. An experienced teacher recently reported that the three key differentiations she pays attention to first are: (1) break it down, (2) repeat, repeat, repeat, (3) make it relevant.

Put into Practice

Informally ask parents, teachers, and students how they feel about differentiated instruction to meet the learning needs of exceptional students. What "hard questions" might you be asked by students without exceptionalities and their parents?

Step 4: Perspectives and Consequences

Take time to reflect on each differentiation from many perspectives. What has your experience been with it? Whereas step 2 focuses on the demands on the students made by your classroom, curriculum, and ways of teaching, it is important at this step to ask: What are the demands this differentiation makes on you? Are they realistic? If you are uncomfortable with a differentiation, it is unlikely that you will continue to use it. To bolster your self-efficacy, start small and build up to your highest aspirations. If you accept that setbacks will occur, you will be better prepared to overcome your disappointment and renew your efforts. To get the most return for your effort, differentiate in ways that are beneficial for many students and that have demonstrated effectiveness. Use observation to learn about the exceptional students' experience of the differentiation. Do the students feel that the opportunities you are offering and the changes you are making are respectful? Do the differentiations draw too much unwanted attention to these students? Can you ensure that the options you offer are productive choices for many students so that everyone feels part of the community? How does the rest of the class view your differentiations? If they become the basis of teasing, then you know you have not achieved your goals. How would the parents of the exceptional student view the differentiations you used? And how would the community look on these adaptations?

Next consider the consequences, intended and unintended, for the exceptional students—learning, drawbacks—and for others affected by the differentiation. What are the consequences of the differentiation for others in the class? Do any dilemmas arise? Are some students providing too much assistance to classmates when they should be completing their own assignments? If you provide an open-ended assessment, you may be disappointed when students capable of writing an essay choose to develop a graphic representation of what they have learned. Giving choice requires that we help students to know themselves and to make good choices for themselves, with an appropriate degree of challenge. In the case at the beginning of this chapter, Mr. Carvello differentiated instruction for Hema and considered the impact on her peers. He developed a rota of willing volunteers, so many of her classmates learned to interact appropriately with Hema without feeling overly responsible for her progress or missing much instructional time. Ongoing assessment will help you to make adjustments as you teach.

Step 5: Teach and Assess the Match

During and following the teaching, assess how well the differentiation overcame the mismatch between student strengths and needs, interests, learning preferences, and prior knowledge, on one hand, and classroom demands, on the other. This analysis will help you decide about altering the differentiation while it takes place and about continuing the differentiation. Persevere and give it time to be effective. You can observe how engaged the students are, ask the students how they find the changes, record marks, analyze errors, and talk with parents.

Choosing and Combining Strategies for Differentiating

Over the years, many approaches have been developed to help teachers focus on how to adapt or differentiate to meet the needs of all students. Many teachers still find an older approach helpful when they are thinking about exceptional learners, especially those with severe disabilities that make their learning experience different from that of most other students. When you find a mismatch between student strengths and the demands of your curriculum and teaching there are three ways to change teaching: (1) teach through the mismatch; (2) teach around the mismatch; and (3) remediate or accelerate in hopes of overcoming the mismatch. These differentiations can be used individually or in combination.

Weblinks

NEW BRUNSWICK: CHALLENGE FOR CREDIT
www.gnb.ca/0000/
publications/curric/Challenge_
for_Credit.pdf

ALBERTA EDUCATION: MAKING A DIFFERENCE: MEETING DIVERSE LEARNING NEEDS WITH DIFFERENTIATED INSTRUCTION
http://education.alberta.ca/
teachers/resources/cross/
making-a-difference.aspx

SPECIAL EDUCATION ASSOCIATION OF BC: FIRST STEPS (TO DIFFERENTIATED INSTRUCTION)
http://seabc.pbworks.com/w/
page/23257896/First%20Steps

ONTARIO MINISTRY OF EDUCATION: LEADING MATH SUCCESS, GRADES 7–12
www.edu.gov.on.ca/eng/
document/reports/numeracy/
numeracyreport.pdf

Teaching Through the Mismatch

Most of the strategies we discuss in this text are means of teaching through the mismatch. They require us to find ways to involve students in the overall teaching for the class. However, there are two other distinct strategies that are more likely to set students apart from the other members of the class. This means we need to approach them in a matter-of-fact way without drawing too much attention to students, or they may not be willing to accept these strategies.

Teaching Around the Mismatch

Strategies for teaching around the mismatch are sometimes called **bypass strategies** because they allow students to succeed in the classroom using alternative means. Samuel bypassed his lack of computation skills with a calculator so he could concentrate on solving problems. Universal design would suggest that using a calculator might be an option provided to all students; that decision depends on what your teaching objectives are. But if you can offer a calculator to many students, then those who really need it may feel more comfortable about using it. Like most bypass strategies, calculator use was successful for Samuel because he was taught to use the calculator proficiently. To teach around spelling disabilities, one might allow some or all students to use a spell checker. Braille bypasses sight to enable reading, but unlike a calculator or spell checker, Braille is only helpful for students without sight. This reminds us that some bypass strategies benefit all while others are person-specific. Bypass strategies that enhance independence are usually preferable (e.g., a spell checker rather than a peer editor, although a peer editor may be a step on the way to independent use of a spell checker).

Remediating or Accelerating to Overcome the Mismatch

A second strategy for overcoming a mismatch is intensive remediation or acceleration. Intensive **remediation** is designed to address basic skills or learning strategies that the student needs and that you believe the student can acquire. A resource teacher may do unison reading with a slow reader or a group of slow readers in grade 9 to help the students increase reading speed so they can comprehend their textbooks. You could tutor four students who have difficulty printing, while the class writes daily journal entries. Intensive intervention in phonological processing can turn non-readers with learning disabilities into readers. Judicious use of remediation can be very effective. An example of **acceleration** (used to move academically advanced students into challenging learning) is teaching a small group of adolescents in your geography class to run a statistical program and analyze Statistics Canada data. They are bored by your unit on immigration, well prepared to take the unit test, and eager to meet this challenge. If this would be an appropriate activity for many students, then it might be a tiered activity that others can choose; but if you believe it is only appropriate for two or three students, then you need to find a way for them to engage in this tiered activity while others choose from a range of other tasks. Some provinces enable high school students to challenge for credit if they believe they have met "all the learning, process, interpersonal, participation objectives or outcomes/requirements of a course" (New Brunswick, 2014; www.gnb.ca/0000/publications/curric/Challenge_for_Credit.pdf).

Put into Practice

Read at least two specialized resources that focus on DI and assessment for students with a specific exceptionality. Choose one from the list below and locate another source yourself; you may use one of the references provided in this text. Consider what, if anything, is unique about differentiating to meet the needs of a student with a specific exceptionality. Discuss with peers who have read different sources.

Gibson, L. (2013). Differentiated instruction and students with learning disabilities. *Advances in Special Education, 24,* 161–183.

Bowen, J.M. (2005). Classroom interventions for students with traumatic brain injuries. *Preventing School Failure, 49*(4), 34–41.

Bianco, M., Carothers, D.E., & Smiley, L.R. (2009). Gifted students with Asperger syndrome: Strategies for strength-based programming. *Intervention in School and Clinic, 44*(4), 206–215.

Gent, P.J. (2009). *Great ideas: Using service learning and differentiated instruction to help your students succeed.* Baltimore, MD: Paul H. Brookes. (students with intellectual disabilities, students with developmental disabilities)

Examples and Non-Examples of DI

Cross-Reference
Chapter I defined accommodations, modifications, and alternative expectations. Consult your local and provincial documents to see if this distinction is made. What terms are used in your province and in your school district?

In addition to recognizing differentiated instruction in practice, it is important that you acknowledge what differentiated instruction does *not* mean. It does not mean doing something different for each student in the class. And it does not mean disorganized and disorderly student activity, with everyone doing what they like. Differentiated instruction does not mean that you must always use groups, maintain the same groups over time, or isolate students who are experiencing difficulty learning. When using differentiated instruction, you can still engage in whole-class activities with all students taking part in the same activity or in variations on an activity.

The next section helps you to identify the many aspects of the classroom that can be adapted or differentiated.

Analyzing Teaching: What You Can Adapt

In Chapter 1 we discussed three forms of adaptations: accommodations (which change how you teach but do not alter the provincial curriculum expectations for the grade); modifications, which refer to changes in what is taught, that is, in grade-level expectations as well as teaching approaches; and alternative expectations, those that are not represented in the curriculum but are appropriate to the student's needs (such as mobility training or social skills not normally taught in the school context) (Ontario Ministry of Education, 2004). At the beginning of this chapter, Samuel and Sally received accommodations to the curriculum, and Hema received modifications as well as having some alternative expectations, such as learning to use the telephone. When you use the ADAPT strategy to analyze and differentiate teaching, you may be struck by how many ways there are to make changes that meet student needs. For example, you can adapt the substance of your teaching (e.g., outcomes, content, cognitive complexity, authenticity, and interest of the task). Or you may find that it makes more sense to change the environment (e.g., seating). You may want to enhance student engagement by changing the method of instruction—through activity-based learning or by changing the form of practise. All these aspects of teaching are closely related and are often called differentiating the process. You can also differentiate the product of learning, which could be a report, debate, poster, brochure, rap song, model, and so forth. Looking at the components that make up teaching enables us to see myriad ways of differentiating for exceptional students.

Tiered instruction is grouping students for instruction based on their prior background knowledge in a given subject area. Richards and Omdal (2007) describe teaching secondary science by tiering. They present the content at varying levels of complexity while using the same process for all students; they found this was especially beneficial for lower level learners. In the case at the beginning of the chapter, this is what Ms. Chiang did when she grouped students by their current level of understanding of the topic, elements of Shakespeare's tragedies. One tier had two groups (of students ready for extensions) while the other tier had one group (of students like Sally who did not completely understand the elements). The Focus on Research box shows how the concept of universal design for learning (UDL) may inform the way we think about differentiation.

Outcomes, Content, Cognitive Complexity, Authenticity, and Interest of Task

Outcomes and these other aspects of teaching are all related to the substance and intent of what is taught. When you change the learning outcomes to something

What do you think?

Read Paul S. George's paper "A Rationale for Differentiating Instruction in the Regular Classroom," published in *Theory into Practice* (2007, 44 (3), pages 185–193). He argues that we differentiate because it is the right thing to do, because it honours diversity and equitable opportunity to learn in heterogeneous classrooms. He makes the case that publicly funded, heterogeneous classrooms are essential for the future of democracy. What do you think of his argument?

Weblinks

ELECTIONS CANADA: CLASSROOM RESOURCES
www.elections.ca (search for "Classroom resources")

HOW TO ORGANIZE AN ELECTION SIMULATION (IN CANADA)
www.studentvote.ca/home.php

radically different from those in the grade-level curriculum that you teach the class, you are setting alternative expectations. This occurs when 14-year-old Adam, who has intellectual disabilities, learns to make a sandwich. However, Sylvia, who is blind, has the geography curriculum accommodated by using raised maps of the province and the guidance of a peer tutor. She may focus on the demographics of the province, which can be accessed on the computer in an auditory form or printed in Braille. Sylvia's outcomes are based on those in the curriculum of the grade level you are teaching. Modifying outcomes for a gifted student may mean including expectations from a higher grade level, for example, conducting a critical analysis of the declining role of landforms in demographic patterns of population. Changes range from minor to large depending on the students' strengths and needs and on classroom demands, but they should always ensure that the pupil learns.

Cognitive complexity refers to the cognitive demands made of the learner. When **authentic tasks** are presented to students in the form in which they occur in society, students usually find these tasks complex. A class staging a mock municipal election would research how to nominate municipal candidates, hold press conferences, and cast and count votes while learning about the issues. An exceptional student could work toward the goal of improving co-operation with peers (on her IEP) as a member of a campaign team. A gifted student might run for mayor. These students are experiencing high cognitive complexity. However, students from other classes who listen to speeches, read newspapers to learn the issues, and cast ballots will be learning about democracy in a concrete way, and not experiencing as much cognitive complexity. Authentic tasks can provide concrete experiences of abstract ideas such as democracy. Cognitively complex challenges help to maintain the interest of gifted students, who often develop deep sensitivities to issues and injustices at an early age (Hartsell, 2006; Malin & Makel, 2012).

Interest comprises an affective interaction between students and tasks. It is often suggested that gifted students follow their interests (e.g., Linnenbrink-Garcia et al., 2013). However, interest also plays an important role in engaging students who are not interested in learning for its own sake—including those with learning disabilities, ADHD, Asperger syndrome, and other exceptionalities. For these students, developing curriculum around interests (in sculpture, trucks, pets, etc.) can produce focused attention and learning (McPhail et al., 2004). I taught a reading comprehension unit that included all my curriculum goals (identifying the main idea and supporting details, reading captions of figures, etc.) and was based on Saskatchewan's driver handbook. The idea came to me as I watched my students struggle to read the content they needed to pass the test for a learner's driving permit. I capitalized on their interest in learning to drive to improve their reading comprehension, and they all secured the coveted permit. Chapter 7 describes the Theory of Self-Determination (Ryan & Deci, 2000), in the section on motivation and rewards, and how it is often helpful to maintain student interest, when a task is not intrinsically motivating, by increasing student feelings of relatedness, competence, and autonomy. This generates an affective interaction between students and tasks.

Environment, Method of Presentation, Pace, and Quantity

Environment has to do with classroom climate and physical layout, which are addressed in Chapter 7. High expectations accompanied by high support make for the best learning environment. To increase your support and encouragement, be

Further Reading on Challenging Gifted Students

Cognitively complex issues, interest, and gifted students:

Hartsell, B. (2006). Teaching toward compassion: Environmental values education for secondary students. *Journal of Secondary Gifted Education,* 17, 265–271.

Trna, J. (2014). IBSE (inquiry-based science) and gifted students. *Science Education International,* 25(1), 19–28.

Malin, J., & Makel, M.C. (2012). Gender differences in gifted students' advice on solving the world's problems. *Journal for the Education of the Gifted,* 35(2), 175–187.

Cross-Reference
Chapter 7 focuses on classroom climate, community, and management—including strategies for creating an environment in which to ADAPT. It also includes a discussion of how to provide encouragement so that students do not lose heart.
Ways to enhance social relations and use co-operative and collaborative learning are elaborated on in Chapter 10.

Further Reading

On differentiation for gifted students:

Powers, E.A. (2008). The use of independent study as a viable differentiation technique for gifted learners in the regular classroom. *Gifted Child Today, 31*(3), 57–65.

Siegle, D. (2015). Using QR codes to differentiate learning for gifted and talented students. *Gifted Child Today, 38*(1), 63–66.

Olthouse, J.M. (2013). Multiliteracies theory and gifted education. *Gifted Child Today, 36*(4), 246–253.

alert to signs of discouragement and remind students of their accomplishments. Giving encouragement is another topic discussed in Chapter 7. You can change the environment by changing seating; this is a useful strategy, although rarely intense enough to make big changes in learning. Remove distractions, glare, and clutter and consider keeping exceptional students near you to help them focus.

You can vary **method of presentation** to the advantage of your whole class. When you present ideas orally, you can use an approach similar to that of Ms. Ash (described in the case study at the beginning of this chapter). She gave students a partially completed outline, modelled how to complete the outline, stopped to allow students to write on their outline, and used methods of direct instruction. Research suggests that most average-achieving students, exceptional students, and English language learners benefit from being directly shown with clear explanations, models, guided practise, independent practise, and feedback in an array of subjects (Al-Darayseh, 2014; Doabler & Fien, 2013; Reutzel et al., 2012; Swanson & Deshler, 2003). Videotaped presentations allow all students to learn about atoms, for example, before reading the textbook on the subject. Guest speakers may capture students' interests. Hands-on learning is often necessary for exceptional learners and helpful for other students. When planning a presentation, run down your list of exceptional students and ask what you expect each of them to learn from the presentation. Then ask what you can ADAPT to ensure they learn. This does not mean planning separate lessons; rather, it means making small changes to the lesson while planning it and while teaching it.

Pace is the rate of presentation of new information or the rate of introduction of new skills. Often exceptional students need new skills to be introduced in small steps and slowly to ensure mastery, and they need concepts to be introduced slowly, with opportunity and time to develop understanding before the next concept. This may mean setting priorities and deleting some concepts or skills for exceptional students. While Ms. Krugly introduced three reading comprehension strategies to her class, the resource teacher taught one comprehension strategy to a group of six exceptional students. Their follow-up activities contained only sequencing exercises. Instead of learning three strategies to a small extent, these six students learned one reading comprehension strategy well and were able to use it when they read. Introducing skills slowly is a helpful and easy differentiation—use fewer new spelling words, and so forth, and expect learning to the same standard as the others in the class. On the other hand, gifted students may need the pace increased and the expectations raised. Strickland (2007), in a clearly laid out "action tool" for teachers, describes identifying the unit goals the student has and has not already mastered. With the student, you have to work out the enrichment or extension activities the student will do instead of participating in regular class activities.

Student Engagement and Activities, Amount of Practise, and Form of Practise

Student **engagement** refers to the extent to which students embrace learning and classroom activities. Students who are disengaged from learning and from the social life of the classroom have little reason to go to school or to co-operate with those around them. It is critical that we engage every student and ensure that every student learns, although what they learn may not always be the same as their peers. A danger of poorly implemented inclusion is that students are only physically present in the classroom without being part of the community or engaged in learning. Students must be cognitively active to be engaged; if you provide choice and make a genuine effort to engage your students, you can expect fewer behaviour problems and less alienation (Bowen & Arsenault, 2008). Allow students to choose their reading material or use three novels of varying levels of difficulty if that means that every student will engage with a book, or place a few students at a listening station with a book on tape and expect every one of them to demonstrate comprehension.

Additional practise is often critical to the learning of exceptional students. Brief reviews of key information or skills may help retention for them and for other students. You can use different follow-up activities; for example, the follow-up activity on blue paper may place pairs at a centre in the classroom after they have completed the practise examples. The yellow follow-up may require students to independently develop challenge questions, and the green follow-up may place students with you for review and practise. Change the colours so that green is not always the "easiest," change the groups so they don't become the stereotyped "buzzards, bluebirds, and owls," and change the group that receives your attention. Differentiating the **form of practise** means accepting oral or written practise or whatever advances the students' learning.

Strickland (2007) describes two tasks that lead students to the same learning goals at the conclusion of a secondary social studies unit. The more complex task asks students, "Using reliable and defensive research, develop a way to show how New World explorers were paradoxes. Include the unit's principles. But also go beyond them." The task that is asked of most students is, "Using the list of resources and list of product options that I have provided, show how two key explorers took chances, experienced success and failure, and brought about both positive and negative change. Provide evidence" (Strickland, 2007, p. 252). If you had students who would struggle with both versions, what could you ask them to do that would be appropriate for them and would still meet the same learning goals as the two tasks already described? Perhaps you could ask these students to focus on one explorer, or direct these students to resources you know they can read or videos they can view on the topic.

Scaffolding and Grouping

Scaffolding is the support that may enable a student to do more with the assistance of a peer or the teacher than he can do independently. **Zone of proximal development (ZPD)** refers to the learning the student is about to undertake that she can already understand with support (Vygotsky, 1996). Exceptional students often benefit from gradually decreasing scaffolding as they internalize what they first do in social situations. This is why **grouping** is seen as such an important strategy in differentiated classrooms, and why collaborative and co-operative learning have appeared as teaching strategies throughout this text. Every resource on differentiating focuses on flexible grouping.

Differentiating Teaching of Listening, Reading, and Writing

Building Listening Skills, Storytelling, and the Use of Environmental Print

We sometimes assume that our students know how to listen, but some may lack this skill and many will benefit from activities that build listening skills. The following strategy is effective in elementary classrooms (Evans & Strong, 1996) and can be

Further Reading on Listening and Literacy

Sharma, M., Dhamani, I., Leung, J., & Carlile, S. (2014). Attention, memory, and auditory processing in 10- to 15-year-old children with listening difficulties. *Journal of Speech, Language, and Hearing Research, 57*(6), 2308–2321.

Hudson, M.E., & Browder, D.M. (2014). Improving listening comprehension responses for students with moderate intellectual disability during literacy class. *Research & Practice for Persons with Severe Disabilities, 39*(1), 11–29.

Fisher, D., & Frey, N. (2014). Speaking and listening in content area learning. *Reading Teacher, 68*(1), 64–69.

Prior, J., & Gerard, M. (2004). *Environmental print in the classroom: Meaningful connections for learning to read.* Newark, DE: International Reading Association.

adapted for secondary school classes. Create a brief narrative account that you think will interest your students. Remind them of three skills for *paying attention*:

1. Look at the person reading or speaking.

2. Sit still.

3. Keep your hands in your lap.

Then focus on *listening skills* by giving a purpose for listening:

1. With younger students, show three pictures of an event in the story, such as the ending. Ask them to listen so they can choose the correct picture of the event.

2. With older students, replace the pictures with three brief sentences or passages. Ask them to listen so they can choose the passage with the viewpoint of a particular character, and so forth.

In a study with older students who experienced difficulty listening, Joffe et al. (2007) demonstrated that teaching them to produce mental images for sentences and stories improved their ability to recount the sentences and stories to which they had listened.

Teach students to recount personal experiences and to listen to each other's accounts. With another adult, model telling a brief personal experience while the other adult models active listening and asks a genuine question. Model restating the question and responding. Switch roles. Next have students in pairs follow your model, switching roles.

Environmental print refers to the common words and symbols of our environment, which represent fast food restaurants, carmakers, and so on. With practise, young children recognize these familiar words in manuscript printing as well as in symbols (Browne, 2007). You can capitalize on this step toward reading with children who acquire literacy slowly and effortfully. Environmental print can also be used in teaching mathematics (e.g., Koellner & Wallace, 2007). The following list offers strategies to take advantage of environmental print:

- Encourage cutting and pasting of symbols from magazines until the child can print the words in a personal journal.

- Use manuscript print under the environmental print symbol to promote recognition of the printed form.

- Post printed signs around the classroom on the window, door, desk, and so forth.

- Post children's names on their desks so the child with developmental disabilities can match names on books to names on desks and distribute books.

- Enlist parents to help their children to use environmental print at home.

Background to Differentiating Teaching of Reading

In April 2000 the National Reading Panel (NRP) in the United States released its findings on teaching reading (www.nationalreadingpanel.org). Their thorough review of the vast literature on teaching reading led them to focus on five components: **phonemic awareness, phonics, fluency, vocabulary**, and **comprehension**. Phonemic or phonological awareness is the awareness of and sensitivity to the smallest units within words—phonemes or sounds. Phonics stresses sound–symbol relationships, helping learners to match the letters of the alphabet to the already-known speech sounds. Fluency contributes to comprehension and involves children reading out loud with speed, accuracy, and proper expression. Vocabulary focuses on children understanding the meaning of words, and reading comprehension is an active process of understanding that requires an intentional and thoughtful interaction between the reader and the text. The report says, "Children at risk of reading failure especially require direct and systematic instruction in these skills, and that instruction should be provided as early as possible. Children in kindergarten and in the first grade respond well to instruction in phonemic awareness and phonics, provided the instruction is delivered in a vibrant, imaginative, and entertaining fashion. Children who experience early difficulty in reading respond well to phonics instruction through the late elementary school years" (National Reading Panel, 2000). Walpole and McKenna (2007) in their book, *Differentiated reading strategies for the primary grades*, provide a clear guide for primary teachers on differentiating reading instruction in each of the components in the NRP Report with a separate chapter for each primary grade.

Differentiating to Promote Learning to Read: Phonological Processing and Balanced Reading Programs

Research indicates that the most critical contributor to fluent word reading is the ability to recognize letters, spelling patterns, and whole words effortlessly and automatically on sight (Uhry, 2013). The best way to develop early reading skills is with explicit instruction and teacher-directed strategy instruction, especially for at-risk children and children with learning disabilities. In a small teacher-led group, students need to practise daily with activities such as letter–sound correspondence bingo, and use onset and rime to practise making words like h-at, b-at, p-at, s-at, and so forth. Researchers (e.g., Willows, 2002) suggest balancing explicit instruction of word-recognition skills (e.g., phonemic awareness) with meaningful reading activities (see also Grenawalt, 2004; Heydon et al., 2004/2005). See Figure 8.1 on teaching phonemic awareness. Phonemic awareness components include:

- sensitivity to, and explicit awareness of, individual sounds that make up words
- demands that children analyze or manipulate only sounds, not meaning
- early skills such as recognizing rhyming, and later skills such as segmenting the sounds in words and synthesizing the sounds in words

Figure 8.1 demonstrates how to teach phonemic awareness.

FIGURE 8.1 TEACHING PHONEMIC AWARENESS

Planning Phoneme Awareness Activities

1. Identify phonemic awareness tasks appropriate for the children you are teaching. In *Phoneme Awareness in Young Children* (1998), Adams and her colleagues provide a wide array of engaging activities to encourage children to play with sounds.

2. Use phoneme sounds, e.g., /sss/ the sound a snake makes, rather than letter names /S/.

3. Use explicit instruction: begin by providing a step-by-step description of the activity and then model what the children are expected to do. Provide practise and feedback.

4. Teach continuant sounds (e.g., /m/, /s/, /l/) by exaggerating such as "sssssnake." Later teach stop consonants (e.g., /t/, /g/, /p/) using rapid repetition such as "/k/-/k/-/k/-/k/-/k/ atie."

5. Teach sounds in the initial position first (*m*at). Then teach sounds in the final position (ma*t*), and last teach sounds in the medial position (m*a*t).

Put into Practice

Drawing on the following materials, develop a plan for teaching phonemic awareness and phonics to all grade 1 students, with more regular practise for those at risk for learning disabilities.

Adams, M.J., Foorman, B.R., Lundberg, I., & Beeler, T. (2006). *Phonemic awareness in young children: A classroom curriculum*. Chatswood, Australia: Elsevier Australia.

McCormack, R.L., & Pasquarelli, S.L. (2010). *Teaching reading: Strategies and resources for grades K-6*. New York, NY: Guilford Press.

Fox, B.J. (2012). *Word identification strategies: Building phonics into a classroom reading program* (5th ed.). Boston, MA: Pearson.

Dollins, C. (2014). Expanding the power of read-alouds. *Young Children, 69*(3), 8–13.

Bursuck, W. (2011). *Teaching reading to students who are at risk or have disabilities: A multi-tier approach* (2nd ed.). Upper Saddle River, NJ: Pearson.

Further Reading

On improving fluency:

Wilson, J.K. (2012). Brisk and effective fluency instruction for small groups. *Intervention in School and Clinic, 47*(3), 152–157.

Madden, M., & Sullivan, J. (2008). *Teaching fluency beyond the primary grades: Strategy lessons to meet the specific needs of upper grade readers.* New York: Scholastic.

Atwater, S. (2014). Fast Track to Fluency: Volunteers promoting oral reading fluency in struggling readers. *English in Texas, 44*(1), 20–25.

Young, C., Mohr, K., & Rasinski, T. (2015). Reading Together: A successful reading fluency intervention. *Literacy Research and Instruction, 54*(1), 67–81.

Lingo, A.S. (2014). Tutoring middle school students with disabilities by high school students: Effects on oral reading fluency. *Education & Treatment of Children, 37*(1), 53–76.

Rasinski, T., & Young, C. (2014). Assisted reading: A bridge from fluency to comprehension. *The New England Reading Association Journal, 50*(1), 1–4.

Teaching Phonics

Phonics, knowledge of individual letter names and sounds, is combined with phonemic awareness. The teaching of phonics should begin with the simple and regular forms and then move to the more complicated irregulars (Starrett, 2006). Teach the more regular consonants like *buh* and *tuh* first, followed by the short vowels that appear in two-thirds of all English words. The *Jolly Phonics* program (Lloyd et al., 1998) is often used to ensure a systematic and engaging introduction of sounds through consonant digraphs (like *sh* in *ship*) and blends (like *bl* in *blends*), followed by long vowels and word patterns. Pattern books, rhymes, songs, and poems can help readers practise letter–sound relationships. Direct instruction, recommended for the teaching of phonics, consists of these steps: show, explain, practise, assess, and transfer. Starrett (2006) offers specific, practical tips and strategies to teach phonics for balanced reading.

Enhancing Fluency

Fluent readers recognize most words rapidly and accurately and focus their attention on making sense of the text (Allor & Chard, 2011). Fluency develops through practise reading, especially reading familiar text. The strategy called repeated reading is particularly effective. Practising and then reading to an authentic audience is a good strategy with readers of all ages. Poor readers in grade 6 can read to buddies in kindergarten, and grade 1 students can read to their parents and younger siblings. Look for creative ways to enable older readers to practise in comfortable contexts where they feel supported and encounter no teasing. In a highly readable paper, Wilson (2012) encourages teachers to provide differentiated, brisk, and effective fluency practise daily to small groups by ensuring students:

1. hear models of fluent oral reading
2. engage in repeated reading
3. receive assisted reading-while-listening, such as reading along with audio
4. focus on phrasing (they can insert slash marks at the end of each phrase)

Madden and Sullivan (2008) provide exemplary lessons that help grade 4 to 6 readers achieve well-paced, expressive oral reading within a diverse classroom. Classic strategies for enhancing fluency include repeated reading and readers' theatre. For a practical report on the role of enhancing fluency (and four other reading processes) in providing effective instruction for struggling adolescent readers, see Roberts et al. (2008).

Differentiating Reading to Learn: Using Textbooks by Adapting, Supplementing, and Bypassing

Whereas in the primary grades, students learn to read, by the junior grades, children are reading to learn (Chall, 1983). In reading to learn, students must comprehend new text, relate new ideas to prior knowledge, and create an elaborate understanding. Inefficient readers often require prompting to attend to their relevant prior knowledge and relate it to their new learning, and they may require assistance with vocabulary and word recognition. Berne and Degener (2012) provide clear descriptions of how to balance brief strategic, differentiated reading lessons with whole-class work, guide reading groups, assess what students need in these flexible groups, and gauge students' understanding as they read. Comprehension is purposeful and active, and teaching should be structured so comprehension occurs before, during, and after reading.

The **scaffolded reading experience (SRE)** is designed for classes with students of varying abilities in reading. It applies the steps of the ADAPT strategy, encouraging teachers to plan by considering (1) the students, (2) the reading selection, and (3) the purpose of the reading. SRE considers three steps in teaching: pre-reading activities, during-reading activities, and post-reading activities. See Table 8.1 for examples. Four instructional concepts within SRE are (1) scaffolding, (2) gradual release of responsibility, (3) zone of proximal development, and (4) the notion of success (Liang, 2011).

Graves and Braaten (1996) describe a grade 7 teacher using SRE with a class of twenty-eight (sixteen typical, six above-average, and six below-average readers). The text was "The King of Storms" (Flatow, 1985), an expository piece about hurricanes in 1500 words and eight sections. The **pre-reading activities** for the entire class included a discussion about the movie *Twister*, a video clip of tornadoes, a discussion of destructive weather the students and their families had experienced, a preview of the text by the teacher, and a contrast of hurricanes and tornadoes.

Then the groups participated in tiered activities with differing amounts of scaffolding. The strong readers received written instructions for **post-reading activities** and began silent reading. The average readers began a vocabulary- and concept-building assignment in small groups and then read. The less-skilled readers worked with the teacher on vocabulary and concepts, and the teacher read half the article aloud. Then, two groups of three students each received instructions to become experts on a designated section of the article. The teacher served as a resource for all students. The skilled readers contrasted the destruction caused by hurricanes and tornadoes and made a chart to show the path hurricanes usually follow and the countries that can be struck by hurricanes. The average-reader groups wrote a summary of a section of the article and created a visual representation. The two groups of less-skilled readers had the same assignment with more scaffolding prior to and during the activity. A few classes later, each group presented its information, and the teacher corrected any misinformation and closed the unit with highlights and video clips of hurricanes. All students had been challenged to learn content and improve their reading comprehension.

TABLE 8.1 POSSIBLE COMPONENTS OF A SCAFFOLDED READING EXPERIENCE

Pre-Reading Activities	During-Reading Activities	Post-Reading Activities
Relating the reading to students' lives	Silent reading	Questioning
Motivating	Reading to students	Discussion
Activating background knowledge	Guided reading	Writing
Building text-specific knowledge	Oral reading by students	Drama
Preteaching vocabulary	Modifying the text	Artistic and non-verbal activities
Preteaching concepts		Application and outreach activities
Pre-questioning, predicting, and direction setting		Reteaching
Suggesting strategies		

Source: Graves, M.F., & Braaten, S. Scaffolded reading experiences: Building bridges to success. *Preventing School Failure*, 40(4), 169 -73. Reproduced by permission of Taylor & Francis LLC (http://www.tandfonline.com)

Phonological Awareness

We have all heard of it, but what is phonological awareness and what role should it play in teaching students experiencing difficulty in learning to read?

One of the most consistent findings to emerge from research on beginning reading is the relationship between phonological awareness and reading acquisition. Converging evidence—that is, the preponderance of evidence—has shown that the phonological domain is causally related to reading acquisition (Uhry, 2013).

Phonological awareness has been called phonological processing, phonemic awareness, and phonological sensitivity. It has been described as the ability to perceive spoken words as a sequence of sounds or the awareness of and access to the sounds of language. It is also defined as the ability to think about and consciously manipulate the sounds in words.

Many learners with reading disabilities experience deficits in the ability to manipulate and use the sounds of language in these ways. The effects are serious and cumulative. In 1994 Stanovich wrote that "children who begin school with little phonological awareness have trouble acquiring alphabetic coding skill and thus have difficulty recognizing words. Reading for meaning is greatly hindered when children are having too much trouble with word recognition" (p. 281). Gradually, not being able to read interferes with learning in other school subjects and can adversely affect many areas of school achievement, something Stanovich called the "Matthew effect" (1986), meaning that the poor get poorer while the rich get richer.

You may be asking when we should teach phonological awareness. Research suggests intervention should be made early because these skills are necessary for children to begin learning to read. It has been suggested that intervention should start prior to formal reading instruction, as a preventive measure. And some studies suggest that the level of proficiency may need to approach that of skilled readers to be optimally effective. Thus, sooner is better, but one can also recommend beginning as soon as the need is recognized.

Five levels of phonological awareness can be taught prior to formal reading instruction. From easiest to hardest, these are

- rhyme (e.g., nursery rhymes)
- oddity tasks (compare and contrast sounds of words for rhyme or alliteration)
- blending or syllable splitting (e.g., "What word would you have if you put these sounds together: /c/, /a/, /t/?")
- phonological segmentation (e.g., "What sounds do you hear in the word *cat*?")
- phoneme manipulation (e.g., add, delete, or move phonemes)

The most important of these dimensions may be explicitly teaching auditory blending and segmenting prior to formal reading instruction. Auditory segmenting involves analyzing and breaking speech down into its component parts. Auditory blending, on the other hand, is synthesizing or recombining speech into whole units. Blending may be a bit easier, but segmentation may be the most closely related to early reading acquisition. Data suggest that training in letter sound knowledge along with phonological awareness (especially blending and segmenting) is the best combination to promote reading acquisition.

D.C. Simmons and her colleagues (1994) described five factors to include when designing instruction to enhance phonological awareness.

1. Focus initially on the auditory features of words without showing the word in alphabetic symbols. Children can move tokens or clap for each individual sound in words, but don't show the words when first teaching children to combine or segment sounds.

2. Focus initially on explicit, natural segments of language. Then later move to more implicit, complex segments. Begin by segmenting sentences into words, words into syllables, and syllables into phonemes. Manipulating sounds at the phonemic level is what is important for beginning reading.

3. Focus initially on words and sounds that are easily distinguished; for example, select words with few phonemes and words with vowel–consonant (VC) or consonant–vowel–consonant (CVC) patterns that can easily be stored in working memory. Proceed to more complex patterns. Choose words with continuous sounds (*s, r*) rather than stop sounds (*p, t*). Later, teach consonant blends in words like *strap*.

4. Scaffold blending and segmenting through explicit modelling. Provide sufficient time and practise for blending and segmenting to become obvious to less proficient learners. Model conspicuous strategies often, over time. Also teach when, where, and how to use blending and segmenting when reading.

5. After learners are proficient with auditory tasks, integrate letter–sound correspondences. This enables students to move from contrived tasks to realistic reading, spelling, and writing. Children can "cut up" unfamiliar words into their smallest pieces, and ask themselves if they know any words that match the combination of sounds in question.

Phonological awareness holds much promise for identifying many of the students who experience difficulty in learning to read. It also offers a means of intervening early to prevent reading disabilities. However, some students' reading disabilities may be caused by other factors (such as naming speed; see de Groot et al., 2015). Also, some students do not respond as well as most to phonological awareness interventions, so it is important to monitor the progress of individual children.

More recently researchers, primarily in the United States, have been focusing on response to intervention (RTI), which defines reading disability as the inability of otherwise typically developing children to respond adequately to high-quality instruction because of an impairment in the phonological processing skills required to learn to read (Fletcher et al., 2005). The RTI model includes procedures for identifying reading disability and for monitoring progress in acquisition of phonemic processing. As well, the model includes a three-tiered approach to intervention, moving from group and less intensive to individual and more intensive interventions as children's literacy learning problems persist. Much remains to be both researched and implemented before RTI will be a regular feature in schools. However, as Uhry (2013) argues, research has made great progress in understanding reading disabilities and interventions.

References

de Groot, B.J.A., Van den Bos, K.P., Minnaert, A., van den Meulen, B. (2015). Phonological processing and word reading in typically developing and reading disabled children: Severity matters. *Scientific Studies of Reading, 19*(2), 166–181.

Fletcher, J.M., Denton, C., & Francis, D. (2005). Validity of alternative approaches for the identification of learning disabilities: Operationalizing unexpected underachievement. *Journal of Learning Disabilities, 38*, 545–552.

Simmons, D.C., Gunn, B., Smith, S.B., & Kameenui, E.J. (1994). Phonological awareness: Applications of instructional design. *LD Forum, 19* (2), 7–10.

Stanovich, K.E. (1986). Matthew effects in reading: Some consequences of individual differences in the acquisition of literacy. *Reading Research Quarterly, 21*, 360–407.

Stanovich, K.E. (1994). Romance and reality. *Reading Teacher, 47*(4), 280–291.

Uhry, J.K. (2013). The role of phonemic awareness in learning to read and spell successfully. *Perspectives on Language and Literacy, 39*(1), 11–16.

Textbooks can be supplemented with guest speakers, videos, field trips, multimedia, trade books, newspapers, and hands-on activities. Remember to provide opportunities for gifted students to challenge one another. To bypass the textbook, look for alternative texts that cover the same topics. Seek **high-interest, low-vocabulary books** for novel study and general reading.

Matthias Tunger/Getty Images

Newspapers can supplement textbooks in many subjects.

Teaching Vocabulary and Comprehension Strategies

Vocabulary and comprehension are intimately related (Walpole et al., 2011). Walpole and her colleagues (2011) provide extensive description of how to implement a research-based reading program in grade 4 and grade 5, including word identification, fluency, vocabulary, and comprehension. They recommend that teachers at these grade levels read aloud to their class, stopping to conduct engaging discussion about vocabulary essential to understanding the story. The idea is to teach vocabulary and comprehension strategies quickly and then to use them flexibly as students discuss content. Some of the comprehension strategies that students need at this age include: comparing-contrasting, contextualizing a story, raising their own confusions, using prior knowledge, inserting themselves into the text, noting how the author constructed the text, questioning, and summarizing. All of these can be taught through reading aloud to your students and conducting engaging discussions that challenge them to use all these strategies. In addition to whole-class instruction, they recommend intensive tier 2 intervention for students whose vocabulary and comprehension lag below grade level.

For some students it is enough to introduce new vocabulary and connect it to their existing language. However, you may need to do more to ensure that many students, including exceptional students, acquire new vocabulary. Carnine and his colleagues (2003) developed an effective and direct way to teach vocabulary with five steps.

1. Choose a range of positive and negative examples to introduce teaching the new word or concept. For the concept of leisure, give examples of watching television, camping, playing tennis, and so on (six examples). Non-examples might include working at a part-time job and running errands for your parents (two non-examples).

2. Use synonyms that the students already know. For *leisure*, you could use the word *play*. State the definition simply and clearly. Leisure is time that is free from work, when you can choose what you want to do.

3. Model or point to positive and negative examples. For the concept of leisure, model telephoning a friend to arrange a game of tennis. Point to pictures of people viewing a painting in a gallery. For non-examples, model going to work and point to pictures of people entering a factory.

4. Ask a series of yes/no questions to help students discriminate examples from non-examples. Ask how they know whether to say yes or no. Ask the students why they answer no to non-examples by using the definition you have taught.

5. Find out whether students can discriminate this concept from others. Is leisure the same as rest? How might they be different? Explore features that are sometimes present in the concept. For example, leisure is sometimes done alone and sometimes done with friends.

After you have taught the vocabulary used in a unit, students can sort words according to criteria you provide or according to criteria generated by the students (which allows you to see how the students are thinking about the content of the unit). Brassell (2009) provides many other examples of differentiating, such as asking groups to choose words to learn and ways to learn them, and predict-o-grams in which students make predictions about how authors use words to tell a story. The research demonstrates that reading comprehension improves when vocabulary is taught explicitly (Beck & McKeown, 2007).

Further Reading

Use books that are high in interest and easy for exceptional students, reluctant readers, and ELL students to read:

D'Ardenne, C. et al. (2013). PLCs in action: Innovative teaching for struggling grade 3–5 readers. *Reading Teacher, 67*(2), 143–151.

Fránquiz, M. (2008). Learning English with high-interest, low-vocabulary literature: Immigrant students in a high school new-arrival center. *English Leadership Quarterly, 30*(3), 5–8.

Blasingame, J. (2007). Books for adolescents. *Journal of Adolescent & Adult Literacy, 50*, 686–686.

Schatmeyer, K. (2007). Hooking struggling readers: Using books they can and want to read. *Illinois Reading Council Journal, 35*(1), 7–13.

Samuels, C.A. (2014, April 23). For challenged readers, custom-tailored texts. *Education Week, 33*(29), 8–9.

Servilio (2009) illustrates how providing choice motivates older students. She offers three tiered tasks for each of reading (read chapters individually, read every other page with a partner, listen to chapters on audio recording and follow along); comprehension (write five or more questions you asked yourself; summarize each chapter in at least five sentences; use the advance organizer to record five events in the chapters); and examples of personal connection tasks (research a major historical figure and his contribution by winning a battle; create rules you would give that figure, write a song to help his troops to remember the rules, and write about why you chose these rules; draw a picture and label the appearance of the characters; and record where in the reading you got your information).

Enhancing Written Expression and Facilitating Note-Taking

To differentiate the writing of **narrative text**, use a series of scaffolded tasks. For those who write fluently and willingly, use only topic prompts. For students who cannot start with a topic prompt, introduce picture prompts and brainstorming about the pictures. Next time try only topic prompts, reintroducing picture prompts only for those who need them. For students who cannot begin from a picture prompt and brainstorming, add a **story-planning sheet** with the following prompts:

- Setting—where and when the story took place
- Main character—the person or persons around whom the problem or conflict revolves
- Character clues—appearance, actions, dialogue, thoughts of character, comments of others
- Problem—conflicts
- Attempts—how the character tries to solve the problem
- Resolution—how the problem gets solved or does not get solved

Students can complete the prompts briefly on the story-planning sheet while brainstorming with a partner and later independently. Those who don't need a planning sheet can use a checklist of these prompts, with the addition of theme, to check that all essential elements are in their narratives. This approach can be adapted to scaffold student writing of notes from a text, lecture, discussion, or video. The principles are to provide no more scaffolding than students need and to gradually move students from peer and teacher support to independence with self-checking. Keep records of the scaffolding that students use each day so you can prompt for more independence. If you copy each degree of scaffolding onto a different colour of paper, you can encourage students to move from yellow to green, and so forth, and see at a glance who is using each degree of scaffolding (see Lutz et al., 2006).

To differentiate the writing of **expository text** or **opinion essays**, teach the entire class to use a series of strategies. Then review the steps in the strategy and scaffold the use of the strategy for students with LD and others who find written expression difficult. Place a poster on the wall where it is visible to all students. Give students who need it their own copy of the strategy to keep at hand.

Monroe and Troia (2006) suggest using a strategy called DARE for planning the writing of an opinion essay:

- **D**evelop a position statement.
- **A**dd supporting arguments.

- **R**eport and refute counterarguments.
- **E**nd with a strong conclusion.

You can also teach a strategy for prompting students to revise their papers. Many students who have difficulty expressing themselves in writing do not understand that revision is expected. For revising, you can try introducing the SEARCH strategy (Ellis & Friend, 1991):

- **S**et goals (did I do that?).
- **E**xamine the paper to see if it makes sense.
- **A**sk if you said what you meant.
- **R**eveal picky errors (are my sentences to long or too short, and did I spell all words correctly?).
- **C**opy over neatly.
- **H**ave a last look for errors.

Finally, for reluctant writers, teach them how to engage in prompted self-regulation, using a self-question like, "What are the steps I follow by myself and with my partner?" or "What is the big issue for me to focus on in my writing today?" or a self-instruction like "I need to try hard to do my best today" (Monroe & Troia, 2006).

Differentiating Teaching of Mathematics

In mathematics, differentiations reduce the mismatch between the student's strengths and needs and curriculum demands. Number sense is foundational for all mathematical learning, followed by fluency in computation and problem solving. Each aspect may need to be differentiated.

Number Sense

Number sense refers to an essential sense of what numbers mean, how to compare numbers, and how to see and count quantities—that is, an understanding of whole numbers, number operations, and number relations. Most children acquire the foundations for this conceptual structure informally through interactions with family and peers before kindergarten. Students with good number sense move effortlessly between quantities in the real world and mathematical expressions, and can represent the same quantity in multiple ways, depending on context and purpose. They see that when they have three cars and five trucks, they have more trucks than cars, without executing a precise numerical operation. Children who have not acquired this sense of numbers require formal instruction to do so (Jordan et al., 2011). Number sense may serve the same function for mathematics as phonological awareness serves for beginning reading—it appears to be essential for later competence. There is increasing evidence relating inadequate number sense to learning disabilities (Desoete et al., 2012).

Griffin and Case (1997) developed an instructional program in number sense, called Rightstart, using three representational systems:

1. conventional math symbols: digits and addition, subtraction, and equal signs
2. a thermometer that shows the number line in a clear vertical direction, so bigger is higher and smaller is lower
3. a representational system that looks like the Candyland board game

What do you think?

Look for a source on teaching students to read and write. Consider the ideas of the author(s) and relate their ideas to what you have learned from experience about the connections between reading and writing in classrooms at the level at which you teach. One source you could consult is

Strickland, D.S., Ganske, K., & Monroe, J.K. (2002). *Supporting struggling readers and writers: Strategies for classroom intervention, 3–6.* Newark, DE: International Reading Association.

Parr, J.M., & McNaughton, S. (2014). Making connections: The nature and occurrence of links in literacy teaching and learning. *Australian Journal of Language and Literacy, 37*(3), 141–150.

Look for other sources to read on the topic, and compare your ideas to the thinking of your peers.

Weblinks

ON NUMBER SENSE AND NUMBER SENSE GAMES:

http://cemc2.math.uwaterloo.ca/mathfrog/english/kidz/Games6.shtml

http://coldlakeelementary.ca (click on math games under Resources to see activities)

http://nzmaths.co.nz/content-tutorials

Students play games comparing quantities and adding one number to another using the three representational systems, with frequent opportunities to make choices and verbalize their understandings and rationales for the strategies they use to solve problems. Jordan et al. (2011) describe an intervention in which kindergarten children play games to recognize and name quantities up to four instantly without counting; associate numerals to quantities; make quantity comparisons; and play the Great Race Game (adapted from Ramani & Siegler, 2008) which uses a spinner (with the numbers one and two) and a ladder beginning with the number one. Children add on the one or two they have spun; so they learn to count on from where they are (e.g., on three, spin two, and count on; when they reach five and have finished, the instructor verbalizes "That's right, five is two after three"). Many researchers have recently shown the effectiveness of interventions teaching number sense to kindergarten children, especially those from high-poverty neighbourhoods (e.g., Dyson et al., 2013; Sood & Jitendra, 2013).

Many teachers use a **hundreds chart** to help students explore number sense at a more complex level. Naylor (2006) provides practical descriptions of five activities for different grade levels using the traditional hundreds chart, with the numbers 1 to 10 in the top row from left to right, with 11 to 20 immediately below, and so on to 100. The activities are (1) chart tour (grades K–2); (2) mystery number (grades 1–3); (3) missing numbers (grades 1–3); (4) multiple patterns (grades 3–5); and (5) least common multiples (grades 5–8). Children can play in groups, choosing or being assigned more difficult tasks as they become more adept at number sense.

Vacc (1995) modified the typical hundreds chart to align its vocabulary and format with the vocabulary and methods used when manipulating numbers. It includes the numbers 0 to 99 and progresses from right to left (see Figure 8.2). It places the numerals 0 through 9 in the "ones" column, the numerals 10 through 19 in the "tens" column, and so on. Vacc recommends that teachers use clear, coloured counters so students can see the numeral under the counter and that they model using a restructured hundreds chart on an overhead transparency. Students manipulate clear, coloured markers on their own hundreds charts to count, match number words and numerals, identify numbers and numerical relationships, and place value. Students can use the chart for numerical patterns, addition, subtraction, multiplication, division,

Further Reading

On number sense and number sense games:

For sample activities from Rightstart, look at *Monographs of the Society for Research in Child Development*, 1996, 6(1/2), 247–249.

Griffin, S. (2004). Teaching number sense. *Educational Leadership*, 61(5), 39–43.

Griffin, S. (2004). Building number sense with number worlds: A mathematics program for young children. *Early Childhood Research Quarterly*, 19(1), 173–180.

Witzel, B.S., Ferguson, C.J., & Mink, D.V. (2012). Strategies for helping preschool through grade 3 children develop math skills. *Young Children*, 67(3), 89–94.

Further Reading

To learn more about the Rightstart program for teaching number sense by Case and Griffin:

Mononen, R., Aunio, P., & Koponen, T. (2014). A pilot study of the effect of Rightstart instruction on early numeracy skills of children with specific language impairment. *Research in Developmental Disabilities*, 35(5), 999–1014.

Griffin, S.A., Case, R., & Siegler, R.S. (1994). Rightstart. In K. McGilly (Ed.), *Classroom lessons: Integrating cognitive theory and practice* (pp. 25–50). Cambridge, MA: MIT Press.

FIGURE 8.2 REVISED HUNDREDS CHART

90	80	70	60	50	40	30	20	10	0
91	81	71	61	51	41	31	21	11	1
92	82	72	62	52	42	32	22	12	2
93	83	73	63	53	43	33	23	13	3
94	84	74	64	54	44	34	24	14	4
95	85	75	65	55	45	35	25	15	5
96	86	76	66	56	46	36	26	16	6
97	87	77	67	57	47	37	27	17	7
98	88	78	68	58	48	38	28	18	8
99	89	79	69	59	49	39	29	19	9

Source: Vacc, N.N. (1995). Gaining number sense through a restructured hundreds chart. *Teaching Exceptional Children*, 28(1), 51. Used by permission.

What do you think?

Why might the hundreds chart modified by Vacc help children? Read the following paper and discuss with your peers:

Vacc, N.N. (1995). Gaining number sense through a restructured hundreds chart. *Teaching Exceptional Children,* 28(1), 50–55.

See the traditional number chart in Naylor, M. (2006). Integrating math in your classroom: From one to one hundred. *Teaching Pre K–8,* (5), 36, 38.

Further Reading

These recent books contain many practical teaching ideas:

Conklin, M. (2012). *It makes sense! Using the hundreds chart to build number sense.* Opa-Locka, FL: Math Solutions (IG Publishing).

Shumway, J.F. (2011). Number sense routines: Building numerical literacy every day in grades K–3. Portland, ME: Stenhouse Pub.

Conklin, M. (2010). *It makes sense! Using ten-frames to build number sense, grades K–2.* Opa-Locka, FL: Math Solutions (IG Publishing).

Further Reading

Montague, M., & Jittendra, A.K. (2006). *Teaching mathematics to middle school students with learning difficulties.* Thousand Oaks, CA: Corwin Press.

Stone, R. (2007). *Best practices for teaching mathematics: What award-winning classroom teachers do.* Thousand Oaks, CA: Corwin Press.

Godfrey, C.J., & Stone, J. (2013). Mastering fact fluency: Are they game? *Teaching Children Mathematics,* 20(2), 96–101.

and prime numbers. For example, to teach place value, say, "Cover the number that is two 'tens' and four 'ones.' Next cover five 'tens' and seven 'ones.'"

For numerical patterns, say, "Begin with zero, count by twos, placing a marker on each number counted. Describe the pattern you have made." Next you can add a prediction component for counting by twos, threes, and so forth. This is a systematic way to develop and enhance number sense. An adapted hundreds chart can also be used to teach patterns for giving change (Perry, 2000). Manipulative models have also been used to build number sense for addition of fractions (Cramer & Henry, 2013).

Computation

Often an effect of math learning disabilities is lack of fluency with **computation** and basic number facts. Teaching older students to use a calculator, a bypass strategy, is usually considered justifiable after you have adapted teaching to increase number fact fluency. Recall Samuel in the case study at the beginning of this chapter. Samuel benefited from being taught to use a calculator because the secondary curriculum demands that he carry out basic calculations in the context of problem solving but provides no more opportunities for learning these basic skills. Samuel, his parents, and his teachers had made every effort earlier in his school career and now accepted that a calculator would enable him to use his cognitive capacity to solve problems rather than to make calculations. Offering calculators to all students (when knowing the multiplication facts is not the focus of the learning) is a differentiation used by increasing numbers of teachers.

When young children are counting the objects in two sets, do not immediately expect them to memorize number facts. Teach them to count on, by naming one number and counting on the other. Model this strategy using fingers, number lines, objects, or the three representational systems suggested by Griffin and Case (1997). For example, for 6 + 3, say, "Six, put your finger on 6 on the number line and put one counter on each of 7, 8, and 9," saying each number as you put the counter on it. Throughout, keep strengthening basic counting skills. Later, teach the child to always start with the larger of the two numbers, remembering that it takes number sense to judge which is larger. This can be called "the trick." Teach the commutative principle by showing that 4 + 5 = 5 + 4. Using arrays can be helpful for this learning (www.eduplace.com/math/mw/background/3/05/te_3_05_overview.html). Encourage students to read number problems aloud and verbalize what they are thinking. Garnett (1992) suggests the order in which addition (and multiplication) facts should be learned (see Figure 8.3). As students become more mature in their strategies, teach them to ask, "Do I just know this one?" and use retrieval strategies whenever possible. Press for speed with a few facts at a time, following the order in Figure 8.3. When students are not using retrieval strategies, encourage them to think out loud, and discuss the strategies children can use with them. Also consider using assistive technology as a means of differentiating the teaching of multiplication. For example, Irish (2002) used computer-assisted instruction and a multimedia software program (Memory Math) to teach students with learning disabilities the basic multiplication facts. The software utilizes keyword mnemonics. Suh and her colleagues (2012) help teachers to review technology and choose a computer application appropriate for teaching number sense, base ten, and calculation. There are many games for mastering fact fluency (see Godfrey & Stone, 2013). Tier 2 interventions have been used to teach number sense and practise of addition and subtraction facts (e.g., Valenzuela et al., 2014).

FIGURE 8.3 ALTERNATIVE TEACHING SEQUENCE FOR ADDITION AND MULTIPLICATION FACTS

Addition

Adding 1 or 0 to any number

(1)	+1 and +0 principles	
(2)	Ties	2+2 3+3 4+4 5+5 6+6 7+7 8+8 9+9
(3)	Ties +1	2+3 3+4 4+5 5+6 6+7 7+8 8+9
(4)	Ties +2	2+4 3+5 4+6 5+7 6+8 7+9
(5)	+10 Principle from 2+10 through 10+10	
(6)	+9 Facts from 2+9 through 9+9 Use the linking strategy (n+10) −1	
(7)	Remaining facts	2+5 2+6 2+7 2+8 3+6 3+7 3+8 4+7 4+8 5+8

Must include major emphasis on the commutative principle (5+6 = 6+5)

Multiplication

(a)   ×1 and ×0 principles

Multiplying any number by 1 or 0

(b)   × 2/2 ×

(c)   × 3/3 ×

(d)   × 9/9 ×

(e)   Perfect squares

   (1 × 1, 2 × 2, 3 × 3, 4 × 4, 5 × 5, 6 × 6, 7 × 7, 8 × 8, 9 × 9, 10 × 10)

(f)   Remaining facts

3 × 4	3 × 6	3 × 7	3 × 8
	4 × 6	4 × 7	4 × 8
		6 × 7	6 × 8
			7 × 8

Must include major emphasis on the commutative principle (5 × 6 = 6 × 5).

Source: Garnett, K. (1992). Developing fluency with basic number facts: Intervention for students with learning disabilities. *Learning Disabilities: Research and Practice, 7,* 210–216. Used by permission.

Marilyn Burns (2007) offers ways to "catch kids up" who lack basic math concepts. Her list reminds us of all the ways we can differentiate the teaching of math:

- pace lessons carefully (deal with confusion as soon as you see it)
- build in a routine of support (model by thinking aloud, then have students work an example with support before working an example alone; check worked examples of those who are unsure of themselves)
- encourage student interaction (so students verbalize and think aloud with a partner)
- make connections explicit (so students build new learning on what they know)
- encourage mental calculations (to improve number sense and efficiency)
- build in vocabulary instruction (before, during, and after teaching a topic)

Put into Practice

Find an example of strategy instruction for teaching the solving of word problems. Follow the steps to teach a friend or student. Here are four resources:

Krawec, J., Huang, J., Montague, M., Kressler, B., & de Alba, A.M. (2013). The effects of cognitive strategy instruction on knowledge of math problem-solving processes of middle school students with learning disabilities. *Learning Disability Quarterly, 36*(2), 80–92.

Jitendra, A.K. et al. (2013). Impact of small-group tutoring interventions on the mathematical problem solving and achievement of third-grade students with mathematics difficulties. *Learning Disability Quarterly, 36*(1), 21–35.

Jitendra, A. (2002). Teaching students math problem solving through graphic representations. *Teaching Exceptional Children, 34,* 34–38.

Gonsalves, N., & Krawec, J. (2014). Using number lines to solve math word problems: A strategy for students with learning disabilities. *Learning Disabilities Research & Practice, 29*(4), 160–170.

Problem Solving, Representation, Symbol Systems, and Application

Many exceptional students experience difficulty solving problems, a focus of recent curriculum reforms. Number sense and computational fluency are essential for **problem solving**. It is difficult to bypass number sense; however, calculators can be used to bypass lack of computational fluency. Research provides many reasons for using calculators as an adaptation for students with a range of disabilities including mild intellectual disabilities (Yakubova & Bouck, 2014):

- Calculators provide all students with practise and success in calculating ratios and solving proportion problems.
- Calculators, including graphing calculators, encourage students to focus on advanced concepts rather than number crunching.
- Calculators make calculations less tedious for exceptional students.
- Calculators allow for the use of real data sets.
- Calculator use increases student confidence, enthusiasm, and number sense.

Classroom teachers who differentiate teaching have developed many strategies to help diverse learners succeed in mathematics. For example, Lee and Herner-Patnode (2007) describe how Deb, a grade 4 teacher, enables students to represent their mathematical understanding. Deb's students keep notebooks in which they use diagrams, graphs, and symbols to define mathematics words in their own ways. She encourages them to connect the vocabulary and meaning to situations that are relevant for them. Creating mathematics-oriented cartoons can provide visual and artistic opportunities for students who struggle with written or verbal strategies (Gay & White, 2002). Poch and colleagues (2015) help educators to discern what instruction students need in order to make a diagram that enables them to represent and solve problems, a helpful accommodation for all students.

There are many simple accommodations that can be offered to all students. Fahsl (2007) describes providing graph paper that helps students to line up the columns in their questions, encouraging students to use a highlighter to draw their attention to the part of a problem or calculation that they find "tricky," providing fact charts (or calculators), manipulatives, and a timer to help with time management. Peshek (2012) provides examples of how teachers can differentiate formative assessment (such as using a learning log of objectives and observation to record student progress daily). She illustrates rubrics that can be developed by teachers to identify student learning of the big ideas in the course. Jitendra et al. (2014) provide a reliable curriculum-based measure of word problem solving for grade 3. These teaching ideas, taken with the other strategies described in this section, suggest that differentiating the teaching of mathematics can be effective. Remember as well the example of Ms. Ash, in the opening case study, who differentiates her math teaching to meet the needs of Samuel, who has a learning disability. In the process she makes learning more effective for all her students. Ms. Ash used a well-researched approach to teaching—advance organizers that make explicit connections between new concepts and previous learning, a structured outline followed by guided practise, and then independent practise (see Steele, 2008, for a description of these and other strategies for helping exceptional students to learn mathematics). Advance organizers can be used effectively in any subject area (Preiss & Gayle, 2006).

Differentiating Teaching in Content Areas: Science, Social Studies and Literature, Visual Arts, Music, Drama, and French

Differentiating Science

Differentiating teaching science to classes that include exceptional students can feel overwhelming because safety and supervision in the science laboratory are intensified (Roy, 2015). For example, blind students and students with low vision require an orientation to the location of equipment and supplies and must be paired with a sighted peer; everyone must be reminded to return equipment to the same location. The visually impaired student can participate by timing phases of an experiment on a Braille watch, making sound observations, or taking readings on a Braille or talking thermometer. A **CCTV** image magnifier enables students with low vision to observe experiments, and handouts can be copied at 129 or 156 percent to allow easier reading. Because few students have visual impairments, it is unlikely that your school laboratory will be stocked with the materials described here. Seek them from another school, the district board office, or a provincial resource centre, or contact the nearest office of the Canadian National Institute for the Blind (CNIB) (www.cnib.ca). Consult resources that guide the science teaching of students who have visual impairment, hearing impairment, and physical disabilities. Concrete suggestions appear in a paper on differentiating science teaching (Fetters et al., 2003). Piggott (2002) describes ways to differentiate science teaching for students with disabilities and for students who are gifted, including an example of differentiating the teaching of electrolysis through enrichment and extension (reading extracts from Faraday's notebooks). Vowell and Phillips (2015) differentiate to teach young children about the three states of matter, while Dotger and Causton-Theoharis (2010) demonstrate how to use choice to differentiate science teaching.

Because about half of exceptional students have learning disabilities and because adaptations that help these students may be effective for all who read below grade level, consider the reading demands of your science text. Look for texts with a lower reading level that provide parallel information or for a website that is more accessible to students who are poor readers. Steele (2008) suggests that teachers differentiate science teaching by using advance organizers, graphic organizer prompts that draw students' attention to connections, examples from everyday life, and visual displays. She suggests differentiating textbook use by providing chapter notes for students who need them to study, teaching students how the chapters of the science text are organized, and summarizing key concepts before and after students read each chapter. UDL is illustrated in a paper by Kurtts et al. (2009) about teaching solubility and concentration. They vary representation (printed and audio lecture notes, science journal, demonstration with an open can of soft drink, explicit instruction); expression (oral, written, artistic); and engagement (partner activity, virtual investigation, website activities).

Differentiating Social Studies and Literature

Reciprocal teaching, which involves instructing students on teaching one another by taking turns leading discussions in small groups, has been advocated as a strategy for DI. Usually the teacher models how to lead the discussion and provides

Further Reading on Differentiating in the Content Areas

Milman, N.B., Carlson,-Bancroft, A., Boogart, A.V. (2014). Examining differentiation and utilization of iPads across content areas in an independent, preK–4th grade elementary school. *Computers in the Schools, 31*(3), 119–133.

Greenwood, S.C. (2010). Content area readers: Helping middle-level students become word aware (and enjoy it!). *Clearing House, 83*(6), 223–229.

Chapman, C., & King, R. (2009). *Differentiated instructional strategies for writing in the content areas* (2nd ed.). Thousand Oaks, CA: Corwin Press.

Ogle, D., Klemp, R., & McBride, B. (2007). *Building literacy in social studies: Strategies for improving comprehension and critical thinking.* Alexandria, VA: Association for Supervision & Curriculum Development.

Weblinks

TELUS WORLD OF SCIENCE EDMONTON
www.odyssium.com

TELUS SPARK: THE NEW SCIENCE CENTRE (CALGARY)
www.sparkscience.ca

SCIENCE NORTH (ONTARIO)
www.sciencenorth.ca

DISCOVERY CENTRE (NOVA SCOTIA)
www.discoverycentre.ns.ca

PHYSLINK.COM (TEACHING RESOURCES FOR PHYSICS AND ASTRONOMY)
www.physlink.com/Education

BC SCIENCE TEACHERS' ASSOCIATION
www.bcscta.ca

scaffolding for the groups as they begin. This teaching approach (Palincsar & Brown, 1984; also see Deshler et al., 2007) has been used from kindergarten to high school. Form groups of four or five students with one or two exceptional students in each group. Choose a different discussion leader for each group daily, beginning with a confident but patient student who will model well for peers. Students read a selection from their textbook (usually three to four pages). With younger students, you might ask them to stop after each paragraph. Each student receives a worksheet until the class is familiar with reciprocal teaching. Allow students to choose to use the worksheet after you make blank paper available. On the worksheet, ask students to think of three good questions about what they have read. Prompt them to list the subheadings and three main points under each subheading. Then have the group go through the strategies of questioning, summarizing, predicting, and clarifying. For example, for the strategy of questioning, help the discussion leader to use *who*, *what*, *where*, *when*, and *why* questions to elicit the key ideas of the passage. Summarizing involves the leader asking the others to provide a summary of the passage, beginning with the early highlights. After one student has answered, the discussion leader can ask others to add or to correct. Clarifying refers to asking questions "whenever we don't understand something." Encourage students to ask questions by emphasizing that anyone who doesn't understand should ask a question. Suggest that passages often leave readers wondering, and that together the group can puzzle these things out. Predicting involves students in considering what comes next. The leader should read out a subheading and ask students to engage in predicting what will appear under this subheading. Discussion of these predictions leads to increased comprehension. A large body of research attests to the effectiveness of reciprocal teaching—for all students, including those with disabilities and reluctant readers (Lederer, 2000; Meenakshi et al., 2007; Slater & Horstman, 2002; van den Bos et al., 2007). Reciprocal teaching has been used in many content areas beyond literature and social studies, including science (Herrenkohl, 2006) and math word problems (Van Garderen, 2004).

Further Reading

Anderson, D., & Cook, T. (2014). Committed to differentiation and engagement: A case study of two American secondary social studies teachers. *Journal of Social Studiers Education Research, 5*(1), 1–19.

Duschl, R.A., Schweinbruber, H.A., & Shouse, A.N. (Eds.). (2015). *Taking science to school: Learning and teaching science in grades K–8.* Washington, DC: National Academies Press. (available at www.nap.edu)

SteveStone/Getty Images

Encourage students to think out loud to you and discuss the strategies they are using.

Another approach involves using children's literature that provides authentic portrayals of children with disabilities. For examples, see Figure 8.4.

Differentiating teaching in any subject, including social studies, can be as straightforward as giving students choices in what they read, the tasks they complete, and the products they produce to demonstrate their learning. Kosky and Curtis (2008) integrated the arts into social studies units and found that what students appreciated most was being given choices in what and how they learned, which increased motivation, especially for students who required differentiated instruction. Web-based learning environments have been created in history (and other subjects) to help teachers create motivating, inquiry-based history units. Okolo and her colleagues (2007) created a virtual history museum (http://vhm.msu.edu) with a vast

Put into Practice

Read one of these sources on reciprocal teaching. With a peer develop a reciprocal teaching activity to try out what you have learned.

Mandel, E., Osana, H., & Venkaatesh, V. (2013). Addressing the effects of reciprocal teaching on the receptive and expressive vocabulary of 1st grade students. *Journal of Research in Childhood Education, 27*(4), 407–426.

Peleaux, J., & Endacott, J. (2013). ReQuest in the secondary history classroom: How does the introduction of purposeful reading technique effect comprehension of text? *Networks: Online Journal for Teacher Research, 15*(1), 1–10.

Stricklin, K. (2011). Hands-on reciprocal teaching: A comprehension technique. *Reading Teacher, 64*(8), 620–625.

FIGURE 8.4 ANNOTATED BIBLIOGRAPHY OF RECENT CHILDREN'S LITERATURE WITH AUTHENTIC REPRESENTATIONS OF DISABILITY TO ENHANCE SOCIAL ACCEPTANCE AND MENTAL HEALTH

In their outstanding paper, Alicja Rieger and Ewa McGrail (2015) describe criteria for choosing children's literature that promotes acceptance and empathy rather than pity, provides positive images of persons with disabilities, describes disabilities and characters realistically, and promotes an attitude of "one of us."

Waiting for No One (2011) by Beverley Brenna, Markham, ON: Red Deer Press (Fitzhenry Whiteside).

With a poignant storyline about the ups and downs of life with *Asperger syndrome*, this Canadian book is suitable for readers from grade 6 into adolescence. The main character, 18-year-old Taylor Jane Simon, struggles for independence, like all adolescents. Has won awards in Canada and the United States.

Wendy on Wheels Saves the Day (2011) by Angela Ruzicka, St. Louis, MO: Angela Ruzicka Publishing.

The author created a character, Wendy, based on her sister who has *spina bifida* and uses a wheelchair. Wendy is an adventurous 10 year old who "rolls through life in her wheelchair" and in this book she helps her friends (a reversal from kids with disabilities being helped by their friends). Suitable from K to grade 3.

Moses Goes to the Circus (2003) by Isaac Millman, Richmond, BC: Raincoast Books (Farrar, Straus and Giroux).

Moses is *hard of hearing* and he and his family are going to the Circus of Senses for children who are hard of hearing or visually impaired. His sister is learning ASL and the book helps us to learn along with her. For K to grade 3, recognized as Outstanding Children's Book about the Disability Experience.

Ben, King of the River (2001) by David Gifaldi, New York, NY: Albert Whitman and Company.

Highly recommended by teachers and parents, this award-winning book is narrated by Chad, the older brother of Ben who has a *developmental disability*. Chad expresses both his frustrations with Ben and Ben's great qualities as a brother and a person—all the action takes place while the family is on a camping trip. There is a page of tips for siblings of children with disabilities written by children. For listeners and readers from K to grade 4.

Do You Remember the Color Blue? Questions Children Ask About Blindness (2000) by Sally Hobart Alexander, New York, NY: Viking Childrens Books (Penguin Young Readers).

In this frank discussion, for grades 4 to 7, Sally answers questions about losing her sight at the age of 26. The thought-provoking questions posed by children about *blindness* have made her think about how she coped with her loss, how to deal with people who don't know how to interact with her, and all the positive changes in her life that she never expected.

collection of artifacts that teachers can use to help students construct compare and contrast charts, cause and effect tables, and so on. Students can engage in a range of written activities, including writing a journal, an essay, a newspaper account, or a letter. Visit similar Canadian websites, including Virtual Museum of New France at the Canadian Museum of Civilization (www.historymuseum.ca/virtual-museum-of-new-france) and Canada and the First World War at Canadian War Museum (www.warmuseum.ca/firstworldwar). The Canadian Museum of Nature also has a Teacher Zone with lesson plans and resources for differentiating (http://nature.ca/education/index_e.cfm).

Concept maps and other explicit structures can help students understand the key relationships between the big ideas in social studies texts. Nesbit and Adesope (2006) reviewed the research on concept maps and report that this flexible teaching approach, which can help to differentiate teaching, has been associated with increased knowledge retention not only in social studies, but in almost every area of teaching and learning, from economics to physics and biology.

Differentiating Visual Arts

The arts may be a great equalizer in education because, regardless of language and ability, music, visual art, and drama are accessible to all, are largely non-verbal, and focus on creativity and self-expression, fundamental aspects of being human (e.g., Cornett, 2006; Gregoire & Lupinetti, 2005). Guay (1993) found that teachers who successfully adapted visual art communicated regularly with resource teachers and other specialists, made rules and expectations explicit, and expected students to help one another. They used clear instructions, repetition when needed by individual students, modelling, and motivational openings to each class. They provided differentiated tasks so students with physical, attentional, and other disabilities had partial or full participation in the class activities (Guay, 1995). De Coster and Loots (2004) have developed a framework for art education for blind students that uses both visual and tactile information. Overall, teachers need to keep in mind some of the fundamental principles of differentiating: teach to developmental needs; treat academic struggle as strength; provide multiple pathways to learning; give formative feedback.

Differentiating Music

Recently, music educators have begun to clarify how music teaching in schools can benefit from differentiated instruction. Christina Grant of Nipissing University and Arlene Lerer of Toronto District School Board (2011) describe how to use many strategies, including small groups, peer coaches, diagnostic assessment, and students' interests to offer respectful options for students. They help teachers to rethink the traditional rehearsal model to encourage students to follow their passion in music and to plan meaningful engagement for all students.

Music can be a challenging area of inclusive education for exceptional students, (Brown & Jellison, 2012). McCord and Watts (2006) describe how to differentiate the instrumental music curriculum for exceptional students, by making a video recording so students can hear the music and see a musician doing the fingering on an instrument like a saxophone simultaneously. McCord and Fitzgerald (2006) provide strategies for matching instruments to students with disabilities; for example, "Strings are a good choice for children with cystic fibrosis and other physical disabilities that affect breathing" (p. 48). They also provide strategies for music reading

Weblinks

NATIONAL INSTITUTE OF ART AND DISABILITIES (SERVES ADULTS WITH DEVELOPMENTAL AND PHYSICAL DISABILITIES)
www.niadart.org

VSA ARTS (FOR PEOPLE WITH DISABILITIES TO LEARN THROUGH, PARTICIPATE IN, AND ENJOY THE ARTS)
www.vsamass.org

such as "Consider highlighting spaces with different colors," and "Simplify parts whenever you can" (McCord & Fitzgerald, 2006, p. 50).

Recent research suggests that music teachers are comfortable accommodating and modifying to meet needs of exceptional learners (Vanweelden & Whipple, 2014). A review of forty years' research demonstrates that many of the studies were conducted in elementary classrooms and social skills were the most likely outcome measures rather than music skills (Jellison & Draper, 2015). Smith (2006) describes techniques for helping reluctant and exceptional students to sing and provides an extensive resource list. All these authors show how the teaching of music can be differentiated to include all students.

Differentiating Drama

Drama involves many means of self-expression, including mime, monologue, tableau, and choral speaking, enabling teachers to negotiate the forms of assignments and self-expression with exceptional students. Differentiations include replacing body movement with facial expression and hand gestures for students in wheelchairs, allowing mime for non-verbal or shy students, and allowing students with learning disabilities to write and perform choral responses rather than monologues. Gifted students can negotiate open-ended assignments. Kronenberg and Blair (2010) provide a clear example of using UDL with multiple means of representation, expression, and engagement in a drama unit on ancient civilizations. The biggest challenge in the relatively unstructured drama classroom may be maintaining the attention of easily distracted exceptional students. Principles of classroom management and approaches for teaching students with ADHD may prove helpful.

Differentiating French

Differentiated instruction is often a necessity in the foreign language classroom, as mixed levels are not uncommon. Teachers of French and French immersion often find that they have to differentiate for exceptional students. They report that motivation is a key factor, especially when

- students have language acquisition and literacy difficulties (e.g., learning disabilities)
- the target language has no personal meaning for the student
- negative socio-political attitudes may be associated with the language
- students lack the basics from previous years' French classes

A recent study conducted in Ontario (Wise & Chen, 2009) showed that an intervention enhanced the phonological awareness of French immersion (FI) students who were at-risk for reading difficulties, much like similar interventions have for children learning to read in English. This suggests that familiar strategies can help exceptional leaners to thrive in FI.

Strategies that may help include an assertive behaviour management plan; twenty-minute blocks of time for activities; and a variety of activities to use the four skill areas of reading, writing, speaking, and listening. Strategies for differentiated instruction in the foreign language classroom include providing learning centres, student choice, and texts at a range of difficulty. Figure 8.5 includes examples of how to use pre-reading and reading strategies while teaching, and how to differentiate for students who have disabilities and for gifted students.

FIGURE 8.5 SCAFFOLDING LEARNING AND MOTIVATION IN THE SECONDARY FRENCH CLASS

Pre-Reading, Teaching, and Assessment of a Chapter in the Text

- Build vocabulary understanding through activities and games.
- Explain context of first reading in English or second language so students are prepared to relate new knowledge to prior knowledge.
- Discuss the purpose, function, and construction of the grammar introduced in the chapter.
- Organize a paired treasure hunt of a grammar concept: pairs of students compete to find all examples of the concept in the reading selection.
- Teach the grammar concept formally with cloze exercises or creation of examples.
- Give a written/oral assignment that features the grammar concept.
- Assess learning through projects, assignments, games, dialogues, listening tests, quizzes, exams.

Differentiations for Students with Disabilities

- Comprehension checks by the teacher; guidance from peer tutor
- Word cues on tests and quizzes
- Open-text exam with a textbook guide to key topics; guide could be created by students by predicting what will be on the exam

Differentiations for Developmentally Advanced Students

- Open-ended projects that allow them to be as creative as they can
- A bonus binder that all students can access when they finish assigned work and earn bonus points by completing challenging puzzles, crosswords, etc.
- Board games in French

Understanding the Learning Difficulties in French Class of Students with LD

- They require much support and encouragement.
- The hardest part for them is understanding the comprehension questions.
- Post a question-word list.
- Teach them to use the words from the question in the answer.
- Teach them to search for the words that appear in the question in the assigned readings in the text.
- For writing, brainstorm sentence starters with the class so no one has a blank sheet.

Source: Developed by Nicole Lévesque, Barrie, Ontario. Used by permission.

Differentiating Homework

Research continues to show that, despite controversy surrounding the topic, completing **homework** is positively related to achievement for students in general education (Chang et al., 2007; Trautwein, 2007). Most classroom teachers assign homework, and many report that exceptional students experience difficulties completing homework. These students may have difficulty focusing their attention, especially if they find the assignment difficult, and tend to show poor time management on long-term projects. Bryan and Burstein (2004) make the case that teachers must share the responsibility for the homework problems experienced by exceptional students because they frequently assign the same homework that has been assigned to the rest of the class, which is too difficult or time-consuming and has not been differentiated for exceptional students. They also argue that teachers must ensure that students properly record assignments and have the necessary materials. For more ideas about assigning meaningful homework, see Vatterott (2010) and Wieman and Arbaugh (2014).

The following guidelines are relevant for students with and without exceptionalities and can be used to facilitate completion of homework by all students:

- Assign work that students already understand so they can deepen their understanding, rather than assigning work they are likely to practise incorrectly.

- Differentiate the amount of work assigned or time for completion so the homework expectation is realistic (e.g., some teachers say 50 minutes maximum homework daily).

- Consider the IEPs of exceptional students, and what is most important for them to learn. This may mean a different homework assignment, but it does *not* mean no homework.

- Motivate students to be more independent through imaginative homework assignments; for students who cannot complete the assignment independently, offer the option of working in pairs.

- Provide rubrics for the content if you assign projects so the emphasis is on knowledge rather than building skills. Assign a poster rather than a model of the solar system. The latter is too time-consuming for what is learned (Vatterott, 2010).

- Discuss the reasons for assigning homework: consolidating classroom learning, increasing independent practise, showing progress to parents, etc.

- Develop predictable routines for homework early in the year, including a self-monitoring tracking system.

- Assign homework early enough in the period that students can try the assignment and ask for help before they leave.

Studies suggest that the families of exceptional students (Mayer & Kelley, 2007) and of ELL students (Brock et al., 2007) can effectively support their children's homework with some direction from the school, making the benefits of homework accessible to students who need to optimize every opportunity to learn. Teachers can differentiate homework, making tasks meaningful and feasible for each student.

Weblinks

FOR DIFFERENTIATED INSTRUCTION IN THE SECOND LANGUAGE CLASSROOM:

FROM THE BLOG OF LUCIE DELABRUERE, A HIGH SCHOOL TEACHER
http://lucie.typepad.com/blog/2006/04/differentiated_.html

COMMUNIQUÉ OF THE LOTE CENTER FOR EDUCATOR DEVELOPMENT IN AUSTIN, TEXAS
www.sedl.org/loteced/communique/n06.pdf

FRENCH IMMERSION IN MANITOBA: A HANDBOOK FOR SCHOOL LEADERS
www.edu.gov.mb.ca/k12/docs/fr_imm_handbook/fr-imm-mb_07.pdf

Further Reading

On differentiating homework for exceptional students:

Mayer, K., & Kelley, M.L. (2007). Improving homework in adolescents with attention-deficit/hyperactivity disorder: Self vs. parent monitoring of homework behavior and study skills. *Child and Family Behavior Therapy, 39*(4), 25–42.

Brosvic, G.M., Dihoff, R.E., Epstein, M.L., & Cook, M.L. (2006). Feedback facilitates the acquisition and retention of numerical fact series by elementary school students with mathematics learning disabilities. *Psychological Record, 56*, 35–47.

Myles, B.S., Ferguson, H., & Hagiwara, T. (2007). Using a personal digital assistant to improve the recording of homework assignments by an adolescent with Asperger syndrome. *Focus on Autism and Other Developmental Disabilities, 22*, 96–99.

Purestock/Getty Images

This high school encouraged students to create a graffiti wall in response to the growth of problematic graffiti throughout the school. Art provides students with an outlet for expressing feelings and ideas and opportunities to develop appreciation as well as skill.

For example, practising number facts with immediate feedback can be particularly effective for students with math learning disabilities (Brosvic et al., 2006), and using a personal digital assistant (PDA) can enable a youth with Asperger syndrome to record homework assignments effectively (Myles et al., 2007). Karen Hume of the Durham District School Board in Ontario reminds teachers that feedback makes homework more effective and that students can self-assess and graph their improvement (2008). Homework is meaningful if it is purposeful, efficient, personalized, doable, and inviting, and enables students to tell teachers what they need help with without penalty (Vatterott, 2010).

Summary

This chapter has described universal design for learning (UDL) and differentiated instruction (DI) and illustrated how teachers can use the ADAPT strategy to analyze and adapt teaching for all students, including exceptional learners. You can ADAPT many aspects of teaching, including substance (outcomes, content, cognitive complexity, authenticity, and task interest), or you can focus on changing the method of presentation, pace, and quantity for exceptional learners. Depending on the strengths and needs of exceptional students, it may be appropriate to ADAPT student engagement and activities, the amount of practise, or the form of practise. Changing any of these aspects of teaching invariably affects other aspects because they are closely linked. Many examples are drawn from practice and research to illustrate differentiating the teaching of listening, reading, writing, mathematics, and the content areas. Differentiating homework is introduced.

Key Terms

acceleration (p. 227)
additional practise (p. 231)
authentic tasks (p. 229)
bypass strategies (p. 227)
CCTV (p. 245)
cognitive complexity (p. 229)
comprehension (p. 232)
computation (p. 242)
concept maps (p. 248)
differentiated instruction (DI) (p. 222)
engagement (p. 230)
environment (p. 229)
expository text (p. 239)
fluency (p. 232)
form of practise (p. 231)

grouping (p. 231)
high-interest, low-vocabulary
    books (p. 237)
homework (p. 250)
hundreds chart (p. 241)
interest (p. 229)
method of presentation (p. 230)
narrative text (p. 239)
number sense (p. 240)
opinion essays (p. 239)
pace (p. 230)
phonemic awareness (p. 232)
phonics (p. 232)
post-reading activities (p. 235)
pre-reading activities (p. 235)

problem solving (p. 244)
reciprocal teaching (p. 245)
remediation (p. 227)
scaffolded reading experience
    (SRE) (p. 235)
scaffolding (p. 231)
story-planning sheet (p. 239)
tiered instruction (p. 228)
three-block model (p. 222)
universal design for learning
    (UDL) (p. 220)
vocabulary (p. 232)
zone of proximal development
    (ZPD) (p. 231)

Challenges for Reviewing Chapter 8

1. List all the aspects of teaching that can be differentiated. Choose one of the opening scenarios of this chapter and see how many of the aspects of teaching in your list can be differentiated to benefit the student in the scenario. How many of these are likely to also benefit other students in the class?

2. Using the opening case of Sally, describe how you would differentiate the teaching of listening, reading, and writing for Sally and other students with similar needs in your classroom. If you teach primary students, create a scenario for Sally in grade 1 and respond to this question for that scenario.

3. Focus on the opening case of Ms. Ash and describe all the ways she differentiates the teaching of math. Create a scenario involving number sense and younger children, and describe how you could differentiate your teaching to benefit your students who are struggling with number sense.

4. Think about a student who might be in one of your classes who is experiencing difficulty in science or social studies, and especially in completing homework in this content area. Describe the thinking process you would engage in to decide how to differentiate both your teaching in this subject and the homework you assign to meet the needs of this student. If you teach secondary students, adjust this question to be relevant for a subject you teach.

Activities for Reviewing Chapter 8 with Your Peers

5. Discuss with your peers how you would like to use the ADAPT strategy to analyze and differentiate teaching. What do you think will be particularly challenging about this process? Particularly rewarding? How can teachers collaborate to enjoy the rewarding aspects and meet the challenges of differentiating teaching?

6. Consider the principles that guide teachers in choosing and combining strategies for differentiating in the classroom. Discuss your ideas with both secondary and elementary teachers. Write a set of steps that you think will help you to differentiate your teaching. Compare them with the steps written by your peers. Why might they be different?

7. Return to the opening cases of Ms. Ash, Hema, and Sally and, with your peers, answer the five questions that follow the cases. What do you learn from these cases?

CHAPTER 9

Differentiating Assessment and Using Assessment to Differentiate Teaching

LEARNER OBJECTIVES

After you have read this chapter, you will be able to:

1. Describe how to use the ADAPT strategy to analyze and differentiate assessment.

2. Describe large-scale assessment in Canada and the accommodations used for exceptional students.

3. Explain how teachers can use classroom assessments to inform differentiated teaching and how rubrics can be used in classroom assessment.

4. Describe adaptations to classroom assessment, including tests, performance assessment, and portfolios.

5. Discuss adaptations and alternatives to report card marks.

Canadian Press Images

S ASHA IS IN GRADE 5 AND HAS ATTENTION DEFICIT HYPERACTIVITY DISORDER AS WELL AS A LEARNING DISABILITY (LD) IN READING. Sasha's teacher, Mr. Sinclair, has been differentiating teaching with the assistance of the resource teacher, and Sasha feels proud of being able to finish most assignments and understanding what is being taught, especially in social studies and science. When Sasha receives his report card in October, he expects it to say he is doing well. He rips it open and sees low grades in every subject. Sasha doesn't understand. He asks the teacher, "Why do you say I'm doing good work and then give me Level I, the lowest grade? I got 8 out of 10 on my science project." How can Mr. Sinclair explain to Sasha that his science project was only six pages long while those of the other students were eight pages long, and that Sasha was allowed to replace some paragraphs with drawings? These adaptations were consistent with Sasha's IEP, which had provided clear guidance for Mr. Sinclair in differentiating teaching. Unfortunately the IEP contained vague information about how to differentiate assessment or grades, and Mr. Sinclair had worried that Sasha would be crushed by his low marks.

BELLE HAS HEARING LOSS AND USES AN FM SYSTEM AND SPEECH-READING TO LEARN IN THE SECONDARY SCHOOL CLASSROOM. She has an IEP that guides her teachers at Oak Ridge Secondary School in differentiating teaching and assessment. Belle's math teacher, Ms. Frost, knows that Belle tires easily and that although she is efficient at speech-reading, it only enables her to catch a fraction of what is said. Belle has math in the last period of the day. Ms. Frost uses a system of frequent oral tests to help students gauge their own learning and prepare for unit tests and term exams. Belle met with Ms. Frost after the first oral test to explain how difficult it was for her to understand the questions and to respond on paper quickly. The two of them reviewed Belle's IEP with the resource teacher. The decision was that Belle would take the tests and do her best, but that the oral quizzes would not contribute to Belle's final grade in the course. The weights of the other assessments—unit tests, homework completion, and term tests—would be increased. Belle felt that this was a fair resolution and was pleased that she could show Ms. Frost that she understood geometry and could use her graphing calculator effectively. However, she worried that other students who disliked the oral quizzes would think it was not fair for her to have different arrangements for calculating her grade.

1. What guidance do teachers need to differentiate assessment for students who have disabilities that interfere with meeting the usual assessment expectations?

2. How can teachers match assessment to the differentiated teaching they are providing for exceptional students?

3. How can teachers prevent students like Sasha and Belle from giving up when effort and improved work are not recognized and rewarded?

4. Why might parents object if schools differentiate assignments and then penalize the students after they do well on what they have been asked to do because their tasks have differed from those of their peers?

Introduction

The subject of this chapter is differentiating or adapting assessment and using assessment data to differentiate teaching. **Assessment** is data collection. It refers to gathering information of many kinds about a student or a group of students, using a variety of tools and techniques. **Large-scale assessment** refers to nationwide, province-wide, or district-wide efforts to provide information about student achievement, usually by means of paper-and-pencil tests. **Classroom assessment** refers to the day-to-day practices adopted by teachers to describe student learning, often through a variety of means, including portfolios, conferences with students, and paper-and-pencil tests. There is no judgment inherent in assessment. It is the act of describing student performance. **Testing** is one form of assessment, normally using a paper-and-pencil test (either designed by the teacher or commercially available) to gather information that describes a student's or group's level of performance. A **high-stakes test** is a test whose results have important consequences for the test taker, such as determining whether the student receives a high school diploma. **Evaluation** involves making judgments and decisions, based on the assessment data that have been gathered, about a student or group of students. **Grading** is a symbolic representation of evaluation, and **reporting** is the way in which evaluation results are communicated.

Using the ADAPT Strategy for Assessment

You need strategies for differentiating or adapting assessment that are effective for exceptional students and efficient for you, and that become a regular part of your planning and teaching. You also need to use assessment data to inform differentiated teaching. In many provinces in Canada, three terms (introduced in Chapter 1 and discussed in Chapter 8) are used in IEPs to refer to changes in expectations, instruction, and assessment:

1. *Accommodations* refer to changes in how a student is taught or assessed, but not in what is taught or assessed; the expectations are drawn from the provincial curriculum at the student's grade level.

2. *Modifications* are changes to what is taught and what is assessed, with the expectations drawn from a different grade level, higher or lower.

3. *Alternate expectations, programs, and assessment* help students acquire knowledge and skills not represented in the curriculum.

You can use the ADAPT strategy introduced in Chapter 1 to differentiate assessment for learners with many exceptionalities, in elementary and secondary schools, and for large-scale and classroom assessment. To recap, the ADAPT strategy has the following five steps:

- Step 1: **A**ccounts of students' strengths and needs
- Step 2: **D**emands of the classroom
- Step 3: **A**daptations
- Step 4: **P**erspectives and consequences
- Step 5: **T**each and assess the match

Large-Scale Assessment and Exceptional Students in Canada

In recent years educators have experienced pressure from governments, parents, and the general public for evidence to show how well schools are preparing Canadian students to compete in the global economy. Pressure arises from the results of international assessment programs that compare our academic achievement with that of other countries, especially countries in the Organisation for Economic Co-operation and Development (OECD) (e.g., *Education Indicators in Canada: An International Perspective*, Canadian Education Statistics Council, 2014). Factors contributing to this pressure also include increasing diversity and the changing role families play in education (Ben Jaafar & Anderson, 2007). It has been said that you can tell what is valued in a society by looking at what is measured in its schools, how that measurement is conducted, and the significance of the decisions made based on that measurement.

In the past, schools in Canada demonstrated accountability by showing that they had conformed to the expected process, identified exceptional students, and written IEPs for those students. However, that has changed in the past fifteen years. In Ontario, for example, schools' IEPs must conform to fourteen standards (Ontario Ministry of Education, 2000a). Alberta also has *Standards for Special Education* (Alberta Learning, 2004), which focus on four topics: access, appropriateness, accountability, and appeals. And 2006 saw the release of *Appropriate Educational Programming in Manitoba: Standards for Student Services,* with expectations in nine areas, including access, early identification, and assessment. Demands for accountability are increasingly focusing on whether the process is producing desired outcomes. In a recent paper, Sonia Ben Jaafar (2006) of the University of Toronto argues that Canada has a unique approach to accountability that reflects our commitment to equitable opportunities to learn and to the Canadian value of social justice. She found that the beliefs of Canadian school leaders were the key factor in determining how they behaved in schools (Ben Jaafar, 2006), in contrast to data on principals in American schools who aligned their practices with state policies irrespective of their beliefs (Ladd & Zelli, 2002). Ben Jaafar calls our unique approach inquiry-based accountability, which means that administrators and educators use assessment information to decide "what to do given the local situation and the demands of the broader context" (2006, p. 69). Large-scale assessment in Canada has been described as providing two kinds of accountability: economic-bureaucratic and ethical-professional (Volante & Ben Jaafar, 2008).

Large-scale assessment plays a different role in education in Canada than in some other countries, like the United States. Don Klinger of Queen's University and his colleagues (2011; Klinger & Wade-Woolley, 2012) describe how student assessment in Canada is closely related to school accountability rather than to the fate of individual students. They examine the School Effectiveness Framework in Ontario and report how schools use assessment information to monitor the effectiveness of their school reform efforts. Addressing this issue, Volante and Cherubini (2010) of Brock University show how some secondary teachers use large-scale assessment results for data-integrated decision making. Every province has a large-scale assessment program and all provinces also participate in the Pan-Canadian Education Indicators Program (PCEIP), which is a joint venture of Statistics Canada and the Council of Ministers of Education, Canada (CMEC). Under the heading of Student Achievement, you can find achievement data for all the provinces and territories (www. statcan.gc.ca/pub/81-582-x/2011001/t-c-g-eng.htm).

Put into Practice

Look for articles in local and national newspapers that reflect the recent demands for assessment to show that Canadian schools are delivering excellence. Discuss with your peers the ways that teachers can support one another and can work with families to reduce the feelings of pressure brought on by these demands.

Further Reading

Consult the provincial documents that guide IEPs in your jurisdiction to see if standards for IEPs have been released or are under development. Check for standards related to adapting large-scale and classroom assessment as well.

Exceptional students are encouraged to participate in the large-scale tests administered in Canada. In their 2009 fact sheet, The Council of Ministers of Education gave four reasons for students being excused from participation in the 2007 Pan-Canadian tests. The students who could be excluded were students who had demonstrated extremely limited abilities, students who could be adversely affected by having to participate, as well as students for whom a school could not make appropriate accommodations, and finally students whose parents requested that they not take part (CMEC, 2009). Students are entitled to the accommodations usually made for them in the classroom, which are not related to the knowledge or skill the test is intended to measure, but change an aspect of test administration. "For example, students who normally had a scribe to write were permitted a scribe for these assessments. Students were given extra time to complete the assessments if they required it in the judgment of the school-based staff" (CMEC, 2003, p. 6). Some of the issues to consider when deciding what accommodations will make a large-scale assessment meaningful for an exceptional learner appear in Figure 9.1.

Cross-Reference
Chapter 2 contains detailed information on IEPs and the role of the teacher in their development and implementation.

FIGURE 9.1 ACCOMMODATIONS TO LARGE-SCALE ASSESSMENT FOR EXCEPTIONAL STUDENTS: ISSUES TO CONSIDER

What is the role of the student's IEP?

- What accommodations for assessment are listed in the student's IEP?
- What accommodations are used for classroom assessment, and are they appropriate for large-scale assessment?
- What accommodations are appropriate for this individual student given the nature of the large-scale test?
- How has the province, school board, or school usually approached such accommodations?
- What information is provided by the province or school board about conditions under which an exceptional student is exempted from large-scale assessment?
- Where must the information about accommodations be recorded when the large-scale assessment is submitted?

When should these adaptations be decided?

- How much time is needed to consult with the student, the parents, and all educators involved in the decisions?
- How much planning and organizing is required to ensure the accommodations are ready?

How are accommodations about setting decided?

- Can the student focus in the presence of thirty classmates?
- Would preferential seating in the classroom be an adequate accommodation?
- Would adaptive equipment be adequate to accommodate the student's needs (e.g., special lighting, pencil grip, keyboarding)?
- Will the student likely distract classmates taking the large-scale assessment?
- Are prompts required to focus the student's attention on the assessment?

How are accommodations about timing decided?

- Can the student work continuously for the length of the assessment?
- Should the student have additional time to complete the assessment?
- Should the student be given periodic supervised rest breaks during the assessment?

(continued)

FIGURE 9.1 *(continued)*

- Does the student's regular medication affect the time of day when the assessment should be administered to the student?
- Does the student's anxiety about a particular subject area suggest that that assessment should be administered last?

How are accommodations of presentation decided?

- Can the student listen to and follow oral instructions?
- Will an interpreter (sign language or oral interpreter) be needed for the student?
- Will a Braille version of the assessment be required?
- Will a large-print version of the assessment be required?
- Will an audio version of the assessment be required?
- Will it be necessary to provide a verbatim reading of the instructions and/or questions? (Interpretation of questions is usually not permitted.)

How are accommodations to response format decided?

- Will it be necessary for the student to answer beside the question rather than in a response booklet?
- Will the student require a computer to complete the response booklet?
- Will it be necessary for responses to be audio-recorded and transcribed?
- Will other assistive devices or technologies be required (e.g., augmentative communication systems)?
- Will verbatim scribing of responses be necessary?

Sources: Thurlow, M.L., Elliott, J.L., & Ysseldyke, J.E. (2003). *Testing students with disabilities: Practical strategies for complying with district and state requirements* (2nd ed.). Thousand Oaks, CA: Sage. Lin, P.-Y. (2010). *Test accommodations in Canadian provincial assessments: Current practices, policies, and research.* www.canadiantestcentre.com/pdfs/AccommodationsPracticeandResearch.pdf

What do you think?

If provincial policies require that large-scale assessment generally adopt the adaptations used in classroom assessment, what are the implications for you, the classroom teacher, and for the adaptations you are expected to make daily?

What do you think?

In 2011 the Queen's University *Education Letter* focused on large-scale testing and ranking: http://educ.queensu.ca/education-letter. David Johnson argued in his paper that the elementary school large-scale assessments by the Education Quality and Accountability Office (EQAO) in Ontario are "great value for money" because they provide a means of comparing schools with students from similar backgrounds. For a different perspective, read the argument by Todd Rogers, in the same publication, that there should be no school rankings under any circumstances because this is not the purpose for which the tests are conducted. What do you think?

There is great diversity in provincial large-scale student assessment (Volante, 2006). Provincial descriptions appear in research papers by Don Klinger and his colleagues (2008), Volante and Ben Jaafar (2008), and Lin (2010).

There are many issues associated with including students with disabilities in large-scale assessment programs. Accommodations to the test format or to the allocation of assisting resources should serve to decrease the effects of the disability in the measurement of the student's knowledge and skills (DeLuca, 2008). All provincial testing programs have policies for providing accommodations. In 2010 Pei-Ying Lin surveyed the test accommodation policies and practices in Canadian provincial assessments. The four main categories of test accommodations that have been found in research were provided. These are changes in

- timing (e.g., extended timing)
- setting (e.g., individual administration)
- presentation modality (e.g., Braille, assistive technology)
- response modality (e.g., scribe)

The policies and procedures that guide accommodation selection were less clear. Educators are expected to make the necessary accommodations that enable exceptional students to participate fairly in all aspects of the assessment to demonstrate their

MBI/Alamy

Students learn together in the classroom and on the volleyball court.

learning. The recent standards for IEPs (Ontario Ministry of Education, 2000a) address "exemptions from provincial assessments" and state that only in rare cases will a student be exempted: essentially when, even with accommodations, the student would not be able to provide evidence of learning on the assessment. A statement must appear in the IEP explaining why the assessment is not appropriate for the student and identifying the ministry or EQAO policy under which the exemption is applied.

Comparison with the United States

In the United States, much has been written about including exceptional students in state and federal high-stakes tests that often determine whether students proceed to the next grade or, at least, contribute substantially to students' report card grades. The issues in the American context that surround the participation of students with disabilities in district and state testing programs are discussed in Lai and Berkeley (2012) and in Yell et al. (2012). Since 2000 exceptional students in the United States have been expected to participate in district and statewide assessment, with or without accommodations, or by using alternative assessments. **Alternative assessments**, which are usually provided only to students in the lowest 1 or 2 percent on measures of cognitive ability, are intended to focus on authentic skills and on assessing experience in community and other real-life environments. Most states use a portfolio or body-of-evidence approach in alternative assessments for these students with severe intellectual disabilities (Salvia & Ysseldyke, 2007). However, there are many challenges associated with this approach, including describing it in terms parents can understand. In Canada, we do not currently offer alternative forms of assessment to students exempted from large-scale assessments.

We have few high-stakes tests, while in the United States, which is the source of much of the research on large-scale and high-stakes tests, schools face a rigorous accountability system dominated by high-stakes testing. Simply put, our contexts are quite different. However, policy-makers in both countries could learn from the cautionary tales told by British researchers (e.g., Rustique-Forrester, 2005) about how increased demands for accountability have resulted in increased dropout rates among exceptional and at-risk students. Many question whether educators can ensure that these assessments are administered fairly and produce valid results for exceptional students. Some of the questions to ask to ensure fairness and validity appear in Figure 9.2.

Summary of Exceptional Students and Large-Scale Assessment in Canada

In summary, your students may be included in large-scale assessment (Lin, 2010). Frequently, exceptional students who have accommodations in their programs are

FIGURE 9.2 ENSURING FAIRNESS AND VALIDITY

To ensure the fairness of standardized assessments and the validity of the results, answer these questions:

1. What test accommodations does the student need to demonstrate her knowledge without interference from her disability?

2. What test accommodations will not change the skill that the test items are assessing?

3. Has the student been provided with adequate opportunities to learn, practise, and apply the knowledge assessed by the test?

4. Has the student been provided with adequate opportunities to develop the necessary test-taking skills?

5. Has the student received adequate information about the testing process and the ways to express his needs during the assessment?

6. What accommodations does the student receive for classroom assessment (these should be identified in the IEP)?

Further Reading

On adapting large-scale assessment for students with a range of exceptionalities:

Salend, S.J. (2008). Determining appropriate testing accommodations. *Teaching Exceptional Children, 40*(4), 14–22.

Edgemon, E.A., Jablonski, B.R., & Lloyd, J.W. (2006). Large-scale assessments: A teacher's guide to making decisions about accommodations. *Teaching Exceptional Children, 38*(3), 6–11.

Olinghouse, N.G., & Colwell, R.P. (2013). Preparing students with learning disabilities for large-scale writing assessments. *Intervention in School and Clinic, 49*(2), 67–76.

Cawthon, S.W., Winton, S.M., Garberoglio, C.L., & Gobble, M.E. (2011). The effects of American sign language as an assessment accommodation for students who are deaf or hard of hearing. *Journal of Deaf Studies and Deaf Education, 16*(2), 198–211.

Kieffer, M.J., Rivera, M., & Francis, D.J. (2012). *Research-based recommendations for the use of accommodations in large scale assessments: 2012 Update (Practical guidelines for the education of ELLs, Book 4)*. Portsmouth, NH: Center on Instruction. (available from ERIC http://eric.ed.gov/ED537635)

included in large-scale assessment and receive the accommodations listed in their IEPs that they receive day to day in the classroom. Those students whose goals are considerably different from their peers and whose IEPs recommend alternative programs (estimated at 1 to 2 percent of the school population) are usually exempt from large-scale assessments. Being familiar with the IEPs of the students you teach will enable you to participate in school-based decisions about the accommodations appropriate for your students on classroom assessments and large-scale assessments.

Classroom Assessment

Changing Conceptions of Classroom Assessment

Teachers spend up to one-third of their professional time on assessment-related activities, and effective assessment can contribute to better learning for all students (Stiggins, 2014). In the last decade, the understanding about classroom assessment held by teachers, ministries and departments of education, and researchers has changed. While schools were once seen as ranking students based on achievement, current policies and practices focus on helping all students to learn, including exceptional students. This changing role of schools has made it imperative that we rethink assessment (Stiggins, 2014).

In the past, teachers and schools relied on **norm-referenced** tests to compare students with peers, while today we increasingly use **criterion-referenced** tests to compare student performance to pre-set standards. The questions to ask include: Who has met the standard? What do we need to do to enable all students to meet the standard (or to do the very best they can)?

The term **summative assessment** has long been used for tests administered after learning is assumed to have taken place. Such tests were intended to provide parents and students with a summary of students' learning and their relative standing. Increasingly, this is called **assessment *of* learning**. Traditionally, **formative assessment** referred to assessment collected during learning which was intended to promote learning and not to simply judge whether students had learned. Increasingly, this is called **assessment *for* learning**.

Further Reading

Locate and read the following Canadian resources on assessment and the dilemmas inherent in both large-scale and classroom assessment in the Canadian context:

DeLuca, C. (2008). Including students with disabilities in large-scale assessment programs. *Exceptionality Education International, 18*(2), 38–50.

Klinger, D., DeLuca, C., & Miller, T. (2008). The evolving culture of large-scale assessment in Canadian education. *Canadian Journal of Educational Administration and Policy, 76*. www.umanitoba.ca/publications/cjeap

Volante, L. (2006). An alternate vision for large-scale assessment in Canada. *Journal of Teaching and Learning, 4*(1), 1–14.

Volante, L. (2010). Assessment of, for, and as learning within schools: Implications for transforming classroom practice. *Action in Teacher Education, 31*, 66–75.

What do you think?

Use the ADAPT strategy to recommend accommodations to large-scale testing for one of the students—Sasha or Belle—described in the cases that open this chapter. Which steps of the ADAPT strategy are most relevant for adapting large-scale assessment? Why?

ASSESSMENT *FOR* LEARNING

Assessment *for* learning is well matched to the demands of teaching in inclusive classrooms and is particularly informative for differentiating instruction. This is because assessment *for* learning takes place while students are learning, as often as necessary, rather than simply at the end. Teachers often interact with students and provide assistance as part of the assessment because the purpose is to figure out how to scaffold the next steps for learning. This kind of responsive assessment depends on your diagnostic skills (King & Chapman, 2011; Stiggins, 2014; Volante, 2010). The emphasis is on creating descriptions that you can use in the next stage of teaching to differentiate learning for your students. Figure 9.3 provides questions to ask yourself when you are using classroom assessment to inform teaching. Doubet (2012) describes how one middle school effectively used collaborative formative assessment—assessment *for* learning—to differentiate instruction to meet the needs of diverse students.

USING ASSESSMENT *FOR* LEARNING TO ENHANCE STUDENT CONFIDENCE AND MOTIVATION

The increasing emphasis on assessment *for* learning in the classroom has implications for students' learning and for their motivation. When students receive feedback that shows them how much they have learned and that communicates the message that the teacher can help them to learn what they didn't know on this assessment, this can contribute to their feelings of success and confidence, and to their believing that they can learn (Stiggins, 2014). Albert Bandura called such confidence **self-efficacy**. His research over thirty years has demonstrated that a strong sense of self-efficacy enables students to feel challenged—not threatened—by difficult tasks, to set goals for themselves, and to persevere (Bandura, 1994, 2011). On the other hand, his research has demonstrated that when students are repeatedly judged by others and by

FIGURE 9.3   QUESTIONS FOR TEACHERS TO ASK THEMSELVES WHEN PLANNING AND USING CLASSROOM ASSESSMENT TO INFORM TEACHING

1. ***What are my students supposed to learn?***
   Consider the curriculum, upcoming provincial tests, and community expectations.

2. ***What have my students learned already?***
   Use continuous evidence to consider the group as a whole, and each student's current place on the continuum of expected learning.

3. ***What do my students still need to learn?***
   Building on your answers to the previous questions, decide what you should focus on next.

4. ***Which students need special services, accommodations, or modifications?***
   Think about those individuals who are not meeting grade level expectations or who need to be taught differently.

5. ***Have my students met the expectations?***
   Compare their learning to grade expectations, and, for exceptional students, compare their learning to expectations in their IEPs.

Source: Hutchinson, N.L., & Martin, A.K. (2012). *Inclusive classrooms in Ontario schools.* Toronto: Pearson Education Canada. Reprinted with permission.

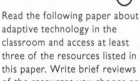

Put into Practice

Read the following paper about adaptive technology in the classroom and access at least three of the resources listed in this paper. Write brief reviews of the resources you choose and exchange reviews with your peers. Try out one resource in a classroom.

Salend, S.J. (2009). Technology-based classroom assessments: Alternatives to testing. *Teaching Exceptional Children, 41*(6), 48–58.

FIGURE 9.4 STRATEGIES FOR ASSESSMENT FOR LEARNING

1. Helping Students to Understand What Good Work Looks Like and to Set Goals
   - *Provide a vision of the learning target in language that students can understand;* For exceptional learners, adjust the language and explain individually
   - *Provide samples of student work along the route to the finished product;* For exceptional learners, make the steps appropriately smaller (or larger for gifted learners)

2. Helping Students to Assess Their Progress
   - *Provide specific descriptive feedback (anecdotal is preferable to numerical) so students know how to improve their work;* For exceptional learners, avoid overwhelming the student with too much feedback
   - *Teach students to provide descriptive feedback for themselves to improve their work;* For exceptional learners, help them to focus on their accomplishments

3. Helping Students to Raise the Quality of Their Work
   - *Draw students' attention to one key attribute of their work at a time, while reminding them that at the end, they will assemble all the pieces;* For exceptional learners, help them to focus on the most attainable change
   - *Teach students to reflect on changes in the quality of their work and on their enhanced abilities;* For exceptional learners, provide clear, concrete evidence of growth

Adapted from Chappuis, J. (2010). *The seven strategies of assessment FOR learning*. Portland, OR: ETS Assessment Training Institute. Stiggins, R. (2009). Assessment FOR learning in upper elementary grades. *Phi Delta Kappan, 90*(6), 419–421.

Source: Hutchinson, N.L., & Martin, A.K. (2012). *Inclusive classrooms in Ontario schools.* Toronto: Pearson Education Canada. Reprinted with permission.

themselves to have failed, they come to doubt their own abilities. Then when confronted with difficult tasks, they tend to dwell on their personal deficiencies and on the hardships they are encountering, rather than concentrating on how to be successful.

To help students build a strong sense of academic self-efficacy, we provide them with frequent information about how they are doing, and we differentiate our teaching based on that information. This helps all students, including exceptional learners, to make progress and recognize and value their progress (Stiggins, 2014).

Figure 9.4 includes a number of strategies that may help you to use assessment *for* learning to ensure that students are, and feel they are, part of the assessment process. Each strategy includes information specific to exceptional students. All students need a clear and realistic target, and work samples can provide concrete examples for students. Continuous feedback should be descriptive and include guidance about what and how to change. It is also important to encourage students to assess their own work and to self-regulate their learning—by describing what they have done well and have done not so well, why they think that is, and by setting goals.

When students begin to self-regulate we are moving into **assessment as learning**, the ultimate goal. "Effective assessment empowers students to ask reflective questions and to consider a range of strategies for learning" (Earl, 2003, p. 44). Teachers in inclusive classrooms face the challenge of finding a balance among the three approaches—assessment *of* learning, assessment *for* learning, and assessment *as* learning—because they all contribute to student learning. Table 9.1 compares these three forms of assessment.

Classroom assessment will help you differentiate your teaching. When you are planning instruction, assessment data can help you determine student needs in relation to specific objectives so you can begin a new instructional unit where the students are and work toward appropriately challenging outcomes (King & Chapman, 2011).

Assessment can guide you when you are in the midst of instruction because you will "constantly gather information to make decisions about when to move on, stop, or change direction" (Lambdin & Forseth, 1996, p. 298). Gathering data while teaching enables you to make in-process decisions about students' levels of mastery as well as their misconceptions, insights, and needs (Stiggins, 2014). If most are progressing well and a few are not, you will use assessment data to provide scaffolding or adapted teaching for those few. However, if most are not progressing well, you may need to make substantial instructional changes. Also consider students' interest in and engagement with the teaching. Such assessment *for* learning can consist of observation, work samples, paper-and-pencil tests, portfolios, as well as students' discussions and questions. You could form new student groups, change your pacing, or change the presentation and content for individuals or for the whole class.

Assessment *of* learning tells you about student mastery of the content and can serve as pre-assessment for the next unit. This information is often reported to parents as well as to students. You must discern to what extent each individual has reached the outcomes, including exceptional students with IEP outcomes, while assessing the effectiveness of your teaching. You may decide to reteach concepts or, in the next unit, to supplement the text with audio for some students and have others write answers in individual words rather than in sentences.

Much has been written recently about the need for constant progress monitoring to improve decision making within a response to intervention (RTI) model. RTI requires schoolwide screening and frequent progress monitoring of targeted learners who are receiving intensive interventions in small groups or individually (Fuchs et al., 2015). Collaborating with peers can help you to use RTI to implement differentiated assessment. All descriptions of RTI emphasize that progress-monitoring data are

TABLE 9.1 COMPARING ASSESSMENT OF, FOR, AND AS LEARNING

	Assessment *of* Learning	Assessment *for* Learning	Assessment *as* Learning
Timing	After learning	Ongoing—before, during learning	During learning
Assessor	Teacher, school district	Teacher, gradually learner	Learner
Comparison	Other students	Standards, expectations	Personal goals
Major Uses	Judging placement, promotion	Making instructional decisions, providing learners with feedback about learning and with motivational support	Self-monitoring, self-regulation, autonomous learning

Adapted from Stiggins, R. (2009), Assessment FOR learning in upper elementary grades. *Phi Delta Kappan, 90*(6), 419–421. Earl. L. (2003), Assessment of learning, for learning, and as learning. In L. Earl (Ed.), *Assessment as learning: Using classroom assessment to maximize student learning*. Thousand Oaks, CA: Corwin Press.

Cross-Reference
In Chapters 1 and 8, references were made to response to intervention (RTI) models that are beginning to appear in provincial documents and to be implemented in some school districts and in some provinces in Canada, such as New Brunswick.

used for decision-making purposes. Data help teachers in making judgments about the success of their instruction for individual students and to determine when additional support is needed or when such intensive instruction is no longer needed. For a clear description of using progress monitoring, see Stecker (2007).

Some teachers find it helpful to develop rubrics. **Rubrics** are descriptions of learning at different levels of development. Many rubrics can be described as **quantitative rubrics**; that is, they identify students with higher achievement as having greater quantities of valued responses:

- Level 1: Includes some of the main ideas
- Level 2: Includes most of the main ideas
- Level 3: Includes all or almost all of the main ideas

However, quantitative rubrics provide little guidance for teachers in adapting teaching. They imply that inadequacies are inherent in students and they fail to focus on the learning that students have accomplished and the challenges that remain.

Qualitative rubrics describe the qualities that characterize learning at various levels and provide students with information about the steps they must take to improve. Table 9.2 shows the components of a qualitative rubric on written expression. Fostaty Young and Wilson (2000) suggest that when you undertake to develop a rubric, you place examples of student work in front of you and analyze the qualities of the work that you view as "okay," "average," and "wow!" or as Levels 1, 2, and 3.

Qualitative rubrics tell you what has been demonstrated, not what is missing. For example, if an exceptional student's work demonstrates that he or she is working at Level 1 for legibility and visual appeal, you would want to emphasize that the student write words and focus on teaching her to leave "white spaces" between the words (see Table 9.2). At the same time, it might be helpful to encourage the pupil to use illustrations to communicate her ideas (see Song et al., 2008, on using cartoons as an alternative learning assessment). For a classmate who is writing full sentences with periods and capitals and who writes only an initial draft, you might focus on planning and sequencing. The student could practise listing ideas and then putting numbers in front of them to improve the order, or, if that proves too abstract, he or could write

TABLE 9.2   COMPONENTS OF A QUALITATIVE RUBRIC UNDER DEVELOPMENT

Elements	Level 1	Level 2	Level 3
Legibility and Visual Appeal	▪ Forms recognizable letters	▪ Letters are grouped and spaced to form words	▪ Words follow in logical sequence
	▪ Initial draft is also the final draft	▪ Creates a final draft from the original	▪ Includes illustrations—used where appropriate
Planning	▪ Researches topic	▪ Sequences ideas	▪ Considers the readers' needs in the planning
	▪ Lists ideas	▪ Identifies sources	
Sentences	▪ Begins sentences with capital letters	▪ Sentences are linked in a coherent order	▪ Uses variety in sentence structure to create effects
	▪ Ends sentences with periods		

Source: Fostaty Young, S.C., & Wilson, R.J. (2000). *Assessment and learning: The ICE approach*. Winnipeg: Portage & Main Press (Peguis Publishers). Reprinted with permission.

Put into Practice

Read "Cartoons, an Alternative Learning Assessment" by Youngjin Song and her colleagues, published in *Science Scope* (January 2008, pages 16–21). Discuss with your peers how to put this alternative assessment strategy into practice in the classes and subjects you teach.

each idea on a card and then try to sequence them in different orders to decide on the best order. A group of academically advanced students who have reached Level 3 on legibility and planning might be taught to use variety in sentence structure to create effects like surprise, suspense, or humour. Qualitative rubrics can help you see who has reached each level that you described and guide you in making decisions about differentiating teaching and about reteaching. Quinlan (2011) has written a practical guide to developing and using rubrics with chapters for each grade, K to 12.

Preparing Students and Parents for Equitable (but Not Necessarily the Same) Assessment

Sometimes you need to differentiate assessment. While most of the class writes a history test in forty-five minutes, Jacob (who has learning disabilities) writes the same test in ninety minutes in the resource room. This is consistent with the accommodations on his IEP—more time in a quiet place. Bonita (who has intellectual disabilities and alternative learning goals) explains to an educational assistant how to travel to local sites that have historic significance, working on two goals on her IEP—learning to travel independently by bus and engaging in conversation with an adult.

What do you say when students or parents ask you why Jacob gets more time, or why Bonita has an oral test? From your first contact with students and parents, refer to your commitment to differentiating teaching and assessment to meet individual student needs. Talk of students as individuals with varying strengths. Explain that exceptional students are included in your classroom because this is the policy of the school, school district, and province. Use examples that make it easy for students and parents to see that this is about fairness. Blind students are taught to read using Braille, and they complete tests in Braille. This does not disadvantage seeing students who don't need Braille. Similarly, research conducted in Canada shows that students without learning disabilities are not disadvantaged when their classmates with learning disabilities receive appropriate accommodations on assessment (e.g., Lesaux et al., 2006). A recent study reports on how universities are beginning to use universal design for learning (UDL) to offer extended time to all students on online assessments, not just to those whose accommodations include extended time due to LD or another disability (Luu, 2015). An experienced teacher offers practical advice about how to implement a redo policy that helps students to reach mastery without alienating any class members (Wormeli, 2011).

It is important that your students and their parents perceive your assessments as fair. When you differentiate assessment, the potential for being perceived as unfair is great, and this could undermine the trusting relationships you have developed with students and parents.

Fairness is a complex concept, especially in discussions about assessment (e.g., Mislevy et al., 2013). Sometimes we treat everyone equally—all children are treated with respect. Sometimes we make decisions based on merit—the child who sings brilliantly plays the lead in the school musical. Sometimes we treat everyone equitably—they receive what they need, like differentiated assessment. If a student objects because Bonita has a different test, explain that this test is as hard for Bonita as theirs is for them. And do your best to make certain that this is the case.

Young children may find these issues hard to understand because they have difficulty putting themselves in someone else's place. Welch (2000) suggests reflecting a student's feelings when the student says that something is unfair; asking the student to write about their feelings; and discussing individually what they have written. Be sensitive to the possibility that the student is telling you they need acknowledgement for their accomplishments too. Also, remember that the students may be right and you may be providing a crutch, that is, more differentiations than are necessary or fair. Be prepared to review your approach and to reconsider the rate at which you are gradually increasing independence and decreasing scaffolding.

Research suggests older students perceive three types of fairness and that the order of importance to these students is (1) interactional fairness, (2) procedural fairness, and (3) fairness of outcomes (Lizzio et al., 2007; Rodabaugh, 1996). These are described in Figure 9.5.

Differentiating Classroom Assessment

Differentiating Learning Outcomes for Exceptional Students

This chapter contains many examples of differentiating learning outcomes for exceptional students. Wormeli (2006, pp. 57–58) describes **tiering assessments**

Further Reading

On differentiating assessment:

Wormeli, R. (2006). *Fair isn't always equal: Assessing and grading in the differentiated classroom*. Portland, ME: Stenhouse Publishers.

Salvia, J., Ysseldyke, J., & Bolt, S. (2013). *Assessment: In special and inclusive education*. Belmont, CA: Wadsworth (Cengage Learning).

Gipe, J. (2010). *Multiple paths to literacy: Assessment and differentiated instruction for diverse learners, K–12*. Toronto: Pearson Education Canada.

King, R.S., & Chapman, C.M. (2011). *Differentiated assessment strategies: One tool doesn't fit all*. Thousand Oaks, CA: Corwin Press.

Blaz, D. (2008). *Differentiated assessment for middle and high school classrooms*. Larchmont, NY: Eye on Education.

FIGURE 9.5   WHAT MIDDLE SCHOOL AND HIGH SCHOOL STUDENTS EXPECT AS FAIR TREATMENT FROM EDUCATORS

Interactional Fairness

■ Neutrality or impartiality; everyone gets their turn and no one is favoured

■ Respectful treatment for everyone; teachers remain calm, discuss private matters in private

■ Consistent concern shown for everyone's well-being in the class; teachers care, listen, are available

■ Actions show integrity, e.g., consistency, truthfulness

■ Propriety; relationships are supportive but not too close; privacy is respected

Fairness in Procedures

■ Assessment that helps all students to learn as well as serving as a means of assigning grades

■ Clear expectations about attendance and concern about students' missed learning due to absence

■ Clear expectations about when students work alone and when students work collaboratively

■ Opportunities for student voice to be heard about procedures including assessment

Fairness in Outcomes

■ Course grades that reflect what students believe they have learned and have earned

■ High expectations and support so all students can show what they know

Adapted from Blaz, D. (2008). *Differentiated assessment for middle and high school classrooms*. Larchmont, NY: Eye on Education. Lizzio, A. et al. (2007). University students' perceptions of a fair learning environment. *Assessment & Evaluation in Higher Education, 32*(2), 195–213. Rodabaugh, R.C. (1996). Institutional commitment to fairness in college teaching. *New Directions for Teaching and Learning, 66*, 37–45.

Source: Hutchinson, N.L., & Martin, A.K. (2012). *Inclusive classrooms in Ontario schools*. Toronto: Pearson Education Canada. Reprinted with permission.

Weblinks

EXAMINE STUDY SKILLS AND STUDY GUIDES AT THE FOLLOWING SITES:

QUEEN'S UNIVERSITY LEARNING STRATEGIES

http://sass.queensu.ca/learningstrategies/tutoring

TIPS ON GETTING TEENS TO DO THEIR HOMEWORK

http://parentingteens.about.com/cs/homeworkhelp/a/homeworktips.htm

TORONTO PUBLIC LIBRARY: KIDSPACE HOMEWORK A TO Z

http://kidsspace.torontopubliclibrary.ca/homeworkmore.html

STUDY GUIDES AND STRATEGIES

www.studygs.net

ELEMENTARY TEACHERS' FEDERATION OF ONTARIO: NOVEL STUDY LINKS

www.nt.net/~torino/novels3.html

Students learn in many contexts, including in co-operative education workplaces and while doing community service.

for advanced students. He suggests you begin with the grade-level task and then raise or lower the challenge level. To increase complexity and challenge, ask students to manipulate information rather than echoing it, to extend the concept to other areas, to critique something against a set of standards, or to incorporate more facets.

Although you are expected to differentiate teaching and assessment for the class as a group and to meet the needs of exceptional learners as much as possible, you are not expected to individualize teaching and assessment for every student. The learning outcomes for exceptional students are guided by their IEPs. Thus you need to consider what outcomes are appropriate for an exceptional student while planning your teaching. These outcomes form the basis for their assessment following teaching, just as curriculum outcomes do for students without exceptionalities. If Sasha, in the case study at the beginning of this chapter, is expected to produce less written work but work of a similar quality to his peers, then this outcome needs to be specified clearly. This differentiated outcome subsequently guides your assessment and grading of Sasha.

Preparing Students for Classroom Tests

You can prepare all students, including exceptional students, for classroom tests. These strategies can be introduced to the whole class, and more practise can be arranged for small groups and individual students as necessary. Most of these strategies can be used in any subject and are particularly helpful for teaching middle school and high school students how to prepare independently.

Cross-Reference
Chapter 1 contains information about RTI (response to intervention).

Creating a study guide shows all students what is most important to study and especially helps those who read slowly and those who have memory problems (Lifvendahl, 2007). Some teachers use practise tests to prepare their students for teacher expectations and test format (Rhone, 2006), and tutoring by a peer, resource teacher, or educational assistant may help. Study buddies or study groups are often acceptable to older students and may also promote social relations (Sloane, 2007). Webquests can be adapted so all students can participate (Skyler et al., 2007).

You can help students analyze their previous tests for typical errors and then group students to explain to each group how to overcome particular kinds of errors. Demonstrate on a projected image the wrong way to answer and put a large stroke through it. Then demonstrate a correct strategy for tackling that type of question. If you solicit ideas from students, provide explicit feedback about whether they are correct or incorrect.

To teach study skills, provide all students with a passage to study and have them work in pairs. Ask the pairs to highlight what is most important in the passage, and ask each pair to come up with a way to remember two parts they highlighted. Show students which sections you think are most important and explain why. Then ask students to give their plans for how to remember the most important information—systematically go through the sections of the passage you highlighted, asking for memory strategies from students. Help them to make connections between ideas to make the content more meaningful and easier to remember.

Develop chunking strategies, ways of grouping information, as well as mnemonics for remembering important lists (Munyofu et al., 2007). A mnemonic imposes an order on information to be remembered using poems, rhymes, jingles, funny sayings, or images. To remember the names of the Great Lakes, for instance, teach your students the mnemonic *HOMES* for Huron, Ontario, Michigan, Erie, Superior.

Concept maps can be developed individually or collaboratively to help students connect ideas (Adesope & Nesbit, 2013; Gao et al., 2007). At the end of a unit, give students a blank concept map with only a few keywords filled in. Ask each student or pair of students to complete a concept map. Then project yours and ask students to discuss how their headings and details differ. Distribute copies of your concept map so students have a good model from which to study and to develop concept maps on other topics.

In a practical article, Dunlosky (2013) describes how to teach students to use study strategies effectively: practise-testing, distributed practise over time, generating explanations, rereading and highlighting, writing summaries, and keyword mnemonics.

Adapting Classroom Tests During Test Construction

All students are likely to benefit from tests that are clearly written. However, some test items that present no difficulties for most students can create problems for exceptional students; they may find the language and format confusing, need to use Braille, or have questions read to them. Figure 9.6 contains a number of

FIGURE 9.6 HOW TO ADAPT CLASSROOM TESTS WHILE YOU ARE CONSTRUCTING THEM

Ten Ways to Adapt Objective Tests

- For non-readers or poor readers, record the questions so they can listen to the questions.
- Lower the reading level by using simpler words and shorter sentences, while retaining the original meaning.
- Ensure that students are familiar with the format of the test by previewing the format with them.
- Supplement written instructions with spoken instructions. Provide examples at the beginning of the test that you have students complete with you guiding them.
- Enlarge the print. Put more white space between questions. Avoid cluttered layout.
- Draw attention to keywords by underlining, using bold font, or highlighting.
- Include fewer items for students who work slowly.
- Place possible options at the bottom of the page for fill-in-the-blanks questions.
- Ensure that students understand how credit and marks will be awarded.
- Give an open-book test or allow students to bring a brief summary (specify allowed length).

Five Ways to Adapt Essay Tests

- Use simpler words and shorter sentences in the question. Draw attention to keywords in the questions (e.g., highlighting, using bold).
- Include information about how many key points you expect and about how credit and marks will be awarded.
- Provide a checklist of ideas to include or a checklist for proofreading depending on students' needs.
- Provide an outline for students to fill in. You can even write the topic sentence of each section.
- Allow additional time for students who work slowly.

suggestions for adapting a classroom test during its construction. Some adaptations could help all students, and you may incorporate them into the test you distribute to the entire class, or you may make an adapted version for a number of students when you construct the original test. You can mark small changes that only apply to one or two students on the student's copy just before you distribute the test or during the test.

Adapting Administration of Classroom Tests

What problems would you anticipate might arise during administration when exceptional students are taking classroom tests? Look to the students' IEPs and your in-school team for guidance. For an objective or short-answer test, students could require additional time or fewer questions, oral administration, a scribe, interpretation of a question, a calculator for problem solving, relevant formulas or definitions, and other external memory aids. For an essay test, extended time or fewer required points in answers may be critical for those who process information slowly. A quiet, distraction-free environment may be necessary. Spell checking can improve the quality of written work. An open-book test may be appropriate to test use of knowledge rather than memory. Even a well-constructed test will fail to demonstrate the knowledge of exceptional students if it is administered inappropriately.

WHAT DO STUDENTS AND TEACHERS THINK ABOUT ACCOMMODATIONS MADE DURING ASSESSMENTS?

There has been a limited amount of research on student and teacher perspectives on the range of assessment accommodations that can be made during the development and administration of classroom and large-scale tests (Oke, 2015). Figure 9.7 provides an annotated bibliography on the views of exceptional students (and their classmates) on assessment accommodations, stigma, and well-being. Assessment accommodations are perceived as less acceptable than accommodations made during teaching. As well, students report stigma and decreased well-being associated with testing accommodations.

The few studies of teacher perspectives suggest that teachers believe accommodations are desirable but not necessarily feasible (Schumm & Vaughn, 1991) and use only a few of the accommodations suggested in IEPs (Gajria et al., 1994). In a survey

FIGURE 9.7 ANNOTATED BIBLIOGRAPHY ON THE VIEWS OF EXCEPTIONAL LEARNERS ON ASSESSMENT ACCOMMODATIONS, STIGMA, AND WELL-BEING

Sometimes students with disabilities are unwilling to accept the assessment accommodations to which they are entitled. They may feel like too much attention is focused on how they are different, may feel deflated by needing accommodations, or may report feeling stigmatized by peers or even teachers for needing accommodations.

Consequences of using testing accommodations: Student, teacher, and parent perceptions of and reactions to testing accommodations (2005) by S.C. Lang, P.J. Kumke, C.E. Ray et al., *Assessment for Effective Intervention, 31*, 49–62.

On a survey, grade 4 and grade 8 students with and without disabilities reported that they perceived using accommodations had a negative effect on students' self-efficacy.

Student preferences for adaptations in classroom testing (2000) by J.S. Nelson, M. Jayanthi, M.H. Epstein, & W.D. Bursuck, *Remedial and Special Education, 21*(1), 41–52.

A survey of middle school students with and without disabilities reported that the preferred accommodation was take-home tests (an invisible accommodation which provides more time for completion); the least preferred accommodation was having test questions read aloud.

Students' perceptions of two hypothetical teachers' instructional adaptations for low achievers (1993) by S. Vaughn, J.S. Schumm, F.J. Niarhos, & J. Gordon, *Teaching and Teacher Education, 9*(1), 107–118.

High school and middle school students, who were interviewed about accommodations, viewed accommodations made during regular instruction positively. However, they were much less positive about accommodations made during tests.

Students' preferences for service delivery: Pull-out, in-class, or integrated models (1989) by A. Heinen & J.R. Jenkins, *Exceptional Children, 55*(6), 516–523.

Students from grades 2, 4, and 5 did not wish to draw peer attention to their skill deficits. The desire to avoid embarrassment increased with age.

Teaching adolescent students with learning disabilities to self-advocate for accommodations (2014) by M.A. Prater, A.S. Redman, D. Anderson, & G.S. Gibb, *Intervention in School and Clinic, 49*(5), 298–305.

High school students with LD were taught to recognize when an accommodation was needed, select an appropriate accommodation, and request and implement the accommodation. They were observed using the accommodations in regular classes, so perhaps teaching self-advocacy can overcome students' feelings of stigma and concerns about well-being.

What do you think?

How might cultural values influence parents' and children's views of fairness and adaptations in assessment? How could you learn about these influences and act on them in an effective and sensitive manner?

study, Jayanthi et al. (1996) reported that teachers thought providing individual help during tests and simplifying test questions were the most helpful accommodations, while the easiest accommodations were providing extra space on tests and allowing open books during testing. More recently, Eisenman et al. (2011) found that high school educators thought the role of the special educator had to be redefined in the general classroom for accommodations to be more effective. Generally, educators at all levels expressed positive views about accommodations but expressed a need for more comprehensive guidance on how to implement them effectively (Oke, 2015; Scanlon & Baker, 2012).

These studies emphasize the importance of not drawing unnecessary and unwanted attention to students receiving assessment accommodations. They also highlight the need for classroom teachers and special educators to collaborate fully so exceptional students receive and accept the assessment accommodations to which they are entitled.

Adapting Scoring or Marking of Classroom Tests

Adapted scoring or marking of classroom tests should be guided by key information in students' IEPs, and you may want to discuss the implications with your principal or in-school team. When you mark objective tests or essay tests, students with disabilities in writing, spelling, or memory should not be penalized for spelling or grammatical errors. You could provide these students with an opportunity to edit their own work before you mark their tests, or you could ask them to indicate the places where they think they have made errors. On essay tests, you may review written responses with students individually and allow students with writing disabilities to elaborate orally on their written responses. You can adapt the marking scheme. Remember the case study of Belle at the beginning of this chapter. Because of her hearing loss, oral quizzes did not count toward her grade in mathematics. It may enhance self-awareness and self-advocacy to show exceptional students how they would have scored without and with the adapted scoring.

Recognize your own assumptions about marking classroom tests and work collaboratively with others who teach the exceptional students in your class. Research has shown that when teachers collaborated to develop personalized grading plans for exceptional students, everyone, including teachers, parents, and students, found the process to be fairer and more effective (Hong & Ehrensberger, 2007; Munk & Bursuck, 2001). Assess students frequently through a variety of means. Give feedback that helps students to improve and remember that effective, informative classroom tests can increase students' self-efficacy and motivation (Segers et al., 2008).

Using Adapted Performance Assessments

Performance assessment usually refers to assessment activities that require students to perform tasks. In studying municipal government, your grade 5 students may read local newspapers, attend a meeting of the municipal council, and invite a councillor to visit the classroom. If you assess what they have learned by asking them to write a letter about a community issue to a local politician, you will be using performance assessment. Grade 11 students in a career development and co-operative education course may learn how to answer interview questions by playing the roles of interviewer and interviewee. If they are assessed by participating in an interview with an unfamiliar adult volunteer, that is performance assessment.

Put into Practice

Consult a source on performance assessment, such as one of these:

Lindsay, D., Rueter, J., & Simpson, C. (2013). Authentic assessment: Establishing a clear foundation for instructional practices. *Preventing School Failure*, 57(4), 189–195.

Hibbard, K.M. (2000). *Performance-based learning and assessment in middle school science.* Larchmont, NY: Eye on Education.

Berman, S. (2008). *Performance-based learning.* Thousand Oaks, CA: Corwin Press.

Luongo-Orlando, K. (2003). *Authentic assessment: Designing performance-based tasks.* Markham, ON: Pembroke Publishers.

VanTassel-Baska, J. (2014). Performance-based assessment: The road to authentic learning for the gifted. *Gifted Child Today*, 37(1), 41–47.

Develop a performance-based task and assessment with an accompanying rubric and make adaptations for an exceptional student (whom you describe in one paragraph).

Characteristics of **authentic assessments** include:

- performance on authentic, engaging, and important problems
- performance on contextualized tasks that represent those expected in the adult world
- real problems with a number of steps that require more than formulaic solutions
- tasks that demand students produce a quality product or performance

For exceptional students, performance assessments can focus on life skills. These students are learning by doing construction in a program designed to keep at-risk students in school. By the end of the semester, they will have built a house.

Performance assessments enable students to show what they know without relying exclusively on reading and writing, and they need not be subject to the same time constraints. Sasha, who has ADHD and reading disabilities, is in the grade 5 class that wrote letters to municipal politicians. Sasha drafted his letter on a computer, read it into an audio recorder, listened to it, and then reorganized the order of the paragraphs. By using a spell checker and grammar checker, he corrected most of the errors and produced a quality product. Because he knows that he speaks better than he writes, Sasha telephoned city hall, made an appointment with the councillor representing his district, and hand-delivered his letter. Sasha demonstrated what he had learned about municipal government and, because he was highly motivated by this assessment, he made differentiations himself.

Sometimes students with disabilities miss the connections between assessments in school and their application to real-world contexts. That is why Sasha's teacher ensured that the letter was written to an adult in municipal government rather than to the teacher. Well-designed performance assessments can help students see these connections (Berman, 2008). This assessment required that Sasha's class learn how to write a persuasive letter, provide specific examples that support an argument, and sequence the parts of a letter. They needed plenty of practise prior to the culminating task. Sasha's teacher recognized that if the process was not engaging, it would become just another test.

Students on alternative programs benefit from performance assessment. Bill, a non-verbal adolescent with autism, is learning to express his agreement and disagreement to unfamiliar adults so he can find employment or volunteer work. A performance assessment might require him to attend a meeting with the manager of a charity shop who requires a volunteer to sweep the floor and to unpack and sort donations. Bill will show the manager that he can communicate agreement and disagreement and can perform the assigned tasks. Bill practises the interview with an educational assistant, sweeps the classroom, and practises sorting a box of housewares daily. The educational assistant attends the workplace meeting with Bill and next term will accompany Bill to his on-the-job training at the charity shop. Performance assessments have great potential for assessing exceptional students in meaningful ways.

Portfolios as Classroom Assessments for Exceptional Learners

Portfolios are collections of student work that show their achievements and their learning over time. They usually contain evidence of reflection and self-evaluation

What do you think?

Read the following paper on researchers' understanding of authentic assessment and performance assessment, and debate with your peers whether the two terms represent the same concept or two distinct concepts.

Frey, B.B., & Schmitt, V.L. (2007). Coming to terms with classroom assessment. *Journal of Advanced Academics, 18*, 402–423.

What do you think?

Read two sources on portfolio assessment. Then consult current documents and websites of the ministry of education in your province. What do you think of the use of portfolios in the assessment of learning of exceptional students?

Denton, D., & Wicks, D. (2013). Implementing electronic portfolios through social media platforms: Steps and student perceptions. *Journal of Asynchronous Learning Networks, 17*(1), 125–135.

Glor-Scheib, S., & Telthorster, H. (2006). Activate your student IEP team member using technology: How electronic portfolios can bring the student voice to life. *Teaching Exceptional Children Plus, 2*(3), Article 1.

Abrami, P.C., & Barrett, H. (2004). Directions for research and development on electronic portfolios. *Canadian Journal of Learning and Technology, 31*(3), 1–15.

Wade, A., Abrami, P.C., & Sclater, J. (2005). An electronic portfolio to support learning. *Canadian Journal of Learning and Technology, 31*(3), 33–50.

Thompson, A.S., & Baumgartner, L. (2008). Exploring portfolios in the elementary classroom with students with disabilities/ exceptionalities: Timely or time-consuming? *Exceptionality Education Canada, 18,* 148–165.

Carothers, D.E., & Taylor, R.L. (2003). The use of portfolios for students with autism. *Focus on Autism and Other Developmental Disabilities, 18,* 121–124.

This student reads from a comic she has written and illustrated as her final assignment in a social studies unit.

that contribute to students' valuing their own work and themselves (British Columbia Ministry of Education, 2004). Electronic portfolios are described by Glor-Scheib and Telthorster (2006). Denton and Wicks (2013) describe using social media platforms to implement electronic portfolios. The following procedures work well for conventional portfolios and can also be applied to electronic portfolios:

- *Collect* in a way that is efficient for your classroom organization.
- *Select* purposefully so the contents show students meeting learning goals.
- *Reflect*—students can write on an introductory page or on sticky notes; or teacher and student can summarize in a conference together.
- *Inspect*—teacher, student, and parents should consider the accomplishments in light of the goals that were set.

Examples of content that might go into a portfolio in reading and writing (with adaptations for exceptional students in brackets) include

- a log of books read with personal reactions to the books (the personal reactions could be captioned drawings or spoken comments)
- an audio recording of the student reading (monthly recordings would show progress for early readers)
- representative responses to pre- and post-reading questions (could change gradually from multiple choice to fill in the blanks to written responses)
- a scrapbook of representative writing samples (increasing in length and complexity)
- notes from conferences with the teacher (ranging from a checklist to a paragraph)
- student-selected best performance in writing of various genres (a limited range of genres)
- teacher-developed qualitative rubrics that show increasing accomplishments in written expression

You may need to teach exceptional students how to select and reflect on portfolio pieces and offer more guidance in the organization of the information. Some exceptional students may not function independently in student–parent conferences and need you to participate rather than being nearby and monitoring. Portfolio assessments that have been used for students with alternative outcomes include a vocational resumé in grade 12, management of a student's own schedule, and engagement in hobbies. Portfolios provide a flexible, individualized approach to capture the learning outcomes of a heterogeneous group of students.

Adaptations and Alternatives to Report Card Marks

One of the most debated questions in education is how student learning should be reported, and even more contentious is the issue of how to adapt report card grades for exceptional students. For examples of how to approach this challenge, see Guskey and Jung (2009, 2012) and Jung and Guskey (2010). Assessments must not discriminate against students with disabilities or serve as disincentives to exceptional students like Sasha, who was described at the beginning of this chapter. But we are aware that grades must also be meaningful to students, parents, teachers, and eventually to post-secondary institutions and employers. Table 9.3 provides examples of grading adaptations that could be used to report grades for exceptional learners across a wide range of exceptionalities and needs, from mild to severe. Be sure to read the policies for your jurisdiction, so you understand which of these options are acceptable in your school.

The first of these options is **changing grading criteria**. Belle's case at the beginning of this chapter demonstrates how you can vary grading weights so students are not disadvantaged by impossible tasks. Adapting curricular expectations must build on the IEP to assess what is expected for the exceptional student. In effect you are using progress on the IEP objectives as the grading criterion (Silva et al., 2005). If you expect Linda, a student with developmental disabilities, to learn to discuss the historical sites in the community, then assess her performance on this outcome. Don't assign a low grade because she cannot write an essay when this was never expected of Linda or taught to her. Grading contracts or modified course syllabi *may* enable you to give students credit for attendance, promptness, effort, co-operative behaviour, and improvement (Munk & Bursuck, 2004). Make the criteria objective and consistent with the IEP, and inform the student and parents about the criteria. Sometimes grading on the basis of improvement motivates students to work hard, attend, and pay attention (Silva et al., 2005).

Further Reading

Read three of the following five papers on grading adaptations for exceptional students and discuss with your peers the most important issues that you think arise on this topic. How do the adaptations advanced by each of these papers differ? And how do the processes recommended for arriving at grading adaptations differ?

Guskey, T.R., & Jung, L.A. (2012). Four steps in grading reform. *Principal Leadership, 13*(4), 22–28.

Jung, L.A., & Guskey, T.R. (2010). Grading exceptional learners. *Educational Leadership, 67*(5), 31–35.

Guskey, T.R., & Jung, L.A. (2009). Grading and reporting in a standards-based environment: Implications for students with special needs. *Theory into Practice, 48*, 53–62.

Munk, D.D., & Bursuck, W.D. (2004). Personalized grading plans: A systematic approach to making the grades of included students more accurate and meaningful. *Focus on Exceptional Children, 36*(9), 1–11.

Silva, M., Munk, D.D., & Bursuck, W.D. (2005). Grading adaptations for students with disabilities. *Intervention in School and Clinic, 41*(2), 87–98.

Salend, S.J. (2005). Report card models that support communication and differentiation of instruction. *Teaching Exceptional Children, 37*(4), 28–34.

TABLE 9.3 EXAMPLES OF GRADING ADAPTATIONS

Change Grading Criteria	Change to Letter and Number Grades	Use Alternatives to Letter and Number Grades
Change weights of elements.	Add written feedback.	Change to pass/fail grades.
Change outcomes from curriculum.	Add log of student accomplishments.	Include checklists of key competencies.
Assign grade based on student improvement.	Add work samples from portfolios.	Include contracts negotiated with individual students.

Changes to letter and number grades may mean clarifying them with a comment that explains the level of the books used in language arts or math. It may be better to make these explanations in a letter stapled to the report card and to also type on the report card that it is valid only if the explanatory letter is attached. What you write on the report about the adapted curriculum and the IEP may be limited by policy and by legislation regarding privacy of information. Learn the provincial, district, and school policies well in advance of the first reporting period. A summary of student activities constitutes a student activity log. This may be particularly beneficial in reporting progress for students on alternative programs.

There are few **alternatives to the letter and number grades** that dominate North American reporting systems. However, some teachers have specified the requirements for tasks in a unit and used qualitative rubrics to assign pass/fail or credit/no credit designations to show that exceptional students have met the minimum requirements for tasks in that unit. Checklists for skills that are taught at

TABLE 9.4 ONTARIO REPORT CARD POLICIES FOR STUDENTS WITH IEPS IN ELEMENTARY AND SECONDARY SCHOOL

Student's IEP	Elementary
Student with an IEP receives only accommodations for a subject/strand	Not necessary or advisable to check the IEP box on the student's report card
Student with an IEP has modified expectations, which vary from the expectations of the regular program for the grade, but are based on the Ontario Curriculum, Grades 1–8	Check the IEP box when it applies to a particular subject or strand. The following statement must appear in the Strengths/Weaknesses/Next Steps section: "The grade/mark for this strand/subject is based on achievement of the expectations in the IEP, which vary from the Grade expectations."
Student has an IEP and expectations are alternatives to the curriculum expectations	An alternative format may be used to record achievement (e.g., the evaluation section of the IEP)

Student's IEP	Secondary
Student with an IEP receives only accommodations for a course	Not necessary or advisable to check the IEP box on the student's report card
Student with an IEP has some learning expectations for a course that are modified from the curriculum expectations but the student is working toward a credit for the course	Check the IEP box
Student with an IEP has learning expectations modified to such an extent that the principal deems a credit will not be granted for the course	Check the IEP box The following statement must be included in the Comments section (with comments about the student's achievement): "This percentage grade is based on achievement of the expectations specified in the IEP, which differ significantly from the curriculum expectations for the course."
Student has an IEP and expectations are alternatives to the curriculum expectations	Check the IEP box The following statement must be included in the Comments section (with comments about the student's achievement): "This percentage grade is based on achievement of the expectations specified in the IEP, which differ significantly from the curriculum expectations for the course." Or an alternative format may be used to record achievement (e.g., the evaluation section of the IEP)

Based on information in: Ontario Ministry of Education. (2008). *Growing success.* Toronto: Ministry of Education; Ontario Ministry of Education. (1998, 1999). Guide to the provincial report card (Grades 1–8/Grades 9–12). Toronto: Ontario Ministry of Education.

Source: Hutchinson, N.L., & Martin, A.K. (2012). *Inclusive classrooms in Ontario schools.* Toronto: Pearson Education Canada. Reprinted with permission.

various grades can help you to communicate the skills that students have mastered, are working on, and have not yet begun to acquire. Often students and parents can understand how much progress the student has made by looking at a checklist or a set of open-ended statements related to curriculum mastery (e.g., recognizes numbers up to seven, or identifies fourteen letters of the alphabet). If this information cannot replace a grade, perhaps it can help to explain a grade. Indicate the skills and knowledge attained compared with those listed in the student's IEP annual outcomes.

Whatever grading adaptations you use, ensure that they are acceptable to your in-school administrators and consistent with the policies and procedures that govern report cards in your province. For example, Table 9.4 outlines Ontario's report card policies for students who have IEPs and shows how complex these policies can be. Be prepared to explain your grading adaptations to the student and parents and collaborate with others who teach the exceptional student (see Farenga & Joyce, 2000; Silva et al., 2005). In all you do, think about how you would want a teacher to report on the progress of your exceptional child and hold yourself to the standards you would expect of others.

Put into Practice

If you are looking for an ongoing source of professional development, consider joining the Council for Exceptional Children and receiving *Teaching Exceptional Children* ten times annually. Visit the website at www.cec.sped.org

Summary

This chapter focused on using assessment to inform differentiated instruction, and on a contentious issue in exceptional education: adapting assessment to report fairly the learning of exceptional students. All teaching and assessment of exceptional students should be guided by the annual outcomes listed in their IEPs and by the descriptions of strengths and needs. We reviewed here how to use the ADAPT strategy to analyze assessment. The chapter described large-scale assessment in Canada and the adaptations used for exceptional students. This was followed by descriptions of how teachers conduct classroom assessment and use it to inform differentiation, and the role of rubrics. There were descriptions of classroom assessment, including tests, performance assessment, and portfolios, and one final topic on adaptations and alternatives to report card marks.

Key Terms

alternative assessment (p. 260)

alternatives to letter and number grades (p. 276)

assessment (p. 256)

assessment as learning (p. 263)

assessment for learning (p. 261)

assessment of learning (p. 261)

authentic assessment (p. 273)

changes to letter and number grades (p. 276)

changing grading criteria (p. 275)

classroom assessment (p. 256)

criterion-referenced (p. 261)

evaluation (p. 256)

fairness (p. 266)

formative assessment (p. 261)

grading (p. 256)

high-stakes test (p. 256)

large-scale assessment (p. 256)

norm-referenced (p. 261)

performance assessment (p. 272)

portfolio (p. 273)

qualitative rubrics (p. 265)

quantitative rubrics (p. 265)

reporting (p. 256)

rubrics (p. 265)

self-efficacy (p. 262)

summative assessment (p. 261)

testing (p. 256)

tiering assessments (p. 267)

Challenges for Reviewing Chapter 9

1. Read the brief descriptions of Sasha and Belle at the beginning of this chapter. Choose one of these students to focus on. This student is in your class, and large-scale assessment will be conducted at your grade level this year. Review the relevant sections of this chapter. Describe the thinking process that you will engage in to decide what accommodations will be appropriate for this student, if any, and describe the way you would advocate for the student if accommodations were needed.

2. Think about a student who might be in one of your classes who needs adaptations to his report card marks. Consider a student who might need alternatives to report card marks. What are the characteristics of these students that make these changes to report card marks appropriate? Review the relevant sections of the chapter and make notes on your ideas.

3. Return to the opening cases of Sasha and Belle and answer the four questions that follow the cases.

Activities for Reviewing Chapter 9 with Your Peers

4. Discuss with your peers the ways in which you can envision teachers using the ADAPT strategy to analyze and adapt assessment. Why is it not enough to simply differentiate instruction without adapting assessment? What challenges do you foresee, and how can you collaborate with your teaching colleagues to overcome them?

5. Write a brief scenario for a class that includes at least one gifted student and one student with a disability; describe the students briefly. Prepare to discuss this scenario, which focuses on teaching that you are likely to do at your grade level, with your peers. Describe how you would conduct assessment so it would inform differentiated teaching. Think about both tiered teaching and other forms of differentiation. Include a qualitative rubric in your discussion of this scenario. Compare your ideas with those of your peers who teach at different levels. Try to identify aspects of thinking about assessment that were common to you and your peers, regardless of grade level.

6. Use the scenario you created for question 2. Assume the role of one member of an in-school team for one of the exceptional students in the scenario. Ask a peer to assume one of the other roles on the team. Discuss adaptations to classroom assessment that you would make to ensure assessment was meaningful for all students in the class, including the exceptional student. Include adaptations to tests, performance assessment, and portfolios, when each of these would need to be adapted. Again, discuss with your peers and compare ideas.

CHAPTER 10

Enhancing Social Relations

Sonya Etchison/123RF

LEARNER OBJECTIVES

After you have read this chapter, you will be able to:

1. Discuss the ways in which social development and social acceptance of exceptional learners are central to inclusion.

2. Describe the role of friendship in the development of exceptional individuals.

3. Discuss elementary and secondary schools as social environments, including schoolwide programs, initiatives for safe schools, and approaches to preventing bullying.

4. Use the ADAPT strategy to analyze the social demands of the classroom and select collaborative and co-operative teaching strategies.

VAL STARTED GRADE 1 IN SEPTEMBER WITH THE CHILDREN WHO HAD BEEN IN HER KINDERGARTEN CLASS AND HAD ATTENDED PRESCHOOL WITH HER. Val participated in an early intervention program, was always encouraged to explore her environment, and is quite adventuresome once she is familiar with her surroundings. Because Val is blind, she does not play much on the equipment in the playground. Some days she asks the teacher on playground supervision to help her get onto a swing, but at recess she usually invites a classmate to stand with her under a tree or to sit with her on a bench. One day, Val's teacher reminds the other children to play games at recess that include Val. Peter and Yamun pipe up that they like to play catch and that Val cannot play "because she can't see the ball." Peter says, "It just wouldn't be safe." On the way out to the playground later in the day, Yamun tells the teacher, "It's kind of boring spending recess with Val. She can't do much. And I don't like when she doesn't look at me. Why does she look at my ear when I'm talking to her?"

LYNN RUSHES INTO THE RESOURCE ROOM WITH HER FRIEND SUPARNA. These two grade 11 students are almost inseparable. Lynn and Suparna both have learning disabilities. They participate together on the school cheerleading squad, and when the two aren't together they are texting. Lynn has severe difficulties with written expression, and she has brought her latest English assignment to the resource room so she can edit it with a peer tutor from grade 12. When I ask Lynn how her day is going, she replies, "Great!" The girls part, promising to meet in the locker room after school. Suparna goes to her history class and Lynn sits down with her peer tutor. Not many people know how severe Lynn's learning disability is—other than her closest friends, her peer tutor, her classroom teachers, and me. As Lynn's resource room teacher and counsellor, I know how hard it is for her to complete her written assignments without "blowing her cover." Lynn leaves class rather than read aloud in front of her peers, works hard with me and with her peer tutor to edit all written work before she submits it, and writes her tests in the resource room where it is quiet and she has extra time. When you ask Lynn why she comes to school, she will tell you, "To be with my friends!"

1. How would you describe the peer relations of Val and Lynn?

2. What should teachers be expected to do to meet the social and friendship needs of students like Val and Lynn?

3. How might the social characteristics and social relations of these students and other exceptional learners affect their learning in inclusive classrooms?

4. What teaching strategies are likely to help exceptional students be part of the social and academic life of the classroom?

5. What school and community resources can a teacher draw on to enhance the social relations of students like Lynn and Val?

Introduction

The focus of this chapter is the **social relationships** of exceptional learners in inclusive classrooms. Through friendships with peers of a similar age, young people experience companionship, support, a sense of belonging, and fun, as well as learning about themselves and the world. However, darker relationships can coexist with brighter ones within children's and adolescents' social networks (Hartup, 2006), and important developmental outcomes are associated with both. In this chapter we think about our role in fostering the friendships, social acceptance, and full participation that are necessary if inclusion is to be more than a placement. The term *social integration* has been used to describe students' full participation in the social interactions of the school community; the term implies that exceptional children are involved in relationships with typically developing peers that are similar in nature to those formed between typically developing youth.

Recent research informs us of the perspectives of youth with disabilities (e.g., Salmon, 2013), of gifted youth (e.g., McHugh, 2006), and of students without disabilities on friendship and on belonging (e.g., Rossetti, 2011). Considering the students' points of view may help you to foster the kinds of friendships that are important for emotional well-being, and to respond constructively when children and adolescents pull back from peers who, for example, don't look them in the eye, like Val in the first of the opening case studies. Many approaches that are used extensively in schools foster social interactions including co-operative learning, collaborative learning, small groups, and activity centres. You can use the ADAPT strategy to analyze the social demands of your classroom organization and of tasks, and compare these demands to student strengths and needs. This chapter provides examples of some of the options for designing the social structure of learning, with examples drawn from current resources, including many Canadian resources.

The Importance of Social Development and Social Acceptance to Inclusion

Chapter 1 describes how participating in all facets of Canadian society, including experiencing **social development** in educational institutions, is a fundamental right of all Canadians. If inclusion means full and valued participation in the life of the classroom, then we need to understand how **social competence** of exceptional students, **social acceptance** by peers, and **friendships** contribute to equity and inclusion. Social competence involves being able to engage in age-appropriate social cognitions and actions (Diamond et al., 2013), while social acceptance refers to the consensual liking or disliking that is directed by the group toward the individual. Friendships are close relationships characterized by reciprocity and commitment between individuals who see themselves as equals (Hartup, 2006). In the next two sections, we focus on the perspectives of exceptional students on their peer relations and on the perspectives of their peers on social relations with exceptional students.

Perspectives of Exceptional Students on Their Peer Relations

What do exceptional students think about their relationships, friendships, and feelings of belonging with their classmates? Only recently have researchers begun to focus on

Further Reading

On social relations and friendship:

Meyer, L.E., & Ostrosky, M.M. (2014). Measuring the friendships of young children with disabilities: A review of the literature. *Topics in Early Childhood Special Education, 34*(3), 186–196.

Chadsey, J., & Han, K.G. (2005). Friendship-facilitation strategies: What do students in middle school tell us? *Teaching Exceptional Children, 38*(2), 52–57.

Bagwell, C., & Schmidt, M.E. (2011). *Friendship in childhood and adolescence.* New York, NY: Guilford.

Diamond, K.E., Huang, H.-H., & Steed, E. (2013). The development of social competence in children with disabilities (2nd ed.). In P. Smith & C. Hart (Eds.), *Wiley-Blackwell handbook of childhood social development* (pp. 627–645). Malden, MA: Blackwell.

Rillotta, F., & Nettelbeck, T. (2007). Effects of an awareness program on attitudes of students without an intellectual disability towards persons with an intellectual disability. *Journal of Intellectual and Developmental Disability, 32*, 19–27.

Karten, T.J. (2010). *Inclusion strategies that work! Research-based methods for the classroom.* Thousand Oaks, CA: Corwin Press. (Contains teaching ideas for a disability awareness program.)

Cross-Reference
In describing the first two steps in the ADAPT strategy, Chapter 1 emphasizes students' social, emotional, and behavioural strengths and needs as well as the social, emotional, and behavioural demands of the classroom.

the voices of exceptional students on this issue. Despite variability in their reports, the importance of feeling connected with peers, with and without disabilities, seems to be a dominant theme. For example, Tom, an adolescent with Asperger syndrome, demonstrated a robust understanding of friendship—as developing when individuals share interests, help one another, and care—when he described his best friend: "He helps me figure out things that I really like, if I'm afraid of something, he helps me get over my fear" (Howard et al., 2006, p. 622). Similarly, adolescents who attended intense programs for gifted and talented youth reported that the greatest benefits were the new friendships formed with peers of similar ability and the feelings of belonging they developed with these "interesting peers" (McHugh, 2006, p. 182).

In a study of grade 5 and 6 students with high-incidence disabilities, Murray and Greenberg (2006) found that students with LD, emotional and behaviour disabilities or exceptionalities (EBD), or mild intellectual disabilities who had positive peer relations in the classroom were less likely to experience emotional and behavioural problems at school. Students who felt supported by teachers were less likely to experience anxiety at school. Studies suggest that exceptional students who feel a sense of belongingness or connectedness enjoy school more and are more likely to be engaged in learning in the classroom.

"Friends are what gets me through school I guess you could say. They're always there to support me . . . friends you tell everything and they're always there, so they're very important" (Lévesque, 1997, p. 73). These are the words of Lynn, the grade 11 student with LD introduced in the case study at the beginning of this chapter. Lynn attends the same Canadian secondary school as Matt, a grade 11 student with LD and ADHD. Contrast Lynn's words with what Matt said when asked how important friends were to him: "Ah just sometimes I just don't know how to relate to a lot of the people anymore. . . . It's not very important I don't think. . . . I know lots of people, but you know like I don't try" (Lévesque, 1997, p. 122).

Whereas Lynn is a popular cheerleader with close friends, Matt is socially isolated and cannot find anyone to listen to him talk about his favourite computer game. Buhrmester (1998; Underwood & Buhrmester, 2007) developed a theory of adolescent friendship characterized by four elements of **interpersonal competence**: initiating and sustaining conversation, initiating plans to spend time with friends outside school, disclosing personal thoughts and empathy, and managing conflict effectively. In interviews and observations, Nicole Lévesque (1997) of Queen's University found that Lynn demonstrated these four competencies, while all four posed a challenge for Matt.

Lynn and Matt's social experiences differ radically, yet both cases demonstrate how peer relations can influence thoughts about school and shape psychosocial development. Lynn's close friendships and positive peer relationships enrich her educational experiences and enhance her self-esteem. Her story is an uplifting illustration of how some

gpointstudio/Shutterstock

Two girls with diabetes are best friends. They both enjoy skating and each understands what the other has to deal with—frequent finger-pricking, taking insulin, and a careful diet.

exceptional students thrive academically, socially, and personally in supportive environments. Matt, on the other hand, stands alone in the halls, cannot carry on a reciprocal conversation, and reports that he had nothing to look forward to when he returned to school after the winter break.

Recently a number of studies have given voice to students with physical disabilities. Adolescents interviewed by Jamieson and her colleagues (2009) described the challenges and rewards of joining activities and finding friends in Canadian high schools. This study found that students' resolve to find a way to participate was strengthened by having close friends at school. Lucy, who is in a wheelchair, attended an inclusive secondary school: "On my first day at the school it was scary because I was worried if I was going to make friends or not. But I made friends straight away" (Curtin & Clark, 2005, p. 205). Marilyn, another student in a wheelchair, described a teacher who told the class about Marilyn, her disability, and her wheelchair and explained that Marilyn would be a full member of the class. Marilyn suggests, "The key to inclusion is making people without disability comfortable with disability, [but also helping them] accept that they have got a responsibility to help remove the barriers" (Ballard & McDonald, 1999, p. 102). These studies highlight how important it is for teachers to promote social relations for all students, including exceptional learners.

Perspectives of Peers on Social Relations with Exceptional Classmates

The research reports a range of **peer perspectives** on relationships with students with disabilities. The case study of Val reflects findings reported by Pat MacCuspie (1996) of Nova Scotia in an interview study about the inclusion of blind students. Classmates tended to describe their friendships with blind elementary school students as based on helping rather than on shared interests or fun, which were the basis for their relationships with non-disabled friends. Some children described the inconveniences of learning with blind children; for example, paired reading was problematic because a Braille reader is slow and pages of Braille are large and awkward. Young children seemed uncomfortable with classmates who did not make eye contact, and some did not understand that blind children could not see at all, but thought they could see less clearly than other people. MacCuspie recommends that teachers be forthright in teaching classmates about the nature of the disability and, for example, explain why a blind child cannot maintain eye contact. Simulation activities and movies have been used to help teachers and students increase their understanding of the challenges faced by students with different (dis)abilities. Figure 10.1 contains information and resources for planning a **(dis)ability awareness program** for your classroom or school.

Many studies have reported that children and adolescents with a range of disabilities tend to have low social status in regular classrooms (e.g., Frostad & Pijl, 2007). **Social status** is based on **sociometric rating**, that is, whether classmates would choose these students as best friends, would choose them to play with, and so forth. Judith Wiener of the University of Toronto and Nancy Heath of McGill University (e.g., Bloom et al., 2007; Wiener & Tardif, 2004) have reported low social status in a number of studies of Canadian children with learning disabilities and emotional and behavioural disorders. A large study of the social networks of four hundred children from grades 2 through 5 showed that the seventeen children with autism or Asperger syndrome experienced lower social status, companionship, and reciprocity

Further Reading

Lindsay, S., & Edwards, A. (2013). A systematic review of disability awareness interventions for children and youth. *Disability and Rehabilitation, 35*(8), 623–646.

Discover together: A disability awareness resource (kit). Department of the Secretary of State of Canada. (Six units examining different exceptionalities, to raise awareness about the competencies of people with disabilities. Recommended for grades K–8. Adapt the recommendations for developing a (dis)ability awareness program appropriate for a secondary school environment. Consider a film festival.)

Safran, S.P. (2000). Using movies to teach students about disabilities. *Teaching Exceptional Children, 32*(3), 44–47.

Ivory, P. (1997), Disabilities in the media: The movies. *Quest, 4*(4). www.mda.org/publications/Quest/q44movies.html.

FIGURE 10.1   (DIS)ABILITY AWARENESS PROGRAMS

Purposes: To foster greater understanding of people with disabilities
To increase students' knowledge about specific disabilities
To increase students' sensitivity toward individuals with disabilities

Develop a program that reflects your local school needs. Invite parents of children with disabilities, older students with disabilities, and adults with disabilities to take part in the planning and in the program.

Adults with disabilities may speak about their disabilities, share feelings, demonstrate how their adapted equipment (e.g., motorized wheelchair, hearing aid) works. Some adults are comfortable to eat lunch with a class of students or sit and talk in the schoolyard at recess as well.

Ask students with and without disabilities to be presenters. They can read from books about children with disabilities, show videos, and act as hosts for adult presenters. These students will benefit from a reflective component to their participation and will appreciate recognition as well.

Locate resources (videos, books, pamphlets, and other community resources). Consult the lists in this book, websites, and community organizations.

Take photographs to remember the occasion, invite the local press, and recognize participants in a school assembly.

Resources to consult:

Center for Disability Information and Referral (Indiana University). Kids' Corner: Have you ever wondered what it's like to have a disability? www.iidc.indiana.edu/cedir/kidsweb

Easter Seals New Brunswick. *Disability Awareness Training CD-ROM.* http://easter-seals.nb.ca/prog_datcd.php

Ison, N., et al. (2010). "Just like you": A disability awareness programme for children that enhanced knowledge, attitudes and acceptance: Pilot study findings. *Developmental Neurorehabilitation, 13*(5), 360–368.

Denti, L.G., & Meyers, S. (1997). Successful ability awareness programs: The key is in the planning. *Teaching Exceptional Children, 29*(4), 52–54.

Rillotta, F., & Nettelbeck, T. (2007). Effects of an awareness program on attitudes of students without an intellectual disability towards persons with an intellectual disability. *Journal of Intellectual and Developmental Disability, 32*, 19–27.

Columna, L., Lieberman, L., Arndt, K., & Yang, S. (2009). Using online videos for disability awareness. *Journal of Physical Education, Recreation, and Dance, 80*(8), 19–24.

Department of the Secretary of State of Canada. *Discover together: A disability awareness resource (kit).* (A teaching kit with six units to raise awareness about the competencies of people with disabilities. Recommended for grades K–8.)

Kirch, S.A., Bargerhuff, M.E., Cowan, H., & Wheatly, M. (2007). Reflections of educators in pursuit of inclusive science. *Journal of Science Teacher Education, 18*, 663–692. (Describes a program for enhancing disability awareness of teachers.)

than their normally developing peers (Chamberlain et al., 2007). Similar findings were reported in an Ottawa study of youth with ADHD (Normand et al., 2013).

Researchers have attempted to understand what might contribute to the low social status of students with disabilities. For example, a study of high school students in Ontario reported the attitudes of almost two thousand grade 9 students toward their peers with disabilities. The majority of students (61 percent) held positive attitudes; however, 21 percent held attitudes that ranged from slightly below neutral to very negative. Dimensions of school culture were related to students' attitudes.

When students perceived that the school encouraged learning for all students rather than competition among students, they viewed peers with disabilities more positively. Positive relationships between teachers and students and positive student relationships were also associated with more positive attitudes (McDougall et al., 2004). Having a friend with a disability also contributed to more positive attitudes. Another study, involving eighty children with a range of disabilities, found that socially accepted children tended to have disabilities that were less likely to affect social problem solving and emotional regulation, whereas children who were socially rejected had disabilities that were more likely to affect social competence (Odom et al., 2006). These two studies suggest that both the characteristics of individual exceptional students and the social contexts we create as teachers contribute to the social status of exceptional students in our classrooms. Many have suggested that social acceptance can be helped by teachers incorporating children's and young adult's literature that portrays persons with disabilities in an authentic, positive manner.

What can you do as a teacher to contribute positively to the social status of exceptional students in your classroom? In 2005, researchers asked students in middle school who had friends with disabilities what teachers could do to increase friendships between students with and without disabilities. The strategies the students suggested included:

1. Put all students in the same classes and provide extra help if some students need it.
2. Provide more information about how students with disabilities are the same as and different from other students.
3. Don't let students make fun of students with disabilities.
4. Create programs all students can have fun doing together.
5. Let us be buddies; use volunteers who are "nice" students.
6. Include students with disabilities in groups in the classroom, rather than in pairs.
7. Let students with disabilities tell us about their disabilities.
8. Create clubs and after-school activities that can include everyone.
9. Let all students take the same buses by using accessible buses. (Chadsey & Han, 2005)

In a study in a British secondary school known for its inclusive practices, Ainscow et al. (1999) learned through interviews what the students thought of the school. "Possibly the most significant and frequently mentioned factor relating to [their] positive feelings [was] . . . the school as a source of social encounters" (p. 141). One student said, "It just seems a lot easier to make friends here—it happens in lessons and free time" (Ainscow et al., 1999, p. 141). Students described positive relationships with teachers and opportunities to pursue individual projects. The researchers reported "relaxed relationships" between males and females, "little or no evidence of racism among the students," and that "students with disabilities are accepted as being just part of the 'normal' school community" (Ainscow et al., 1999, p. 141). They described a blind student who talked straightforwardly with her classmates about her disability and the disabilities of others.

These adolescents defended the practice of including exceptional students. One told the researchers, "I don't see why they shouldn't be in the school because they're just normal, just people same as all of us. They should all have the same chance as anyone else should have" (Ainscow et al., 1999, p. 148). These studies suggest that teachers can foster the perception of exceptional students as valued classmates and

What do you think?

Why do you think parents of exceptional children might be concerned when classmates see their relationship with the exceptional student as primarily based on helping rather than on reciprocal enjoyment of each other's company? How can teachers encourage children (or adolescents) with and without disabilities to see themselves as equals in their relationships?

Put into Practice

Researchers have reported that some schools tend to be inclusive communities where there are many positive reports of friendships, social relations, and respect among students, including exceptional students. Look for a school that is developing such a reputation and make naturalistic observations of the students, teachers, and administrators in that school. What can you learn from such observations about how to create an inclusive community in your classroom and school?

Cross-Reference
Chapter 7 provides teachers with many ideas for developing a positive classroom climate to foster interaction among all students, including exceptional learners.

can teach so that everyone experiences the benefits of being included. You can minimize students' sense that disabilities are foreign and exotic and can help make everyone comfortable with disability. Providing information and eliminating mystery about the exceptionality can go a long way. Treating exceptional students much as you treat everyone else is also essential. There are implications for parents too.

Long-term friendships appear to provide considerable benefits to exceptional students, as do family connections outside school. Families of exceptional children may need to take an active role in initiating play opportunities with neighbouring families in the early years so that children without disabilities feel comfortable alongside the exceptional child (Hall & McGregor, 2000). Parents consider social skills, emotional skills, and friendship to be priority outcomes for their children with disabilities (e.g., Petrina et al., 2015). The next section describes the importance of friendship to development and elaborates on why teachers and parents should make the effort to foster such friendships.

The Role of Friendship in the Development of Exceptional Individuals

Social competence and social acceptance are important for all children and adolescents. Friendship has been called the most human relationship. Social skills and competencies are acquired in both close friendships and general peer group relationships. Intimacy skills are more likely to develop in friendships, and skills like leadership and feelings of inclusion are more likely to develop in peer relations.

Research suggests that children and adolescents who experience poor peer adjustment are at greater risk for criminality and dropping out of school (e.g., Bukowski et al., 2004). Social skills are increasingly important to successful participation in the workplace (Hutchinson et al., 2008). Researchers have shown that social co-operation also contributes to cognitive development. Vygotsky (1978) wrote that "social relations or relations among people . . . underlie all higher functions and their relationships" (p. 163). He argued that all learning is first carried out between the individual and others in the environment. In these social interactions, the individual gradually internalizes what he has been doing, saying, and thinking. Speech and dialogue are thought to be important mediators of internalization (Ostad & Sorenson, 2007). Dialogues that lead to developmental change involve finely tuned co-ordinations between the child and another person, and occur within the **zone of proximal development** between the child's independent problem solving and what the child can do with adult guidance or in collaboration with more capable peers. Conversation or modelling is helpful, especially when it is focused on one another's strategies and reasoning (Del Favero et al., 2007).

Do children co-operate better with friends than with non-friends? Children and adolescents want to have their friends as co-operative partners at school, and co-operation increases their liking for one another (Kutnick & Kington, 2005). When children do school tasks with friends, they interact more, pay more attention to equity rules, and discuss mutually beneficial outcomes more (e.g., Zajac & Hartup, 1997). Azmitia and Montgomery (1993) reported that friends learn more, especially when they give differing points of view and try to find the best solution or combine elements of more than one perspective, as long as they remain task-focused. Recent studies suggest that it is most effective to initially allow students to choose their partners or groups, enabling friendship groups to work collaboratively, but that, once students experience success

Cross-Reference
Chapter 2 includes a section on educational assistants and their roles in educating students with disabilities in inclusive classrooms. You may remember that the issue was raised of educational assistants sometimes coming between children with disabilities and their classmates. How might that situation contribute to the level of social competence and social acceptance of exceptional students? What can you do as a classroom teacher to ensure that exceptional students benefit from the actions of educational assistants and are not socially disadvantaged?

working with friends, they can transfer that positive attitude to working with acquaintances (e.g., Hanham & McCormick, 2009). A recent review cites evidence from more than thirty years that attests to the effectiveness of co-operative learning for helping students to learn with their friends and to learn and build better relationships with peers who differ from them in (dis)ability or race (Schul, 2011).

Children and adolescents whose ability to express themselves is limited to individual words or nods are likely to be disadvantaged in cognitive development and learning. Friends usually show mutual understanding of one another's needs and capacities, and this probably helps them provide responses that are within each other's zone of proximal development, even if each is different in level of development (Steiner-Bell, 2005). The reciprocity, or "give and take," that characterizes friendships usually involves sharing and self-disclosure. This may foster open dialogue, willingness to exchange ideas, and constructive feedback. Companions who trust one another are freer to disagree, more readily believe the information they receive, and are more effective at communicating with one another (Azmitia et al., 2005). These characteristics have been observed in friendships of both adolescents and children. All these characteristics are likely to contribute to the social interaction required for cognitive development. Thus, friendships appear to contribute to the social and cognitive development of students.

Elementary and Secondary Schools as Social Environments

Schools are highly social environments in which students spend the day working and playing with their classmates. Classic studies (e.g., Vaughn, 1991) and more recent research (e.g., Hutchinson et al., 2004; Normand et al., 2013) suggest that it is important to enhance both the social competence of youth with exceptionalities and their social acceptance by peers because neither alone is sufficient. Teachers must create a context where co-operation, community, and peer support thrive. This means informal teaching of social competence and acceptance of diversity with the entire class and making your thinking apparent to the students (Northfield & Sherman, 2004).

Informal Teaching: Climate and Role Models

Teachers create positive and inclusive climates in their classrooms by showing respect for all members of the class and making all students feel that their presence counts. They interact with all students in ways that communicate caring and acceptance. This includes avoiding teasing and sarcasm, communicating high expectations for all students to be successful, and supporting students to reach those high expectations. Students learn their manner of treating their fellow students from you. This means that you must provide good models and demand that students behave similarly. When there are difficulties, you can respond by "seizing the moment" and negotiating with the group. When you make your thinking apparent to students, you provide a model of deciding, acting, and explaining that promotes both social competence and social acceptance, without patronizing. Classrooms that are organized by the teacher as inclusive, caring, prosocial learning communities are more likely to be safe for all students and to enhance the competence of all students—those with and without disabilities (Cefai, 2007).

> **Cross-Reference**
> Chapter 7 contains considerable information on informal teaching of social expectations and social acceptance; it also provides many strategies for creating an inclusive classroom that is a community.

Further Reading

Strategies to facilitate development of social competence and social acceptance

Circle of friends:

James, A., & Leyden, G. (2010). Putting the circle back into Circle of Friends. *Educational and Child Psychology, 27*(1), 52–63.

Videotherapy:

Dole, S., & McMahan, J. (2005). Using videotherapy to help adolescents cope with social and emotional problems. *Intervention in School and Clinic, 40*(3), 151–155.

School-based mentoring:

Smith, C.A., & Stormont, M.A. (2011). Building an effective school-based mentoring program. *Intervention in School and Clinic, 47*(1), 14–21.

Social networking websites:

Morgan, J.J. (2010). Social networking web sites: Teaching appropriate social competence to students with emotional and behavioral disorders. *Intervention in School and Clinic, 45*(3), 147–157.

Facilitating Friendships

You may feel that it is beyond your responsibilities as a teacher to facilitate friendships among your students. However, facilitating friendships may make the classroom a better place for everyone, including you. Figure 10.2 shows some of the steps that you can take.

Research has been conducted and programs have been developed to enhance the friendship and conversational skills of students with many of the exceptionalities described in Chapters 3, 4, and 5. Examples include:

- children with attention deficit hyperactivity disorders (DuPaul & Weyandt, 2006)
- children and adolescents with autism (Palmen et al., 2008)
- children with Asperger syndrome (Crooke et al., 2008)
- youth with Williams syndrome (Klein-Tasman & Albano, 2007)
- children with physical disabilities (Clarke & Wilkinson, 2008)
- young children with a range of disabilities (Terpstra & Tamura, 2008)
- children with fetal alcohol spectrum disorders (Laugeson et al., 2007)

Intensive programs like those listed above may require the participation of a resource teacher, occupational therapist, or social worker, but many teaching strategies can serve as friendship interventions. These teaching strategies include "getting-to-know-you" activities early in the year, literature with friendship themes, discussions of alliances in history, and discussions on ways to express emotions. Some teachers have demonstrated that international videoconferencing and regular email contact can be used to help students with multiple or severe disabilities to meet new people and work as a group to communicate with these overseas friends (O'Rourke et al., 2011). Use modelling, guided practise, and independent practise to teach social skills so students can conduct themselves appropriately in your classroom, in assembly, on a field trip, or during videoconferences. Encourage pairs of students who you think might form friendships to learn together. Be vigilant; when you see friendships developing and appropriate social behaviour occurring, provide acknowledgment and support.

For students who experience mental health challenges or behaviour problems or are lonely, set friendship goals. With young children, meet individually and ask who the student would like to get to know. Goals might include learning the other child's name, sharing a toy or game, or working together at an activity centre. With older

FIGURE 10.2   WHAT CAN YOU DO TO FACILITATE FRIENDSHIPS?

- During the early years, you can provide a structured and supervised social program that can help children practise relationships.
- In the middle years, it helps to provide activities that encourage prosocial interaction during unstructured times of the day when some children may be excluded. At this age, children choose friends on the basis of personality and interests, and friendships become increasingly stable. Boys may form gangs, while girls tend to form small, intimate groups.
- During preadolescence, involving students in co-operative and collaborative activities gives you an opportunity to teach social skills as part of your curriculum. At this age, helping and confiding usually replace playing, and many students need assistance with conversational skills.
- When teaching adolescents, it is important to remember that you are helping to develop leadership and good citizenship in your students through your example. Adolescents are seeking role models. Their friendships are about trust, intimacy, and the sharing of deeply personal thoughts. These close friendships are complemented by membership in larger groups identified by taste in music, clothing, and vernacular expressions.

Weblinks

ABOUT ADOLESCENTS AND PEER RELATIONS:

FOCUS ADOLESCENT SERVICES
http://focusas.com/PeerInfluence.html

FRIENDSHIPS—HELPING YOUR CHILD THROUGH EARLY ADOLESCENCE (US DEPARTMENT OF EDUCATION)
www2.ed.gov/parents/academic/help/adolescence/part9.html

DEALING WITH PEER PRESSURE
http://kidshealth.org/teen/your_mind/friends/peer_pressure.html

students, you may be able to set goals for participation in an extracurricular activity or group. Teach students to handle rejection by considering what they should say if the peer they approach turns them down. Structure social times, such as recess and lunch periods, by forming groups that include isolated students. Create peer buddy programs, ask socially able students to include a shy child in their conversation. Ensure that the presence of an adult, such as an educational assistant, does not interfere in fledgling conversations or friendships. Help parents be aware of opportunities for their child to interact with children outside school. See the boxed feature Theory and Research Highlights from Educational Psychology: The Construct of Friendship. Figure 10.3 provides an annotated bibliography on the role of social relations and friendship in the mental health of children and adolescents, particularly those with disabilities.

Weblinks

MANY SCHOOLS HAVE WEBSITES. VISIT THE WEBSITES OF BIRCHWOOD INTERMEDIATE SCHOOL IN PEI AND LASALLE COMMUNITY COMPREHENSIVE HIGH SCHOOL IN QUÉBEC. LOOK AT THEIR CODES OF CONDUCT. THEN SEARCH FOR THREE OTHER SCHOOLS WHOSE WEBSITES INCLUDE CODES OF CONDUCT. THINK ABOUT HOW THESE CODES OF CONDUCT COMPARE TO WHAT SHOULD APPEAR IN SUCH A CODE. DISCUSS WITH YOUR PEERS.

BIRCHWOOD INTERMEDIATE SCHOOL IN PEI
www.edu.pe.ca/birchwood/code.htm

LASALLE COMMUNITY COMPREHENSIVE HIGH SCHOOL IN QUÉBEC
http://lcchs.lbpsb.qc.ca/documents/Agenda.pdf

FIGURE 10.3 ANNOTATED BIBLIOGRAPHY ON THE ROLE OF SOCIAL RELATIONS AND FRIENDSHIP IN THE WELL-BEING AND MENTAL HEALTH OF CHILDREN AND ADOLESCENTS

Children and adolescents make decisions about their social relationships and their choice of friends based on many characteristics of their peers. This means that some children may be stigmatized, an issue that challenges teachers as they focus on creating inclusive classrooms that are healthy places for everyone to participate. It also means that friendships can have negative as well as positive impacts on well-being and mental health depending on who is chosen as a friend. And some students with disabilities may be vulnerable if acceptance has eluded them.

Supporting Interethnic and Interracial Friendships Among Youth to Reduce Prejudice and Racism in Schools: The Role of the School Counselor (2014/2015) by Cinzia Pica-Smith & Timothy A. Poynton, *Professional School Counseling, 18*(1), 82–89.

Initiatives by school counsellors and educators that promote positive intergroup (interracial and interethnic) friendships can have both individual and systemic effects on students' experience of their school. These initiatives have been shown to reduce prejudice and enhance social, emotional, and cultural competence.

To Dwell Among Gamers: Investigating the Relationship Between Social Online Game Use and Gaming-Related Friendships (2014) by Emese Domahidi, Ruth Festl, & Thorsten Quandt, *Computers in Human Behavior, 35*, 107–115.

Adults worry about gamers retreating from direct social interactions. German researchers found that online gaming may contribute to community for gamers; those who are online the most do tend to rely most on online friendships. However, generally, gamers used the game to spend time with old friends and make new friends online but tended to have good friends offline as well.

The Friendship Study: An Examination of Weight-Based Stigmatization During the Elementary and Middle School Years (2014) by Holly Spencer Kihm, *Journal of Family and Consumer Sciences, 106*(2), 37–42.

Children may stigmatize peers who are overweight. When shown drawings of children and asked who they would they would choose as friends, there was bias against overweight children.

Best Friend and Friendship Group Influence on Adolescent Nonsuicidal Self-Injury (2013) by Jianing You, Min Pei Lin, Kei Fu, & Freedom Leung, *Journal of Abnormal Child Psychology, 41*(6), 993–1004.

Youth whose best friends engaged in nonsuicidal self-injury (NSSI) were more likely to begin to engage in NSSI over time. Students who already had NSSI tended to join peer groups with other members also engaging in NSSI. This study shows the dark side of friendship during the adolescent years.

Friendship Intimacy, Close Friend Drug Use, and Self-Medication in Adolescence (2014) by Julia M. Shadur & Andrea M. Hussong, *Journal of Social and Personal Relationships, 31*(8), 997–1018.

This study found that adolescents who reported lower friendship intimacy and negative relationships with peers were more likely to engage in substance use. Those who reported that their close friends used drugs were also more likely to use drugs but not to self-medicate. Again, youth without friends appear to be vulnerable.

Weblinks

ONTARIO'S PREMIER'S SAFE SCHOOLS AWARDS
www.edu.gov.on.ca/eng/safeschools/award.html

RECIPIENTS OF THE 2013–2014 ONTARIO PREMIER'S AWARDS FOR ACCEPTING SCHOOLS

AGNES TAYLOR PUBLIC SCHOOL – PEEL DISTRICT SCHOOL BOARD

BLESSED TERESA OF CALCUTTA CATHOLIC ELEMENTARY SCHOOL – HAMILTON-WENTWORTH CATHOLIC DISTRICT SCHOOL BOARD

BLESSED TRINITY CATHOLIC SECONDARY SCHOOL – NIAGARA CATHOLIC DISTRICT SCHOOL BOARD

DR. G.W. WILLIAMS SECONDARY SCHOOL – YORK REGION DISTRICT SCHOOL BOARD

ÉCOLE ÉLÉMENTAIRE CARREFOUR DES JEUNES – CONSEIL SCOLAIRE VIAMONDE

ERINDALE SECONDARY SCHOOL – PEEL DISTRICT SCHOOL BOARD

ST. DAVID CATHOLIC SCHOOL BOARD – SUDBURY CATHOLIC DISTRICT SCHOOL BOARD

ST. EDMUND CAMPION CATHOLIC SECONDARY SCHOOL – DUFFERIN PEEL CATHOLIC DISTRICT SCHOOL BOARD

ST. JOSEPH SECONDARY SCHOOL – DUFFERIN PEEL CATHOLIC DISTRICT SCHOOL BOARD

STANLEY MILLS PUBLIC SCHOOL – PEEL DISTRICT SCHOOL BOARD

VALLEY VIEW PUBLIC SCHOOL – DURHAM DISTRICT SCHOOL BOARD

The Construct of Friendship

Much has been written about the nature of friendship by philosophers, psychologists, and educators. While it has been called "the most human relationship," there have been calls recently for friendship research to focus on revealing the dynamics of friendship, positive and negative (Bukowski & Sippola, 2005). Many researchers have suggested that friendship has both a deep structure and a surface structure. By deep structure, they mean friendship's essence or meaning—mutuality and reciprocity. The need for enjoyable companionship is filled by friendship; these are the rewarding and pleasurable aspects of friendship. Surface structure refers to the social exchanges within the reciprocal, companionable relationship, but when these exchanges are fraught with difficulty, friendship can create our greatest problems and anxieties (Bukowski et al., 2006).

Some writers have observed that friendship seems to be harder for exceptional adolescents than for children or adults (Tipton et al., 2013). What might make friendship particularly elusive for exceptional adolescents? According to developmental theorists, at every age there are preoccupying concerns to which people must attend. In early childhood, friendships meet the need for equality-based exchange relationships (Brett & Willard, 2002), and adolescence is characterized by concerns with self-clarification, self-validation, and obtaining assistance to cope (Buhrmester & Prager, 1995). These concerns shape the surface structure of friendship and its social exchanges; for example, young children play beside or with one another, and are often more focused on the play than on themselves. Adolescents "hang out," self-disclose, engage in supportive problem solving, and seek self-defining activities with friends (Buhrmester, 1998). Buhrmester argues that four interpersonal competencies follow from these developmental concerns that are essential for dyadic friendships during the adolescent years:

a) initiating and sustaining conversation
b) making plans to spend time together
c) self-disclosing personal thoughts and providing emotional support
d) working through conflicts

Friends are most often of a similar age and preoccupied with similar developmental issues. Friendships provide unique opportunities to wrestle with issues of most concern to both individuals. This may not be the case when exceptional adolescents are cognitively or socially less mature, or more mature, than their non-disabled peers—they may have few common pressing issues. That friends wrestle with common issues suggests that adolescents need at least one supportive

peer (who is accepting, understanding, and dependable) to help them deal with preoccupying concerns.

Buhrmester (1990) found that for adolescents from 13 to 16 years of age there were strong relations between their reports of close relationships with friends, their interpersonal competence, and their self-reported social adjustment. This is one of many studies of adolescents in the general population that shows that having quality friendships is central to developing social competence.

There appear to be different "cultures" for male and female relations during adolescence. Interactions between female adolescents focus on building interpersonal connections. This means that adolescent females report more frequent interactions of an intimate and supportive nature with female friends than do males with male friends (Maccoby, 1990). However, recent research shows that females are also more likely to engage in co-rumination, repeatedly focusing on problems and dwelling on negative affect; this disclosure process has been related to depression in adolescent females (Rose et al., 2005). This suggests that not all close adolescent-female friendships have positive effects.

Interactions between adolescent males focus more on agentic concerns and less on communal ones. They have been described as "side-by-side" interactions because they focus on doing things together, mainly sports and competitive games (Wright, 1982). Their supportive discussions often focus on the accomplishments of sports teams and individuals. Such interactions may meet needs for achievement, recognition, and power. Studies show that close male-adolescent friendships can also produce negative effects. Dishion and his colleagues found that at-risk boys reinforce the deviant behaviours of friends, a process that has been called deviancy training (Dishion et al., 1999). The more friends laugh at deviant behaviour, the more it increases over time (Dishion et al., 2004). In the case of both co-rumination and deviancy training, the interactions between adolescents are friendly and intimate to the outside observer; only an examination of the content of the exchanges and attention to the follow-up shows the dark side of such friendships.

When we think about how we can structure classrooms, social organizations, and family events to facilitate healthy friendships for children—and especially for adolescents—with exceptionalities, it may be important to consider what developmental needs friendship may address for all the individuals involved, and to think about how socializing contexts may differ for adolescents according to gender. In an ethnographic study of three young people with developmental syndromes, Karin Steiner-Bell of Queen's University (2004) described an adolescent boy with Down syndrome whose friendships were based on sports with other males of a similar age with similar disabilities. His family involved him in school activities, sports teams, and the Special Olympics. He could initiate and sustain conversations and resolve conflicts with same-age peers and with adults in his neighbourhood.

An adolescent male with Asperger syndrome had few adolescent friends and considered his father to be his best friend. He also played computer simulation games with his sisters. His family lived in a remote location and he rarely participated in community activities. He was not strong on any of Buhrmester's four competencies, but he had particular difficulty recognizing and communicating feelings. A young adult woman with Williams syndrome (a rare genetic disorder characterized by developmental delay coupled with strong language skills) had friends with disabilities and friends without disabilities as well as a boyfriend within the disabled community. She reported finding friendships easier during her adult years—when she was able to meet people outside school who shared her interests in music, art, and book clubs. She showed greater strengths in all four of Buhrmester's competencies than did the two adolescent boys.

Case studies like those developed by Steiner-Bell help us to combine what we know about disabilities with recent work on the psychological construct of friendship to enhance the social relations of exceptional adolescents.

References

Brett, B., & Willard, W.W. (2002). The origins of reciprocity and social exchange in friendships. *New Directions for Child and Adolescent Development, 95*, 27–40.

Buhrmester, D. (1990). Intimacy of friendship, interpersonal competence, and adjustment during preadolescence and adolescence. *Child Development, 61*, 1101–1111.

Buhrmester, D. (1998). Need fulfilment, interpersonal competence, and the developmental contexts of early adolescent friendship. In W.M.

Bukowski, A.F. Newcomb, & W.W. Hartup (Eds.), *The company they keep: Friendship in childhood and adolescence* (2nd ed.) (pp. 158–185). New York: Cambridge University Press.

Buhrmester, D., & Prager, K. (1995). Patterns and functions of self-disclosure during childhood and adolescence. In K.J. Rotenberg (Ed.), *Disclosure processes in children and adolescents* (pp. 10–46). New York: Cambridge University Press.

Bukowski, W.M., Adams, R.E., & Santo, J.B. (2006). Recent advances in the study of development, social and personal experience, and psychopathology. *International Journal of Behavioral Development, 30*, 26–30.

Bukowski, W.M., & Sippola, L.K. (2005). Friendship and development: Putting the most human relationship in its place. *New Directions for Child and Adolescent Development, 109*, 91–97.

Dishion, T.J., McCord, J., & Poulin, F. (1999). When interventions harm: Peer groups and problem behavior. *American Psychologist, 54*, 755–764.

Dishion, T.J., Nelson, S.E., & Bullock, B. (2004). Premature adolescent autonomy: Parent disengagement and deviant process in the amplification of problem behavior. *Journal of Adolescence, 27*, 515–530.

Maccoby, E.E. (1990). Gender and relationships: A developmental account. *American Psychologist, 45*, 513–520.

Rose, A.J., Schwartz, R.A., & Carlson, W. (2005). *An observational assessment of co-rumination in the friendships of girls and boys.* Paper presented at the Society for Research in Child Development, Atlanta, GA.

Steiner-Bell, K. (2004). *Social understanding in the friendships of persons with a developmental syndrome.* Unpublished doctoral thesis, Queen's University, Kingston, Ontario.

Tipton, L.A., Christensen, L., & Blacher, J. (2013). Friendship quality in adolescents with and without an intellectual disability. *Journal of Applied Research in Intellectual Disabilities, 26*, 522–532.

Wright, P.H. (1982). Men's friendships, women's friendships and the alleged inferiority of the latter. *Sex Roles, 8*, 1–20.

Safe Schools

Violence is a societal problem that reaches into schools. Children and adolescents need to learn and socialize with their classmates in safe and secure environments—and those with disabilities are more likely than their peers to experience bullying and other forms of violence at school (e.g., Dalton, 2011; Redmond, 2011). Ministries of education across Canada have undertaken initiatives to make schools safer. For example, in 2007 Ontario brought in Progressive Discipline and School Safety, which includes policies and procedures related to hate propaganda and other forms of behaviour motivated by hate or bias. Schools are expected to respond to inappropriate behaviour in the most appropriate way rather than with automatic suspensions and expulsions. Bullying was added to the list of infractions that can lead to suspension. All schools were required to develop and implement a schoolwide progressive discipline policy (www.edu.gov.on.ca/eng/safeschools/discipline.pdf) that takes a whole-school approach, using a continuum of intervention supports and consequences and strategies that advance positive student behaviour and character development. Ontario also presents the Premier's Safe and Accepting Schools Awards annually. The winning schools for 2013–2014 are listed in Weblinks, and the nomination form can be seen at www.edu.gov.on.ca/eng/safeschools/nominate.html. One winning school is profiled in Figure 10.4. Notice the emphasis on social acceptance of students with disabilities and on mental health. This school also won in 2010–2011.

Schoolwide Approaches and Teachers' Roles

Chapter 6 focuses on ways to create a classroom community and a positive climate for learning with your students. The social climate of the school also contributes to the social climate of your classroom. Important aspects of the social environment in a school can be influenced by **schoolwide approaches**. The most effective violence-reduction programs involve students in many ways (Horner et al., 2010). Some schools adopt schoolwide anti-bullying programs that guide teachers, foster consistency, and ensure a high rate of teacher and peer response to bullying incidents. Research suggests this is necessary to make a school safe for all, including the most vulnerable students. Your school may have adopted a code of conduct that is to be

FIGURE 10.4   DESCRIPTION OF DR. G.W. WILLIAMS SECONDARY SCHOOL, AURORA, YORK REGION DISTRICT SCHOOL BOARD, A WINNER OF THE PREMIER'S SAFE SCHOOLS AWARD, 2013–2014

Healthy minds, open hearts

Increasing student involvement by choosing school priorities and resources for initiatives that will help all students feel safe and included has been an ongoing challenge for Dr. G.W. Williams. Some students with various exceptionalities were reluctant to participate in events or deliver announcements. Knowing these challenges, the school wanted to promote the importance of healthy living, safety, and well-being in a caring, inclusive learning environment in a variety of ways that included:

- In cooperation with the local public health unit, fire departments, police services, traffic safety, and the Canadian Mental Health Association, dedicated Safety Week and Mental Health Week campaigns were held to raise awareness of mental health and substance abuse issues. Also a "Think Empathy" week promoted bullying awareness and Mothers Against Drunk Driving (MADD) held an assembly with senior students to discuss the hazards of drunk driving.

- Through a partnership with local grocers, "The Food for Learning" program offered students access to healthy snacks in the guidance department any time during school hours. To further promote healthy food choices for students, two Subsidized Salad Weeks were held which offered salads at reduced prices.

- Special inclusion and celebration events like Purple Day were held where the team joined forces with the Gay-Straight Alliance to show support for the school's LGBTQ community.

The school's safety and inclusion initiatives have made it a positive place that offers students the resources they need to overcome social and emotional challenges and lead happier, healthier lives. The Subsidized Salad Weeks quadrupled the sales of salads at the cafeteria. The Safe and Inclusive Schools Team has also made a significant difference in the engagement, visibility, and leadership skills of the school's students with mild intellectual disabilities.

Safe Schools Ontario: www.edu.gov.on.ca/eng/safeschools/award.html

applied in every part of the school. If you look at the website for LaSalle Community Comprehensive High School (in Weblinks), you will see that the schoolwide code of conduct extends to how students communicate online and to cyberbullying.

CODE OF CONDUCT

Many provinces have developed codes of conduct or adopted policies requiring codes of conduct. For example, Nova Scotia Education (2008) sets out standards of behaviour in the *Provincial School Code of Conduct and Code of Conduct Guidelines*. British Columbia provides a resource called *The Building Blocks of Safe, Caring and Orderly Schools*. Manitoba's resource is *Safe and Caring Schools*. Saskatchewan adopted *Caring and Respectful Schools*. A **code of conduct** clearly identifies school rules and acceptable student behaviours. The best ones are short and easy to understand, with clearly stated consequences for actions, and involve students and the community in designing and committing to the code. The code should include only rules that will be enforced consistently (Fenning et al., 2004). It informs students, teachers, parents, and others what kind of behaviour is expected of students at a particular school. As we become an increasingly "wired" society, students can exploit technology to deliberately antagonize and intimidate those they see as vulnerable, including students who are overweight or small in size, are sensitive, or have disabilities (Willard, 2007). Thus codes of conduct should be designed to prevent cyberbullying. A copy of the code of conduct should be sent to parents at the start of every school year and distributed to students and staff. Birchwood Intermediate School in Prince Edward Island has its code of conduct on its website (www.edu.pe.ca/birchwood/code.htm). The code consists of five items, the first being, "I will respect myself, and other people's rights, personal space and feelings." The code of conduct for LaSalle Community Comprehensive High School (http://lcchs.lbpsb.qc.ca/documents/Agenda.pdf) has seven sections covering respect for self, others, property, and safety, as well as punctuality, regular attendance, and preparation for class. It includes the rationale for each item and the possible consequences of non-compliance. Figure 10.5 describes the characteristics usually associated with an effective code of conduct. Researchers have suggested that schools integrate proactive discipline practices into codes of conduct (e.g., Fenning et al., 2004) and recognize the academic needs of many students who violate behaviour codes and the need to teach the expected behaviours explicitly each school year. They also recommend a description of the positive reward system for expected behaviours and acknowledgment of the roles of key stakeholders.

To make the code of conduct meaningful, discuss it with your students, ensure everyone understands its purpose and expectations, and seek agreement from students to follow it. You may appreciate the presence of the principal or vice-principal in your classroom for at least part of this discussion. For teachers to follow through consistently, there must be a shared understanding based on discussion by the staff, agreement on what actions will be taken following common incidents, and agreement on emergency responses to violence and aggression (Reinke et al., 2006).

A code of conduct is only one strategy to improve the social environment of a school. Principals and teachers must lead by example, ensuring that their actions serve as positive models for students in how we treat one another. Quick and Normore (2004) argue that leadership in any endeavour is a moral task—but even more so for educational leaders because "everyone is watching, especially the students" (p. 336).

Put into Practice

Develop a code of conduct for your classroom. Make three lesson plans for introducing the code and two for reviewing it with your class.

Further Reading

Daunic, A.P., et al. (2000). Schoolwide conflict resolution and peer mediation programs. *Intervention in School and Clinic, 36*(2), 94–100.

Colvin, G. (2007). *Seven steps for developing a proactive schoolwide discipline plan: A guide for principals and leadership teams.* Thousand Oaks, CA: Corwin Press.

Graham, S. (2011). What educators need to know about bullying. *Educational Horizons, 89*(2), 12–15.

FIGURE 10.5 CHARACTERISTICS OF AN EFFECTIVE CODE OF CONDUCT

A code of conduct should

1. explain the rules of student behaviour

2. clearly define roles, rights, and responsibilities of persons involved in the school setting, including teachers, administrators, and support staff, as well as parents and police

3. describe consequences for misbehaviour

4. say that striking another person may be considered a criminal act and dealt with as such (especially in secondary school)

5. say that every student has a right to be safe and secure from threats and harassment, including cyberbullying and cyberthreats

6. include a policy against crimes of property, racism, sexual harassment, and sexual assault

7. include proactive discipline practices

What do you think?

While many researchers have advocated involving students in all aspects of generating a code of conduct to achieve a safer and more positive school climate, others have argued that codes of conduct marginalize those who do not conform easily and are intended to produce docile citizens and workers. Read the following papers by Paula Denton of the University of the Massachusetts and Rebecca Raby of Brock University to decide what you think.

Denton, P. (2003). Shared rule-making in practice: The Jefferson committee at Kingston High School. *American Secondary Education,* 31(3), 66–96.

Raby, R. (2005). Polite, well-dressed and on time: Secondary school conduct codes and the production of docile citizens. *Canadian Review of Sociology and Anthropology,* 42, 71–91.

To engage in **moral leadership**, educational leaders must enhance the sense of community within the school, and create traditions that symbolically represent the values and culture of the school community. This means being aware of their own values, translating these into action, and exemplifying their commitment in their behaviour. Educators who embody moral leadership will develop policies and demonstrate behaviour that is free from bullying and intervene if they observe or receive reports of bullying by anyone, anywhere in the school (Smith et al., 2008).

Schoolwide Behaviour Management Systems

Schoolwide behaviour management systems are comprehensive approaches to managing behaviour throughout a school (Colvin, 2007) which include but go beyond the approaches already discussed. They are process-based models in which collaborative teams of teachers, administrators, parents, and students work together to obtain consensus. Rosenberg and Jackman (2003) describe the PAR model:

- **P**revent troubling behaviour.
- **A**ct, or respond, to rule compliance and non-compliance consistently.
- **R**esolve the issues that underlie troubling behaviour.

The model includes systematic, collaborative work to arrive at a coherent framework, which includes a mission statement, a code of conduct or set of rules and expectations, consequences for compliance and non-compliance, crisis management, strategies for resolution (e.g., social skills instruction, peer mediation), as well as ongoing parent and family involvement and effective instruction and accommodations. Rosenberg and Jackman illustrate how to develop, implement, and evaluate a PAR action plan. Recently a number of descriptive studies have reported on the successful implementation of **schoolwide positive behaviour support (SWPBS)** (Horner et al., 2010) in a wide array of diverse schools, including urban middle schools, urban elementary schools, and alternative schools. SWPBS is a prevention-oriented approach that defines and teaches behaviour expectations, rewards appropriate behaviour, and integrates support for individuals, groups, and the whole school.

PREVENTING BULLYING

Cross-Reference
Chapter 6 includes a framework for analyzing equity incidents in the classroom that could be used to decide how to intervene to prevent future incidents of bullying and cyberbullying. Chapter 7 focuses on what you can do to create and maintain a positive climate in your classroom. Reviewing Chapter 7 while you are reading this chapter may help you to develop strategies for your class while working with your colleagues for a schoolwide approach.

Research suggests that students who are harassed and bullied are more likely to exhibit aggression and anti-social behaviour that might interfere with their participation in learning activities (Rusby et al., 2005), and bullied students tend to have lower levels of achievement (Beran et al., 2008). Studies like these contribute to educators' concerns that, for all students, including exceptional students, there are close ties among social acceptance, social development, and learning. Thus, for more than a decade the provinces have been developing and promoting policies to prevent bullying, like *Keeping Our Schools Safe* (New Brunswick, 2000) and *Anti-Bullying Strategy* (Saskatchewan Learning, 2005). Manitoba has created checklists that can be used to help students identify concerns about bullying and harassment (e.g., www.edu.gov.mb.ca/k12/specedu/guidance/pdf/Secondary_Student_Checklist.pdf). Children and adolescents with disabilities have suggested that schools need to offer programs of disability awareness and develop networks of peer support, while teachers need to listen to students with disabilities without drawing attention to them (Lindsay & McPherson, 2012).

Schoolwide programs are the most effective response to bullying because it is a problem that occurs in the school's social environment as a whole (Nickerson et al., 2013). "**Bullying** is a form of abuse at the hands of peers that can take different forms at different ages" (Craig et al., 2007, p. 465). These forms include physical, emotional, verbal, and cyberbullying. **Cyberbullying** is a form of psychological cruelty perpetrated virtually, and refers to threats, insults, and demeaning messages spread through the Internet or by cellphone. Sometimes it takes the form of exclusion when students create a list of users whose messages are blocked from joining online groups such as chat rooms. Particularly devastating are chat rooms that have been set up to receive mean-spirited postings about a classmate. While cyberthreats and cyberbullying often take place away from school, we cannot ignore their potential for destroying students' safety and well-being twenty-four hours a day, in school and out of school (Willard, 2007). Recent research suggests that mental health, particularly depression in adolescent females, mediates a link between cyberbullying and suicide (Bauman et al., 2013).

Children and adolescents who lack social skills and do not pick up on social cues are among those likely to be victims of all forms of bullying, and exceptional students often lack social skills and miss social cues (Cummings et al., 2006; Luciano & Savage, 2007). Beran (2006) reported that students' and teachers' reports of what constitutes bullying are not highly correlated. These studies remind us how challenging dealing with bullying can be for educators. Your efforts to prevent students in your class from bullying or being bullied will likely be more effective if your school has a schoolwide anti-bullying program.

All students must understand that bullying is unacceptable. Thus, every class in a school should participate in a consistent program that emphasizes that bullying and cyberbullying and students who bully will be dealt with. All teachers and students need to recognize bullying. The characteristics of verbal, emotional, and physical bullying as well as cyberbullying should be portrayed around the school, in assemblies, and in classrooms in language that all students can understand. Everyone, adults and children, must have strategies for responding.

The Olweus Bullying Prevention Program is described at www.clemson.edu/olweus. This well-researched program integrates school-level components that include schoolwide rules against bullying, with classroom-level components like regular class meetings to reinforce the schoolwide rules, and with individual-level components (interventions with those who are bullied, those who bully, and parents). The program includes teacher guides, booklets, and videos.

Wendy Craig of Queen's University and Debra Pepler of York University lead the Canadian Initiative for the Prevention of Bullying (www.prevnet.ca). The network has many partners and is known as PREVNet. PREVNet offers toolkits for education, assessment, and intervention. These researchers argue that bullying is closely related to development and is about children's and adolescents' relationships. They suggest that intervention strategies must involve the wider community, including parents and other adults, and must help children and adolescents to intervene effectively. They recognize that bullies as well as victims require support and that relationship problems require relationship solutions (Craig et al., 2010). PREVNet's website includes tip sheets that parents, teachers, and students can download.

To respond effectively to bullying, children must be confident that they have the backing of adults. PREVNet research suggests that teachers respond only about 10 percent of the time. When students judge teachers as effective at responding to bullying, then students engage in less bullying and more reporting of bullying to the

Anti-Bullying and Anti-Violence Programs

There are many websites available to help you and your school tackle bullying on a schoolwide basis. Most of these Canadian sites also provide links to other international sites.

London (Ontario) Family Court Clinic:

www.lfcc.on.ca/bully.htm

This site contains extensive information about bullying for parents and teachers. The highly readable information is an excerpt from the second edition of *A.S.A.P.: A School-based Anti-violence Program*, which is available from the London Family Court Clinic. It consists of a video and sixty-five lessons.

Bully Beware Programs (British Columbia):

www.bullybeware.com

This site contains information about a video (*Bully Beware*), books (*Take Action Against Bullying* and *How Parents Can Take Action Against Bullying*), and posters that can be used around the school to support the anti-bullying program. There are also tips and news articles from Canadian newspapers and magazines about bullying incidents in our schools and communities.

Bullying.org (children at Banded Peak School in Bragg Creek, Alberta, and their teacher, William Belsey):

www.bullying.org

This site was started after the shooting at W.R. Myers High School in Taber, Alberta, when stories emerged that the accused had been bullied. A group of grade 1 to 8 students who met to provide peer support grew into www.bullying.org, which attempts to help young people help each other. Not only can you and your students learn by visiting this site, but you may be inspired to commit to an online project that would ensure that your students internalize and live the lessons you are learning together.

Stop Cyberbullying:

www.cyberbullying.ca

This site was started by the developers of www.bullying.org, Bill Belsey and his students. It contains practical suggestions about combating cyberbullying, including lobbying the telecommunications industry about the problem.

PREVNet:

www.prevnet.ca

This combined research and practice website focuses on promoting relationships and eliminating violence. Based at Queen's University and York University, it involves many of the leading researchers in Canada in the field of bullying and a wide range of organizations and agencies.

Olweus Bullying Prevention Program:

www.clemson.edu/olweus

This is the North American website at Clemson University for the most researched anti-bullying program, developed by Dan Olweus of Norway.

teacher (Veenstra et al., 2014). This means that teachers can play an effective role in reducing bullying.

We must also teach all students, including exceptional students who use alternative forms of communication, to report incidents that occur to them or others. Children need to role-play and practise proactive and prosocial responses to bullying. Figure 10.6 provides teachers with strategies for helping students to respond to bullying. You can use resources like this one to devise student activities for practise. You may also need to coach your students to include all classmates in their activities, and to support victims, report incidents, and take part in role-playing to practise leadership and citizenship (Olweus, 2003). It is critical to prevent ostracization or victimization of students who report bullying. Figure 10.7 introduces a strategy called ABC—TELL NOW, which you can use to help children, and students of all ages with intellectual disabilities, to learn how to report incidents of cyberbullying.

Strong programs to improve the school environment also involve individualized interventions with violent, bullying, and at-risk students (Olweus, 2003). If children in your class are identified as bullies, you may be asked to participate in interventions with a counsellor. This will help you to be consistent with these specialists in your preventive and responsive dealings to prevent them bullying.

FIGURE 10.6 HELPING STUDENTS RESPOND TO BULLYING

- Help students to recognize when they should seek adult intervention.
- Encourage children and adolescents to come forward and report bullying and cyberbullying early, before the emotional effects become too great. Remind them that by seeking adult help they will help to create an atmosphere where people can feel safe instead of feeling frightened and insecure because they might be bullied.
- Be aware of the signs of bullying, and support children and adolescents who experience bullying. Avoidance, including avoiding school, may be a sign that a child is being bullied. Watch for students who experience stomach aches, headaches, and depressive symptoms or who are victims of exclusion, including virtual exclusion.
- Monitor exchanges between more powerful and less powerful students closely. If you don't expect to see a particular pair of students interacting, then ensure that you are aware of the nature of their interactions. Remember that bullying can be physical, verbal, emotional, or virtual. Be vigilant, because the longer bullying goes on, the harder it will be to put an end to it.
- Watch for signs of responses to bullying. Girls are more likely to use relationship skills to try to deal with bullying, while boys are more likely to resort to violence or retaliation.
- Provide children and youth who are bullied with effective strategies. Help them to recognize healthy and unhealthy relationships (even friends can engage in bullying). And encourage students to report bullying immediately.
- Help those who are bullied to walk away and try not to show the bully that she has succeeded in creating upset or anger. Help students to practise their replies to things that they may be teased or bullied about (unusual name, glasses, hearing aid, etc.) so they can give the impression it doesn't bother them. And encourage students to report bullying immediately.
- Create a positive social climate in which all are valued, teach students your expectations, enforce your expectations for healthy relationships between classmates, help students to develop healthy peer relationships, and respond to bullying and cyberbullying consistently and in accord with the protocol about which students have been informed.

Sources: Stones, R. (2005). *Don't pick on me: How to handle bullying* (3rd ed.). Markham, ON: Pembroke Publishers. Craig, W., Pepler, D., & Blais, J. (2007) Responding to bullying: What works? *School Psychology International, 28*, 465–477. Beale, A.V., & Hall, K.R. (2007). Cyberbullying: What school administrators (and parents) can do. *Clearing House, 81*(1), 8–12.

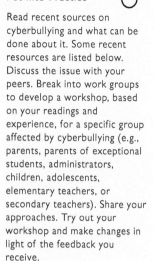

Put into Practice

Read recent sources on cyberbullying and what can be done about it. Some recent resources are listed below. Discuss the issue with your peers. Break into work groups to develop a workshop, based on your readings and experience, for a specific group affected by cyberbullying (e.g., parents, parents of exceptional students, administrators, children, adolescents, elementary teachers, or secondary teachers). Share your approaches. Try out your workshop and make changes in light of the feedback you receive.

Examples of sources:

Willard, N.E. (2007). *Cyberbullying and cyberthreats: Responding to the challenge of online social aggression, threats, and distress.* Champaign, IL: Research Press.

Beale, A.V., & Hall, K.R. (2007). Cyberbullying: What school administrators (and parents) can do. *Clearing House, 81*(1), 8–12.

Brunner, J., & Lewis, D. (2007). Ten strategies to address bullying. *Principal Leadership (High School Ed.), 7*(9), 73–75.

Diamanduros, T., & Downs, E. (2011). Creating a safe school environment: How to prevent cyberbullying at your school. *Library Media Connection, 30*(2), 36–38.

FIGURE 10.7 TEACHING STUDENTS A STRATEGY FOR REPORTING CYBERBULLYING

Cyberbullying is an increasing problem in schools in North America and around the world. The first advice usually given to teachers, parents, and other responsible administrators is that students must be encouraged and supported to report any form of bullying, including cyberbullying.

Even children and adolescents who know how to report are reluctant to do so for fear of retaliation. We can respond to those fears by acting on student reports decisively and fairly, speaking individually with the victim immediately, and providing emotional support. Then we must move to have the bully receive the appropriate response according to the school's code of conduct. It is more effective to deal with bullies individually, even if a number of them are involved in an incident, because they may find strength in numbers. It is also important to ensure that other students who may have been bystanders see you support the bullied student and deal with the bully.

ABC—TELL NOW, is a strategy for teaching students who don't know how to report bullying to recognize what is happening to them and to report it to an adult. It is appropriate to teach children and students with intellectual disabilities, of any age, to use their ABCs to TELL NOW.

Post the strategy in the classroom in large print, review it frequently, and teach older pupils to support children and students with intellectual disabilities in using the strategy.

Sample Poster to Hang in the Classroom

ABC—TELL NOW

Am I hurt?
By computer or cellphone?
Cause it was mean?

TELL an adult **NOW**

Strong intervention programs for students who are bullied involve teachers in ongoing co-operative learning activities that reduce social isolation. They increase adult supervision at key times such as recess and lunch because most bullying occurs out of the sight of teachers and adult volunteers. Increasing supervision, with other schoolwide components, contributes to reducing bullying. Reducing bullying through schoolwide efforts contributes to a school in which social relations can grow between exceptional students and their classmates. You can also introduce peer tutoring and co-operative and collaborative learning in your classroom.

ANOTHER PERSPECTIVE ON WHAT SOME HAVE CALLED THE "EPIDEMIC OF BULLYING"

Recently, Emily Bazelon (2013) in her book, *Sticks and Stones: Defeating the Culture of Bullying and Rediscovering the Power of Character and Empathy,* has questioned our widespread use of the term *bullying*. She reminds us that Dan Olweus (1993) laid out three criteria for identifying bullying: (a) verbal, physical, or social aggression; (b) that it is repeated over time; and (c) that it involves a power differential. Bazelon suggests that some of what we have come to call bullying in recent years is actually conflict between children or adolescents which adults should help them learn to deal with, some is what she found young people referred to as "drama," and some is actually criminal behaviour (such as rape or texting or posting sexually explicit photos). Bazelon argues that only a small percentage of students engage in bullying and that it is important that we avoid sending the mistaken message that 'everyone is doing it,' which may make students feel that 'it is OK, after all everyone is doing it.' She makes the case that, if we distinguish these various forms of behaviour and actively treat those who bully and engage in each of the other behaviours in a way that is appropriate and effective, we may accomplish more to make schools safe and instructive contexts in which students learn to care for others. Some believe it is time to look for fresh perspectives on bullying including this controversial point of view.

Put into Practice

Review the ADAPT strategy in Chapter 1. Use it to devise a peer teaching approach to promote social development, social acceptance, and academic learning of an exceptional student.

Using the ADAPT Strategy to Analyze Social Demands in the Classroom: Peer Teaching and Collaborative Learning

You can use the ADAPT strategy to analyze the social demands of classroom organization and tasks and compare these demands with student strengths and needs. There may be opportunities for students to learn from one another through peer teaching, as well as through collaborative and co-operative learning.

Peer Teaching

Peer teaching has been called peer tutoring, peer-assisted learning, and peer-mediated instruction. Essentially it involves peers as teaching partners. Research shows that students benefit in many different arrangements of peer teaching (e.g., Stenhoff & Lignugaris/Kraft, 2007; Topping et al., 2012). For example, after middle school students with and without learning disabilities worked in tutoring dyads to teach each other vocabulary in language arts, the students with LD functioned at a level similar to their peers without LD; teachers reported the procedures were easy to implement and engaged the students (Hughes & Fredrick, 2006). Peer tutoring has also been an effective intervention for improving reading comprehension of low achievers and for English language learners (Miller et al., 2010; Lague & Wilson, 2011). However, typically about 10 percent of students do not respond to even the most successful peer-mediated instruction, suggesting the need for more intensive, individualized interventions for a small number of students, as discussed in Chapter 1 (Fuchs & Fuchs, 2005).

Some programs enable students with disabilities to take the role of tutor. Blackbourn and Blackbourn (1993) described how an adolescent with moderate developmental disabilities taught a grade 1 non-disabled child who needed individual teaching and practise adding and subtracting numbers up to nine with manipulatives. The tutor was skilled in addition and subtraction of up to three-digit numbers. A teacher modelled how he was to praise the tutee and provided task sheets for them to work on. The grade 1 student improved in mathematics and the tutor became more responsive to learning new mathematics. Both increased in self-confidence. This study illustrates findings consistently reported: both tutors and tutees benefit; students with and without disabilities can benefit from tutoring and from being tutored (e.g., Topping et al., 2012); and peer tutoring is effective for students with mild disabilities in secondary settings as well as for younger learners (e.g., Stenhoff & Lignugaris/Kraft, 2007).

Further Reading

Gillies, R.M., Ashman, A., & Terwel, J. (Eds.). (2007). *The teacher's role in implementing cooperative learning in the classroom*. New York: Springer. (This edited volume provides practical illustrations drawn from the author's research on how teachers can use co-operative and collaborative learning.)

Gillies, R.M. (2007). *Cooperative learning: Integrating theory and practice*. Thousand Oaks, CA: Sage. (Contains planning guides and scripts that are helpful for in-service and pre-service teachers.)

Udvari-Solner, A., & Kluth, P. (2007). *Joyful learning: Active and collaborative learning in inclusive classrooms*. Thousand Oaks, CA: Corwin Press. (Presents techniques for using differentiation and collaborative learning at the elementary and secondary levels. Includes reproducible handouts.)

Littleton, K., Miell, D., & Faulkner, D. (Eds.). (2004). *Learning to collaborate, collaborating to learn*. New York: Nova Science. (Focuses on understanding the nature of productive talk and joint work. Identifies the most important aspects of interaction between learners.)

Coelho, E. (2007). *Adding English: A guide to teaching in multilingual classrooms*. Don Mills, ON: Pippin. (A Canadian resource for meeting the needs of culturally diverse students by an educator known for her writing about collaborative learning.)

Learning in pairs is good preparation for co-operative and collaborative learning in groups.

Cathy Yeulet/123RF

Using Co-operative and Collaborative Learning to Meet Academic and Social Goals

Enhancing social development and acceptance requires sufficient opportunities to practise these skills in a supportive environment. You may have heard students say that they prefer to learn social skills while learning "relevant and practical information." These perspectives point to integrating social skills enhancement into the ongoing curriculum within the classroom. **Collaborative learning** methods include co-operative learning and problem solving in pairs and groups. These grouping methods usually involve students of varying abilities and skills, that is, heterogeneous groupings rather than homogeneous groupings.

The essence of collaboration is the construction of shared meanings for conversations, concepts, and experiences. Collaborative learning methods have been successful in improving academic performance of students of varying ages, grades, subjects, and abilities. Research has demonstrated a couple of key characteristics of collaborative learning that make it highly effective. Students are more likely to be successful when

1. they are instructed in well-structured, cognitively oriented programs (e.g., Gillies et al., 2007).

2. they are required as part of their group work to give and receive explanations for answers and ideas suggested in discussion (Gillies & Haynes, 2011).

During collaborative learning, students tend to reproduce teacher discourse and to meet the expectations communicated by the teacher (Webb et al., 2006). This means that if you want students to verbalize their thinking, ask questions, and provide explanations, you must structure the activities, model these ways of thinking and acting, and be clear in communicating these expectations to your students.

Classroom teachers have reported that collaborative learning is effective in meeting the needs of exceptional students included in their classes, but that it works better for some students than for others. The major benefits for exceptional students, teachers report, are improved self-esteem, a safe learning environment, and better classroom success rates and products (Gillies & Haynes, 2011). The primary modification for exceptional students is selecting suitable partners for them. Teachers have observed that collaborative learning gives exceptional students greater voice and participation in classroom activities. There are a number of simple techniques you can use, starting on the first day of class, to facilitate collaborative learning and a more interactive classroom.

Planning for Formal Teaching of Collaboration

Choose a collaborative strategy when you intend to promote positive peer support, social acceptance, and social competence, and especially when the knowledge can be best learned through the contributions of many learners. Figure 10.8 shows the planning decisions that go into designing collaborative learning.

There are many examples of lesson plans for collaborative learning (e.g., Udvari-Solner & Kluth, 2007). There are also excellent models of planning collaborative teaching for classes that include students with special needs (Villa et al., 2007) with techniques ranging from simple to complex. These sources contain forms for all aspects of the planning and execution of collaborative teaching.

TTYPA

A simple method to use during a lecture, film, or reading is called **TTYPA**, or "turn to your partner and . . . " The teacher stops and tells the students to "Turn to your partner and. . . introduce yourself. . . describe a time when you . . . Then switch roles." It is useful for making connections between prior learning and a new topic. To ensure that all students understand what to do, use TTYPA for the first partner to describe the instructions and the second partner to describe the first two steps. Such interdependence is easy to achieve and is good preparation for more complex collaborative activities.

PAIRED PARTNERS: THINK ALOUD

In **partners thinking aloud**, you model thinking aloud and ensure that the students understand what is expected of them. One student is the problem solver and the other the monitor. The problem solver thinks aloud throughout the task, and the monitor cues the "self-talk" of the solver by asking questions such as, "What is your goal?" "Does this make sense?" "Why?" Then they switch roles.

FIGURE 10.8 PLANNING DECISIONS IN DESIGNING COLLABORATIVE LEARNING

1. Academic goals for the group as a whole and adaptations or modifications of goals for exceptional students
2. Social goals for the group and for exceptional students
3. Communicating both sets of goals and teaching, rather than assuming, social skills
4. The type of interaction between students to meet these goals
5. The collaborative learning technique to promote such interaction
6. Membership of student groups
7. Room arrangement
8. Structure of positive interdependence so students get the following messages: We sink or swim together. Do your work; we are counting on you. How can we help each other to do better?
9. Student roles to use
10. Monitoring student performance
11. Guidelines for intervening in poorly functioning groups (as little as possible; with questions rather than answers)
12. Individual accountability (during monitoring or in the products)
13. Introducing the lesson, fostering collaboration
14. How students obtain closure on the content and feedback, and reflect on the social skills
15. Evaluating the learning and reflecting on the process

Co-operative learning has been used extensively to promote interdependence in inclusive classrooms. Co-operative learning by a group of students requires

- positive interdependence (a sense of sink or swim together)
- tasks that require everyone's efforts for group success (each has to contribute and learn)
- interpersonal skills (communication, trust, leadership, decision making, and conflict resolution)
- face-to-face interaction and processing (reflecting on how well the team is functioning and how to function even better)
- feedback on social processes in the group (www.co-operation.org)

Students work together to accomplish shared goals. They are assigned to small groups and instructed to ensure that all members of the group learn the assignment. Students discuss material, help one another understand it, and encourage one another to work hard. Check individual accountability and learning frequently. You can use this approach for a brief discussion to kick off an activity or in an entire curriculum unit. You can accept one product from the whole group and give group members a grade based on this product or devise a combination of individual and group assessment. Assigning roles ensures that everyone participates (for example, the checker ensures that each member understands, the encourager urges members to speak up, the recorder writes down the ideas of the group, the reporter reports to the rest of the class, etc.). Johnson and Johnson (2004) wrote that the elements that promote higher achievement and liking among students include high-quality reasoning strategies, constructive management of conflict over ideas, and feelings of psychological support and acceptance. Research suggests that co-operative learning strategies that incorporate individual accountability and group rewards are more likely to improve the achievement of students with disabilities (Nyman-McMaster & Fuchs, 2002).

The jigsaw strategy, described in Figure 6.3, is a structured co-operative learning approach.

Teaching Students to Collaborate

How can you learn to use co-operative learning strategies successfully? In their paper "Learning to cooperate: A teacher's perspective," Sonnier-York and Stanford (2002) describe how one teacher learned to use co-operative learning. They recount the importance of teaching students how to work together (assume nothing!) and of making each group member accountable for contributing to completion and quality. They describe how teachers must observe and mediate (but not control students) while making observational notes that can be used to inform instructional decisions. Students need to see their products completed and exhibited and to take part in highly varied co-operative tasks. And, finally, Sonnier-York and Stanford recommend that you evaluate your progress and increasingly integrate co-operative learning across the curriculum. You can use ADAPT and observation to decide which behaviours and social skills students need most. For the most important social skills (such as giving everyone a chance to talk, listening actively, and providing explanations), students need practise. They will probably require effective role models (you can model or use a paired teaching strategy), and you will need to help

Further Reading

Children with autism and Asperger syndrome experience particular challenges because lack of social competence is at the heart of their disability (Chapter 4 contains a section on characteristics of students with autism and Asperger syndrome). The following two papers focus specifically on enhancing the social competence and social acceptance of these students:

Boutot, E.A. (2007). Fitting in: Tips for promoting acceptance and friendships for students with autism spectrum disorders in inclusive classrooms. *Intervention in School and Clinic, 42,* 156–161.

Webb, B.J., Miller, S.P., Pierce, T.B., Strawser, S., & Jones, W.P. (2004). Effects of social skill instruction for high-functioning adolescents with autism spectrum disorders. *Focus on Autism and Other Developmental Disabilities, 19,* 53–62.

A boy with autistic spectrum disorder walks with his service dog who keeps him safe by preventing him from running toward water. The dog also helps to break down social barriers and acts as an ambassador for ASD.

them persist in the face of deterrents. In her book, *Designing Groupwork: Strategies for the Heterogeneous Classroom* (1998), Elizabeth Cohen provides several examples of activities and games to help students acquire group-work skills (also see Cohen et al., 2004).

Begin with simple, short activities that provide frequent occasions for participation. Try participation in pairs through TTYPA, think-pair-share (shown in Figure 6.3), and think aloud pairs and progress to short co-operative learning activities such as group work on a five-minute mystery. You will learn to form groups and intervene effectively by practising with simple, short collaborative activities.

Researchers describe using collaborative approaches to teach middle school students to understand literature. Blum and his colleagues (2002) used literature circles and found that students with special needs accurately assessed their reading difficulties and perceived an improvement in their reading skills. Hindin and her colleagues (2001) used a supported literacy approach to help poor readers participate in high-level conversations and rehearse the reading and thinking processes that good readers use. Fitch and Hulgin (2007) demonstrated the effectiveness of collaborative learning

Weblinks

HOAGIES' GIFTED EDUCATION PAGE
www.hoagiesgifted.org/play
_partner.htm

CHILDREN'S LITERATURE WEB GUIDE
www.acs.ucalgary.ca/~dkbrown/
index.html

CONSIDER THE CHALLENGES WHEN
GIFTED STUDENTS FEEL MORE
COMFORTABLE WITH OLDER
FRIENDS. LOOK FOR OTHER
WEBSITES, BOOKS, AND ARTICLES
THAT FOCUS ON ENHANCING THE
SOCIAL RELATIONS AND FRIENDSHIPS
OF CHILDREN AND ADOLESCENTS
WHO ARE GIFTED.

Cross-Reference

Chapter 8 describes differentiating
or adapting teaching to meet
adapted and modified goals of
exceptional students, and Chapter 9
focuses on adapting assessment.

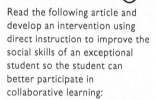

Put into Practice

Read the following article and
develop an intervention using
direct instruction to improve the
social skills of an exceptional
student so the student can
better participate in
collaborative learning:

Johns, B.H., Crowley, P., &
Guetzloe, E. (2005). The central
role of teaching social skills.
*Focus on Exceptional Children,
37*(8), 1–8.

Read the following article and
make a plan for supplementing
the direct instruction for this
student with other strategies
(e.g., using children's or
adolescent literature to teach
social skills and to establish
friendships).

Church, K., Gottschalk, C.M., &
Leddy, J.N. (2003). 20 ways to
. . . Enhance social and friendship
skills. *Intervention in School and
Clinic, 38*, 307–310.

---

assessment through dialogue (CLAD), a procedure in which students collaboratively completed multiple choice quizzes using dialogue and critical thinking to reach consensus and received immediate feedback. Students who participated in CLAD made large gains in reading, including reading comprehension. These researchers recommend activities that are culturally relevant, interactive, responsive, and collaborative, and that provide a window into students' thinking and extend students' background knowledge.

Challenges to Collaborative Learning

There are a number of challenges to collaborative learning. We cannot assume that discussion or collaboration is an unproblematic way to help students attain higher-order thinking or greater social competence. Teachers report that assessment is a major challenge (Gillies & Boyle, 2010). Co-operative activities in which all students in a group receive the same grade can result in unfair evaluation outcomes if some students have not contributed, or if some knew all the content before the unit began. Occasionally, a student may become dependent on the more able members of a co-operative group. Exceptional students and gifted students in inclusive classrooms are more likely to experience these drawbacks. You may have to provide alternative evaluation criteria for some students and modified or adapted goals and activities for some exceptional students. Johnson and Johnson (2004) describe methods teachers can use to promote group responsibility and individual accountability when assessing students in groups. For example, they suggest that teachers must structure effective groups and make an assessment plan. You can use groups to assess individual performances by observing individuals or using individual tests; simply put, students learn it in a group and perform it alone. You can also assess group performances through group products (e.g., case discussions, dramatic or musical productions, and group investigations). You can structure peer assessment (for immediate and detailed formative feedback) and self-assessment (which contributes to students' setting their own goals and monitoring their progress toward these goals).

To meet these challenges, monitor group interaction. Focus on the needs of exceptional students when creating groups. Gifted students can benefit from being placed in a collaborative group with gifted peers, where they can challenge one another and pursue advanced tasks (Winebrenner, 2007). In areas where they are far ahead of the rest of the class, they may be too impatient to be supportive and good models for the lowest achievers. Use heterogeneous groups as much as possible, but consider the best group composition for meeting the academic and social goals of each lesson. Usually students who are academically competent (not necessarily gifted), socially competent, and patient make the best partners or group members for exceptional students. Once you know who these students are, you can form groups by putting one of them in each corner of the room and distributing the rest of the class into the four groups (Taylor, 2008).

For a variety of reasons, secondary school teachers often find it more challenging to adopt collaborative learning. Secondary school teachers often feel pressure to "cover the curriculum," and peers may not always be able to make learning clear and explicit enough for exceptional learners to succeed. However, many teachers find that the gains in motivation, reasoning, and self-directedness more than compensate for the time required to teach students to work collaboratively, especially

Children and adolescents with physical disabilities learn to sail.

when students work together on meaningful tasks, such as oral history interviews with recent immigrants in a history course (Lattimer & Riordan, 2011) or on designing and implementing a virtual museum in language arts (Ho et al., 2011). In upper years, students may be competing for entry to post-secondary education and scholarships. Some adolescents show a low tolerance for diversity (Cobia & Carney, 2002). Collaborative groups can focus the frustration of group members on students who contribute less than their share when the collaborations are unsuccessful.

Cohen and her colleagues (1990) suggest that groups can be dominated by high-status members who may not pay attention to the contributions of low-status members. They make recommendations for minimizing the impact of status problems:

1. Teach students to listen, take turns, and assume various roles. Emphasize process as much as content, gradually shifting the emphasis to content.

2. Use stimulating materials and activities that are not entirely dependent on reading. These may include diagrams, videos, audio recordings, case studies, and authentic documents.

3. Build on student experience, beyond that typically used in the classroom, with authentic tasks. Bestow status on students who may have had part-time jobs and excel at negotiating resolutions in conflicts, etc. Look for ways to use student expertise (also see Cohen, 1998; Cohen et al., 2004).

4. Collaborate with colleagues, seek professional development, and keep an account of your experiences to share with colleagues.

Although there are challenges, there are also benefits in social development and social acceptance when you use collaborative teaching approaches in the classroom.

Summary

Social development and social acceptance are critical to inclusion because they refer to exceptional students' ability to take part in the social and academic life of the classroom and to their acceptance by classmates. Both exceptional students and their peers without disabilities have expressed an array of views on inclusion and the social processes that accompany it. Friendship is probably much more important to learning than we have understood in the past, enabling students to gradually internalize the ideas they are challenged with by their peers. Both elementary and secondary schools are social environments, and schoolwide approaches can ensure that schools are inviting and safe for all students. As a teacher, you can analyze social demands and choose a wide range of collaborative and social approaches to learning to enhance social relations.

Key Terms

bullying (p. 295)
co-operative learning (p. 302)
code of conduct (p. 293)
collaborative learning (p. 300)
cyberbullying (p. 295)
(dis)ability awareness program
    (p. 283)
friendships (p. 281)
interpersonal competence (p. 282)

moral leadership (p. 294)
partners thinking aloud (p. 301)
peer perspectives (p. 283)
peer teaching (p. 299)
schoolwide approaches (p. 292)
schoolwide behaviour management
    systems (p. 294)
schoolwide positive behaviour
    support (SWPBS) (p. 294)

social acceptance (p. 281)
social competence (p. 281)
social development (p. 281)
social status (p. 283)
sociometric rating (p. 283)
social relationships (p. 281)
TTYPA (p. 301)
zone of proximal development
    (p. 286)

Challenges for Reviewing Chapter 10

1. Why are social development and social acceptance of exceptional learners so important to the inclusion of these students? What role can the classroom teacher play—in an elementary school, in a secondary school—in promoting social development and social acceptance of exceptional learners?

2. Create a fuller description of Val, the blind grade 1 student described in the case at the beginning of this chapter, and, using the ADAPT strategy, analyze the social demands of math class and of recess for this student. Select collaborative and co-operative teaching strategies to help deal with each of these situations. Refer to sources identified in this chapter as well as the information provided in this chapter.

3. Lynn, the young woman with learning disabilities in the opening case, is in your secondary class. Using the ADAPT strategy, analyze the social demands made of Lynn by your typical lesson. Select collaborative and co-operative teaching strategies to help deal with each of the challenges that you identify. Refer to sources identified in this chapter as well as the information provided in this chapter.

4. Return to the opening cases of Val and Lynn and answer the five questions that follow the cases.

Activities for Reviewing Chapter 10 with Your Peers

5. Identify the role of friendship in the lives of students with and without exceptionalities, and particularly its role in their lives at school. Discuss with your peers why it is important for you to be aware of the role of friendship in the development of exceptional individuals. Compare and contrast the role teachers can play in the secondary classroom with the role that they can play in an elementary classroom.

6. Prepare to assume the role of one of the members of a team that has been assembled in your school to prevent cyberbullying. The team includes three members of the teaching staff, two parents, a guidance counsellor, the president of the student council, and the principal, who will chair the meetings. You want to advocate for a schoolwide approach, but you know that at least one member thinks that approach will take too long to organize, and the needs are immediate. What resources would you use to prepare for the meetings, what points would you make in the meetings, and why do you think these contributions are important? Role-play this scenario with your peers, assuming the roles of the eight members of the team.

CHAPTER 11

Enhancing Transitions for Exceptional Children and Youth

LEARNER OBJECTIVES

After you have read this chapter you will be able to:

1. Describe the importance of transitions in the life of exceptional children and youth.

2. Discuss the role of parent advocacy and self-advocacy in inclusive education and successful transitions.

3. Describe strategies for enhancing transitions during the school day for all students and especially for exceptional students.

4. Discuss the importance of working collaboratively with families during the transition into school for children with disabilities.

5. Describe the role teachers can take in the transition from school to school for exceptional learners.

6. Discuss the issues inherent in transition from school to the workplace and from school to further education for exceptional students.

Angela Hampton Picture Library/Alamy

BOBBY IS A 5-YEAR-OLD BOY WHO IS TRANSITIONING FROM A PLAYGROUP IN HIS RURAL COMMUNITY INTO KINDERGARTEN IN HIS NEIGHBOURHOOD SCHOOL. He lives on a farm with his parents and an older brother who attends the same school. Bobby has developmental disabilities and is delayed in all aspects of development, including language, fine and gross motor skills, and attention. He has a serious health condition that was brought under control with medication about a year before Bobby began kindergarten. Bobby loves to play with his classmates and joins in every game they will allow him to play. Sometimes he disrupts their play because he is less mature and can "act a bit silly" according to some of the other children. When that happens, which is rare, they tell Bobby he can't play. All the children know Bobby from playgroup and they enjoy his enthusiasm; according to his kindergarten teacher, she and the other children "just treat Bobby like one of the class." His teacher says, "At this age, he doesn't need many accommodations" and "I advocate for Bobby whenever I feel the school is not providing him with what he needs." When Bobby began kindergarten, his mother was pleased that he was included in a regular class. But as the year went on, she noticed that the other children were learning the sounds of the letters, speaking in more complex sentences, and attending to the teacher for longer periods of time. She became concerned: "Just being there is not enough; I want Bobby to be learning what all the other kids are learning."

ANNETTE IS IN GRADE 4. Her next transition will come after grade 5, when she must move from her neighbourhood school, Avon Elementary, to a middle school across town. Annette hates change, unpredictability, and chaos. She has Asperger syndrome. Her family started working with the kindergarten teacher eight months before her transition from preschool to Avon Elementary. To get Annette ready for the move from Avon to Brown Middle School, her family and teacher have made a plan to start a full year ahead. In September of grade 5, Annette will start going to Brown for an hour per week, then two hours, with a gradual increase. By the end of grade 5, Annette will know her homeroom teacher and her resource teacher at Brown, the location of both their rooms, as well as how to eat in the cafeteria, how to borrow a book from the library, and how to use a combination lock. This kind of troubleshooting should help Annette to make the transition without the stress and overreaction that can cause her to fight or flee and hide. Annette's IEP for grade 5 focuses as much on preparing her for the transition as on academic learning. Everyone agrees that if the transition is smooth, Annette can begin learning as soon as she arrives at Brown. Without a smooth transition, her first year will probably be disastrous.

JUSTIN IS 18 AND IN HIS LAST MONTH OF HIGH SCHOOL. He attends a focused career development program for at-risk youth in an upholstery shop (these programs are sometimes called career academies). The upholstery shop is located within a high school, and is run by a classroom teacher, Nick, who serves as the workplace supervisor and teaches credit courses to the students learning upholstery. Nick is a qualified upholsterer who worked in an upholstery business before becoming a teacher. The two-year upholstery program has provided Justin and his classmates with hands-on experience in designing, cutting, sewing, and installing upholstery. In a month, Justin will begin a full-time job working as an upholsterer. He remembers how he felt two years ago when he saw his choices as either applying to a focused program or dropping out of school like so many of his friends. Justin was struggling to complete the assignments in his grade 10 courses. He was bored, skipping school, and beginning to be "a regular in the vice-principal's office." Justin loves cars but he had taken a mechanics course in his old high school, and he knew he didn't want to spend his life under a car. However, he loved the idea of making the inside of old cars as good as new. And that is what Justin will be doing at an automotive repair business in just one month. He says he can hardly wait to leave school and start "my first real job; pretty good for a guy who almost dropped out!"

1. Why are transitions so critical to many exceptional and at-risk students? What do the case studies of Bobby, Annette, and Justin have in common?

2. What can teachers do to help students like Bobby, Annette, and Justin (and their families) so these students will be successful in their transitions into school, transitions from school to school, and transitions out of school?

3. What kinds of strategies can teachers teach students like Bobby, Annette, and Justin so they can be as independent as possible in their learning?

4. Describe how schools have become more focused on the needs of exceptional students for life in the community since the emphasis shifted to inclusion.

5. What strategies do Bobby, Annette, Justin, and other exceptional students require in order to be aware of their own strengths and needs and to advocate for themselves?

Introduction

Cross-Reference
How does this chapter relate to the ADAPT strategy in Chapter 1?

This chapter focuses on enhancing **transitions** for exceptional students and at-risk students, including transitions into school, transitions during the school day, transitions between schools, and transitions out of school to further education or to the workplace. Bobby, Annette, and Justin—who have developmental disabilities, have Asperger syndrome, and are at-risk for dropping out, respectively—are facing transitions and need strategies to help them function independently to meet the demands of school and life. This chapter prepares you for helping exceptional students to successfully navigate the many transitions that are part of life at school.

The Importance of Transitions in the Lives of Exceptional Children and Youth

Cross-Reference
Chapter 4 contains characteristics and strategies specific to students with Asperger syndrome.

Throughout this text you have read about teachers and parents working together to ensure opportunities for social, academic, and community participation of learners with exceptionalities. Participating in school and in life outside school requires that we adjust to change and make transitions. These experiences can be daunting for any of us, but usually they pose even greater challenges for exceptional children and youth. If you look back to Chapters 3, 4, and 5, you will see that many of the descriptions of characteristics of exceptional students refer to students requiring advance warning of changes in their schedules, benefiting from consistency and predictable routines, and experiencing difficulties when they must adjust to change.

Many provincial departments and ministries of education have developed handbooks and resources for teachers and families that focus on enhancing transitions for exceptional students. Similarly, many organizations have provided extensive information about how to support the transition of exceptional young children into school from early childhood education, generally recognizing that these transitions require increased sensitivity and support. Some of these resources are listed in Figure 11.1.

There are a number of actions that parents can take on behalf of their young children and that older students can take for themselves or with their parents to enhance transitions. It is critical for parents and students to inform themselves, discuss the upcoming transition, and make plans that anticipate the possible challenges and the ways in which they can respond productively. It is also important that parents and older students are prepared to advocate for what they believe is best. The next section focuses on the role of advocacy and self-advocacy in the transitions of exceptional and at-risk learners. This is followed by sections on transitions during the school day, transition into school, and transition into junior high and secondary school. There is also a section on transition from school to further education and the workplace. The closing section discusses why successful transitions are vital for inclusion in the community, in the workplace, and in society.

FIGURE 11.1   TRANSITION RESOURCES FOR TEACHERS AND FAMILIES

Transitions for Exceptional Students

- Transition Planning for Students with Special Needs (Nova Scotia Department of Education, 2005)
- Transition Planning: A Resource Guide (Ontario Ministry of Education, 2002)
- A Resource for the Transition of Students with Exceptionalities from School to Work or Post-Secondary Education and Adult Life (New Brunswick Department of Education, 2001)
- Transition Planning Guide for Students with Disabilities and Their Families (Alberta Education, 2010)

Transitions into School

- Victorian Early Years Learning and Development Framework (State Government Victoria, Australia; www.education.vic.gov.au)
- Getting Ready for Kindergarten (Toronto District School Board; for parents; available in twenty-four languages; www.tdsb.on.ca)

Transitions for All Students

- Managing School Transitions: Promising Practices in Alberta's Schools (A Support Resource) (Alberta Education, 2009)

The Role of Advocacy and Self-Advocacy in Inclusive Education and Transitions

Partnerships between parents or guardians and schools are critical to the inclusive education of children and adolescents with disabilities. Teachers can enhance these partnerships by considering the parents' perspective and listening actively to them (Bacon & Causton-Theoharis, 2013). Most home-school partnerships include **parent advocacy**, and, increasingly, exceptional students are learning to advocate for themselves. Advocacy occurs whenever people speak on behalf of themselves or others and present or defend a position. Understanding advocacy can help us to respond constructively, without making promises we cannot keep about program or placement, and can help teachers and parents to feel that they are allies in seeking what is best for exceptional students and in helping the students to seek this for themselves.

Parent Advocacy

Parents have extensive knowledge about their children, based on years of experience, and often see themselves as experts about their children. When they have effective communication skills, they can share this knowledge with educators. Historically, parents have advocated primarily for inclusive placements for their children and for accommodations in the classroom (Trainor, 2010). Trainor's interviews with parent advocates showed that most focused primarily on advancing the needs of their own children, while a few reported working to advance change for all students with disabilities or for all students with a particular disability. Recent Canadian studies report similar findings to Trainor's about the frustrations of parents who know their children well but understand less about the IEP process. Such parents report being less effective as change agents and advocates because they are not sure what can appear on an IEP or what classroom accommodations they can advocate for

Further Reading

About parent advocacy:

Wischnowski, M., & Cianca, M. (2012). A new script for working with parents. *Phi Delta Kappan, 93*(6), 34–37.

Trainor, A. (2010). Diverse approaches to parent advocacy during special education home-school interactions. *Remedial and Special Education, 31*(1), 34–47.

Duquette, C., Fullarton, S., Orders, S., & Robertson-Grewal, K. (2011). Insider, outsider, ally, or adversary: Parents of youth with learning disabilities engage in educational advocacy. *International Journal of Special Education, 26*(3). www.internationaljournalofspecialeducation.com

Hutchinson, N.L., Pyle, A., Villeneuve, M., Dods, J., Dalton, C., & Minnes, P. (2014). Understanding parent advocacy during the transition to school of children with developmental disabilities: Three Canadian cases. *Early Years: An International Journal, 34*(4), 348–363.

Autin, D. (2014). Preparing for the new school year: Tips and tools! *Exceptional Parent, 44*(5), 54–55.

(Hutchinson et al., 2014). As educators, our role includes assisting parents who need information about these issues, particularly drawing their attention to information on the school district's website and to brochures, handbooks, and community organizations that can supplement the clear, accurate information that we provide about IEPs and student and parent rights (Autin, 2014).

Some parent advocates have described schools as patronizing when they attempt to teach already well-informed parents about their own children. This reminds us how important it is to ask questions and listen before "jumping in" with unnecessary and redundant information. Schools have also been seen to limit the discussion about what is possible for children, especially for those with severe disabilities, by focusing on the child's deficits and on what the school can do for the child rather than considering the child's strengths and the unique contributions the exceptional child can make to the classroom (Sheldon, 2012).

In a series of interview studies with parents of students with fetal alcohol syndrome, gifted students, and students with learning disabilities, Cheryl Duquette of University of Ottawa and her colleagues have found that parent advocacy can be seen in four dimensions: awareness, seeking information, presenting the case, and monitoring (Duquette et al., 2007; Duquette et al., 2011a; Duquette, et al., 2011b). Awareness refers to parents recognizing how their child is different from others, and seeking information refers to parents learning about their child's strengths and weaknesses and about the school system. Presenting the case includes the communication, meetings, and advocacy that take place with educators, while monitoring refers to such activities as ensuring the accommodations in the IEP are provided as intended. Although parents usually began with awareness, most engaged in all four dimensions simultaneously throughout their child's school career. Some parent advocates became insiders to the school system by assuming roles like school trustee, while most reported feeling that they advocated from the position of outsider.

Self-Advocacy

Unlike many parents, exceptional learners are insiders to what goes on at school—and to their own exceptionalities. The challenges they face, as advocates, tend to be associated with their age and their communication abilities. They must become aware, well-informed, effective communicators who can negotiate with adults for what they need; can inform others much older than themselves about what they can contribute; and can monitor the ongoing situation. **Self-advocacy** is usually seen as an aspect of self-determination. There are two major theories of **self-determination**. Ryan and Deci (2000; Deci & Ryan, 2008) have formulated self-determination theory (SDT), which argues that having a sense of autonomy, competence, and relatedness enables any individual, including exceptional individuals, to be self-determining. Wehmeyer, in contrast, has focused on self-determination as a form of activism that enables individuals with disabilities to make successful transitions and to take charge of their own lives (e.g., Wehmeyer & Abery, 2013). Wehmeyer's framework has been closely associated with research on self-advocacy.

Self-advocacy refers to the ability to speak up for what we need and want. Test and his colleagues developed a model of self-advocacy for students with disabilities (2005). The two basic "tools" in their model of self-advocacy are knowledge of self and knowledge of rights. The third component is communication of these two kinds of knowledge, and the final component is leadership enabling a person to advocate for others as a group with common concerns. For students with disabilities who do

Put into Practice

Military families may need additional support when one parent is deployed overseas in a dangerous mission and the remaining parent must advocate for an exceptional child while functioning as a single parent and fearing for the safety of the deployed partner. *Exceptional Parent*, a magazine for parents of exceptional children, has many articles on the experiences of military families. Read two or three of these insider perspectives and try to locate a military family willing to talk about these experiences. With your peers, generate a list of questions you might ask this family and a list of issues that are specific to the situation of military families. You might want to begin by reading:

Agoratus, L., Autin, D., & Kinsell, M. (2013). The military family support 360 project. *Exceptional Parent, 43*(7), 62–63.

not incidentally acquire knowledge of self, or self-awareness, this must be taught explicitly. Schreiner (2007) urged educators to include self-advocacy goals on students' IEPs. Examples of IEP goals appear in Figure 11.2.

Recently developed programs help students, including those with developmental disabilities, to advocate for themselves. Kleinert and her colleagues (2010) report on a program with three phases in which students (a) select a personal goal, (b) develop an action plan to reach that goal, and (c) self-evaluate progress and adjust the plan or goal as needed. This program included young children and learners with severe disabilities. For details, consult the program website for the Kentucky Youth Advocacy Project (www.kyap.org). The goal book available on this website helps teachers to coach even young students through a process of identifying their supporters; what they can do independently; and what they need help with, enjoy doing, dislike, do well, don't do well, or would like to change. It breaks down the process of goal setting and identifying which steps to follow to make increasingly greater progress toward the self-identified goal. Goals for young children have included "Learn to tell my teacher I need to go somewhere to cool down," and for middle school students, "Use a communication board to talk to people," while high school students' goals have included "Initiate conversations" and "Do something in nursing after graduation; check out the two-year nursing program at the community college." Hart and Brehm (2013) have developed a similar model with ten steps which uses role-playing and offers a more sophisticated approach for students with mild disabilities.

Another program uses self-advocacy to implement a behaviour management plan for adolescents (Sebag, 2010). It puts the students in charge of identifying their struggles with their conduct at school. The student takes the lead in identifying a strategy to tackle the struggle and in monitoring and reflecting on progress, while the teacher serves as the coach or facilitator. The five steps include:

Further Reading

About self-determination and its application for students with disabilities:

Ryan, R.M., & Deci, E.L. (2000). Self-determination theory and the facilitation of intrinsic motivation, social development, and well-being. *American Psychologist, 55*, 68–78.

Deci, E.L., & Ryan, R.M. (2008). Self-determination theory: A macrotheory of human motivation, development, and health. *Canadian Psychology, 49*(3), 182–185.

Wehmeyer, M., & Abery, B. (2013). Self-determination and choice. *Intellectual and Developmental Disabilities, 51*(5), 399-411.

Wehmeyer, M. (1999). A functional model of self-determination: Describing developing and implementing instruction. *Focus on Autism and Other Developmental Disabilities, 15*, 106–116.

Dryden, E.M., Desmarais, J., & Arsenault, L. (2014). Effectiveness of the IMPACT: Ability program to improve safety and self-advocacy skills in high school students with disabilities. *Journal of School Health, 84*(12), 793–801.

Luckner, J.L., & Sebald, A.M. (2013). Promoting self-determination of students who are deaf or hard of hearing. *American Annals of the Deaf, 158*(3), 377–386.

FIGURE 11.2   GOALS FOR SELF-ADVOCACY TO INCLUDE ON STUDENTS' IEPS

- The student will describe the nature of his accommodations and/or modifications listed in the IEP.
- The student will describe the characteristics associated with her exceptionality.
- The student will describe how these characteristics influence his learning in the classroom.
- The student will describe situations that she finds challenging in the school environment.
- The student will communicate effectively about what would help him to handle the challenges encountered.
- The student will set personal goals for behaviours she wishes to acquire (or wishes to change).
- The student will describe personal strengths to use to reach the goals he has set.
- The student will list steps in an action plan to reach her personal goals.
- The student will describe a means of assessing whether he has completed the steps in the action plan and reached the goal.

Sources: Schreiner, M.B. (2007). Effective self-advocacy. *Intervention in School and Clinic, 42*(5), 300–304. Kleinert, J.O., Harrison, E., Fisher, T., & Kleinert, H. (2010). "I can" and "I did": Self-advocacy for young students with developmental disabilities. *Teaching Exceptional Children, 43*(2), 16–26. Sebag, R. (2010). Behavior management through self-advocacy. *Teaching Exceptional Children, 42*(6), 22–29.

- Weekly report that includes daily reports on conduct (completed by student and teacher)
- Student-teacher conference to review and reflect on weekly reports
- Developing goals and strategies together, with student taking the lead role and advocating for an approach the student believes can be successful
- Follow-up conference of student and teacher in which student, coached by teacher if necessary, leads review of progress
- Adjustments to goal and strategy and ongoing implementation of the plan

Recent Canadian research has demonstrated that self-advocacy is particularly important when adolescents and young adults with disabilities enter workplaces in which they must negotiate accommodations. They are only entitled to accommodations when they inform employers of their disabilities and of their needs. Case studies of two youths with learning disabilities, who did not acknowledge their disabilities in the workplace and were unsuccessful without accommodations, reported that the employers would have provided accommodations if the students had negotiated for them (Versnel et al., 2008). A case study of a young woman with physical disabilities demonstrated the advantages of her negotiating her own accommodations rather than simply receiving accommodations (Hutchinson et al., 2008). Similar findings about the importance of self-advocacy in the workplace were reported for two at-risk youth (DeLuca et al., 2010). While self-advocacy is critical for major transitions like transitions from school to work, it is also important for students negotiating the many small transitions within the school day, from one activity or location to another.

Transitions During the School Day

Many times during the school day, and even during each brief lesson, transitions are made between activities, sometimes called **activity transitions**. If time for teaching and learning is lost at each of these transitions, then the day includes much less time on task and less learning. Research on transitions during the school day has been conducted on classes of young children, of adolescents, and of adult learners and, in recent years, has often focused on what is needed by exceptional students. What is clear is that teachers can teach their classes to transition smoothly and, then, can focus on what is needed in addition to ensure that exceptional learners are part of those smooth transitions.

A recent analysis of transitions in a class of second-language adult learners highlighted the jointly negotiated nature of classroom discourse. The teacher responded to questions and interruptions during transitions, making them conversational so they contributed to the learning of the class, while still maintaining orderly transitions (Jacknick, 2011). Research suggests that effective teachers:

(a) prepare their students for transitions by warning them a transition is approaching
(b) begin and end transitions with clear verbal and non-verbal signals about their expectations
(c) give brief, logical instructions during transitions
(d) wait for students to follow instructions before continuing
(e) stay focused and are not distracted by minor extraneous matters
(f) are aware of what all students are doing during transitions
(g) teach students how to transition

For specific suggestions on how to prepare students for transitions, see Figure 11.3.

It may be helpful to have young children sing during transitions (Mathews, 2012)—for example, a cleanup song that signals the start of cleanup time and is sung throughout this activity, or a consistent song to mark the beginning of circle time. Physical movement has also been shown to promote smooth transitions. Orlowski and Hart (2010) provide examples of young children doing yoga poses (like mountain and downward dog) to get ready for a new activity.

Some specific strategies are helpful for all students but are absolutely essential for exceptional learners—the most prominent of these is the **visual schedule** (Thelen & Klifman, 2011). Post a schedule for the class in a prominent place where all can see it; include a schedule for the entire day or period and another which shows the steps within each activity (post it for each activity as it begins). For exceptional learners, individualize this so it uses symbols or pictures or speak to individual exceptional students and check that they know what is coming, as is suited to these students' needs. While the data show that visual schedules, both static and video, are especially helpful for students with autism spectrum disorder (ASD) (e.g., Banda et al., 2009; Cihak & Ayres, 2010; Pierce et al., 2013), they are also helpful for other exceptional learners. Be sure you find the means that works best for each exceptional student. Often it is helpful to give an indication of how much time remains until a transition. Some teachers show this by moving a pointer along a line, by posting the number of minutes remaining, or by showing three large buttons and removing them at intervals until, when they remove the last button, students know it is time to change activities.

Teach the whole class how to transition and then take the time to teach exceptional students using the strategies that you know are effective for their learning. Smooth transitions are key to productive and engaging classrooms—places where teachers and students want to be.

While we most often think of transition as referring to the move from secondary school into post-secondary endeavours, there are also considerable challenges associated with the move from preschool to elementary school and from elementary or junior high into secondary school. As we saw in the case of Annette, issues can also arise in the transition to junior high or middle school.

FIGURE 11.3 PREPARING STUDENTS FOR SMOOTH TRANSITIONS

- Provide explicit instruction in how students should transition.
- Make behavioural expectations clear so they will be understood by all students.
- Provide a rationale for your expectations.
- Give examples by modelling what is expected.
- Provide non-examples yourself (never have students practise incorrectly).
- Remind students of expectations immediately prior to transitions.
- Pay attention to correct behaviour.
- Quickly redirect inappropriate behaviour without drawing attention to it.
- Engage in active supervision during transitions.
- Individualize transition instruction for exceptional students.
- Post visual schedules for the class.
- Use individualized visual schedules for exceptional students when required.

Transition into School

For children with disabilities, a successful **transition to school** and early social inclusion are important to later functioning and well-being. Parents serve as key informants and facilitators in the promotion of inclusion for their young, exceptional children. Families often perceive a loss of support associated with the move from early childhood education (ECE) into elementary school. Most parents' experience of ECE and of therapies and other services in the preschool years is of a **family-centred approach** where parents are essentially the clients (Villeneuve et al., 2013). In the cases of children with complex conditions, there may be ten to twenty service providers during the preschool years, and many of these will change or cease to provide services when the child begins school.

What schools recognize and must communicate effectively to parents is that transition is a process and not an event. In most provinces, transition planning meetings are held in the spring prior to entry to kindergarten; for example, New Brunswick Department of Education recommends that such preparations begin in February, seven months prior to the start of school. Parents are invited to these "planning" meetings, as are the exceptional child's key service providers. Recent Canadian research documents the experiences of three families over a twelve-month period in which their children with developmental disabilities transitioned into kindergarten (Hutchinson et al., 2014). These researchers observed **transition planning meetings**. While parents reported providing considerable information about their child at the transition planning meeting in spring, the families did not feel that the school provided adequate information at that meeting about the plans for the child's program or services. The school, however, viewed the meeting as an opportunity to receive, rather than provide, information, and then developed plans to meet the child's needs based on the information they had received that day.

In a study of a preschool resource teacher, Amy, who was considered exemplary by parents and kindergarten teachers, Hutchinson and Schmid (1996) found that this teacher described herself as an advocate who focused on the needs of individual exceptional children and on creating partnerships. She felt responsible for the transition from ECE to elementary school, and her strategies included:

- Invite kindergarten and grade 1 teachers to the preschool to observe an exceptional student, rather than relying on information presented in a case conference.
- Record on videotape the exceptional child at the preschool and give the video to the parents to take to the kindergarten teacher.

Put into Practice

Choose an exceptionality and discuss with your peers the challenges that students with that exceptionality are likely to experience during transitions. Search for resources that provide guidance to meet the transition needs of those students. Share resources with your peers, who have each chosen a different exceptionality.

Examples of resources for students with ASD:

Cihak, D.F., & Ayres, K.M. (2010). Comparing pictorial and video-modeling activity schedules during transitions for students with autism spectrum disorders. *Research in Autism Spectrum Disorders, 4*, 763–771.

Banda, D.R., Grimmett, E., & Hart, S.L. (2009). Activity schedules: Helping students with autism spectrum disorders in general education classrooms manage transition issues. *Teaching Exceptional Children, 41*(4), 16–21.

Hume, K., Sreckovic, M., Snyder, K., Carnahan, R. (2014). Smooth transitions: Helping students with autism spectrum disorder navigate the school day. *Teaching Exceptional Children, 47*(1), 35–45.

This boy ran away one week after starting at a new school. Transitions can be tough. When asked why, he said, "School is too hard."

Getty Images

Hobbies such as competing in plowing matches can turn into careers. Rebecca Woodman, at 15, competed in the 1998 International Plowing Match.

What do you think?

Look for a source on teaching students to read and write. Consider the ideas of the author(s) and relate their ideas to what you have learned from experience about the connections between reading and writing in classrooms at the level at which you teach. One source you could consult is Strickland, D.S., Ganske, K., & Monroe, J.K. (2002). *Supporting struggling readers and writers: Strategies for classroom intervention, 3–6.* Newark, DE: International Reading Association. Look for other sources to read on the topic, and compare your ideas to the thinking of your peers.

- Provide in-service to school staff (especially in rural schools where they had not previously taught a child with a particular exceptionality).

- Record on videotape a parent of a child with an unusual or severe disability (e.g., a feeding machine), explaining the child's condition in non-technical terms for the teacher.

The strategies used by Amy fostered continuity and treated parents as partners. Amy described the transition between preschool and elementary school as "really important because the child can get lost in the shuffle." The Canadian case studies described above highlight the complexity of the transition process and the large number of professionals involved with each exceptional child and the family.

We all know that transitions can be stressful. As a kindergarten or grade 1 teacher, you can ensure that you are knowledgeable about your exceptional students before they arrive so that the level of stress is as low as possible for you, the student, and the family (Burke & Hodapp, 2014). And remember that families are usually accustomed to more intense and frequent communication with their child's ECE teachers and service providers than you can provide. Perhaps a communication book will enable school and home to conduct a regular conversation. It may help to be strategic in calling home with positive news as well as concerns. Make parents feel that they are partners in the transition process but remind them that the kindergarten classroom is quite different from the ECE setting. Explaining these things to parents before school begins and reminding them at the start of the school year may help to promote realistic expectations and effective communication. The transition from kindergarten to grade 1 receives little attention, but research suggests that entering grade 1 can also be a challenging transition for exceptional learners and their families. The academic demands of the curriculum and the need for independence increase, while instructional support for learning decreases.

Transition into Junior High School and into Secondary School

What about the transition to middle school, junior high school, or secondary school—the change from spending the school day with one teacher to adjusting to a different teacher every period of the day? This is likely to be stressful for any exceptional students for whom change causes fear. The actions taken by the family and teacher of Annette, described in a case study at the beginning of this chapter, are designed to minimize the trauma of her upcoming transition. This girl with Asperger syndrome will have gradually learned to meet the most challenging social expectations of her new school before she begins classes there. Because her biggest challenges are the social expectations associated with learning in classrooms, these were made the focus of her IEP for the year during which she was being prepared for the transition. Her classroom and resource teachers at Avon Elementary have worked as an effective team with Annette, her parents, and the resource teacher at Brown Middle School. An older girl, Marie, who took an interest in Annette while she was visiting Brown, offered to serve as a peer tutor and teach Annette to open her combination lock. Schools with peer tutor programs can supplement the efforts of teachers to welcome new exceptional students. Marie, who has LD, remembers how difficult her move to Brown was and appreciates the help she received from her peer tutor. Recent research suggests that another means of enhancing social adjustment across the transition to high school is to involve students with disabilities in organized activities like sports and community service activities that help them to develop friendships (Bohnert et al., 2013).

As a classroom teacher, you do not have to develop and execute **transition plans** alone. Draw on the resources of the in-school team. Joan Versnel (2005a) of Dalhousie University in Halifax implemented a transition program for grade 6 students making the transition to junior high school. Students with and without disabilities and their parents reported that the program helped students to participate fully in a transition meeting and to handle the challenges of junior high school. Look for resources within the school and the community. For example, the Community Living Association or Spina Bifida Association may be willing to help, and the Canadian National Institute for the Blind (CNIB) has mobility specialists to help blind students learn their new environment. The most efficient way to enhance independence during the transitions of exceptional students is to ensure that these goals and strategies are in the student's IEP at least during the final year before they make the transition. Then a whole team, including parents and the student, will be making student independence a priority over the year.

Unsuccessful high school transitions contribute to dropout rates and low achievement (Herlihy, 2007). Students who have experienced either academic or behavioural challenges in grade 8 are more likely to experience both in high school, and the presence of problem behaviour nearly always interferes with academic learning (McIntosh et al., 2008). The same study suggests that up to 35 percent of grade 9 students need additional support in one or both areas. Studies that identify the factors which contribute most to dropping out point to the transition into grade 9 and what happens during that year as being critical (Neild et al., 2008). And some groups of students are particularly vulnerable during the transition to high school, including inner city adolescents, those who are in foster care or have identified disabilities, and those who do not establish a feeling of connectedness with the school and with at least one teacher (Crouch et al., 2014; Geenen & Powers, 2007; Turner, 2007). Adolescents who perceive that their teachers are fair and care about them are more likely to be engaged in school and less likely to initiate risky behaviours, including drug use, excessive use of alcohol, or violent behaviour (McNeely & Falci, 2004). When students feel that we, their teachers, support them, it generates a sense of belonging, which contributes to their succeeding in school and reduces their involvement in health-risk behaviours. The message for us is clear—we must connect with our students, especially at the points of transition.

Further Reading

On Asperger syndrome:

Myles, B., & Simpson, R.L. (2003). *Asperger syndrome: A guide for educators and parents* (2nd ed.). Austin, TX: Pro-Ed.

Kiker Painter, K. (2006). *Social skills groups for children and adolescents with Asperger's syndrome*. London, UK: Jessica Kingsley.

Betts, S., Betts, D., & Gerber-Eckard, L. (2007). *Asperger syndrome in the inclusive classroom: Advice and strategies for teachers*. London: Jessica Kingsley.

Bolick, T. (2004). *Asperger syndrome and adolescence: Helping preteens and teens get ready for the real world*. Gloucester, MA: Fair Winds Press.

Sicile-Kira, C. (2006). *Adolescents on the autism spectrum: A parent's guide to the cognitive, social, physical, and transition needs of teenagers with autism spectrum disorders*. New York: The Berkley Publishing Group.

Kutscher, M.L. (2014). *Kids in the syndrome mix of ADHD, LD, autism spectrum, Tourette's, anxiety and more* (2nd ed.). London: Jessica Kingsley Publishers.

Put into Practice

Visit the websites of the provincial departments of education. Record the transition documents and other information you have learned about transition. Which provinces make this information readily available? You could share this task with your peers and share resources as well.

Transition from School to Further Education and the Workplace

Put into Practice

Read two of the resources listed below and then talk with your peers who have read different sources. Arrange to visit a community agency that serves individuals with disabilities and their families to learn about the ways in which they are able to provide equity tools such as computer and assistive technology devices. Why might such devices assist some students to make transitions?

Specht, J., Howell, G., & Young, G. (2007). Students with special education needs in Canada and their use of assistive technology during the transition to secondary school. *Childhood Education, 83*, 385–396.

Lancioni, G.E., O'Reilly, M.F., Singh, N.N., Sigafoos, J., Oliva, D., & Severini, L. (2008). Enabling two persons with multiple disabilities to access environmental stimuli and ask for social contact through microswitches and a VOCA. *Research in Developmental Disabilities: A Multidisciplinary Journal, 29*, 21–28.

Asselin, S.B. (2014). Learning and assistive technologies for college transition. *Journal of Vocational Rehabilitation, 40*(3), 223–230.

When we speak of transition, we are most often referring to the **transition to post-secondary education (PSE)** or to the workplace. This is the transition for which we have been preparing students with disabilities and at-risk youth in our inclusive education system and our academic and social programs. This is the transition on which data are collected and judgments are made about the school system and our efforts as educators—by organizations within Canada, such as Statistics Canada (Gilmore, 2010), and by global organizations [e.g., Organisation for Economic Co-operation and Development (OECD), 2014]).

Helping Exceptional Students to Transition to College and University with a Focus on Mental Health and Well-Being

Many students find it challenging to make a successful transition from the security of a familiar secondary school, usually in their own neighbourhood, to a college or university, often far from home and family. However, this process can be even more daunting for exceptional students. Each year, increasing numbers of exceptional students tackle this challenge of transitioning to post-secondary education (PSE). And their families and high school teachers are a major source of support and encouragement during the application phase, the preparation phase, and the early days of PSE. By helping young people anticipate the challenges, we can help them to meet the challenges. One big change they can anticipate is that others will no longer be responsible for their learning or their advocacy; the demands for independence will be great in PSE. They will have to be in charge of

Students gain workplace skills in career-focused secondary programs.

their own learning (Connor, 2012). Figure 11.4 includes strategies specifically for helping students with disabilities to prepare for the transition to PSE.

One of the fastest growing concerns on college and university campuses is mental health issues experienced by PSE students, and this is accompanied by large growth in the number of students with psychiatric and other mental health conditions, including depression, anxiety disorder, bipolar disorder, and others (Venville et al., 2014). Students with disabilities are at increased risk of experiencing mental health difficulties (McMillan & Jarvis, 2013). Students can often access peer mentors as well as formal services on campus and mental health services in the community. In order to ensure continuity, students who have been receiving services prior to leaving home will have to arrange appointments and meet service providers well ahead of beginning their program in a new community. They are best to choose campuses that encourage participation of all students in campus activities and that have well-developed student crisis support. The transition from adolescence to adulthood requires youth with psychiatric and mental health concerns to set goals and choose the supports that will help them to reach those goals; choice of peers can be particularly influential when the family and its support are not nearby. This transition is considered to be unique because of the potential for extensive changes in nearly all aspects of

FIGURE 11.4 STRATEGIES FOR HELPING STUDENTS WITH DISABILITIES TO PREPARE FOR THE TRANSITION TO POST-SECONDARY EDUCATION

- Discuss differences between high school and PSE.
- Inform students that they are responsible for disclosing their disability in PSE if they wish to receive services and accommodations.
- Help them to be comfortable with informing others about their disability.
- Encourage them to contact the Disability Services Office early to ensure they have an assessment completed prior to the start of their first year in PSE.
- Help students to identify their strengths and weaknesses.
- Encourage them to discuss with PSE academic advisors the course load that is right for them.
- Urge them to attend any preparatory events their PSE institution offers to familiarize students with disabilities with the campus.
- Help students to enrol in one PSE course during high school, if possible.
- Help them to develop study skills during their high school years.
- Encourage them to seek support groups on their PSE campus for students with similar challenges. This is especially important for students who have experienced mental health challenges.
- Remind them to ask if they can be assigned a note-talker and can access class notes on a course website.
- Help them to practise self-advocacy throughout their high school years.
- Encourage them to become savvy and independent technology users prior to starting PSE.
- Remind them that many students find the transition to PSE difficult; so persevere!

Sources: Gil, L.A. (2007). Bridging the transition gap from high school to college. *Teaching Exceptional Children, 40*(2), 12–15. Connor, D.J. (2012). Helping students with disabilities transition to college: 21 tips for students with LD and/or ADD/ADHD. *Teaching Exceptional Children, 44*(5), 16–25. Belch, H.A. (2011). Understanding the experiences of students with psychiatric disabilities: A foundation for creating conditions of support and success. *New Directions in Student Services, 134*, 73–94.

Further Reading

About helping students to handle the social and emotional challenges of transitions to ensure good mental health:

Lantieri, L., & Goleman, D. (2008). *Building emotional intelligence: Techniques to cultivate inner strength in children.* Louisville, CO: Sounds True.

Panju, M. (2008). *7 successful strategies to promote emotional intelligence in the classroom.* Harrisburg, PA: Continuum International.

Burke, K. (2008). *What to do with the kid who. . . . Developing cooperation, self-discipline, and responsibility in the classroom.* Thousand Oaks, CA: Corwin Press.

Jamieson, J., & Jamieson, C. (2012). *Managing Asperger syndrome at college and university: A resource for students, tutors, and support services.* (2nd ed.). Abingdon, UK: Routledge.

Madriaga, M. (2010). 'I avoid pubs and the student union like the plague': Students with Asperger syndrome and their negotiation of university spaces. *Children's Geographies, 8*(1), 39–50.

life in a relatively short period of time, combined with the possibility of so many different life paths that could be followed. Figure 11.5 describes recent sources relevant for understanding post-secondary students who are experiencing mental health challenges.

Two other groups of exceptional students who are attending PSE in growing numbers are youth with learning disabilities (LD) and with attention deficit hyperactivity disorder (ADHD). For these students, your guidance when they are in secondary school can enable them to develop effective study habits and strategies. Given that they usually need more time than their peers to complete the required reading and writing, it is critical that they learn good time management and block time to complete readings, study for tests, and prepare written assignments (Connor, 2012; Peters, 2011). Whereas secondary schools are expected to offer accommodations to exceptional learners, PSE students must request accommodations and must advocate for themselves. As we have discussed, they should get considerable practise of self-advocacy in the relative safety of their high school. Because colleges and universities tend to use memory-based means of assessment, it may be essential for PSE students with LD or ADHD to seek advice on their campus about how to use memory-based strategies to prepare for mid-term and final tests. Most colleges and universities offer

FIGURE 11.5   ANNOTATED BIBLIOGRAPHY OF RECENT SOURCES ON UNDERSTANDING THE NEEDS OF STUDENTS EXPERIENCING CHALLENGES WITH MENTAL HEALTH IN POST-SECONDARY SETTINGS

Educators have many questions about referring students to mental health services, either before or after they arrive in PSE. These resources help us to understand the issues and the process.

Policy on Preventing Discrimination Based on Mental Health Disabilities and Addictions (2014) by Ontario Human Rights Commission.

This recent publication provides clear, user-friendly guidance on how to resolve human rights matters related to mental health in a range of contexts, including schools and PSE.

Exploring Pretreatment Expectancies in a Campus Mental Health Setting: The Validation of a Novel Expectancies Measure (2014) by Nicki Aubuchon-Endsley & Jennifer Callahan, *Journal of College Counseling, 17,* 64–78.

Because an individual's expectancies are related to their outcomes of mental health treatment, this research reports on a valid measure of expectancies and suggests that it is critical for educators to know about and to inform students about the process they can expect in a campus mental health setting.

Exploring How Perceived Threat and Self-Efficacy Contribute to College Students' Use and Perceptions of Online Mental Health Resources (2014) by Christopher McKinley & Erin Ruppel, *Computers in Human Behavior, 34,* 101–109.

Many educators encourage young people to seek support through online support groups for mental health challenges; this study confirmed that, in general, feeling vulnerable contributed to youth joining online groups and self-efficacy predicted greater trust of online groups.

The Role of University Support Services on Academic Outcomes for Students with Mental Illness (2014) by Andrea Simpson & Kerry Ferguson, *Education Research International,* http://dx.doi.org/10.1155/2014/295814.

Students who registered with a university's disability services office (DSO) were found to experience academic benefits compared to their academic average in the year prior to registering. Students can benefit from their instructors encouraging them to register with DSO in the university.

study strategy courses and online resources, but students need to anticipate that they will need this kind of support and sign up early. Otherwise, they may fail their first tests before they register for study skills or study strategy workshops. Recent Canadian research demonstrates that students with learning disabilities who enrolled in a "university success" course received higher grades than those who did not (Reed et al., 2009). These courses have also been shown to be helpful to university students without LD and to provide psychosocial and mental health benefits, such as increased confidence and self-efficacy (Kennett & Reed, 2009; Reed et al., 2011).

Students with hearing loss, vision loss, or physical disabilities may need guidance during the secondary years to select institutions for PSE that are well equipped to meet their needs. Some colleges and universities offer much more extensive support programs for students with these low-incidence disabilities than other institutions (Hyde et al., 2009; Targett et al., 2013). A recent Canadian study suggests that high school students with visual impairments need specialized information during the post-secondary recruitment process because recruitment materials must be accessible for them and available accommodations must be explained. High school teachers suggested that, while all students can become better prepared for college or university by making a trip to the institutions they are considering, such visits are essential for students who have low vision or are blind. Before visiting a campus, they should request and arrange to meet instructors, and to have their questions answered about living arrangements, academic requirements, mobility orientation, and accommodations (Reed & Curtis, 2011). Canadian secondary teachers and counsellors who responded to this survey emphasized the need to help students with visual impairments to become more independent during high school because of the big changes in expectations that accompany enrolment in PSE: "If we could temper that shock somehow during the first few weeks at a college or university (in the first year), it would be helpful" (Reed & Curtis, 2011, p. 556). It is important to remember that students with disabilities are more likely to experience mental health issues during transitions to unfamiliar learning environments.

What about students with intellectual disabilities or developmental disabilities—can they attend PSE? Canada has been a leader in developing **inclusive post-secondary education (IPSE)** programs that enable youth with intellectual or developmental disabilities to continue learning after they have exceeded the provincial age limit for receiving services in secondary school. For example, the University of Alberta led the way when parents of young adults with DD and ID and their allies collaborated with the university to create an inclusive on-campus program in 1987 (Weinkauf, 2002). Students with ID and DD usually audit courses, taking one or two at a time, and do not accumulate credits toward a degree. Many universities offer such programs, usually to small numbers of participants who receive support services from the university or from a community agency. Programs in BC are described in a report by Mosoff et al. (2009), and a paper by Wintle (2012) provides a rich description in a multiple perspective case study of the experience of Francine, a young woman with ID attending a drama education class in the faculty of education in an Ontario university. The teacher candidates in the course described their growth while seeing Francine as a member of the class and a friend, and the instructor described how she used differentiated instruction (DI) to ensure Francine's participation. Francine found the course stimulating and valued social as well as academic learning opportunities. Wherever you teach in Canada, you can probably find a college or university with an IPSE program in your region of the province.

What do you think?

Exceptional students report that they are often bullied when they transition to new contexts where they have not yet developed relationships or found allies. Should we teach children and adolescents how to respond when they are bullied, or should we put all our energy into preventing bullying?

Further Reading on Supporting Transitions

Wehmeyer, M., & Webb, K. (Eds.). (2011). *Handbook of adolescent transition education for youth with disabilities.* New York, NY: Routledge, Taylor & Francis Group.

Shaw, S.F., Madaus, J.W., & Dukes, L.L. (Eds.). (2010). *Preparing students with disabilities for college success: A practical guide to transition planning.* Baltimore, MD: Brookes Pub.

Applequist, K.L., Mears, R., & Loyless, R. (2009). Factors influencing transition for students with disabilities: The American Indian experience. *International Journal of Special Education, 24*(3), 45–56.

Prior, S. (2013). Transition and students with twice exceptionality (giftedness and a disability). *Australasian Journal of Special Education, 37*(1), 19–27.

Cheney, D. (2012). Transition tips for educators working with students with emotional and behavioral disabilities. *Intervention in School and Clinic, 48*(1), 22–29.

Henninger, N.A., & Taylor, J.L. (2014). Family perspectives on a successful transition to adulthood for individuals with disabilities. *Intellectual and Developmental Disabilities, 52*(2), 98–111.

Further Reading

On high school programs for transition to PSE:

McEachren, A.G., & Kenny, M.C. (2007). Transition groups for high school students with disabilities. *The Journal for Specialists in Group Work, 32*(2), 165–177.

Naugle, K., Campbell, T.A., & Gray, N.D. (2010). Post-secondary transition model for students with disabilities. *Journal of School Counseling, 8,* 1–31.

Gil, L.A. (2007). Bridging the transition gap from high school to college. *Teaching Exceptional Children, 40*(2), 12–15.

IPSE has been shown to increase the likelihood of youth with ID and DD gaining employment or ongoing volunteer roles in their communities (Yamamoto et al., 2014), and is considered one part of the transition of youth with ID and DD to adult roles in their communities.

Because research has shown that students with any disability are less likely than their peers to attend PSE and, when they do, less likely to receive a degree (Erickson et al., 2010), strategies and models have been developed to enable high school educators to prepare these students (e.g., Gil, 2007). One model emphasizes the importance of high school educators (a) knowing and informing students about the rights of students with disabilities, (b) promoting student self-advocacy, (c) collaborating with parents and other professionals, and (d) using community resources (Naugle et al., 2010). One specific recommendation that has proven effective is for school counsellors to conduct small transition groups (following individual screening interviews for suitability) in conjunction with individual career counselling. The emphases for discussion include awareness of self and others, self-determination and self-advocacy, making the right PSE choice, negotiating admissions, accessing support services, choosing a major, and making new connections (McEachern & Kenny, 2007). The research suggests that the support and encouragement of high school teachers and counsellors can make a great difference to the transitions of exceptional youth to PSE; transition is not an event but a process.

Helping Exceptional Students to Transition to Work

Exceptional students leaving high school may **transition to work** indirectly, through PSE, which provides them with an opportunity to acquire social and academic learning and maturity as well as other career-enhancing skills. Or they may transition to work directly. There are many jobs that do not require PSE education or training, but which require short-term or on-the-job training. However, youth with disabilities and youth at risk of leaving school early require support and preparation for this school-to-work transition.

Even before the most recent economic downturn, youth worldwide were experiencing high levels of unemployment, up to three times as high as adults in many countries and twice as high as adults in Canada (International Labour Organization, 2006). Among the groups most vulnerable to **social exclusion** as young adults are those with disabilities and at-risk youth who have left school early without acquiring workplace qualifications (Anuncibay, 2007). Others include youth who are in care (Geenen & Powers, 2007) or have been living in poverty or other conditions that have demanded a high level of resilience throughout their high school years.

Work-based education (WBE), in its many forms, is one of the solutions most frequently recommended in research as well as in reports by international agencies (Wiesner et al., 2003; Quintini et al., 2007). WBE refers to educational and other interventions (based in schools, colleges, and agencies) for high school students and young adults. These programs facilitate learning by placing young people in supervised practica in workplace contexts for all or part of their educational programs. Learning experiences in WBE include workplace mentoring, paid work experience, unpaid work experience, job shadowing, career academies or focused vocational programs, apprenticeships, and co-operative education (co-op). Co-op education is the most widely used WBE approach in Canada.

To be well prepared for WBE and transition to work following school, youth need opportunities for career development, including self-awareness/career awareness, career exploration, and career experiences.

Career Development and Career Education for Exceptional Individuals

Career development recognizes that career aspirations develop gradually over time and require experiences and reflection on those experiences (Lindstrom et al., 2011). For exceptional individuals, most would agree that career development begins in childhood and extends through adolescence into the adult years (Hutchinson et al., 2008; Morningstar, 1997). Super's (Super et al., 1996) lifespan theory of career development suggests adolescence should be spent focusing on career exploration rather than preparation for a specific occupation. He has stressed the need for planned exploration, experience, and evaluated trial experience in workplaces to develop career maturity and planfulness. Most career education programs for adolescents with disabilities include three components: (1) self-awareness/career awareness, (2) career exploration, and (3) career experiences.

Recent research on the social cognitive career theory (SCCT), developed by Lent et al. (1999), has been used to understand career development and work-based education (WBE) in minority students (e.g., Gushue, 2006) and in students with disabilities (e.g., Punch et al., 2005). This approach to career development assumes that we are agents of and influence our own experiences and development. It focuses on attributes of the individual, contextual factors, and behaviour, as well as on how these three aspects interact with and influence one another. Case studies reported by Hutchinson et al. (2008) demonstrated the applicability of SCCT for understanding how youth with disabilities negotiate accommodations in WBE so they can participate fully and learn by doing. Naomi, who has spastic cerebral palsy, was able to negotiate the removal of barriers that might have interfered with her reaching her goals. She formed links between her interests and her career-related goals. Through her experiences in and reflections on WBE, she formed positive, realistic self-efficacy. Naomi wanted to become a travel agent and to help people with disabilities to travel without barriers. At the end of her final interview, Naomi offered, "Anything worthwhile takes a bit of risk . . . I think people should go for what they want," adding, "People need to know what they want" (Hutchinson et al., 2008, p. 131). Naomi's WBE program facilitated self-awareness/career awareness, career exploration, and career experiences.

Developing Self-Awareness and Career Awareness

Self-awareness refers to knowing oneself, developing a picture of the kind of person one is. For students with disabilities, self-awareness includes understanding the characteristics associated with their disability—their personal strengths and needs as well as their interests, preferences, and abilities. Career awareness refers to students' understanding of all aspects of adult responsibilities and roles, and the nature and meaning of work. This includes the incredible range of ways in which adults engage in paid work; volunteer and unpaid work; and other pursuits, including leisure activities, child rearing, and citizenship. Self-awareness and career awareness are often associated with the developmental tasks of adolescence. Many provinces include

What do you think?

M. Nagler and A. Nagler's (1999) *What's stopping you: Living successfully with disability* (Toronto: Stoddart) is a comprehensive Canadian manual for self-advocacy that focuses more on adults than on adolescents and children. Although this is an older source, it provides classic advice. What would you ask the authors if you had an opportunity to meet them? For a different perspective, read A. Boylan (2008), *Advocacy for children and young adults* (McGraw-Hill Education [Open University Press of the UK]) or C.M. Oliver, J. Dalrymple, and C. Booth's (2008) *Developing advocacy for children and young people: Current issues in research, policy and practice* (Jessica Kingsley). Again, what would you ask the authors if you could meet them?

Further Reading

On career development for children:

Watson, M., & McMahon, M. (2005). Children's career development: A research review from a learning perspective. *Journal of Vocational Behavior, 67*(2), 119–132.

Cassidy, R.A. (2007). The benefits of a comprehensive K–12 career development system. *Techniques: Connecting Education and Careers, 82*(4), 44–46.

Stott, K.A., & Jackson, A.P. (2005). Using service learning to achieve middle school comprehensive guidance program goals. *Professional School Counseling, 9*(2), 156–159.

courses on career development and co-operative education in the secondary curriculum, which include a component on self-awareness. The Canadian program *Pathways* (Hutchinson & Freeman, 1994) includes a module called "Knowing About Yourself, Knowing About Careers."

Career Exploration

Career exploration, actions that teach about possible careers and adult roles, can take many forms. Engaging in imaginative play, reading, watching films, playing on teams, and developing hobbies and interests all contribute to career exploration. When parents say that their exceptional adolescents have too much homework and cannot take part in extracurricular activities, you may want to speak up. These after-school pursuits are critical in helping young people to engage in career exploration. You may have known a gifted young woman who chaired the public relations committee in secondary school and began to consider a career in marketing. Or you may have known a boy with developmental disabilities who cooked for the school fair and asked if he could visit a cafeteria to learn about possible careers in food preparation. Students must reflect on the exploration or experience and relate it to themselves. Questions students can ask include:

- Did I enjoy doing that, and why?
- How good was I at that?
- How confident do I feel about doing it again?
- Why was that so interesting?
- Is this something that makes me feel "in my element"?
- If I were to do this every day, how would I feel about it?

You can contribute to career exploration at any grade level by including discussions of the application of the knowledge you are teaching. When your students study history, you can point out how history is used to create lifelike settings for films and television programs and invite a historian to tell your students what she does. When studying design and technology, discuss with students how engineers, technicians, and construction workers on the teams that design and build bridges apply this kind of knowledge. Invite an array of individuals who work with people, including occupational therapists, child-care workers, and bus drivers. Remember that chefs and pharmacists are applied chemists.

When you focus on the connections between the curriculum and possible careers, you engage your students in career exploration. Encourage students to ask questions; consult books and websites; and learn about the educational qualifications, demands, wages, and dangers of the careers that interest them. Many provinces have extensive websites intended to help adolescents and young adults to secure the information they need to make informed decisions (e.g., SaskNetWork; www.sasknetwork.gov.sk.ca). Provide opportunities for children and adolescents to interview adults in careers that intrigue them. Encourage wide exploration of many possibilities rather than premature narrowing to one or two careers.

Individualized transition plans provide youth with disabilities with systematic opportunities to gradually become aware of their own strengths and weaknesses and to develop career maturity. Using case-study research, Hutchinson and her colleagues (2008) reported on the experiences of two adolescents—one with physical disabilities (Naomi) and one with intellectual disabilities (Max)—negotiating workplace accommodations during co-operative education. In the travel agency where she obtained work experience, Naomi, who has already been introduced in this chapter, negotiated physical accommodations, social and cognitive accommodations, and teaching-and-learning accommodations. She formed links between her interests and her career-related goals, as well as acquiring positive, realistic self-efficacy and outcome expectations. In his placement in a lumber store, Max received the same types of accommodations as Naomi but had only a small role in negotiating them. He also experienced difficulty translating his vague career goals into actions. Also using case-study research, Lindstrom and Benz (2002) reported on the career trajectories of young women with learning disabilities following their graduation from high school. It took many of them a number of years to establish stable, productive careers. In two recent case studies, Chris DeLuca and colleagues at Queen's University (2010) reported on two at-risk youth, Tim and Ashley, who thrived in WBE, developed resiliency, and each secured full-time employment within one year of completing a structured WBE program that included work experience designed to facilitate their transitions. Both had been disengaged by regular school programs; Ashley had returned to school after dropping out and Tim had avoided dropping out by choosing WBE.

Career counselling is an important part of preparation for transition to work, whether it is direct transition or indirect transition to work through PSE. However, career counselling may need to be differentiated to meet individual student needs.

Recently, career counsellors have begun to recognize that conventional career counselling may not meet the needs of Aboriginal youth because it is based on a world view not shared by many Aboriginals, and counsellors who lack cultural awareness may not recognize what is important to Aboriginals in career-life planning. Anne Charter and her colleagues in Manitoba developed a program, called *Career Counselling for Aboriginal Youth: The Journey Inward; the Journey Outward*, with advice and assistance from four Manitoba First Nations communities. Rod McCormick from the University of British Columbia, a member of the Mohawk nation, and two colleagues produced a career-life planning model for First Nations people called *Guiding Circles* (McCormick et al., 2002).

Why Career Development Is Critical to the Participation of Youth in the Labour Market

Career development has become a critical issue for at-risk youth and youth with disabilities for a number of reasons. Recent international reviews suggest that contributing factors to high youth unemployment include the disengagement of youth from education as well as a changing labour market that can no longer absorb young workers with minimal qualifications (McGinty & Brader, 2005). Enabling youth, including those with disabilities, to access the labour market is very important for the well-being of these individuals and of our country.

Labour market information provides those working and aspiring to work with details about current and projected demand for labour services and supply of labour services in the economy. Thus, youth who express interest in work that takes advantage of their numerical abilities could learn about the demand for mathematics teachers, actuarial professionals, chartered accountants, mathematics professors, and mathematical engineers. The same kind of information is available about any cluster of ability-related occupations. Online resources make it easy to access labour market information.

Weblinks

LABOUR MARKET INFORMATION (JOB BANK)
www.jobbank.gc.ca/home-eng.do?lang=eng

LABOUR FORCE SURVEY, STATISTICS CANADA
www.statcan.gc.ca (SEARCH FOR LABOUR FORCE SURVEY)

JOBPOSTCANADA.COM
www.jobpostcanada.com/generalsites.htm

MANITOBA WORKINFONET
http://mb.workinfonet.ca

LEARNING TOOLS (CONFERENCE BOARD OF CANADA)
www.conferenceboard.ca/topics/education/learning-tools.aspx

Further Reading

On self-determination and self-advocacy:

Astromovich, R.L., & Harris, K. (2007). Promoting self-advocacy among minority students in school counseling. *Journal of Counseling and Development, 85*(3), 269–276.

McCarthy, D. (2007). Teaching self-advocacy to students with disabilities. *About Campus, 12*(5), 10–16.

Chambers, C.R., Wehmeyer, M.L., Saito, Y., Lida, K.M., Lee, Y., & Singh, V. (2007). Self-determination: What do we know? Where do we go? *Exceptionality, 15*(1), 3–15.

National Council on Disability. (2014). *Understanding disabilities in American Indian and Alaska Native communities. Toolkit Guide.* Washington, DC: National Council on Disability. (Available at www.ncd.gov.)

Wood, W.M., Karvonen, M., Test, D.W., Browder, D., & Algozzine, B. (2004). Promoting student self-determination skills in IEP planning. *Teaching Exceptional Children, 36*(3), 8–16.

Pearl, C. (2004). Laying the foundation for self-advocacy: Fourth graders with learning disabilities invite their peers into the resource room. *Teaching Exceptional Children, 36*(3), 44–49.

Parents, teachers, and employers often assume that career exploration and decision making are easy for gifted students, who have high academic achievement and many abilities, and can access information easily (Maxwell, 2007). However, research suggests that as many as half of academically advanced students experience difficulties and want help with career counselling, exploration, and decision making (Paterson, 2006). Meredith Greene (2006), a former teacher in Nova Scotia, reviewed the psychological and emotional issues that affect career choice for gifted adolescents including indecision, pressure from others, lack of career role models, and lack of meaningfulness or personal challenge in careers.

Some of these issues differentially affect gifted males, females, and minorities. For example, gifted females often experience uncertainty about their abilities and their interests during the adolescent years, while males are more likely to pursue linear career paths toward high-status careers from adolescence into the early adult years (Maxwell, 2007). Many gifted youth from culturally diverse backgrounds have a deep concern for their communities and limit their career interests to careers that would be of service there, while grappling with implicit messages from their communities that they may fail to achieve their goals. Whiting (2006) identifies issues specific to black males, Assouline and her colleagues (2010) focus on the counselling needs of students who are twice exceptional, those who are gifted and also have a disability, while Burney and Cross (2006) identify counselling needs of gifted students who live in poverty in rural settings.

Career exploration is a complex and lengthy process of seeking and reflecting on information and experience, setting goals and monitoring progress toward them, and changing direction and pursuing alternatives. There are many competencies and perspectives that young people need to develop and embrace to progress in career development, and many of these can be enhanced through career experience.

Career Experience

Career experience refers to the opportunities adolescents have to try out and experience aspects of the working role that is expected of adults. Some describe this as the reality testing of the understanding developed through career exploration. In Canada the most common forms of career experiences that occur within school programs are co-operative education and work experience. Both the Canadian Labour Force Development Board and the Advisory Council on Science and Technology have recommended co-operative education as a central component of the transition to work. Provincial ministries of education have increased their focus on co-operative education, for example Nova Scotia has developed Options and Opportunities (O_2). Part-time jobs also offer youth career experiences, although they say they take jobs to earn and WBE opportunities to learn (Hutchinson et al., 2008).

CO-OPERATIVE EDUCATION AND WORKPLACE LEARNING

Co-operative education (co-op), in which schools co-operate with employers, involves students in extended periods of time in a workplace (often around one hundred hours over a school term) while enrolled in full-time study. Typically students also engage in classroom orientations to the workplace and in reflective seminars. This is the most common form of WBE in Canada. **Workplace experience** is usually of shorter duration, ranging from a one-day job-shadowing experience to a few half-day visits within the context of a credit course. A review of the co-op education and career education policies across Canada at the end of the 1990s showed that all provinces and territories provide co-op education and/or workplace experiences and referred directly to the provision of accommodations in co-op education and workplace learning for exceptional students. There were also frequent references to the needs of at-risk students (Hutchinson et al., 1999).

Research suggests that adolescents with disabilities can benefit from co-op and career education (Hutchinson et al., 2008), as can youth who are at risk for dropping out (DeLuca et al., 2010). These students often learn well in structured, hands-on, experiential settings—often much better than in traditional classrooms. In a study of college and university students from four programs, Chin and his colleagues (2000) found that over 95 percent of those who had *and* had not taken co-op education in secondary school recommended it to others. Their reasons for taking co-op education were often combinations of career exploration and career experiences—for example, wanting to try out careers that interested them and use the information to help them decide whether to pursue a particular career. A review of representative curriculum documents from school districts in Ontario (Hutchinson et al., 2001) showed that school districts saw co-op education as a means of helping students make connections between the classroom and the world of work, as well as a means of career exploration and career experiences.

Marcel Jancovic/Shutterstock

I want the same things as other people—to work and to live on my own.

Research conducted in the United States with students with various disabilities suggests that vocational or on-the-job training during the high school years for a particular entry-level job is premature (e.g., Stuart & Smith, 2002). Morningstar (1997) recommends a balanced program of career development that includes opportunities to develop career maturity and self-determination through meaningful work experiences that are primarily for learning, not simply on-the-job-training. Morningstar describes an ideal program that is much like co-op education as it is practised in Canada and other forms of WBE available in Canadian provinces. Encourage your exceptional students and their parents to consider co-op education as an integral part of their secondary school years. In our research at Queen's University with adolescents in co-op education, we have learned that co-op stretches adolescents—with and without disabilities—in ways that we had not imagined (e.g., DeLuca et al., 2010).

It is important that education for exceptional students include opportunities for them to dream about their futures and to become enthusiastic about being valued and making the transition to assuming adult roles, because "the specific nature of a youth's dream is less important than the enthusiasm dreaming generates for goal achievement" (Powers et al., 1996, p. 12).

Summary

This chapter has focused on enhancing transitions for exceptional students and at-risk students, including transitions into school, transitions during the school day, transitions between schools, and transitions out of school to further education or to the workplace. There are a number of actions that teachers and parents can take on behalf of their young children and that older students can take for themselves or with their parents to enhance the experience of transition. It is critical for parents and students to inform themselves, discuss the upcoming transition, and make plans that anticipate the possible challenges and the ways in which the family can respond productively. It is also important that parents and older students are prepared to advocate for what they believe is best. The topics of advocacy and self-advocacy were addressed in the transitions of exceptional and at-risk learners.

Key Terms

activity transitions (p. 315)

career counselling (p. 327)

career development (p. 325)

career experience (p. 328)

career exploration (p. 326)

co-operative education (co-op) (p. 328)

family-centred approach (p. 317)

inclusive post-secondary education (IPSE) (p. 323)

labour market information (p. 327)

parent advocacy (p. 312)

self-advocacy (p. 313)

self-awareness (p. 325)

self-determination (p. 313)

social exclusion (p. 324)

transition planning meeting (p. 317)

transition plans (p. 319)

transition to post-secondary education (PSE) (p. 320)

transition to school (p. 317)

transition to work (p. 324)

transitions (p. 311)

visual schedule (p. 316)

workplace experience (p. 328)

Challenges for Reviewing Chapter 11

1. Why is your role so important, as a classroom teacher, in helping exceptional students (those in elementary as well as those in secondary school) to become more independent learners?

2. Identify the actions a teacher can take to make transitions for exceptional learners as smooth as possible. Focus on transitions for students in the context in which you teach—elementary or secondary. Think of all the kinds of transitions you can, and identify what you can do.

3. Describe the actions you would take when teaching a class that includes either Annette or Justin, discussed in the cases at the beginning of the chapter, to ensure that all students' career development is enhanced. Then describe the way you would accommodate the needs of Annette or Justin and the resources that you would help this student access in order to ensure career development is differentiated and appropriate to the student's needs.

Activities for Reviewing Chapter 11 with Your Peers

4. Prepare to assume the role of the classroom teacher of an exceptional student on a school-based team (or the role of a parent, principal, or resource teacher) for a meeting about Bobby, Annette, or Justin, described in the opening cases of this chapter. List (a) the resources you would use to prepare for a discussion about this student making the described transition, (b) the resources you would use to prepare for a discussion about this transition, (c) the contributions you would make in the meeting on the discussion about this transition, and (d) how the actions you suggest could enhance the student's independence. Participate with your peers in the role-play of the school-based team meeting about this student.

5. Return to the opening cases of Bobby, Annette, and Justin. Answer the questions that follow the cases in discussion with your peers.

6. Choose an exceptionality and choose a transition discussed in this chapter. Make a list of relevant resources and a list of tips for your peers. Exchange with your peers so that you each assemble a collection of tips and resources. Together consider how similar your suggestions are and what is unique in your lists of tips that is tailored to the type of transition or the specific exceptionality. Generate some general guidelines for transition questions that follow the cases.

Conclusion

Thriving as a Teacher

Every one of us can remember the day we realized that we were actually teaching! We had realized a dream and were embarking on a totally new adventure. Exhilarating, daunting, and very emotional! And the rollercoaster ride continues, with a crazy mix of ups and downs. How can we ensure that we thrive and take care of our mental health—and not simply survive—in our chosen profession, especially in our early days as a teacher?

Succeeding as a Beginning Teacher

This conclusion is not about exceptional children and adolescents. This conclusion is about you. It is about how you can thrive as a teacher. The word *thriving* conjures up accomplishment, satisfaction, and prosperity. Teachers enter the profession with high expectations, a vision of the future, and a mission to educate children and adolescents. Years of research suggest that effective and rewarding teaching is most apt to be accomplished by optimistic and self-confident teachers. Studies that focused on teachers who were successful in their beginning years found that they seemed to be particularly high in self-confidence and energy levels. All these teachers had a number of characteristics in common, including a deep commitment to teaching, genuine caring for students, and the goals to become better teachers and to learn more (Cochran-Smith, 2006; Venter & Pohan, 2011). Research has found that beginning teachers need both a positive outlook and the support of their colleagues and administrators to succeed, and that these personal and contextual factors interact in complex and idiosyncratic ways (Beltman et al., 2011).

Teachers who have a greater belief in their ability to teach have been found to be more likely to (a) try different ways of teaching, (b) be businesslike by being organized in their teaching and fair and firm in their dealings with students, and (c) be enthusiastic about teaching. Those who believed strongly that students benefit from school experiences were also high in confidence and enthusiasm about teaching (for a thorough review, see Beltman et al., 2011). The picture that emerges suggests that some personal characteristics, such as commitment, self-confidence, and a positive outlook, contribute to thriving in teaching. These are things over which you have some control. As well, some aspects of the teaching environment, such as colleague and administrator support as well as opportunities to contribute to school decision making, over which you exert less control, may also be critical, especially in the early years. Figure C-1 was prepared by an early-career teacher at the conclusion of her first year teaching secondary school French and English.

Teachers cite many rewarding aspects of their work that contribute to their positive outlook. In an Ontario study many years ago teachers reported that the three most satisfying aspects of teaching involved their relationships with their students. These were (a) experiencing good rapport and relationships with young people;

FIGURE C-1   SURVIVAL SKILLS FOR THE FIRST-YEAR TEACHER: HOW TO STAY WELL AND ENJOY BEING A TEACHER

- Find a mentor—a department head or an experienced teacher—who can offer another perspective on the daily dilemmas you face.
- Find a friend—a new teacher like yourself—so you can support one another and talk out your problems and potential solutions.
- Meet resource teachers and guidance staff—as soon as you arrive at your school, learn about the available resources.
- Don't be afraid to borrow resources—replenish the department files or your colleagues' files with your own creations.
- Make a sick-day plan—include lesson plans, the required materials, class seating plan, attendance list, and instructions, just in case.
- Keep lines of communication open with parents.
- Maintain a page for each student—document telephone calls made to parents, calls received, conversations with resource personnel, behaviour observation notes, etc.
- Maintain (or ask designated students to maintain) a logbook of each day's lesson and copies of extra handouts so that absent students can be responsible for finding and catching up on missed work.
- Before you start teaching, set your policy on washroom breaks, late assignments, attendance, truancy, lates, your behaviour plan, methods for getting the students' attention, etc. Discuss these with a mentor so that your policies are consistent with the school's code of behaviour, and adapt them as required as the year progresses.
- Remember that you need time to develop all the creative activities that make your classes exciting and rewarding to teach. Develop a manageable number each week (e.g., one or two), borrow when necessary, and accept that some ideas will have to wait until the next time you teach this unit.
- Take off Friday night and at least one full day on the weekend to recharge for the next week.

Source: Prepared by N. Lévesque, a classroom teacher in Barrie, Ontario. Used by permission.

(b) recognizing that students are suddenly understanding or enjoying their lessons; and (c) seeing student success, achievement, and satisfaction. These rewards of teaching reflect the reasons that many teachers give for choosing their profession: "I enjoy children" and "I love history and really want to pass my love of learning on to others." The next most frequently mentioned reward was interacting with and receiving support from colleagues (King et al., 1988). The same themes persist in recent interview studies of teachers (e.g., Moore Johnson & The Project on the Next Generation of Teachers, 2007). I encourage you to consider what you need to thrive as an educator.

Being a Change Agent

Like many other professions, teaching in the current era is caught in the throes of massive and continual change. Michael Fullan (2013) of the University of Toronto describes how change has been introduced into Canadian schools without regard for the impact it has on teachers' daily lives. Almost all change, even when we embrace the innovation, results in feelings of loss and grief (Browning, 2008). Change also makes teachers feel incompetent (or less competent than when they were doing what they knew well) and creates confusion and conflict. Unless each of these issues is matched with an appropriate response, change is unlikely to succeed and we may endanger our well-being.

"Teachers vastly underestimate their power to change things" (Sarason, 1993, p. 6). In a perceptive analysis of what it takes to be a change agent, Donna Patterson (1996), a teacher from Saskatchewan, suggested that teachers focus on self-care first and then on political astuteness, planning, effective conflict resolution, and humour. With these strengths, teachers can become agents of change in their own classrooms, lead by example, and earn the respect of their colleagues for their ideas. Recently both Roffey (2015) and Watson (2014) have written about the need for similar positive approaches when teachers work collaboratively to bring about schoolwide change. Figure C-2 offers advice for teachers working to make change and make their classes more inclusive. Collegial relationships and a culture that encourages teachers to care for one another while learning together empower teachers to become agents of change for their schools (Lukacs & Galluzzo, 2014).

Handling Stress and Staying Well

In the past few decades the helping professions in many countries have experienced the loss of talented and capable members. Thirty years ago Bryan Hiebert of the University of Calgary summarized the research on teacher stress in Canada (1985). Canadian teachers reported a variety of stressors but referred most often to work overload (or pace of work) and student discipline problems or challenges in interacting with students whose lives were complex. Across all the studies, representing all parts of the country, the problems usually seemed to involve some form of personal interaction or time-management concerns. A more recent study by Jennifer Lawson (2008) of the University of Manitoba focused on women administrators in high-poverty community schools, and the two issues raised in Hiebert's report persist—the pace of the demands and the challenges and complexities of the lives of children and their families, in this case, in high-poverty communities.

FIGURE C-2 YOU CAN BE A CHANGE AGENT

- Take care of yourself while working for change by making sure you have support, both social and instrumental support.
- Things take time; trust the process; trust yourself; remain positive and patient.
- Respect others who have views different from yours; anticipate and accept that you will make mistakes.
- Remember that working steadily will help you reach your goals; encourage yourself and acknowledge the encouragement of others.
- Be a team player; use your strengths and encourage others to use their strengths so you can work together to reach your mutual goals.
- Be an example of what you are striving for; keep the means consistent with the goals.
- Anticipate that you are taking risks; be alert to feedback that you can provide for yourself and that you will inevitably receive from others.
- Approach every challenge as a learner; work to understand the full meaning and implications of the dilemmas you experience as you strive for meaningful change.

Since Hiebert's report in 1985 the pressures on Canadian classroom teachers have, if anything, increased with the growing diversity in Canadian classrooms, including the inclusion of exceptional students in regular classrooms. Inclusion and increasing diversity can involve many of the factors that contribute to teaching being rewarding (e.g., satisfaction in seeing students "get it," collaboration with colleagues) or being stressful (increased workload, discipline problems, lack of administrative support).

What is stress, and how can you, as a beginning teacher, cope well with this challenge and be a resilient teacher? Much has been written about stress and burnout in educators, and many definitions have been used. One of the most widely cited perspectives on teacher burnout describes three dimensions—emotional exhaustion (which may underlie the other two), depersonalization, and feelings of low personal accomplishment. While we may not find it easy to define stress or burnout, we can probably all think of examples from our personal experiences as teachers. Listen to Maria describe to her support group what she found when she returned to her grade 5 class after recess on the afternoon of October 19:

> I am soooo frustrated. I was late getting to my room yesterday because I had separated four students who were fighting on the playground. I felt my blood pressure soar when I yelled at them, avoided taking any random punches, and led them to the principal's office—only to find the office empty. I couldn't leave them alone, on the verge of tearing each other apart, could I? So I worried about the fights that might be breaking out in my class. And fretted that someone might pick on Josh, who has childhood rheumatoid arthritis and is frail and vulnerable. After what seemed like an eternity, the principal's secretary came strolling down the hall. When I asked her where the principal was, she laughed and pointed toward my room. How could I have forgotten? He was in my room waiting to observe me teaching.
>
> In the excitement, it had slipped my mind completely. All I could think of then was, "What an idiot he will think I am! I knew I should have asked someone to switch recess duty with me. Why did no one volunteer? They knew I had an observation." By then I was angry with the whole staff! I was so nervous that my hands were wet, my throat was dry, and my mind was blank. I always feel inadequate when I am evaluated. Especially when it is the first evaluation—I can't seem to stay calm, even though I have taught for five years. I asked myself, "What was the lesson I planned to teach?" I had to look in my daybook to jog my memory; the lesson involved a complex explanation, hands-on practice, and follow-up written practice in adding fractions. Why did I not choose something simpler? I must have been trying to show off and impress him with my up-to-date methods. I fumbled my way through the explanation, forgot to do the hands-on activity, and had to explain the written activity about a thousand times. To almost every student individually. By the time my principal left, my stomach was almost sick. I dread receiving the evaluation. Even I think I should be fired.

Maria went on to explain to the members of her group that she had moved to this downtown school in September when her partner was transferred to the city from a small town. She found that the teachers were not as friendly as in her previous school and the children fought all the time in the schoolyard, "like gang warfare." Maria's partner was rarely home because he was adjusting to a new job, and her preschool children hated the new daycare, begging every morning to go to Sue's, the home of their previous child minder. To finish her story, Maria added with emphasis, "I'm so stressed!"

Few of us would disagree with Maria's assessment of the situation. This sounds like a case of many threats that together exceed Maria's coping strategies. However, there was reason to be optimistic. To begin to take control of the situation, Maria had called the number on a poster the first day it was tacked on the bulletin board in the staff room. The poster said

Feel stressed? Need support?

New group starting September 30 at Eastside Teachers' Centre.

Call today!

That is how Maria came to be telling eight strangers about her most frustrating day at work.

Focusing on Your Well-Being

Recently researchers have studied the stress of large numbers of teachers in Britain and North America. They suggest that stress is triggered and sustained by the cognitive processes we choose to use when we perceive a threat, is affected by the emotions we experience, and affects our health (Gold & Roth, 2014). This means that stress affects all our well-being. We make decisions about how we will cope with a threat; when our coping mechanisms are successful, distress is minimized and we may even feel a positive type of stress (eustress). However, when our coping mechanisms are not adequate, we experience negative emotions and feel threatened, and our immune system is affected, which may result in illness. While this all sounds menacing, there are many strategies teachers can use to handle their stressors and learn new coping mechanisms (see Figure C-3).

In the *Professional Health* program (Gold & Roth, 2014), problem solving is the focus and personal and professional needs are the content. Teachers are urged to go beyond stress management and focus on their underlying problems and needs. While we all need skills to survive the immediate challenges, we may also need psychological support to grow over the long term and to develop professional

FIGURE C-3 STEPS FOR TEACHERS IN UNDERSTANDING AND RESPONDING TO STRESS

1. Identify and acknowledge the causes of stress in your life.
   (a) Professional causes of stress
   (b) Personal causes of stress
2. Identify your feelings and your emotional reactions to these feelings.
3. Become aware of the unmet needs behind your feelings.
   (a) Emotional-physical needs
   (b) Psycho-social needs
   (c) Personal-intellectual needs
4. Learn stress-reduction strategies.
   (a) Identify what you can and cannot change.
   (b) Change your beliefs and actions in situations you can control.
   (c) Choose your reaction to situations you cannot control (you can control your reaction).
   (d) Use assertive communication to say no in a constructive way.
   (e) Use relaxation techniques.
   (f) Take charge of your physical health through nutrition, sleep, and exercise.
   (g) Seek social support.

health. Otherwise, we could be continuously engaged in stress management when what we need is to gain self-control. Maria found that her teacher support group helped her become aware of the factors that were causing difficulties and getting in the way of her teaching. She recognized her feelings, her stressors, and her own abilities to deal with them. She realized how much she had needed to belong to a group of teachers whom she could talk to for support. Gold and Roth report that teachers begin to withdraw after they feel isolated from their colleagues. Visit other teachers' classrooms, arrange exchanges, or find a support group like the one Maria found.

Two contrasting conceptual approaches have been used to understand the stressful experiences of teachers and other professionals in caring professions. Burnout (Mantilla & Diaz, 2012; Maslach, 2003), occurring gradually, is characterized by feelings of emotional exhaustion and depersonalization, and reduced feelings of personal accomplishment at work, causing teachers to distance themselves from their students. In contrast, compassion fatigue (Hoffman et al., 2007) is conceptualized as secondary traumatization through the ongoing act of compassion, and is thought to emerge suddenly, characterized by feelings of helplessness, isolation, and disorientation.

Teachers are sometimes surprised to learn that they need to keep mentally active to deal with stress. While teaching offers the promise of intellectual stimulation, it is easy for us to become buried in paperwork and spend the evenings marking, rather than reading about innovative teaching approaches or attending stimulating cultural events. However, discovering new ideas contributes to our personal intellectual needs. For example, Gold and Roth (2014) encourage teachers to embrace intellectual challenges so they can thrive at work: enrol in professional development or graduate courses, take out a subscription to a concert series, or learn to weave. This is intellectually stimulating and helps you to meet new soulmates. It also allows you to become a novice and renew empathy for your students who are not experts in everything that is taught in the classroom.

Being a Teacher Who Makes a Difference

This book has examined the many facets of teaching and including exceptional children in our classrooms—so they may take their places in Canadian society. In this Conclusion, we have briefly looked at and discussed teachers who thrive on challenge, change students' lives, and are never forgotten. This is the kind of teacher we aspire to be—a teacher who touches the lives of children or adolescents and who matters. When I read the obituary published in *The Globe and Mail* on August 3, 1999 (Carlucci), I wished I had known Ben Sheardown. I close this book by introducing you to this teacher who made a difference for so many.

FIGURE C-4 LOOKING BACK ON THE LIFE OF A TEACHER WHO HELPED HUNDREDS OF STUDENTS

Ben Sheardown died of cancer at the age of 55. He was a teacher, guidance counsellor, father, husband, and athlete in Whitehorse. His partner, Cathy, said she wasn't surprised that more than 1000 people paid tribute to Ben. Nor was she surprised that their cards, letters, and tributes covered an entire wall. What surprised her was *how much Ben had mattered* to so many people.

After Ben died, the local newspaper printed letters to the editor from around the world. These letter writers credited Ben with changing their lives and, in some cases, saving their lives. Cathy Sheardown said, "I'm getting numerous cards in the mail that start out, 'You don't know me but . . .' and they're telling me, 'If it wasn't for Mr. Sheardown, I would never have become who I am or never been able to do what I've done; I certainly wouldn't have gone through school.'" She continued, "He affected a ton of people in different ways, never, ever taking the credit and letting [the kids] almost believe it was their idea" (Carlucci, 1999, p. A17). Former students expressed over and over that Ben Sheardown was there for them, even when they felt that nobody else cared about them. He gave them a second chance, and many told stories of this compassionate teacher giving them third and fourth chances.

In the last year of his life, Ben Sheardown was inducted into the Yukon Sports Hall of Fame. He almost refused to accept the award because he thought maybe it was given out of pity to a man with a terminal illness. With the help of his family and friends, he came to see the award as a tribute to those who helped him accomplish great things in his lifetime, as well as to him. Even as a busy teacher, he pursued a healthy lifestyle. He played hockey (helping the Yukon to win gold in the Arctic Winter Games in 1972) and basketball. He ran, biked, swam, and took part in Nordic skiing. In winter, he was often seen riding his bike or taking his dog, Tacumsa, on long walks through downtown trails. The photograph on his memorial service showed him with Tacumsa in the shadow of a hilltop called the King's Throne near Kathleen Lake, a pristine area on the cusp of Kluane National Park.

Jim Perry first met Ben Sheardown when they were both 10 years old. Jim had just moved to Whitehorse from Ireland. He remembered Ben as reaching out to the new kid and described how they became lifelong friends. Jim Perry travelled thousands of kilometres to speak at Ben Sheardown's memorial service. "This memorial was a true indication of the kind of support and the number of lives he touched. Ben left a huge footprint on many hearts." This was a teacher who brought out the best in others and truly made a difference.

Adapted from: Carlucci, M. (1999). Life story: Helped hundreds of youngsters. *The Globe and Mail*, August 3, p. A17.

Glossary

A

Aboriginal cultures Aboriginal peoples are nations, that is, political and cultural groups, with values and lifeways distinct from those of other Canadians.

Aboriginal elders The senior members of an Aboriginal community who are respected and looked to for wisdom.

academic tasks as punishment The practice of assigning students additional homework or lines to write as a punishment.

acceleration An approach for educating gifted students that allows them to move through the curriculum in an area of strength at an accelerated pace or to work at the next grade level.

accommodations Changes to how a student is taught, including such things as teaching strategies, supports, and alternate formats, when the outcomes are consistent with the student's grade placement.

acquired brain injury (ABI) See *traumatic brain injury (TBI)*.

activity transitions Transitions between activities in the classroom, between lessons, or between distinct parts of lessons.

ADAPT A systematic strategy for adapting teaching to include exceptional learners consisting of five steps: **A**ccounts of students' strengths and needs; **D**emands of the classroom; **A**daptations; **P**erspectives and consequences; **T**each and assess the match.

adaptive behaviour Areas of participation in the life of the community in which individuals with developmental disabilities may be delayed (e.g., communication, leisure, self-care, social skills).

additional practise Providing more opportunities for exceptional learners to practise what has been taught and to develop full understanding of ideas, procedures, etc.

advocate A person who represents or champions the cause of another.

alcohol-related neurodevelopmental disorder (ARND) Formerly called fetal alcohol effects (FAE). A lifelong birth defect due to prenatal exposure to alcohol without facial or growth abnormalities; however, learning and behaviour deficits are enduring.

allergy An abnormal reaction to a normal substance (e.g., peanuts).

alternative assessment Assessment that focuses on authentic skills and experiences in real-life environments, for example, portfolios in contrast to traditional testing formats.

alternative expectations Related to the development of skills deemed essential to learning in areas not represented in the curriculum policy documents.

alternatives to letter and number grades Typically consist of pass/fail or credit/no credit designations, rather than specific letter or number grades.

American Sign Language (ASL) A manual language system that has its own rule-governed syntactic system.

amplification The process of enhancing sound, usually through the use of hearing aids or FM (frequency modulation) systems.

anaphylactic shock See *anaphylaxis*.

anaphylaxis A sudden, severe allergic reaction that causes breathing difficulties; death can occur within minutes unless an injection is administered.

antidepressants Medications for managing attention deficit hyperactivity disorder.

applied or workplace stream A secondary school program intended to prepare adolescents for entering the workforce rather than for formal post-secondary education.

Asperger's disorder or Asperger's syndrome (AS) Previously defined as severe and sustained impairment in social interaction with restricted, repetitive patterns of behaviour, interests, and activities, with no significant delays in language acquisition or cognitive development; now part of autistic disorders on the spectrum of ASD.

assessment Data collection, gathering information of many kinds about a student or a group of students, using a variety of tools and techniques.

assessment *as* learning Assessment that enables students to learn to be reflective and self-regulating, and links their own learning and self-assessment.

assessment *for* learning Assessment that is well matched to the demands of teaching in inclusive classrooms and is particularly helpful for differentiating teaching for exceptional learners and others who need tailored instruction. Takes place during learning with teachers providing feedback (formerly called formative assessment).

assessment *of* learning Assessment administered after learning is assumed to have taken place, intended to provide students and parents with a summary of the students' learning and relative standing (formerly called summative assessment).

asthma Obstructed airways that hinder the flow of air in and out of the lungs; an attack is characterized by persistent wheezing, tightness in the chest, and excess phlegm, and can be life threatening.

attention deficit hyperactivity disorder (ADHD) A persistent pattern of inattention and impulsiveness or of hyperactivity or of both that hinders social, academic, and vocational expectations.

authentic assessment Assessment on tasks that are engaging, contextualized, and represent those expected in the adult world.

authentic tasks Learning activities close to real-world tasks, usually involving problems that are engaging, contextualized, and represent those expected in the adult world.

autism spectrum disorder (ASD) Disorders characterized by varying degrees of impairment in three areas: communication skills, social interactions, and repetitive and stereotyped patterns of behaviour. Four previously separate disorders are now considered to be within ASD.

autistic disorder Characterized by deficits in communication and social interaction, as well as restrictive, repetitive behaviours, interests, and activities.

B

blind Characterized by loss of sight and use of auditory and tactile sources of information to replace sight.

Braille A system of raised dots that can be read by touch by persons who are blind.

brain injury Damage to brain tissue, often as a result of a blow to the head or an accident that can cause physical difficulties (e.g., paralysis) and cognitive problems (e.g., memory loss).

bullying A pattern of actions that involves an imbalance of power, a victim who is upset, and a bully who shows a lack of compassion; can take many forms, including physical, emotional, and verbal.

bypass strategies Teaching and learning approaches that allow students to gain access to, practise, or demonstrate learning of the curriculum in alternative ways.

C

Canadian Charter of Rights and Freedoms This bill of rights is entrenched in the Constitution of Canada and guarantees the civil rights of everyone in Canada; was signed into law in 1982.

cancer A malignant tumour or growth of body cells.

career counselling Providing guidance to help students recognize their strengths and responsibilities as they mature, including teaching about the nature and meaning of work.

career development Growing understanding of changing roles and responsibilities, including adult responsibilities, roles, and the nature and meaning of work.

career experience Opportunities for students to acquire experience related to workplaces and adult responsibilities.

career exploration Actions undertaken deliberately or for their own sake that teach about possible careers and adult roles.

case coordinator Person responsible for ensuring that the various services required by an exceptional student are co-ordinated; sometimes parents assume this role.

CCTV Closed-circuit television system consisting of a digital camera and display so that anything placed in front of the camera is magnified on the display to allow visually impaired people to see things that are far away—such as a demonstration at the front of a classroom—or read a book or look at a photograph.

cerebral palsy (CP) A group of disorders impairing body movement and muscle co-ordination as a result of an interference in messages between the brain and the body.

changes to letter and number grades Clarifying with a comment to indicate that a student may be using a textbook that is below the actual grade level of the class or to explain the reading level of books used in language arts.

changing grading criteria Varying grading weights so exceptional students are not disadvantaged by an impossible task; for example, students who are hard of hearing do not have part of their grade determined by the results of oral pop quizzes.

checkpoints Checklists for students to complete at quarter and halfway points of long-term assignments to show progress and receive feedback.

child abuse Physical abuse (use of force on a child's body), emotional abuse (persistent attacks on a child's sense of self), sexual abuse (any sexual exploitation) by an adult or another child, or neglect of a child by parent or caregiver.

child–teacher relationships How teachers treat children contributes to children's socio-emotional development, including treating children with respect and getting to know their interests, strengths, and needs.

chromosomal abnormalities Chromosomes contain genes with the chemical codes that direct cell function; aberrant chromosomes are those with abnormal numbers or structures.

chronic health condition A qualified medical practitioner has certified that a student requires medical procedures, excluding administration of medication only, to ensure the health and safety of the student while in school or requires ongoing special education interventions due to the student's limited school attendance or because the condition adversely affects the student's educational performance.

classroom assessment Day-to-day practices adopted by teachers to describe student learning through portfolios, conferences with students, paper and pencil tests, etc.

classroom procedures Efficient ways of moving all members of a class through the day or the period that are consistent with the teacher's goals and follow from the rules (e.g., transitions and distribution of materials).

climate The general feeling created in a classroom; positive classroom climate usually is thought to develop when people treat each other with respect.

code of conduct Brief guidelines that clearly identify school rules and acceptable student behaviours and contain consequences.

cognitive abilities Processes and knowledge, including vocabulary, verbal fluency, retention, generalizing, making abstractions, organizing, and planning.

cognitive complexity The cognitive demands made of the learner by teaching and learning in the classroom.

cognitive disabilities Challenges in processes and knowledge including making abstractions; often characterize developmental disabilities.

cognitive strategies Plans and processes designed to accomplish learning or solve problems.

colitis See *ulcerative colitis (UC)*.

collaboration Teachers and other professionals learning from each other's experiences and working in teams where all members feel that their contributions are valued.

collaborative learning Teaching approaches that include cooperative learning and problem solving in pairs and groups and that usually involve student groups of varying abilities and skills, that is, heterogeneous groupings.

communication disorders Refers to exceptionalities in speech or language or both. Speech is disordered when it deviates so far from the speech of other people that it calls attention to itself, interferes with communication, or causes the speaker or listeners distress. Language is disordered when student has impairment in expressive or receptive language.

communication exceptionalities Refers to exceptionalities that are primarily characterized by interfering with effective communication, including speech and language disorders and students who are deaf or hard of hearing.

community A group of people who have shared interests and who mutually pursue the common good.

community agreements Four guidelines for students to use in developing a sense of community in the classroom: attentive listening, appreciation/no put-downs, the right to pass when given an opportunity to speak, and mutual respect (*Tribes,* Gibbs, 2001).

community-based Education that focuses on relating what is learned in school to what occurs in the community; often learning takes place in the community as well as in the school.

community circle The gathering of all students in a class in a large circle where each student is given an opportunity to present herself in a structured way and to reflect on what is happening in her world (*Tribes,* Gibbs, 2001).

comprehension Reading comprehension is an active process of understanding that requires an intentional and thoughtful interaction between the reader and the text.

computation Mathematical skill and understanding in using the four basic operations to combine numbers.

concept maps Graphic organizers that show relationships among concepts as well as essential characteristics of the concepts.

concrete-to-representational-to-abstract (CRA) A sequence of instruction that takes students through Concrete hands-on instruction with manipulative objects, then through pictorial Representations of those manipulatives, to learning through Abstract notation including operational symbols.

consistency In classroom management, maintaining the same expectations from day to day and applying the same consequences when students fail to meet expectations while honouring adaptations for exceptional students.

contract A behaviour management technique involving a written agreement that states what the teacher and the student agree to do, and specifies the positive rewards and the consequences for failing to live up to the agreement.

co-operative education (co-op) A form of work-based education, used widely in Canada, that involves students learning in workplaces as well as in classrooms; may be paid or unpaid, usually for course credit.

co-operative learning A teaching approach that involves students in learning with peers in small groups, taking roles, and working interdependently.

corporal punishment Punishing a student for misbehaving by striking the student or threatening to strike the student.

creativity Demonstrated by students contributing ideas, transforming and combining ideas, asking questions, and being curious.

criterion-referenced Data in which a student's work is compared to expected outcomes.

Crohn's disease (CD) A chronic inflammatory disease of the intestines.

cultural awareness Sensitivity when one makes the effort to become aware and respectful of the beliefs, values, and lives of members of other cultural groups.

culturally diverse backgrounds Used to refer to students who are not from the majority Anglo-European culture.

culturally relevant pedagogy Teaching approaches designed to respect the culture, life experience, and learning needs of culturally diverse students.

culturally responsive teaching (CRT) Teaching that involves using teaching materials and instructional strategies that respect the culture, life experience, and learning needs of each student and recognize the contribution each student has made to the community and learning of the classroom.

cyberbullying A form of psychological cruelty perpetrated virtually. Refers to threats, insults, and demeaning messages spread through the Internet or by cellphone.

cystic fibrosis (CF) Increasingly severe respiratory problems and extreme difficulty in digesting nutrients from food.

D

deaf Characterized by hearing loss that interferes with the acquisition and maintenance of the auditory skills necessary to develop speech and oral language and causes one to use visual sources of information to replace hearing.

Deaf community Many adults who are deaf describe themselves as a cultural minority and use the term *Deaf* to designate cultural group membership; the common language is American Sign Language (ASL).

depression Refers to a state of low mood which is not necessarily a sign of mental illness but may contribute to self-hurting and suicide if prolonged and untreated.

developmental disabilities The development of cognitive abilities and adaptive behaviours at a much slower rate than normal, which results in significant limitations in these areas at mild and severe levels.

developmentally advanced See *gifted.*

diabetes A condition in which the pancreas fails to produce a sufficient amount of the hormone insulin for proper sugar absorption in the body, which may place restrictions on physical activity.

diabetes emergency kit A ration package containing juice, raisins, or dextrose, often carried by an individual with diabetes and sometimes kept in a central location in a school to be used by students with diabetes in an emergency.

differentiated instruction (DI) Acknowledges that students differ in interests, learning profile, and level of functioning and alters teaching to address these differences.

(dis)ability awareness programs Programs developed to foster greater understanding of people with disabilities, to increase students' knowledge about specific disabilities, and to increase students' sensitivity toward individuals with disabilities.

discrepancy A controversial method of identifying a learning disability by establishing a difference between ability (usually measured by an intelligence test) and achievement in one or more of the following areas: reading, writing, language acquisition, mathematics, reasoning, or listening.

diversity Variation in culture, ability, and values that characterizes modern Canadian society.

domains Areas, such as overall intellect, leadership, creativity, or the arts, where gifted students excel.

double-deficit hypothesis Refers to deficits in both phonemic awareness and rapid naming.

Down syndrome A genetic defect causing limitations in physical and cognitive development; physically, children with Down syndrome have low muscle tone and a generalized looseness of the ligaments.

Duchenne muscular dystrophy (DMD) A musculoskeletal condition with marked physical degeneration that occurs during the school years.

dyscalculia Learning disabilities in arithmetic, especially calculations.

dysgraphia Learning disabilities in writing.

dyslexia Learning disabilities in reading.

E

echolalia Speech that is an immediate imitation of that of some other speaker.

educational assistant (EA) Paraprofessional assigned to work with one or more exceptional students in a classroom or to support a teacher's work with an entire class while monitoring the exceptional students and offering them support at key moments.

emotional or behaviour exceptionality Usually characterized by dysfunctional relationships at home and/or school and at least one of aggression, negative psychological states, and social problems; usually behaviour differs markedly and chronically from accepted norm and interferes with student's own learning and learning of others.

encouragement Giving courage or spurring someone on, which can be particularly helpful in alleviating the discouragement experienced by exceptional students when challenged to participate and learn in inclusive classrooms.

enforcing a rule In teaching classroom rules, enforcement usually follows demonstration and practise and refers to the follow-up and feedback provided by teachers to commend students when they follow the rules and to ensure that consequences are applied when students fail to follow the rules.

engagement The extent to which students embrace learning and throw themselves into the activities of the classroom.

English as a second language (ESL) Students who have learned a language other than English as their first language and must acquire English as a second language, often in the context of school; programs designed to teach English to these students.

English language learner (ELL) students Students from diverse cultures who speak English as a second language.

environment Context of learning, composed of both classroom climate and physical layout.

enzyme supplements Medication taken by a person with cystic fibrosis before a meal or snack to replace pancreatic enzymes that the body does not produce and that are essential to digestion.

epilepsy A neurological disorder that occasionally produces brief disturbances in normal electrical functions of the brain that lead to sudden, brief seizures that vary in nature and intensity from person to person.

epinephrine Adrenalin; administered in the event of an anaphylactic allergic reaction; can be life saving.

EpiPen® Brand name of an easily administered form of adrenalin often carried by children who have allergies and anaphylactic reactions.

equal participation The United Nations' (1993) *Standard Rules on the Equalization of Opportunities for Persons with Disabilities* targeted eight areas for equal participation in the local community, including education, health, employment, and social services.

equality rights In Canada, the equality rights that apply to education are contained in section 15(1) of the Charter: "Every individual is equal before and under the law and has a right to the equal protection and equal benefit of the law without discrimination based on race, national or ethnic origin, colour, religion, sex, age, or mental or physical disability."

equity Equity education means tailoring teaching to challenge inequities and discrimination.

evaluation Making decisions based on the assessment data that have been gathered about a student or group of students; on an IEP this refers to procedures the in-school team will use to demonstrate accountability by showing that the student is making reasonable progress.

exceptional students Learners who are gifted as well as students with disabilities; used interchangeably with terms like *students with special needs* to describe students in need of special education programs.

executive function Defined in many ways, but generally refers to those cognitive processes needed to sustain problem-solving toward a goal and responsible for higher level action control such as directing, connecting, and organizing information.

expository text Content-area text with the purpose of providing information, in contrast to narrative text, which tells a story.

expulsion Permanent removal of a student from the classroom as a consequence of the student behaving inappropriately, violating the code of conduct, etc.

F

fairness Refers to just treatment, which means same treatment in some contexts and equitable (but different) treatment in other contexts.

family-centred approach Teaching and service provision that focuses on the family as the client as well as the student. Typically seen during the pre-school years and less after children begin school.

feedback Helpful information given to assist with improvement in learning or performance.

fetal alcohol effects (FAE) This term is no longer in wide use but appears in older publications; see *alcohol-related neurodevelopmental disorder (ARND)*.

fetal alcohol spectrum disorder (FASD) Lifelong birth defects characterized by physical and physiological abnormalities due to prenatal exposure to alcohol causing delays in development, central nervous dysfunction, learning problems, and possible facial abnormalities.

fetal alcohol syndrome (FAS) Physical and physiological abnormalities due to prenatal exposure to alcohol causing delays in development, central nervous dysfunction, a characteristic pattern of facial features, and learning problems.

fluency Contributes to comprehension and refers to children reading out loud with speed, accuracy, and proper expression.

form of practise Allowing students to engage in oral or written practise or another form of practise that advances their learning; can be adapted for exceptional students.

formal assessment Assessment using standardized tests. These could include an intelligence test; behaviour observation checklists; vision, hearing, or language assessments; and medical tests.

formative assessment Assessment conducted during learning, intended to promote learning and not simply to judge whether students have learned (presently referred to as assessment *for* learning).

frequency modulation (FM) systems With a classroom FM system, the carrier wave is transmitted through the air by frequency modulation from a teacher-worn microphone to a student-worn FM receiver; students with hearing impairments can hear the teacher clearly from any location in the classroom.

friendships Close relationships characterized by reciprocity, that is, give and take, and by commitment between individuals who see themselves as equals.

functional curriculum Outcomes for a student are based on life skills such as shopping, banking, and cooking.

G

generalized seizures Epileptic seizures that involve the whole brain.

gifted Exceptionally high abilities in one or several areas, including specific academic subjects, overall intellect, leadership, creativity, or the arts.

grading Symbolic representation of evaluation or judgments based on assessment data, often in the form of letter grades, percentages, or performance levels.

grouping The practice of deliberately placing students in learning or working groups; used extensively in co-operative and collaborative learning approaches.

H

hard of hearing Partial hearing loss that interferes with the acquisition and maintenance of the auditory skills necessary to develop speech and oral language; use visual sources of information to supplement or replace hearing.

head injury See *traumatic brain injury (TBI)*.

hearing aids Systems that amplify all sounds, worn in the ear.

hearing status Description of one's ability to hear; used to describe the parents of children who are deaf.

heritage language The language of one's ancestors; heritage language programs help children learn and maintain their parents' first language.

high blood sugar (hyperglycemia) An abnormally high amount of sugar in the bloodstream; usually associated with diabetes.

high functioning autism (HFA) Describes people with autistic disorder who are deemed to be cognitively high functioning but with delay in development of speech and language as well as deficits in social interaction.

high-interest, low-vocabulary books Written materials designed to interest and engage students while using simple vocabulary and uncomplicated sentence structure.

high-stakes tests Tests that influence whether students proceed to the next grade or graduate.

high task commitment Found in students who work hard and need little external motivation, especially in areas that interest them.

holding pattern A strategy teachers use when they have a misbehaving student wait (in the office, at the side of the classroom, immediately outside the door) until the teacher is available to meet and talk with the student.

homeless Those who have experienced the loss of their home are often thrust away from community, friends, and support systems.

homework Tasks assigned to students by their teachers to be completed at home.

homophobia Discrimination against people who are gay or lesbian that often takes the form of taunts, ridicule, and physical assaults.

hundreds chart A chart containing the numbers from 1 to 100 or 0 to 99 in rows and columns; used to help students learn the meaning of place value and relationships among numbers.

hydrocephalus A condition characterized by an excessive accumulation of cerebrospinal fluid in the brain due to an obstruction of its flow.

hyperactivity Characterized by fidgeting, squirming, moving constantly, talking excessively, and finding it challenging to play or work quietly.

hypersensitive Tendency to be extremely sensitive to sensory stimuli, such as touch, and to engage in unusual behaviour to obtain a particular sensory stimulation.

I

Identification, Placement, and Review Committee (IPRC) In Ontario, this committee, consisting of the teacher, special educators, administrators, and parents, meets to consider whether a child is exceptional and recommends a placement prior to the IEP meeting.

immigrant A person who has come to Canada as a permanent resident from a foreign country.

impulsivity Characteristics include blurting out answers before the teacher has finished asking a question, not waiting for one's turn, and interrupting other students.

inattentiveness Characterized by ignoring details, making careless errors, having trouble concentrating and staying on task while working or playing.

inclusion The social value and policy that persons with disabilities are entitled to full participation in all aspects of Canadian society, including education.

inclusive post-secondary education (IPSE) Programs that enable youth with intellectual or developmental disabilities to continue learning in post-secondary institutions after they have exceeded the provincial age limit for receiving services in secondary school.

individual education plan (IEP) A written plan developed for an exceptional student that describes the accommodations, modifications, and services to be provided.

individual program plan (IPP) The form that an IEP takes in some provinces (e.g., Alberta, Nova Scotia).

individual support services plan (ISSP) The form that an IEP takes in Newfoundland and Labrador, where a number of government departments collaborate to provide integrated services.

inflammation A localized physical condition with heat, swelling, and pain.

informal assessment Testing carried out by the classroom teacher or the resource teacher that provides information about an exceptional student's current level of functioning.

informal conference A behaviour management technique in which a teacher and student meet to define the problem clearly, generate solutions together, and agree on what each will do to implement the solution.

information processing The human mind's activity of taking in, storing, and using information.

in-school suspension Student attends school, completes work, but spends the day in a suspension room away from peers and social interaction.

in-school teams Solution finding groups whose purpose is to provide a forum for dialogue by parents, teachers, and other professionals about the needs of exceptional students.

intellectual disabilities (ID) Refer to an individual's functioning within the community and limitations in both intelligence and adaptive skills.

intelligence Ability or abilities to acquire and use knowledge for solving problems and adapting to the world.

interest An affective interaction between students and tasks.

interpersonal competence The abilities needed for friendships, including initiating and sustaining conversation, initiating plans to spend time with friends outside of school, disclosing personal thoughts and empathy, and managing conflict effectively.

"invisible" classroom management Techniques used by teachers to increase students' appropriate behaviour so that they rarely have to draw attention to inappropriate behaviour.

J

juvenile arthritis (JA) A chronic arthritic condition with continuous inflammation of one or more joints, stiffness, pain, and possible involvement of the eyes.

L

labour market information Details about current and projected demand for labour services and about supply of labour services in the economy.

language impairment Language is disordered when a student has impairment in expressive or receptive language.

large-scale assessment Nationwide, province-wide, or district-wide efforts to provide information about student achievement, usually by means of paper and pencil tests.

learned helplessness The expectation, based on previous experiences with a lack of control, that all one's efforts will lead to failure.

learning and behaviour exceptionalities Exceptionalities that are often apparent in the school context, if not before, that affect how students learn and regulate their own behaviour in a classroom context.

learning disabilities (LD) Dysfunctions in processing information that may occur in reading, writing, or arithmetic calculations; often defined as a discrepancy between ability and achievement despite average or above-average intelligence.

leukemia A type of cancer that forms in the bone marrow, causing abnormal white blood cell development.

low blood sugar (hypoglycemia) The condition in which there is an abnormally low amount of sugar in the bloodstream; a complication of diabetes.

low-key interventions Minimal actions taken by teachers to respond to minor misbehaviours so that the teachers' actions do not disrupt the flow of the class and to de-escalate rather than raise the stakes.

M

manipulatives Learning materials children can handle to aid learning, such as counters when adding in arithmetic.

medical conditions Chronic health conditions include medical conditions like asthma, juvenile arthritis, and diabetes for which children receive ongoing medical treatment.

mental health Refers to a state of well-being in which an individual realizes his potential, can cope with the normal stresses of life, and is able to contribute to the community.

metacognition Knowledge and monitoring of our own thinking.

method of presentation The means used to communicate information to students, including oral, visual, videorecorded demonstration, live demonstration, and hands-on techniques.

mild intellectual disability (MID) A less severe level of intellectual disability; individuals often learn successfully in regular classrooms and attain considerable independence.

modifications Changes made to the content of the learning expectations, making them substantially different from the prescribed curriculum for the student's grade placement, and specifically selected to meet the exceptional student's needs in accordance with the IEP.

monitoring The process of the teacher being alert and responsive to student action as part of classroom management.

moral leadership Refers to an approach to school leadership that emphasizes acting on personal and community values.

muscular dystrophy (MD) A group of muscle disorders characterized by progressive weakness and wasting away of the voluntary muscles that control body movement.

musculoskeletal conditions Chronic health conditions that affect the muscles and the skeleton and that can affect all aspects of a student's life (e.g., muscular dystrophy and juvenile arthritis).

N

naming speed Describes how quickly individuals can name aloud objects, pictures, colours, or symbols (letters or digits). Variations in naming speed in children provide a strong predictor of their later ability to read. Sometimes called rapid naming.

narrative text Written expression that is intended to tell a story.

natural consequences Punishment in which a student suffers the logical outcome of a misbehaviour (e.g., a student removing pencil marks from a desk after writing on the desk).

needs Areas in which an exceptional student has relatively weak abilities and skills that need to be developed or bypassed in her education by drawing on or compensating with areas of relative strength; schools often focus on academic, social/emotional, and behavioural needs in preparing a student's IEP.

neglect Omission on the part of parent or caregiver to provide a child with the basic necessities such as food, clothing, shelter, adequate supervision, or medical care.

nervous system impairment Results of damage or dysfunction of the brain or spinal cord that may have occurred before, during, or after birth; examples of exceptionalities are cerebral palsy, spina bifida, epilepsy, Tourette syndrome, brain injury, and fetal alcohol syndrome.

neurological dysfunction See *nervous system impairment*.

norm-referenced Data in which a student's work is compared to the work of other students who are comparable in age or grade.

norms for classroom interaction Expectations and rules about how students will initiate interactions with and respond to one another: effective communication and respectful interaction in conversation and discussion.

number sense Essential sense of what numbers mean, how to compare numbers, and how to see and count quantities in the world around us.

O

open-ended assignment Students are given options for completing an assignment and decide how far to take their learning.

opinion essays A form of writing in which personal opinion is expressed through a position statement and subsequently supported by arguments that justify the position taken.

organic cause Physical or physiological basis for a disability.

P

pace The rate of presentation of new information or rate of introduction of new skills.

parent advocacy The experience of parents speaking on behalf of their exceptional children and often on behalf of others as well.

parent–teacher conferences Formal meetings of parents and teachers at regular intervals during the school year and more frequent informal discussions that can build a productive partnership.

partial fetal alcohol syndrome (pFAS) Less obvious and seemingly milder than fetal alcohol syndrome with few or no facial abnormalities; however, learning and behaviour deficits are enduring.

partial seizures Epileptic seizures that involve one area of the brain; there may be strange sensations, possibly accompanied by inappropriate movements such as plucking at clothes or books, smacking the lips, or aimless wandering but without complete consciousness being lost.

partners thinking aloud A collaborative learning activity in which students work in pairs, alternating roles of teacher and learner with the learner thinking aloud and the teacher offering prompts and feedback; can be used for guided practise.

peer perspectives The views of classmates on their relationships with children and adolescents with disabilities, in the literature on social relationships of exceptional children.

peer teaching Has been called peer tutoring, peer-assisted learning, and peer-mediated instruction; refers to students helping one another to learn by serving as peer teaching partners.

performance assessment Assessment that provides opportunities for students to demonstrate directly their ability to combine and use their knowledge, skills, and habits of mind.

perseveration Repeating an activity.

personal program plan (PPP) The form that the IEP takes in some provinces (e.g., Saskatchewan).

phonemic awareness Sensitivity to and explicit awareness of individual sounds that make up words, which demands that children analyze or manipulate the sounds (includes early skills such as recognizing rhyming and later skills such as segmenting and synthesizing the sounds in words).

phonics Stresses sound–symbol relationships, helping learners to match the letters of the alphabet to the already known speech sounds.

physical disabilities A range of conditions restricting physical movement or motor abilities as a result of nervous system impairment, musculoskeletal conditions, or chronic medical disorders.

physical exceptionalities See *physical disabilities*.

physical space The physical layout and areas of a classroom that can make it inviting, accessible, and efficient (including arrangement of furniture, audiovisual equipment, visual aids, etc.).

portfolio A collection of the student's work in an area showing growth, self-reflection, and achievement.

positive behavioural supports An approach to dealing with problem behaviours that focuses on the remediation of deficient contexts documented to be the source of the problems, with the emphasis on altering the environment before a problem behaviour occurs or teaching appropriate behaviours as a strategy for eliminating the need for problem behaviours to be exhibited.

post-reading activities Activities following individual, paired, or group reading of an assigned piece of text; usually include application of what has been read and a review of learning by the teacher.

poverty Insufficient access to the basic goods, services, and opportunities accepted as necessary for a decent standard of living in Canada, as defined by the Canadian Council on Social Development and Statistics Canada.

prenatal exposure to alcohol Maternal use of alcohol during pregnancy.

pre-reading activities Activities that occur prior to individual, paired, or group reading of an assigned piece of text and usually include an introduction to the topic and the vocabulary and a preview of the text by the teacher.

pre-referral intervention Actions taken by a teacher, possibly with the aid of a resource teacher, after the teacher has voiced concerns about a student and before the student has been referred for formal assessment.

preteaching The technique of preparing exceptional students, frequently used with students who are deaf or hard of hearing, by teaching them the vocabulary and concepts prior to introducing new material to the entire class.

preventers Anti-inflammatory drugs taken regularly to prevent and treat inflammation in persons with asthma.

principles of fairness See *fairness*.

pro-act The actions of teachers effective at classroom management who appear to respond to misbehaviour at a moment's notice; they actually anticipate and act almost before the behaviour occurs (Henley, 2006).

problem solving Using generic or ad hoc methods in an orderly manner to find solutions to problems.

problem-solving approach A behaviour management technique in which the teacher asks students questions about what they think the problem was, what they did to contribute to the problem, how they can make amends, and how they can prevent the problem from recurring, and then the teacher follows up.

progress monitoring Regular collection of data to compare a student's academic progress on specific skills to previous achievement and to the goals set for the student.

progressive discipline policy A sequence of gradually more stern responses from classroom detention to in-school suspension.

prosocial behaviours Voluntary behaviours, intended to benefit others and contribute to the social functioning of a group.

puffer A small device that delivers medication in a premeasured amount to persons with asthma; sometimes called an inhaler.

punishment A response or consequence aimed at decreasing the likelihood of an inappropriate behaviour.

Q

qualitative rubrics Descriptions of learning that characterize learning at various levels and provide students with information about the next steps they must tackle in order to improve.

quantitative rubrics Descriptions of learning that identify that students with higher achievement have greater quantities of valued responses such as some of the main ideas, most of the main ideas, or all of the main ideas.

R

rapid naming (or rapid automatized naming (RAN)) Describes how quickly individuals can name aloud objects, pictures, colours, or symbols (letters or digits). Variations in naming speed in children provide a strong predictor of their later ability to read. Sometimes called *naming speed*.

reading comprehension Reading skill involving understanding the meaning of what has been read.

reasons why students act the way they do Students may act in ways that seem inappropriate to teachers for many reasons. Teachers need to try to understand the reasons rather than make assumptions or take it personally.

reciprocal teaching A teaching approach that involves enabling students to teach one another by taking turns leading discussion in small groups; usually the teacher models how to lead the discussion and provides scaffolding for the groups as they begin.

refugee A person who has left his home country and seeks refuge in Canada from war, persecution, or a natural disaster.

relationships While students' relationships and social interactions with peers are important, so are their relationships and social interactions with teachers. Students say the most important thing they need at school are teachers willing to "be there" for them.

relievers Rescue medications to relax the muscles of the airways and provide quick relief of breathing problems for persons with asthma.

remediation Intensive instruction, to address basic skills in an area in which a student has needs, that can be carried out with an individual or a small group in the classroom or in a resource room.

remission Temporary disappearance of the symptoms of a health condition or disease.

Report of the Royal Commission on Aboriginal Peoples (RCAP) In 1991 four Aboriginal and three non-Aboriginal commissioners were appointed to investigate Aboriginal issues and advise the federal government; one of their major recommendations was to end assimilation of Aboriginal peoples.

reporting The way in which evaluation results are communicated, including individual student report cards, which can be computer generated or written by teachers.

resilient students Generally resilience is thought to refer to positive adaptation in the face of adversity; recent research suggests we emphasize the need for individuals to exercise enough personal agency to navigate, or make their way to, the resources they require to meet their needs and to negotiate for what they need, and the importance of families, communities, and schools enabling such agency.

resource teacher A special educator who supports teachers and exceptional students, usually by consulting with teachers and offering some direct services to exceptional students, either in the classroom or in the resource room; can have many titles, including learning assistance teacher, learning program teacher, tutor, and curriculum resource teacher.

response to intervention (RTI) A way of thinking about how we can intervene before students fail by intensifying and improving teaching for struggling learners.

restorative justice Challenges students to hold themselves and each other accountable to right wrongs, as individuals and as a group.

reward systems Teachers give students as a group or as individuals tokens or points in a systematic way for appropriate behaviour or work.

right to pass Students having the right to choose the extent to which they will participate in a group activity that requires sharing personal information; teachers acknowledge a pass by saying, "That is fine," and offer a second chance for those who passed (used in community circle; *Tribes,* Gibbs, 2001).

rubrics Descriptions of learning at different levels of development; can be quantitative or qualitative descriptions.

rules Expressions of what can and cannot be done in the classroom that are brief and specific, positively worded, and clearly understood by students.

S

scaffolded reading experience (SRE) Designed for classes with students of varying abilities in reading, it involves teachers in adapting the three steps of pre-reading, reading, and post-reading activities by providing varying degrees of support so all students can learn.

scaffolding Support for learning and problem solving; can be clues, reminders, encouragement, breaking the problem into parts, or anything that enables a student to grow in independence as a learner.

school-based team A team of teachers, specialists, and administrators that problem solves about students experiencing academic or behaviour difficulties and decides whether students should be individually assessed for an IEP.

schoolwide approach A program that is adopted, implemented, and enforced throughout a school; for example, a code of conduct or anti-bullying policy that is applied in every part of the school.

schoolwide behaviour management systems Comprehensive behaviour management systems that are adopted collaboratively and consistently throughout a school and tend to lead to positive outcomes in behaviour.

schoolwide positive behaviour support (SWPBS) A prevention-oriented approach that defines and teaches behaviour expectations, rewards appropriate behaviour, and integrates support for individuals, groups, and the whole school.

seizures Brief bursts of electrical activity in the brain.

self-advocacy An individual's ability to effectively communicate, convey, negotiate, or assert her own interests, desires, needs, and rights.

self-awareness Knowing about oneself; developing a picture of the kind of person one is.

self-care The personal care activities that maintain hygiene and health.

self-concept Our perceptions about ourselves.

self-efficacy One's judgment of one's own ability to complete a specific task or reach a specific goal.

self-determination The abilities, motivation, and volition that enable people to define goals for themselves and to take and sustain the initiative to reach those goals.

self-monitoring A strategy in which students are taught to check whether they have performed targeted behaviours.

self-regulation Learners proactively monitoring, directing, and regulating their behaviour to achieve self-set goals of acquiring knowledge and expanding expertise, with the emphasis on autonomy and control by the individual.

severe intellectual disabilities Includes those previously described as moderate, severe, or profound disabilities, spanning a range of abilities from those who can acquire academic skills to those who require assistance with self-care.

sexual harassment Includes put-downs and negative comments made about gender or sexual preference, sexist jokes, and calling someone gay or lesbian.

shunt A mechanism installed to drain the fluid that builds up with hydrocephalus, for reabsorption in individuals with spina bifida.

signal The means used by teachers to obtain and maintain the attention of students, including flicking the lights, raising a hand, rhythmic clapping or speaking, or even blowing a whistle in the gymnasium; usually taught to classes at the beginning of term.

simple absence seizure (petit mal) This generalized seizure occurs in children; they stare or daydream for 5 to 15 seconds and there may be small muscle movements in the face, the eyes may roll up or to one side, and the child may be confused about the seconds "missed."

social acceptance The response and evaluation by peers of students' social behaviours, including approving of their behaviours, considering them to be members of the group, and including them in social and learning activities.

social competence See *social development*.

social development The ability to implement developmentally appropriate social behaviours that enhance one's interpersonal relationships without causing harm to anyone.

social exclusion Students not experiencing inclusive environments where they feel like they belong and are part of the group.

social relationships Friendships, peer relations, and romantic relationships that change with development; for example, by middle childhood, children choose friends on the basis of personality and interests and friendships become increasingly stable.

social status A rating of a child's or adolescent's popularity with their classmates, that is, how well they are liked.

social stories Describe a situation from the perspective of a student, direct the student to do the appropriate behaviour, and are in the first person; developed by Gray (2002) for children with autistic disorder.

sociometric rating A system of collecting data by asking children to indicate which classmates they would choose as best friends, to play with, etc., and which they would not choose; enables researchers to develop ratings of popularity or social status for individual students.

special education programming Programs or services designed to accommodate students whose educational needs cannot adequately be met through the use of regular curriculum and services only.

special education plan (SEP) The term used in New Brunswick for an IEP.

speech and language disorders These exceptionalities refer to problems encountered in the oral production of language and/or impairment in the use or comprehension of spoken language that interfere with communication.

speech impairment Speech is disordered when it deviates so far from the speech of other people that it calls attention to itself, interferes with communication, or causes the speaker or listeners distress.

speech-reading The skill of understanding speech by watching the lips and face; sometimes called lip-reading.

spina bifida A condition developed prenatally that disturbs proper development of the vertebrae or spinal cord and results in varying degrees of damage to the spinal cord and nervous system.

stimulants A class of medications (e.g., Ritalin) commonly used as treatment for ADHD.

story-planning sheet Scaffolding to help students create narrative text that includes prompts such as the following: setting, main character, character clues, problem, attempts to solve the problem, and resolution.

strengths Areas in which an exceptional student has relatively strong abilities and skills on which to draw in compensating or learning in areas of relative weakness; schools often focus on academic, social/emotional, and behavioural strengths in preparing a student's IEP.

structure A high level of organization, support, and predictability that can benefit exceptional learners in the classroom.

student support plan (SSP) Required by the Northwest Territories if a student has a modified education plan based on outcomes in the NWT curriculum.

summative assessment Tests administered after learning was presumed to have taken place, intended to provide students and their parents with a summary of the students' learning and relative standing (presently referred to as assessment *of* learning).

suspension Temporary removal of a student from the classroom (for a day or more) as a consequence of the student behaving inappropriately, violating the code of conduct, etc.

T

teacher–student relationships How teachers treat children contributes to children's socio-emotional development, including treating children with respect and getting to know their interests, strengths, and needs.

testing A form of assessment, normally using a paper and pencil test (either designed by the teacher or commercially available) to gather information that describes a student's or a group's level of performance.

theory of mind The notion that others think, feel, and know; Lombardo and Baron-Cohen (2011) hypothesized that people with autistic disorder do not have a theory of mind.

thinking aloud Teachers or peers can make the invisible visible by verbalizing their thoughts and showing students how to use a strategy, solve a problem, etc.

three-block model An approach to universal design for learning with three distinct parts: (a) creating community, (b) planning for diversity through differentiated instruction, (c) systems and structures for inclusion, such as policies.

tics Involuntary, rapid, sudden muscular movements; uncontrollable vocal sounds; and inappropriate words (seen in Tourette syndrome).

tiered instruction Teaching one concept or lesson, but meeting different learning needs by varying aspects such as the presentation, task, materials, and product.

tiering assignments Presenting assessment at varying levels of complexity on the same content for all students; often matched with tiered instruction that groups students based on their current understanding.

tonic-clonic (grand mal) seizure In this generalized seizure, the individual sometimes gives a sharp cry before falling to the floor, the muscles stiffen then begin to jerk rhythmically, and there may be loss of bladder control, some breathing difficulty, and saliva may gather at the mouth.

Tourette syndrome (TS) A neurological disorder involving motor tics and uncontrollable vocal sounds or inappropriate words that are often accompanied by obsessions and hyperactivity.

transient lifestyle A way of living adopted by homeless people who move from shelter to shelter; often seen in adolescents who have left home.

transition plan A formal, written plan that some provinces require, for students with an IEP, to ensure that preparation for post-secondary endeavours begins early in the high school years.

transition planning meeting A meeting with a student, the family, educators, and service providers to plan the services, placement, etc. that a student will receive following the transition from one level or type of schooling to another.

transition to post-secondary education (PSE) The process of moving from secondary school to the next level of education (formal or informal).

transition to school The experience of young children moving from pre-school contexts, such as formal ECE programs or informal experiences, into school (usually to kindergarten).

transition to work The process of adolescents and young adults moving from school contexts (secondary or post-secondary) to the world of work.

transitions Changes experienced in the experience of schooling (can take many forms).

traumatic brain injury (TBI) Occurs when an external force traumatically injures the brain. Causes include falls, vehicle accidents, sports injuries, and violence.

TTYPA A collaborative learning activity in which a teacher stops and tells the students to "turn to your partner and . . . introduce yourself, or . . . describe a time when you . . ." Then the students switch roles.

Twinject Brand name of an easily administered epinephrine injection for the emergency treatment of those with severe allergies, including anaphylactic reactions.

U

ulcerative colitis (UC) A form of inflammatory bowel disease in which the area of the gastrointestinal tract that is affected is the large intestine, that is, the colon.

universal design for learning (UDL) The design of instructional materials and activities that allows the learning goals to be achievable by individuals with wide differences in their abilities to see, hear, speak, move, etc. by means of flexible curricular materials and activities designed to include alternatives for students with diversity in abilities and backgrounds.

V

verbal reprimand Punishment in which a student is reminded of the classroom rules; the most effective reprimands are immediate, unemotional, brief, and backed up with a time out or loss of privileges.

visual impairment Disability characterized by partial or complete loss of sight and use of auditory and tactile sources of information to supplement or replace sight.

visual schedule A representation of the day's activities in order, in pictorial form, especially helpful for pre-literate students.

vocabulary The kind and level of language used in oral and written expression to communicate meaning to students; can also refer to the kind and level of language used in oral and written expression by students.

voice synthesizer Converts information typed or scanned into a computer into speech.

W

wheezing Breathing with an audible chesty, whistling sound; a symptom of an asthma episode.

workplace experience Involves students for brief periods of time in a workplace (ranging from one-day job-shadowing experiences to a few half-day visits) within the context of a credit course.

Z

zone of proximal development (ZPD) Distance between a child's development as shown in independent problem solving and the level of potential development as determined through problem solving with adult guidance or collaboration with more capable peers; from the work of Vygotsky.

References

A'Bear, D. (2014). Supporting the learning of children with chronic illness. *Canadian Journal of Action Research, 15*(1), 22–39.

Aburn, G., & Gott, M. (2014). Education given to parents of children newly diagnosed with acute lymphoblastic leukemia: The parent's perspective. *Pediatric Nursing, 40*(5), 243–256.

Adams, L.D., & Kirova, A. (2007). *Global migration and education.* Mahwah, NJ: Lawrence Erlbaum Associates.

Adams, M., Foorman, B., Lundberg, I., & Beeler, T. (1998). *Phoneme awareness in young children.* Toronto, ON: Irwin Publishing.

Adelman, H.S., & Taylor. L.L. (2006). *The school leader's guide to student learning supports: New directions for addressing barriers to learning.* Thousand Oaks, CA: Corwin.

Adesope, O., & Nesbit, J. (2013). Animated and static concept maps enhance learning from spoken narration. *Learning and Instruction, 27,* 1–10.

Ainscow, M., Booth, T., & Dyson, A. (1999). Inclusion and exclusion in schools: Listening to some hidden voices. In K. Ballard (Ed.), *Inclusive education: International voices on disability and justice* (pp.139–151). London, UK: Falmer Press.

Akinbami, L.J., Moorman, J.E., Garbe, P.L., & Sondik, E.J. (2009). Status of childhood asthma in the United States, 1980–2007. *Pediatrics, 123*(3), S131–S145.

Alber, S.R., & Heward, W.L. (1997). Recruit it or lose it: Teaching students to recruit contingent teacher attention. *Intervention in School and Clinic, 5,* 275–282.

Alberta Education. (n.d.). *Differentiated Instruction: An Introduction.* Retrieved from http://education.alberta.ca/media/1233952/4_ch1%20intro.pdf

Alberta Education. (2010a). *Making a difference: Meeting diverse learning needs with differentiated instruction.* Edmonton, AB: Government of Alberta, Education.

Alberta Learning. (2002). *First Nations, Métis and Inuit education policy framework: A progress report.* Edmonton, AB: Alberta Learning.

Alberta Learning. (2004). *Standards for special education.* Edmonton, AB: Alberta Learning.

Al-Darayseh, A. (2014). The impact of using explicit/implicit vocabulary teaching strategies on improving students' vocabulary and reading comprehension. *Theory and Practice in Language Studies, 4*(6), 1109–1118.

Ališauskaitė, I., & Butkienė, D. (2013). Emotion perception from situation: Comparing the abilities of children with intellectual disability and children with regular development. *Special Education, 2,* 37–46.

Allor, J.H., & Chard, D.J. (2011). A comprehensive approach to improving reading fluency for students with disabilities. *Focus on Exceptional Children, 43*(5), 1–12.

Alvi, S., Scott, H., & Stanyon, W. (2010). "We're locking the door": Family histories in a sample of homeless youth. *Qualitative Report, 15*(5), 1209–1226.

American Psychiatric Association (APA) (2000/2004). *Diagnostic and statistical manual of mental disorders* (4th ed., *DSM-IV-TR*). Washington, DC: APA.

American Psychiatric Association (APA) (2013). *Diagnostic and statistical manual of mental disorders* (5th ed., *DSM-5*). Washington, DC: APA.

Anderson, K. (2004). Speaking from the heart: Everyday storytelling and adult learning. *Canadian Journal of Native Education, 28,* 123–129.

Anderson, K.M. (2007). Differentiating instruction to include all students. *Preventing School Failure, 51*(3), 49–54.

Anderson, K.L., & Goldstein, H. (2004). Speech perception benefits of FM and infrared devices in children with hearing aids in a typical classroom. *Speech and Language Services in Schools, 35,* 169–184.

Andersson, U. (2010). Skill development in different components of arithmetic and basic cognitive functions: Findings from a 3-year longitudinal study of children with different types of learning difficulties. *Journal of Educational Psychology, 102*(1), 115–134.

Anuncibay, R. (2007). Social, personal and educational constraints on access to employment among groups at risk of social exclusion: Contributions from an employment observatory. *Journal of Vocational Education and Training, 59*(4), 435–449.

Armstrong, M.I., Birnie-Lefcovitch, S., & Ungar, M.T. (2005). Pathways between social support, family well being, quality of parenting, and child resilience: What we know. *Journal of Child and Family Studies, 14*(2), 269–281.

Arnett, A., Pennington, B., Willcutt, E., DeFries, J., & Olson, R. (2015). Sex differences in ADHD symptom severity. *Journal of Child Psychology & Psychiatry, 56*(6), 632–639.

Arvio, M., & Sillanpaa, M. (2003). Prevalence, aetiology and comorbidity of severe and profound intellectual disability in Finland. *Journal of Intellectual Disability Research, 47*(2), 108–112.

Assouline, S.G., Nicpon, M.F., & Whiteman, C. (2010). Cognitive and psychosocial characteristics of gifted students with written language disability. *Gifted Child Today, 54*(2), 102–115.

Atleo, S. (2013). Open letter to the Minister of Aboriginal Affairs and Northern Development Canada. Ottawa, ON.

AuCoin, A., & Porter, G. (2013). The role of the resource teacher in an inclusive setting. *Education Canada, 53*(2), 24–27.

Autin, D. (2014). Preparing for the new school year: Tips and tools. *Exceptional Parent, 44*(5), 54–55.

Axelrod, P. (2015). Banning the strap: The end of corporal punishment in Canadian schools. *Education Canada, 55*(1), online.

Azano, A., & Tuckwiller, E.D. (2011). GPS for the English classroom: Understanding executive dysfunction in secondary students with autism. *Teaching Exceptional Children, 42*(6), 38–45.

Azmitia, M., Ittel, A., & Radmacher, K. (2005). Narratives of friendship and self in adolescence. In N. Way & J.V. Hamm (Eds.), The experience of close friendships in adolescence. *New Directions for Child and Adolescent Development,* (107), 23–39.

Azmitia, M., & Montgomery, R. (1993). Friendship, transactive dialogues, and the development of scientific reasoning. *Social Development, 2,* 202–221.

Azzopardi, A. (2011). Conceptualising discursive communities: Developing community in contemporary society. *International Journal of Inclusive Education, 15*(1), 179–192.

Baboudjan, N., Corrigan, S., Grant, N., Lavender, J., & Sullivan, N. (Spring, 2011). Creating positive space. *Education Forum (of OSSTF), 37*(2), 24–27.

Bacon, J.K., & Causton-Theoharis, J. (2013). "It should be teamwork": A critical investigation of school practices and parent advocacy in special education. *International Journal of Inclusive Education, 17*(7), 682–699.

Baker, J.M. (2005). How homophobia hurts children: Nurturing diversity at home, at school, and in the community. Florence, KY: Routledge.

Baldwin, L., Omdal, S.N., & Pereles, D. (2014). Beyond stereotypes: Understanding, recognizing, and working with twice-exceptional learners. *Teaching Exceptional Children, 47*(4), 216–225.

Ballard, K., & McDonald, T. (1999). Disability inclusion and exclusion: Some insider accounts and interpretations. In K. Ballard (Ed.), *Inclusive education: International voices on disability and justice* (pp. 97–115). London, UK: Falmer Press.

Banda, D.R., Grimmett, E., & Hart, S.L. (2009). Activity schedules: Helping students with autism spectrum disorders in general education classrooms manage transition issues. *Teaching Exceptional Children, 41*(4), 16–21.

Bandura, A. (1994). *Self-efficacy in changing societies.* New York, NY: Cambridge University Press.

Bandura, A. (2011) Entry in *Concise Corsini encyclopedia of psychology and behavioral science.* Wiley online library.

Bangou, F., & Fleming, D. (2014, Spring). Citizenship, becoming, literacy and schools: Immigrant students in a Canadian secondary school. *Our Schools/Our Selves,* 91–99.

Barger, R.H. (2009). Gifted, talented, and high achieving. *Teaching Children Mathematics, 16*(3), 154–161.

Barker, J. (2005). *Evaluating Web pages: Techniques to apply and questions to ask.* http://www.lib.berkeley.edu/TeachingLib/Guides/Internet/Evaluate.html

Barkley, R.A. (2010). Against the status quo: Revising the diagnostic criteria for ADHD. *Journal of the American Academy of Child and Adolescent Psychiatry, 49*(3), 205–207.

Barkley, R.A. (2012). *Executive functions: What they are, how they work, and why they evolved.* New York, NY: Guilford Press.

Barnes, M., Faulkner, H., Wilkinson, M., & Dennis, M. (2004). Meaning construction and integration in children with hydrocephalus. *Brain and Language, 89,* 47–56.

Barnes, M., & Wade-Woolley, L. (2007). Where there's a will there are ways to close the achievement gap for children with learning difficulties. *Orbit Magazine, 37*(1), 9–13.

Barnes, M., Wilkinson, M., Khemani, E., Boudesquie, A., Dennis, M., & Fletcher, J. (2006). Arithmetic process in children with spina bifida: Calculation accuracy, strategy use, and fact retrieval fluency. *Journal of Learning Disabilities, 39*(2), 174–187.

Barr, H.M., & Streissguth, A.P. (2006). *Fetal alcohol syndrome.* Toronto, ON: Brookes.

Basch, C.E. (2011). Asthma and the achievement gap among urban minority youth. *Journal of School Health, 81*(10), 606–613.

Bauer, K., Iyer, S., Boon, R., & Fore, C. (2010). 20 ways for classroom teachers to collaborate with speech-language pathologists. *Intervention in School and Clinic, 45*(5), 333–337.

Bauman, S. (2010). School counselors and survivors of childhood cancer: Reconceptualizing and advancing the cure. *Professional School Counseling, 14*(2), 156–164.

Bauman, S., Toomey, R.B., & Walker, J.L. (2013). Associations among bullying, cyberbullying, and suicide in high school students. *Journal of Adolescence, 36,* 341–350.

Bazelon, E. (2013). Sticks and stones: Defeating the culture of bullying and rediscovering the power of character and empathy. New York, NY: Random House.

Beal-Alvarez, J.S., Lederberg, A.R., & Easterbrooke, S.R. (2012). Grapheme-phoneme acquisition of deaf preschoolers. *Journal of Deaf Studies and Deaf Education, 17*(1), 39–60.

Beck, I.L., & McKeown, M.G. (2007). Increasing young low-income children's oral vocabulary repertoires through rich and focused instruction. *Elementary School Journal, 107,* 251–273.

Belanger, J., & Gagné, F. (2006). Estimating the size of the gifted/talented population from multiple identification criteria. *Journal for the Education of the Gifted, 30*(2), 131–163.

Bell, D. (2004). *Sharing our success: Ten case studies in Aboriginal schooling.* Kelowna, BC: Society for the Advancement of Excellence in Education.

Bell, N. (2013). Just do it: Anishinaabe culture-based education. *Canadian Journal of Native Education, 36*(1), 36–58.

Bellanti, C. (2011). Meeting the needs of children with ADHD in the classroom. *The Brown University Child and Adolescent Behavior Newsletter, 27*(12), 1, 5–6.

Beltman, S., Mansfield, C., & Price, A. (2011). Thriving not just surviving: A review of research on teacher resilience. *Educational Research Review, 6,* 185–207.

Ben Jaafar, S. (2006). From performance-based to inquiry-based accountability. *Brock Education, 16,* 62–77.

Ben Jaafar, S., & Anderson, S. (2007). Policy trends and tensions in accountability for educational management and services in Canada. *Alberta Journal of Educational Research, 53*(2), 207–228.

Bennett, S., Good, D., & Kumpf, J. (2003). *Educating educators about ABI: Resource book.* St. Catharines, ON: Ontario Brain Injury Association.

Bennett, S., Weber, K., & Dworet, D. (2008). *Special education in Ontario schools* (6th ed.). St. David's, ON: Highland Press.

Bennett, T., Szatmari, P., et al. (2014). Language impairment and social competence in preschoolers with autism spectrum disorders: A comparison of DSM-5 profiles. *Journal of Autism and Developmental Disabilities, 44*(11), 2797–2808.

Beran, T.N. (2006). A construct validity study of bullying. *Alberta Journal of Educational Research, 52,* 241–250.

Beran, T.N., Hughes, G., & Lupart, J. (2008). A model of achievement and bullying: Analyses of the Canadian National Longitudinal Survey of Children and Youth data. *Educational Research, 50,* 25–39.

Berg, D.H. (2006). *Role of processing speed and working memory in children's mental addition,* (Unpublished doctoral thesis). Queen's University, Kingston, ON.

Berg, D.H. (2008). Working memory and arithmetic calculation in children: The contributory roles of processing speed, short-term memory, and reading. *Journal of Experimental Child Psychology, 99*(4), 288–308.

Berg, D.H., & Hutchinson, N.L. (2010). Cognitive processes that account for mental addition fluency differences between children typically achieving in arithmetic and children at-risk for failure in arithmetic. *Learning Disabilities: A Contemporary Journal, 8*(1), 1–20.

Berliner, D.C. (2009). *Poverty and potential: Out-of-school factors and school success.* Boulder, CO: Education and the Public Interest Center and Education Policy Research Unit. Retrieved at http://epicpolicy.org/publication/poverty-and-potential

Berman, S. (2008). *Performance-based learning: Aligning experiential tasks and assessment to increase learning.* Thousand Oaks, CA: Corwin Press.

Berne, J., & Degener, S.C. (2012). *Strategic reading groups: Guiding readers in the middle grades.* Thousand Oaks, CA: Corwin (Sage).

Berninger, V.W., & May, M.O. (2011). Evidence-based diagnosis and treatment for specific learning disabilities involving impairments in written and oral language. *Journal of Learning Disabilities, 44*(2), 167–183.

Berninger, V.W., Rutberg, J.E., Abbott, R.D., Garcia, N., Anderson-Younstrom, M., Brooks, A., & Fulton, C. (2006). Tier 1 and tier 2 early intervention for handwriting and composing. *Journal of School Psychology, 44*(1), 3–30.

Berry, R.A.W. (2006). Inclusion, power, and community: Teachers and students interpret the language of community in an inclusive classroom. *American Educational Research Journal, 43,* 489–529.

Bertrand, J. (2009). Interventions for children with fetal alcohol spectrum disorders (FASDs). *Research in Developmental Disabilities, 30*, 986–1006.

Bevans, K., Crespo, R., Forrest, C., Louis, T., & Riley, A. (2011). School outcomes of children with special health care needs. *Pediatrics, 128*(2), 303–312.

Billot, J., Goddard, J.T., & Cranston, N. (2007). How principals manage ethnocultural diversity: Learnings from three countries. *International Studies in Educational Administration, 35*(2), 3–19.

Bjorquist, E., Nordmark, E., & Hallstrom, I. (2015). Living in transition: Experiences of health and well-being and the needs of adolescents with cerebral palsy. *Child: Care, Health & Development, 41*(2), 258–265.

Blackbourn, V.A., & Blackbourn, J.M. (1993). An adolescent with moderate mental disabilities tutors a 1st-grade, nondisabled child. *Teaching Exceptional Children, 25*(4), 56–61.

Blasco, P.M., Saxton, S., & Gerrie, M. (2014). The little brain that could: Understanding executive function in early childhood. *Young Exceptional Children, 17*(3), 3–18.

Bloom, E.L., & Heath, N. (2009). Recognition, expression, and understanding facial expressions of emotion in adolescents with nonverbal and general learning disabilities. *Journal of Learning Disabilities, 43*(2), 180–192.

Bloom, E.L., Karagiannakis, A., Toste, J.R., Heath, N.L., & Konstantinopoulos, E. (2007). Severity of academic achievement and social skills deficits. *Canadian Journal of Education, 30*, 911–930.

Blum, H.T., Lipsett, L.R., & Yocom, D.J. (2002). Literature circles: A tool for self-determination in one middle school inclusive classroom. *Remedial and Special Education, 23*(2), 99–108.

Blumberg, S.J., Foster, E.B., & Frasier, A.M. (2007). Design and operation of the National Survey of Children's Health. *Vital Health Statistics, 1*, 23–39.

Boccanfuso, C., & Kuhfeld, M. (March, 2011). Multiple responses, promising results: evidence-based, nonpunitive alternatives to zero tolerance. *Research-to-Results Brief: Child Trends, 2011*(09). Retrieved from www.childtrends.org/Files/Child_Trends-2011_03_01_RB_AltToZeroTolerance.pdf

Boggan, M., Bifuh-Ambe, E., Harper, S., & Smith, I. (2009). Viva Saskatchewan! Improving school district teacher induction programs in the Katrina states by stealing ideas from our international neighbors. *Research in Higher Education Journal, 7*(1), 56–65.

Bohnert, A.M., Aikins, J.W., & Arola, N.T. (2013). Regrouping: Organized activity involvement and social adjustment across the transition to high school. *New Directions for Child and Adolescent Development, 140*, 57–75.

Bondy, E., Ross, D. D., Gallingane, C., & Hambacher, E. (2007). Creating environments of success and resilience: Culturally responsive classroom management and more. *Urban Education, 42*, 326–348.

Borowsky, I.W., Ireland, M., & Resnick, M.D. (2001). Adolescent suicide attempts: Risk and protectors. *Pediatrics, 107*(3), 485–493.

Bouck, E. (2013). Factors impacting receipt of a functional curriculum. *Education and Training in Autism and Developmental Disabilities, 48*(4), 522–530.

Bouck, E., & Satsangi, R. (2014). Evidence-base of a functional curriculum for secondary students with mild intellectual disability: A historical perspective. *Education & Training in Autism & Developmental Disabilities, 49*(3), 478–486.

Bouck, E., Satsangi, R., & Muhl, A. (2013). Using audio recorders to promote independence in grocery shopping for students with intellectual disability. *Journal of Special Education Technology, 28*(4), 15–26.

Bourget, B., & Chenier, R. (2007). *Mental Health Literacy in Canada: Phase One Report Mental Health Literacy Project*. Ottawa, ON: Canadian Alliance on Mental Illness and Mental Health.

Bowen, G.M., & Arsenault, N. (2008). It's all about choice. *Science Teacher, 75*(2), 34–37.

Bower, J.M., van Kraayenoord, C., & Carroll, A. (2015). Building social connectedness in schools: Australian teachers' perspectives. *International Journal of Educational Research, 70*, 101–109.

Bradford, S., Shippen, M., Alberto, P., Houchins, D., & Flores, M. (2006). Using systematic instruction to teach decoding skills to middle school students with moderate intellectual disabilities. *Education & Training in Developmental Disabilities, 41*(4), 333–343.

Brassell, D. (2009). Dare to differentiate: Vocabulary strategies for all students. *New England Reading Association Journal, 44*(2), 1–6.

Bray, M. Kehle, T., Loftus, G., Grigerich, S., & Nicholson, H. (2008). Children with asthma: Assessment and treatment in school settings. *Psychology in the Schools, 45*(1), 63–73.

Brazeau, C., & Charmly, S. (2014). *Hurt, help, healing, hope: Rethinking Canada's residential school history* (Primary resource teaching guide for the Ontario Curriculum, 2013, Grade 8 History; lesson plans and resources). Kingston, ON: QSpace at Queen's University. Retrieved at http://hdl.handle.net.proxy.queensu.ca/1974/12331

Brendtro, L., Brokenleg, M., Van Bockern, & Bluebird, G. (1990). *Reclaiming youth at risk: Our hope for the future*. Bloomington, IN: Solution Tree.

Brendtro, L., Bokenleg, M., & Van Bockern, S. (2014). Environments where children thrive: The Circle of Courage model. *Reclaiming Children & Youth, 23*(3), 10–15.

Brethwaite, K.S. (1996). Keeping watch over our children: The role of African Canadian parents on the education team. In K. S. Brethwaite & C. E. James (Eds.), *Educating African Canadians* (pp. 107–130). Toronto, ON: James Lorimer & Co.

Briand, P. (2011). *Multiple perspectives on the connection between temporary conductive hearing loss and reading development* (Unpublished Master's thesis). Queen's University, Kingston, ON.

Brislin, D.C. (2008). Reaching for independence: Counseling implications for youth with spina bifida. *Journal of Counseling and Development, 86*, 34–38.

British Columbia Education. (2006). *Manual of policies, procedures, and guidelines*. Victoria, BC: Ministry of Education.

British Columbia Ministry of Education. (2004). *Provincial student assessment program*. Victoria, BC: British Columbia Ministry of Education.

British Columbia Ministry of Education. (2006). *Shared learnings*. Victoria, BC: Author.

British Columbia Ministry of Education. (2011). *Special education services: A manual of policies, procedures and guidelines*. Victoria, British Columbia Ministry of Education.

British Columbia Ministry of Education. (2012). *Manual of policies, procedures, and guidelines (Section C)*. Victoria, BC: Ministry of Education.

British Columbia Special Education Branch. (2008). *Special education services: A manual of policies, procedures, and guidelines*. Victoria, BC: Queen's Printer for British Columbia. Retrieved from http://www.bced.gov.bc.ca/specialed/ppandg/toc.htm

Brock, C.H., Lapp, D., Flood, J., Fisher, D., & Keomghee, T.H. (2007). Does homework matter? An investigation of teacher perceptions about homework practices for children from nondominant backgrounds. *Urban Education, 42*, 349–372.

Brosvic, G.M., Dihoff, R.E., Epstein, M.L., & Cook, M.L. (2006). Feedback facilitates the acquisition and retention of numerical fact series by elementary school students with mathematics learning disabilities. *Psychological Record, 56*, 35–47.

Brown, L. (2008, May 20). Serving students in culturally clustered schools. *The Toronto Star*. Retrieved from http://www.thestar.com/life/health_wellness/2008/05/20/serving_students_in_culturally_clustered_schools.html

Brown, L.S., & Jellison, J.A. (2012). Music research with children and youth with disabilities and typically developing peers: A systematic review. *Journal of Music Therapy, 49*(3), 335–364.

Brown, T., & Amundson, N. (2010). Youth experience of trying to get off the street: What has helped and hindered? *Canadian Journal of Counselling and Psychotherapy, 44*(2). Retrieved from http://cjc-rcc.ucalgary.ca/cjc/index.php/rcc/article/view/389

Browne, A. (2007). *Teaching and learning communication, language and literacy.* Thousand Oaks, CA: Sage/Paul Chapman.

Browne-Dianis, J. (2011). Stepping back from zero tolerance. *Educational Leadership, 69*(1), 24–28.

Browning, F.C. (2008). Synchronizing loss with life over a life span: A dynamic perspective. *Adultspan: Theory Research and Practice, 7*(1), 26–31.

Brownlie, F., & King, J. (2000). *Learning in safe schools: Creating classrooms where all students belong.* Markham, ON: Pembroke Publishers.

Bryan, T., & Burstein, K. (2004). Improving homework completion and academic performance: Lessons from special education. *Theory Into Practice, 43*(3), 213–219.

Buchanan, D., Colton, P., & Chamberlain, K. (2010). *Making a difference: An educator's guide to child and youth mental health problems* (3rd ed.). Hamilton, ON: Offord Centre for Child Studies, McMaster University.

Bucks, R., Hawkins, K., Skinner, T., Horn, S., Seddon, P., & Home, R. (2009). Adherence to treatment in adolescents with cystic fibrosis: The role of illness perceptions and treatment beliefs. *Journal of Pediatric Psychology, 34*(8), 893–902.

Buggey, T. (2007). A picture is worth: Video self-modeling applications at school and at home. *Journal of Positive Behavior Interventions, 9,* 151–158.

Buhrmester, D. (1998). Need fulfillment, interpersonal competence, and the developmental contexts of early adolescent friendship. In W.M. Bukowski, A.F. Newcomb, & W.W. Hartup (Eds.), *The company they keep: Friendship in childhood and adolescence* (pp. 158–185). New York, NY: Cambridge University Press.

Bukowski, W.M., Rubin, K.H., & Parker, J.G. (2004). Social competence: Childhood and adolescence. In N.J. Smelser & P.B. Baltes (Eds). *International encyclopedia of the social and behavioral sciences* (pp. 14258–14264). Oxford, UK: Elsevier.

Bukowski, W.M., & Sippola, L.K. (2005). Friendship and development: Putting the most human relationship in its place. *New Directions for Child and Adolescent Development, 109,* 91–97.

Burd, L., Fisher, W., & Kerbeshian, J. (1987). A prevalence study of pervasive developmental disorders in North Dakota. *Journal of the American Academy of Child and Adolescent Psychiatry, 26*(5), 700–703.

Burge, P., Ouellette-Kuntz, H., Box, H., & Hutchinson, N. L. (2008, December 3). A quarter century of inclusive education for children with intellectual disabilities in Ontario: Public perceptions. *Canadian Journal of Educational Administration and Policy, 87.* Retrieved from http://www.umanitoba.ca/publications/cjeap/currentissues.html

Burgstahler, S., & Chang, C. (2009). Promising interventions for promoting STEM fields to students who have disabilities. *Review of Disability Studies: An International Journal, 5*(2), 29–47.

Burke, M.M., & Hodapp, R.M. (2014). Relating stress of mothers of children with developmental disabilities to family-school partnerships. *Intellectual and Developmental Disabilities, 52*(1), 13–23.

Burney, V.H., & Cross, T.L. (2006). Impoverished students with academic promise in rural settings. *Gifted Child Today, 29*(2), 14–21.

Burns, E., & Martin, A. (2014). ADHD and adaptability: The roles of cognitive, behavioural, and emotional regulation. *Australian Journal of Guidance & Counselling, 24*(2), 227–242.

Burns, M. (2007, November). Nine ways to catch kids up: How do we help floundering students who lack basic math concepts? *Educational Leadership,* 16–21.

Cakmak, A., & Bolukbas, N. (2005). Juvenile rheumatoid arthritis: Physical therapy and rehabilitation. *Southern Medical Journal, 98*(2), 212–216.

Caldarella, P., Shatzer, R.H., & Gray, K.M. (2011). The effects of school-wide positive behavior support on middle school climate and student outcomes. *RMLE Online: Research in Middle Level Education, 35*(4), 1–14.

Callen, P.J. (2009, April). The power of acceptance. *Exceptional Parent Magazine,* 78–79.

Campaña, L., & Ouimet, D. (2015). iStimulation: Apple iPad use with children who are visually impaired, including those with multiple disabilities. *Journal of Visual Impairment & Blindness, 109*(1), 67–72.

Campbell, D.S., Serff, P., & Williams, D. (1994). *BreakAway company.* Toronto, ON: Trifolium Publishing.

Canadian Diabetes Association Clinical Practice Guidelines Expert Committee. (2008). Canadian Diabetes Association clinical practice guidelines for the prevention and management of diabetes in Canada. *Canadian Journal of Diabetes, 32* (suppl. 1), S150–S161.

Canadian Education Statistics Council. (2014). *Education indicators in Canada: An international perspective.* Ottawa, ON: Statistics Canada.

Canadian Teachers' Federation. (2009, March). *Issue brief on teacher assistants.* Ottawa, ON: Canadian Teachers' Federation.

Canitano, R., & Vivanti, G. (2007). Tics and Tourette syndrome in autism spectrum disorders. *Autism, 11,* 19–28.

Canney, C., & Byrne, A. (2006). Evaluating circle time as a support to social skills development: Reflections on a journey in school-based research. *British Journal of Special Education, 33*(1), 19–24.

Carlucci, M. (1999, August 3). Life story: Helped hundreds of youngsters. *The Globe and Mail,* p. A17.2.

Carnahan, C.R., Williamson, P.S., & Christman, J. (2011). Linking cognition and literacy in students with autism spectrum disorder. *Teaching Exceptional Children, 43*(6), 54–62.

Carnahan, C.R., Williamson, P., Clarke, L., & Sorenson, R. (2009). A systematic approach for supporting paraeducators in educational settings: A guide for teachers. *Teaching Exceptional Children, 41*(5), 34–43.

Carnine, D.W., Kameenui, E.J., Silbert, J., & Tarver, S.G. (2003). *Direct instruction reading* (4th ed.). Rutherford, NJ: Prentice Hall.

Caro, D.H., McDonald, J.T., & Willms, J.D. (2009). Socio-economic status and academic achievement trajectories from childhood to adolescence. *Canadian Journal of Education, 32*(3), 558–590.

Carr, E.G. (2006). SWPBS: The greatest good for the greatest number, or the needs of the majority trump the needs of the minority? *Research and Practice for Persons with Severe Disabilities, 31,* 54–56.

Carr, P.R., & Lund, D.E. (Eds.). (2007). *The great white north? Exploring whiteness, privilege, and identity in education.* Rotterdam, the Netherlands: Sense Publishers.

Carter, J. & Leschied, A. (2010). Maintaining mental health and youth justice-involved students in mainstream education: Implications for Ontario's new mandatory requirement for school attendance. *Education & Law Journal, 19*(3), 169–201.

Cassidy, W. (2005). From zero tolerance to a culture of care. *Education Canada, 45*(3), 40–42.

Castagno, A.E., & Brayboy, B.M.J. (2008). Culturally responsive schooling for Indigenous youth: A review of the literature. *Review of Educational Research, 78*(4), 941–993.

Cefai, C. (2007). Resilience for all: A study of classrooms as protective contexts. *Emotional and Behavioral Difficulties, 12*(2), 119–134.

Chadsey, J., & Han, K.G. (2005). Friendship facilitation strategies: What do students in middle school tell us? *Teaching Exceptional Children, 38*(2), 52–57.

Chafouleas, S.M., McDougal, J.L., Riley-Tillman, T.C., Panahon, C.J., & Hilt, A.M. (2005). What do daily behavior report cards (DBRCs) measure? An initial comparison of DBRCs with direct observation for off-task behavior. *Psychology in the Schools, 42*, 669–676.

Chafouleas, S.M., Riley-Tillman, T.C., & Sassu, K.A. (2006). Acceptability and reported use of daily behavior report cards among teachers. *Journal of Positive Behavior Interventions, 8*, 174–182.

Chall, J.S. (1983). *Stages of reading development.* New York, NY: McGraw Hill.

Chamberlain, B., Kasari, C., & Rotheram-Fuller, E. (2007). Involvement or isolation? The social networks of children with autism in regular classrooms. *Journal of Autism and Developmental Disorders, 37*, 230–242.

Chang, M., Singh, K., & Mo, Y. (2007). Science engagement and science achievement: Longitudinal models using NELS data. *Educational Research and Evaluation, 13*, 349–371.

Chappuis, J. (2014). Thoughtful assessment with the learner in mind. *Educational Leadership, 71*(6), 20–26.

Charles, C.M., & Charles, M.G. (2004). *Classroom management for middle-grade teachers.* Boston, MA: Pearson Allyn & Bacon.

Chaturvedi, A., Gartin, B.C., & Murdick, N.L. (2011). Tourette syndrome: Classroom implications. *Physical Disabilities: Education and Related Services, 30*(1), 53–66.

Chin, P., Munby, H., Hutchinson, N.L., & Steiner-Bell, K. (2000). Meeting academic goals: Post-secondary students' intentions for participating in high school co-operative education programs. *Journal of Vocational Educational Research, 25,* 126–154.

Chitiyo, M., Makweche-Chitiyo, P., & Park, M. (2011). Examining the effect of positive behaviour support on academic achievement of students with disabilities. *Journal of Research in Special Education Needs, 11*(3), 171–177.

Christianson, A.L., Zwane, M.E., Manga, P., Rosen, E., Venter, A., Downs, D., & Kromberg, J.G.R. (2002). Children with intellectual disability in rural South Africa: Prevalence and associated disability. *Journal of Intellectual Disability Research, 46*(2), 179–186.

Chung, K.K.H., & Tam, Y.H. (2005). Effects of cognitive-based instruction on mathematics problem solving by learners with mild intellectual disabilities. *Journal of Intellectual and Developmental Disabilities, 30*(4), 207–216.

Cihak, D.F., & Ayres, K.M. (2010). Comparing pictorial and video-modeling activity schedules during transitions for students with autism spectrum disorders. *Research in Autism Spectrum Disorders, 4*, 763–771.

Ciullo, S., Falcomata, T., & Vaughn, S. (2015). Teaching social studies to upper elementary students with learning disabilities: *Graphic organizers and explicit instruction. Learning Disability Quarterly, 38*(1), 15–26.

Clarke, M., & Wilkinson, R. (2008). Interaction between children with cerebral palsy and their peers 2: Understanding initiated VOCA-mediated turns. *Augmentative and Alternative Communication, 24*(1), 3–15.

Clay, D.L. (2007). Culturally competent interventions in schools for children with physical health problems. *Psychology in the Schools, 44*, 389–396.

Cleverley, K., & Kidd, S. (2011). Resilience and suicidality among homeless youth. *Adolescence, 34*(5), 1049–1054.

Cobia, D.C., & Carney, J.S. (2002). Creating a culture of tolerance in schools: Everyday actions to prevent hate-motivated violent incidents. *Journal of School Violence, 1*, 87–103.

Cochran-Smith, M. (2006). *Stayers, leavers, and dreamers: Why people teach and why they stay: The Barbara Biber Lecture.* New York, NY: Bank Street College of Education.

Codjoe, H. (2006). The role of an affirmed black cultural identity and heritage in the academic achievement of African-Canadian students. *Intercultural Education, 17*(1), 33–54.

Cohen, E. (1998). *Designing groupwork: Strategies for the heterogeneous classroom* (2nd ed.). New York, NY: Teachers College Press.

Cohen, E., Brody, C.M., & Sapon-Shevin, M. (2004). *Teaching cooperative learning: The challenge for teacher education.* Albany, NY: State University of New York Press.

Cohen, E., Lotan, R., & Catanzarite, L. (1990). Treating status problems in the cooperative classroom. In S. Schlomo (Ed.), *Cooperative learning: Theory and research* (pp. 203–229). New York, NY: Praeger.

Coles, C.D., Strickland, D.C., Padgett, L., & Bellmoff, L. (2007). Games that "work": Using computer games to teach alcohol-affected children about fire and street safety. *Research in Developmental Disabilities, 28*, 518–530.

Colvin, G. (2007). *Seven steps for developing a proactive schoolwide discipline plan: A guide for principals and leadership teams.* Thousand Oaks, CA: Corwin Press.

Connor, D.J. (2012). Helping students with disabilities transition to college: 21 tips for students with LD and/or ADD/ADHD. *Teaching Exceptional Children, 44*(5), 16–25.

Constantini, L. (2013). Parent engagement: Building trust between families and schools. *Education Canada, 53*(2), 48–50.

Conti-Ramsden, G., & Durkin, K. (2008). Language and independence in adolescents with and without a history of specific language impairment (SLI). *Journal of Speech, Language and Hearing Research, 51*(1), 70–83.

Conway, C.M. (2006). Navigating through induction: How a mentor can help. *Music Education Journal, 92*, 56–60.

Cooper, H.L., & Nichols, S.K. (2007). Technology and early Braille literacy: Using the Mountbatten Pro Brailler in primary-grade classrooms. *Journal of Visual Impairment and Blindness, 101*, 22–31.

Cornett, C.E. (2006). Center stage: Arts-based read-alouds. *The Reading Teacher, 60*, 234–240.

Coughlin, J., & Montague, M. (2011). The effects of cognitive strategy instruction on the mathematical problem solving of adolescents with spina bifida. *Journal of Special Education, 45*(3), 171–183.

Council of Ministers of Education, Canada. (2003). *2002 Report on reading and writing assessment: School achievement indicators program.* Toronto, ON: Council of Ministers of Education, Canada.

Council of Ministers of Education, Canada. (2009). *Pan-Canadian assessment program for 13-year olds (PCAP-13 2007): Fact sheet.* Toronto, ON: Council of Ministers of Education, Canada.

Craig, W., Pepler, D., & Blais, J. (2007). Responding to bullying: What works? *School Psychology International, 28*, 465–477.

Craig, W.M., Pepler, D.J., Murphy, A., McCuaig-Edge, H. (2010). What works in bullying prevention? In E.M. Vernberg & B.K. Biggs (Eds.), *Preventing and treating bullying and victimization* (pp. 215–241). New York, NY: Oxford University Press.

Cramer, K., & Henry, A. (2013). Using manipulative models to build number sense for addition of fractions. *Yearbook (National Council of Teachers of Mathematics), 75*, 365–371.

Cranston, J. (2011). Relational trust: The glue that binds a professional learning community. *Alberta Journal of Educational Research, 57*, 59–72.

Crooke, P.J., Hendrix, R.E., & Rachman, J.Y. (2008). Brief report: Measuring the effectiveness of teaching social thinking to children with Asperger syndrome (AS) and high functioning autism (HFA). *Journal of Autism and Developmental Disorders, 38*(3), 581–591.

Crouch, R., Keys, C.B., & McMahon, S.D. (2014). Student-teacher relationships matter for school inclusion: School belonging, disability, and school transitions. *Journal of Prevention and Intervention in the Community, 42*(1), 20–30.

Crowchief-McHugh, D., Yellowhorne-Breaker, K., Weasel Fat-White, E. (2000). *A handbook for Aboriginal parents of children with special needs.* Edmonton, AB: Special Education Branch, Alberta Department of Education.

Crudden, A. (2012). Transition to employment for students with visual impairments: Components for success. *Journal of Visual Impairment and Blindness, 106*(7), 389–399.

Cuccaro, C., & Geitner, G. (2007). Lunch and recess: The "eye of the storm": Using targeted interventions for students with behavioral problems. *Teaching Exceptional Children Plus, 3*(4). Retrieved from http://escholarship.bc.edu/education/tecplus/vol3/iss4/art2

Cummings, J.G., Pepler, D.J., Mishna, F., & Craig, W. (2006). Bullying and victimization among students with exceptionalities. *Exceptionality Education Canada, 16,* 193–222.

Curtin, M., & Clark, G. (2005). Listening to young people with physical disabilities' experiences of education. *International Journal of Disability, Development and Education, 52,* 195–214.

Cutuli, J.J., Desjardins, C.D., Herbers, J.E., Long, J. D., Heistad, D., Chan, C.-K., Hinz, E., & Masten, A. S.. (2013). Academic achievement trajectories of homeless and highly mobile students: Resilience in the context of chronic and acute risk. *Child Development, 84*(3), 841–857.

Dalton, C. (2011). Social-emotional challenges experienced by students who function with mild and moderate hearing loss in educational settings. *Exceptionality Education International, 21*(1), 28–45.

Dalton, C., Hutchinson, N.L., & Dods, J. (2009). *Creating positive learning environments: A review of the literature prepared for the MISA Professional Network Centre* (Unpublished report). Faculty of Education, Queen's University, Kingston, ON.

Damini, M. (2014). How the group investigation model and the six-mirror model changed teachers' roles and teachers' and students' attitudes towards diversity. *Intercultural Education, 25*(3), 197–205.

Daniel, Y., & Bondy, K. (2008). Safe schools and zero tolerance: Policy, program, and practice in Ontario. *Canadian Journal of Educational Administration and Policy, 70,* 1–20. Retrieved from http://umanitoba.ca/publications/cjeap/pdf_files/daniel.pdf

Davis, M., & Guthrie, J. (2015). Measuring reading comprehension of content area texts using an assessment of knowledge organization. *Journal of Educational Research, 108*(2), 148–164.

Dean, J. (2014). *Review of Minister's Directive of Inclusive Schooling.* Retrieved from www.ece.gov.nt.ca/files/ERI/independent_review_of_inclusive_schooling_2014.pdf

Deci, E.L., & Ryan, R.M. (2008). Self-determination theory: A macrotheory of human motivation, development, and health. *Canadian Psychology, 49*(3), 182–185.

De Coster, K., & Loots, K. (2004). Somewhere in between touch and vision: In search of meaningful art education for blind individuals. *International Journal of Art and Design Education, 23*(3), 326–334.

Dei, G.J.S. (2003). *Anti-racism education: Theory and practice.* Black Point, NS: Fernwood.

Delaine, B. (2010). Talk medicine: Envisioning the effects of Aboriginal language revitalization on Manitoba schools. *First Nations Perspective, 3,* 65–88. Retrieved from http://www.mfnerc.org/images/stories/FirstNationsJournal/Volume3/journal_vol3.pdf

Del Favero, L., Boscolo, P., Vidotto, G., & Vicentini, M. (2007). Classroom discussion and individual problem-solving in the teaching of history: Do different instructional approaches affect interest in different ways? *Learning and Instruction 17,* 635–657.

DeLuca, C. (2008). Issues in including students with disabilities in large-scale assessment programs. *Exceptionality Education International, 18*(2), 38–50.

DeLuca, C., Hutchinson, N.L., deLugt, J., Beyer, W., Thornton, A., Versnel, J., Chin, P., & Munby, H. (2010). Learning in the workplace: Fostering resilience in disengaged youth. *Work: A Journal of Prevention, Assessment & Rehabilitation, 36,* 305–319.

DeLuca, C., Hutchinson, N.L., Versnel, J., Dods, J., & Chin, P. (2012). Bridging school and work: A person-in-context model for enabling resilience in at-risk youth. In S. Billett, G. Johnson, S. Thomas, C. Sim, S. Hay, & J. Rya (Eds.), *Experiences of school transitions: Policies, practice and participants* (pp. 43–69). New York, NY: Springer.

de Lugt, J.S. (2012). *Learning to read: What it really means* (Unpublished paper). Queen's University, Kingston, Ontario.

Denton, D., & Wicks, D. (2013). Implementing electronic portfolios through social media platforms: Steps and student perceptions. *Journal of Asynchronous Learning Networks, 17*(1), 125–135.

DePaepe, P., Garrison-Kane, L., & Doelling, J. (2002). Supporting students with health needs in schools: An overview of selected health conditions. *Focus on Exceptional Children, 35*(1), 1–24.

Duquette, C., Fullarton, S., Orders, S., & Robertson-Grewal, K. (2011). Insider, outsider, ally, or adversary: Parents of youth with learning disabilities engage in educational advocacy. *International Journal of Special Education, 26*(3), 124–141.

Duquette, C., Orders, S., Fullarton, S., & Robertson-Grewal, S. (2011). Fighting for their rights: Advocacy experiences of parents of children identified with intellectual giftedness. *Journal of the Education of the Gifted, 34*(3), 488–512.

Duquette, C., Stodel, E., Fullarton, S., & Hagglund, K. (2007). Secondary school experiences of individuals with foetal alcohol spectrum disorder: Perspectives of parents and their children. *International Journal of Inclusive Education, 11*(5–6), 571–591.

Deshler, D., Palincsar, A.S., Biancarosa, G., & Nair, M. (2007). *Informed choices for struggling adolescent readers: A research-based guide to instructional programs and practices.* Newark, DE: International Reading Association.

Desoete, A., Ceulemans, A., De Weerdt, F., & Pieters, S. (2012). Can we predict mathematical learning disabilities from symbolic and non-symbolic comparison tasks in kindergarten? Findings from a longitudinal study. *British Journal of Educational Psychology, 82*(1), 64–81.

Desoete, A., & De Weerdt, F. (2013). Can executive functions help us to understand children with mathematical learning disorders and to improve instruction? *Learning Disabilities: A Contemporary Journal, 11*(2), 27–39.

Dessemontet, R., Bless, G., & Morin, D. (2012). Effects of inclusion on the academic achievement and adaptive behavior of children with intellectual disabilities. *Journal of Intellectual Disability Research, 56*(6), 579–587.

Devecchi, C., & Rouse, M. (2010). An exploration of the features of effective collaboration between teachers and teaching assistants in secondary schools. *Support for Learning, 25*(2), 91–99.

Dewey, J. (1916). *Democracy and education: An introduction to the philosophy of education.* New York, NY: Macmillan.

Diamond, K.E., Huang, H.-H., & Steed, E. (2013). The development of social competence in children with disabilities (2nd ed.). In P. Smith & C. Hart (Eds.), *Wiley-Blackwell handbook of childhood social development* (pp. 627–645). Malden, MA: Blackwell.

Dickason, O.P., & Newbigging, W. (2010). *A concise history of Canada's First Nations* (2nd ed.). Don Mills, ON: Oxford University Press.

DiClementi, J.D., & Handelsman, M.M. (2005). Empowering students: Class-generated course rules. *Teaching of Psychology, 32,* 18–21.

Dillabough, J-A., Wang, E., & Kennelly, J. (2005). Ginas, thugs, and gangstas: Young people's struggles to "become somebody" in working class urban Canada. *Journal of Curriculum Theorizing, 21*(2), 83–108.

Dimling, L.M. (2010). Conceptually based vocabulary intervention: Second graders' development of vocabulary words. *American Annals of the Deaf, 155*(4), 425–448.

Dirks, E., Spyer, G., van Lieshout, E., de Sonneville, L. (2008). Prevalence of combined reading and arithmetic disabilities. *Journal of Learning Disabilities, 41*(5), 460–473.

Doabler, C.T., & Fien, H. (2013). Explicit mathematics instruction: What teachers can do for teaching students with mathematics difficulties. *Intervention in School and Clinic, 48*(5), 276–285.

Dods, J.C. (2012). *Hearing the words "Hi Nick": The critical role that school-based relationships play in supporting the learning and well-being of youth who have experienced trauma* (Unpublished paper). Queen's University, Kingston, ON.

Dods, J. (2014). *Ideas about why people act the way they do* (Unpublished document). Queen's University, Kingston, ON.

Donaldson, J.B., & Zager, D. (2010). Mathematics interventions for students with high functioning autism/Asperger's syndrome. *Teaching Exceptional Children, 42*(6), 40–46.

Dooley, J., Gordon, K.E., Dodds, L., & MacSween, J. (2010). Duchenne muscular dystrophy: A 30-year population-based incidence study. *Clinical Pediatrics, 49*(2), 177–179.

Dotger, S., & Causton-Theoharis, J. (2010). Differentiation through choice: Using a think-tac-toe for science content. *Science Scope, 33*(6), 18–23.

Doubet, K.J. (2012). Formative assessment jump-starts a middle grades differentiation initiative. *Middle School Journal, 43*(3), 32–38.

Douglas, D. (2004). Self-advocacy: Encouraging students to become partners in differentiation. *Roeper Review, 26*(4), 223–238.

Downing, J. E., & Peckham-Hardin, K. D. (2007). Inclusive education: What makes it a good education for students with moderate to severe disabilities? *Research & Practice for Persons with Severe Disabilities, 32*, 16–30.

Dragone, M.A., Bush, P.J., Jones, J.K., & Bearison, D.J. (2002). Development and evaluation of an interactive CD-ROM for children with leukemia and their families. *Patient Education and Counseling, 46*, 297–307.

Duffy, J., Wareham, S., & Walsh, M. (2004). Psychological consequences for high school students of having been sexually harassed. *Sex roles, 50*(11/12), 811–821.

Dunlosky, J. (2013). Strengthening the student toolbox: Study strategies to boost learning. *American Educator, 37*(3), 12–21.

Dunn, L. (1968). Special education for the mildly retarded: Is much of it justifiable? *Exceptional Children, 35*, 5–22.

DuPaul, G.J., & Weyandt, L.L. (2006). School-based intervention for children with attention deficit hyperactivity disorder: Effects on academic, social, and behavioral functioning. *International Journal of Disability, Development and Education, 53*, 161–176.

DuPaul, G.J., Weyandt, L.L., & Janusis, G.M. (2011). ADHD in the classroom: Effective intervention strategies. *Theory Into Practice, 50*(1), 35–42.

Duffy, J., Wareham, S., & Walsh, M. (2004). Psychological consequences for high school students of having been sexually harassed. *Sex roles, 50*(11/12), 811–821.

Duquette, C. (2007). Becoming a role model: Experiences of Native student teachers. *Alberta Journal of Educational Research, 53*(4), 387–400.

Dworet, D., & Maich, K. (2007). Canadian school programs for students with emotional/behavioral disorders: An updated look. *Behavioral Disorders, 33*(1), 33–42.

Dyson, L. (2010). Unanticipated effects of children with learning disabilities on their families. *Learning Disability Quarterly, 33*, 43–55.

Dyson, N., Jordan, N., & Glutting, J. (2013). A number sense intervention for low-income kindergarteners at risk for mathematics difficulties. *Journal of Learning Disabilities, 46*(2), 166–181.

Earl, L. (2003). Assessment of learning, for learning, and as learning. In *Assessment as learning: Using classroom assessment to maximize student learning* (pp. 34–47). Thousand Oaks, CA: Corwin Press.

Early, C. (2005, Summer). Meeting the needs of ESL/ELD learners in the classroom. *ETFO Voice*, 21–24.

Eaton v. Brant (County) Board of Education. (1995). 22 O.R. (3d) 1 O.C.A.

Edmunds, A. (1999). Acquiring learning strategies. *Teaching Exceptional Children, 31*(4), 69–73.

Edmunds, A. (2008). ADHD assessment and diagnosis in Canada: An inconsistent but fixable process. *Exceptionality Education Canada, 18*(2), 3–23.

Egodawatte, G., McDougall, D., & Stoilescu, D. (2011). The effects of teacher collaboration in grade 9 applied mathematics. *Educational Research for Policy & Practice, 10*, 189–209.

Eisenman, L.T. (2007). Social networks and careers of young adults with intellectual disabilities. *Intellectual and Developmental Disabilities, 45*(3), 199–208.

Eisenman, L.T., Pleet, A.M., Wandry, D., & McGinley, V. (2011). Voices of special education teachers in an inclusive high school: Redefining responsibilities. *Remedial and Special Education, 32*, 91–94.

Ellis, E.S., & Friend, P. (1991). Adolescents with learning disabilities. In B.Y.L. Wong (Ed.), *Learning about learning disabilities* (pp. 505–561). San Diego, CA: Academic Press.

Ellison, L.F., & Wilkins, K. (2009). *Cancer prevalence in the Canadian population* (Statistics Canada Report 82-003). Ottawa, ON: Statistics Canada.

Emerson, R.W., Holbrook, M.C., & D'Andrea, F.M. (2009). Acquisition of literacy skills by young children who are blind. *Journal of Visual Impairment and Blindness, 103*(10), 610–624.

Emme, M.J., Kirova, A., Kamau, O., & Kosanovich, S. (2006). Ensemble research: A means for immigrant children to explore peer relationships through photonovela. *Alberta Journal of Educational Research, 52*(3), 160–181.

Emmer, E.T., & Evertson, C.M. (2013). *Classroom management for middle and high school teachers*. Boston, MA: Allyn & Bacon.

Erasmus, G. (1996). Quoted in the Royal Commission on Aboriginal People: *Highlights from the Report*. Government of Canada.

Erickson, W., Lee, C.G., & von Schrader, S. (2010). *2008 Disability status reports: United States*. Ithaca, NY: Cornell University. Retrieved from http://digitalcommons.ilr.cornell.edu/edicollect/1285

Erkolahti, R., & Ilonen, T. (2005). Academic achievement and the self-image of adolescents with diabetes mellitus type-1 and rheumatoid arthritis. *Journal of Youth and Adolescence, 34*, 199–205.

Espelage, D.L., & Swearer, S.M. (2010). A social-ecological model for bullying prevention and intervention: Understanding the impact of adults in the social ecology of youngsters. In S.R. Jimerson, S.M. Swearer, & D.L. Espelage (Eds.), *Handbook of bullying in schools: An international perspective* (pp. 61–72). New York, NY: Routledge.

Evans, D.D., & Strong, C.J. (1996). What's the story? Attending, listening, telling in middle school. *Teaching Exceptional Children, 28*(3), 58–61.

Faggella-Luby, M.N., & Deshler, D.D. (2008). Reading comprehension in adolescents with LD: What we know; what we need to learn. *Learning Disabilities Research & Practice, 23*(2), 70–78.

Fahsl, A. (2007). Mathematics accommodations for all students. *Intervention in School and Clinic, 42*(4), 198–203.

Farenga, S., & Joyce, B. (2000). Preparing for parents' questions. *Science Scope, 23*(6), 12–14.

Felesena, M.D. (2013). Does your district have a progressive discipline policy? *Education Digest, 79*(1), 39–42.

Fenning, P.A., Pulaski, S., & Gomez, M. (2012). Call to action: A critical need for designing alternatives to suspension and expulsion. *Journal of School Violence, 11*(2), 105–117.

Fenning, P., Theodos, J., Benner, C., & Bohanon-Edmonson, H. (2004). Integrating proactive discipline practices into codes of conduct. *Journal of School Violence, 3*(1), 45–61.

Fenstermacher, K., Olympia, D., & Sheridan, S.M. (2006). Effectiveness of a computer-facilitated interactive social skills training program for boys with attention deficit hyperactivity disorder. *School Psychology Quarterly, 21*(2), 197–224.

Fetters, M., Pickard, D.M., & Pyle, E. (2003). Making science accessible: Strategies to meet the needs of a diverse student population. *Science Scope, 26*(5), 26–29.

Fien, H., Santoro, L., Baker, S.K., & Park, Y., et al. (2011). Enhancing teacher read alouds with small-group vocabulary instruction for students with low vocabulary in first-grade classrooms. *School Psychology, 40*(2), 307–318.

Findlay, S. (2010). The problem of punishment. *Social and Legal Studies, 19*(2), 256–258.

Fitch, E.F., & Hulgin, K.M. (2007). Achieving inclusion through CLAD: Collaborative learning assessment through dialogue. *International Journal of Inclusive Education, 7*, 1–17.

Flanagain, W.C. (2007). *A survey: The negative aspects of in and out of school suspensions and alternatives that promote academic achievement.* (ERIC Document Reproduction Service No. ED 499538).

Flatow, I. (1985). The king of storms. In M.W. Aulls & M.F. Graves (Eds.), *In another world* (pp. 57–63). New York, NY: Scholastic.

Fletcher, J.M., Lyon, G.R., Fuchs, L.S., & Barnes, M.A. (2007). *Learning disabilities: From identification to intervention.* New York, NY: Guilford Press.

Foley, D. (2012). Ultimate classroom management handbook: A veteran teacher's instant techniques for solving adolescent student misbehavior. St. Paul, MN: Just Works.

Fombonne, E. (2007). Epidemiological surveys of pervasive developmental disorders. In F. R. Volkmar (Ed.), *Diagnosis and definition of autism and other pervasive developmental disorders* (pp. 33–68). Cambridge, UK: Cambridge University Press.

Fombonne, E., Zakarian, R., Bennett, A. Meng, L., & McLean-Heywood, D. (2006). Pervasive developmental disorders in Montreal, Quebec, Canada: Prevalence and links with immunizations. *Pediatrics, 118*(1), 139–150.

Fostaty Young, S.F., & Wilson (R.J.). (2000). *Assessment and learning: The ICE approach.* Winnipeg, MB: Portage & Main Press (Peguis Publishers).

Foster, J., & Matthews, D. (2012). *Troubling times: How parents and teachers can help children understand and confront adversity. From Being smart about gifted children: A guidebook for parents and educators.* Tuscon, AZ: Great Potential Press. Retrieved from www.sengifted.org/articles_social/FosterMatthews_TroublingTimes.shtml

Fowler, M., & McCabe, P.C. (2011). Traumatic brain injury and personality change. *Pediatric School Psychology: Communiqué, 39*(7), 4–10.

Frijters, J.C., Lovett, M.W., Steinbach, K.A., Wolf, M., Sevcik, R.A., & Morris, R. (2011). *Neurocognitive predictors of reading outcomes for children with reading disabilities. Journal of Learning Disabilities, 44*(2), 150–166.

Frostad, P., & Pijl, S.J. (2007). Does being friendly help in making friends? The relation between the social position and social skills of pupils with special needs in mainstream education. *European Journal of Special Needs Education, 22*, 15–30.

Fuchs, D., & Fuchs, L.S. (2005). Peer-assisted learning strategies: Promoting word recognition, fluency, and reading comprehension in young children. *Journal of Special Education, 39*, 34–44.

Fuchs, D., Hale, J.B., & Kearns, D.M. (2011). On the importance of a cognitive processing perspective: An introduction. *Journal of Learning Disabilities, 44*(2), 99–104.

Fuchs, L., Fuchs, D., & Hamlett, C. (2015). Republication of "Curriculum-based measurement: A standardized, long-term goal approach to monitoring student progress." *Intervention in School and Clinic, 50*(3), 185–192.

Fullan, M. (2013). *The new meaning of educational change* (electronic book text). New York, NY: Teachers College Press.

Gable, R.A., Hendrickson, J.M, Tonelsom, S.W., & Acker, R.V. (2002). Integrating academic and non-academic instruction for students with emotional/behavioral disorders. *Education and Treatment of Children, 25*, 459–475.

Gaetz, S., Donaldson, J., Richter, T., & Gulliver, T. (2013). *The state of homelessness in Canada.* Toronto, ON: Canadian Homelessness Research Network Press.

Gajiria, M., Salend, S.J., & Hemrick, M.A. (1994). Teacher acceptability of testing modifications for mainstreamed students. *Learning Disabilities Research and Practice, 9*(4), 236–243.

Galway, T.M., & Metsala, J.L. (2011). Social cognition and its relation to psychosocial adjustment in children with nonverbal learning disabilities. *Journal of Learning Disabilities, 44*(1), 33–49.

Ganz, J.B., Boles, M., Goodwyn, F.D., & Flores, M. (2014). Efficacy of handheld electronic visual supports to enhance vocabulary in children with ASD. *Focus on Autism and Other Developmental Disabilities, 29*(1), 3–12.

Ganz, J. B., Earles-Vollrath, T., & Cook, K. (2011). Video modeling: A visually based intervention for children with autism spectrum disorder. *Teaching Exceptional Children, 43*(6), 8–19.

Gao, H., Shen, E., Losh, S., & Turner, J. (2007). A review of studies on collaborative concept mapping: What have we learned about the technique and what is next. *Journal of Interactive Learning Research, 18*, 479–492.

Garay, S.V. (2003). Listening to the voices of deaf students: Essential transition issues. *Teaching Exceptional Children, 35*(4), 44–48.

Garnett, K. (1992). Developing fluency with basic number facts: Intervention for students with learning disabilities. *Learning Disabilities: Research and Practice, 7*, 210–216.

Gathering strength: Canada's Aboriginal action plan. (1998). Ottawa, ON.

Gay, A.S., & White, S.H. (2002). Teaching vocabulary to communicate mathematically. *Middle School Journal, 34*(2), 33–38.

Gay, G. (2000). *Culturally responsive teaching: Theory, research, and practice.* New York, NY: Teachers College Press.

Geddes, K.A. (2010). Using tiered assignments to engage learners in advanced placement physics. *Gifted Child Today, 33*(1), 32–40.

Geenen, S., & Powers, L.E. (2007). "Tomorrow is another problem": The experiences of youth in foster care during their transition into adulthood. *Children and Youth Services Review, 29*, 1085–1101.

Gehret, J. (1991). *Eagle eyes: A child's view of attention deficit disorder.* Fairport, NY: Verbal Images Press.

Gentry, M., & Fugate, C.M. (2012). Gifted native American students: Underperforming, underidentified, and overlooked. *Psychology in the Schools, 49*(7), 631–646.

Gentry, M., Peters, S.J., & Mann, R.L. (2007). Differences between general and talented students' perceptions of their career and technical education experiences compared to their traditional high school experiences. *Journal of Advanced Academics, 18*(3), 372–401.

Giangreco, M.F., Suter, J.C., & Doyle, M.B. (2010). Paraprofessionals in inclusive schools: A review of recent research. *Journal of Educational and Psychological Consultation, 20*, 41–57.

Gibbons, E. (2015). Supporting deaf and hard-of-hearing students in the schools. *Contemporary School Psychology, 19*, 46–53.

Gibbs, J. (2001). *Tribes: A new way of learning and being together*. Windsor, CA: CenterSource Systems.

Gibbs, J. (2006). *Reaching all by creating tribes learning communities*. Windsor, CA: CenterSource Systems.

Gil, L.A. (2007). Bridging the transition gap from high school to college. *Teaching Exceptional children, 40*(2), 12–15.

Gill, V. (2007*). The ten students you'll meet in your classroom: Classroom management tips for middle and high school teachers*. Thousand Oaks, CA: Corwin Press.

Gillberg, C., & Fernell, E. (2014). Autism plus versus autism pure. *Journal of Autism and Developmental Disabilities, 44*, 3274–3276.

Gillies, R.M., Ashman, A., & Terwel, J. (Eds.). (2007). *The teacher's role in implementing cooperative learning in the classroom*. New York, NY: Springer.

Gillies, R.M., & Boyle, M. (2010). Teachers' reflections on cooperative learning: Issues of implementation. *Teaching and Teacher Education, 26*(4), 933–940.

Gillies, R.M., & Haynes, M. (2011). Increasing explanatory behavior, problem-solving, and reasoning within classes using cooperative group work. *Instructional Science, 39*, 349–366.

Gilliland, H. (1999). *Teaching the Native American*. Dubuque, IA: Kendall/Hunt Publishing Co.

Gilman, R., Huebner, E.S., & Furlong, M.J. (Eds.). (2009). *Handbook of positive psychology in schools*. New York, NY: Routledge.

Gilmore, J. (2010). Trends in dropout rates and the labour market outcomes of young dropouts. *Education Matters: Insights on Education, Learning and Training in Canada, 7*(4).

Glor-Scheib, S., & Telthorster, H. (2006). Activate your student IEP team member using technology: How electronic portfolios can bring the student voice to life. *Teaching Exceptional Children Plus, 2*(3), Article 1.

Godfrey, C.J., & Stone, J. (2013). Mastering fact fluency: Are they game? *Teaching Children Mathematics, 20*(2), 96–101.

Gokiert, R.J., Ford, D.M., & Ali, M. (2014). Creating inclusive parent engagement practices. *Multicultural Education, 21*(3/4), 23–27.

Gold, Y., & Roth, R.A. (2014). *Teachers managing stress and preventing burnout: The professional health solution* (electronic book text). London, UK: Taylor & Francis.

Goodman, A. (2008). Student-led, teacher-supported conference: Improving communication across an urban school district. *Middle School Journal, 39*(3), 48–54.

Goodwin, A.K., & King, S.H. (2002). *Culturally responsive parental involvement*. New York, NY: AACTE Publications.

Gordon, M. (2012). Children coping with illness: In their own words. *Canadian Children, 37*(1), 31–39.

Goulet, L.M., & Goulet, K.N. (2014). *Teaching each other: Nehinuw concepts and Indigenous pedagogies*. Vancouver, BC: UBC Press.

Government of Canada. (2008). *Advancing the Inclusion of Persons with Disabilities* (4th ed.). Ottawa, ON: Author.

Graetz, J.E., Mastropieri, M.A., & Scruggs, T.E. (2006). Using video self-modeling to decrease inappropriate behavior. *Teaching Exceptional Children, 38*(5), 43–48.

Grant, C., & Lerer, A. (2011, Fall). Revisiting the traditional classroom band model: A differentiated perspective. *Canadian Music Educator, 24–27*.

Grant, R., Delany, G., Goldsmith, G., Shapiro, A., & Redlener, I.E. (2013). Twenty-five years of child and family homelessness: Where are we now? *American Journal of Public Health, 103*(S2), e1–e10.

Graves, M.F., & Braaten, S. (1996). Scaffolded reading experiences: Bridges to success. *Preventing School Failure, 40*, 169–173.

Gray, C.A. (2002). *My social story book*. London, UK: Jessica Kingsley Publishers.

Greene, M.J. (2006). Helping build lives: Career and life development of gifted and talented students. *Professional School Counseling, 10*(1), 34–42.

Gregoire, M.A., & Lupinetti, J. (2005). Support diversity through the arts. *Kappa Delta Pi Record, 41*(4), 159–163.

Grenawalt, V. (2004). Going beyond the debate: Using technology and instruction for a balanced reading program. *Teacher Librarian, 32*(2), 12–16.

Gresham, F.M. (2002). Teaching social skills to high risk children and youth: Preventive and remedial strategies. In M.R. Schinn, H.M. Walker, & G. Stoner (Eds.), *Interventions for academic and behavior problems II: Preventative and remedial approaches* (2nd ed., pp. 403–432). Washington, DC: National Association of School Psychologists.

Gresham, F.M., & Vellutino, F.R. (2010). What is the role of intelligence in the identification of specific learning disabilities: Issues and clarifications. *Learning Disabilities Research & Practice, 25*(4), 194–206.

Grieve, A.J., Tluczek, A., Racine-Gilles, C.N., Laxova, A., Albers, C.A., & Farrell, P.M. (2011). Associations between academic achievement and psychosocial variables in adolescents with cystic fibrosis. *Journal of School Health, 81*(11), 713–720.

Griffin, S., & Case, R. (1997). Re-thinking the primary school math curriculum: An approach based on cognitive science. *Issues in Education, 3*, 1–49.

Gronneberg, J. (2008). A UDL twist on classic texts. *Special Education Technology Practice, 10*(4), 33–37.

Guay, D.M. (1993). Cross-site analysis of teaching practices: Visual art education with students experiencing disabilities. *Studies in Art Education, 34*(3), 222–232.

Guay, D.M. (1995). The sunny side of the street: A supportive community for the inclusive art classroom. *Art Education, 48*(1), 51–56.

Gumpel, T.P. (2007). Are social competence difficulties caused by performance or acquisition deficits? The importance of self-regulatory mechanisms. *Psychology in the Schools, 44*(4), 351–372.

Guo, Y. (2010). Meetings without dialogue: A study of ESL parent–teacher interactions at secondary school parents' nights. *School Community Journal, 20*(1), 121–140.

Gupta, R., & Kar, B.R. (2010). Specific cognitive deficits in ADHD: A diagnostic concern in differential diagnosis. *Journal of Child and Family Studies, 19*(6), 778–786.

Gurney, J.G., Fritz, M.S., Ness, K.K., Sievers, P., et al. (2003). Analysis of prevalence trends of autism spectrum disorder in Minnesota. *Archives of Pediatric and Adolescent Medicine, 157*(7), 622–627.

Gushue, G.V. (2006). The relationship of ethnic identity, career decision-making self-efficacy and outcome expectations among Latino/a high school students. *Journal of Vocational Behavior, 68*(1), 85–95.

Guskey, T.R., & Jung, L.A. (2009). Grading and reporting in a standards-based environment: Implications for students with special needs. *Theory Into Practice, 48*, 53–62.

Guskey, T.R., & Jung, L.A. (2012). Four steps in grading reform. *Principal Leadership, 13*(4), 22–28.

Guthrie, J., McRae, A., Coddington, C., Lutz Klauda, Wigfield, A., Barbosa, P. (2009). Impacts of comprehensive reading instruction on diverse outcomes of low- and high-achieving readers. *Journal of Learning Disabilities, 42*(3), 195–214.

Hale, J.B., Alfonso, V., Berninger, V., Bracken, B., et al. (2010). Critical issues in response-to-intervention, comprehensive evaluation, and specific learning disabilities identification and intervention: An expert white paper consensus. *Learning Disability Quarterly, 33*(3), 223–236.

Haley, A. N., & Watson, D. C. (2000). In-school literacy extension: Beyond in-school suspension. *Journal of Adolescent and Adult Literacy, 43,* 654–661.

Hall, A. (2014). Beyond the author's chair. *Reading Teacher, 68*(1), 27–31.

Hall, L.J., & McGregor, J.A. (2000). A follow-up study of the peer relationships of children with disabilities in an inclusive school. *Journal of Special Education, 34,* 114–126.

Hall, P.S. (2013). A new definition of punishment. *Reclaiming Children and Youth, 21*(4), 22–26.

Hamilton, R., & Moore, D. (2004). Education of refugee children: Documenting and implementing change. In R. Hamilton & D. Moore (Eds.), *Educational interventions for refugee children* (pp. 106–116). London, UK: Routledge Falmer.

Hampton, E. (1995). Toward a redefinition of Indian education. In M. Battiste & J. Barman (1995) (Eds.), *First Nation education in Canada: The circle unfolds* (pp. 5–46). Vancouver, BC: UBC Press.

Hanham, J., & McCormick, J. (2009). Group work in schools with close friends and acquaintances: Linking self-processes with group processes. *Learning and Instruction, 19,* 214–227.

Hannah, C.L., & Shore, B.M. (2008). Twice-exceptional students' use of metacognitive skills on a comprehension monitoring task. *Gifted Child Quarterly, 52*(1), 3–18.

Hardy, M.I., McLeod, J., Minto, H., Perkins, S.A., & Quance, W.R. (1971). *Standards for education of exceptional children in Canada: The SEECC Report.* Toronto, ON: Leonard Crainford.

Hare, C. (2014). New project aims to tackle diabetes in schools. *ATA News, 49*(2). Retrieved from www.teachers.ab.ca/Publications/

Harlacher, J.E., Roberts, N.E., & Merrell, K.W. (2006). Classwide interventions for students with ADHD. *Teaching Exceptional Children, 39*(2), 6-12.

Hart, J.E., & Brehm, J. (2013). Promoting self-determination: A model for training elementary students to self-advocate for IEP accommodations. *Teaching Exceptional Children, 45*(5), 40–48.

Hartsell, B. (2006). Teaching toward compassion: Environmental values education for secondary students. *Journal of Secondary Gifted Education, 17,* 265–271.

Hartup, W.W. (2006). Relationships in early and middle childhood. In A.L. Vangelisti & D. Perlman (Eds.), *The Cambridge handbook of personal relationships* (pp. 177–190). New York, NY: Cambridge University Press.

Heath, N.L., McLean-Heywood, D., Rousseau, C., Petrakos, H., Finn, C.A., & Karagiannakis, A. (2006). Turf and tension: Psychiatric and inclusive communities servicing students referred for emotional and behavioural difficulties. *International Journal of Inclusive Education, 10*(4–5), 335–346.

Heath, N., Roberts, E., & Toste, J. (2013). Perceptions of academic performance: Positive illusions in adolescents with and without learning disabilities. *Journal of Learning Disabilities, 46*(5), 402–412.

Heck, K., Subramaniam, A., & Carlos, R. (2010). *The Step-It-Up-2-Thrive theory of change.* Davis, CA: 4-H Center for Youth Development, University of California. Retrieved from http://www.ca4h.org/files/4046.pdf

Helfman, E. (1992). *On being Sarah.* Morton Grove, IL: Albert Whitman and Company.

Hendriksen, J., Poysky, J., Schrans, D., et al. (2009). Psychosocial adjustment in males with Duchenne muscular dystrophy. *Journal of Pediatric Psychology, 34*(1), 69–78.

Henley, M. (2006). *Classroom management: A proactive approach.* Upper Saddle River, NJ: Pearson Merrill Prentice Hall.

Herlihy, C. (2007). *Toward ensuring a smooth transition into high school.* Washington, DC: National High School Center.

Herrenkohl, L.R. (2006). Intellectual role taking: Supporting discussion in heterogeneous elementary science classes. *Theory Into Practice, 45*(1), 47–54.

Herrman, D., Thurber, J., Miles, K., & Gilbert, G. (2011). Childhood leukemia survivors and their return to school: A literature review, case study, and recommendations. *Journal of Applied School Psychology, 27*(3), 252–275.

Heydon, R., Hibbert, K., & Iannacci, L. (2004/2005). Strategies to support balanced literacy approaches in pre- and inservice teacher education. *Journal of Adolescent and Adult Literacy, 48*(4), 312–319.

Hiebert, B. (1985). *Stress and teachers: The Canadian scene.* Toronto, ON: Canadian Education Association.

Hill, C. (2003). The role of educational assistants: Are they influencing inclusive practices? *Alberta Journal of Educational Research, 49,* 1–4.

Hill, D., & Flores, M. (2014). Comparing the Picture Exchange Communication System and the iPad™ for communication of students with autism spectrum disorder and developmental delay. *Tech Trends: Linking Research and Practice to Improve Learning, 58*(3), 45–53.

Hindin, A., Cobb Morocco, C., & Mata Anguila, C. (2001). "This book lives in our school": Teaching middle school students to understand literature. *Remedial and Special Education, 22,* 204–213.

Hinshaw, S.P., Owens, E.B., Sami, N., & Fargeon, S. (2006). Prospective follow-up of girls with attention-deficit/hyperactivity disorder into adolescence: Evidence for continuing cross-domain impairment. *Journal of Consulting and Clinical Psychology, 74*(3), 489–499.

Ho, C.M.L., Nelson, M.E., & Mueller-Wittig, W. (2011). Design and implementation of a student-generated virtual museum in a language curriculum to enhance collaborative multimodal meaning-making. *Computers & Education, 57*(1), 1083–1097.

Hobbs, J. (2011). Inclusive education: Lessons from Quebec's English sector. *Education Canada, 51*(4), 20–23.

Hobbs, J. (2015). Inclusive education: Lessons from Quebec's English sector. *Education Canada, 55*(2). Retrieved from http://www.cea-ace.education-canada

Hoffman, S., Palladino, J., & Barnett, J. (2007). Compassion fatigue as a theoretical framework to help understand burnout among special education teachers. *Journal of Ethnographic & Qualitative Research, 2*(1), 15–22.

Hong, B., & Ehrensberger, W. (2007). Assessing the mathematical skills of students with disabilities. *Preventing school failure, 52*(1), 41–47.

Hopkins, L., Wadley, G., Vetere, F., Fong, M., & Green, J. (2014). Utilising technology to connect the hospital and the classroom: Maintaining connections using tablet computers and a 'Presence' app. *Australian Journal of Education, 58*(3), 278–296.

Horner, R.H., Sugai, G., & Anderson, C.M. (2010). Examining the evidence base for school-wide positive behavior support. *Focus on Exceptional Children, 42*(8), 1–14.

Hoskin, J., & Fawcett, A. (2014). Improving the reading skills of young people with Duchenne muscular dystrophy in preparation for adulthood. *British Journal of Special Education, 41*(2), 172–190.

Howard, B., Cohn, E., & Orsmond, G.I. (2006). Understanding and negotiating friendships: Perspectives from an adolescent with Asperger syndrome. *Autism, 10,* 619–627.

Howe, R.B., & Covell, K. (2011). Countering disadvantage, promoting health: The value of children's human rights education. *Journal of Educational Thought, 45*(1), 59–85.

Howlin, P. (2007). The outcome in adult life for people with ASD. In F. R. Volkmar (Ed.), *Diagnosis and definition of autism and other pervasive developmental disorders* (pp. 269–306). Cambridge, UK: Cambridge University Press.

Huerta, M., Bishop, S.L., Duncan, A., Hus, V., & Lord, C. (2012). Application of DSM-5 criteria for autism spectrum disorder to three samples of children with DSM-IV diagnoses of pervasive developmental disorders. *American Journal of Psychiatry, 169*(10), 1056–1064.

Hughes, C. (2011). Effective instructional design and delivery for teaching task-specific learning strategies to students with learning disabilities. *Focus on Exceptional Children, 44*(2), 1–16.

Hughes, C., Golas, M., Cosgriff, J., Brigham, N., Edwards, C., & Cashen, K. (2011). Effects of a social skills intervention among high school students with intellectual disabilities and autism and their general education peers. *Research and Practice for Persons with Severe Disabilities, 36*(1), 46–61.

Hughes, E., Witzel, B., Riccomini, P., Fries, K., & Kanyongo, G. (2014). Meta-analysis of algebra interventions for learners with disabilities and struggling learners. *Journal of the International Association of Special Education, 15*(1), 36–47.

Hughes, T.A., & Fredrick, L.D. (2006). Teaching vocabulary with students with learning disabilities using classwide-peer tutoring and constant time delay. *Journal of Behavioral Education, 15*, 1–23.

Hume, K. (2008). *Start where they are: Differentiating for success with the young adolescent.* Toronto: Pearson Education Canada.

Hume, K., & Odem, S. (2007). Effects of an individual work system on the independent functioning of students with autism. *Journal of Autism and Developmental Disorders, 37*, 1166–1180.

Hurlbutt, K.S., & Handler, B.R. (2010). High school students with Asperger syndrome: A career path binder project. *Intervention in School & Clinic, 46*(1), 46–50.

Hutchinson, N.L. (2004). *Teaching exceptional children and adolescents: A Canadian casebook.* (2nd ed.) Toronto: Prentice Hall.

Hutchinson, N.L. (2007). *Inclusion of exceptional learners in Canadian schools: A practical handbook for teachers* (2nd ed.). Toronto, ON: Pearson Prentice Hall.

Hutchinson, N.L., Chin, P., Munby, H., Mills de Espana, W., Young, J., Edwards, K.L. (1999). How inclusive is co-operative education in Canada? Getting the story and the numbers. *Exceptionality Education Canada, 8*(3), 15–43.

Hutchinson, N.L., & Freeman, J.G. (1994). *Pathways: Knowing about yourself, knowing about careers.* Scarborough, ON: Nelson Canada.

Hutchinson, N.L., Freeman, J.G., & Berg, D.H. (2004). Social competence of adolescents with learning disabilities: Interventions and issues. In B.Y.L. Wong (Ed.), *Learning about learning disabilities* (3rd ed., pp. 415–448). New York, NY: Academic Press.

Hutchinson, N.L., Munby, H., Chin, P., Edwards, K.L., Steiner-Bell, K., Chapman, C., Ho, K., & Mills de España, W. (2001). The intended curriculum in co-operative education in Ontario secondary schools: An analysis of school district documents. *Journal of Vocational Educational Research, 26*, 103–140.

Hutchinson, N.L., Pyle, A., Villeneuve, M., Dods, J., Dalton, C., & Minnes, P. (2014). Understanding parent advocacy during the transition to school of children with developmental disabilities: Three Canadian case studies. *Early Years: An International Research Journal, 34*(4), 348–363.

Hutchinson, N.L., & Schmid, C. (1996). Perceptions of a resource teacher about programs for preschoolers with special needs and their families. *Canadian Journal of Research in Early Childhood Education, 5*(1), 73–82.

Hutchinson, N.L., Versnel, J., Chin, P., & Munby, H. (2008). Negotiating accommodations so that work-based education facilitates career development for youth with disabilities. *Work: A Journal of Prevention, Assessment & Rehabilitation, 30*, 123–136.

Hyde, M., Punch, R., & Power, D. (2009). The experiences of deaf and hard of hearing students at Queensland University: 1985–2005. *Higher Education Research & Development, 28*(1), 85–98.

International Labour Organization. (2006). *Global employment trends for youth.* Geneva, Switzerland: Author.

Irish, C. (2002). Using peg- and keyword mnemonics and computer assisted instruction to enhance basic multiplication performance in elementary students with learning and cognitive disabilities. *Journal of Special Education Technology, 17*, 29–40.

Irwin, M., & Elam, M. (2011). Are we leaving children with chronic illness behind? *Physical Disabilities: Education & Related Services, 30*(2), 67–80.

Iseman, J.S., & Naglieri, J.A. (2011). A cognitive strategy instruction to improve math calculation or children with ADHD and LD: A randomized controlled study. *Journal of Learning Disabilities, 44*(2), 184–195.

Ivison, J. (December 8, 2011). Education is key to life after Attawapiskat. *National Post.* Retrieved from http://fullcomment.nationalpost.com/2011/12/08/john-ivison-education-is-key-to-life-after-attawapiskat

Jacknick, C.M. (2011). Breaking in is hard to do: How students negotiate classroom activity shifts. *Classroom Discourse, 2*(1), 20–38.

Jacobson, L.T., & Reid, L.R. (2010). Improving the persuasive essay writing of high school students with ADHD. *Exceptional Children, 76*(2), 157–174.

James, C. (2012). *Life at the intersection: Community, class and schooling.* Halifax, NS: Fernwood Publishing.

James, S., & Freeze, R. (2006). One step forward, two steps back: Immanent critique of the practice of zero tolerance in inclusive schools. *International Journal of Inclusive Education, 10*(6), 581–594.

Jamieson, M., Hutchinson, N.L., Taylor, J., Fallon, K., Berg, D., & Boyce, W. (2009). Friendships of adolescents with physical disabilities attending inclusive high schools. *Canadian Journal of Occupational Therapy, 76*(5), 368–378.

Jamieson, J., Zaidman-Zait, A., & Poon, B. (2011). Family support needs as perceived by parents of preadolescents and adolescents who are deaf or hard of hearing. *Deafness & Education International, 13*(3), 110–130.

Jansen, S., van der Putten, A., & Vlaskamp, C. (2013). What parents find important in the support of a child with profound intellectual and multiple disabilities. *Child: Care, Health & Development, 39*(3), 432–441.

Jayanthi, M., Epstein, M.H., Polloway, E.A., & Bursuck, W.D. (1996). A national survey of general education teachers' perceptions of testing adaptations. *The Journal of Special Education, 30*(1), 99–115.

Jellison, J.A., & Draper, E. (2015). Music research in inclusive school settings: 1975 to 2013. *Journal of Research in Music Education, 62*(4), 325–331.

Jeynes, W.H. (2007). The relationship between parental involvement and urban secondary school student academic achievement. *Urban Education, 42*, 82–110.

Jimenez, B.A., Lo, Y., & Saunders, A.F. (2012). The additive effects of scripted lessons plus guided notes on science quiz scores of students with intellectual disabilities and autism. *The Journal of Special Education, 20*, 1–14.

Jimerson, S.R., Swearer, S.M., & Espelage, D.L. (2010). *Handbook of bullying in schools: An international perspective.* New York, NY: Routledge.

Jitendra, A.K., Dupuis, D., & Zaslofsky, A. (2014). Curriculum-based measurement and standards-based mathematics: Monitoring the arithmetic word problem-solving performance of third grade students at risk for mathematics difficulties. *Learning Disability Quarterly, 37*(4), 241–251.

Jitendra, A.K., & Star, J.R. (2011). Meeting the needs of students with learning disabilities in inclusive mathematics classrooms: The role of schema-based instruction on mathematical problem solving. *Theory Into Practice, 50*(1), 12–19.

Joffe, V.L., Cain, K., & Maric, N. (2007). Comprehension problems in children with specific language impairment: Does mental imagery training help? *International Journal of Language and Communication Disorders, 42*, 648–664.

Johnsen, S.K., Parker, S., & Farah, Y. (2015). Providing services for students with gifts and talents within a response-to-intervention framework. *Teaching Exceptional Children, 47*(4), 226–233.

Johnson, D.W., & Johnson, R.T. (2004). *Assessing students in groups: Promoting group responsibility and individual accountability.* Thousand Oaks, CA: Corwin Press.

Johnson, J., & Reid, R. (2011). Overcoming executive function deficits in students with ADHD. *Theory Into Practice, 50*(1), 61–67.

Johnson, L. (2011). *Teaching outside the box: How to grab your students by their brains.* San Francisco, CA: Jossey-Bass.

Jones, E.A., Neil, N., & Feeley, K. (2014). Enhancing learning for children with Down syndrome. In R. Faragher & B. Clarke (Eds.), *Educating learners with Down syndrome.* New York, NY: Routledge.

Jones, M.G., Minogue, J., Oppewal, T., Cook, M.P., & Broadwell, B. (2006). Visualizing without vision at the microscale: Students with visual impairments explore cells with touch. *Journal of Science Education and Technology, 15*, 345–351.

Joong, P., & Ridler, O. (2005). School violence: Perception and reality. *Education Canada, 45*(4), 61–63.

Jordan, A., Glenn, C., & McGhie-Richmond, D. (2010). The Supporting Effective Teaching (SET) project: The relationship of inclusive teaching practices to teachers' beliefs about disability and ability, and about their roles as teachers. *Teaching and Teacher Education, 26*(2), 259–266.

Jordan, N.C., Dyson, N., & Glutting, J. (Fall, 2011). *Developing number sense in kindergarteners at risk for learning difficulties in mathematics.* Society for Research on Educational Effectiveness.

Jordan, N., Glutting, J., Ramineni, C., & Watkins, M. (2010). Validating a number sense screening tool for use in kindergarten and first grade: Prediction of mathematics proficiency in third grade. *School Psychology Review, 39*(2), 181–195.

Jung, L.A., & Guskey, T.R. (2010). Grading exceptional learners. *Educational Leadership, 67*(5), 31–35.

Kadivar, P., YarYari, F., & Niyazi, E. (2010). The effects of strategy-focused writing instruction for students with learning disability. *International Journal of Learning, 17*(10), 419–426.

Kagan, R.S., Joseph, L., Dufresne, C., et al. (2003). Prevalence of peanut allergy in primary-school children in Montreal, Canada. *Journal of Allergy and Clinical Immunology, 112*(6), 1223–1228.

Kagan, S. (2013). *Cooperative learning structures.* San Clemente, CA: Kagan Publishing.

Kanevsky, L. (2011). A survey of educational acceleration practices in Canada. *Canadian Journal of Education, 34*(3), 153–180.

Kanevsky, L., & Clelland, D. (2013). Accelerating gifted students in Canada: Policies and possibilities. *Canadian Journal of Education, 36*(3), 229–271.

Kaplan, S.N. (2008). Curriculum consequence: If you learn this, then . . . *Gifted Child Today, 31,* 41–42.

Kappelman, M.D., Rifas-Shiman, S.L., et al. (2007). The prevalence and geographic distribution of Crohn's disease and ulcerative colitis in the United States. *Clinical Gastroenterology, 5*(12), 1424–1429.

Karalunas, S.L., & Huang-Pollock, C.L. (2011). Examining relationships between executive functioning and delay aversion in attention deficit hyperactivity disorder. *Journal of Clinical Child & Adolescent Psychology, 40*(6), 837–847.

Katz, J. (2012). *Teaching to diversity: The three-block model of universal design.* Winnipeg, MB: Portage & Main Press.

Kaufman, M. (2005). *Easy for you to say: Questions and answers for teens living with chronic illness or disability* (2nd ed.). Buffalo, NY: Firefly.

Kaul, T. (2011). Helping African American children self-manage asthma: The importance of self-efficacy. *Journal of School Health, 81*(1), 29–33.

Kennett, D.J., & Reed, M.J. (2009). Factors influencing academic success and retention following a 1st-year post-secondary success course. *Educational Research and Evaluation, 15*(2), 153–166.

Kidd, S., & Evans, D. (2011). Home is where you draw strength and rest: The meaning of home for houseless young people. *Youth & Society, 43*(2), 752–773.

Kidder, A. (2011). Parent advocacy: The good, the bad, and the ugly. *Education Canada, 51*(4). Retrieved from www.cea-ace.ca/education-canada/article/parent-advocacy-good-bad-and-ugly

Kim, Y.Y. (2001). *Becoming intercultural: An integrative theory of communication and cross-cultural adaptation.* Thousand Oaks, CA: Sage.

King, A.J.C., Warren, W., & Peart, M. (1988). *The teaching experience.* Toronto, ON: Ontario Secondary School Teachers' Federation.

King, R.S., & Chapman, C.M. (2011). *Differentiated assessment strategies: One tool doesn't fit all.* Thousand Oaks, CA: Corwin Press.

Kirby, J.R., Georgiou, G.K., Martinussen, R., & Parrila, R. (2010). Naming speed and reading: From prediction to instruction. *Reading Research Quarterly, 45*(3), 341–362.

Kirst, M., Frederick, T., & Erickson, P.G. (2011). Concurrent mental health and substance use problems among street-involved youth. *International Journal of Mental Health and Addiction, 9*, 543–553.

Klassen, R. (2002). The changing landscape of learning disabilities in Canada: Definitions and practice from 1989–2000. *School Psychology International, 23*, 199–219.

Klassen, R. (2007). Using predictions to learn about the self-efficacy of early adolescents with and without learning disabilities. *Contemporary Educational Psychology, 32*(2), 173–187.

Klassen, R., & Lynch, S.L. (2007). Self-efficacy from the perspective of adolescents with LD and their specialist teachers. *Journal of Learning Disabilities, 40*(6), 494–507.

Kleinert, J.O., Harrison, E., Fisher, T., & Kleinert, H.. (2010). "I can" and "I did": Self-advocacy for young students with developmental disabilities. *Teaching Exceptional Children, 43*(2), 16–26.

Klein-Tasman, B.P., & Albano, A.M. (2007). Intensive, short-term cognitive-behavioral treatment of OCD-like behavior with a young adult with Williams syndrome. *Clinical Case Studies, 6*(6), 483–492.

Klinger, D.A., DeLuca, C., & Miller, T. (2008). The evolving culture of large-scale assessment in Canadian education. *Canadian Journal of Educational Administration and Policy, 76*, 5. Retrieved from https://www.umanitoba.ca/publications/cjeap/articles/klinger.html

Klinger, D., Maggi, S., & D'Angiulli, A. (2011). School accountability and assessment: Should we put the roof up first? *Educational Forum, 75*(2), 114–128.

Klinger, D., & Wade-Woolley, L. (2012). *Supporting low-performing schools in Ontario, Canada: Case study.* Toronto, ON: Ministry of Education.

Kluth, P. (2004). Autism, autobiography, and adaptations. *Teaching Exceptional Children, 36*(4), 42–47.

Koellner, K., & Wallace, F. (2007). Alternative uses for junk mail: How environmental print supports mathematics literacy. *Mathematics Teaching in the Middle School, 12,* 326–332.

Kogan, M.D., Blumberg, S.J., Schieve, L.A., Boyle, C.A., Perrin, J.M., Ghandour, R.M., & Van Dyck, P.C. (2009). Prevalence of parent-reported diagnosis of autism spectrum disorder among children in the US, 2007. *Pediatrics, 124,* 1–9.

Korat, O. (2010). Reading electronic books as a support for vocabulary, story comprehension and word reading in kindergarten and first grade. *Computers & Education, 55,* 24–31.

Kosky, C., & Curtis, R. (2008). An action research exploration integrating student choice and arts activities in a sixth grade social studies classroom. *Journal of Social Studies Research, 32*(1), 22–27.

Kottler, J.A., & Kottler, E. (2006). *Counseling skills for teachers.* Thousand Oaks, CA: Corwin Press.

Koutsoklenis, A., & Theodoridou, Z. (2012). Tourette syndrome: School-based interventions for tics and associated conditions. *International Journal of Special Education, 27*(3), 213–223.

Kozey, M., & Siegel, L.S. (2008). Definitions of learning disabilities in Canadian provinces and territories. *Canadian Psychology, 49*(2), 162–171.

Kraus, J.F. (1986). The relationship of family income to the incidence, external causes, and outcomes of serious brain injury, San Diego County, California. *American Journal of Public Health, 76*(11), 1345–1347.

Kronenberg, D., & Blair, K. (2010). Sixth-graders bring ancient civilizations to life through drama. In D. Glass, B. Henderson, & L. Barnum (Eds.), *The contours of inclusion: Inclusive arts teaching and learning.* The International Organization on Arts and Disability. Retrieved from www.eric.ed.gov/PDFS/ED522677.pdf

Kurtts, S., Matthews, C.E., & Smallwood, T. (2009). (Dis)solving the differences: A physical science lesson using universal design. *Intervention in School and Clinic, 44*(3), 151–159.

Kutash, K., Duchnowski, A.J., & Lynn, N. (2006). *School-based mental health: An empirical guide for decision-makers.* Miami, FL: University of South Florida, Research and Training Center for Children's Mental Health.

Kutnick, P., & Kington, A. (2005). Children's friendships and learning in school: Cognitive enhancement through social interaction? *British Journal of Educational Psychology, 75,* 521–538.

Lacasse, A., & Mendelson, M. (2006). The perceived intent of potentially offensive sexual behaviors among adolescents. *Journal of Research on Adolescence, 16*(2), 229–238.

Ladd, H. F., & Zelli, A. (2002). School-based accountability in North Carolina. *Educational Administration Quarterly, 38,* 494–529.

Lague, K.M., & Wilson, K. (2011). Peer tutors improve reading comprehension. *Education Digest, 76*(7), 56–58.

Lai, S., & Berkeley, S. (2012). High-stakes test accommodations: Research and practice. *Learning Disability Quarterly, 35*(3), 158–169.

Laird, G. (2007). *Shelter: Homelessness in a growth economy.* Calgary, AB: Sheldon Chumir Foundation for Ethics in Leadership.

Lam, C.S.M. (1996). The green teacher. In D. Thiessen, N. Bascia, & I. Goodson (Eds.), *Making a difference about difference: The lives and careers of racial minority immigrant teachers* (pp. 15–50). Toronto, ON: Garamond Press.

Lambdin, D.V., & Forseth, C. (1996). Seamless assessment /instruction = good teaching. *Teaching Exceptional Children Mathematics, 21*(1), 294–298.

Landrum, T.J., & Sweigart, C.A. (2014). Simple, evidence-based interventions for classic problems of emotional and behavioral disorders. *Beyond Behavior, 23*(3), 3–9.

Lane, K.L., Wehby, J., & Barton-Arwood, S.M. (2005). Students with and at risk for emotional and behavioral disorders: Meeting their social and academic needs. *Preventing School Failure, 49*(2), 6–9.

Langberg, J., & Becker, S. (2012). Does long-term medication use improve the academic outcomes of youth with attention-deficit/hyperactivity disorder? *Clinical Child and Family Psychology Review, 15*(3), 215–233.

Langer, E.C. (2007). *Classroom discourse and interpreted education: What is conveyed to deaf elementary school students* (Unpublished doctoral dissertation). University of Colorado at Boulder.

Larivee, B. (2006). *Authentic classroom management: Creating a learning community and building reflective practice* (2nd ed.). Boston, MA: Pearson Allyn & Bacon.

Lattimer, H., & Riordan, R. (2011). Project-based learning engages students in meaningful work. *Middle School Journal, 43*(2), 18–23.

Laugeson, E.A., Paley, B., Schonfeld, A.M., Carpenter, E.M., Frankel, F., & O'Connor, M.J. (2007). Adaptation of the children's friendship training program for children with fetal alcohol spectrum disorders. *Child and Family Behavior Therapy, 29*(3), 57–69.

Law, M., King, G., King, S., Kertoy, M., Hurley, P., Rosenbaum, P., Young, N., & Hanna S. (2006). Patterns of participation in recreational and leisure activities among children with complex physical disabilities. *Developmental Medicine and Child Neurology, 48,* 337–342.

Lawson, J. (2008). Women leaders in high-poverty community schools: Work-related stress and family impact. *Canadian Journal of Education, 31*(1), 55–77.

Learning Disability Association of Canada (LDAC). (2002). Official definition of learning disabilities: Adopted by the Learning Disabilities Association of Canada January 30, 2002 (re-endorsed March 2, 2015). Retrieved from http://www.ldac-acta.ca

Learning Disability Association of Ontario (LDAO). (2001). Definitions of LDs. Retrieved from www.ldao.ca

Lederer, J.M. (2000). Reciprocal teaching of social studies in inclusive elementary classrooms. *Journal of Learning Disabilities, 33,* 91–106.

Lee, H.J., & Herner-Patnode, L.M. (2007). Teaching mathematics vocabulary to diverse groups. *Intervention in School & Clinic, 43*(2), 121–126.

Lee, S.I., Schachar, R.J., Chen, S.X., Ornstein, T.J., Charach, A., Barr, C., & Ickowicz, A. (2008). Predictive validity of DSM-IV and ICD-10 criteria for ADHD and hyperkinetic disorder. *Journal of Child Psychology & Psychiatry & Allied Disciplines, 49*(1), 70–78.

Lent, R.W., Hackett, G., & Brown, S.D. (1999). A social cognitive view of school-to-work transition. *Career Development Quarterly, 47,* 297–311.

Lepofsky, M.D. (1996). A report card on the *Charter's* guarantee of equality to persons with disabilities after 10 years—what progress? What prospects? *National Journal of Constitutional Law, 7,* 263–431.

Lerna, A., Esposito, D., Conson, M., & Massagli, A. (2014). Long-term effects of PECS on social-communicative skills of children with autism spectrum disorders: A follow-up study. *International Journal of Language and Communication Disorders, 49*(4), 478–485.

Lesaux, N.K., Pearson, M.R., & Siegel, L.S. (2006). The effects of timed and untimed testing conditions on the reading comprehension performance of adults with reading disabilities. *Reading and Writing, 19*(1), 21–48.

Lévesque, N.L. (1997). *Perceptions of friendships and peer groups: The school experiences of two adolescents with learning disabilities* (Unpublished master's thesis). Queen's University, Kingston, ON.

Levin, D.E. (2003). *Teaching young children in violent times: Building a peaceable classroom.* Cambridge, MA: Educators for Social Responsibility.

Levin, B. (2008). These may be good times: An argument that things are getting better. In C. Sugrue (Ed.), *The future of educational change: International perspectives* (pp. 34–47). New York, NY: Routledge.

Levine, T.H., & Marcus, A.S. (2010). How the structure and focus of teachers' collaborative activities facilitate and constrain teacher learning. *Teaching and Teacher Education: An International Journal of Research and Studies, 26*(3), 389–398.

Lewis, A., & Parsons, S. (2008). Understanding of epilepsy by children and young people with epilepsy. *European Journal of Special Education Needs, 23*(4), 321–335.

Lewis, R., & Burman, E. (2006). Providing for student voice in classroom management: Teachers' views. *International Journal of Inclusive Education, 1,* 1–17.

Lewis, S. (1992). *Report on race relations.* Toronto, ON: Government of Ontario.

Lewthwaite, B., Owen, T., Doiron, A., Macmillan, B., & Renaud, R. (2014a). Our stories about teaching and learning: A pedagogy of consequence for Yukon First Nation settings. *Interchange, 44,* 105–128.

Lewthwaite, B., Owen, T., Doiron, A., Renaud, R., & Macmillan, B. (2014b). Culturally responsive teaching in Yukon First Nation settings: What does it look like and what is its influence? *Canadian Journal of Educational Administration and Policy, 55*(April 10, 2014).

Liang, L.A. (2011). Scaffolding middle school students' comprehension and response to short stories. *Research in Middle Level Education (RMLE Online), 34*(8), 1–16. Retrieved from http://www.nmsa.org

Lifvendahl, S. (2007). Pursuing rigor at the middle level. *Principal Leadership, 8*(1), 30–33.

Lin, P.-Y. (2010). *Test accommodations in Canadian provincial assessments: Current practices, policies, and research.* Retrieved from http://www.canadiantestcentre.com/PDF//AccommodationsPracticeandResearch.pdf

Lindberg, J.A., & Swick, A.M. (2006). *Common-sense classroom management for elementary school teachers* (2nd ed.). Thousand Oaks, CA: Corwin Press.

Lindsay, S., & McPherson, A.C. (2012). Strategies for improving disability awareness and social inclusion of children and young people with cerebral palsy. *Child: Care, Health and Development, 38*(6), 809–816.

Lindsay, S., Proulx, M., Scott, H., & Thomosn, N. (2014). Exploring teachers' strategies for including children with autism spectrum disorder in mainstream classrooms. *International Journal of Inclusive Education, 18*(2), 101–122.

Lindstrom, L.E., & Benz, M.R. (2002). Phases of career development: Case studies of young women with learning disabilities. *Exceptional Children, 69,* 67–83.

Lindstrom, L., Doren, B., & Miksch, J. (2011). Waging a living: Career development and long-term employment outcomes for young adults with disabilities. *Exceptional Children, 77*(4), 423–434.

Linnenbrink-Garcia, L., Patall, E., & Messersmith, E. (2013). Antecedents and consequences of situational interest. *British Journal of Educational Psychology, 83*(4), 591–614.

Liu, C-C., & Hong, Y-C. (2006). Providing hearing-impaired students with learning care after classes through smart phones and the GPRS network. *British Journal of Educational Technology, 38*(4), 727–741.

Livingstone, A-M., Celemencki, J., & Calixte, M. (2014). Youth participatory action research and school improvement: The missing voices of black youth in Montreal. *Canadian Journal of Education, 37*(1), 283–307.

Lizzio, A., Wilson, K., & Hadaway, V. (2007). University students' perceptions of a fair learning environment: A social justice perspective. *Assessment & Evaluation in Higher Education, 32*(20), 195–213.

Lloyd, S., Wernham, S., Jolly, C., & Stephen, L. (1998). *Jolly phonics.* Chigwell, UK: Jolly Learning.

Lombardo, M.V., & Baron-Cohen, S. (2011). The role of the self in mindblindness in autism. *Consciousness & Cognition, 20*(1), 130–140.

Long, C., Downs, C.A., Gillette, B., Kills in Sight, L., & Iron-Cloud Konen, E. (2006). Assessing cultural life skills of American Indian youth. *Child Youth Care Forum, 35,* 289–304.

Long, L., MacBlain, S., & MacBlain, M. (2008). Supporting students with dyslexia at the secondary level: An emotional model of literacy. *Journal of Adolescent and Adult Literacy, 51*(2), 124–134.

Lucas, B., & Smith, A. (2004). *Help your child to succeed: The essential guide for parents.* Markham, ON: Pembroke Publishers.

Luciano, S., & Savage, R.S. (2007). Bullying risk in children with learning difficulties in inclusive educational settings. *Canadian Journal of School Psychology, 22,* 14–31.

Luckner, J.L., & Cooke, C. (2010). A summary of the vocabulary research with students who are deaf or hard of hearing. *American Annals of the Deaf, 155*(1), 38–67.

Luecking, R.G. (2011). Connecting employers with people who have intellectual disability. *Intellectual and Developmental Disabilities, 49*(4), 261–273.

Lukacs, K.S., & Galluzzo, G.R. (2014). Beyond empty vessels and bridges: Toward defining teachers as the agents of school change. *Teacher Development, 18*(1), 100–106.

Lundberg, I., & Reichenberg, M. (2013). Developing reading comprehension among students with mild intellectual disabilities: An intervention study. *Scandinavian Journal of Educational Research, 57*(1), 89–100.

Lutz, S.L., Guthrie, J.T., & Davis, M.H. (2006). Scaffolding for engagement in elementary school reading instruction. *Journal of Educational Research, 100,* 3–20.

Luu, K. (2015). *The use of online quizzes to support learning and planning in an undergraduate course* (Unpublished PhD dissertation). Queen's University, Kingston, ON.

Maberly, D.A.L., Hollands, H., Chuo, J., et al. (2006). The prevalence of low vision and blindness in Canada. *Eye, 20,* 341–346.

MacCuspie, P.A. (1996). *Promoting acceptance of children with disabilities: From tolerance to inclusion.* Halifax, NS: Atlantic Provinces Special Education Authority.

Mackenzie, S. (2011). 'Yes but …': Rhetoric, reality and resistance in teaching assistants' experiences of inclusive education. *Support for Learning, 26*(2), 64–71.

Madden, M., & Sullivan, J. (2008). *Teaching fluency beyond the primary grades: Strategy lessons to meet the specific needs of upper-grade readers.* New York, NY: Scholastic, Inc.

Mady, C., & Arnett, K. (2009). Inclusion in French Immersion in Canada: One parent's perspective. *Exceptionality Education International, 19*(2), 37–49.

McCaleb, S.P. (1995). *Building communities of learners: Collaboration among teachers, students, families, and community.* Mahwah, NJ: Lawrence Erlbaum.

Maehler, C., & Schuchardt, K. (2011). Working memory in children with learning disabilities: Rethinking the criterion of discrepancy. *International Journal of Disability, Development and Education, 58*(1), 5–17.

Magro, K. (2006/2007). Overcoming the trauma of war: Literacy challenges of adult learners. *Education Canada, 47*(1), 70–74.

Malin, J., & Makel, M.C. (2012). Gender differences in gifted students' advice on solving the world's problems. *Journal for the Education of the Gifted, 35*(2), 175–187.

Mandali, S.L., & Gordon, T.A. (2009). Management of type 1 diabetes in schools: Whose responsibility? *Journal of School Health, 79*(12), 599–601.

Mantilla, J., & Diaz, M. (2012). Development and validation of a measuring instrument for burnout syndrome in teachers. *The Spanish Journal of Psychology, 15*(3), 1456–1465.

Markoulakis, R., Scharoun, S., Bryden, P., & Fletcher, P. (2012). An examination of handedness and footedness in children with high functioning autism and Asperger syndrome. *Journal of Autism and Developmental Disorders, 42*(10), 2192–2201.

Martell, G.A. (2008). Why saving a seat is not enough: Aboriginal rights and school community councils in Saskatchewan. . *First Nations Perspective, 1*. Retrieved from http://www.mfnerc.org/index.php?option=com_content&task=category&sectionid=14&id=92&Itemid=116&Itemid=117

Martinussen, R., & Major, A. (2011). Working memory weaknesses in students with ADHD: Implications for instruction. *Theory Into Practice, 50*(1), 68–75.

Marton, I., Wiener, J., Rogers, M., Moore, C., & Tannock, R. (2009). Empathy and social perspective taking in children with attention-deficit/hyperactivity disorder. *Journal of Abnormal Child Psychology, 37*(1), 107–118.

Maslach, C. (2003). Job burnout: New directions in research and intervention. *Current Directions in Psychological Science, 12*(5), 189–192.

Mason, L.H., Harris, K.R., & Graham, S. (2011). Self-regulated strategy development for students with writing difficulties. *Theory Into Practice, 50*(1), 20–27.

Mathews, S.E. (2012). Singing smoothes classroom transitions. *Dimensions of Early Childhood, 40*(1), 13–17.

Matilla, M-L., Kielinen, M., et al. (2007). An epidemiological and diagnostic study of Asperger syndrome according to four sets of diagnostic criteria. *Journal of the American Academy of Child and Adolescent Psychiatry, 46*, 636–646.

Mattatall, C. (2008, June). *Gauging the readiness of Canadian school districts to implement responsiveness to intervention.* Paper presented at the annual meeting of the Canadian Society for the Study of Education, Vancouver, BC.

Matthews, D.J., & Dai, D.Y. (2014). Gifted education: Changing conceptions, emphases and practice. *International Studies in Sociology of Education, 24*(4), 335–353.

Matthews, M.S., & Kirsch, L. (2011). Evaluating gifted identification practice: Aptitude testing and linguistically diverse learners. *Journal of Applied School Psychology, 27*(2), 155–180.

Maxwell, M. (2007). Career counseling is personal counseling: A constructivist approach to nurturing the development of gifted female adolescents. *Career Development Quarterly, 55*(3), 206–224.

Mayer, K., & Kelley, M.L. (2007). Improving homework in adolescents with attention-deficit/hyperactivity disorder: Self vs. parent monitoring of homework behavior and study skills. *Child and Family Behavior Therapy, 39*(4), 25–42.

McBee, M., Shaunessy, E., & Matthews, M. (2012). Policy matters: An analysis of district-level efforts to increase the identification of underrepresented learners. *Journal of Advanced Academics, 23*(4), 326–344.

McCafferty, S.G., Jacobs, G.M., & DaSilva Iddings, C. (Eds.). (2006). *Cooperative learning and second language teaching.* Cambridge, UK: Cambridge University Press.

McCartney, E., Boyle, J., & Ellis, S. (2015). Developing a universal reading comprehension intervention for mainstream primary schools within areas of social deprivation for children with and without language-learning impairment: A feasibility study. *International Journal of Language & Communication Disorders, 50*(1), 129–135.

McClintock, B., Pesco, D., & Martin-Chang, S. (2014). Thinking aloud: Effects on text comprehension by children with specific language impairment and their peers. *International Journal of Language and Communication Disorders, 49*(6), 637–648.

McConaughy, S.H., Volpe, R.J., Antshel, K.M., Gordon, M., & Eiraldi, R.B. (2011). Academic and social impairments of elementary school children with attention deficit hyperactivity disorder. *School Psychology Review, 40*(2), 200–225.

McCord, K., & Fitzgerald, M. (2006). Children with disabilities playing musical instruments: With the right adaptations and help from teachers and parents, students with disabilities can play musical instruments. *Music Educators Journal, 92*(4), 46–52.

McCord, K., & Watts, M.H. (2006). Collaboration and access for our children: Music educators and special educators together: When music educators and special educators work together, all students are likely to benefit. *Music Educators Journal, 92*(4), 26–31.

McCormick, R.M., Amundsen, N.E., & Poehnell, G. (2002). *Guiding circles: An Aboriginal guide to finding career paths.* Saskatoon, SK: Aboriginal Human Resources Development Council of Canada.

McCue, H.A. (2000). *The learning circle: Classroom activities on First Nations in Canada.* Ottawa, ON: Indian and Northern Affairs Canada.

McCue, H.A. (2004). *An overview of federal and provincial policy trends in First Nations education.* Retrieved from http://chiefs-of-ontario.org/

McDougall, J., DeWit, D.J., King, G., Miller, L., & Killip, S. (2004). High school-aged youths' attitudes toward their peers with disabilities: The role of school and student interpersonal factors. *International Journal of Disability, Development and Education, 51*, 287–313.

McEachern, A.G., & Kenny, M.C. (2007). Transition groups for high school students with disabilities. *The Journal for Specialists in Group Work, 32*(2). 165–177.

McGinty, S., & Brader, A. (2005). Educational disengagement: A review of international, Australian and state policy responses. In A. Pandian, M.K. Kabilan, & S. Kaur (Eds.), *Teachers, practices, and supportive cultures* (pp. 25–35). Serdang: Universiti Putra Malaysia Press. Retrieved from http://www.andybrader.com/downloads/educationaldisengagement.pdf

McHugh, M.W. (2006). Governor's schools: Fostering the social and emotional well-being of gifted and talented students. *Journal of Secondary Gifted Education, 17*(3), 50–58.

McIntosh, K., Flannery, K.B., Sugai, G., Braun, D.H., & Cochrane, K.L. (2008). Relationships between academics and problem behavior in the transition from middle school to high school. *Journal of Positive Behavior Intervention, 10*(4), 243–355.

McIntosh, K., MacKay, L.D., Andreou, T., Brown, J.A., Mathews, S., Gietz, C., & Bennett, J.L. (2011). Response to intervention in Canada: Definitions, the evidence base, and future directions. *Canadian Journal of School Psychology, 28*(1), 18–43.

McKay, S., Gravel, J.S., & Tharpe, A.M. (2008). Amplification considerations for children with minimal or mild bilateral hearing loss and unilateral hearing loss. *Trends in Amplification, 12*(1), 43–54.

McKinney, S. (2014). The relationship of child poverty to school education. *Improving Schools, 17*(3), 213–216.

McLeod, S., & Harrison, L.J. (2009). Epidemiology of speech and language impairment in a nationally representative sample of 4- to 5-year-old children. *Journal of Speech, Language, and Hearing Research, 52*, 1213–1229.

McManus, V., & Savage, E. (2010). Cultural perspectives of interventions for managing diabetes and asthma in children and adolescents from ethnic minority groups. *Child: Care, Health & Development, 36*(5), 612–622.

McMillan, J.M., & Jarvis, J.M. (2013). Mental health and students with disabilities: A review of the literature. *Australian Journal of Guidance and Counselling, 23*(2), 236–251.

McNeely, C., & Falci, C. (2004). School connectedness and the transition into and out of health-risk behavior among adolescents: A comparison of social belonging and teacher support. *Journal of School Health, 74*(7), 284–292.

McPhail, J.C., & Pierson, J.M., Goodman, J., & Noffke, J.B. (2004). Creating partnerships for complex learning: The dynamics of an interest-based apprenticeship in the art of sculpture. *Curriculum Inquiry, 34*, 463–493.

Meadan, H., Ostrosky, M.M., Triplett, B., Michna, A., & Fettig, A. (2011). Using visual supports with young children with autism spectrum disorder. *Teaching Exceptional Children, 43*(6), 28–37.

Meenakshi, G., Jitendra, A.K., Sood, S., Sacks, G. (2007). Improving comprehension of expository text in students with LD: A research synthesis. *Journal of Learning Disabilities, 40*, 210–225.

Menear, K.S., & Smith, S. (2011). Teaching physical education to students with autism spectrum disorders. *Strategies, 24*(3), 21–24.

Mergler, M., Vargas, K., & Caldwell, C. (2014). Alternative discipline can benefit learning. *Phi Delta Kappan, 96*(2), 25–30.

Meyer, E.J. (2010). Transforming school cultures. *Gender and Sexual Diversity in Schools, 10*(2), 121–139.

Miedijensky, S., & Tal, T. (2009). Embedded assessment in project-based science courses for the gifted: Insights to inform teaching all students. *International Journal of Science Education, 31*(18), 2411–2435.

Mihalas, S., Morse, W.C., Allsopp, D.H., & Alvarez McHatton, P. (2009). Cultivating caring relationships between teachers and secondary students with emotional and behavioral disorders. *Remedial and Special Education, 30*(2), 108–125.

Miller, D., Topping, K., & Thurston, A. (2010). Peer tutoring in reading: The effects of role and organization on two dimensions of self-esteem. *British Journal of Educational Psychology, 80*(3), 417–433.

Miller, P., Pavlakis, A., Lac, V., & Hoffman, D. (2014). Responding to poverty and its complex challenges: The importance of policy fluency for educational leaders. *Theory Into Practice, 53*, 131–138.

Ministère de l'Éducation. (1999). *Adapting our schools to the needs of all students.* Québec, QC: Gouvernement du Québec.

Ministère de l'Éducation. (2000). *Students with handicaps, social maladjustments or leaning difficulties: Definitions.* Québec, QC: Gouvernement du Québec.

Mislevy, R.J., Haertel, G., Cheng, B., Ructtinger, L., DeBarger, A., Murray, E. et al. (2013). A "conditional" sense of fairness in assessment. *Educational Research and Evaluation, 19*(2–3), 121–140.

Mo, Y., & Singh, K. (2008). Parents' relationships and involvement: Effects on students' school engagement and performance. *Research in Middle Level Education Online, 31*(10), 1–11.

Mohan, E., & Shields, C.M. (2014). The voices behind the numbers: Understanding the experiences of homeless students. *Critical Questions in Education, 5*(3), 189–202.

Molnar, B.E., Cerda, M., Roberts, A.L., & Buka, S.L. (2008). Effects of neighborhood resources on aggressive and delinquent behaviors among urban youths. *American Journal of Public Health, 98*(6), 1086–1093.

Monroe, B.W., & Troia, G.A. (2006). Teaching writing strategies to middle school students with disabilities. *Journal of Educational Research, 100*, 21–33.

Montague, M., Ebdrs, C., & Dietz, S. (2011). Effects of cognitive strategy instruction on math problem solving of middle school students with learning disabilities. *Learning Disability Quarterly, 34*(4), 262–272.

Moore Johnson, S., and the Project on the Next Generation of Teachers. (2007). *Finders and keepers: Helping new teachers survive and thrive in our schools.* San Francisco, CA: Jossey-Bass.

Morcom, L. (2014). Determining the role of language and culture in First Nations schools: A comparison of the First Nations Education Act with the policy of the Assembly of First Nations. *Canadian Journal of Educational Administration and Policy, 163*(September 19, 2014).

Morgan, P.L., Farkas, G., Tufis, P.S., & Sperling, R.S. (2008). Are reading and behavioral problems risk factors for each other? *Journal of Learning Disabilities, 41*(5), 417–436.

Morningstar, M. E. (1997). Critical issues in career development and employment preparation for adolescents with disabilities. *Remedial and Special Education, 18*, 307–320.

Morris, C., & Sharma, U. (2011). Facilitating the inclusion of children with visual impairment: Perspectives of itinerant support teachers. *Australasian Journal of Special Education, 35*(2), 191–203.

Morris, R.C., & Howard, A.C. (2003). Designing an effective in-school suspension program. *Clearing House, 76*, 156–159.

Morrison, W., & Peterson, P. (2013). *Schools as a setting for promoting positive mental health: Better practices and perspectives* (2nd ed.). Toronto, ON: Pan-Canadian Joint Consortium for School Health.

Mosoff, J., Greenholtz, J., & Hurtado, T. (2009). *Assessment of inclusive post-secondary education for young adults with developmental disabilities.* Ottawa, ON: Canadian Council on Learning.

Munk, D.D., & Bursuck, W.D. (2001). Preliminary findings on personalized grading plans for middle school students with learning disabilities. *Exceptional Children, 67*, 211–234.

Munk, D.D., & Bursuck, W.D. (2004). Personalized grading plans: A systematic approach to making the grades of included students more accurate and meaningful. *Focus on Exceptional Children, 36*(9), 1–12.

Munyofu, M., Swain, W.J., Ausman, B.D., Lin, H., Kidwai, K., Dwyer, F. (2007). The effect of different chunking strategies in complementing animated instruction. *Learning Media and Technology, 32*, 407–419.

Muratori, M., & Smith, C. (2015). Guiding the talent and career development of the gifted individual. *Journal of Counseling & Development, 93*(2), 173–182.

Murray, C., & Greenberg, M.T. (2006). Examining the importance of social relationships and social contexts in the lives of children with high incidence disabilities. *Journal of Special Education, 39*, 220–233.

Myles, B.S., Ferguson, H., & Hagiwara, T. (2007). Using a personal digital assistant to improve the recording of homework assignments by an adolescent with Asperger syndrome. *Focus on Autism and Other Developmental Disabilities, 22*, 96–99.

Nachshen, J.S., Garcin, N., & Minnes, P. (2005). Problem behavior in children with intellectual disabilities: Parenting stress, empowerment and school services. *Mental Health Aspects of Developmental Disabilities, 8*, 105–114.

Nachshen, J.S., & Minnes, P. (2005). Empowerment in parents of school-aged children with and without developmental disabilities. *Journal of Intellectual Disability, 49*, 889–904.

Naraian, S. (2011). Seeking transparency: The production of an inclusive classroom community. *International Journal of Inclusive Education, 15*(9), 955–973.

Nation, K., Cocksey, J., Taylor, J., & Bishop, D. (2010). A longitudinal investigation of early reading and language skills in children with poor reading comprehension. *Journal of Child Psychology & Psychiatry, 51*(9), 1031–1039.

National Indian Brotherhood/Assembly of First Nations. (1972). *Indian control of Indian education.* Retrieved from http://64.26.129.156/call-toaction/Documents/ICOIE.pdf

National Institute for Mental Health. (n.d.). www.nimh.nih.gov/health/topics/child-and-adolescent-mental-health/index.shtml

National Reading Panel. (2000). *Teaching children to read.* Retrieved from http://www.nichd.nih.gov/publications/pubs/nrp/documents/report.pdf

National Reading Panel. (2010). *Report of the National Reading Panel.* Retrieved from www.nichd.nih.gov/publications/nrp/report.cfm

Naugle, K., Campbell, T.A., & Gray, N.D. (2010). Post-secondary transition model for students with disabilities. *Journal of School Counseling, 8,* 1–31.

Naylor, M. (2006). Integrating math in your classroom: From one to one hundreds. *Teaching Pre-K to 8, 36*(5), 36–37.

Neild, R.C., Stoner-Eby, S., & Furstenberg, F. (2008). Connecting entrance and departure: The transition to ninth grade and high school dropout. *Education and Urban Society, 40*(5), 543–569.

Nel, N., Kempen, M., & Ruscheinski, A. (2011). Differentiated pedagogy as inclusive practice: The "learn not to burn" curriculum for learners with severe intellectual disabilities. *Education as Change, 15*(2), 191–208.

Nesbit, J., & Adesope, O. (2006). Learning with concept and knowledge maps: A meta-analysis. *Review of Educational Research, 76*(3), 413–448.

New Brunswick. (2000). *Keeping our schools safe.* Retrieved at www.gnb.ca/0000/publications/ss/keepschoolsafe.pdf

New Brunswick Department of Education. (2002b). *Positive learning environment policy.* Fredericton, NB: New Brunswick Department of Education.

New Brunswick Department of Education. (2014, January). *Challenge for credit.* Retrieved from www.gnb.ca/0000/publications/curric/Challenge_for_Credit.pdf

Newfoundland and Labrador Department of Education. (2006). *Safe and caring schools policy.* St. John's, NL: Government of Newfoundland.

Newfoundland and Labrador Department of Education and Early Childhood Development. (2010). *Roles of teachers in inclusive schools.* Retrieved from http://www.ed.gov.nl.ca/edu/k12/inclusion.html

Newland, L. (2014). Supportive family contexts: Promoting child well-being and resilience. Early *Child Development and Care, 184*(9/10), 1136–1346.

Nickerson, A.B., Corbnell, D.G., Smith, J.D., & Furlong, M.J. (2013). School antibullying efforts: Advice for education policymakers. *Journal of School Violence, 12,* 268–282.

Niskar, A.S. (2001). *Estimated prevalence of noise-induced hearing threshold shifts among children 6 to 19 years of age.* Atlanta, GA: National Centre for Environmental Health, Centers for Disease Control and Prevention.

Noddings, N. (1996). On community. *Educational Theory, 46,* 245–267.

Normand, S., Schneider, B., Lee, M., Maisonneuve, M.-F., Chupetlovska-Anastasova, A., Kuehn, S., & Robaey, P. (2013). Continuities and changes in the friendships of children with and without ADHD: A longitudinal observation study. *Journal of Abnormal Child Psychology, 41,* 1161–1175.

Normand, S., Schneider, B., Lee, M., Maisonneuve, M.-F., Kuehn, S., & Robaey, P. (2011). How do children with ADHD (mis)manage their real-life dyadic friendships? A multi-method investigation. *Journal of Abnormal Child Psychology, 39*(2), 293–305.

Northfield, S., & Sherman, A. (2004). Acceptance and community building in schools through increased dialogue and discussion. *Children and Society, 18,* 291–298.

Nottingham Chaplin, P. K., Baldonado, K., & Ramsey, J. (2014). Children's vision health. *Exchange, 217,* 36–41.

Nova Scotia Education. (2008). *Provincial School Code of Conduct and Code of Conduct Guidelines.* Halifax, NS: Nova Scotia Education.

Nowacek, E.J., & Mamlin, N. (2007). General education teachers and students with ADHD: What modifications are made? *Preventing School Failure, 51*(3), 28–35.

Nyman-McMaster, K., & Fuchs, D. (2002). Effects of cooperative learning on the academic achievement of students with learning disabilities: An update on Tateyama-Sniezek's review. *Learning Disabilities Research & Practice, 17,* 107–117.

O'Brien, B.E., Wolf, M., & Miller, L.T. (2011). Orthographic processing efficiency in developmental dyslexia: An investigation of age and treatment factors at the sublexical level. *Annals of Dyslexia, 61*(1), 111–135.

O'Connor, M., Howell-Meurs, S., Kvalsvig, A., & Goldfeld, S. (2015). Understanding the impact of special health care needs on early school functioning: A conceptual model. *Child: Care, Health & Development, 41*(1), 15–22.

Odom, S.L., Zercher, C., Li, S., Marquart, J., & Sandall, S. (2006). Social acceptance and social rejection of young children with disabilities in inclusive classes. *Journal of Educational Psychology, 98,* 807–823.

Ogilvie, C.R. (2011). Step by step: Social skills instruction for students with autism spectrum disorder using video models and peer mentors. *Teaching Exceptional Children, 43*(6), 20–26.

Oke, D. (2015). *When the consumers lose their appetites: A literature review on the usage of accommodations at the high school level* (Unpublished paper). Queen's University, Kingston, ON.

Okolo, C., Englert, C., Bouck, E., & Heutsche, A. (2007). Web-based history learning environments: Helping all students learn and like history. *Intervention in School and Clinic, 43*(1), 3–11.

Olson, H.C., Jirikowic, T., Kartin, D., & Astley, S. (2007). Responding to the challenge of early intervention for fetal alcohol spectrum disorders. *Infants and Young Children, 20,* 172–189.

Olweus, D. (1993). *Bullying at school: What we know and what we can do.* Oxford, UK: Blackwell.

Olweus, D. (2003, March). A profile of bullying. *Educational Leadership,* 2–17.

Ontario Ministry of Education. (2000a). *Individual education program: Standards for development, program planning, and implementation.* Toronto, ON: Ontario Ministry of Education. Retrieved from http://www.edu.gov.on.ca/eng/general/elemsec/speced/iep/iep.html

Ontario Ministry of Education. (2001a). *Special education: A guide for educators.* Toronto: Ontario Ministry of Education. Retrieved from www.edu.gov.on.ca/eng/general/elemsec/speced/guide/specedhandbooke.pdf

Ontario Ministry of Education. (2001b). *Special education: A guide for educators.* Toronto, ON: Ontario Ministry of Education. Retrieved from www.edu.gov.on.ca/eng/general/elemsec/speced/guide/specedhandbooke.pdf

Ontario Ministry of Education. (2004). *Memorandum no. 127.* Toronto, ON: Ontario Ministry of Education.

Ontario Ministry of Education. (2005). *Education for all (The report of the expert panel on literacy and numeracy instruction for students with special education needs, kindergarten to grade 6).* Toronto, ON: Queen's Printer for Ontario.

Ontario Ministry of Education. (2007). *Safe Schools Act.* Toronto, ON: Ontario Ministry of Education.

Ontario Ministry of Education. (2013). *Learning for all: A guide to effective assessment and instruction for all students, kindergarten to grade 12.* Toronto, ON: Ontario Ministry of Education. Retrieved at http://www.edu.gov.on.ca/eng/general/elemsec/speced/LearningforAll2013.pdf

Ontario Ministry of Education (2014, August 26). *Policy/Program Memorandum No. 8.* Toronto, ON: Ontario Ministry of Education.

Ontario Ministry of Education. (2014). *Safe and Accepting Schools.* Toronto, ON: Ontario Ministry of Education.

Ontario Public Health. (2000). *Ontario Public Health and Epidemiology Report, Volume 11*(5). Toronto, ON: Ontario Public Health.

Ontario Secondary School Teachers' Federation (OSSTF). (1995). *The joke's over*. Toronto, ON: OSSTF.

Organisation for Economic Co-operation and Development (OECD). (2014, September). *OECD employment outlook: How does Canada compare?* Retrieved at http://www.oecd.org/canada/EMO-CAN-EN.pdf

Orlowski, M.A., & Hart, A. (2010, September). Including movement during routines and transitions. *Young Children*, 88–93.

O'Rourke, S.L., Martin, M., Brown, L., Bauer, W., Dobbins, M., Schaeffer, A., Cartin, D., Pollard, C., & Byrne, D. (2011). International friendships for students with special needs. *Teaching Exceptional Children, 43*(4), 8–15.

Orpinas, P., & Horne, A.M. (2010). Creating a positive school climate and developing social competence. In S.R. Jimerson, S.M. Swearer, & D.L. Espelage (Eds.), *Handbook of bullying in schools: An international perspective* (pp. 49–60). New York, NY: Routledge.

Ostad, S.A., & Sorensen, P.M. (2007). Private speech and strategy-use patterns. *Journal of Learning Disabilities, 40*, 2–14.

Osterman, K.F. (2000). Students' need for belonging in the school community. *Review of Educational Research, 70*(3), 323–367.

Ozer, D., Baran, F., Aktop, A., Nalbant, S., Aglamis, E., & Hutzler, Y. (2011). Effects of a Special Olympics unified sports soccer program on psycho-social attributes of youth with and without intellectual disability. *Research in Developmental Disabilities, 33*, 229–239.

Palincsar, A.S., & Brown, A. (1984). Reciprocal teaching of comprehension- fostering and comprehension-monitoring activities. *Cognition and Instruction, 1*, 117–175.

Palmen, A., Didden, R., & Arts, M. (2008). Improving question asking in high-functioning adolescents with autism spectrum disorders. *Autism, 12*(1), 83–98.

Palmer, H. (1997). ... But where are you really from? Stories of identity and assimilation in Canada. Toronto, ON: Sister Vision.

Paquette, J., & Fallon, G. (2014). In quest of indigeneity, quality, and credibility in Aboriginal post-secondary education in Canada: Problematic contexts and potential ways forward. *Canadian Journal of Administration and Policy, 165*(October 29, 2014).

Parent, A. (2011). "Keep us coming back for more": Urban Aboriginal youth speak about wholistic education. *Canadian Journal of Native Education, 34*(1), 28–48.

Parhar, N., & Sensoy, S. (2011). Culturally relevant pedagogy redux: Canadian teachers' conceptions of their work and its challenges. *Canadian Journal of Education, 34*(2), 189–198.

Paterson, K.M. (2006). Differentiated learning: Language and literacy projects that address diverse classrooms. Markham, ON: Pembroke Pub. Ltd.

Patterson, D. (1996). Becoming a change agent in your elementary classroom. In J. Andrews (Ed.), *Teaching students with diverse needs: Elementary classrooms* (pp. 14–37). Scarborough, ON: Nelson Canada.

Pederson, J.E., & Digby, A.D. (Ed.). (2014). *Secondary schools and cooperative learning: Theories, models, and strategies*. (Electronic book distributed by MyLibrary).

Pedersen, K.S., & Kitano, M.K. (2006). Designing a multicultural literature unit for gifted learners. *Gifted Child Today, 29*(2), 38–49.

Perkins-Dock, R., Battle, T., Edgerton, J., & McNeill, J. (2015). A survey of barriers to employment for individuals who are deaf. *Journal of the American Deafness & Rehabilitation Association, 49*(2), 66–85.

Perry, B.K. (2000). Patterns for giving change and using mental mathematics. *Teaching Children Mathematics, 7*(4), 196–199.

Peshek, S. (2012, Spring). Assessment and grading in a differentiated mathematics classroom. *Ohio Journal of School Mathematics, 65,* 45–50.

Peters, J. (2011). *Transition skills of first-year college students with learning disablities* (Unpublished Ed.D. dissertaton). Walden University.

Peterson, J. (2015). School counselors and gifted kids: Respecting both cognitive and affective. *Journal of Counseling & Development, 93*(2), 153–162.

Petrina, N., Carter, M., & Stephenson, J. (2015). Parental perceptions of the importance of friendship and other outcome priorities in children with autism spectrum disorder. *European Journal of Special Needs Education, 30*(1), 61–74.

Pewewardy, C., & Hammer, P.C. (2003). Culturally responsive teaching for American Indian students. *ERIC Digest*, ED482325.

Pfannenstiel, K.H., Bryant, D., Bryant, D.P., Bryant, B.R., & Porterfield, J. (2015). Cognitive strategy instruction for teaching word problems to primary-level struggling students. *Intervention in School and Clinic, 50*(5), 291–296.

Philpott, D. (2007). Assessing without labels: Inclusive education in the Canadian context. *Exceptionality Education Canada, 17*(3), 3–34.

Philpott, D.F., & Cahill, M. (2007). *A pan-Canadian perspective on the professional knowledge base of learning disabilities* (Unpublished paper). Memorial University of Newfoundland, St. John's, NL.

Philpott, D.F., & Dibbon, D. (2007). A review of the literature on Newfoundland and Labrador's model of Student Support Services: A global perspective on local practice (Appendix G, Literature review). In *Focusing on students: A report of the ISSP & Pathways Commission* (pp. 177–219). St. John's, NL: ISSP & Pathways Commission.

Pianta, R.C. (2006). Classroom management and relationships between children and teachers: Implications for research and practice. In C.M. Evertson & C.S. Weinstein (Eds.), *Handbook of classroom management: Research, practice, and contemporary issues* (pp. 685–710). Mahwah, NJ: Erlbaum.

Pickens, J., & Dymond, S. (2014). Special education directors' views of community-based vocational instruction. *Research & Practice for Persons with Severe Disabilities, 39*(4), 290–304.

Pierce, J.M., Spriggs, A.D., Gast, D.L., & Luscre, D. (2013). Effects of visual activity schedules on independent classroom transitions for students with autism. *International Journal of Disability, Development & Education, 60*(3), 253–269.

Pieretti, R., Kaul, S., Zarchy, R., & O'Hanlon, L. (2015). Using a multimodal approach to facilitate articulation, phonemic awareness, and literacy in young children. *Communication Disorders and Literacy in Young Children, 36*(3), 131–141.

Piggott, A. (2002). Putting differentiation into practice in secondary science lessons. *School Science Review*, 83 (305), 65–71.

Pike, D. (2010). Creating and supporting LGBTQ positive space groups in the Hamilton-Wentworth District School Board: A resource guide for secondary school administrators, teachers and support staff. Retrieved from www.sprc.hamilton.on.ca/reports.php

Pike, D. (2012, Summer). The gift of positive space groups: A transformation for LGBTQ students. *Education Canada*, 28–32.

Poch, A.L., van Garderen, D., & Scheuermann, A. (2015). Students' understanding of diagrams for solving word problems: A framework for assessing diagram proficiency. *Teaching Exceptional Children, 47*(3), 153–162.

Pohl, A. (1997, April). Teaching Native studies. *OPSTF News*.

Porter, G., & Aucoin, A. (2011). *Strengthening inclusion, strengthening schools*. Fredericton, NB: New Brunswick Department of Education. Retrieved from http://www.gnb.ca/0000/publications/comm/InclusionActionPlanReport.pdf

Poth, C., Pei, J., Job, J., & Wyper, K. (2014). Toward intentional, reflective, and assimilative classroom practices with students with FASD. *Teacher Educator, 49*(4), 247–264.

Powers, L.E., Sowers, J., Turner, A., Nesbitt, M., Knowles, A., & Ellison, R. (1996). *Take charge*. Portland, OR: Oregon Health Sciences University.

Preddy, L.B. (2009). Reaching advanced readers in the middle grades. *School Library Media Activities Monthly, 25*(10), 19–21.

Preiss, R.W., & Gayle, B.M. (2006). A meta-analysis of the educational benefits of employing advanced organizers. In B.M. Gayle, M. Allen, M., R.W. Preiss, & N. Burrell, *Classroom communication and instructional processes: Advances through meta-analysis*. Mahwah, NJ: Lawrence Erlbaum.

Prevatt, F.F., Heffer, R.W., & Lowe, P.A. (2000). A review of school reintegration programs for children with cancer. *Journal of School Psychology, 38*, 447–467.

Prince Edward Island Department of Education and Early Learning. (2001). *Minister's Directive No. MD 2001-08 Special Education.* Retrieved from www.gov.pe.ca/eecd

Pugh, R., & Chitiyo, M. (2012). The problem of bullying in schools and the promise of positive behaviour supports. *Journal of Research in Special Education Needs, 12*(2), 47–53.

Punch, R., Creed, P., & Hyde, M. (2005). Predicting career development in hard-of-hearing adolescents in Australia. *Journal of Deaf Studies and Deaf Education, 10*(2),146–160.

Quick, P.M., & Normore, A.H. (2004). Moral leadership in the 21st century: Everyone is watching—especially the students. *The Educational Forum, 68*(4), 336–347.

Quinlan, A.M. (2011). *A complete guide to rubrics: Assessment made easy for teachers of K–college* (2nd ed.). Blue Ridge Summit, PA: Rowman & Littlefield.

Quintini, G., Martin, J.P., & Martin, S. (2007). *The changing nature of the school-to-work transition process in OECD countrs*. WDA-HSG Discussion Paper No. 207-2. Retrieved from http://ssrn.com/abstract=1884070

Rakow, S. (2007). All means all: Classrooms that work for advanced learners. *Middle Ground, 11*(1), 10–12.

Ramani, G.B., & Siegler, R.S. (2008). Promoting broad and stable improvements in low-income children's numerical knowledge through playing number board games. *Child Development, 79*(2), 375–394.

Ramsay, J. (2007). *A case study of an effective working relationship involving an educational assistant and an educator* (Unpublished master's thesis). Queen's University, Kingston, ON.

Randolph, J.J. (2007). Meta-analysis of the research on response cards: Effects on test achievement, quiz achievement, and off-task behavior. *Journal of Positive Behavior Interventions, 9*, 113–128.

Raver, C.C., Jones, S.M., Li-Grining, C.P., Metzger, M., Champon, K.M., & Sardin, L. (2008). Improving preschool classroom processes: Preliminary findings from a randomized trial implemented in head start settings. *Early Childhood Research Quarterly, 23*, 10–26.

Redmond, S.D. (2011). "Expose the bully." Retrieved at scottdouglasredmond.wordpress.com/tag/expose-the-bully

Reed, M., & Curtis, K. (2011, September). High school teachers' perspectives on supporting students with visual impairments toward higher education: Access, barriers, and success. *Journal of Visual Impairment and Blindness*, 105(9) 548–559.

Reed, M.J., Kennett, D.J., Lewis, T., & Lund-Lucas, E. (2011). The relative benefits found for students with and without learning disabilities taking a first-year university preparation course. *Active Learning in Higher Education, 12*(2), 133–142.

Reed, M.J., Kennett, D., Lewis, T., Lund-Lucas, E., Stallberg, C., & Newbold, (2009). The relative effects of university success courses and individualized interventions for students with learning disabilities. *Higher Education Research and Development, 28*(4) 385–400.

Regan, K., & Page, P. (2008). Character building: Using literature to connect with youth. *Reclaiming Children and Youth, 16*(4), 37–43.

Reilly, C., & Ballantine, R. (2011). Epilepsy in school-aged children: More than just seizures? *Support for Learning, 26*(4), 144–151.

Reinke, W.M., Herman, K.C., & Tucker, C. (2006). Building and sustaining communities that prevent mental disorders: Lessons from the field of education. *Psychology in the Schools, 43*, 313–329.

Reis, S.M., & Renzulli, J.S. (2010). Is there still a need for gifted education? *An examination of current research. Learning and Individual Differences, 20*(4), 308–317.

Reiss, J. (2008). *102 content strategies for English language learners: Teaching for academic success in grades 3–12*. Upper Saddle River, NJ: Pearson/Merrill Prentice Hall.

Reithaug, D. (1998a). *Orchestrating academic success by adapting and modifying programs*. West Vancouver, BC: Stirling Head Enterprises.

Reithaug, D. (1998b). *Orchestrating positive and practical behaviour plans*. West Vancouver, BC: Stirling Head Enterprises.

Renzulli, J.S. (2008). Teach to the top: How to keep high achievers engaged and motivated. *Instructor, 117*(5), 34–38.

Report of the Royal Commission on Aboriginal Peoples (RCAP). (1996). Ottawa, ON.

Reschly, A.L., Huebner, E.S., Appleton, J.J., & Antaramian, S. (2008). Engagement as flourishing: The contribution of positive emotions and coping to adolescent' engagement at school and with learning. *Psychology in the Schools, 45*(5), 419–431.

Reutzel, D.R., Petscher, Y., & Spichtig, A.N. (2012). Exploring the value added of a guided, silent reading intervention: Effects on struggling third-grade readers' achievement. *Journal of Educational Research, 105*(6), 404–415.

Reynolds, C. (2004, December 27). Children of war. *Maclean's, 118*(1).

Rhone, A.E. (2006). Preparing minority students for high-stakes tests: Who are we cheating? *Childhood Education, 82*, 233–237.

Richards, M.R.E., & Omdal, S.N. (2007). Effects of tiered instruction on academic performance in a secondary science course. *Journal of Advanced Academics, 18*(3), 424–453.

Ridgway, A., Northup, J., Pellegrin, A., LaRue, R., & Hightshoe, A. (2003). Effects of recess on the classroom behavior of children with and without attention-deficit hyperactivity disorder. *School Psychology Quarterly, 18*(3), 253–268.

Ridosh, M., Braun, P., Roux, G., Bellin, M., & Sawin, K. (2011). Transition in young adults with spina bifida: A qualitative study. *Child: Care, Health & Development, 37*(6), 866–874.

Rieger, A., & McGrail, E. (2015). Exploring children's literature with authentic representations of disability. *Kappa Delta Pi Record, 15*(1), 18–23.

Rissman, B. (2011). Nonverbal learning disability explained: The link to shunted hydrocephalus. *British Journal of Learning Disabilities, 39*(3), 209–215.

Roberts, C.A., & Lazure, M.D. (1970). *One million children: A national study of Canadian children with emotional and learning disorders*. Toronto, ON: Leonard Crainford.

Roberts, G., Torgeson, J.K., Boardman, A., & Scammacca, N. (2008). Evidence-based strategies for reading instruction of older students with learning disabilities. *Learning Disabilities Research and Practice, 23*(2), 63–69.

Roberts, J. (2006). *First Nations, Inuit, and Metis peoples: Explaining their past, present, and future* (Teachers' resource). Toronto, ON: Edmond Montgomery Publications.

Robertson, C., Watt, M-J., & Yasui, Y. (2007). Changes in the prevalence of cerebral palsy for children born very prematurely with a population-based program over 30 years. *Journal of the American Medical Association, 297*(24), 2733–2740.

Robinson, D.H., Funk, D.C., Beth, A., & Bush, A.M. (2005). Changing beliefs about corporal punishment: Increasing knowledge about ineffectiveness to build more consistent moral and informational beliefs. *Journal of Behavioral Education, 14,* 117–139.

Robinson, K. (2015). *Secondary school teachers' perception of educational roles that enhance the inclusion of exceptional students* (Unpublished master's thesis). Queen's University, Kingston, ON.

Rodabaugh, J. (1996). Institutional commitment to fairness in college teaching. *New Directions for Teaching and Learning, 66,* 37–45.

Roffey, S. (2015). Becoming an agent of change for school and student well-being. *Educational & Child Psychology, 32*(1), 21–30.

Rosenberg, M., & Jackman, L. (2003). Development, implementation, and sustainability of comprehensive school-wide behavior management systems. *Intervention in School and Clinic, 39*(1), 10–21.

Rossetti, Z.S. (2011). That's how we do it: Friendship work between high school students with and without autism or developmental disability. *Research and Practice for Persons with Severe Disabilities, 36*(1–2), 23–33.

Rosetti, Z.S., & Goessling, D.P. (2010). Paraeducators' roles in facilitating friendships between secondary students with and without autism spectrum disorders or developmental disabilities. *Teaching Exceptional Children, 42*(6), 64–70.

Ross, S.W., & Horner, R.H. (2009). Bully prevention in positive behavior support. *Journal of Applied Behavior Analysis, 42*(4), 747–759.

Rothstein, R. (2008, April). Whose problem is poverty? *Educational Leadership, 65*(7), 8–13.

Rotter, K.M. (2004). Simple techniques to improve teacher-made instructional materials for use by pupils with disabilities. *Preventing School Failure, 48*(2), 38–43.

Roy, K. (2015). The cutting edge of safety. *Science Scope, 38*(6), 62–63.

Rubie-Davies, C.M. (2007). Classroom interactions: Exploring the practices of high- and low-expectation teachers. *British Journal of Educational Psychology, 77*(2), 289–306.

Runciman, S. (2012). *Breaking the cycle of violence: An exploration into dating violence prevention curriculum* (Unpublished MEd thesis). Queen's University, Kingston, Ontario.

Rusby, J.C., Forrester, K.K., Biglan, A., & Metzler, C.W. (2005). Relationships between peer harassment and adolescent problem behaviors. *Journal of Early Adolescence, 25,* 453–477.

Russell, V., & Solomon, S. (2004). Addressing homophobic bullying in the elementary classroom. *Orbit, 34*(2). Retrieved from http://individual.utoronto.ca/steven_solomon/resources.html

Rustique-Forrester, E. (2005). Accountability and the pressure to exclude: A cautionary tale from England. *Education Policy Analysis Archives, 13*(26). Retrieved from http://epaa.asu.edu/epaa/v13n26

Ryan, J.B., Hughes, E.M., Katsiyannis, A., McDAniel, M., & Sprinkle, C. (2011). Research-based educational practices for students with autism spectrum disorders. *Teaching Exceptional Children, 43*(3), 56–64.

Ryan, R.M., & Deci, E.L. (2000). Self-determination theory and the facilitation of intrinsic motivation, social development, and well-being. *American Psychologist, 55*(1), 68–78.

Ryder, J.F., Tunmer, W.E., & Greaney, K.T. (2008). Explicit instruction in phonemic awareness and phonetically based decoding skills as an intervention strategy for struggling readers in whole language classrooms. *Reading and Writing: An Interdisciplinary Journal, 21,* 349–369.

Sacks, G., & Kern, L. (2008). A comparison of quality of life variables for students with emotional and behavioral disorders and students without disabilities. *Journal of Behavioral Education, 17*(1), 111–127.

Saewyc, E.M., Skay, C. L., Pettingell, S.L, Reis, E.A., Bearinger, L., Resnick, M., Murphy, A., & Combs, L. (2006). Hazards of stigma: The sexual and physical abuse of gay, lesbian, and bisexual adolescents in the United States and Canada. *Child Welfare, 85*(2), 195–213.

Salleh, N.M., Jelas, Z.M., & Zainal, K. (2011). Assessment of social skills among visually impaired students. *International Journal of Learning, 17*(12), 89–97.

Salmon, N. (2013). "We just stick together": How disabled teens negotiate stigma to create lasting friendship. *Journal of Intellectual Disability Research, 57*(4), 347–358.

Salvia, J. & Ysseldyke, J. (2007). *Assessment in special and inclusive education* (10th ed.). Boston, MA: Houghton Mifflin.

Samaroo, J., Dahya, N., & Alidina, S. (2013). Exploring the challenges of conducting respectful research: Seen and unforeseen factors within urban school research. *Canadian Journal of Education, 36*(3), 438–457.

Sankar-DeLeeuw, N. (2007). Case studies of gifted kindergarten children part II: The parents and teachers. *Roeper Review, 29,* 93–99.

Santor, D., Short, K., & Ferguson, B. (2009). *Taking mental health to school: A policy-oriented paper on school-based mental health for Ontario.* Ottawa, ON: Children's Hospital of Eastern Ontario.

Sanzo, M. (2008). The child with arthritis in the school setting. *Journal of School Nursing, 24*(4), 190–196.

Sarason, S.B. (1993). *You are thinking of teaching? Opportunities, problems, realities.* San Francisco, CA: Jossey-Bass.

Saskatchewan Education. (2004). *Caring and respectful schools: Ensuring student well-being.* Regina, SK: Saskatchewan Education.

Saskatchewan Learning. (2005). *Anti-bullying strategy.* Retrieved at http://education.gov.sk.ca/anti-bullying-strategy

Saunders, G., Page, H., & Wood, G. (2011). Great science for autistic students. *Science Scope, 35*(3), 20–23.

Saunders, J. (2012). The support of deaf students in the transition between further education and school into higher education. *Deafness & Education International, 14*(4), 199–216.

Scanlon, D., & Baker, D. (2012). An accommodation model for the secondary inclusive classroom. *Learning Disability Quarterly, 35*(4), 212–224.

Scheffler, R.M., Brown, T., Fulton, B., Hinshaw, S., Levine, P., & Stone, S. (2009). Positive association between attention-deficit/hyperactivity disorder medication use and academic achievement during elementary school. *Pediatrics, 123,* 1273–1279.

Schechter, R., & Grether, J.K. (2008). Continuing increases in autism reported to California's developmental service system: Mercury in retrograde. *Archives for General Psychiatry, 65*(1), 19–24.

Schohl, K., Van Hecke, A., Carson, A.M., Dolan, B., Karst, J., & Stevens, S. (2014). A replication and extension of the PEERS intervention: Examining effects on social skills and social anxiety in adolescents with autism spectrum disorders. *Journal of Autism and Developmental Disorders, 44,* 532–545.

Schreiner, M.B. (2007). Effective self-advocacy. *Intervention in School and Clinic, 42*(5) 300–304.

Schul, J.E. (2011). Revisiting an old friend: The practice and promise of cooperative learning for the twenty-first century. *The Social Studies, 102,* 88–93.

Schumm, J.S., & Vaughn, S. (1991). Making adaptations for mainstreamed students: General classroom teachers' perspectives. *Remedial and Special Education, 12*(4), 18–27.

Sebag, R. (2010). Behavior management through self-advocacy. *Teaching Exceptional Children, 42*(6), 22–29.

Segers, M., Gijbels, D., & Thurlings, M. (2008). The relationship between students' perceptions of portfolio assessment practice and their approaches to learning. *Educational Studies, 34*(1), 35–44.

Servilio, K.L. (2009). You get to choose! Motivating students to read through differentiated instruction. *Teaching Exceptional Children Plus, 5*(5), Article 5. Retrieved from http://escholarship.bc.edu/education/tecplus/vol5/iss5/art5

Shane, H., Laubscher, E., Schlosser, R., Flynn, S., Sorce, J., & Abramson, J. (2012). Applying technology to visually support language and communication in individuals with autism spectrum disorders. *Journal of Autism and Developmental Disorders, 42*(6), 1228–1235.

Shaver, D., Marschark, M., Newman, L., & Marder, C. (2014). Who is where? Characteristics of deaf and hard-of-hearing students in regular and special schools. *Journal of Deaf Studies & Deaf Education, 19*(2), 2013–219.

Shaw, S., Glaser, S., Stern, M., Sferdenschi, C., & McCabe, P. (2010, March). Responding to students' chronic illnesses. *Principal Leadership,* 12–16. Retrieved from www.nasponline.org

Shaw, S.R., & McCabe, P.C. (2008). Hospital-to-school transition for children with chronic illness: Meeting the new challenges of an evolving health care system. *Psychology in the Schools, 45,* 74–87.

Shaywitz, S.E., Morris, R., & Shaywitz, B.A. (2008). The education of dyslexic children from childhood to young adulthood. *Annual Review of Psychology, 59,* 451–475.

Sheetz, A.H., Goldman, P., Millett, K., et al. (2004). Guidelines for managing life-threatening food allergies in Massachusetts schools. *Journal of School Health, 74*(5), 155–160.

Sheldon, E. (2012). *Parent advocacy literacy and self-determination theory* (Unpublished paper). Queen's University, Kingston, ON.

Shin, M., Besser, L., Siffel, C., et al. (2010). Prevalence of spina bifida among children and adolescents in 10 regions in the United States. *Pediatrics, 126*(2), 274–279.

Shogren, K., Lang, R., Machalicek, W., Rispoli, M., & O'Reilly, M. (2011). Self- versus teacher-management of behavior for elementary school students with Asperger syndrome: Impact on classroom behavior. *Journal of Positive Behavior Interventions, 13*(2), 87–96.

Short, K., Ferguson, B., & Santor, D. (2009). *Scanning the practice landscape in school-based mental health in Ontario.* Paper prepared for The Provincial Centre of Excellence for Child and Youth Mental Health at Children's Hospital of Eastern Ontario (CHEO). Ottawa, ON: CHEO.

Siegel, L.S. (1999). Issues in the definition and diagnosis of learning disabilities. *Journal of Learning Disabilities, 32,* 304–319.

Siegle, D. (2005). Six uses of the internet to develop students' gifts and talents. *Gifted Child Today, 28*(2), 30–36.

Silva, M., Munk, D.D., & Bursuck, W.D. (2005). Grading adaptations for students with disabilities. *Intervention in School & Clinic, 41*(2), 87–98.

Simeonsdotter Svensson, A., Pramling Samuelsson, I., Hellstrom, A-L., & Jenholt Nolbris, M. (2014). Experiences of SKYPE communication in education and research: Data collection concerning young children with long-term illness. *Early Childhood Development & Care, 184*(7), 1017–1030.

Simpson, R.L. (2005). Evidence-based practices and students with autism, spectrum disorders. *Focus on Autism and Other Developmental Disabilities, 20,* 140–149.

Simpson, C.G., Gaus, M.D., Garcia Biggs, M.J., & Williams, J. (2010). Physical education and implications for students with Asperger's syndrome. *Teaching Exceptional Children, 42*(6), 48–56.

Skyler, A.A., Higgins, K., & Boone, R. (2007). Strategies for adapting webquests for students with learning disabilities. *Intervention in School and Clinic, 43*(1), 20–28.

Slater, W.H., & Horstman, F.R. (2002). Teaching reading and writing to struggling middle school and high school students: The case for reciprocal teaching. *Preventing School Failure, 46,* 163–166.

Sloane, M.W. (2007). First grade study groups deepen math learning. *Young Children, 62*(4), 83–89.

Smith, J. (2006). Every child a singer: Techniques for assisting developing singers: All children can sing if you take the time to teach them. *Music Educators Journal, 93*(2), 28.

Smith, P.K., & Slonje, R. (2010). Cyberbullying: The nature and extent of a new kind of bullying, in and out of school. In S.R. Jimerson, S.M. Swearer, & D.L. Espelage (Eds.), *Handbook of bullying in schools: An international perspective* (pp. 249–262). New York, NY: Routledge.

Smith, P.K., Smith, C., Osborn, R., & Samara, M. (2008). A content analysis of school anti-bullying policies: Progress and limitations. *Educational Psychology in Practice, 24,* 1–12.

Smith, T.E.C., Polloway, E.A., Patton, J.R., Dowdy, A.A., McIntyre, L.J., & Francis, G.C. (2008). *Teaching students with special needs in inclusive settings* (3rd Canadian ed.). Toronto, ON: Pearson Education Canada.

Smith, W.J. (1992). Special education policy in Quebec: Evolution or status quo? *Education Canada, 32*(1), 40–48.

Sofronoff, K., Dark, E., & Stone, V. (2011). Social vulnerability and bullying in children with Asperger syndrome. *Autism, 15,* 355–372.

Solish, A., Perry, A., & Minnes, P. (2010). Participation of children with and without disabilities in social, recreational and leisure activities. *Journal of Applied Research in Intellectual Disabilities, 23,* 226–236.

Solomon, R.P. (1996). Creating an opportunity structure for Blacks and other teachers of colour. In K.S. Brethwaite & C.E. James (Eds.), *Educating African Canadians* (pp. 216–233). Toronto, ON: James Lorimer & Co.

Song, Y., Heo, M., Krumenaker, L., & Tippins, D. (2008). Cartoons, an alternative learning assessment. *Science Scope,* 16–21.

Sonnier-York, C., & Stanford, P. (2002). Learning to cooperate: A teacher's perspective. *Teaching Exceptional Children, 34*(6), 40–44.

Sood, S., & Jitendra, A.K. (2013). An exploratory study of a number sense program to develop kindergarten students' number proficiency. *Journal of Learning Disabilities, 46*(4), 328–346.

Soukup, M., & Feinstein, S. (2007). Identification, assessment, and intervention strategies for deaf and hard of hearing students with learning disabilities. *American Annals of the Deaf, 152*(1), 56–62.

Spencer, V., Evmenova, A., Boon, R., & Hayes-Harris, L. (2014). Review of research-based interventions for students with autism spectrum disorders in content area instruction: Implications and considerations for classroom practice. *Education and Training in Autism and Developmental Disabilities, 49*(3), 331–353.

Sprouls, K., Mathur, S.R., & Upreti, G. (2015). Is positive feedback a forgotten classroom practice? Findings and implications for at-risk students. *Preventing School Failure, 59*(3), 153–160.

Stanovich, K.E. (2005). The future of a mistake: Will discrepancy measurement continue to make the learning disabilities field a pseudoscience? *Learning Disability Quarterly, 28*(2), 103–115.

Staples, K.E., & Dilberto, J.A. (2010). Guidelines for successful parent involvement. *Teaching Exceptional Children, 42*(6), 58–63.

Starrett, E.V. (2006*). Teaching phonics for balanced reading* (2nd ed.). Thousand Oaks, CA: Corwin.

Statistics Canada (2006) *Census trends.* Retrieved from www12.statcan.ca/english/census06/

Statistics Canada. (2011a). *Aboriginal peoples in Canada: First Nations, People, Metis and Inuit* (National Household Survey). Ottawa, ON: Author. Retrieved from http://www12.statcan.gc.ca

Statistics Canada. (2011b). *Immigration and ethnocultural diversity* (National Household Survey). Ottawa, ON: Author. Retrieved from http://www12.statcan.gc.ca

Stecker, P.M. (2007). Using progress monitoring with intensive services. *Teaching Exceptional Children, 40*(5), 52–57.

Steele, M.M. (2008). Helping students with learning disabilities succeed. *Science Teacher, 75*(3), 38–42.

Steiner-Bell, K. (2005). *Social understanding in the friendships of persons with a developmental syndrome* (Unpublished doctoral dissertation). Queen's University, Kingston, ON.

Stelmach, B. (2009). A non-Aboriginal researcher's retrospective of a study on Aboriginal parent involvement. *First Nations Perspective, 2*. Retrieved from http://www.mfnerc.org/index.php?option=com_content&task=category&sectionid=14&id=101&Itemid=116&Itemid=120

Stenhoff, D.M., & Lignugaris/Kraft, B. (2007). A review of the effects of peer tutoring on students with mild disabilities in secondary settings. *Exceptional Children, 74*, 8–30.

Stiggins, R. (2014). Improve assessment literacy outside of schools too. *Phi Delta Kappan, 96*(2), 67–72.

Story, M., Mueller, J., & Mace, R. (1998). *The universal design file: Designing for people of all ages and abilities.* Raleigh, NC: North Carolina State University, Center for Universal Design.

Stough, L.M., & Palmer, D.J. (2003). Special thinking in special settings: A qualitative study of expert special educators. *The Journal of Special Education, 38*, 174–186.

Strickland, C.A. (2007). *Tools for high quality differentiated instruction.* Alexandria, VA: Association for Supervision and Curriculum Development.

Stuart, C.H., & Smith, S.W. (2002). Transition planning for students with severe disabilities: Policy implications for the classroom. *Intervention in School and Clinic 37*(4), 234–236.

Sugai, G., & Horner, R.H. (2008). What we know and need to know about preventing problem behavior in schools. *Exceptionality, 16*(2), 67–77.

Suh, J., Seshaiyer, P., Freeman, P., & Baker, C. (2012). Modeling 10-ness using Tech-knowledgy. *Teaching Children Mathematics, 18*(9), 574–578.

Sullivan, A., Klingbeil, D., & Van Norman, E. (2013). Beyond behavior: Multilevel analysis of the influence of sociodemographics and school characteristics on students' risk of suspension. *School Psychology Review, 42*(1), 99–114.

Super, D.E., Savicka, M.L., & Supe, C.M. (1996). The life-span, life-space approach to careers. In D. Brown, L. Brooks, & Associates (Eds.) *Career choice and development* (3rd ed., pp. 121–178). San Francisco: Jossey-Bass.

Swanson, H.L., & Deshler, D. (2003). Instructing adolescents with learning disabilities: Converting a meta-analysis to practice. *Journal of Learning Disabilities, 36*, 124–135.

Szatmari, P., Bryson, S.E., Boyle, M.H., & Duku, E. (2003). Predictors of outcome among high functioning children with autism and Asperger syndrome. *Journal of Child Psychology and Psychiatry, 44*(4), 520–528.

Tannock, R. (2007). The educational implications of attention deficit hyperactivity disorder. What works? Research into practice. Research Monograph No. 3. Toronto: Literacy and Numeracy Secretariat & the Ontario Association of Deans of Education. Retrieved from www.edu.gov.on.ca/eng/literacynumeracy/inspire/research/what-Works.html

Tannock, R., & Martinussen, R. (2001, November). Reconceptualizing ADHD. *Educational Leadership*, 20–25.

Targett, P., Wehman, P., West, M., Dillard, C., & Cifu, G. (2013). Promoting transition to adulthood for youth with physical disabilities and health impairments. *Journal of Vocational Rehabilitation, 39*(3), 239–239.

Taylor, J.A. (2008). Social competence and collaborative guided inquiry science activities: Experiences of students with learning disabilities (Unpublished doctoral thesis). Queen's University, Kingston, ON.

Tejero Hughes, M., & Parker-Katz, M. (2013). Integrating comprehension strategies into social studies instruction. *Social Studies, 104*(3), 93–104.

Tellez-Zenteno, J.F., Pondal-Sordo, M., Matijevic, S., & Wiebe, S. (2004). National and regional prevalence of self-reported epilepsy in Canada. *Epilepsia, 45*(12), 1623–1629.

Terpstra, J.E., & Tamura, R. (2008). Effective social interaction strategies for inclusive settings. *Early Childhood Education Journal, 35*, 405–411.

Test, D.W., Fowler, C.H., Wood, W.M., Brewer, D.M., & Eddy, S. 2005). A conceptual framework of self-advocacy for students with disabilities. *Remedial and Special Education, 26*(1), 43–54.

Tews, L., & Lupart, J. (2008). Students with disabilities' perspectives of the role and impact of paraprofessionals in inclusive education settings. *Journal of Policy and Practice in Intellectual Disabilities, 5*(1), 39–46.

Thelen, P., & Klifman, T. (2011, July). Using daily transition strategies to support all children. *Young Children*, 92–98.

Thomson, D.L. (2010). Beyond the classroom walls: Teachers' and students' perspectives on how online learning can meet the needs of gifted students. *Journal of Advanced Academics, 21*(4), 662–712.

Thompson, H.A. (Fall, 2011). Criminalizing kids: The overlooked reason for failing schools. *Dissent Magazine*. Retrieved from www.dissent-magazine.org/issue/?issue=176

Thornberg, R. (2006). Hushing as a moral dilemma in the classroom. *Journal of Moral Education, 35*, 89–104.

Tomlinson, C.A. (1999). *The differentiated classroom: Responding to the needs of all learners.* Alexandria, VA: Association for Supervision and Curriculum Development.

Tomlinson, C.A. (2010, February). Sometimes we must rethink our theories and learn how to teach … one kid at a time. *Educational Leadership*, 12–16.

Tomlinson, C.A. (2014). *The differentiated classroom: Responding to the needs of all learners* (2nd ed.). Alexandria, VA: Association for Supervision and Curriculum Development.

Topping, K.J., Thurston, A., McGavock, K., & Conlin, N. (2012). Outcomes and process in reading tutoring. *Educational Research, 54*(3), 239–258.

Touchette, N. (2000). Kids and type 2: Type 2 diabetes, the kind that only adults used to get, is on the rise among America's youth. *Diabetes Forecast, 53*(11), 79.

Trainor, A. (2010). Diverse approaches to parent advocacy during special education home–school interactions: Identification and use of cultural and social capital. *Remedial and Special Education, 31*(1), 34–47.

Trautwein, U. (2007). The homework-achievement relation reconsidered: Differentiating homework time, homework frequency, and homework effort. *Learning and Instruction, 17*, 372–388.

Tretter, T.R. (2010). Systematic and sustained: Powerful approaches for enhancing deep mathematical thinking. *Gifted Child Today, 33*(1), 16–26.

Triplett, C.F., & Hunter, A. (2005). Talking circle: Creating community in our elementary classrooms. *Social Studies and the Young Learner, 18*(2), 4–8.

Trocmé, N., Fallon, B., MacLaurin, B., Sunha, V., Black, T., et al. (2010). *Canadian incidence study of reported child abuse and neglect 2008: Major findings.* Ottawa, ON: Public Health Agency of Canada.

Trudel, T.M., Scherer, M., & Elias, E. (2011). Understanding traumatic brain injury: An introduction. *Exceptional Parent Magazine*, July, 33–37.

Tsai, L.Y. (2012). Sensitivity and specificity: DSM-IV versus DSM-5 criteria for autism spectrum disorder. *American Journal of Psychiatry, 169*(10), 1009–1011.

Tsai, L.Y. (2013). Asperger's disorder will be back. *Journal of Autism and Developmental Disabilities, 43*, 2914–2942.

Turner, S.L. (2007). Preparing inner-city adolescents to transition into high school. *Professional School Counseling, 10*(3)–252.

Twemlow, S.W., Fonagy, P., & Sacco, F.C. (2010). The etiological cast to the role of the bystander in the social architecture of bullying and violence in schools and communities. In S. R. Jimerson, S. M. Swearer, & D. L. Espelage (Eds.), *Handbook of bullying in schools: An international perspective* (pp. 73–86). New York, NY: Routledge.

Tymms, P., & Merrell, C. (2011). ADHD and academic attainment: Is there an advantage in impulsivity? *Learning and Individual Differences, 21*(6), 753–758.

Udvari-Solner, A., & Kluth, P. (2007). *Joyful learning: Active and collaborative learning in inclusive classrooms.* Thousand Oaks, CA: Corwin Press.

Uhry, J.K. (2013). The role of phonemic awareness in learning to read and spell successfully. *Perspectives on Language and Literacy, 39*(1), 11–16.

Underwood, M., & Buhrmester, D. (2007). Friendship features and social exclusion: An observational study examining gender and social context. *Merrill-Palmer Quarterly, 53*, 412–438.

Ungar, M. (2000). Drifting toward mental health: High-risk adolescents and the process of empowerment. *Youth & Society, 32*(2), 228–252.

Ungar, M. (2004). A constructionist discourse on resilience: Multiple contexts, multiple realities among at-risk children and youth. *Youth & Society, 35*(3), 341–365.

Ungar, M. (2006). *Strengths-based counseling with at-risk youth.* Thousand Oaks, CA: Corwin Press.

Ungar, M. (2007). The beginnings of resilience: A view across cultures. *Education Canada, 47*(3), 28–32.

United Nations Educational, Scientific, and Cultural Organization (UNESCO). (2014). *UNESCO atlas of the world's languages in danger.* Retrieved from http://www.unesco.org/culture/languages-atlas/index.php

United Nations Enable. *Rights and Dignity of Persons with Disabilities.* Retrieved from www.un.org/disabilities

Uwah, C., McMahon, H.G., & Furlow, C.F. (2008). School belonging, educational aspirations, and academic self-efficacy among African-American male high school students: Implications for school counselors. *Professional School Counseling, 11*(5), 296–305.

Vacc, N.N. (1995). Gaining number sense through a restructured hundreds chart. *Teaching Exceptional Children, 28*(1), 50–55.

Valenzuela, V.V., Gutierrez, G., & Mambros, K.M. (2014). Response to intervention: Using single-case design to examine the impact of tier 2 mathematics interventions. *School Psychology Forum, 8*(3), 144–155.

Valo, S., & Tannock, R. (2010). Diagnostic instability of DSM-IV ADHD subtypes: Effects of informant source, instrumentation, and methods for combining symptom reports. *Journal of Clinical Child and Adolescent Psychology, 38*(6), 749–760.

Van den Bos, K.P., Nakken, H., Nicolay, P.G., & van Houten, E.J. (2007). Adults with mild intellectual disabilities: Can their reading comprehension ability be improved? *Journal of Intellectual Disability Research, 51*, 835–849.

van Deur, P. (2011). Views of gifted elementary students about self-directed learning. *Gifted & Talented International, 26*(1/2), 111–120.

Van der Molen, M.J., Henry, L.A., & Van Luit, J.E.H. (2014). Working memory development in children with mild to borderline intellectual disabilities. *Journal of Intellectual Disability Research, 58*(7), 637–650.

Van Garderen, D. (2004). Reciprocal teaching as a comprehension strategy for understanding mathematical word problems. *Reading and Writing Quarterly, 20*, 225–229.

van Schie, P., Siebes, R., Dallmeijer, A., Schuengel, C., Smits, D-W., Gorter, J., & Becher, J. (2013). Development in social functioning and communication in school-aged (5–9 years) children with cerebral palsy. *Research in Developmental Disabilities, 34*(12), 4485–4494.

Vanweelden, K., & Whipple, J. (2014). Music educators' perceived effectiveness of inclusion. *Journal of Research in Music Education, 62*(2), 148–160.

Vatterott, C. (2010, Summer). Hallmarks of good homework. *Educational Leadership*, 10–15.

Vaughn, S. (1991). Social skills enhancement in students with learning disabilities. In B.Y.L. Wong (Ed.), *Learning about learning disabilities* (pp. 407–440). San Diego, CA: Academic Press.

Veenstra, R., Lindenberg, S., Huitsing, G., Sainio, M., & Salmivalli, C. (2014). The role of teachers in bullying: The relation between antibullying attitudes, efficacy, and efforts to reduce bullying. *Journal of Educational Psychology, 106*(4), 1135–1143.

Venter, H., & Pohan, C. (2011). Five care principles for a thriving career. *New Teacher Advocate, 18*(3), 4–5.

Venville, A., Street, A.F., & Fossey, E. (2014). Good intentions: Teaching and specialist support perspectives of student disclosure of mental health issues in post-secondary education. *International Journal of Inclusive Education, 18*(11), 172–1188.

Versnel, J.J. (2005a). *Self-advocacy for the transition of early adolescents to junior high school* (Unpublished doctoral thesis). Queen's University, Kingston, ON.

Versnel, J. (2005b). *Transition preparation program: Linking motivation and learning strategies for youth facing challenging transitions* (Unpublished Ph.D. dissertation). Faculty of Education, Queen's University, Kingston, ON.

Versnel, J., Hutchinson, N.L., Munby, H., & Chin, P. (2008). Work-based learning for adolescents with learning disabilities: Creating a context for success. *Exceptionality Education Canada, 18*, 113–134.

Villa, R.A., Nevin, A., & Thousand, J.S. (2007). *Differentiating instruction: Collaborative planning and teaching for universally designed learning.* Thousand Oaks, CA: Corwin Press.

Villegas, A.M., & Lucas, T. (2007). The culturally responsive teacher. *Educational Leadership, 64*(6), 28–33.

Villeneuve, M., Chatenoud, C., Hutchinson, N.L., Minnes, P., et al. (2013). The experience of parents as their children with developmental disabilities transition from early intervention to kindergarten. *Canadian Journal of Education, 36*(1), 4–43.

Villeneuve, M., & Hutchinson, N.L. (2012). Enabling outcomes for students with developmental disabilities through collaborative consultation. *Qualitative Report, 17*(Art. 97), 1–29. Retrieved from http://www.nova.edu/sss/QR/QR17/villeneuve.pdf, http://www.nova.edu/ssss/QR

Volante, L. (2006). An alternate vision for large-scale assessment in Canada. *Journal of Teaching and Learning, 4*, 1–14.

Volante, L. (2010). Assessment of, for, and as learning within schools: Implications for transforming classroom practice. *Action in Teacher Education, 31*, 66–75.

Volante, L., & Ben Jaafar, S. (2008). Educational assessment in Canada. *Assessment in Education: Principles, Policy & Practice, 15*(2), 201–210.

Volante, L., & Cherubini, L. (2010). Understanding the connections between largescale assessment and school improvement planning. *Canadian Journal of Educational Administration and Policy, 115.* Retrieved from http://www.umanitoba.ca/publications/cjeap

Vowell, J., & Phillips, M. (2015). All aboard! The Polar Express is travelling to science: Understanding the states of matter while differentiating instruction for young learners. *Science Activities, 52*(1), 1–8.

Vuijk, P., Hartman, E., Scherder, E., & Visscher, C. (2010). Motor performance of children with mild intellectual disability and borderline intellectual functioning. *Journal of Intellectual Disability Research, 54*(11), 955–965.

Vygotsky, L. (1978). *Mind in society.* Cambridge, MA: Harvard University Press.

Vygotsky, L.S. (1996). *Thought and language* (Revised). Cambridge, MA: MIT Press.

Walker, A., & Nabuzoka, D. (2007). Academic achievement and social functioning of children with and without learning difficulties. *Educational Psychology, 27*(5), 635–654.

Walpole, S., & McKenna, M.C. (2007). *Differentiated reading strategies for the primary grades*. New York, NY: Guilford Pub.

Walpole, S., McKenna, M.C., & Philippakos, Z.A. (2011). *Differentiated reading instruction in grades 4 and 5: Strategies and resources*. New York, NY: Guilford.

Watson, C. (2014). Effective professional learning communities? The possibilities for teachers as agents of change in schools. *British Educational Research Journal, 40*(1), 18–29.

Watson, G., & Bellon-Harn, M. (2014). Speech-language pathologists and general educator collaboration: A model for tier 2 service delivery. *Intervention in School and Clinic, 49*(4), 237–243.

Watson, M., & Battistich, V. (2006). Building and sustaining caring communities. In C.M. Evertson & C.S. Weinstein (Eds.), *Handbook of classroom management: Research, practice, and contemporary issues* (pp. 53–280). Mahwah, NJ: Erlbaum.

Webb, N.M., Nemer, K.M., & Ing, M. (2006). Small group reflections: Parallels between teacher discourse and student behavior in peer-directed groups. *The Journal of the Learning Sciences, 15*, 63–119.

Webster, M.L., & Valeo, A. (2011). Teacher preparedness for a changing demographic of language learners. *TESL Canada Journal, 28*(2), 105–128.

Weenie, A. (2009). Toward an understanding of the ecology of indigenous education. *First Nations Perspective, 2*. Retrieved from http://www.mfnerc.org/index.php?option=com_content&task=category&sectionid=14&id=101&Itemid=116&Itemid=120

Wehmeyer, M., & Abery, B.H. (2013). Self-determination and choice. *Intellectual & Developmental Disabilities, 51*(5) 399–411.

Weil, M. (2011). Listen up! *THE Journal, 38*(7), 16–19.

Weinkauf, T. (2002). College and university? You've got to be kidding: Inclusive post-secondary education for adults with intellectual disabilities. *Crossing Boundaries: An Interdisciplinary Journal, 1*(2), 28–37.

Weinstein, C.S., Tomlinson-Clarke, S., & Curran, M. (2004). Toward a conception of culturally responsive classroom management. *Journal of Teacher Education, 55*, 25–38.

Weisz, J.R., Sandler, I.N., Durlak, J.A., & Anton, B.S. (2005). Promoting and protecting youth mental health through evidence-based prevention. *American Psychologist, 60*(6), 628–648.

Welch, A. B. (2000). Responding to student concerns about fairness. *Teaching Exceptional Children, 33*(2), 36–40.

Welch, M.E. (2010). *Differences in student misbehaviour after completing in-school suspension between rural high school and suburban high school students* (Unpublished doctoral dissertation). University of Southern Mississippi, Hattiesburg.

Whalon, K., & Hart, J. (2011). Children with autism spectrum disorder and literacy instruction: An exploratory study of elementary inclusive settings. *Remedial and Special Education, 32*(3), 243–255.

White, K., Budai, J., Mathew, D., Rickson Deighan, M., & Gill, H. (2012). Educators' perspectives about a public school district's Aboriginal education enhancement agreement in British Columbia. *Canadian Journal of Native Education, 35*(1), 42–62.

White, M. (2010). Students are not to blame. *Our schools/our selves, 19*(2), 113–127.

Whiting, G.W. (2006). Enhancing culturally diverse males' scholar identity: Suggestions for educators of gifted students. *Gifted Child Today, 29*(3), 46–50.

Whitley, J., Lupart, J.L., & Beran, T. (2007). The characteristics and experiences of Canadian students receiving special education services for a learning disability. *Exceptionality Education Canada, 17*(3), 85–109.

Whitley, J., Lupart, J.L., & Beran, T. (2009). The characteristics and experiences of Canadian students receiving special education services for emotional/behavioural difficulties. *Exceptionality Education Canada, 19*(1), 14–31.

Whitney, J., Leonard, M., Leonard, W., Carmelio, M., & Carmelio, V. (2005). Seek balance, connect with others, and reach all students: High school students describe a moral imperative for teachers. *The High School Journal, 89*(2), 29–39.

Wideman-Johnston, T. (2011). *The academic journey of students with chronic gastrointestinal illness: Narratives from daughters and their mothers* (Unpublished Master's thesis). Nipissing University, North Bay, ON.

Wieman, R., & Arbaugh, F. (2014). Rethinking homework: Best practices that support diverse needs. *Mathematics Teaching in the Middle School, 29*(3), 160–165.

Wiener, J., & Tardif, C. (2004). Social and emotional functioning of children with learning disabilities: Does special education placement make a difference? *Learning Disabilities Research and Practice, 19*, 20–32.

Wiesnert, M., Vondracek, F.W., Capaldi, D., & Porfeli, E. (2003). Childhood and adolescent predictors of early adult career pathways. *Journal of Vocational Behavior, 63*(3), 305–328.

Wihak, C., & Merali, N. (2007). Racial/cultural identity: Transformation among school-based mental health professionals working in Nunavut. *Canadian Journal of Education, 30*(1), 291–322.

Willard, N.E. (2007). *Cyberbullying and cyberthreats: Responding to the challenge of online social aggression, threats, and distress*. Champaign, IL: Research Press.

Williams, L., Henderson, M., & Marcuse, G. (1998). *First Nations: The circle unbroken: The teacher's guide (videos 5, 6, 7)*. Montreal, QC: National Film Board of Canada.

Williams, T., Connolly, J., Pepler, D., & Craig, W. (2005). Peer victimization, social support, and psychosocial adjustment of sexual minority adolescents. *Journal of Youth and Adolescents, 34*(5), 471–482.

Williamson, P., Carnahan, C., & Jacobs, J. (2012). Reading comprehension profiles of high-functioning students on the spectrum: A grounded theory. *Exceptional Children, 78*(4), 449–469.

Willms, J.D. (2002a). Vulnerable children: Findings from Canada's National Longitudinal Study of Children and Youth. Edmonton, AB: University of Alberta Press.

Willms, J.D. (2002b). Vulnerable children and youth: Findings from Canada's National Longitudinal Study of Children and Youth. *Education Canada, 42*(3), 40–43.

Willows, D. (2002). The balanced literacy diet. *School Administrator, 59*, 30–33.

Wills, C., & Bradshaw, L. (2013). *Empowering voices for student success: Embedding restorative practice and circle process in school culture*. Brockville, ON: Upper Canada School District.

Wilson, J.K. (2012). Brisk and effective fluency instruction for small groups. *Intervention in School and Clinic, 47*(3), 152–157.

Winebrenner, S. (2007). *Teaching gifted kids in the regular classroom: Strategies and techniques every teacher can use to meet the academic needs of the gifted and the talented* (3rd ed.). Minneapolis, MN: Free Spirit.

Wintle, J. (2012). A multiple perspective case study of a young adult with intellectual disabilities participating in a pre-service teacher education class. *Exceptionality Education International, 22*(1), 37–54.

Winzer, M. (2007). *Children with exceptionalities in Canadian classrooms* (7th ed.). Toronto: Pearson Education Canada.

Wise, N., & Chen, X. (2009). Early identification and intervention for at-risk readrs in French immersion. *Work works? Research into Practice, 18*, Ontario's Literacy and Numeracy Secretariat.

Wise Berninger, V. (2012). Strengthening the mind's eye. *Principal, 91*(5), 28–31.

Witzel, B., & Clarke, B. (2015). Focus on inclusive education: Benefits of using a multi-tiered system of supports to improve inclusive practices. *Childhood Education, 91*(3), 215–219.

Witzel, B.S., Riccomini, P.J., & Schneider, E. (2008). Implementing CRA with secondary students with learning disabilities in mathematics. *Intervention in School and Clinic, 43*(5), 270–276.

Wolfe, D.A., Crooks, C.C., Chiodo, D., & Jaffe, P. (2009). Child maltreatment, bullying, gender-based harassment, and adolescent dating violence: Making the connections. *Psychology of Women Quarterly, 33*(1), 21–24.

Wolff Heller, K., Mezei, P.J., & Thompson, M.J. (2008). Meeting the assistive technology needs of students with Duchenne muscular dystrophy. *Journal of Special Education Technology, 23*(4), 15–23.

Wolffe, K., & Kelly, S. (2011). Instruction in areas of the expanded core curriculum linked to transition outcomes for students with visual impairments. *Journal of Visual Impairment & Blindness, 105*(6), 340–349.

Wolford, P.L., Heward, W.L., & Alber, S.R. (2001). Teaching middle school students with learning disabilities to recruit peer assistance during cooperative learning group activities. *Learning Disabilities: Research and Practice, 16*, 161–173.

Womack, S.A., Marchant, M., & Borders, D. (2011). Literature-based social skills instruction: A strategy for students with learning disabilities. *Intervention in School and Clinic, 46*(3), 157–164.

Woolfolk Hoy, A., & Weinstein, C.S. (2006). Student and teacher perspectives on classroom management. In C.M. Evertson & C.S. Weinstein (Eds.), *Handbook of classroom management: Research, practice, and contemporary issues* (pp. 181–220). Mahwah, NJ: Erlbaum.

World Health Organization (WHO). (1980). *International classification of impairments, disabilities, and handicaps.* Geneva, Switzerland: WHO.

World Health Organization (WHO). (2010). *International classification of functioning, disability, and health* (ICF). Geneva, Switzerland: WHO. Retrieved from http://www.who.int/classifications/icf/en

Wormeli, R. (2006). Fair isn't always equal: Assessing and grading in the differentiated classroom. Portland, ME: Stenhouse Pub.

Wormeli, R. (2011). Redos and retakes done right. *Educational Leadership, 69*(3), 22–26.

Xin, Y.P., Grasso, E., Dipipi-Hoy, C.M., & Jitendra, A. (2005). The effects of purchasing skill instruction for individuals with developmental disabilities: A meta-analysis. *Exceptional Children, 71*, 379–402.

Yakubova, G., & Bouck, E.C. (2014). Not all created equally: Exploring calculator use by students with mild intellectual disability. *Education and Training in Autism and Developmental Disabilities, 49*(1), 111–126.

Yamamoto, K.K., Stodden, R.A., & Folk, E.D.R. (2014). Inclusive postsecondary education: Reimagining the transition trajectories of vocational rehabilitation clients with intellectual disabilities. *Journal of Vocational Rehabilitation, 40*(1), 59–71.

Yates, S. (1994). *Nobody knows.* Winnipeg, MB: Gemma B. Publishing.

Yell, M., Katsiyannis, A., Collins, J., & Losinski, M. (2012). Exit exams, high-stakes testing, and students with disabilities: A persistent challenge. *Intervention in School and Clinic, 48*(1), 60–64.

Yildiz, A., Baltaci, S., & Güven, B. (2011). Metacognitive behaviours of the eighth grade gifted students in problem solving process. *New Educational Review, 26*(4), 248–260.

Yohani, S.C., & Larsen, D.J. (2009). Hope lives in the heart: Refugee and immigrant children's perceptions of hope and hope engendering sources during early years of adjustment. *Canadian Journal of Counselling and Psychotherapy, 43*(4). Retrieved from http://cjc.synergiesprairies.ca/cjc/index.php/rcc/article/viewArticle/631

Yssel, N., Adams, C., Clarke, L.S., & Jones, R. (2014). Applying an RTI model for students with learning disabilities who are gifted. *Teaching Exceptional Children, 46*(3), 42–52.

Yu, J.A., Babikian, T., & Asarnow, R.F. (2011). Academic and language outcomes in children after traumatic brain injury: A meta-analysis. *Exceptional Children, 77*(1), 263–281.

Zafar, A. (2010, October 27). Three provinces get failing grades on ADHD. *CBC News.* Retrieved from www.cbc.ca/news/health/story/2010/10/27/adhd-schools.html

Zajac, R.J., & Hartup, W.W. (1997). Friends as coworkers: Research review and classroom implications. *Elementary School Journal, 98*, 3–13.

Zebehazy, K., & Smith, T. (2011). An examination of characteristics related to the social skills of youths with visual impairments. *Journal of Visual Impairment & Blindness, 105*(2), 84–95.

Zentall, S., Kuester, D., & Craig, B. (2011). Social behavior in cooperative groups: Students at risk for ADHD and their peers. *Journal of Educational Research, 104*(1), 28–41.

Zuger, S. (2007). The deadly PB & J. *Instructor, 117*(2), 53–55.

Zuvekas, S.H., & Vitiello, B. (2012). Stimulant medication use in children: A 12-year perspective. *American Journal of Psychiatry, 169*(2), 160–166.

Name Index

Note: Entries for tables and figures are followed by *t* and *f*, respectively.

New Brunswick Department of Education and Early Childhood Development, 6

New Yorker, 29

Newbigging, W., 156, 157

Newcomb, A.F., 291

Newfoundland and Labrador Department of Education, 99, 124

Newfoundland and Labrador Department of Education and Early Childhood Development, 14

Newland, L., 180

Niarhos, F.J., 271

Nichols, S.K., 41

Nickerson, A.B., 295

Nicklin, J.M., 206

Niesyn, M., 197

Nixon, D., 88

Normand, S., 78, 287

Normore, A.H., 293

North West Territories Education, Culture and Employment, 10

Northfield, S., 287

Nottingham Chaplin, P.K., 129

Nova Scotia Education, 293, 312

Nowacek, E.J., 78, 79

Nylund, C., 83

O

Obenchain, K.M., 189

Obradovic, 178

Obradovic, J., 179

O'Brien, B.E., 69

O'Connor, M., 131, 132

O'Connor, M.J., 139

Odem, S., 111

Odom, S.L., 285

O'Driscoll, C., 76

Ogilvie, C.R., 110

Ogle, D., 245

Oh, S., 62

Oke, D., 271, 272

Okolo, C., 247

Olinghouse, N.G., 261

Oliva, D., 320

Oliver, C.M., 325

Olson, H.C., 138, 139

Olszewski-Kubilius, P., 59

Olthouse, J.M., 230

Olweus, D., 297, 298

Omdal, S.N., 59, 228

Ontario Human Rights Commission, 322

Ontario Ministry of Community Services, 96

Ontario Ministry of Education, 6, 12, 46, 53, 67, 68, 76, 96, 121, 168, 202, 228, 257, 260, 276, 312

Ontario Secondary School Teachers' Federation, 173

Orders, S., 312

O'Reilly, M.F., 320

Organisation for Economic Co-operation and Development, 320

Orlowski, M.A., 316

O'Rourke, S.L., 288

Orpinas, P., 188, 208

Osana, H., 247

Ostad, S.A., 286

Osterman, K.F., 170

Ostrosky, M.M., 281

Ouimet, D., 130

Owens, J., 75

Oxford, R.L., 172

Ozer, D., 105

Ozonoff, S., 108, 109

P

Padden, C.A., 128

Padgett, L., 139

Page, P., 88

Paley, B., 139

Palikara, O., 112

Palincsar, A.S., 246

Palmen, A., 288

Palmer, D., 38

Palmer, D.J., 72

Palmer, G., 22

Palmer, H., 164

Panju, M., 321

Papadopoulos, G., 60, 61

Paquette, J., 163

Paradis, J., 172

Parent, A., 159

Parhar, N., 165, 166, 167

Park, M., 211

Parker, S.L., 59

Parker-Katz, M., 73

Parr, J.M., 240

Parrila, R., 60, 61

Parsons, S., 135

Pasquarelli, S.L., 233

Paterson, K.M., 328

Patterson, D., 334

Pavlakis, A., 177

Pearl, C., 328

Pearson, J., 177

Peckham-Hardin, K.D., 106

Pedersen, K.S., 63

Pederson, J.E., 167, 173

Peleaux, J., 247

Pepler, D., 296, 297

Pereles, D., 59

Perkins-Dock, R., 128

Perner, J., 22

Perry, B.K., 242

Perry, Jim, 338

Perry, N., 37

Perry, N.E., 37, 38

Peshek, S., 244

Peterborough Victoria Northumberland and Clarington Catholic District School Board, 48, 49

Peterkin, A., 174

Peternel, G., 59

Peters, J., 322

Peterson, J., 62

Peterson, P., 83

Petrina, N., 286

Pewewardy, C., 193

Pfannenstiel, K.H., 73

Pfiffner, L., 76

Phillips, M., 245

Philpott, D., 11, 12

Philpott, D.F., 15, 66

Phongaksom, S., 18

Pianta, R.C., 191

Pica-Smith, C., 289

Pickens, J., 104

Pierce, J.M., 316

Subject Index

Note: Entries for tables and figures are followed by *t* and *f*, respectively.